Europe and the Mediterranean as Linguistic Areas

Studies in Language Companion Series (SLCS)

This series has been established as a companion series to the periodical *Studies in Language.*

Volume 88

Europe and the Mediterranean as Linguistic Areas. Convergencies from a historical and typological perspective
Edited by Paolo Ramat and Elisa Roma

Europe and the Mediterranean as Linguistic Areas

Convergencies from a historical and typological perspective

Edited by

Paolo Ramat

Elisa Roma
University of Pavia

John Benjamins Publishing Company
Amsterdam / Philadelphia

The paper used in this publication meets the minimum requirements of American National Standard for Information Sciences – Permanence of Paper for Printed Library Materials, ANSI z39.48-1984.

Library of Congress Cataloging-in-Publication Data

Europe and the Mediterranean as linguistic areas : convergencies from a historical and typological perspective / edited by Paolo Ramat, Elisa Roma.

p. cm. -- (Studies in language companion series, ISSN 0165-7763 ; v. 88)

Includes bibliographical references and index.

1. Europe--Languages. 2. Areal linguistics. I. Ramat, Paolo II. Roma, Elisa.

P380.E796 2007

409.4--dc22 2007014514

ISBN 978 90 272 3098 0 (Hb; alk. paper)

John Benjamins Publishing Co. · P.O. Box 36224 · 1020 ME Amsterdam · The Netherlands
John Benjamins North America · P.O. Box 27519 · Philadelphia PA 19118-0519 · USA

Table of contents

List of the contributors

Giorgio Banti
Università 'L'Orientale'
Napoli
gibanti@unior.it

Sonia Cristofaro
Università degli Studi
Pavia
crison@unipv.it

Pierluigi Cuzzolin
Università degli Studi
Bergamo
pierluigi.cuzzolin@unibg.it

Federica Da Milano
Università 'La Bicocca'
Milano
federica.damilano@unimib.it

Paolo Di Giovine
Università 'La Sapienza'
Roma
paolo.digiovine@uniroma1.it

Sara Flamini
Università 'La Sapienza'
Roma.
saraflamini@yahoo.it

Silvia Luraghi
Università degli Studi
Pavia
silvia.luraghi@unipv.it

Anna Giacalone Ramat
Università degli Studi
Pavia
annaram@unipv.it

Gianguido Manzelli
Università degli Studi
Pavia
manzelli@unipv.it

Caterina Mauri
Università degli Studi
Pavia
caterinamauri@hotmail.com

Ignazio Mauro Mirto
Università degli Studi
Palermo
ignazio.mirto@libero.it

Heike Necker
Universität Zürich
hnecker@gmx.de

Marianna Pozza
Università 'La Sapienza'
Roma
marianna.pozza@alice.it

Paolo Ramat
Università degli Studi
Pavia
paoram@unipv.it

Elisa Roma
Università degli Studi
Pavia
elisa.roma@unipv.it

Domenica Romagno
Università degli Studi
Pisa
d.romagno@ling.unipi.it

Andrea Sansò
Università degli Studi
Pavia
sanso@humnet.unipi.it

Thomas Stolz
Universität Bremen
stolz@uni-bremen.de

Foreword

Paolo Ramat

The present volume is a collection of papers which originated from a research project ('Europa e Mediterraneo dal punto di vista linguistico: storia e prospettive' – 'Europe and the Mediterranean from a linguistic point of view: history and prospects') funded in the years 2003–2005 by the Italian Ministry of Education, University and Research (Ministero dell'Istruzione, dell'Università e della Ricerca, MIUR Code: RBN01X7E7) as part of a more general research program ('FIRB' strategic program 'Eredità e prospettive nelle Scienze Umane' – 'Legacies and prospects in the Human Sciences').[1]

In the introduction to a recently published collection of papers, Matras, McMahon and Vincent (2006: xv) write that

1. Four Universities cooperated in the research project: the University of Pavia (coordinator: Sonia Cristofaro), the University of Pisa (coordinator: Romano Lazzeroni), the University of Rome 'La Sapienza' (coordinator Paolo Di Giovine), and the Università per Stranieri di Siena (coordinator: Marina Benedetti). The main coordinator at the national level was Paolo Ramat (University of Pavia).

The papers were presented and discussed at one of the three plenary meetings held in Pisa (2003), Pavia (2004), and Siena (2006). Other papers originating from the research have appeared in or are in press for various journals. The list of publications issued from the research project which is given at the end of this foreword shows the breadth of interests (both synchronic and diachronic) tied to the main theme of the research. A choice was necessary in order to enhance the coherence of the volume and not to exceed the number of pages the Publisher had calculated for the volume. The choice was agreed among the coordinators of the four research teams.

Finally Thomas Stolz, who is a well-known specialist on areal typology and linguistic areas, was invited to contribute a paper which ties up with the topics of this volume.

Last but certainly not least I wish to thank all the colleagues who acted as anonymous referees for the first drafts of the chapters included in this volume. Each chapter has been reviewed by at least two well-known linguists – and the final version which is now published has gained a lot from their suggestions and criticisms. The referees were: Anders Ahlqvist, Giorgio Banti, Marina Benedetti, Giuliano Bernini, Walter Bisang, Giuliana Fiorentino, Martin Haspelmath, Christian Lehmann, Romano Lazzeroni, Konstanze Jungbluth, Marija Koptjevskaja Tamm, Paolo Martino, Alessandro Mengozzi, Michele Prandi, Ignazio Putzu, Elisa Roma, Rosanna Sornicola, Theo Vennemann, Johan van der Auwera and myself.

> [e]diting a volume on linguistic areas is both a fascinating and a worrisome undertaking, for essentially the same reason: 'linguistic area' is a rather ill-defined and amorphous notion. [. . .] It is precisely because of the potential collision between the need for clear and detailed description on the one hand, and theoretical and definitional considerations on the other, that we feel this volume is so timely.

We too have the same feeling and we hope that this book will contribute to the general discussion on what may be considered a linguistic area.

The starting point of our project has been the historical fact that the populations of Europe and the Mediterranean area have been in contact during millennia. These contacts cannot have been without effects on the languages spoken in these areas. Consequently, the general aim of the project has been the study of several structural similarities displayed by European and Mediterranean languages in order to ascertain whether these similarities are due to language contact or other factors such as genetic inheritance or general typological tendencies. Reconstructing how the similarities were brought into existence means mapping the history of contacts and cultural exchanges in the concerned areas. Therefore, the methodological key words of the project and of this book are *areal typology* and *linguistic area*.

There are two main different ways of approaching areal typology, although both of them result in mapping on geographical charts the phenomena they scrutinize (see for instance in this collection the papers by A. Giacalone and A. Sansò, or C. Mauri).

According to Östen Dahl (2001: § 1) "Areal typology [. . .] is the study of patterns in the areal distribution of typologically relevant features of languages". Thus, the starting point is here a linguistic feature that we know to be important from the point of view of general typology – say, the basic word order (WO). In other words areal typological research would be guided by the geographical distribution of linguistic phenomena. In the case of WO the linguist has to check the areal distribution of the six theoretically possible WOs on a world wide scale. The mapping of the different WOs will probably hint at a non-random distribution and will make it possible to speak, e.g., of VSO and SOV-areas, whereby the distribution of VSO languages might, in a diachronic perspective, represent a residual survival of a previously larger VSO diffusion, as happened to the Semitic languages of Ethiopia when they borrowed the Cushitic SOV order. G. Banti shows in this volume that Harari, the south-easternmost Ethiosemitic language, has, over time, developed an OV morphosyntax as an effect of the Cushitic and Omotic substratum and adstratum. Auxiliaries thus shifted from a preverbal position (which is the most frequent in the older Geʿez texts), to a postverbal position (see Bisang 2006 and also Sőrés and Marchello-Nizza 2005, who refer to the shift VO → OV in Afro-Asiatic languages of Ethiopia, although many traits of these languages have maintained the VO-type[2]). On the other hand Maltese developed a quite non-Arabic periphrastic passive probably under the influence of the Romance languages (in particular Sicilian).

Dahl's approach, which is shared by other typologists and for the sake of clarity could be labeled 'purely distributional approach', has guided the compilation of the remarkable *World Atlas of Language Structures* (Oxford Univ. Press 2005). The Atlas contains many maps on a world-wide scale, each of which illustrates a specific feature, e.g. the pronominal and adnominal demonstratives which show three main types: identity, as in English [*I don't like this* and *this man*]; difference, as in French [*Donne-moi ce livre-là et garde celui-ci pour toi*]; different inflectional features, as in Turkish [*Ali bun-u*$_{\text{DEM.PRO.ACC.}}$ *unut-amı-yor* "Ali is unable to forget it" vs. *bu*$_{\text{DET}}$ *gazette-yi*$_{\text{ACC}}$ "this newspaper": see Diessel 2005: 174]. The third type, which on a world scale is instantiated only by a minority of languages, shows a strong concentration in the Caucasian area: Lezgian, Georgian, Kabardian and the not very distant Turkish and Persian languages. It is an easy guess that this relatively rare typological feature has spread from a center to the neighboring languages. If other relevant features confirmed this geographical distribution, then we could speak of a typological area. (And, indeed, Caucasian languages are often regarded as an example of a linguistic area, or 'Sprachbund'.)

As I said before, our approach is, by contrast, based on the assumption that some geographical areas are 'per se' historical-cultural – and hence also linguistic – contact-zones: we could label it as 'historical typological approach'. The task of the linguist is in this case to verify how large and deep are the isoglosses unifying the languages of a given area. This assumption is of course not without problems: how should the Mediterranean area or the Baltic one be defined? There is no doubt that Marseille, Barcelona and Beirut belong to the Mediterranean area. But what about Lyon, Madrid or Damascus? How far can we push the concept of a 'Mediterranean area'? The problem shifts again from a geographical to a more cultural-linguistic dimension. It is evident that the historical perspective may help a lot in defining the cultural and linguistic ties between Madrid or Damascus and the Mediterranean. This means that research on language contacts and linguistic areas has to be conducted by way of a bi- or pluralistic approach. This is what many contributors to the present volume have tried to do.

2. Sörés and Marchello-Nizza note also that the change in the order of the two basic elements, V and O, does not necessarily entail the Determinatum/Determinans changes which are usually hierarchically connected with the basic WO change. There are languages, like Georgian, with a VO (i.e. Determinatum+Determinans) order but Rel+N and ADJ+Standard order in comparative constructions (i.e. Determinans+Determinatum). From an areal typological point of view this is an important point, which can explain many of the typological 'inconsistencies' we find in a large number of languages.

According to this general frame, contributions span over a wide range of topics, both diachronically and synchronically, mainly focusing on morphosyntactic phenomena. Consequently, both (historical) descriptive grammars and questionnaires have been used wherever and whenever possible. This twofold approach to linguistic data is not always usual in typological research. The subject matter of each chapter reflects, of course, the main interests of the author(s). So, although the final choice of the contributions (cp. Note 1) was done according to the above mentioned key words 'areal typology' and 'linguistic area', one cannot expect to find a systematic discussion of all the aspects concerning the topics announced in the title of the volume.

We find studies concerning the evolution of the verbal structure in some ancient Indo-European and Semitic linguistic traditions, along with researches on relative clause strategies in the languages nowadays spoken in Europe. An example of the first strategy is the paper by Di Giovine, Flamini and Pozza (*The Internal Structure of Verbal Stem in the Germanic Languages*). The verb structure in the ancient languages of the I.-E. domain may be threefold, i.e. characterized either by endomorphic stems with internal morphemes (Ablaut, infixes) and/or reduplication; or by "mixed" stems (i.e. with both internal and external morphemes); or finally by exomorphic stems (i.e. only with external morphemes: suffixes, prefixes, compound tenses). Continuing a previous analysis of some eastern I.-E. languages (Vedic, epic and classical Sanskrit, Avestic and Old Persian: cp. De Angelis and Di Giovine, in press) the Authors show, on the basis of an accurate statistical calculus, that also the Germanic languages share the same shift from internal morphology of the verbal conjugation to an external one. Under this point of view also the loss of reduplication (e.g. Goth. *haíhait, faífāh, saíslēp*) can be seen as a drift towards right-suffixation, which may finally lead to compound tenses.

This is an meaningful step for placing the data into an appropriate frame, both typologically and historically – a step which could be labeled 'dynamic typology' in the Greenbergian sense. The evidence which points to a right-shift for morphemes (i.e. from endomorphism to exomorphism, up to periphrastic forms) is not limited to the verbal system, but is in keeping with a general trend of many I.-E. languages (especially VO Western European languages).

On the other hand, other papers have examined a large range of European and Mediterranean languages, instead of concentrating on the analysis of a particular (sub)family and its diachronic evolution. They have tried to sketch the present situation and map it onto the picture general cross-linguistic typological studies have acquired at the world-level. Obviously, these papers have a basically synchronic approach and are based on descriptive grammars and questionnaires.

Cristofaro and Giacalone Ramat present a general overview of the various relativization strategies found in the languages of Europe and focus on a number of semantic and pragmatic phenomena about the relativization of syntactic roles which are intrinsically less accessible to relativization, such as indirect object, possessor and oblique. Particular attention is paid to roles not included in the Accessibility Hierarchy of Keenan and Comrie 1977, namely circumstantials of time. Givón (1990: 679) has argued that time nouns occur most often as circumstantials, and thus their occurrence in relative clauses is, so to say, expected and need not be signaled by any specific morphosyntactic means.

Spanish

(1)	a.	*La*	*vez*	***que***	*fui*	*allí*	*llovió*
		the	time	REL	I.was	there	it.rained

"The time I went there it rained"

In fact, one of the primary functions of a relative clause is grounding, that is making referents relevant to the ongoing conversation by explicitly relating them to given referents in discourse. But time nouns (like the generic *la vez*) usually do not function as relevant referents and topics for further conversation. They just provide a temporal setting for the main event (in our example *llovió*). Hence, it is not so important to specify the role of the relativized item in the relative clause at the morphological level, and many strategies do not provide a syntactic specification. On the contrary in

(2)	*Todos y cada uno*	*de*	*los días*	***en***	***que***	*nos*	*vimos*	*llovió*
	each	of	the days	in	REL	RECPR	we.met	it.rained

"On each of the days we met it rained"

todos y cada uno de los dias is an important discourse topic and therefore the time reference is specified via the temporal/local preposition *en.*

Thus, Cristofaro and Giacalone argue that, more generally, the patterns observed in the relativization of time circumstantials can be accounted for in terms of the discourse relevance of the item being relativized. Typological observations lead to pragmatic and parsing strategies considerations. From the areal viewpoint it has to be noticed that the observed patterns hold for all the languages taken into account, but are implemented in different ways in individual languages. Differences reflect geographical factors, with a noticeable contrast between Western and Eastern Europe.

Complementary to Cristofaro and Giacalone's inquiry is the in-depth study by E. Roma on relativization patterns attested at various stages in the Celtic languages of the British Isles. She looks for aspects in the evolution that may be connected with contact phenomena in both the history of Celtic languages and the history of English. No relative pronoun agreeing with its antecedent in grammatical features such as Gender or Number does ever appear in Insular Celtic languages. Like many other European and non-European languages (see Jespersen 1927: III, 108–111, and Cristofaro and Giacalone, this volume), Modern Celtic Languages resorts to an analytic strategy by way of an anaphoric resumptive pronoun. Further, as far as English is concerned, gapping, as in *the man I love*, and preposition stranding as in *the man I am in love with*, have been often considered as due to Celtic substrate influence, as nothing similar can be found in Continental Indo-European languages. But the Scandinavian languages — Icelandic, Danish, Swedish and Norwegian — have this construction, and this has been considered an argument against the hypothesis of Celtic influence.

First of all, Roma notes that Celtic and English relative clause strategies have become more similar to each other during the centuries the languages have been in contact in the British Isles, though Celtic languages still maintain their peculiarities (initial mutations in the first place). Irish has grammaticalized an unstressed invariable relative particle originally made up of a demonstrative stem, and has generalized a sort of preposition stranding. English, on its turn, has spread out an invariable marker (OE *þe*, ModE *that*). In particular, the Old English strategy for temporal and locative circumstantials looks quite similar to the Welsh one: invariable particle *þe* but no resumptive pronoun:

(3) King Alfred's Orosius 5.30 (Vezzosi 1998: 227)
on þæm fiftan geare þe Marius wæs consul
on DET.SG.DAT fifth year-DAT REL M. was consul
"on the fifth year that Marius was consul"

Roma underlines an important point when discussing possible Celtic – Anglo-Saxon contacts. Consider the following example

(4) Gospels, John VII.39, Lindisfarne ms. (Northumbr.)
of gaste þone-ACC "of the spirit that...."
Gospels, John VII.39, Corpus ms. (West-Saxon)
be þam-DAT *gaste þe* "by the spirit that....."

The relative particle *þe* is invariable because an inflected demonstrative is preposed to the head noun. This restriction is unparalleled in other ancient I.-E. languages and, most importantly, in Germanic languages, where the demonstrative stem has taken up relative functions. Therefore, Roma concludes:

> "I believe this is one of the few points where Celtic influence could be worth considering, as the phenomenon is somehow restricted in time and does not seem to correspond to any language-internal drift."

As for stranding, it is the preferred option with some prepositions (*mid, on, to, ymb, in(ne)*) since the time of the oldest West-Saxon texts:

(5) AWH p. 369 (ca1065; Bourcier 1977: 286, 566)
ic kiþe eow þat ic habbe gegefen
I announce-PRS.1SG 2PL.DAT that I have-PRS.1SG give-PST.PTCP

Criste *&* *Scē* *Petre* *into* *Westmunstre*
Christ-DAT and St. Peter-DAT into W.-DAT
ðet *cotlif* *ic* *wœs* *geboran* *inne*
DET.N.SG.ACC hamlet I be-PST.1SG born in
'I proclaim to you that I have given to Christ and St. Peter in Westminster, the small village I was born in'.

The evolution of Celtic features in English proceeds Northwards and Eastwards. This is in keeping with the historical facts since the most Celtic-influenced area, excluding of course Cornwall and Wales, is in the South-West of England.

From a general point of view, i.e. in terms of language contacts, early structural transfers from Celtic into English (or, to quote another example, from Dravidian into Indo-Aryan languages) represent the expected pattern. On the other hand, Celtic loanwords in English are not as frequent as English loanwords in the Celtic languages.

I have dealt with the results both of Cristofaro / Giacalone's and Roma's inquiries in some length in order to underline how the two approaches are both complementary and necessary. We need large-scale comparisons (although in the present case they are mainly limited to European and Mediterranean languages) but also in-depth diachronic analyses based on texts. As already said above, the tools required are different but not mutually exclusive: on the one hand the researcher is in need of consulting grammars and if possible to use questionnaires to submit to native speakers. On the other hand literary written traditions play necessarily a major role.

Some other papers go along the lines sketched in Cristofaro and Giacalone. This is the case of C. Mauri's study on *Conjunctive, disjunctive and adversative constructions in Europe: Some areal considerations* which concludes also with some areal considerations and interesting maps. A large sample of European languages is analyzed with respect to non-European languages, in order to find features which might characterize Europe as a more or less homogeneous area. The outcome of the analysis is the highly interesting existence of a corrective, counterexpectative area exemplified by the German contrast

(6) a. *Ich habe viel Durst, aber ich mag keinen Orangensaft*
I have much thirst, but I like no orange-juice
"I am very thirsty, but I don't like orange juice".

versus

b. *Peter studiert nicht in seinem Zimmer, sondern spielt er im Garten*
P. studies not in his room but plays he in.the garden
"Peter is not studying in his room, but he's playing in the garden".

Other languages, too, have different markers for the corrective and the counterexpectative contrast: Basque, Spanish (but not Portuguese), Swedish, Finnish,

Estonian, Lithuanian, Russian, Bulgarian, Chechen, Rumanian, Serbo-Croatian, Hungarian. In the Central-Western part of Europe, many languages have a general adversative marker used for both the counterexpectative and the corrective contrast, like Italian (*ma*), French (*mais*), Dutch (*maar*), English (*but*), etc. However, the general conclusion is that the European area shows, in spite some internal cross-linguistic variation, a high degree of structural homogeneity in the conjunctive, disjunctive and adversative constructions, especially if compared to non-European data.

Also the analysis by Federica Da Milano on demonstratives in the languages of Europe moves along similar lines.[3]

It has to be said that members of the research groups had already been trained in this kind of analysis in previous large researches such as EUROTYP and MEDTYP:[4] in a way, the project whose fruits we present in this volume is a continuation and fusion of these two research programs. See for instance Manzelli's inquiry on the expression of inalienability and emphatic pronominal possession in European and Mediterranean languages [e.g. Maced. *majka mi moja* 'my mummy': inalienable possession; Hung. *a házam* vs. *az én házam*, Turk. *evim* vs. *benim evim* "my house", whereby the second construct expresses emphasis: "my own house"]. Manzelli considers the morphosyntactic strategies and their historical changes in languages spanning from the Scandinavia to the Mediterranean and looks also at possible connections among areally contiguous languages that belong to different language families and are often typologically distant.

Da Milano's analysis of demonstratives operates in parallel text 'corpora' (in the present case Harry Potters' translations in many languages). This is an approach with many advantages and some disadvantages. The advantages consist in that the same content (i.e. semantic) problems are tackled by different languages with their own morphosyntactic strategies: this enables contrastive analyses which may lead to interesting generalizations and/or implicative hierarchies. The disadvantages consist mainly in the risk that translations may be biased by the original text and not reflect the 'natural' strategies of the target language.

However the nowadays trendy approach to parallel texts is by no means new: for instance, there exists a long tradition of comparing the Bible in different

---

3. See also her PhD dissertation on spatial deixis in European languages, issued from the MEDTYP project (Da Milano 2005).

4. See the nine volumes published in the series 'Empirical Approaches to Language Typology' 20: EUROTYP, 1-9, Mouton de Gruyter, Berlin / New York and, respectively, *Mediterranean Languages.* Papers from the MEDTYP workshop held in Tirrenia, June 2000., ed. by P. Ramat and Th. Stolz. Brockmeyer, Bochum 2002.

languages, and in these cases the impact of the original text may be particularly strong. Though limited to a threefold comparison among Gothic, Latin and Old Church Slavonic the analysis conducted by P. Cuzzolin and S. Luraghi is firmly in this tradition. The Authors show how translations can transfer some culture-specific concepts and habits into a different culture, in which they can be integrated. They concentrate on the translations from the Greek original of a number of prepositions, and they of course underline the difference obtaining between on the one side the Latin translation which could rely on a long-standing literary tradition and, on the other side, the Gothic and Slavonic texts which had no written standard tradition to rely on. When a clear translation equivalent is not available, translators are forced to work out different strategies depending on the context. For instance, the Greek preposition *epí* is translated in many different ways. To be noted that as in the previous case of Celtic-Anglo-Saxon contacts the Authors focus on morphosyntactic structures; they are not concerned with loanwords borrowed from Greek in Latin, Gothic and Old Church Slavonic. As is well-known these three languages are plenty of Christian loanwords, but lexical borrowings are not the point in the present collection of papers: rather, its aim has been to uncover deeper possible contacts, at the level of morphology and syntax . To use the title of Cuzzolin and Luraghi's paper, it is possible mediating culture through language, even when we study morphosyntactic contact-induced facts.

The particular stress on syntactic phenomena we find in most of the papers reflects the 'state of the art' in typology.

Another kind of contrastive analysis is offered by I. M. Mirto and H. Necker who study complex noun determiners (CND) in Italian and German, whith some incursions into English. They compare constructs such as

(7) *una marea di parenti lontani* (lit.: a tide of distant relatives)

with

(8) *ein Haufen von entfernten Verwandten* (lit.: a heap of distant relatives)

both meaning "so many distant relatives" with the same structure:

(9) <DET1 N1 *of* N2>

Nouns as *marea* "tide" or *Haufen* "heap" have peculiar patterns, both syntactically and semantically. N1 (*marea*, *Haufen*) works as a function-word rather than as a content-word, i.e. they have lost their lexical meaning and are no longer referential. CNDs exist in English too and are called 'classifier constructions', 'measure noun constructions', and 'measure *phrases*'. See examples like

(10) *Tom drank a finger of whisky*

(11) *They shared a shower of honors,*

whereby

(10) b. *Tom drank a finger*

would make no sense and

(11) b. *They shared a shower*

would have a completely different meaning.

I cannot enter into the accurate discussion of the parameters which determine the semantic and syntactic behaviour of CNDs in the three languages analysed by Mirto and Necker, such as entailments, selection restrictions, verbal number agreement, lack of referentiality. But it has to be underlined the importance of an inquiry in a particular domain which has been mostly neglected in linguistic literature. It would be interesting to enlarge this kind of analysis to other Euro-Mediterranean languages.

When studying particular facts it is also possible to detect some sub-areas (see above with reference to Manzelli's inquiry). Some lesser self-evident typological phenomena are highlighted in this collection of papers, such as the Mediterranean diffusion of the prepositional accusative, i.e. the type *este abogado escondió a muchos prisioneros* "this lawyer hid many prisoners". The matter has already been discussed in a number of previous studies,[5] but without introducing the parameters which govern its distribution, as is now suggested by D. Romagno. It is commonly said that the preposition marks animate direct objects. But cases like

(12) *la nodriza educa el niño* "the nurse raises/educates the child"

versus

(13) *la nodriza ha matado al niño* "the nurse killed the child"

show that the object animacy does not suffice to predict the presence or the absence of the preposition *a*. What is different in (12) and (13) is the verb semantics: *matar* is a highly telic verb that affects its object to a high degree while *educar* is a lowly telic verb, which can also leave its object partially not affected. Object agentivity (and its being affected) is a relevant parameter for having prepositional

5. On the so-called Differential Object Marking (DOM), also considered from a diachronic point of view, see von Heusinger and Kaiser 2005, with further bibliographical references. Von Heusinger and Kaiser compare different Spanish Bible translations, from the 14th century up to *La Biblia de las Américas* (20th century): e.g. *hasta parir Ø siete* [scil. *hijos*] *la estéril* (16th and 17th cent.) vs. *Aun la estéril da a luz a siete* [scil. *hijos*] (*La Biblia de las Américas*) "She who was barren has borne seven children".

objects, along with verb telicity. A third parameter is the individualized, non-generic nature of the object. Compare

(14) *Achille ha matado a̲ Hector* "Achille killed Hector"

versus

(15) *Achille mata Ø̲ enemigos* "Achille kills enemies" (i.e he is a killer of enemies).

Moreover, Romagno rapidly has a look at the behavior of Sardinian, Sicilian, Calabrian, Maltese and also Rumanian. She finds that the three parameters which determine the presence/absence of the prepositional object marking are more or less operative in a central Mediterranean area — and Rumanian. Maltese is likely to have imported the Romance construct from Sicily (though Borg and Mifsud 2002: 36–41, mention that in Spanish Arabic we have prepositional objects. And also Biblical Aramaic and Late Biblical Hebrew, Eastern Arabic modern dialects such as Lebanese or Syriac do know prepositional objects according to more or less the same parametric constraints: human referents, saliency, individualization or personification; definiteness).

However, it is very important to observe that the same parameters operate also outside this area. Comparison with Farsi shows that object individuation, object agentivity, verbal telicity play a decisive role in the choice of the object syntactic construction. As already said, Eastern Arabic dialects, Biblical Aramaic and Late Biblical Hebrew seem to apply the same parameters. One would be inclined to think that the same cognitive parameters are operative also in distant languages.

This last observation raises a basic, not yet answered question: The problem whether the isoglosses are due to language contact or are a spontaneous typological evolution, or even a mixture of both factors, is the ever returning problem in this kind of research. I will come back to the issue at the end of this foreword.

But let us come back to the areal typological discussion. The existence of sub-areas in such large territories including Europe and the Mediterranean countries was, so to say, expected from the outset and is in keeping with the results of analogous investigations conducted in the Circum-Baltic areas[6] and even in the Circum-Mediterranean countries, which belong also to Europe (Spain, France, Italy, Greece and the Balkan area). There is no compact 'Euro-Mediterranean Sprachbund', no uninterrupted 'Euro-Mediterranean linguistic area' in the sense that the languages of this area, even if genetically unrelated, would share a significant number of contiguous structural features, not found in the neighboring languages outside this area. In other words, it is not possible to identify a general

6. See Dahl and Koptjevskaja-Tamm 2001. See also Heine / Kuteva 2005, where Meso-America and the Balkans are labeled (p. 177) 'macro-areas'.

dividing line between Euro-Mediterranean languages and languages beyond this line. However, there are a number of isoglosses involving two or more Euro-Mediterranean languages and each phenomenon has to be scrutinized independently. The linguistic continuum does not know sharp limits: e.g. Turkish, which doubtlessly belongs to the Mediterranean space, has many ties with and borrowings from Farsi, since Turkey has been in contact with the Persian culture for centuries. Consequently, the aim of this volume is not to sketch a 'typological profile of the Euro-Mediterranean languages' but simply to present and discuss features which may be typologically relevant in a cross-linguistic perspective embracing the Mediterranean and/or European languages (cp. also above on the choice of the contributions to this volume).

Some other typologically interesting facts are highlighted in the present collection of papers, which tie just some of the Euro-Mediterranean languages and delineate sub-areas of this vast territory. A. Giacalone Ramat and A. Sansò present a study concerning the indefinite *man*-constructions, as German ***Man** muss bezahlen, wenn **man** die Packung aufreisst* "One must pay if one opens the package", Swed. ***Man** gör vad **man** kan,* French ***On** fait ce qu'**on** peut* "One does what one can". Semantically, the construction is an agent defocusing strategy, i.e. it is used when the speaker wants to background the agent of an action. From the point of view of its areal distribution

> [t]he results [. . . .] show that *man*-constructions are a widespread phenomenon across Europe: these constructions show up consistently in the so-called "Charlemagne area" [as defined in the EUROTYP volumes, see van der Auwera 1998: P.R.], and tend to diffuse eastwards to West and South Slavonic languages, whereas East Slavonic languages do not present clear instances of this construction type. Moving more eastward, these constructions appear only sporadically in the languages of the Caucasus, while being absent also from Arabic varieties in the south (except [again!: P.R.] Maltese). The areal distribution of *man*-constructions allows us to consider them as a yet unnoticed areal feature of the Standard Average European area.

The more so, as on a world scale and contrary to the above discussed case of prepositional object marking, the construct seems to be quite rare.

Notice also that even inside Europe the construct seems to be recessive: historical data prove that its distribution in older times included more languages than today (especially in Germanic and Romance). For instance, Old Italian and Old English knew this construction:

(16) *Potrebbe già **l'uomo** **opporre contra me e dicere che. . .*** (Dante, *Vita Nuova*, 12, 17)
'One could in fact argue against me (i.e. against what I said) and say that. . .'

(17) *swa **man** byrð lytle cyld* = ***ut solet homo gestare parvulum filium suum*** (Deut. 1, 31)
'As a man / one bears his little child'

On the other hand, the eastward expansion towards the Slavonic area appears to be a quite recent phenomenon, and *man*-constructions in Slavonic languages are possibly an 'incipient category'. To cope with this apparent discrepancy the Authors suggest a two-wave model of diffusion, which singles out two historical periods in which the diffusion of these constructions is likely to have taken place. Thus the link between areal distribution, historical developments, and general typological considerations is explicitly affirmed: a not minor result of the inquiry.

This complex of problems is afforded by Th. Stolz who deals with the (apparent) opposition "iconicity vs. non-iconicity" on a world-wide scale. This opposition has also an areal dimension, as has been shown by Stolz himself in a previous article (Stolz 2004; cp. also Stolz and Sansò, in press): Reduplication is wide-spread among the languages of the world to express, among other things, verbal plurality, number marking etc. However, the reduplication of an adjective or an adverb to express its superlative (e.g. Port. *rico rico* "very rich", Ital. *piccolo piccolo* "very small", Alban. *rëndë-rëndë* "very serious", Sard. *abellu abellu* "very slow(ly)"=Turk. *yavaş yavaş*, Gk. *kontá kontá* "very near(ly)", spoken Arab. *El-lêle di hîja awîle awîle* "This night is very long", etc.) seems to have a Mediterranean diffusion, not shared by more Northern European languages: it is impossible to say **nice nice*, or Russian **milyĭ milyĭ* for "very nice". Also the expression of a distributive meaning via the simple reduplication of the lexeme, without building a Prepositional Phrase seems to be characteristic of the Mediterranean area (see Malt. *ħabbat bieb bieb* "to knock to every door", Turk. *alay alay gelmek* "to arrive by flocks"; Gk. *bḗma bḗma* = Ital. *passo passo* "step by step" [not **step step* !], etc.).[7] This does not mean that other languages in the world may not share this feature (cp., e.g., the Turk. example with the Quechua construct *ubiha ubiha* "a flock of sheep", collective from *ubiha* "sheep"(sing.), whose plural is *ubihakuna*). But of course it does not make sense to compare the Mediterranean with the Andes in an areal perspective. The only possible explanation is that the same semantic, cognitive strategy has been applied independently in different areas.

Thus we come back to the central problem, already alluded to. The problem of how to delimitate a typologically significant linguistic area has been tackled many times by many linguists (see Ramat 1998). S. Cristofaro (2000) clearly affords the

7. A similar picture of fragmentary diffusion which does not permit to speak of a 'Sprachbund' phenomenon has been presented by N. Grandi (2002) in the frame of the already mentioned MEDTYP program. Grandi has shown that evaluative constructions (augmentatives, diminutives, pejoratives etc.) reveal in the Mediterranean countries a not random geographical distribution, with an original spreading area to be centered in the Iberian peninsula and in the areas where Latin and Greek were spoken in ancient times. Moroccan Arabic and Berber Tamazight presumably took over evaluative constructions from Spain, whereas Maltese and the Southern Slavonic languages adopted the Latin and the Greek model.

question of what features should be considered as truly areal, how many should they be; which features should on the contrary be considered as general (natural and unmarked) typological evolution. Th. Stolz (see, among other papers, Stolz 2002 in the frame of the discussion concerning a Mediterranean 'Sprachbund') underlines the necessity of having clear-cut borders. A 'well-behaving' Sprachbund should be clearly delimited against the surrounding territories. But unfortunately this does not seem to be the case for Europe and even less for the Mediterranean.

Times have elapsed since the above quoted contributions, but the problem is still there, as evidentiated also by the already quoted volume edited by Yaron Matras et al. (2006). There is no a priory way to decide for the existence or not existence of a Sprachbund. The answer can in my opinion be found only via considering step by step individual problems and patiently putting together the pieces of the puzzle. Further inquiries will be therefore needed in order to shed more light in this much debated and crucial question. We believe that the synchronic as well as the diachronic data many articles in the present volume have made use of is the right way to come nearer to the solution. We hope that the papers of this volume may represent a further contribution to the general discussion.

A noticeable achievement of the research has been the creation of a database in order to document the typological variation across Europe and the Mediterranean: the phenomena that have been scrutinized have been stored in the so-called 'Pavia Typological Database' (PTD). This PTD is now available on the WEB (*http://www.unipv.it/paviatyp/*). The PTD is made up of different modules documenting the typological phenomena which have been studied and presented in this volume as well as other important facts which are currently under scrutiny: it is in fact an ever-growing repository which may be usefully confronted with other existing databases. A. Sansò has presented the idea, the methods and the first results of the database in various occasions. References are given below in the list of publications produced in the frame of the research project.

Finally very special thanks go to my coeditor, Elisa Roma, who shared with me the not easy task to check the final versions of the chapters, looking among other things at how much these versions accepted and took advantage of the suggestions done by the anonymous referees — or also refused them. Without her skillful and competent help the editing of this volume would have lasted many months more.

References

Bisang, W. 2006. Linguistic areas, language contact and typology: Some implications from the case of Ethiopia as a linguistic area. In Y. Matras et al. (eds), 75–98.

Borg, A. & Mifsud, M. 2002. Maltese object marking in a Mediterranean context. In P. Ramat & T. Stolz (eds), 33–46.

Bourcier, G. 1977. *Les propositions relatives en vieil-anglais.* Paris: Champion.

Cristofaro, S. 2000. Linguistic areas, typology and historical linguistics: An overview with particular respect to Mediterranean languages. In *Languages in the Mediterranean area. Typology and convergence. Il progetto MEDTYP*, S. Cristofaro & I. Putzu (eds), 65–81. Milano: FrancoAngeli.

Dahl, Ö. 2001. Principles of areal typology. In *Language typology and language universals*, M. Haspelmath , E. König, W. Oesterreicher & W. Raible (eds), Vol II: 1456–1470. Berlin: De Gruyter.

Dahl, Ö. & Koptjevskaja-Tamm, M. (eds). 2001. *Circum-Baltic languages.* 2 Vols. Amsterdam: John Benjamins.

Da Milano, F. 2005. *La deissi spaziale nelle lingue d'Europa.* Milano: FrancoAngeli.

De Angelis, A. & Di Giovine, P. In press. Il mutamento tipologico nella funzionalità dei morfemi verbali: Le lingue germaniche e l'indo-iranico. In *Typological change in the morphosyntax of the Indo-European languages, Proceedings of the congress held in Viterbo, 25–26 January 2002*, G. Banti, P. Di Giovine & P. Ramat (eds). München: Lincom.

Diessel, H. 2005. Pronominal and adnominal demonstratives. In *The world atlas of language structure*, M. Haspelmath, M.S. Dryer, D. Gil & B. Comrie (eds), 174–177. Oxford: OUP.

Givón, T. 1990. *Syntax: A functional-typological introduction.* Vol. II. Amsterdam: John Benjamins.

Grandi, N. 2002. *Morfologie in contatto. Le costruzioni valutative nelle lingue del Mediterraneo.* Milano: FrancoAngeli.

Heine, B. & Kuteva, T. 2005. *Language contact and grammatical change.* Cambridge: CUP.

Heusinger, K. von & Kaiser, G. 2005. The evolution of differential object marking in Spanish. In *Proceedings of the workshop 'Specificity and the Evolution / Emergence of Nominal Determination in Romance* [Arbeitspapier 119], K. von Heusinger et al. (eds), 33–69. Konstanz: Fachbereich Sprachwissenschaft, Univ. Konstanz.

Jespersen, O. 1922–1931. *A modern English grammar.* Heidelberg: Carl Winter.

Keenan, E. L. & Comrie, B.1977. Noun phrase accessibility and universal grammar. *Linguistic Inquiry* 8: 63–99.

Matras, Y., McMahon, A. & Vincent, N. (eds). 2006. *Linguistic areas. Convergence in historical and typological perspective.* Houndmills: Palgrave.

Ramat, P. 1998. Typological comparison and linguistic areas: Some introductory remarks. *Language Sciences* 20: 227–240.

Ramat, P. & Stolz, T. (eds) 2002. *Mediterranean languages. Papers from the MEDTYP workshop, Tirrenia, June 2000.* Bochum: Universitätsverlag Brockmeyer.

Sörés, A. & Marchello-Nizza, C. 2005. Typologie diachronique: Une nouvelle hypothèse pour le changement de type "OV" > "VO". In *Linguistique typologique*, G. Lazard & C. Moyse-Faurie (eds), 261–287. Villeneuve d'Ascq: Presses Universitaires Septentrion.

Stolz, T. 2002. No *Sprachbund* beyond this line! On the age-old discussion of how to define a linguistic area. In P. Ramat & T. Stolz (eds), 259–281.

Stolz, T. 2004. A new Mediterraneism. Word iteration in areal perspective. *Mediterranean Language Review* 15: 1–47.

Stolz, T. and Sansò, A. In press. The Mediterranean area revisited. Word-iteration as a potential Mediterraneism. *Orbis.*

van der Auwera, J. 1998. Conclusion. In *Adverbial constructions in the languages of Europe*, J. van der Auwera (ed.), 813–836. Berlin: de Gruyter.

Vezzosi, L. 1998. *La sintassi della subordinazione in anglosassone.* Perugia: Edizioni Scientifiche Italiane.

Other publications which derive from the research project 'Europa e Mediterraneo dal punto di vista linguistico: storia e prospettive' (stand as 31st December 2006):

1. Benedetti, M. 2005. Dispersioni formali del medio indoeuropeo. In *Acquisizione e mutamento di categorie linguistiche.* Atti del Convegno Internaz. della Società Ital. di Glottologia (Perugia, ottobre 2003). Roma, Il Calamo: 95–119.
2. Da Milano, F. 2005. *La deissi spaziale nelle lingue d'Europa* [Materiali linguistici 51]. Milano: FrancoAngeli.
3. Da Milano, F. 2004. Le domande sì/no nelle lingue del Mediterraneo. *Archivio Glottol. Ital.* 89: 3–40.
4. Da Milano, F. In press. Demonstratives in parallel texts: A case study. *Sprachtypologie und Universalienforschung*, special issue: *Parallel texts: Using translational equivalents in linguistic typology*, M. Cysouw & B. Wälchli (eds).
5. Da Milano, F. Forthcoming. The systems of demonstratives in the languages of Europe from a typological point of view. In M. Miestamo & B. Wälchli (eds), *TypDiss.*
6. De Angelis, A. 2004. Forme di «tmesi» nel greco omerico, la legge di Wackernagel, e un caso di rianalisi sintattica. In *Dialetti, dialettismi, generi letterari e funzioni sociali*, G. Rocca (a c. di), Atti del V Colloquio Intern. di Linguistica greca, Alessandria, Edizioni dell'Orso: 179–214.
7. Lazzeroni, R. 2005. Fra mondo indiano e mondo mediterraneo: categorie scalari e gradi di comparazione. *Archivio Glottol. Ital.* 90: 3–18.
8. Lazzeroni, R. 2006. La codifica dell'allativo in greco e in ittita. Contributo allo studio di un'area linguistica circumegea. *Archivio Glottol. Ital.* 91: 106–111.
9. Luraghi, S. In press. Possessive constructions in Anatolia, Hurrian, Urartean, and Armenian as evidence for language contact. In Proceedings of the International Conference *Hittites and their Neighbors* (Atlanta, Sept. 2004).
10. Luraghi, S. In press. The evolution of local cases and their grammatical equivalent in Greek and Latin. In *The role of semantics and pragmatics in the development of case*, J. Barðdal & S. Celliah (eds). Amsterdam: John Benjamins.
11. Mauri, C. (2006). Combinazione e contrasto: i connettivi congiuntivi e avversativi nelle lingue d'Europa. *Archivio Glottol. Ital.* 91: 166–202.
12. Meini, L. 2004. Le interrogative indirette con *si* in latino: Modello greco o sviluppo autonomo? *Studi e Saggi Linguistici* 42: 153–171.
13. Pieroni, S. 2004. Lat. *iste*: alla ricerca di una pertinenza. In *Per Alberto Nocentini. Ricerche linguistiche*, A. Parenti (a c. di), 167–188. Firenze : Alinea.
14. Pieroni, S. In press. Per un ordinamento paradigmatico dei dimostrativi. Spunti dal latino. In *Atti della giornata di Linguistica latina (Venezia, maggio 2004).*
15. Romagno, D. 2005. La codificazione degli attanti nel Mediterraneo romanzo: Accordo del participio e marcatura dell'oggetto. *Archivio Glottol. Ital.* 90: 90–113.
16. Romagno, D. 2006. Gradiente di transitività e codifica dell'oggetto. Dall'accusativo preposizionale al partitivo. *Archivio Glottol. Ital.* 91: 203–222.
17. Rovai, F. 2005. L'estensione dell'accusativo in latino tardo e medievale. *Archivio Glottol. Ital.* 90: 54–89.
18. Rovai, F. In press. Manifestazioni di sub-sistemi tipologici attivi in latino. *Archivio Glottol. Ital.*
19. Sansò, A. 2003. Typological databases: A new approach. In *Proceedings of the 17me Congrès International des Linguistes ('CIL 17')*, E. Hajičová, A. Kotěšovcová & J. Mírovský (eds), Prague: Matfyzpress. (CD-ROM).

20. Sansò, A. 2004. MED-TYP: A typological database for Mediterranean languages. In *Proceedings of the 4th International Conference on Language Resources and Evaluation* (LREC 2004: Lisboa, May 2006), M.T. Lino et al. (eds), 1157–1160. Lisboa: Porto Editora.
21. Sansò, A. In press. Documenting variation across Europe and the Mediterranean. The Pavia typological database. In *Proceedings of the 5th International Conference on Language Resources and Evaluation* (LREC 2006: Genova, May 2006).

Trends in the diachronic development of Semitic verbal morphology*

Giorgio Banti

Five languages belonging to two different Semitic language groups, namely Koranic Arabic, Egyptian Cairene Arabic, Maltese, Geᶜez and Harari are examined in order to assess the diachronic development of three areas of their verbal morphology: (a) how many inflectional classes can be distinguished in the Basic Form and in different derived forms, (b) how many stems they have for marking tense and mood distinctions, and (c) how the Imperfect and Jussive inflectional prefixes are vocalized. Because of the complexity of Semitic verbal systems, only the Basic Form and the derived D-, L-, *t*D- and *t*L-forms of strong triradical roots are examined.

Within this strictly defined sample of languages and inflectional paradigms, a marked difference is observed between how the Arabic languages and the Ethio-Semitic ones develop through time in the three above areas.

1. Introduction

The development through time of a specific area of Semitic verbal morphology, namely the internal vowel alternations that mark the main tenses and moods, is discussed in this paper in the typological perspective originally set out at least by Sapir (1921) and recently developed by Di Giovine and others (De Angelis and Di Giovine in print; Di Giovine, Flamini and Pozza in print) for Indo-European verbs. According to this approach, a typological distinction is drawn between stem-internal or "endomorphic" morphological processes such as vowel alternations, infixation, or reduplication, and stem-external or "exomorphic" morphological processes that rely on suffixation, prefixation, or multi-word morphology,

* The author thanks all those who helped him with their advice and their patience in preparing this paper. The following people deserve a particular mention: Riccardo Contini, Paolo di Giovine, Paolo Ramat, and the two anonymous referees who made their comments on this paper prior to its being accepted for publication. Obviously, only this author should be blamed for any mistake or misunderstanding.

i.e., compound tenses. Indo-European verbs typically behave synchronically in varied ways, but a clear-cut trend can be observed through time, from the older languages where verbs with stem-internal morphology occur more frequently, to the younger languages where stem-external morphology prevails and verbs with endomorphic stems are reduced to a small and generally non-productive class, that is frequently treated as "irregular" in grammatical decriptions.

Semitic verbs behave in this regard in a more uniform way, in the sense that the sort of variation they display depends from the class of their roots: "strong" (i.e., regular) triradical roots, "strong" quadriradical roots, "weak" roots with *w* and *y* as their first consonant (I*w* and I*y* roots), as their second consonant (II*w* and II*y* roots), or as their third consonant (III*w* and III*y* roots), "weak" roots with similar second and third consonants (II = III roots aka roots *secundae geminatae*), or minor language-specific classes such as "weak" roots with *n* as their first consonant (I*n* roots) in East and West Semitic, etc. (cf. Goldenberg 1994, 1997, 2005; Ratcliffe 1998). The verbs that belong to each of these classes behave basically in the same way within each language, and even the sort of variation that occurs across different classes of roots does not involve typological differences. For instance, Koranic Arabic strong triradical roots like *QTL* 'kill' have the same stem before vocalic suffixes like *-a* and *-u* as well as before consonantal suffixes like 3.f.pl. *-na*, while weak II*w* roots like *QWL* 'say' have different stems in these cases, e.g., *qāl-* before vocalic *-a* but *qul-* before consonantal *-na* in the Active Perfect, and *-qūl-* before vocalic *-u* but *-qul-* before consonantal *-na* in the Active Imperfect.

(1) Koranic Arabic: "strong" triradical root *QTL* 'kill', "weak" II*w* root *QWL* 'say'

Active Perfect

3.sg.m.	*qatal-a* 'he killed'	*qāl-a* 'he said'
3.pl.f.	*qatal-na* 'they (f.) killed'	*qul-na* 'they (f.) said'

Passive Perfect

3.sg.m.	*qutil-a* 'he was killed'	*qīl-a* 'he was said'
3.pl.f.	*qutil-na* 'they (f.) were killed'	*qil-na* 'they (f.) were said'

Active Imperfect

3.sg.m.	*ya-qtul-u* 'he kills'	*ya-qūl-u* 'he says'
3.pl.f.	*ya-qtul-na* 'they (f.) kill'	*ya-qul-na* 'they (f.) say'

Passive Imperfect

3.sg.m.	*yu-qtal-u* 'he is killed'	*yu-qāl-u* 'he is said'
3.pl.f.	*yu-qtal-na* 'they (f.) are killed'	*yu-qal-na* "they (f.) are said'

Accordingly, it is not possible to distinguish verbs with a (prevailingly) stem-internal morphology from verbs with a (prevailingly) stem-external morphology in a Semitic language. Yet it is possible to assess whether a stem-internal morphological feature in an early attested Semitic language also occurs in a later attested language of the same linguistic group, or is replaced by a stem-external one. For instance, internal passives like Koranic Arabic *qutila* 'he was killed' in (1) and *kutiba* 'it was written' in (2.a) have disappeared in many modern Arabic dialects, cf. Fischer and Jastrow (1980), Durand (1995). Among them, Maltese now uses for the passive either the derived verb *inkiteb* – i.e., the *n*G- or 7th form that is derived by prefixing *n*- to the root – or multi-word constructions like *kien miktub* in (2.c), formed by the Perfect of 'be' and the Passive Participle of the lexical verb. (Maltese even has passive multi-word constructions like *ġie miktub* 'it was written', lit. 'it came written', with the Perfect of 'come').

(2) a. Koranic Arabic
Kutiba *^{c}alay-kum aṣ-ṣiyāmu.*
it.was.written.PASS for-you the-fasting
'Fasting has been prescribed for you' (lit. 'it has been written for you the fasting'). (*Kor.* 2,183)

b. Maltese
Il-ktieb inkiteb.
the-book it.was.written
'The book was written.'

c. Maltese
Il-ktieb kien miktub mitt sena ilu.
the-book it.was written one.hundred year ago
'The book was written one hundred years ago.'

Derived verbs of the *n*G-form also occur in Koranic Arabic, usually as reflexive-passive derivatives from transitive verbs, but the loss of internal passives like *kutiba* is a clear instance of loss of stem-internal morphology, just as the development of phrases like *kien miktub* and *ġie miktub* into full-fledged passive forms is an instance of stem-external morphology. As already pointed out above, many other modern Arabic dialects don't have internal passives and use derived verbs like Maltese *inkiteb* (*n*G-form) or Cairene Arabic *'itkatab* (*t*G-form, a derived form that does not occur in Koranic Arabic) as their major passive forms. This can be construed as an instance of shift from stem-internal morphology to a more stem-external one, since the two derived verbs are formed by extending the root by means of a prefix, respectively *n*- and *t*-, rather than by internal vowel change. However, it can be argued that only Maltese developed multi-word passives like *kien miktub* 'it was written' or *ġie miktub* 'id.', under the influence of Romance multi-word passives like Italian *fu scritto* and *venne scritto* (cf. e.g., Aquilina 1979: 97).

This paper is going to discuss the diachronic development of internal tense and mood vowel alternations in languages belonging to two groups of Semitic languages, namely Arabic and Ethio-Semitic. In doing so, it will also try to assess whether typologically different development paths can be linked to the different histories of language contacts they have had. For both groups there are well-documented languages from the middle of the 1st millennium CE, respectively Koranic Arabic and Ge^{c}ez. The first, namely Arabic as it is attested in the Koran, is a literary language of the 6th–7th centuries CE that was canonized in the subsequent three centuries. Indeed it was only with Ibn Mujāhid (d. 936 CE) that fixed and complete versions of the Koran became available (for further details cf., e.g., Owens 2006: 5 ff.). Koranic Arabic is thus certainly different from how the people of the northern Arabian Peninsula spoke in their ordinary lives in the 6th and 7th centuries, even though it is not easy to tell exactly how much it differed (cf. Fischer 1982 a and 1982 b, and especially Owens 2006 for an updated assessment of the question). Geᶜez, on the other hand, is the language of the great inscriptions of the Axumite kings who ruled in northern Ethiopia between the 3rd and the 6th centuries CE, and of the Christian literature that flourished there starting from the 4th century. It became the classical language of the Ethiopian Church that still uses it as its liturgical language, but there are no reasons for thinking it to have differed substantially from the spoken language of the Axum area in its earliest centuries. Koranic Arabic and Geᶜez cannot be taken as the direct ancestors *strictu senso* of the modern Arabic dialects and, respectively, of the modern Ethio-Semitic languages. Indeed, these originated from spoken varieties, not from the literary and written ones, and there are good reasons for thinking (a.) that there was a good deal of variation in spoken pre-diasporic Arabic of the 6th–7th centuries out of which the modern Arabic dialects that are spoken today developed in the subsequent centuries. As for Geᶜez, (b.) several authors have shown that, on the one hand, its earliest documents display a considerable degree of variation that was levelled out later when it was normalized as the classical written language of Christian Ethiopia (cf. Bausi 2005) and, on the other hand, especially southern Ethio-Semitic displays a number of divergent features that cannot be derived directly from Geᶜez and have to be construed as indicating that the language or group of varieties from which at least part of the modern Ethio-Semitic languages developed was partly different from Geᶜez (cf. Garbini 1972, Goldenberg 1977). Nevertheless, these two well-attested old languages will be taken here as representatives of the earliest documented stages of the two language groups. Indeed, they appear to have been considerably more similar to each other than any modern Arabic dialect now is to any modern Ethio-Semitic language.

As representatives of the contemporary stages of these two language groups, two well-described Mediterranean Arabic dialects shall be taken into consideration here, i.e., Cairene Arabic and Maltese, together with Harari, the south-easternmost Ethio-Semitic language. The main substrate language of Cairene Arabic has been Coptic, that was still strongly VSO like the older stages of Ancient Egyptian. In its inflectional morphology Coptic was a noun incorporating language, and still had many processes that involved stem-internal vowel alternations; for instance, the strong biliteral verb *kōt* 'build' had a qualitative (aka stative) *kēt*, the strong triradical verb *rōht* 'strike' had instead a qualitative *raht*, etc. (cf. e.g., Reintges

2004: 204 ff.). Coptic verb morphology had been thoroughly renewed in the first millennium BCE, and verbs occurred just with two or, in some instances, three different stems, while most inflectional morphology involved chains of prefixed and, more rarely, suffixed morphemes that had developed through the grammaticalization of inflected auxiliaries, pronouns, particles, etc. During the Middle Ages and still now Cairo has been a major cultural hub, and has attracted people from all over the Arabic-speaking world and beyond. Several other varieties of spoken Arabic, as well as Turkish have thus been adstrate languages for Cairene Arabic, while Classical Arabic has been acting as a superstrate language ever since the arrival of Islam to Egypt. Maltese instead, as argued by Brincat (2003), probably has had no substrate language at all, because the archipelago was almost completely depopulated when Arabic-speaking groups arrived in the 9th century. Yet from the end of the 11th century Malta has been politically separated from north Africa, and its population was converted to Christianity. As a result of this Maltese has not had Classical Arabic as a superstrate language during the last thousand years, but displays the effects of massive contact with Sicilian and written Italian as adstrate and superstrate languages. Since 1800, when Malta became first a British protectorate and after some years a part of the British Empire, also English has acted upon Maltese as an adstrate and superstrate language.

On the other hand, Harari is the language of the urban population of the walled city of Harar in eastern Ethiopia, that has been the major centre of Islamic learning in the Horn of Africa for the last five centuries. The language is known in two historical stages: Old Harari in poetic and prosa texts written in Arabic script since the 16th century, and modern Harari spoken today in Harar and by the Harari diaspora in other Ethiopian cities and abroad. Cerulli (1936: 440) argued that Harari had a "sostrato Sidama" that could be easily identified in its lexicon "dove le parole di origine Sidama sono molte e concernono concetti fondamentali". Leslau (1963: 11) confirmed the presence of a sizable amount of "Eastern Sidamo" words, but these etymologies have not been checked yet in the light of the present much better knowledge of the Cushitic lexicon, in order to assess whether they are really to be identified as Highland East Cushitic (HEC) etyma as Cerulli and Leslau claimed. The nearest HEC language is now spoken ca. 400 km south-west of Harar, but the present distribution of languages in central Ethiopia is largely the result of two major events of the 14th, 15th and 16th centuries CE. The first of them were the long wars between Christian and Moslem states, that culminated in the campaigns of the Moslem leader Aḥmad bin Ibrāḥīm al-Ġāzī, also known as the *Grañ* 'the Lefthanded' (d. 1543). These wars devastated and depopulated large stretches of central Ethiopia and weakened both the Christian and the Moslem states. The second major event was the ensuing spread of Oromo-speaking groups into central, western and eastern Ethiopia, who assimilated much of the pre-existing local populations.

The present distribution of the Gurage and HEC languages as compact clusters in south-central Ethiopia is probably a result of these two major events. Another one is the virtual disappearance of the Ḥarla, who are mentioned as one of the major ethnic groups of eastern Ethiopia in historical sources of the 14th, 15th and especially 16th centuries. All the HEC languages are now consistently SOV languages, and there are no reasons for thinking that they were not so in the past. In the last five centuries Harari has been surrounded mainly by Oromo and Somali, two typologically inconsistent East Cushitic languages that have an SOV order at clause level, but N-GEN, N-ADJ, and N-REL linear orders within NP's. In their inflectional morphology, both the HEC languages and Oromo have no stem-internal vowel alternations: their stems are only subject to reduplication and to sandhi rules at their junctures with the inflectional morphemes, that tend to cluster to the right of them. For instance, the Eastern Oromo verb *dhuuguu* 'drink' has in its Perfect 3.SG.M. *dhuug-e*, 3.SG.F. *dhuuyd-de*, 1.PL. *dhuuyn-ne*, in its Imperfect 3.SG.M. *dhuug-a*, 3.SG.F. *dhuuyd-di*, 1.PL. *dhuuyn-na*, etc., all from the stem *dhuug-* (cf. Owens 1985: 70). Somali has instead several cases of internal vowel alternations, beside frequent occurrences of reduplication both to the left and to the right of stems; yet a majority of its verbs are inflected as in Oromo and in the HEC languages, i.e., with an invariable stem followed by inflectional morphemes. Harari has also been in contact with other southern Ethio-Semitic languages, especially Argobba that survived until the 19th century in a cluster of settlements to the south and west of Harar, and Amharic that acquired a strong adstrate and superstrate role after the city was conquered by Menelik in 1887 and incorporated into the Ethiopian empire. Arabic has been however the major superstrate language for Harari already in its early stages, as shown by the presence of scores of Arabic words already in the earliest Old Harari texts.

2. The development of internal vowel alternations in Arabic and Ethio-Semitic

It is well known that the Semitic languages have a complex system of verb derivation whereby several derived forms – also known as "verbal stems", "verbal measures", Arabic *'awzān*, or Hebrew *binyānīm* – are obtained from a primary verb, noun or adjective by different procedures such as geminating the second root consonant, adding a *t* before or after the first root consonant, adding an *n* before the first root consonant, etc., or combinations of them. The system changes according to the language and in different stages of the same language, cf. Contini (in print). Some examples of the main nine verbal forms of Koranic Arabic are given in (3), cf. Penrice (1873) and ᶜAbd al-Bāqī (1995). It should be noted that no root actually has all the theoretically possible derived forms, and that internal passives can be formed from all the nine forms listed below. (Even from intransitive verbs it is always possible to form an internal passive used as as an impersonal form, like *Kor.* 11,110 *fa-ḫtulifa fī-hi* 'but people disagreed about it', lit. 'but-it.was.disagreed about-it').

(3) The main verbal forms of Koranic Arabic

Basic Form (aka Form I, Grundstamm, G)	*kataba* 'write'; *ᶜalima* 'know'.
Doubled Form (aka Form II, Doppelungsstamm, D)	*ᶜallama* 'teach' ← *ᶜalima* G 'know'; *ġallaqa* 'close several things' ← *ġalaqa* G 'close'.
Long-Vowel Form (aka Form III, Langvokalstamm, L)	*qātala* 'fight' ← *qatala* G 'kill'; *kātaba* 'give a slave a contract of freedom' ← *kataba* G 'write'.
Causative Form (aka Form IV, C)	*'aḫraǧa* 'bring out, cast forth' ← *ḫaraǧa* G 'go out, go forth'; *'aṣlaḥa* 'pacify' ← *ṣulḥ* n. 'peace'.
Doubled Form with *t*- prefix (aka Form V, *t*D)	*taᶜ allama* 'know (because one has been taught)' ← *ᶜallama* D 'teach'; *takabbara* 'be proud, regard oneself as big' ← *kabbara* D 'regard as big, praise'.
Long-Vowel Form with *t*-prefix (aka Form VI, *t*L)	*taqātala* 'fight among each other' ← *qātala* L 'fight'; *takātaba* 'write to each other' ← *kataba* G 'write'.
Form with *n*- prefix (aka Form VII, *n*G)	*'insalaḫa* 'be taken away from, come to an end' ← *salaḫa* G 'take away from';
Form with -*t*- infix (aka Form VIII, G*t*)	*'iǧtamaᶜa* 'come together, meet' ← *ǧamaᶜa* G 'bring together, join'.
Form with *st*- prefix (aka Form X, *st*G)	*'istaḫraǧa* 'take out, take forth' ← *'aḫraǧa* C 'bring out, cast forth'; *'istaġfara* 'ask someone's pardon' ← *ġafara* G 'pardon'.

It appears that in the G-form the root consonants undergo no modification as in *ᶜalima.* In the D-form the second root consonant is geminated, e.g., *ᶜallama*; it is basically an intensive and a factitive-causative form. The L-form has a long *ā* between the first and the second root consonants, e.g., *kātaba*; it is frequently a reciprocal form. The C-form has in Arabic an *'a*- prefix in the perfect, e.g., *'a-ḫraǧa*; it is generally a causative-factitive form. The *n*G-form has an *n*- before the first root consonant, as in *'in-salaḫa*; it generally is a reflexive-passive form. The G*t*-form has a -*t*- infixed after the first root consonant, as in *'iǧ-t-amaᶜa*; it is generally a reflexive or middle form. Three forms combine two derivational marks. The *t*D is a reflexive or middle form with *t*- prefixed to the D-form, e.g., *ta-ᶜallama*; the *t*L is a reflexive or middle form with *t*- prefixed to the L-form, e.g., *taqātala.* The *st*G-form is etymologically a C*t*-form derived from a causative with the old *s*- prefix that is well attested in other Semitic languages; it is generally a reflexive-causative form whose precise nuance of meaning varies considerably according to the semantics of the individual root. For instance, the *st*G-verb *'ista-ḫrağa* 'take out, take forth' has a clear semantic connection with the C-verb *'a-ḫrağa* 'bring out, cast forth'.

Each of the different verbal forms has its own inflectional patterns, that frequently also vary according to the class of the verb root. For instance, the C-form of a III*w* weak root inflects differently from the C-form of a strong root. For obvious reasons it is not possible to look here into all the derived forms of all the root classes of the five languages that are discussed in this paper. Rather, only the G-, D-, L-, *t*D- and *t*L-forms of strong triradical roots shall be examined. These five forms are well attested not only in Koranic Arabic, in Cairene Arabic and in Maltese, but also in Geᶜez and in Harari. It shall be seen, however, that in Harari two of them developed along their own ways. It has also to be pointed out that the derivational opposition between G-, D- and L-forms had been lost in Ethio-Semitic already in its earliest attestations: Geᶜez D- and L-verbs lack a G-form from which they may be derived, and have to be regarded as primary verbs from which *t*- and other forms are derived. Nevertheless, the D- and L-forms, as well as the *t*D- and *t*L-forms, are inflectionally different from the G-form in Ethio-Semitic. In addition to this the Ethio-Semitic languages don't have internal passives such as Koranic Arabic *kutiba* 'it has been written'.

Whatever the class of their root, Arabic verbs oppose in the inflectional paradigms of several forms a perfect stem (Pf-stem), an imperfect/jussive stem (ImpfJu-stem), and an imperative stem (Impt-stem). The Pf-stem occurs in the Perfect, that is inflected by means of person suffixes. The ImpfJu-stem occurs in the Imperfect, the Subjunctive, the Jussive, and the two Imperfect Energetic tenses. (i.e., Energetic I, Energetic II), whereas the Impt-stem is used in the Imperative, the Imperative Energetic I, and Imperative Energetic II. The tenses and moods with the ImpfJu-stem are inflected by means of person prefixes and suffixes; the Impt-stem takes only person suffixes. In Cairene Arabic and Maltese this general pattern remains unchanged, even though all the Energetic tenses and the distinction between Imperfect, Subjunctive and Jussive are lost. For obvious reasons of space, only the Perfect, the Imperfect, the Jussive and the Imperative of a Koranic Arabic G-verb of a strong triliteral root like *KTB* 'write' are given in (4.a), while the Perfect, the Imperfect – also used in contexts where Koranic Arabic uses the Subjunctive and the Jussive – and the Imperative of the same verb in Cariene Arabic and in Maltese are shown in (4.b) and (4.c).

Differently from Arabic, the Ethio-Semitic languages have two different stems in their Imperfect vs. their Jussive (notice that the Jussive is often improperly called Subjunctive in Geᶜez grammars), e.g., Geᶜez *-lammǝd-* Impf-stem with geminated second root consonant and *-a-ǝ-* vowels, vs. *-lmad-* Ju-stem with *-CCVC-* syllabic structure and an *a* vowel, that alternates with *ǝ* in other G-stem classes.

Harari lost distinctive consonant gemination, but still distinguishes an Impf-stem *-lamdi-* from a Ju-stem *-lmad-*. The Impf-stem has a *CVCCi* syllable structure, *a* after its first root consonant and final non-palatalising *-i* in forms that don't have the inflectional suffixes 2.SG.F. *-i* or 2-3.PL. *-u*; the Ju-stem has a *-CCVC-* syllable structure and *a* after its second root consonant. Having separate stems in the Imperfect and the Jussive is usually regarded as an archaism, because it also occurs in Akkadian, in traces in Biblical Hebrew, and in the Modern South Arabian languages (cf. Marrassini 2003 and Voigt 2004 most recently, *pace* Cohen 1959 and 1984). The Imperative in Geᶜez and Harari has a stem that is apparently a phonologically conditioned alternant of the Ju-stem, because both languages don't allow two-consonant clusters at the beginnings of words, nor three-consonant clusters word-internally; accordingly, Harari alternates *yalmad* 'he should learn!' with *a-ylimad* 'he should not learn!' with the same stem *-limad* as the Imperative *limad* 'learn!'. (Notice that the Harari Jussive 2.SG. and 2.PL. only occur in negative forms with the prefix *a-*, like *a-tlimad* 'you should not learn!, etc.). But for the opposition between an Imperfect stem (Impf-stem) and a Jussive stem (Ju-stem) the inflectional systems of Geᶜez and Harari are not much different from the Arabic ones, as shown in (4.d) and (4.e). It should also be pointed out here that the alternatons between *lamad-*, *lamat-* and *lamaš-* in the Harari Pf-stem are due to sandhi with the initial consonants of the suffixes. Palatal *ǧ* in Harari 2.SG.F. like *tilamǧi* is due to a more complex palatalization of *d* and other coronals induced by the inherited *-i*-suffix (cf. Geᶜez *təlammədi* etc.). This palatalisation may also affect the first or second root consonant as in *tišabri* 'you (f.) break' *vs. tisabri* 'you (m.) break', *tikačbi* 'you (f.) write' vs. *tikatbi* 'you (m.) write', or even *tišaǧǧi* 'you (f.) prostrate' vs. *tisagdi* 'you (m.) prostrate' (cf. Leslau 1958: 18, 26).

(4) a. Koranic Arabic Perfect, Imperfect, Jussive and Imperative of *kataba* 'write' (active G-form, strong root)

	Perfect	Imperfect	Jussive	Imperative
1.SG.	***katab**-tu*	*'a-**ktub**-u*	*'a-**ktub***	
2.SG.M.	***katab**-ta*	*ta-**ktub**-u*	*ta-**ktub***	***'uktub***
2.SG.F.	***katab**-ti*	*ta-**ktub**-īna*	*ta-**ktub**-ī*	***'uktub**-ī*
3.SG.M.	***katab**-a*	*ya-**ktub**-u*	*ya-**ktub***	
3.SG.F.	***katab**-at*	*ta-**ktub**-u*	*ta-**ktub***	
2.DU.	***katab**-tumā*	*ta-**ktub**-āni*	*ta-**ktub**-ā*	***'uktub**-ā*
3.DU.M.	***katab**-ā*	*ya-**ktub**-āni*	*ya-**ktub**-ā*	
3.DU.F.	***katab**-atā*	*ta-**ktub**-āni*	*ta-**ktub**-ā*	
1.PL.	***katab**-nā*	*na-**ktub**-u*	*na-**ktub***	
2.PL.M.	***katab**-tum*	*ta-**ktub**-ūna*	*ta-**ktub**-ū*	***'uktub**-ū*
2.PL.F.	***katab**-tunna*	*ta-**ktub**-na*	*ta-**ktub**-na*	***'uktub**-na*
3.PL.M.	***katab**-ū*	*ya-**ktub**-ūna*	*ya-**ktub**-ū*	
3.PL.F.	***katab**-na*	*ya-**ktub**-na*	*ya-**ktub**-na*	

b. Cairene Arabic Perfect, Imperfect (also used as Jussive) and Imperative of *katab* 'write' (G-form, strong root)

	Perfect	Imperfect (/Jussive)	Imperative
1.SG.	***katab***-*t*	*'a*-***ktib***	
2.SG.M.	***katab***-*t*	*ti*-***ktib***	***'iktib***
2.SG.F.	***katab***-*ti*	*ti*-***ktib***-*i*	***'iktib***-*i*
3.SG.M.	***katab***	*yi*-***ktib***	
3.SG.F.	***katab***-*it*	*ti*-***ktib***	
1.PL.	***katab***-*na*	*ni*-***ktib***	
2.PL.	***katab***-*tu*	*ti*-***ktib***-*u*	***'iktib***-*u*
3.PL.	***katab***-*u*	*yi*-***ktib***-*u*	

c. Maltese Perfect, Imperfect (also used as Jussive) and Imperative of *kiteb* 'write' (G-form, strong root)

	Perfect	Imperfect (/Jussive)	Imperative
1.SG.	***ktib***-*t*	*ni*-***kteb***	
2.SG.	***ktib***-*t*	*ti*-***kteb***	***ikteb***
3.SG.	***kiteb***	*ji*-***kteb***	
3.SG.F.	***kitb***-*et*	*ti*-***kteb***	
1.PL.	***ktib***-*na*	*ni*-***ktb***-*u*	
2.PL.	***ktib***-*tu*	*ti*-***ktb***-*u*	***iktb***-*u*
3.PL.	***kitb***-*u*	*ji*-***ktb***-*u*	

d. Ge^{c}ez Perfect, Imperfect, Jussive and Imperative of *lamada* 'be accustomed to, learn' (G-form, strong root)

	Perfect	Imperfect	Jussive	Imperative
1.SG.	***lamad***-*ku*	*'ə*-***lamməd***	*'ə*-***lmad***	
2.SG.M.	***lamad***-*ka*	*tə*-***lamməd***	*tə*-***lmad***	***ləmad***
2.SG.F.	***lamad***-*ki*	*tə-lamməd-i*	*tə*-***lmad***-*i*	***ləmad***-*i*
3.SG.M.	***lamad***-*a*	*yə*-***lamməd***	*yə*-***lmad***	
3.SG.F.	***lamad***-*at*	*tə*-***lamməd***	*tə*-***lmad***	
1.PL.	***lamad***-*na*	*nə*-***lamməd***	*nə*-***lmad***	
2.PL.M.	***lamad***-*kəmu*	*tə*-***lamməd***-*u*	*tə*-***lmad***-*u*	***ləmad***-*u*
2.PL.F.	***lamad***-*kən*	*tə*-***lamməd***-*ā*	*tə*-***lmad***-*ā*	***ləmad***-*ā*
3.PL.M.	***lamad***-*u*	*yə-lamməd-u*	*yə*-***lmad***-*u*	
3.PL.F.	***lamad***-*ā*	*yə*-***lamməd***-*ā*	*yə*-***lmad***-*ā*	

e. Harari Perfect, Imperfect, Jussive and Imperative of *lamada* 'be accustomed to, study' (G-form, strong root)

	Perfect	Imperfect	Jussive	Imperative
1.SG.	***lamat***-*ḫu*	*i*-***lamd***-*i*	*na*-***lmad*** ~ -*n*-***limad***	
2.SG.M.	***lamat***-*ḫi*	*ti*-***lamd***-*i*	-*t*-***limad***	***limad***
2.SG.F.	***lamaš***-*ši*	*ti*-***lamǧ***-*i*	-*t*-***limaǧ***-*i*	***limaǧ***-*i*
3.SG.M.	***lamad***-*a*	*yi*-***lamd***-*i*	*ya*-***lmad*** ~ -*y*-***limad***	
3.SG.F.	***lamat***-*ti*	*ti*-***lamd***-*i*	*ta*-***lmad*** ~ -*t*-***limad***	
1.PL.	***lamad***-*na*	*ni*-***lamd***-*i*	*na*-***lmad*** ~ -*n*-***limad***	
2.PL.	***lamat***-*ḫu*	*ti*-***lamd***-*u*	-*t*-***limad***-*u*	***limad***-*u*
3.PL.	***lamad***-*u*	*yi*-***lamd***-*u*	*ya*-***lmad***-*u* ~ -*y*-***limad***-*u*	

2.1 The development of internal vowels in the G-forms of strong triradical roots

Koranic Arabic verbs don't occur only with *-a-a-* vowels – like *kataba* 'he wrote' – in the Pf-stems of their active G-forms: some transitive action verbs like *šariba* 'drink' and several stative and psychological verbs like *ḥasiba* 'suppose' have *i* as their second stem vowel, and a number of stative-qualitative verbs have *u* like *ḥasuna* 'be nice, be beautiful'. The ImpfJu-stems of the active G-forms from strong roots may occur with either *a*, *i* or *u* as their stem vowels, but there are some general trends that can be observed: Pf-stems with the pattern *CaCaC-* like *katab-* have frequently ImpfJu-stems with the pattern *-CCuC-* like *-ktub-*, stems with the liquids *l* and *r* as their second or third root consonants often have *i* like *yaḥmilu* 'he transports', while laryngeals and pharyngeals as second or third root consonants tend to be associated with *a* like *yağ^{c}alu* 'he puts, he makes'; on the other hand, *CaCiC-* Pf-stems generally have *-CCaC-* ImpfJu-stems. There are however a few exceptions like *ḥasiba* 'suppose' with *-CCiC-*. Pf-stems with the pattern *CaCuC-* tend to have stative-qualitative meanings. They are mostly used with a generic present time reference, and don't seem to occur in forms with ImpfJu-stems in the Koran. The ancient grammarians state however that they have *-CCuC-* ImpfJu-stems. The Impt-stems of active G forms correlate systematically with the vowels of the ImpfJu-stems: *-CCuC-* ImpfJu-stems have *'uCCuC-* imperatives, whereas *-CCaC-* and *-CCiC-* ImpfJu-stems have *'iCCaC-* and, respectively, *'iCCiC-* imperatives. This is shown in (5.a) and (5.b), together with the vocalisation of the inflectional prefixes of the Imperfect and the Jussive (cf. Gaudefroy-Demombynes and Blachère 1937; Fischer 1972; Denz 1982).

(5) a. Koranic Arabic strong triradical roots: Pf-, ImpfJu- and Impt-stems of the active G form

	Pf-stem	ImpfJu-stem	Impt-stem
'write'	***katab-***	***Ca-ktub-***	***'uktub-***
'trasport'	***ḥamal-***	***Ca-ḥmil-***	***'iḥmil-***
'put, make'	***ğa^{c}al-***	***Ca-ğ^{c}al-***	***'iğ^{c}al-***
'drink'	***šarib-***	***Ca-šrab-***	***'išrab-***
'suppose'	***ḥasib-***	***Ca-ḥsib-***	***'iḥsib-***
'be beautiful'	***ḥasun-***	(***Ca-ḥsun-***)	(***'uḥsun-***)

b. The above data as a matrix

Ca-CCuC-, *'uCCuC-*	+		(+)
Ca-CCiC-, *'iCCiC-*	+	+	
Ca-CCaC-, *'iCCaC-*	+	+	
	CaCaC-	*CaCiC-*	*CaCuC-*

Cairene Arabic appears to preserve the Koranic Arabic system rather well. The two major differences are (i.) the complete assimilation of the two stem vowels in the

Pf-stem, as in *širib* vs. old *šariba* 'drink', or *ṣuġur* vs. old *ṣaġura* 'become small', and (ii.) having *i* rather than *a* in the person prefixes, a phenomenon that old grammarians already reported for some early varieties of Arabic. The status of the two types *Cu-CCuC/'uCCuC-* vs. *Ci-CCuC-/'iCCuC-* is controversial: according to Mitchell (1962: 70 f.) they are two optional variants, whereas Woidich (2006: 62 f.) doesn't describe them as variants. Interestingly, there are a number of instances of causative or factitive verbs with *CaCaC-* Pf-stems that co-occur with stative verbs with *CiCiC-* or *CuCuC-* Pf-stems, such as *taʿab* 'cause to be tired' vs. *tiʿib* 'become tired', or *ġalab* 'defeat' vs. *ġulub* 'lose, be defeated'. Some of them are residues of Active vs. Passive pairs, other ones are residues of pairs of Active G-stems vs. Active C-stems that have been integrated into the stem system of the G-form when the internal passives and the entire C-form were lost in Cairene Arabic.

(6) a. Cairene Arabic strong triradical roots: Pf-, ImpfJu- and Impt-stems of the G-form

	Pf-stem	ImpfJu-stem	Impt-stem
'enter'	*daḫal-*	*Cu-dḫul-*	*'udḫul-*
'write'	*katab-*	*Ci-ktib-*	*'iktib*
'open'	*fataḥ-*	*Ci-ftaḥ-*	*'iftaḥ-*
'drink'	*širib-*	*Ci-šrab-*	*'išrab-*
'get out'	*nizil-*	*Ci-nzil-*	*'inzil-*
'keep silent'	*sikit-*	*Ci-skut-*	*'iskut-*
'become small'	*ṣuġur-*	*Ci-ṣġar-*	*'iṣġar-*

b. The above data as a matrix

Cu-CCuC-, 'uCCuC-	+		
Ci-CCiC-, 'iCCiC-	+	+	
Ci-CCaC-, 'iCCaC-	+	+	+
Ci-CCuC-, 'iCCuC-		+	
	CaCaC-	*CiCiC-*	*CuCuC-*

Differently from Cairene Arabic, Maltese expanded the older system of inflectional classes of the G-stems into sixteen different inflectional classes, resulting from the association of six different types of Pf-stems with eight different types of ImpfJu- and Impt-stems (cf. Aquilina 1965, 1973; Vanhove 1993; Borg and Azzopardi 1997). The preconsonantal forms of the Pf-stems still preserve the three original vowels *a*, *i* and *o* < *u*, but the combined action of stress, the vowel shifts induced by guttural, emphatic or liquid consonants, and analogy produced a considerably more complex system. Aquilina (1979: 97) points out that also Maltese still has a few residues of old internal passives that have been incorporated into the new system of inflectional classes. Most of them belong to the *CoCoC* ~ *Co-CCoC* class, like *ħoloq* 'be created' vs. *ħalaq* 'create', and *għolob* 'become emaciated' vs. *għaleb* 'overcome'.

(7) a. Maltese strong triradical roots: Pf-, ImpfJu- and Impt-stems of the G-form

	Pf-stems	ImpfJu-stems	Impt-stems
'enter'	*daħal, daħl-V, dħal-C*	*Ci-dħol, Ci-dħl-u*	*idħol, idħl-u*
'strike'	*ħabat, ħabt-V, ħbat-C*	*Ca-ħbat, Ca-ħbt-u*	*aħbat, aħbt-u*
'laugh'	*daħak, daħk-V, dħak-C*	*Ci-dħak, Ci-daħk-u*	*idħak, idaħk-u*
'have breakfast'	*fatar, fatr-V, ftar-C*	*Co-ftor, Co-ftr-u*	*oftor, oftr-u*
'open'	*fetaħ, fetħ-V, ftaħ-C*	*Ci-ftaħ, Ci-ftħ-u*	*iftaħ, iftħ-u*
'approach'	*resaq, resq-V, ersaq-C*	*Ce-rsaq, Ce-rsq-u*	*ersaq, ersq-u*
'paint'	*żebagħ, żebgħ-V, żbagħ-C*	*Ci-żbogħ, Ci-żbgħ-u*	*izbogħ, iżbgħ-u*
'spend'	*nefaq, nefq-V, nfaq-C*	*Co-nfoq, Co-nfq-u*	*onfoq, onfq-u*
'write'	*kiteb, kitb-V, ktib-C*	*Ci-kteb, Ci-ktb-u*	*ikteb, iktb-u*
'be silent'	*siket, sikt-V, skit-C*	*Ci-skot, Ci-skt-u*	*iskot, iskt-u*
'think'	*ħaseb, ħasb-V, ħsib-C*	*Ca-ħseb, Ca-ħsb-u*	*aħseb, aħsb-u*
'kill'	*qatel, qatl-V, qtil-C*	*Co-qtol, Co-qtl-u*	*oqtol, oqtl-u*
'deliver'	*ħeles, ħels-V, ħlis-C*	*Ce-ħles, Ce-ħils-u*	*eħles, eħils-u*
'understand'	*fehem, fehm-V, fhim-C*	*Ci-fhem, Ci-fhm-u*	*ifhem, ifhm-u*
'drink'	*xorob, xorb-V, xrob-C*	*Ci-xrob, Ci-xorb-u*	*ixrob, ixorb-u*
'dream'	*ħolom, ħolm-V, ħlom-C*	*Co-ħlom, Co-ħolm-u*	*oħlom, oħolm-u*

b. The above data as a matrix

Ca-CCaC, aCCaC	+					
Ca-CCeC, aCCeC				+		
Ce-CCaC, eCCaC			+			
Ce-CCeC, eCCeC					+	
Ci-CCaC, iCCaC	+		+			
Ci-CCeC, iCCeC		+			+	
Ci-CCoC, iCCoC	+	+	+			+
Co-CCoC, oCCoC	+		+	+		+
	CaCaC	*CiCeC*	*CeCaC*	*CaCeC*	*CeCeC*	*CoCoC*

In Geᶜez the merger of short **i* and **u* into *ə*, that frequently disappeared under the appropriate stress environment, produced a two-way opposition between *a* and *ə* in the vowel that followed the second root consonant in the Perfect, the Jussive and the Imperative. In most cases the Ju- and Impt-stems with *ə* occur with Pf-stems that have *CaCaC-* before vocalic endings like *nagar-a* 'speak', while Pf-stems with *CaCC-* before vocalic endings like *labs-a* 'he wore' have *a* in their Ju-and Impt-stems. A third class of G-stems has both kinds of Ju- and Impt-stems even though they have *CaCaC-* with vocalic endings, like *lamad-a* 'he learnt'. Finally, there are a few verbs that can occur with both types of Pf-stems as well as with both types of Ju- and Impt-stems (cf. Lambdin 1978; Weninger 2001; Tropper 2002).

(8) a. Ge[c]ez strong triradical roots: Pf-, Impf-, Ju- and Impt-stems of the G-form

	Pf-stem	Impf-stem	Ju-stem	Impt-stem
'speak'	*nagar-*	*Cə-naggər-*	*Cə-ngər-*	*nəgər-*
'wear, clothe'	*labs-V, labas-C*	*Cə-labbəs-*	*Cə-lbas-*	*ləbas-*
'learn'	*lamad-*	*Cə-lamməd-*	*Cə-lmad-* ~ *Cə-lməd-*	*ləmad-* ~ *ləməd-*

b. The above data as a matrix

Cə-CaCCəC, Cə-CCəC-, CəCəC-	+	
Cə-CaCCəC, Cə-CCaC-, CəCaC-		+
Cə-CaCCəC, Cə-CCəC-~Cə-CCaC-, CəCəC-~CəCaC-	+	+
	CaCaC-V	*CaCC-V*

The system of G-stems of Ge[c]ez is further simplified in Harari, where all the G verbs from strong triradical roots inflect in the same way, i.e., according to a single inflectional class. It has to be pointed out, however, that Old Harari texts appear to have traces of the older *CaCC-V* in verbs with a guttural as their third root consonant, e.g., *malḥ-o* 'they chose him' beside *malaḥ-o* in the Song of the Four Caliphs, aka *zikri* of [c]Abdalmālik (cf. Wagner 1983: 302, Banti 2005: 75 f.), or *ṭal[c]u* 'they hated' in the *Kitāb al-farāyiḍ* (cf. Cerulli 1936: 358 f.). It is only in Modern Harari that the system was simplified as shown in (9). It should be noticed, however, that a new vocalic distinction has been introduced in the inflectional prefixes of the Jussive. Whereas Ge[c]ez has *Cə-* prefixes, i.e., *'ə- tə- yə- nə-*, both in the Imperfect and in the Jussive, Harari has *i- ti- yi- ni-* < *'ə- tə-* etc. only in the Impf., but new prefixes with *a*, i.e., *ta- ya- na-*, in the Jussive. The difference between the two paradigms is thus expressed not only by the opposition between the two stems, *-lamdi-* vs. *-lmad-* ~ *-C-limad-*, but also by the opposition between the vowels of the inflectional prefixes.

(9) a. Harari strong triradical roots: Pf-, Impf-, Ju- and Impt-stems of the G-form

	Pf-stem	Impf-stem	Ju-stem	Impt-stem
'learn'	*lamad-*	*Ci-lamdi-*	*Ca-lmad-* ~ *-C-limad-*	*limad-*

b. The above data as a matrix

Ci-CaCCi, Ca-CCaC- (~ -C-CiCaC-), CiCaC-	+
	CaCaC-

2.2 The development of internal vowels in the D-, L-, *t*D- and *t*L-forms of strong triradical roots

The derived forms generally show much less class variation than the G-forms in all stages of Arabic and in Ge[c]ez as well. This is a pattern that already occurs in the oldest Semitic languages for which there are extensive data regarding the vowels of their verbal forms, namely Akkadian, Biblical Hebrew and Aramaic; it thus appears to be an inherited pattern. (For Harari see below). In Koranic Arabic the D- and L-forms have different vowel patterns in their Pf-stems vs. their ImpfJu- and

Impt-stems, whereas the middle forms, i.e., the *t*D- and *t*L-forms have the same vowels throughout. It should also be noted that the vowels of the inflectional prefixes differ: *u* in the D- and L-forms vs. *a* in the *t*D- and *t*L-forms as in the G-form. Differently from the Imperatives of the G-form, those of these four derived forms have the same syllable structures as the ImpfJu-stems. This is because only the ImpfJu-stem of the G-stem has an initial two-consonant cluster that has to be resolved by adding a *'V-* syllable before it when it occurs word-initially (cf. Gaudefroy-Demombynes and Blachère 1937; Fischer 1972; Denz 1982).

(10) a. Koranic Arabic strong three-consonant roots: active D-form

	Pf-stem	ImpfJu-stem	Impt-stem
'teach'	***ᶜallam-***	***Cu-ᶜallim-***	***ᶜallim-***

b. Koranic Arabic strong three-consonant roots: active L-form

'fight'	***qātal-***	***Cu-qātil-***	***qātil-***

c. Koranic Arabic strong three-consonant roots: active *t*D-form

'know'	***taᶜallam-***	***Ca-taᶜallam-***	***taᶜallam-***

d. Koranic Arabic strong three-consonant roots: active *t*L-form

'fight each other'	***taqātal-***	***Ca-taqātal-***	***taqātal-***

Differently from Koranic Arabic, Cairene Arabic developed two classes of D- and *t*D-stems, one with *i* and the other with *a* after the second root consonant. According to Woidich (2006: 67 f.) *a* generally occurs when the second or third root consonant is *r*, an emphatic consonant or a guttural, i.e., *ḫ*, *ġ*, *ḥ*, *ᶜ* and *'*, but not *h*. This does not occur with the L- and *t*L-forms, that always have *i* in that position. The vowels of the derived *t*-verbs are the same as those of their corresponding D- or L-verbs. It should also be noted that the vocalization of the inflectional prefixes is *i* throughout as in the G-form, and that the vowels of the stems are the same in the Pf-, the ImpfJu- and the Impt-stems not only in the *t*D- and *t*L-forms, but also in the D- and the L-forms. Analogical levelling has thus considerably reduced the internal vowel alternations in these derived stems.

(11) a. Cairene Arabic strong three-consonant roots: D-form

	Pf-stem	ImpfJu-stem	Impt-stem
'talk to'	***kallim-***	***Ci-kallim-***	***kallim-***
'break *tr.*'	***kassar-***	***Ci-kassar-***	***kassar-***

b. Cairene Arabic strong three-consonant roots: L-form

'notice'	***lāḥiẓ-***	***Ci-lāḥiẓ-***	***lāḥiẓ-***

c. Cairene Arabic strong three-consonant roots: *t*D-form

'talk, speak'	***'itkallim-***	***Ci-tkallim-***	***'itkallim-***
'break *intr.*'	***'itkassar-***	***Ci-tkassar-***	***'itkassar-***

d. Cairene Arabic strong three-consonant roots: *t*L-form

'be noticed'	***'itlāḥiẓ-***	***Ci-tlāḥiẓ-***	***'itlāḥiẓ-***

Maltese developed a rather complex system of stem classes especially for its D- and *t*D-forms, and even the L- and *t*L-forms have more stem classes than in Koranic and Cairene Arabic. However, the vowels of the derived *t*-form verbs are always like those of their corresponding D- or L-form verb, like *kisser* 'he broke' and *tkisser* 'it was broken', or *ħares* 'he protected' and *tħares* 'it was protected'. Within each derived stem class there has been a thorough levelling between the Pf-, the ImpfJu- and the Impt-stems as in Cairene Arabic. For the sake of simplicity the different stem alternants that occur before vowel and consonant inflectional suffixes have not been reported in (12), since the basic workings of the Maltese system have already been shown in (4.c) and in (7.a). For instance, the D-verb *kisser* 'break *tr.*' has 1-2.SG. *kissir-t*, 3.SG.M. *kisser* and 3.SG.F. *kissr-et* in its Perfect, and accordingly 2.PL. *kissr-u* in its Imperative; the *t*D verb *tkabbar* 'grow proud' has 1-2.SG. *tkabbar-t*, 3.SG.M. *tkabbar*, 3.SG.F. *tkabbr-et* in its Perfect and 2.PL. Impt. *tkabbr-u*, etc. (cf. Aquilina 1965, 1973; Vanhove 1993; Borg and Azzopardi 1997).

(12)				
a.	Maltese strong three-consonant roots: D-form			
		Pf-stem	ImpfJu-stem	Impt-stem
	'break *tr.*'	*kisser-*	*C-/i-kisser-*	*kisser-*
	'lend'	*sellef-*	*C-/i-sellef-*	*sellef-*
	'divide, disperse'	*ferraq-*	*C-/i-ferraq-*	*ferraq-*
	'grow, increase'	*kabbar-*	*C-/i-kabbar-*	*kabbar-*
	'train'	*ħarreġ-*	*C-/i-ħarreġ-*	*ħarreġ-*
b.	Maltese strong three-consonant roots: L-form			
	'bless'	*bierek-*	*C-/i-bierek-*	*bierek-*
	'protect'	*ħares-*	*C-/i-ħares-*	*ħares-*
c.	Maltese strong three-consonant roots: *t*D-form			
	'break *intr.*'	*tkisser-*	*Ci-tkisser-*	*tkisser-*
	'borrow'	*issellef* (<*t-s-*)	*C-/i-ssellef-*	*issellef-*
	'be dispersed'	*tferraq-*	*C-/i-tferraq-*	*tferraq-*
	'grow proud'	*tkabbar-*	*C-/i-tkabbar-*	*tkabbar-*
	'be trained'	*tħarreġ-*	*C-/i-ħarreġ-*	*tħarreġ-*
d.	Maltese strong three-consonant roots: *t*L-form			
	'be blessed'	*tbierek-*	*C-/i-tbierek-*	*tbierek-*
	'be protected'	*tħares-*	*C-/i-tħares-*	*tħares-*
	'fight'	*tqabad-*	*C-/i-tqabad-*	*tqabad-*

Ge^{c}ez is strikingly similar to Koranic Arabic in its having different stems in the D- and L-forms, but substantially a single stem with *a* after its second root consonant in the *t*D- and *t*L-forms. The *ə* after the second root consonant in the Impf-, Ju- and Impt-stems of the D- and L-forms originated most likely from **i*, because of the evidence of Arabic and, for the D-forms, Biblical Hebrew and Aramaic. It should be pointed out that D-verbs, as well as the *t*D-verbs that derive from them, distinguish their Impf-stems from their Ju- and Impt-stems: after the first root consonant the Imperfect has *ē*, while the Jussive and the Imperative have *a* (cf. Lambdin 1978; Weninger 2001; Tropper 2002).

(13) a. Ge^cez strong three-consonant roots: D-form

	Pf-stem	Impf-stem	Ju-stem	Impt-stem
'sanctify'	*qaddas-*	*Cə-qēddəs-*	*Cə-qaddəs-*	*qaddəs-*

b. Ge[c]ez strong three-consonant roots: L-form

	Pf-stem	Impf-stem	Ju-stem	Impt-stem
'bless'	*bārak-*	*Cə-bārək-*	*Cə-bārək-*	*bārək-*

c. Ge[c]ez strong three-consonant roots: *t*D-form

	Pf-stem	Impf-stem	Ju-stem	Impt-stem
'be sanctified'	*taqaddas-*	*Cə-tqēddas-*	*Cə-tqaddas-*	*taqaddas-*

d. Ge[c]ez strong three-consonant roots: *t*L-form

	Pf-stem	Impf-stem	Ju-stem	Impt-stem
'be blessed'	*tabārak-*	*Cə-tbārak-*	*Cə-tbārak-*	*tabārak-*

The peculiar pattern of the Ge[c]ez D- and *t*D-stems, that distinguish their Impf-stem by having *ē* after the first root consonant, seems to be an innovation of Ethio-Semitic, that lacks clear parallels in other groups of Semitic languages. Tigre and Amharic use the Ju- and Impt-stem also for the Imperfect, e.g., Tigre D Pf-stem *mazzan-* 'weigh' vs. Impf-, Ju- and Impt-stem *-mazzən-*, Amharic D Pf-stem *fälläg-* 'want' vs. Impf-, Ju- and Impt-stem *-fälləg-*; this is probably due to analogical levelling. Instead *ē* spread to the Pf-stem in Argobba, that now has, e.g., D Pf-stem *beddäl-* 'wrong' vs. Impf-stem *-beddəl-* Ju-stem *-bäddəl-*. In Harari D- and *t*D-verbs *ē* after the first root consonant spread not only to the Perfect, but also to the Jussive and the Imperative. (See also Leslau 1951: 224 f. on the question of the D stems in Ethio-Semitic). Since Harari also lost consonant gemination the old D- and *t*D-verbs have actually become through analogical and phonological change a new type of L- and *t*L-verbs, namely L*ē*- and *t*L*ē*-verbs respectively. They remain clearly different from the inherited L- and *t*L-verbs that have *ā* instead of *ē*, and that should therefore be called more appropriately L*ā*- and *t*L*ā*-verbs in this language. Harari introduced a new distinction between its Impf- and its Ju- and Impt-stems of the D-form – but not of the *t*D-form – by raising *ē* to *ī* in the Imperfect: Impf. 3.G.M. *yi-bīrqi* is thus now distinguished from Jussive 3.SG.M. *ya-bērqi* not only because of the vowel of its inflectional prefix, but also by having *ī* rather than *ē* after its first root consonant. The different vocalizations of the second root consonants in the Impf-, Ju- and Impt-stems in the Ge[c]ez D- and L-forms vs. the *t*D- and *t*L-stems is preserved in Harari also after the loss of *ə in unstressed open internal syllables, as shown by the difference between the Jussive 3.SG.M. forms *ya-bērqi* 'he should embellish' and *yagāgri* 'he should roast' vs. *ya-tbēraq* 'it should be embellished' and *ya-tgāgar* 'it should be roasted', respectively.

(14) a. Harari strong three-consonant roots: D-form > Lē-form

	Pf-stem	Impf-stem	Ju-stem	Impt-stem
'embellish'	*bēraq-*	*Ci-bīrqi-*	*Ca-bērqi-* ~ *-C-bērqi-*	*bērqi-*

b. Harari strong three-consonant roots: Lā-form

	Pf-stem	Impf-stem	Ju-stem	Impt-stem
'roast'	*gāgar-*	*Ci-gāgri-*	*Ca-gāgri-* ~ *-C-gāgri-*	*gāgri-*

c. Harari strong three-consonant roots: *t*D-form > Lē-form

	Pf-stem	Impf-stem	Ju-stem	Impt-stem
'be embellished'	*tabēraq-*	*Ci-tbēraq-*	*Ca-tbēraq-* ~ *-C-tabēraq-*	*tabēraq-*

d. Harari strong three-consonant roots: *t*Lā-form

	Pf-stem	Impf-stem	Ju-stem	Impt-stem
'be roasted'	*tagāgar-*	*Ci-tgāgar-*	*Ca-tgāgar-* ~ *-C-tgāgar-*	*tagāgar-*

3. Conclusions

It has already been mentioned above in § 2.2 that the marked difference between having a higher number of inflectional classes in the G-form vs. the derived forms is an inherited pattern that already occurs in older Semitic languages like Akkadian, Biblical Hebrew and Aramaic. It is well preserved in the Arabic group even in languages that tend to develop a high number of inflectional classes. Indeed, Maltese has 16 different inflectional classes in its G-form, but 5 in its D- and *t*D-forms, 2 in its L-form and 3 in its *t*L-form. In Ethio-Semitic phonological change, i.e., the merger of short **i* and **u* into *ə*, reduced the number of possible inflectional classes: in Geᶜez there are just 3 of them in the G-form, plus a fourth class of verbs that can optionally have either of the two Pf-stem types and of the two Impf-, Ju- and Impt-stem types. It has been seen above that Harari still preserved the two types of Pf-stems in its older stage, but generalized the disyllabic Pf-stems in its modern stage, and thus has a single inflectional class also in its G-form. Like Koranic Arabic, Geᶜez and Harari have only one inflectional class for each of the four derived stems that have been examined above.

Also the distinctions between the different tense and mood stems of each inflectional class develop in markedly different ways in Arabic and in Ethio-Semitic. These two language groups differed from each other already in their earliest attested stages, because Geᶜez preserved a separate Impf-stem, while Koranic Arabic lost it and used the inherited Ju-stem also for its Imperfect. In their subsequent developments, Arabic languages such as Cairene Arabic and Maltese have preserved in their G-forms the difference between the Pf-stem and the ImpfJu-stem, as well as the Impt-stem, but have generalized a single stem for the Perfect, the Imperfect-Jussive and the Imperative in the derived forms. Geᶜez distinguished its Impf-stem from its Ju- and Impt-stems not only in its G-form, but also in its D- and *t*D-forms, while its L- and *t*L-forms had a single stem for their Imperfect, Jussive and Imperative paradigms. In addition to this, the *t*L-form used the same stem also for its Perfect, and was thus the only form that used a single stem for its four major tenses and moods. Distinctiveness of the Impf-stem is preserved by Harari not only in its G-form, but also in its L*ē*- form that renews the inherited D-form, whereas the L*ā*-form and the *t*L*ā*-forms preserve their Ge[c]ez patterns in having a single stem for the Imperfect, Jussive and Imperative and, respectively, the same stem in the four tenses and moods.

In addition to this, it should also be observed that the vocalizations of the inflectional prefixes behave differently. Koranic Arabic has *a* in its G- and its two *t* forms, i.e., the *t*D- and the *t*L-form, but *u* in its D- and L-forms. Cairene Arabic has generalized *i* everywhere but for the *Cu-dḫul-* class of the G-form. It has already been mentioned above that having *i* is an old dialectal feature that spread to most of the modern dialects; *u* in *Cu-dḫul-* is an innovation, possibly due to analogy with the classes that have *-i-i-* like *Ci-ktib-* and *Ci-nzil-*. Maltese developed a more complex pattern whereby any vowel but *u* may occur in the inflectional prefix of its G-form, while all its derived forms have *i* alternating with Ø. Ge[c]ez has *ə* everywhere both in its G- and its derived forms, while Harari has introduced a new distinction between having *i* in the inflectional prefixes of the Imperfect and *a* in the Jussive, that has been extended also to all its derived forms.

The generalizations that can be suggested for these three areas of internal morphology of the verbal systems of the five languages that have been discussed in this paper are summed up in (15):

(15) a. Number of inflectional classes:
- The Arabic languages increase their number both in the G- and in the derived forms.
- The Ethio-Semitic languages tend to reduce them in the G-form, and have only one class for each of the derived forms already in Ge[c]ez.

b. Having separate tense and mood stems:
- The Arabic languages keep separate Pf-stems in the G-form, but extend stem uniformity, i.e., having a single stem for all tenses and moods, from the derived *t*-forms to the D- and L-forms.
- The Ethio-Semitic languages preserve separate Pf-, Impf- and Ju-/Impt-stems in the G-form. Harari keeps this also in its new L*ē*-form that has developed out of the inherited D-form. The L-form distinguishes the Pf-stem from an Impf-, Ju- and Impt-stem both in Ge[c]ez and in Harari. Ge[c]ez has a single stem for the four tenses and moods only in the *t*L*ā*-form, but Harari extends this also to its *t*L*ē*-form. The tendency towards stem uniformity is thus distinctively less marked than in the Arabic languages.

c. Vocalization of the inflectional prefixes of the Imperfect and the Jussive:
- The Arabic languages unify through time the vocalization of the inflectional prefixes in the derived forms, but tend to diversify it in the G-form: Koranic Arabic had *a* in all the classes of its G-form, Cairene Arabic has just the *Cu-dḫul-* class that differs from the other classes, while Maltese has an extremely diversified system.
- The Ethio-Semitic languages start with Geᶜez that has *ə* everywhere, while Harari has introduced a new vocalization of the Jussive that distinguishes this mood from the Imperfect also in those derived stems that use for them a single stem, i.e., the L*ā*-, the *t*L*ē*- and the *t*L*ā*-forms. The Ethio-Semitic languages tend thus to diversify in a markedly different way than the Arabic languages.

With regard to the questions raised in the Introduction of this paper, it appears that endomorphy, as represented by stem-internal vowel alternations, is well alive in both language groups. Yet it tends to be reduced in the Arabic languages, much less so in the Ethio-Semitic languages. On the other hand, the Arabic languages, and especially Maltese display a marked tendency to increase the number of inflectional classes by differentiating their internal vocalization, i.e., by an endomorphic marking. The developments of the inflectional prefixes are ambiguous, in the sense that prefixes are by definition stem-external, yet they are differentiated by introducing alternations in their internal vowel, i.e., by means of an internal morphological process that closely resembles endomorphic morphology.

Finally, it seems to the present author that linking these divergent developments of Arabic, and specifically of the two Mediterranean Arabic languages, vis-a-vis Ethio-Semitic to their different histories of language contacts is not straightforward. Other aspects of their grammar, and particularly of their verbal systems, correlate quite easily with their typological contexts. For instance, it has already been seen in the Introduction that the development of quite un-Arabic multi-word passives in Maltese is likely to have been influenced by the Romance multi-word passives; instead, the postverbal auxiliaries and the processes of grammaticalization on the right peripheries of verbal groups in Harari are typologically linked to its now prevailingly OV syntax, that is due to its long contacts with OV Cushitic languages. The only morphological feature of the Mediterranean Arabic languages that may be linked to contacts with other languages that had much less stem-internal morphology is their extending stem-uniformity to all the derived forms. Yet Koranic Arabic already had it in its *t*D- and *t*L-forms, and what happened in Cairene Arabic and in Maltese can also be explained as an analogical extension due to internal causes only, i.e., to drift *à la* Sapir (1921). Two other features that may be due to contact are the clear-cut tendency of Harari to have only one inflectional class also in the G-stem – not only in the derived stems as in Koranic Arabic and in

Ge^cez – and its marking the Imperfect and Jussive in all forms with two distinctive sets of inflectional prefixes. Indeed, the HEC languages, Oromo and Somali have separate sets of inflectional suffixes – vs. the inflectional prefixes of Harari – in their Imperfect anf Jussive paradigm, and display almost no allomorphy in the inflectional suffixes of their verbal systems. Furthermore, these Cushitic languages have no inflectional class variation in verbs that belong to the same derivational group, unless the variation is due to sandhi. Also in these two instances, however, analogical change may have been due just to internal developments rather than to contact.

References

ᶜAbd al-Bāqī, M.F. 1995. *Al-muᶜǧam al-mufahras li-'alfāẓ al-Qur'ān al-karīm.* Beirut: Dār el-Fikr.

Aquilina, J. 1965. *Maltese.* London: The English Universities Press.

Aquilina, J. 1973. *The stucture of Maltese.* Msida: The Royal University of Malta.

Aquilina, J. 1979. *Maltese Arabic comparative grammar.* Malta: Interprint Limited and Socialist People's Libyan Arab Jamahiriya.

Banti, G. 2005. Remarks about the orthography of the earliest *ᶜajamī* texts in Harari. In *Scritti in onore di Giovanni M. D'Erme*, vol. I, M. Bernardini & N. Tornesello (eds), 75–102. Naples: Università degli Studi di Napoli "L'Orientale".

Bausi, A. 2005. Ancient features of Ancient Ethiopic. *Aethiopica. International Journal of Ethiopian and Eritrean Studies* 8: 149–169.

Borg, A. & Azzopardi-Alexander, M. 1997. *Maltese.* London: Routledge.

Brincat, G. 2003. *Malta. Una storia linguistica.* Udine & Genoa: Centro Internazionale sul Plurilinguismo and Le Mani-Microart's Edizioni.

Cerulli, E. 1936. *Studi etiopici I. La lingua e la storia di Harar.* Rome: Istituto per l'Oriente.

Cohen, D. 1959. Renouvellement des modes du verbe. Exemples observés dans l'évolution des langues sémitiques méridionales. *Scientia* 94: 166–172.

Cohen, D. 1984. *La phrase nominale et l'évolution du système verbal en sémitique.* Leuven: Éditions Peeters.

Contini, R. In print. Un incrocio di categorie verbali: I temi derivati nelle lingue semitiche. In *Categorie del verbo: Diacronia, teoria, tipologia (Atti del XXXI Convegno Annuale della SIG, Pisa SNS, 26–28 ottobre 2006).* Roma: Il Calamo.

De Angelis, A. & Di Giovine, P. In print. Il mutamento tipologico nella funzionalità dei morfemi verbali: Le lingue germaniche e l'indo-iranico. In *Typological change in the morphosyntax of the Indo-European languages*, G. Banti, P. Di Giovine & P. Ramat (eds). Munich: Lincom.

Denz, A. 1982. Die Struktur des klassischen Arabisch. In *Grundriß der arabischen Philologie*, Vol. I: *Sprachwissenschaft*, W. Fischer (ed.), 58–82. Wiesbaden: Dr. Ludwig Reichert Verlag.

Durand, O. 1995. *Introduzione ai dialetti arabi.* Milano: Centro Studi Camito-Semitici.

Fischer, W. 1972. *Grammatik des klassischen Arabisch.* Wiesbaden: Otto Harrassowitz.

Fischer, W. 1982a. Das Altarabische in islamischer Überlieferung: Das Klassische Arabisch. In *Grundriß der arabischen Philologie*, Vol. I: *Sprachwissenschaft*, W. Fischer (ed.), 37–50. Wiesbaden: Dr. Ludwig Reichert Verlag.

Fischer, W. 1982b. Frühe Zeugnisse des Neuarabischen. In *Grundriß der arabischen Philologie*, Vol. I: *Sprachwissenschaft*, W. Fischer (ed.), 83–95. Wiesbaden: Dr. Ludwig Reichert Verlag.

Fischer, W. & Jastrow, O. (eds). 1980. *Handbuch der arabischen Dialekte* [Porta Linguarum Orientalium N.S. 16]. Wiesbaden: Harrassowitz.

Garbini, G. 1972. *Le lingue semitiche: Studi di storia linguistica.* Naples: Istituto Universitario Orientale.

Gaudefroy-Demombynes, M. & Blachère, R. 1937. *Grammaire de l'arabe classique.* Paris: G.P. Maisonneuve.

Goldenberg, G. 1977. The semitic languages of Ethiopia and their classification. *BSOAS* 40: 461–507.

Goldenberg, G. 1994. Principles of semitic word-structure. In *Semitic and Cushitic studies*, G. Goldenberg & S. Raz (eds), 29–64. Wiesbaden: Harrassowitz. (Reprinted in: G. Goldenberg. 1998. *Studies in Semitic linguistics*, 10–45. Jerusalem: The Magnes Press, The Hebrew University).

Goldenberg, G. 1997. Conservative and innovative features in Semitic languages. In *Afroasiatica neapolitana* [Studi Africanistici, Serie Etiopica 6], A. Bausi & M. Tosco (eds), 3–21. Naples: Istituto Universitario Orientale.

Goldenberg, G. 2005. Semitic triradicalism and the biradical question. In *Semitic studies in honour of Edward Ullendorff*, G. Khan (ed.), 9–25. Leiden: Brill.

Lambdin, T.O. 1978. *Introduction to Classical Ethiopic (Geʿez)* [Harvard Semitic Studies 24] Ann Arbor MI: Scholars Press.

Leslau, W. 1951. Archaic features in South Ethiopic. *Journal of the American Oriental Society* 71: 212–230.

Leslau, W. 1958. *The verb in Harari (South Ethiopic).* Berkeley CA: University of California Press.

Leslau, W. 1963. *Etymological dictionary of Harari.* Berkeley CA: University of California Press.

Marrassini, P. 2003. Sur le sud-sémitique: Problèmes de définition. In *Mélanges David Cohen*, J. Lentin & A. Lonnet (eds), 461–470. Paris: Maisonneuve & Larose.

Mitchell, T.F. 1962. *Colloquial Arabic. The living language of Egypt.* London: The English Universities Press.

Owens, J. 1985. *A grammar of Harar Oromo* [Kuschitische Sprachstudien 4]. Hamburg: Helmut Buske.

Owens, J. 2006. *A linguistic history of Arabic.* Oxford: OUP.

Penrice, J. 1873. *A dictionary and glossary of the Ko-rân.* London. (1993[5] by Curzon Press, Richmond, Surrey).

Ratcliffe, R. 1998. *The broken plural problem in Arabic and comparative Semitic: Allomorphy and analogy in non-concatenative morphology.* Amsterdam: John Benjamins.

Reintges, C.H. 2004. *Coptic Egyptian (Sahidic dialect). A learner's grammar.* Cologne: Rüdiger Köppe.

Sapir, E. 1921. *Language.* New York NY: Harcourt, Brace & Co.

Tropper, J. 2002. *Altäthiopisch. Grammatik des Geʿez mit Übungstexten und Glossar.* Münster: Ugarit-Verlag.

Vanhove, M. 1993. *La langue maltaise.* Wiesbaden: Harrassowitz.

Voigt, R. 2004. Die Entwicklung des Aspektsystem vom Ursemitischen zum Hebräischen. *Zeitschrift der Deutschen Morgenländischen Gesellschaft* 154: 35–55.

Wagner, E. 1983. *Harari-Texte in arabischer Schrift* [Äthiopistische Forschungen 13]. Wiesbaden: Franz Steiner.

Weninger, S. 2001. *Das Verbalsystem des Altäthiopischen.* Wiesbaden: Harrassowitz.

Woidich, M. 2006. *Das Kairenisch-Arabische. Eine Grammatik* [Porta Linguarum Orientalium 22]. Wiesbaden: Harrassowitz.

Demonstratives in the languages of Europe

Federica Da Milano

The definition of 'demonstrative' used in this research is based on Diessel's study (1999): in particular, semantic and pragmatic features of demonstratives have been the main topic of this study.

I have compiled a questionnaire for the elicitation of the data. Because demonstratives seem to straddle the boundaries between semantics and pragmatics, two parameters have been considered: distance (semantic parameter) and the reciprocal orientation between speaker and hearer (pragmatic parameter). The questionnaire including 48 pictures is based on the notion of "dyad of conversation" (Jungbluth 2001).

The results have been visualized by typological maps and checked also by the use of parallel texts.

The research shows that also systems that at a first glance seem to be relatively simple can vary in a very subtle way in their conditions of use.

1. Introduction

The aim of this paper is to give a typological description of the systems of demonstratives in the languages of Europe from a synchronic point of view.

The first problem that arises at the beginning of a typological research is a clear definition of the object under investigation. Haspelmath (1997: 9) underlines the importance of a definition that has to be both functional and formal: "Typological investigations are usually based on a combined functional-formal definition of their domain of inquiry".

As far as the semantic-functional characteristics are concerned, demonstratives generally cover specific pragmatic functions – they are often used to address the attention of the hearer – and they are characterized by specific semantic features.

As far as formal characteristics are concerned, demonstratives are deictic expressions used for particular syntactic functions: they are used as independent pronouns, they can co-occur with a noun in a noun-phrase, they can function as verbal modifiers and they can cover the position of subject/topic in copulative or non-verbal sentences (Diessel 1999). The notion used in this analysis includes not only determiners and pronouns, but also place adverbs, as English *here/there*, by Fillmore (1982) already labelled 'demonstrative adverbs'.

Semantic and pragmatic features are the specific object of this analysis, considering semantic typology "a subfield of linguistics which has a special interest for the psycholinguistic study of the interface between language and other aspects of cognition" (Max Planck Institute for Psycholinguistics, Nijmegen, Annual Report 2000, Project Space).

Demonstratives can codify both qualitative and relational features: this analysis considers only relational features but, while Diessel (1999) considers five features, namely distance, elevation, visibility, geography and movement, my hypothesis is that only distance is a really basic feature, universally codified in demonstratives: in fact, sometimes demonstratives lexicalize not only the deictic dimension, but they combine it with other spatial features that are not deictic in a strict sense (that is, not directly related to the deictic center).

Deixis is at the boundary between semantics and pragmatics: conventional meanings (the domain of semantics) and pragmatic implicatures due to the context (the pragmatic domain) are intertwined in demonstratives. For this reason, the two parameters used for this analysis, namely distance and the reciprocal orientation of the speaker and the addressee, belong to semantics and pragmatics, respectively.

In descriptive grammars, terms like 'proximal/distal' or 'near/far from the speaker' are usually used to define the meaning of demonstratives. However, these definitions are only an approximation of a complex semantic domain. In particular, an important point concerns the distinction we find in the literature between the so-called 'distance-oriented' systems and 'person-oriented' systems. The question is: is that a real distinction, or are they two instantiations of a more general system?

Traditional studies considered only the orientation of a single participant in the conversation, namely the speaker; only in recent years the research has taken into account other factors, as the reciprocal orientation of the speaker and the hearer. Hanks (1990) underlines the problems and the limitations of the notion of 'egocentricity' traditionally used in the studies on deixis; Janssen (2004) considers the importance of the 'perspective', which is of central importance in the analysis of deictic phenomena: he defines the 'vantage point' which is common to the speaker and the addressee as 'speaker.hearer centric' or 'sociocentric'.

2. Methodology

This analysis adopts the 'conversational approach' proposed by Jungbluth (2001a, b; 2005). She introduces the notion of 'dyad of conversation' which is based on the physical orientation of the speaker and the hearer in their interaction.

In natural contexts, there are several ways in which speaker and addressee can be oriented one regarding the other:

face-to-face conversation:

< >
Speaker Hearer

where the speaker and the hearer are one in front of the other;

face-to-back conversation:

< <
Speaker Hearer

where the speaker is behind the hearer; and

side-by-side conversation:

Speaker <
Hearer <

where the speaker and the hearer are side-by-side looking in the same direction.

While the first configuration is well-known in linguistics, the others are generally not taken into account, but they turn out to be very useful to investigate the way in which demonstratives are used in interaction.

The analysis is based on data obtained from descriptive grammars compared with data collected via a questionnaire: moreover, a confirmation of the data is derived from a parallel corpus, namely the translations of the book "Harry Potter and the Chamber of Secrets" by Rowling (see Section 4).

The definition of my typological questionnaire follows the 'EUROTYP Guidelines':

> A typological questionnaire will in the following be understood to be any questionnaire which is used with the aim of collecting parallel information about the members of a set of languages. As many typological studies have already shown, the use of questionnaires presents some problems, one of which is the scarce naturalness of the answers, in comparison to spontaneous productions. However, questionnaires also have many advantages, first of all the possibility of a cross-linguistic comparability: "[...] one may ask how anyone could ever be so stupid as to choose translations as a basis for an investigation of language use. The simple answer is that it is the only realistic method for large-scale data collection in typologically oriented linguistic research" (Dahl 1985: 50).[1]

In order to allow the cross-linguistic comparison with other typological data on the same topic, the questionnaire has been adapted to other typological questionnaires on deixis. In particular, the models have been: Benedetti et al. (2000) (Med-Typ Project); 'The 1999 Demonstrative Questionnaire: THIS and THAT in comparative perspective' (Wilkins, Max Planck Institite for Psycholinguistics, Nijmegen); Jungbluth (2001a, b).

Given the topic under investigation, all the questionnaires are based on pictures. Nevertheless, they show some differences, which we cannot deal with here because of space limitations (see Da Milano 2005: 47–70).

1. The same utterance is quoted in Ricca (1993: 62) and Bernini/Ramat (1992: 72).

The questionnaire (see Appendix) is composed of 48 pictures:[2]

Table 1. The structure of the questionnaire

	face-to-face conversation	*face-to-back conversation*	*side-by-side conversation*
1 object	1–15	22–27	37–42
3 objects	16–18	28–33	43–45
the moon	19–21	34–36	46–48

The informants have been native-speakers of the languages considered in the sample, namely Basque, Bulgarian, Catalan, Czech, Danish, Dutch, English, Finnish, French, German, Hungarian, Italian, Modern Greek, Norwegian, Polish, Portuguese, Russian, Sardinian, Serbo-Croatian, Spanish, Swedish and the Italian variety spoken in Tuscany.

3. The data

Considering distance as the basic feature of demonstratives, a first, general distinction could be made between three-term and two-term systems, both as determiners/ pronouns and adverbs are concerned. But beyond this general classification, the data allow to find very subtle differences: data show the importance of the role of the addressee. In particular, it is possible to identify a distinction between 'dual-anchored type systems' and 'addresse-anchored type systems'. In the former type, the medial term is used both to refer to something near the addressee and to something at a middle distance from the speaker. Spanish and Basque seem to belong to this type.[3]

In the literature, Spanish and Basque are described sometimes as 'person-oriented' systems, sometimes as 'distance-oriented' systems (Alonso 1968, Casares 1959, Carrera-Díaz 1997, Patrick/Zubiri Ibarrondo 2001). The data collected through the questionnaire clearly show the fact that the medial term, the determiner *ese* for Spanish (ex. 1), the adverb *hor* for Basque (ex. 2), are used both to refer to something near the addressee and to something at a middle distance from the speaker.[4]

2. The numbers correspond to the pictures.

3. Because of space limitations, only few cases can be described here. For further details, see Da Milano 2005.

4. A clarification about the representation of the data: uncinate parentheses are used to indicate the reciprocal orientation of the speaker and the hearer (S = speaker, H = hearer, DET = determiner, ADV = adverb); the standard fonts are used for the proximal terms, the italic fonts for the medial terms, the underlined fonts for the distal terms.

(1) Spanish
DET
face-to-face
1 object (pictures: 1–7)

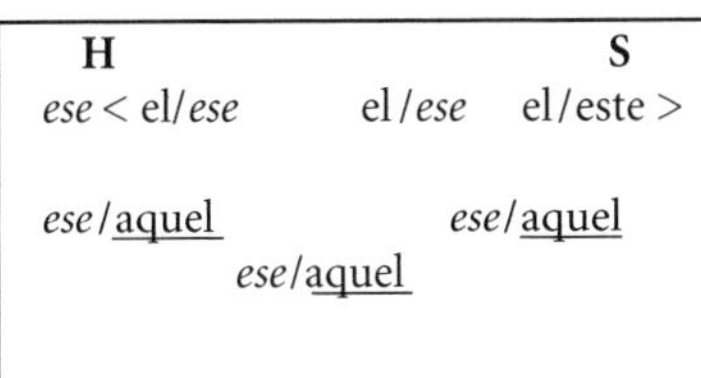

(2) Basque
ADV
side-by-side
1 object (pictures: 40–42; 46–48)

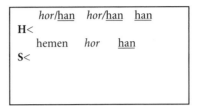

hor/han hor/han han
H<
hemen hor han
S<

Other three-term systems considered in the sample, namely Sardinian and Tuscan, belong to another sub-group. They are 'addressee-anchored type systems': in these systems, the medial term – the determiner *cussu* (ex. 4) and the adverb *inguni* (ex. 3) for Sardinian and the determiner *codesto* (ex. 5) and the adverb *costì* (ex. 6) for Tuscan – can be used only to refer to something near the addressee, while they cannot be used to refer to something at a middle distance from the speaker.

(3) Sardinian
ADV
face-to-face
1 object (pictures: 8–15; 19–21)

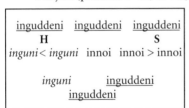

inguddeni inguddeni inguddeni
H S
inguni < inguni innoi innoi > innoi
inguni inguddeni
inguddeni

(4) Sardinian
DET
face-to-back
1 object (pictures: 22–23)

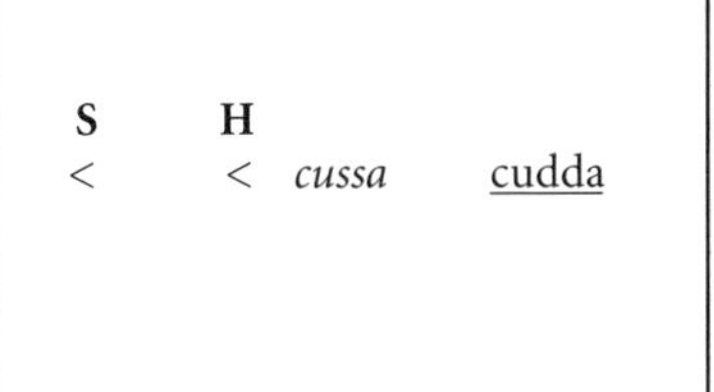

(5) Tuscan
DET
face-to-face
1 object (pictures: 1–7)

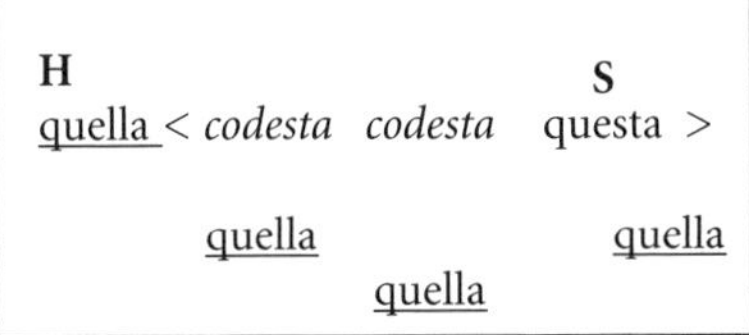

(6) Tuscan
ADV
side-by-side
3 objects (pictures: 43–45)

H<
qui lì là
S<

The data gathered about French demonstrative adverbs confirm the tendency outlined by the grammars concerning the large diffusion of the distal term *là:* "It should be noted also that usage of the proximal and distal demonstratives heavily favours the latter, particularly in speech" (Harris 1988: 221).

In the traditional analysis, *ici* is considered as the proximal term and *là* as the distal one. The role of *là-bas* has received little attention so far. *Là-bas*, originally a deictic used to refer to something far and below compared to the origo, now simply means 'at a big distance'. The same could be partially said about the Italian *laggiù*, which in some contexts has lost the spatial indication on the vertical axis. Nevertheless, the Italian adverb cannot be considered as a 'basic' term, because it is perfectly replaceable by *là* (Benedetti & Ricca 2002).

The data clearly show the diffusion of the French adverb *là*. As shown in (7) and (8), *ici* can always be replaced by *là*. The opposition is now between *là* and *là-bas*, with the former referring to a generic space shared by the interlocutors and the latter referring to something outside the common area. It is interesting to note the use of *là-bas* referring to the moon: the term has lost its specification on the vertical axis:

(7) French
ADV
side-by-side
1 object (pictures: 40–42; 46–48)

là-haut là-haut (tout) là-bas
là-bas
H<
ici/*là* là-bas là-bas
S<

(8) French
ADV
side-by-side
3 objects (pictures: 43–45)

H<
ici /*là* *là* là-bas
S<

As for Italian, the opposition *qui/qua, lì/là* is often discussed in the literature (Brodin 1970, Hottenroth 1983, Gaudino-Fallegger 1992, Vanelli 2001).

The data seem to support the hypothesis according to which the opposition between *lì* and *là*, traditionally considered to be based on vagueness (Vanelli 1992), is now becoming a contrast based on distance: *lì* refers to something nearer than *là* (Benedetti & Ricca 2002). As one can see in (9), Italian shows a three-term adverb system (*qui/lì/là*):

(9) Italian:
ADV
side-by-side
3 objects (pictures: 43–45)

H<
qui *lì* là
S<

Two-term systems have traditionally been considered to codify a symmetric opposition based on distance ('proximal' vs. 'distal'), with the speaker as the origo. Moreover:

> [...] the notions of 'proximal' and 'distal' that are semantically encoded by *this* and *that* cannot be considered spatial in the strict sense of the term because they do not

> specify objectively measurable distances; rather, they are technically neutral with respect to actual spatial extent.
> It is therefore appropriate to treat the notions as abstract semantic features. Together, they constitute a closed language–internal Saussurean system in which each notion is defined not with reference to real concrete space but instead in opposition to the other notion (Saussure 1916; Ruhl 1989) (Kemmerer 1999: 52).

As far as two-term systems are concerned, it is necessary to introduce the notion of markedness, which is crucial for the classification of the systems.

Markedness is an asymmetric relation among occurrences established by different parameters such as frequency, semantic generality (Greenberg 1966) and use in neutral contexts. Unmarked terms are more frequent and semantically more general. They are used in neutral contexts and expressed by shorter and/or morphologically simpler forms. Marked terms are in opposition to the unmarked ones for each parameter. In his typological survey on demonstratives in the languages of the world, Dixon underlines "The question of markedness requires careful examination, in each individual language" (Dixon 2003: 93–94).

Because of space limitations, I will give only some examples based on the data collected through the questionnaire (for further details, see Da Milano 2005).

In the literature, the meaning of the English demonstratives is based on the opposition between proximity (*this*) and distance (*that*), but Lakoff, for example, points out: "Everyone is aware, of course, that their use goes beyond their standard English-textbook definition as forms used to point to objects in the real world, and to identify them as (literally) near to or distant from participants in a conversation" (Lakoff 1974: 345).

The data clearly show a predominant use of the distal terms, the determiner *that* and the adverb *there*:

(10) English
ADV
face-to-face
1 object (pictures: 8–15; 19–21)

there there there there
H S
< there there here > here
there there
there

(11) English
DET
side-by-side
1 object (pictures: 37–39)

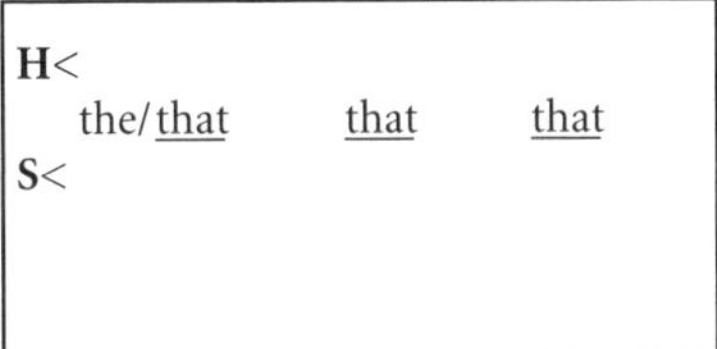

The systems of demonstratives of Norwegian, Swedish, Danish and Dutch belong to the same sub-group: these languages use more often the distal term, which can be considered to be the unmarked term of the opposition:

(12) Norwegian
ADV
side-by-side
1 object (pictures: 40–42; 46–48)

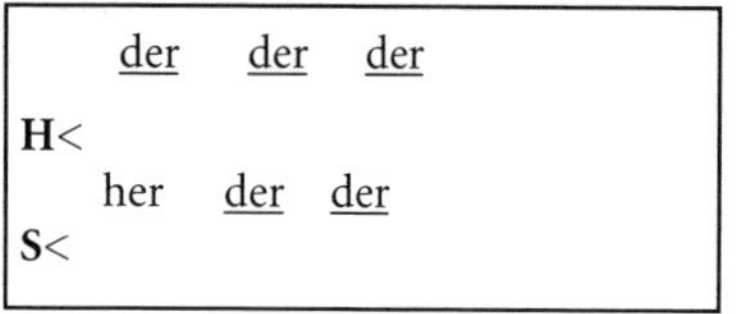

(13) Swedish
ADV
side-by-side
1 object (pictures: 40–42; 46–48)

där där där (borta) H< här där där borta S<

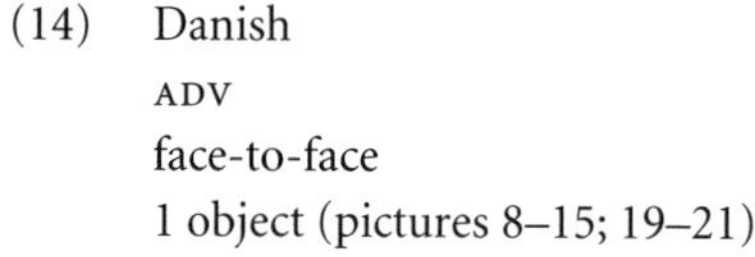

(14) Danish
ADV
face-to-face
1 object (pictures 8–15; 19–21)

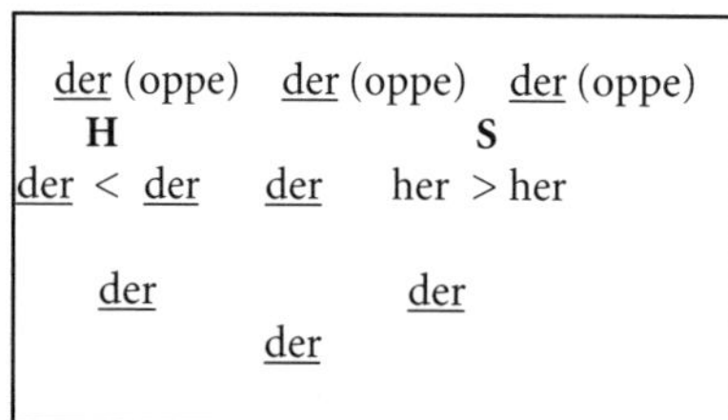

(15) Dutch
DET
face-to-face
1 object (pictures: 1–7)

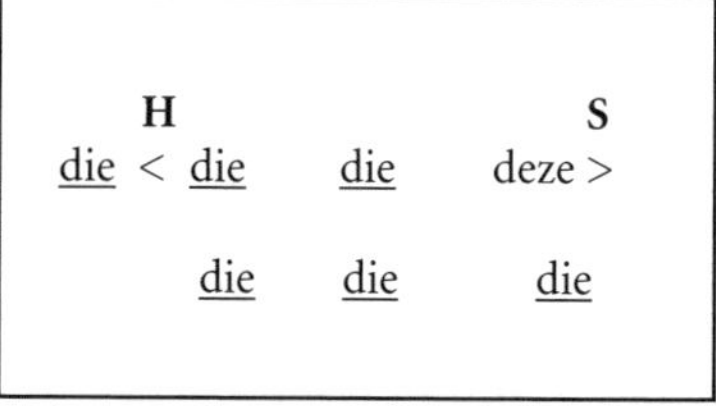

Italian demonstrative determiners are described in different ways in grammars: Gaudino-Fallegger (1992) claims that *questo*, the proximal term, is unmarked and *quello* is the marked term; for Agozzino (1985), on the contrary, the marked term would be *questo*.

The data collected through the questionnaire show a widespread use of the distal *quello*, which could be considered the unmarked term: Italian belongs to the same subgroup of English, Swedish, Norwegian, Danish and Dutch.

(16) Italian
DET
face-to-face
1 object (pictures: 1–7)

(17) Italian
DET
side-by-side
1 object (pictures: 37–39)

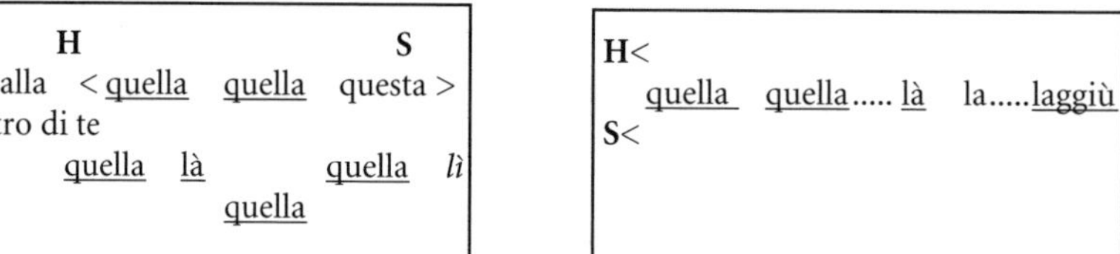

Another subgroup which has been identified through the analysis of the data collected by means of the questionnaire includes Polish, Hungarian, Czech, Russian, Modern Greek and Bulgarian. These languages contrast an unmarked term with a distal term.

Their behavior seems to be mirror-like to that exhibited by English, Danish, Dutch, Italian, Norwegian and Swedish.

(18) Polish
DET
face-to-face
1 object (pictures: 1–7)

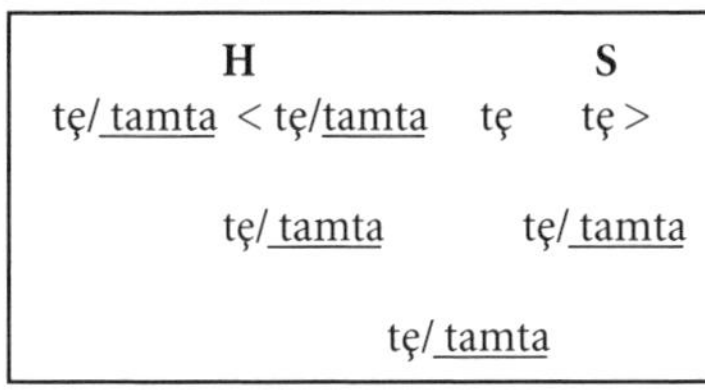

(19) Hungarian
DET
side-by-side
1 object (pictures: 37–39)

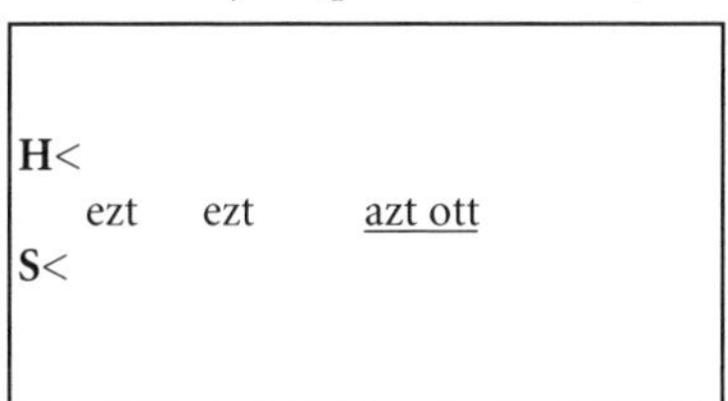

(20) Czech
ADV
face-to-face
1 object (pictures: 8–15; 19–21)

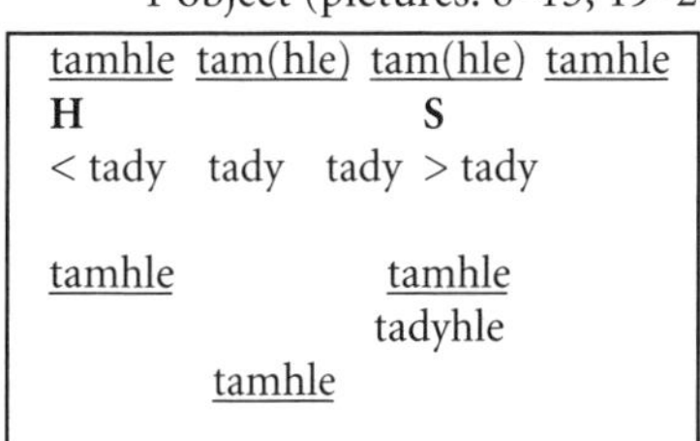

(21) Modern Greek
ADV
face-to-face
1 object (pictures: 8–15; 19–21)

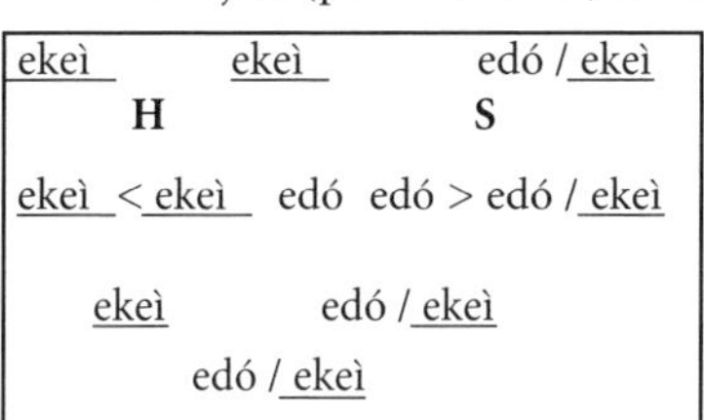

(22) Bulgarian
DET
face-to-back
1 object (pictures: 22–23)

S H
< < tazi tazi

To sum up, these languages seem to use the two terms of their opposition in a different way: the so-called distal term is the marked member, while the proximal term is neutral and it is used in many contexts if there is no need to specify distance. Moreover, as is the case in Czech, these unmarked forms could develop article-like functions (Cummins 1998; Trovesi 2004).

Finally, French and German demonstrative determiners show a tendency toward the reduction to one term. In the literature, French and German are described in different ways. As far as French is concerned, its system of demonstratives is sometimes considered as having only one term, *ce* (Lavric 1997), sometimes two terms, namely *celui-ci* and *celui-là*, and finally even three terms, if *là-bas* is taken into account (Frei 1944). In (23) the way in which demonstrative adverbs function has been described; as far as demonstrative determiners are concerned, French uses only one term, *ce*, which can be reinforced by a demonstrative adverb:

(23) French
DET
side-by-side
1 object (pictures: 37–39)

H<
la la/cette.....(là-bas) la/cette .... là-bas
S<

German shows a similar behavior. While traditional descriptions consider German as having a three-term system (Ehrich 1982), Diessel describes the German system in a way which could also be applied to French:

> There are, however, a few languages in my sample in which some demonstratives are distance-neutral. For instance, though German has three adverbial demonstratives – *hier* 'here', *da* 'there', and *dort* 'there' – it employs a single demonstrative pronoun: *dies* 'this/that' [. . .]. Demonstratives such as German *dies* are typologically uncommon [. . .] I will treat them as demonstratives for two reasons: first like distance-marked demonstratives, distance-neutral demonstratives are commonly used to orient hearer in the surrounding situation, and second they can always be reinforced by demonstratives that are marked for distance if it is necessary to differentiate between two or more referents (Diessel 1999: 2).

(24) German
DET
face-to-face
1 object (pictures: 1–7)

S		**H**	
<den/diesen/den...hier	den/diesen/den...*da*	den/diesen/den...*da*>den/diesen/den da	
den/diesen/den...*da*		den/diesen/den...*da*	
	den/diesen/den...*da*		

4. The parallel corpus

The core of the analysis is represented by the data gathered through the questionnaire; in order to check the generalizations obtained by the collected data, a corpus of parallel texts has been used, consisting of translations of the same book – "Harry Potter and the Chamber of Secrets" by J.K. Rowling – in various European languages (this topic is discussed in Da Milano (forthcoming)).[5]

On the one hand, I have chosen a book of the Harry Potter's serie because of the availability of translations in many languages; on the other hand, because the writing and conversational style of the book is very realistic. The conversation is very natural and colloquial and includes a lot of dialogues, i.e. contexts in which demonstratives are frequently employed in their exophoric use. A parallel corpus based on the translations of the same Harry Potter book has been used for a typological study on epistemic possibility in Slavonic languages (van der Auwera/Schalley/Nuyts 2005). Moreover, Stolz (forthcoming) has used another book of the Harry Potter's series – "Harry Potter and the Philosopher's stone" – to investigate possessive relations in the languages of Europe.

The use of translations in linguistic research is problematic: the phenomenon of interference from the source language is well known (Gellerstam 1996). But this does not mean that translations must be ignored: translational equivalents can be a very useful tool in linguistic research.

An example could be represented by a recent contrastive study on spatial demonstratives in English and Chinese (Wu 2004): one set of data has been obtained via an experimental procedural task (jigsaw puzzle task), the other one from a corpus formed by two pieces of narrative discourse ('Winnie-The-Pooh' and 'Baohulu de Mimi') with their Chinese and English translations, respectively: "Parallel texts make it possibile to observe how demonstrative reference in one language is signalled in the other within basically similar or identical propositions. As parallel texts put the discourse contextual factors largely in control, the behaviour of the demonstratives can be observed and compared in a focused manner" (Wu 2004: 26).

In the original text of my corpus all the occurrences of deictic uses of demonstratives have been isolated and for each of the sentences the translational equivalents have been searched for. The total set of sentences with both demonstrative determiners/pronouns and demonstrative adverbs amounts to 83. Parallel texts, used as a control test of data obtained through the questionnaire, mainly confirm the typological generalizations, as it can be seen from the examples below.

Determiners and pronouns concerning the data from the questionnaire allowed classifying the languages into eight different types, four three-term demonstrative systems and four two-term demonstrative systems (see Sections 3 and 6).

In dual-anchored type systems (represented by Basque and Spanish) the medial term is used both to refer to something near the addressee and to something at a

5. Languages of the translations: Basque, Catalan, Czech, Dutch, French, German, Hungarian, Italian, Polish, Spanish.

medium distance away from the speaker (ex. 1–2). The following example from the parallel text shows a clear context in which the intended referent is near the addressee:[6]

(25) Harry, glancing over, saw Malfoy stoop and snatch up something. Leering, he showed it to Crabbe and Goyle, and Harry realised that he'd got Riddle's diary.
  a. 'Give *that* back' said Harry quietly. [English 258[7]]
  b. '¡Devuélveme *eso*!' – le dijo Harry en voz baja. [Spanish 204]
  c. 'Itzuli *hori*!' – esan zion Harryk isilka. [Basque 201]

English, which has a two-term system, always uses the distal/unmarked term, whereas Spanish and Basque use the medial term.

As far as two-term systems are concerned, Norwegian, Danish, Dutch, English and Northern Italian (ex. 12–17) show an opposition between a proximal term and an unmarked one; the following examples show that English and Dutch exhibit a clear preference for the use of the distal term in situations unmarked for proximity:

(26) a. Tie *that* round the bars,' said Fred, throwing the end of a rope to Harry. [English 32]
  b. 'Hier, knoop *dat* om de tralies', zei Fred, die Harry een touw toewierp. [Dutch 23]

(27) a. 'Is *that* supposed to be music?' Ron whispered. [English 144]
  b. 'Moet *dat* muziek voorstellen?' fluisterde Ron. [Dutch 100]

The reverse case was also attested in the questionnaire study: Polish, Russian, Czech, Hungarian, Bulgarian and Modern Greek treat the proximal demonstrative as the unmarked case, in contrast to a marked distal (ex. 18–22). In the examples (28) and (29) from the parallel texts, English uses the unmarked distal form; however, in Polish, Czech and Hungarian the unmarked proximal term is used:

(28) a. 'Tie *that* round the bars,' said Fred, throwing the end of a rope to Harry. [English 32]
  b. 'Przywiąż *to* do kraty', powiedział Fred, rzucając Harry'emu koniec liny. [Polish 32]
  c. To úž mu Fred pohotově házel konec provazu a vyzval Harryho: 'Uvaž ho kolem *té* mříže!' [Czech 27]
  d. '*Ezt* kösd rá a rácsra', szólt Fred, és egy kötelet dobott oda Harrynek. [Hungarian 30]

(29) Dumbledore reached across to Professor McGonagall's desk, picked up the blood-stained silver sword and handed it to Harry. [...]
  a. 'Only a true Gryffindor could have pulled *that* out of the Hat, Harry', said Dumbledore simply. [English 358]

6. For other examples from the parallel texts, see Da Milano (forthcoming).

7. Numbers behind the citations refer to the pages of the editions consulted.

b. 'Tylko prawdziwy Gryfon mógł wyciagnąć *ten* miecz z tiary' rzekł profesor Dumbledore. [Polish 347–348]
c. '*Ten*hle meč mohl z klobouku vytáhnout jedině ten, kdo do Nebelvíru opravdu patří', řekl prostě Brumbál. [Czech 280]
d. '*Ezt* csak olyan ember húzhatta elő a süvegből, aki ízig-vérig griffendéles' szólt Dumbledore. [Hungarian 309]

As the results obtained via the questionnaire have shown, and the parallel texts seem to confirm, French and German show a tendency to use only one term, *celà/ça* and *der/die/das*, respectively. In most examples, the two languages use only this demonstrative, as is illustrated here:

(30) a. 'Tie *that* round the bars,' said Fred, throwing the end of a rope to Harry. [English 32]
b. 'Attache *ça* aux barreaux', dit Fred qui lança à Harry l'extrémité d'une corde. [French 30]
c. 'Schnür *das* um die Gitterstäbe', sagte Fred und warf Harry das Ende eines Seils zu. [German 29]

(31) a. 'Can I have *that*?' interrupted Draco, pointing at the withered hand on its cushion. [English 60]
b. 'Est-ce que je peux avoir *ça*?' coupa Drago, en montrant du doigt la main desséchée posée sur le coussin. [French 58]
c. 'Kann ich *die* haben?', unterbrach Draco und deutete auf die verwitterte Hand auf dem Kissen. [German 56]

Demonstrative adverbs are concerned also in the case of a first classification between two-term and three-term systems. As shown in Section 3, Spanish and Basque have been classified as dual-anchored systems: example (32) shows a context in which the speaker points very clearly to a space near the addressee and in this context Spanish and Basque use the medial term:

(32) a. Dear Ron, and Harry if you're *there*, [English 53]
b. Querido Ron, y Harry, si estás *ahí*, [Spanish 45]
c. Ron maitea, eta Harry ere bai, *hor* baldin badago: [Basque 43]

German has a system with a contrast among proximal, medial and distal terms (*hier*, *da*, *dort*); however, the examples (33)–(34) show the widespread use of the adverb *da*, indicating that *da* is becoming the default demonstrative adverb.

(33) a. 'Oh, Ron, there won't be anyone in *there*', said Hermion. [English 170]
b. 'Ach Ron, *da* wird niemand drin sein', sagte Hermine. [German 162]

(34) a. There was an ugly sort of wardrobe to his left, full of the teachers' cloaks. 'In *here*. Let's hear what it's all about. [English 315]
b. Zu seiner Rechten stand ein hässlicher Kleiderschrank voller Lehrerumhänge. '*Da* rein. Hören wir erst mal, was eigentlich los ist. [German 301]

From the data obtained with the French translation of Harry Potter, it is also possible to observe the widespread use of the adverb *là*, progressively replacing *ici* (ex. 7–8). Examples (35) and (36) show contexts in which the places referred to are clearly near the speaker: in these cases, English uses the proximal term *here*, while French uses the (formerly) distal *là*:

(35) a. 'What're you doing *here*?' [English 218]
b. 'Qu'est-ce que vous faites *là*?' [French 215]

(36) a. 'I'm *here*!' came Ron's muffled voice from behind the rockfall. [English 326]
b. 'Je suis *là*!' répondit la voix étouffée de Ron, derrière l'amas de rocs. [French 319]

As shown in (9), in Italian a system of demonstrative adverbs is attested that shows a tendency to develop a contrast among three terms; parallel texts seem to confirm this behavior:

(37) a. 'It's *over there*, it got washed out'.
Harry and Ron looked under the sink, where Myrtle was pointing.
A small, thin book lay there. [English 249]
b. 'Eccolo *lì*, si è bagnato tutto!'
Harry e Ron guardarono sotto il lavandino, nella direzione indicata da Mirtilla. Per terra c'era un libriccino [Italian 208]

(38) a. 'Ron – *that* girl who died. Aragog said she was found in a bathroom', said Harry, ignoring Neville's snuffling snores from the corner. 'What if she never left the bathroom? What if she's still *there*?' [English 304]
b. 'Ron…la ragazza che è morta. Aragog ha detto che fu trovata in un gabinetto' disse Harry ignorando Neville che russava fragorosamente dall'altra parte della stanza. 'E se non fosse mai uscita dal gabinetto? E se fosse ancora *là*?' [Italian 253–254]

Finally, as far as two-term systems of demonstrative adverbs are concerned, as previously shown (Section 3), Norwegian, Danish, English and Dutch show a system in which the distal term is unmarked:

(39) a. 'HARRY! What d'yeh think yer doin' down *there*?' [English 62]
b. 'HARRY! Wat mot dat *daar*?' [Dutch 44]

while Polish, Russian, Czech, Hungarian, Bulgarian and Modern Greek have two-term demonstrative systems in which the proximal demonstrative is unmarked; also in these cases, the parallel corpus seems to confirm the generalizations obtained through the questionnaire. In contexts in which English uses the distal adverb *there*, Polish, Czech and Hungarian use the proximal term, as exemplified in (40)–(41):

(40) a. 'HARRY! What d'yeh think yer doin' down *there*?' [English 62–63]
b. 'HARRY! Cholibka, a co ty *tutaj* robisz?' [Polish 61]
c. 'HARRY! Prosím tě, co *tady* pohledáváš?' [Czech 51]
d. 'HARRY! Mi a cickafarkat keresel te *itt*?' [Hungarian 55]

(41) a 'Wait *there*', he called to Ron. [English 327]
b. Poczekaj *tutaj*!' zawołał do Rona. [Polish 318–319]
c. 'Počkej *tady*!' křykl na Rona. [Czech 256]
d. 'Várj meg *itt*' kiáltott át Ronnak. [Hungarian 283]

5. Conclusions

As it can be seen on Map (1) and Map (2), systems which traditionally have been considered homogeneous at a deeper analysis show relevant differences; we have to keep in mind that

> Perhaps right at the outset the reader should be warned that cross-linguistic data on deictic categories is not as good as one would expect, given that core deictic expressions are readily identifiable. One problem is that the meaning of deictic expressions is usually treated as self-evident in grammatical descriptions and rarely properly investigated, and a second problem is that major typological surveys (which perforce rely on those descriptions) have largely yet to be done (but see Cysouw 2001, Diessel 1999) (Levinson 2004: 32)

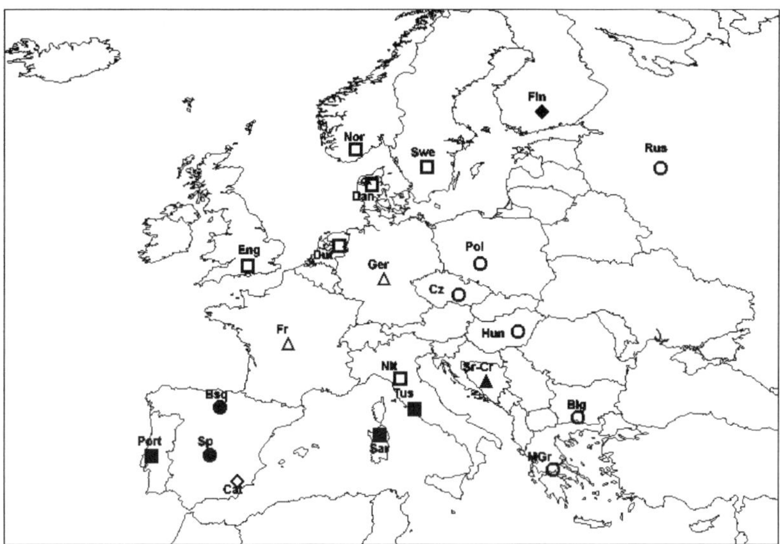

○ unmarked/distal contrast
□ proximal/unmarked contrast
△ toward one-term system
◇ prototypic. dyad-oriented system
● dual-anchored type system
■ addressee-anchored type system
▲ toward reduction
◆ not prototypic. dyad-oriented

Map 1. Areal distribution of the systems of demonstrative determiners/pronouns in the languages of Europe.

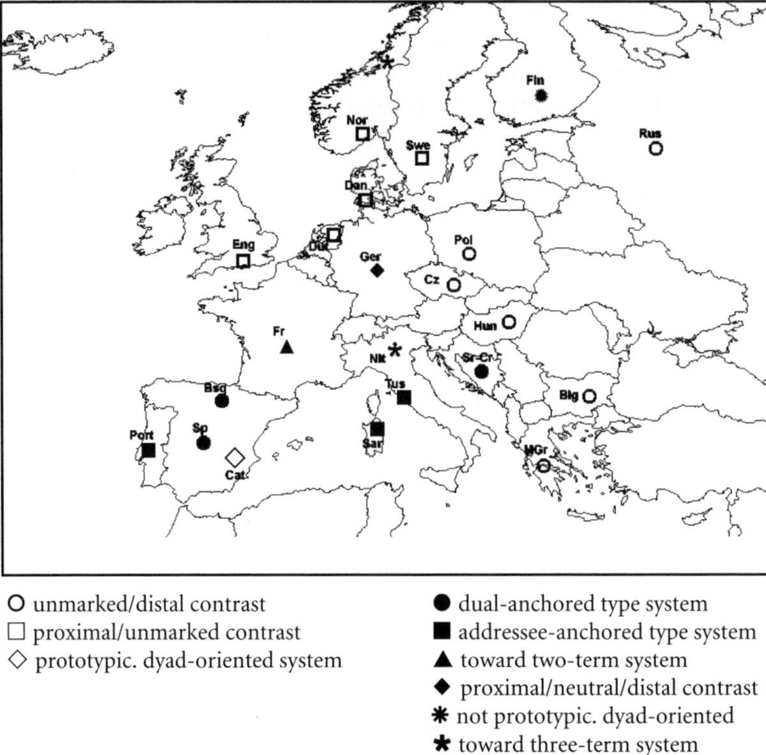

Map 2. Areal distribution of the systems of demonstrative adverbs in the languages of Europe.

The theoretical model which has been used in this analysis, based on the notion of 'dyad of conversation', has turned out to be very useful to investigate apparently negligible (and in many descriptions neglected) nuances in the structure of demonstrative systems. This was particularly needed in a field of research where communicative factors play a relevant role and whose influence in the way in which the system is structured is analysable with difficulty. The reciprocal orientation of the speaker and the hearer seems to have a fundamental relevance in analysing a phenomenon in which factors of the communicative situations are absolute.

It can be seen from the maps that there is a lack of isomorphism between the systems of demonstrative determiners/pronouns on the one hand and the systems of demonstrative adverbs on the other hand. The systems of adverbs show a more complex articulation. This seems to be a well established typological tendency: "Perhaps one can hazard the generalizations that speaker-centered degrees of distance are usually (more) fully represented in the adverbs than the pronominals" (Levinson 2004: 43).

To sum up, from the observation of the maps, it has been possible to identify three sub-groups: the first one includes French, German, Dutch and Northern Italian, which show a similar behavior and constitute, not accidentally, the so-called 'Charle-Magne Sprachbund' (van der Auwera 1998); the second subgroup is formed by the languages of central-eastern Europe, and two of these languages (Bulgarian and Modern Greek) belong to the so-called 'Balkan Sprachbund' (Banfi 1985; 1991); finally, the last subgroup includes Basque, Spanish, Portuguese, Tuscan, Sardinian, Serbian-Croatian; they belong to the Mediterranean area, which does not constitute a real linguistic area (Ramat/Stolz 2002), but which, nevertheless, shows interesting phenomena of convergence.

It is also possible to individuate characteristic elements of the areal model 'center-periphery' (Dahl 2002), which represents the diffusion of a linguistic phenomenon from a cultural, economic and/or politic center, represented in this case by the French-German area. For example, we can find a significant parallelism between the German demonstrative *der* and the Czech demonstrative *ten*. Moreover, it is necessary to underline the typological rarity (Diessel 1999; 2005) shown by French and German. The tendency toward the reduction to one demonstrative determiner (French *ce* and German *der*), neutral for distance, which is very unusual from a typological point of view, is a behavior which could confirm the existence of a European Sprachbund whose nucleus is represented precisely by French and German.

References

Agozzino, D. 1985. Analisi delle strutture informative nel parlato. In *Sintassi e morfologia della lingua italiana d'uso. Teorie e applicazioni descrittive*, A. Franchi De Bellis & L.M. Savoia (ed.), 19–32. Roma: Bulzoni.

Alonso, M. 1968. *Gramática del español contemporaneo.* Madrid: Guadarrama.

Banfi, E. 1985. *Linguistica balcanica.* Bologna: Zanichelli.

Banfi, E. 1991. *Storia linguistica del sud-est europeo.* Milano: Franco Angeli.

Benedetti, M. et al. 2000. The systems of deictic place adverbs in the Mediterranean, handout MedTyp Workshop, Tirrenia (PI), June, 1–3 2000.

Benedetti, M. & Ricca, D. 2002. The systems of deictic place adverbs in the Mediterranean. In P. Ramat & T. Stolz (eds), 13–32.

Bernini, G. & Ramat, P. 1992. *La frase negativa nelle lingue d'Europa.* Bologna: Il Mulino.

Bernini, G. & Ramat, P. 1996. *Negative sentences in the languages of Europe: A typological approach.* Berlin: Mouton de Gruyter.

Brodin, G. 1970. *Termini dimostrativi toscani. Studio storico di morfologia sintassi e semantica.* Lund: C.W.K. Gleerup.

Bühler, K. 1934. *Sprachtheorie.* Stuttgart: Fischer (Italian translation: 1983. *Teoria del linguaggio.* Roma: Armando Editore).

Carrera Díaz, M. 1997. *Grammatica spagnola.* Bari: Laterza.

Casares, J. 1959. *Diccionario ideológico de la lengua española.* 2nd edn., Barcelona: Gustavo Gili.

Cysouw, M. 2001. The paradigmatic structure of person marking. PhD Dissertation, University of Nijmegen.

Cysouw, M. & Wälchli, B. (eds). Forthcoming. Parallel texts: Using translational equivalents in linguistic typology. Special Issue of *STUF.*

Cysouw, M., Biemann, C. & Ongyerth, M. Forthcoming. Using Strong's numbers in the Bible to test an automatic alignment of parallel texts. In M. Cysouw & B. Wälchli (eds).

Cummins, G.M. 1998. Definiteness in Czech. *Studies in Language* 22(3): 567–596.

Dahl, Ö. 1985. *Tense and aspect systems.* Oxford: Blackwell.

Dahl, Ö. 2002. Principles of areal typology. In M. Haspelmath, E. König, W. Oesterreicher & W. Raible (eds), 1456–1470.

Da Milano, F. 2005. *La deissi spaziale nelle lingue d'Europa.* Milano: Franco Angeli.

Da Milano, F. Forthcoming. Demonstratives in parallel texts: A case study. In M. Cysouw & B. Wälchli (eds).

Diessel, H. 1999. *Demonstratives. Form, function and grammaticalization.* Amsterdam: John Benjamins.

Diessel, H. 2005. Distance contrasts in demonstratives. In *The world atlas of language structures,* M. Haspelmath, M.S. Dryer, D. Gil & B. Comrie (eds), 170–173. Oxford: OUP.

Dixon, R.M.W. 2003. Demonstratives. A cross-linguistic typology. In *Studies in Language* 27: 61–112.

Enfield, N.J. 2003. Demonstratives in space and interaction. Data from Lao speakers and implications for semantic analysis. *Language* 79: 82–117.

Ehrich, V. 1982. Da and the system of spatial deixis in German. In J. Weissenborn & W. Klein (eds), 43–63.

Eurotyp Guidelines, www.lotschool.nl/Research/ltrc/eurotyp/

Fillmore, C.J. 1982. Towards a descriptive framework for spatial deixis. In *Speech, place and action. Studies in deixis and related topics,* R.J. Jarvella & W. Klein (eds), 31–59. Chichester: Wiley.

Frei, H. 1944. Systèmes de déictiques. *Acta Linguistica* 4: 111–129.

Gaudino-Fallegger, L. 1992. *I dimostrativi nell'italiano parlato.* Wilhelmsfeld: Gottfried Egert.

Gellerstam, M. 1996. Translation as a source for cross-linguistic studies. In *Languages in contrast: Papers from a symposium on text-based cross-linguistic studies,* K. Aijmer, B. Altenberg & M. Johansson (eds), 53–62. Lund: Lund University Press.

Greenberg, J. 1966. *Universals of Language.* 2nd edn., Cambridge MA: The MIT Press.

Hanks, W.F. 1990. *Referential practice. Language and lived space among the Maya.* Chicago IL: University of Chicago Press.

Harris, M. 1988. French. In *The romance languages,* M. Harris & N. Vincent (eds), 209–245. London: Croom Helm.

Haspelmath, M. 1997. *Indefinite pronouns.* Oxford: Clarendon Press.

Hottenroth, P.-M. 1983. Die Bezeichnung räumlicher Verhältnisse. I. Deixis.II. Präpositionen. In *Bausteine für eine italienische Grammatik,* C. Schwarze, 11–169. Tübingen: Narr.

Imai, S. 2003. Spatial deixis. PhD Dissertation, State University of New York at Buffalo.

Janssen, T. 2004. Deixis and reference. In *Morphologie/morphology. Ein internationales Handbuch zur Flexion und Wortbildung /An international handbook on inflection and word formation,* G. Booij, C. Lehmann & J. Mugdan (eds), in collaboration with W. Kesselheim & S. Skopeteas, 983–998. Berlin: Mouton de Gruyter.

Jungbluth, K. 2001a. Deictics in the dyad of conversation. Findings in the romance languages, handout 23. Jahrestagung der DGfS *Sprache und Kognition*, Leipzig, February 28th – March, 2nd 2001.

Jungbluth, K. 2001b. Data and deictics: Demonstratives in Spanish, Portuguese and Catalan, Sonderforschungsbereich 441, International Conference on Linguistic Data Structures, Tübingen, February 22–24 2001.

Jungbluth, K. 2005. *Pragmatik der Demonstrativpronomina in den iberoromanischen Sprachen.* Tübingen: Niemeyer.

Kemmerer, D. 1999. 'Near' and 'far' in language and perception. *Cognition* 73: 35–63.

Kryk, B. 1987. *On deixis in English and Polish. The role of demonstrative pronouns.* Frankfurt: Peter Lang.

Lakoff, R. 1974. Remarks on this and that. In *Papers from the tenth regional meeting of the Chicago Linguistic Society*, M.W. La Galy, R.A. Fox & A. Bruck, 345–356.

Lavric, E. 1997. 'Ese reino movible' – Spanische, Französische und deutsche Demonstrativa. In *Studien zum romanisch-deutschen und innerromanischen Sprachvergleich*, G. Wotjak (ed.), 515–543. Frankfurt: PeterLang.

Levinson, S.C. 2004. Deixis and pragmatics. In *The Handbook of pragmatics*, L. Horn & G. Ward (eds), 97–121. Oxford: Blackwell.

Meira, S. 2003. 'Addressee effects' in demonstrative systems: The cases of Tiriyó and Brazilian Portuguese. In *Deictic conceptualization of space, time and person*, F. Lenz (ed.), 3–11. Amsterdam: John Benjamins.

Nichols, J. 1992. *Linguistic diversity in space and time.* Chicago IL: University of Chicago Press.

Patrick, J.D. & Zubiri Ibarrondo, I. 2001. *A student grammar of Euskara.* Munich: Lincom.

Ramat, P. & Stolz, T. (eds). 2002. *Mediterranean languages. Papers from the MEDTYP workshop. Tirrenia, June 2000.* Bochum: Universitätsverlag Dr.N. Brockmeyer.

Ricca, D. 1993. *I verbi deittici di movimento in Europa: una ricerca interlinguistica.* Firenze: La Nuova Italia.

Ruhl, C. 1989. *On monosemy.* Albany NY: State University of New York Press.

Saussure, F. 1916. *Cours de linguistique générale.* Payot: Paris.

Stolz, T. Forthcoming. Harry Potter meets Le Petit Prince: On the usefulness of parallel literary corpora in crosslinguistic investigations. In M. Cysouw & B. Wälchli (eds).

Trovesi, A. 2004. *La genesi di articoli determinativi. Modalità di espressione della definitezza in ceco, serbo-lusaziano e sloveno.* Milano: Franco Angeli.

Van der Auwera, J. (ed.) 1998. *Adverbial constructions in the languages of Europe.* Berlin: Mouton de Gruyter.

Van der Auwera, J., Schalley, A. & Nuyts, J. 2005. Epistemic possibility in a Slavonic parallel corpus – a pilot study. In *Modality in Slavonic languages. New perspectives*, B. Hansen & P. Karlík (eds), 201–217. Munich: Otto Sagner.

Vanelli, L. 1992. *La deissi in italiano.* Padova: Unipress.

Vanelli, L. 2001. La deissi. In *Grande grammatica italiana di consultazione*, L. Renzi, G. Salvi & C. Cardinaletti (eds), 259–468. Bologna: Il Mulino.

Weissenborn, J. & Klein, W. (eds). 1982. *Here and there. Cross-linguistic studies on deixis and demonstration.* Amsterdam: John Benjamins.

Wilkins, D.P. 1999. The 1999 demonstrative questionnaire: 'THIS' and 'THAT' in comparative perspective. In *Manual for the 1999 Field Season*, D.P. Wilkins (ed.), 1–24. Nijmegen: Max Planck Institute.

Wu, Yi'an. 2004. *Spatial demonstratives in English and Chinese. Text and cognition.* Amsterdam: John Benjamins.

Appendix – The questionnaire

face-to-face
1 object

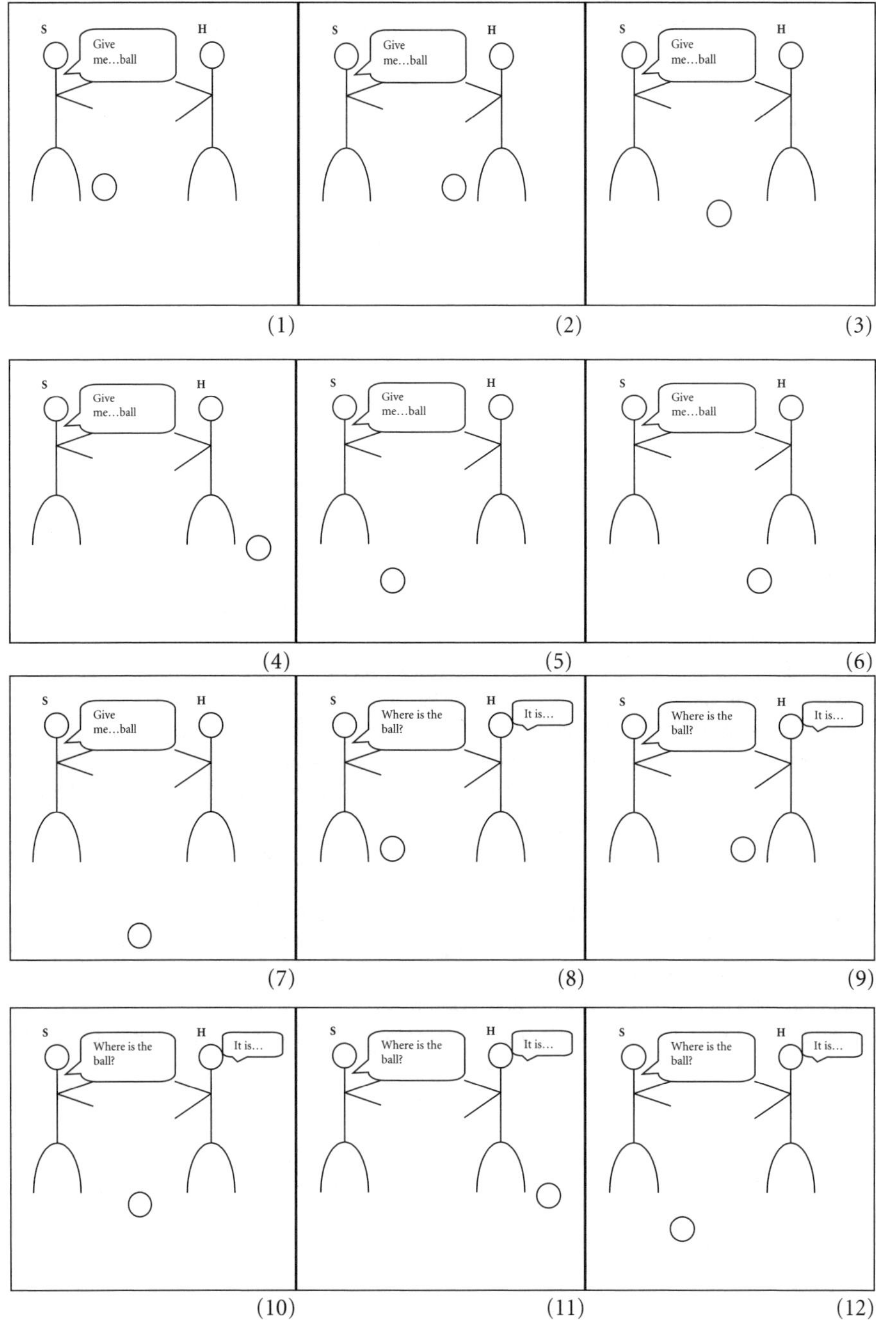

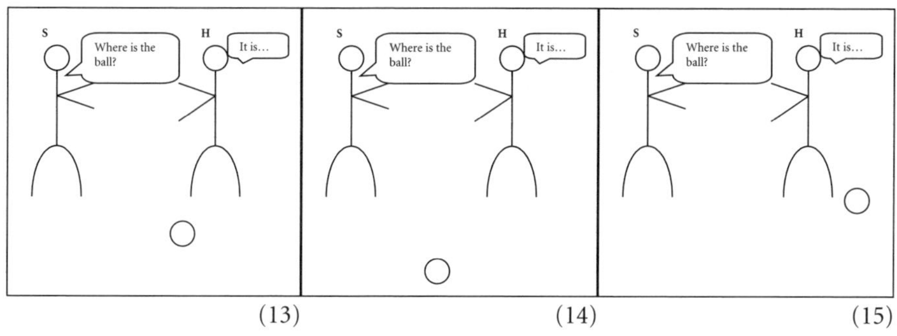

(13) (14) (15)

face-to-face
3 objects

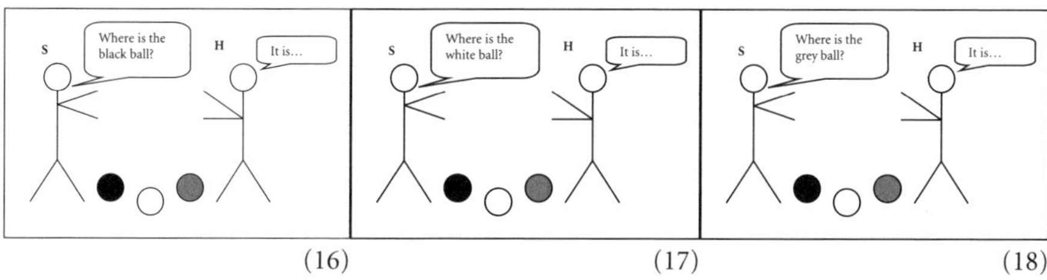

(16) (17) (18)

face-to-face
the moon

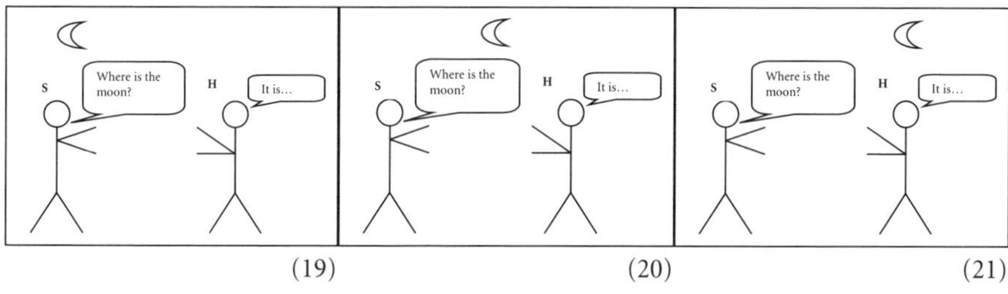

(19) (20) (21)

face-to-back
1 object

(22) (23) (24)

(25) (26) (27)

face-to-back
3 objects

(28) (29) (30)

(31) (32) (33)

face-to-back
the moon

(34) (35) (36)

side-by-side
1 object

(37) (38) (39)

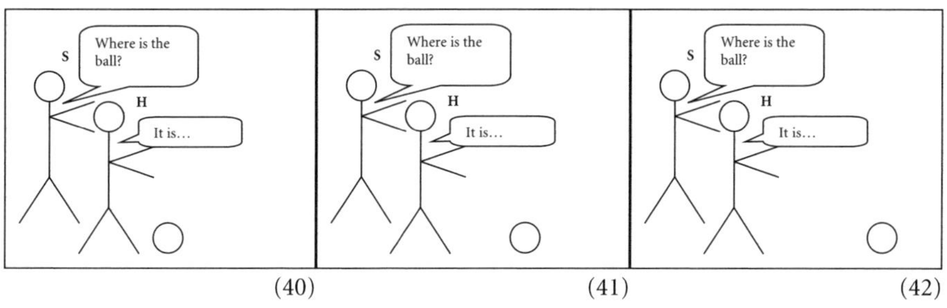

(40) (41) (42)

side-by-side
3 objects

(43) (44) (45)

side-by-side
the moon

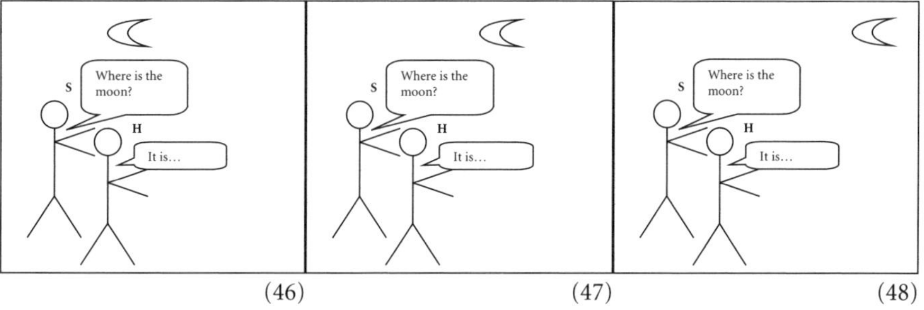

(46) (47) (48)

Internal structure of verbal stems in the Germanic languages

Paolo Di Giovine, Sara Flamini and Marianna Pozza[1]

The authors summarize the first significant results in order to verify to what extent the European languages of the Indo-European family are concerned by a typological change in verb morphology: a shift from a more conservative stage, where morphemes are either strongly integrated within the root or "root expansions", towards a stage where functionality shifts to suffixal morphemes. By means of recapitulatory tables, the paper sets out the method of analysis and the results achieved in the Germanic area, beginning with Gothic and Anglo-Saxon. In spite of common opinion, the evidence that both languages are quite innovative in their trend to exomorphism emerges from the ratio between endomorphic/mixed stems and exomorphic stems: the Gothic index is 0,430 (0,445), the Anglo-Saxon one is 0,531, which means a stage by far less archaic than the Indo-Aryan (1,777 to 0,965) and the Avestan one (0,665).

1. Introductory remarks

1.1. This paper is a chapter of a major research which aims at calculating the place held by the European languages of the I.E. family in a typological scale ranging from internal verb morphology to external verb morphology. According to a proposal dating back to Sapir (1921: 67 ff.) and recently developed by Silvestri (2003: 223 ff.), the typology of verb structure in the ancient languages of the I.E. domain[2] can be labelled as follows:

a. endomorphic stems: internal morphemes (Ablaut, infixes) and/or reduplication (which is an endomorphic morpheme according to De Angelis and Di Giovine 2006, § 1);
b. "mixed" stems: both internal and external morphemes;
c. exomorphic stems: only external morphemes (suffixes, prefixes, periphrastic forms).

---

1. Paolo Di Giovine is responsible for §§ 1.1, 1.2, 2.3–2.6, 3.3, 3.5, 3.6, Sara Flamini for §§ 1.3, 2.1, 3.1, Marianna Pozza for §§ 2.2, 3.2, 3.4.

2. On word structure in the I.E. languages see Belardi 1993: 535 ff.

1.2. A quite satisfactory way of calculating the development index from A-pattern to C-pattern has been previously pointed out (De Angelis and Di Giovine 2006, which includes general and typological references). The ratio between archaic stems (A- and largely B-patterns) and innovative stems (C-pattern) is processed by means of such a fraction: (A+B)/C – from a mathematical point of view, a quotient is the best way to stress a difference, however small it may be.

> A quotient ≥ 1 means that the analysed language is rather conservative, as to verb structure.
> A quotient < 1 marks a partially innovative language.
> A quotient < 0,50 marks a strongly innovative language.

Terms of comparison are highly useful in a research like this one, especially from the point of view of a typological analysis. A set of indexes previously processed with reference to some Eastern I.E. languages (De Angelis and Di Giovine 2006) pointed up a quick shift towards exomorphism within both Old Indo-Aryan (Vedic 1,777 > epic and class. Sanskrit 0,965) and Old Iranian (Gāthic 1,390 > late Avestan 0,665).

Now, we are going to focus our attention on the European languages, beginning with the Germanic languages. First of all, the analysis will affect an Eastern language, Gothic, and a Western language, Anglo-Saxon, both of them quite ancient – apart from runes, Gothic is the oldest historical language within the Germanic group (Ramat 1988: 26 ff.).

1.3. A wide-ranging diachronic comparative analysis needs selectioning a homogeneous sample, which can be obtained from LIV-indexes (Rix 2001). Therefore, within the Germanic group we decided to take into account all the Gothic and Anglo-Saxon verbs which are likely to derive from an Indo-European source (verbal root).

In fact, Anglo-Saxon requires a further precaution: Anglo-Saxon verbs are mentioned in LIV whenever any Gothic verb coming from the same root is missing, otherwise they are not included at all (so we may at first select only 125 Ags. verbs vs. 228 Goth. verbs). That is why our research had to complete the Anglo-Saxon sample – to the final extent of 283 verbs – by means of the Anglo-Saxon verbs which etymologically correspond to the Gothic ones mentioned in LIV-indexes (see Feist 1939; Holthausen 1963; Seebold 1970; Jarosch 1995–).

2. Morphological typology in Gothic verb inflection

2.1. An investigation affecting the whole set of the Gothic verbs having an Indo-European etymology can rely on a few lexicographical sources, nevertheless quite exhaustive. The best source is the Gothic "Thesaurus" (de Tollenaere and Jones 1976), which can be integrated – as to inflection patterns and diachronic remarks – by means of a couple of excellent etymological dictionaries (Feist 1939; Lehmann 1986).

2.2. According to common opinion (Braune 1961; Kieckers, 1928; Krahe 1967; Krause 1968), the Gothic inflectional categories should be filed under the following labels:

a. tense-stems
   present (weak verbs, strong verbs, preterite-present verbs, athematic verbs)
   preterite (weak, strong, pertaining to preterite-present verbs);
b. actionality-stems:
   causative, iterative … → present stem (weak)
   perfect → present stem (preterite-present verbs), strong preterite stem;
c. moods (secondary, they have to be ranked under present resp. preterite stems);
d. passive: it is a plain present stem, with a medial ending (e.g. III pl.: actv. _nimand_: passv. _nimanda_; actv. _nasjand_ : passv. _nasjanda_);
e. participle (present, preterite), infinitive: nominal forms of verb-inflection, on the whole not to be included in the reckoning (with a few exceptions, see § 2.3).

The structural labels (**_endomorphic_**, **mixed**, _exomorphic_) to be attributed to the inflectional categories of the Gothic verb system are shown in the following tables[3] – see § 2.3 for a comment on debatable choices:

Table 1. Gothic strong verbs

Class		Present		Preterite SG.		Preterite PL.		[Pret.participle]
I	*-ĕ-	_-beitan_	***-ŏ-**	**_-bait_**	*-Ø-	**_-bitun_**	*-Ø-	_-bitans_
II	*-ĕ-	_tiuhan_	***-ŏ-**	**_tauh_**	*-Ø-	**_taúhun_**	*-Ø-	_taúhans_
III	*-ĕ-	_-bindan_	***-ŏ-**	**_-band_**	*-Ø-	**_-bundun_**	*-Ø-	_-bundans_
		waírþan		**_warþ_**		**_waúrþun_**		_waúrþans_
		briggan		**_brāhta_** (< *branhta-), **_brāhtēdun_**				
IV	*-ĕ-	_niman_	***-ŏ-**	**_nam_**	***-ē-**	**_nēmun_**	*-Ø-	_numans_
		baíran		**_bar_**		**_bērun_**		_baúrans_
V	*-ĕ-	_giban_	***-ŏ-**	**_gab_**	***-ē-**	**_gēbun_**	*-ĕ-	_gibans_
		lisan		**_las_**		**_lēsun_**		_lisans_
VI	*-ŏ-	_sakan_	***-ō-**	**_sōk_**	***-ō-**	**_sōkun_**	*-ŏ-	_sakans_
	*-ă-	(**_standan_**)	(***-ā-**)	**_stōþ_**	(***-ā-**)	**_*stōþun_**	*-ă-	_(standans)_
VII	*-ē-	_lētan_	***-ō-**	**_laílōt_**	***-ō-**	**_laílōtun_**	*-ē-	_lētans_
Red	I	_haitan_		**_haíhait_**		**_haíhaitun_**		_haitans_
upl.	II	_aukan_		**_aíauk_**		**_*aíaukun_**		_etc._
	III	_fāhan_		**_faífāh_**		**_*faífāhun_**		
	IV	_*slēpan_		**_saíslēp_**		**_saíslēpun_**		
	V	_*flōkan_		**_*faíflōk_**		**_faíflōkun_**		

3. As to Gmc. verb structure we follow the traditional outline, see Prokosch 1939; Meillet 1949; Krahe 1969; van Coetsem and Kufner 1972; Fullerton 1977; Bammesberger 1986 (further details in Kuryłowicz 1975).

Table 2. Gothic weak verbs

Class	[Inf.]	Present	Pret.	coming from:
I	*-jan*	*no Ablaut, themat.* (-ja-*suff.*)	*-ida*	a) *-*yo/e*-verbs b) *-*éyo/e*-iterat./intens. and caus. c) denominatives
II	*-ōn*	*no Ablaut, athemat.* (-ō-*suff.*)	*-ōda*	a) *-*ā(yo/e)*-suff. verbs b) denominatives
III	*-an*	*no Ablaut* (-a[i]-*suff.*)	*-aida*	a) primary verbs b) *-*ē(y)*-suff. verbs c) denominatives
IV	*-nan*	*no Ablaut*	***-nōda***	a) inchoat. *-*nā*-,*-*nə*-deverbat. b) inchoat. *-*nā*-,*-*nə*-denomin.

Table 3. Gothic preterite-presents

Class	Present SG.		Present PL.		Preterite	
I	***-ŏ-**	***wait***	***-Ø-**	***witun***	*-*to*-	*wissa*
II	***-ŏ-**	***daug***	***-Ø-**	****dugun***	*-*to*-	**duhta*
III	***-ŏ-**	***kann***	***-Ø-**	***kunnun***	*-*to*-	*kunþa*
IV	***-ŏ-**	***skal***	***-Ø-**	***skulun***	*-*to*-	*skulda*
V	***-ŏ-**	***mag***		[***magun*** < SG.]	*-*to*-	*mahta*
VI	***-ŏ-**	***-mōt***		–	*-*to*-	*-mōsta*

Table 4. Gothic athematic verbs

Present SG.	Present PL.	Preterite	
ist	***sind***		
(wiljau)	*(wileina)*	*-*to*-	*wilda*

From the point of view of inflection, we can say that Gothic verb consists of:

- 4 classes showing present stems of weak verbs (Krämer 1971)
- 7 classes showing present stems of strong verbs
- relics of athematic present stems
- 6 classes showing (present stems of) preterite-present verbs[4]
- 4 classes showing preterite stems of weak verbs
- 7 classes showing preterite stems of strong verbs
- 5 classes showing reduplicated preterite stems
- 6 classes showing (weak) preterite stems of preterite-present verbs.

4. On the origin of the Gmc. preterite-presents see Birkmann 1987.

2.3. Apart from a majority of clear-cut cases – Gothic verb classification is by far plainer than the Anglo-Saxon one, § § 3.2, 3.3 –, there are a couple of debatable choices:

- whether including or not nominal stems (participle, infinitive), whenever no verbal stem is available for a given root (we think that the former option is safer);
- how to weigh up the present stems of strong verbs. No doubt they are thematic forms, so they have to be labelled as exomorphic (we prefer not to consider the present stem of a strong verb as being apophonically subordinate to preterite).

2.4. Data processing implies a preliminary detailed production of the whole sample taken into account (that is to say, all Gothic verbs having an Indo-European source). An example is given below (*w.* = weak; *s.* = strong; a hyphen marks the beginning of prefixed forms):

Table 5. Gothic data-processing (partial sample)

Verbs	A-stems (endom.)	B-stems (mixed)	C-stems (exom.)
-geig(g)an (ga-) *w. III*			*pres.* -geiga- *pret.* -geigaida-
-geisnan (us-) *w. IV*		*pret.* -geisnōda-	
giban (af-, at-, fra-, us-) *s. V*	*pret.* gaf / gēbun		*pres.* giba-
-gildan (fra-, us-) *s. III*			*pres.* -gilda-
-ginnan (du-) *s. III*	*pret.* -gann / -gunnun		*pres.* -ginna-
-gitan (bi-) *s. V*	*pret.* -gat / -gētun		*pres.* -gita-
giutan (ufar-) *s. II*			*pres.* giuta-

2.5. The following table shows the figures pertaining to Gothic verb structure:

Table 6. Shift from endomorphism to exomorphism: Gothic figures

	Gothic			
Sample: 228 roots	total number	stems / roots	total number broadened with participles	stems / roots
A. endomorphic stems	99	0,434	107	0,469
B. "mixed" stems	6	0,026	6	0,026
C. exomorphic stems	236	1,035	263	1,154
a) pres. of weak verbs	69			
b) pret. of weak verbs and pret.-pres.	65			
c) pres. of strong verbs	102			
Average stem number (A + B + C)/228		1,495		1,649
Typological index: (A+B)/C	0,445 [< 0,50]		0,430 [< 0,50]	

2.6. As shown in the table, results are quantitatively significant. The sample extent of Gothic proves to be quite good (228 verbs) in comparison to the rich sample of Indo-Aryan (519; actually 454 in Saṁhitās, 410 in epic, class. Sanskrit), comparable with Avestan (± 250), sharply better than Old Persian (32).

Our findings are twofold:

a. there is a high percentage of strong verbs (including reduplicated verbs), in comparison with the roots of I.E. origin (125 or 126 out of 228, that is 55%); further, we have to add 13 preterite-presents (5,7%), one athematic verb and one irregular verb. Weak verbs do not reach 40% of the whole sample (87 or 88, that is 38,4%);

b. the index of shift from endomorphism to exomorphism in Gothic is 0,445 (excluding nominal stems) or 0,430 (including nominal stems, whenever no further data are available). It is lower than the quotients worked out with reference to a set of Eastern Indo-European languages (see above, § 1.2), with the exception of Old Persian (0,391).

3. Morphological typology in Anglo-Saxon verb inflection

3.1. When a similar investigation affects the whole set of the Anglo-Saxon verbs having an Indo-European etymology, the Old English lexicographical sources turn out to be by far richer and more complex than the Gothic ones. The best source is still Bosworth and Toller's *Anglo-Saxon Dictionary* (Bosworth and Toller 1882–98 + Toller 1908–21). We have integrated and brought up-to-date its data by means of *DOEC* (*The Dictionary of Old English Corpus in Electronic Form*). Minor sources have been Borden 1982; Holthausen 1963 (etymological) and a set of grammars (Brunner 1965; Campbell 1959; Pilch 1970; Sievers 1968; Stark 1982), all of them useful as to inflection patterns.

3.2. According to common opinion (see the above-mentioned grammars), the Anglo-Saxon inflectional categories should be filed under the following labels, parallel to those given in 2.2 for Gothic (both for Anglo-Saxon and for Gothic the starting point is the excellent I.E. categorization in Hoffmann 1970: 19 ff.; see also Kuryłowicz 1964; Watkins 1969):

a. tense-stems
    present (weak verbs, strong verbs, preterite-present verbs, athematic verbs)
    preterite (weak, strong, pertaining to preterite-present verbs);
b. actionality-stems
    causative, iterative … → present stem (weak);
    perfect → present stem (preterite-present verbs), strong preterite stem;
c. moods (secondary, they have to be ranked under present resp. preterite stems);
d. passive: a single form, *hatte* "he/she was called, his/her name was";
e. participle (present, preterite), infinitive: nominal forms of verb-inflection, on the whole not to be included in the calculation.

The structural labels (***endomorphic***, ***mixed***, exomorphic) to be attributed to the inflectional categories of the Anglo-Saxon verb system are shown in the following tables (further remarks in notes and in § 3.3):

Table 7. Anglo-Saxon strong verbs

Class	Present		Preterite SG.		Preterite PL.		[Pret. PT.]	
I	*-ĕ-	*drīfan*	*-ŏ-	***drāf***	*-Ø-	***drifon***	*-Ø-	*-drifen*
II	*-ĕ-	*bēodan*	*-ŏ-	***bēad***	*-Ø-	***budon***	*-Ø-	*-boden*
		brūcan		***brēac***		***brucon***		*-brocen*
III	*-ĕ-	*bindan*	*-ŏ-	***band (bond)***	*-Ø-	***bundon***	*-Ø-	*-bunden*
		helpan		***healp (halp)***		***hulpon***		*-holpen*
		weorpan		***wearp***		***wurpon***		*-worpen*
		berstan		***bærst***		***burston***		*-borsten*
	*-Ø-	*murnan*		***mearn***		***murnon***		*-mornen*
IV	*-ĕ-	*beran*	*-ŏ-	***bær***[ii]	*-ē-	***bǣron***[iv]	*-Ø-	*-boren*
		niman[i]		***nōm, nam***[iii]	***nōmon, nāmon***[v]			*-numen*
V	*-ĕ-	*metan*	*-ŏ-	***mæt***[viii]	*-ē-	***mǣton***	*-ĕ-	*-meten*
		giefan[vi]		***geaf***		***gēafon***		*-giefen*
		sittan[vii]		***sæt***		***sǣton***		*-seten*
VI	*-ŏ-	*faran*	*-ō-	***fōr***	*-ō-	***fōron***	*-ŏ-	*-faren*
		hebban		***hōf***		***hōfon***	*-hafen (-hæfen)*	
	*-ă-	***standan***	(*-ā-)	***stōd***	(*-ā-)	****stōdon***	*-ă-	*-standen (-stonden)*
reduplicated (Angl.)		*hātan*	*-Ø-	***heht***				*-hāten*
		(ond)rēdan		***(ond)reord***				*(ond)-rēden*
		lācan		***leolc***				*-lācen*
		lētan		***leort***				*-lēten*
red. lost I		*hātan*	-ē-	***hēt***	*-ē-	***hēton***		*-hāten*
		blandan (blondan)		***blēnd***		***blēndon***		*-blanden (-blonden)*
red. lost II		*stealdan*	-ēo-	***stēold***	-ēo-	***stēoldon***		*-stealden*
		bēatan		***bēot***		***bēoton***		*-bēaten*
		hrōpan		***hrēop***		***hrēopon***		*-hrōpen*
		blāwan		***blēow***		***blēowon***		*-blāwen*

i This form shows a regular raising of **-e-* to *-i-* before *-m-*.

ii Such a development is shared by West Saxon and mostly Northumbrian; Kentish – and seldom Northumbrian – have a *-e-*coloured vowel (e.g. *ber* etc.).

iii The *nōm* pattern is chiefly Anglian. In West Saxon it is residual, early replaced by *nam* (an innovation by analogy with III class: Brunner 1965: 301).

iv Such a development is West Saxon; Northumbrian and Kentish show a different outcome, *-ē-* (e.g. *bēr* etc.).

v The late *nāmon* pattern has perhaps arisen by analogy, but the mechanism of such an innovation is not clear at all.

vi *giefan* and *gietan* show the regular effects of vowel split after a palatal consonant (Brunner 1965: 302; Sievers 1968: 293 § 391 n. 2).

vii It is a *-ja-*present stem, with *-e-*Umlaut to *-i-*.

viii Such a development is shared by West Saxon and mostly Northumbrian; Kentish – and seldom Northumbrian – have a *-e-*coloured vowel (e.g. *met* etc.).

Table 8. Anglo-Saxon weak verbs

Class	[Infin.]	Present	Preterite	coming from:
I	*-(i)an*	*no Ablaut, themat.* (-(i)a-*suff.*)	*-de (-te);* *-ede*	a) *-*yo/e-* primary verbs b) *-*éyo/e*-iterat./intens. and caus. c) denominatives
II	*-ian*	*no Ablaut, themat.* (*-ōja- > -ia-*suff.*)	*-ode (-ude),* *-ade*[i]	a) *-*ā(yo/e)*-verbs b) denominatives
III	*-(e)an*	*no Ablaut, themat.* (*-(ē)ja- > -(i)a-*suff.*)	*-de*	a) primary verbs b) *-*ē(y)*-verbs c) denominatives

i *-ade*-suffix is normal in Anglian, but it is rare in West Saxon (where *-ode*, from an earlier *-ude*, is the most frequent one).

Table 9. Anglo-Saxon preterite-presents[5]

Class	Present SG.		Present PL.		Preterite	
I	***-ŏ-**	***wāt*** ***āh***	*-Ø-	***witon*** [***āgon*** < SG.]	*-*to-*	*wisse-*, *wiste-* [*āhte-* < SG.]
II	***-ŏ-**	***dēag (dēah)***	*-Ø-	***dugon***	*-*to-*	*dohte-*
III	***-ŏ-**	***con(n), can(n)*** ***ðearf***	*-Ø-	***cunnon*** ***ðurfon***	*-*to-*	*cūðe-* *ðorfte-*
IV	***-ŏ-**	***sceal(l)*** ***mon, man***	*-Ø-	***sculon, sceolon*** ***munon***	*-*to-*	*sculde-* *munde-*
[V]		–		–		–
VI	***-ō-**	***mōt***		***mōton***	*-*to-*	*mōste-*

Table 10. Anglo-Saxon athematic verbs

Present SG.	Present PL.	Preterite
eom	***sint, sind***	(*wesan*, ft. V*: wæs*)
bīom (bēo)	***bēoð, biðun***[i]	(*wesan*, ft. V*: wæs*)
dōm	***dōð***	***dyde***
gā	***gāð***	[*ēode*]
wille (< optat.)	*willað*	*-to- *wolde*

i Plural forms like *biðun* are not rare in Northumbrian, while *bēoð*, together with its variant *bīoð*, is the normal one in West Saxon (where I sing. *bēo* is an innovation which quickly gains ground at the expense of *bīom*: Brunner 1965: 354 f.).

5. See Tellier 1962.

From the point of view of inflection, we can say that Anglo-Saxon verb consists of:

- 3 classes showing present stems of weak verbs
- 6 classes showing present stems of strong verbs
  relics (4 verbs) of athematic present stems (Lühr 1985: 25 ff.)
- 5 classes showing (present stems of) preterite-present verbs
- 3 classes showing preterite stems of weak verbs
- 6 classes showing preterite stems of strong verbs
  relics of reduplicated preterite stems (Anglian)[6]
- 2 classes with early loss of reduplication (replaced with a root vowel *-ē-* or *-ēo-*)
- 5 classes showing (weak) preterite stems of preterite-present verbs.

3.3. A few questions need a preliminary answer before any reckoning:

- whether including or not nominal stems (participle, infinitive), when no verbal stem is available for a given root. This problem is not so relevant as in Gothic, because Anglo-Saxon has a very rich corpus. If – as I would prefer – we choose to include them, then we shall add three cases only: inf. *gengan*, pret. ptc. *brugen* and pres. ptc. *scūdende*;
- how to weigh up the present stems of strong verbs. As shown above (§ 2.3), they are thematic forms, so they have to be labelled as exomorphic (despite any reduction or loss of final vowels already in early Anglo-Saxon);
- how to weigh up "mixed" stems (vowel change and suffix(es)): when a vowel change depends on context (such as in *recc(e)an* "narrate" vs. pret. *reahte*, with vowel split before *h*), there is no question of "mixed" stems; on the contrary, a plain "mixed" stem occurs whenever there is infixation or ancient apophony or some early – Proto-Germanic – change (e.g. *ðenc(e)an* "think" vs. pret. *ðōhte*, where the long vowel reflects a Proto-Germanic development of I.E. **-anh-*).

3.4. The whole Anglo-Saxon sample was taken into account in a way similar to that carried out for Gothic:

Table 11. Anglo-Saxon data-processing (partial sample)

Verbs	A-stems (endom.)	B-stems (mixed)	C-stems (exom.)
standan (ā-, æt-, and-, be-, for-, fore-, ge-, in-, of-, ofer-, on-, oð-, tō-, ðurh-, under-, wið-, wiðer-, ymb-) *s. VI*	*pret.* stōd / stōdon	*pres.* stand(e)- (stond(e)-)	
-stealdan (ā -, on-) *red. II*	*pret.* stēold		*pres.* -steald(e)-
stelan (be-, for-, ge-) *s. IV*	*pret.* stæl / stǣlon		*pres.* stel(e)-
stenan (ā -) *s. IV*	*pret.* stæn / stǣnon		*pres.* sten(e)-
stencan (tō-) *w. I*			*pres.* stenc(e)- *pret.* stencte-

6. See Karstien 1921, Bech 1969–71 (further details in Beeler 1978: 5 ff.; van Coetsem 1990).

3.5. The following table shows the Anglo-Saxon figures:

Table 12. Shift from endomorphism to exomorphism: Anglo-Saxon figures

	Anglo-Saxon	
Sample: 283 roots	**total number**	**stems / roots**
A. endomorphic stems	189	0,668
B. "mixed" stems	6	0,021
C. exomorphic stems	367	1,301
a) pres. of weak verbs	93	
b) pret. of weak verbs and pret.-pres.	105	
c) pres. of strong verbs	169	
Average stem number (A + B + C) / 283		1,986
Typological index:		
(A+B)/C	0,531 ([> 0,50])	

3.6. As shown in the table, results are quantitatively significant. As expected, the sample extent of Anglo-Saxon (283 verbs) is somewhat better than the Gothic one (228) and sharply better than the Old Persian one (32). It is comparable with Avestan (250) and not far from the excellent sample of Indo-Aryan (519; actually 454 in Saṁhitās, 410 in epic, class. Sanskrit).

Our achievements are a meaningful step forward in the direction of placing the data into an appropriate frame both typologically and historically.

i. There is a high percentage of strong verbs (including reduplicated verbs), in comparison with the roots of I.E. origin (169 out of 283, that is 59,7%, vs. 55% in Gothic); further, we have to add 11 preterite-presents (3,9%) and 4 athematic verbs. Weak verbs (99) reach 35%, vs. 40% in Gothic.
ii. "Mixed" pattern is quite exceptional both in Anglo-Saxon and in Gothic: this is a common Germanic feature, which typologically conflicts with Eastern I.E. languages. Endomorphism is restricted to root preterites and preterito-presents (0,67 in Anglo-Saxon, 0,47 in Gothic), and this figure is more or less the same as the Vedic one. We can infer that Anglo-Saxon and Gothic – we may suggest: the Germanic languages at all – have a structural drift in order to reduce or even to avoid any morpheme-piling in verbal stems.
iii. Endomorphism looks like expanding in Anglo-Saxon, by means of a new set of long-vowel preterites in classes V and VI of strong verbs and classes I and II of (no longer) reduplicating verbs (Di Giovine 1996: 121 ff.).[7] But in the latter ones

7. See also Ross 1967; Meid 1971: 52 ff., 102 ff.; Polomé 1983: 870 ff.; Bammesberger 1986: 66 f.; 1988: 55 ff.; van Coetsem 1990: 101; Schmidt 1991: 137.

an endomorphic mark (long vowel) replaces another endomorphic mark (reduplication), and in the former ones it replaces another apophonic change. That is to say, Anglo-Saxon does not substantially differ from the other ancient I.E. languages. The later partial drift towards strong verbal inflection in Middle and Modern English (Bybee and Slobin 1982) is – so to speak – another kettle of fish and needs a specific explanation (excellent remarks in Ramat 2005: 162 ff.; further bibliography in Wiese, forthcom.).

iv. We argue that there are at least three evidences which point at a right-shift of morphemes (from endomorphic stems to exomorphic stems, that is from left – reduplication, apophony – towards right – suffixes):
   - "mixed" stems, where a weak preterite suffix is secondarily added to a strong stem (§ 3.3);
   - weak preterite stems in the (later) preterite of preterite-present verbs (Tellier 1962; Birkmann 1987);
   - at least 7 examples of originally strong verbs (*murnan, rǣdan/rēdan, sceððan/sceaðan, slǣpan, stīgan, sweltan, ðēon*), which turn out to have weak (suffixed) preterites too, even though sometimes in sporadic or dialectal recurrences, as shown in the table (weak stems in bold types):

Table 13. Shift from endomorphic (strong) inflection to exomorphic (weak) inflection in Anglo-Saxon

Verb	Endomorphic stems	Mixed stems	Exomorphic stems
murnan (be-) *s. III (w.)*	*pret.* mearn / murnon		*pres.* murn(e)- **pret. murnde-**
rǣdan, rēdan (ā-, and-, be-, for-, ge-, mis-, ofer-, under-, wið-) *red. > red. I (> w.)*	*pret. a)* reort (A.); *b)* rēd / rēdon (WS.)		*pres.* rǣd(e)- **pret. rǣdde-**
sceððan, sceaðan (ge-) *w. I, s. VI*	*pret.* scēod		*pres.* sceðð(e)- sceað(e)- **pret. sceðede-**
slǣpan (ge-, on-) *red. I (> w.)*	*pret.* slēp / slēpon		*pres.* slǣp(e)- **pret. slēpte-, slēpde-**
stīgan (ā-, fore-, ge-, ofer-) *s. I (w.)*	*pret.* stāh (stāg) / stigon		*pres.* stīg(e)- **pret. stīg(e)de-** (North.)
sweltan (ā-, for-, ge-) *s. III (w.)*	*pret.* swealt (sweolt) / swulton		*pres.* swelt(e)- **pret. swelte-, swælte-** (rare)
ðēon (for-, fore-, ge-, mis-, ofer-, on-) *s. I (III), (w.)*	*pret.* ðēah, ðāh / ðigon; ðungon		*pres.* ðēo- **pret. ðēode** (rare)[i]

i See Sievers 1968: 321 (n. 18).

v. The index of shift from endomorphism to exomorphism in Anglo-Saxon is 0,531. Here are the data available in comparison with other Indo-European groups (Old Indo-Aryan and Old Iranian):

Anglo-Saxon:	0,531
Gothic:	0,430 (0,445)
Vedic:	1,777
epic, class. Sanskrit:	0,965
Avestan (total):	0,665 (late Av.: 0,442; Gāthic: 1,390)
Old Persian:	0,391.

An important – although provisional – conclusion is to be drawn from the above outlined Gothic and Anglo-Saxon developments. In spite of appearances, at least two important Germanic languages show a clear drift towards exomorphism. This conclusion is even more reliable if compared with a set of well-known similar developments which take place in other European (Indo-European) languages, such as Slavic and Romance languages. The following steps of our research are expected to boost the results we have just sketched on the basis of Gothic and Anglo-Saxon.

References

Bammesberger, A. 1986. *Der Aufbau des germanischen Verbalsystems.* Heidelberg: Winter.

Bammesberger, A. 1988. Der indogermanische Aorist und das germanische Präteritum. In *Languages and cultures. Studies in honor of Edgar C. Polomé,* M.A. Jazayery & W. Winter (eds), 55–62. Berlin: Mouton de Gruyter.

Bech, G. 1969. *Das germanische reduplizierte Präteritum.* København: Munksgaard (*Hist.-Fil. Meddel. udg. af det Kgl. Danske Videnskab Selskab* 44 [1969–71], 1).

Beeler, M. 1978. Verbal reduplication in Germanic and Indo-European. *Pacific Coast Philology* 13: 5–10.

Belardi, W. 1993. Sulla tipologia della struttura formale della parola nelle lingue indoeuropee. *Rendiconti Accademia Lincei* s. IX, 4(4): 535–570.

Birkmann, T. 1987. *Präteritopräsentia,* Tübingen: Niemeyer.

Borden, A.R. 1982. *A comprehensive Old-English dictionary.* Lanham MD: University Press of America.

Bosworth, J. & Toller, T.N. 1882–98. *An Anglo-Saxon dictionary.* Oxford: OUP (*on line*: www.ling.upenn.edu/~kurisuto/germanic/oe_bosworthtoller_about.html# images).

[Bosworth, J. -] Toller, T.N. *An Anglo-Saxon dictionary. Supplement.* → Toller 1908–21.

Braune, W. 1961. *Gotische Grammatik.* 16th edn., E.A. Ebbinghaus (ed.). Tübingen: Niemeyer.

Brunner, K. 1965. *Altenglische Grammatik.* 3rd edn., Tübingen: Niemeyer.

Bybee, J.L. & Slobin, D.I. 1982. Rules and schemas in the development and use of the English past tense. *Language* 58: 265–289.

Campbell, A. 1959. *Old English grammar.* Oxford: Clarendon Press.

van Coetsem, F. & Kufner, H.L. 1972. *Toward a grammar of Proto-Germanic.* Tübingen: Niemeyer.

van Coetsem, F. 1990. *Ablaut and reduplication in the Germanic verb.* Heidelberg: Winter.

De Angelis, A. & Di Giovine, P. 2006. Il mutamento tipologico nella funzionalità dei morfemi verbali: Le lingue germaniche e l'indo-iranico. In *Typological change in the morphosyntax of the Indo-European languages, Proceedings of the Congress held in Viterbo 25–26 January 2002.* München: Lincom.

Di Giovine, P. 1996. Sul preterito a vocalismo radicale lungo nelle lingue indoeuropee "occidentali". *Linguistica Baltica* 4 (*Kuryłowicz Memorial Volume, Analecta Indoeuropaea Cracoviensia,* II), 115–129. Cracow: Universitas.

DOEC: di Paolo Healey, A. (ed.), *The dictionary of Old English corpus in electronic form.* Ann Arbor MI: University of Michigan Press.

Feist, S. 1939. *Vergleichendes Wörterbuch der gotischen Sprache.* 3rd edn. Leiden: Brill.

Fullerton, G.L. 1977. *Historical Germanic verb morphology.* Berlin: de Gruyter.

Hoffmann, K. 1970. Das Kategoriensystem des indogermanischen Verbums. *Münchener Studien zur Sprachwissenschaft* 28: 19–41.

Holthausen, F. 1963. *Altenglisches etymologisches Wörterbuch.* 2nd edn. Heidelberg: Winter.

Jarosch, J.J. 1995. *Rekonstruierendes und etymonomisches Wörterbuch der germanischen starken Verben.* Weiden: Schuch.

Karstien, C. 1921. *Die reduplizierten Perfekta des Nord- und Westgermanischen.* Gießen: Münchowsche Universitätsdruckerei.

Kieckers, E. 1928. *Handbuch der vergleichenden gotischen Grammatik.* München: Hueber.

Krahe, H. 1967. *Historische Laut- und Formenlehre des Gotischen.* 2nd edn., E. Seebold (ed.). Heidelberg: Winter.

Krahe, H. 1969. *Germanische Sprachwissenschaft,* II. 7th edn., W. Meid (ed.). Berlin: de Gruyter.

Krämer, P. 1971. *Die Präsensklassen des germanischen schwachen Verbums* [IBS 5]. Innsbruck: Institut für Sprachwissenschaft der Universität.

Krause, U. 1968. *Handbuch des Gotischen.* 3rd edn., München: Beck.

Kuryłowicz, J. 1964. *The inflectional categories of Indo-European.* Heidelberg: Winter.

Kuryłowicz, J. 1975. Zur Vorgeschichte des germanischen Verbalsystems. In *Festgabe Wolfgang Steinitz* (Berlin/O. 1965), 242–247, repr. in *Esquisses linguistiques, II,* 376–381. München: Fink.

Lehmann, W.P. 1986. *A Gothic etymological dictionary.* Leiden: Brill.

Lühr, R. 1985. Reste der athematischen Konjugaton in den germanischen Sprachen. In *Das Germanische und die Rekonstruktion der Indogermanischen Grundsprache,* J. Untermann & B. Brogyanyi (eds), 25–90. Amsterdam: John Benjamins.

Meid, W. 1971. *Das germanische Praeteritum. Indogermanische Grundlagen und Ausbreitung im Germanischen* [IBS 3]. Innsbruck: Institut für Sprachwissenschaft der Universität.

Meid, W. 1978. Osservazioni sul perfetto indoeuropeo e sul preterito forte germanico. *Incontri linguistici* 4(1): 31–41.

Meillet, A. 1949. *Caractères généraux des langues germaniques.* 3rd edn., 1926, 7th edn., Paris: Hachette.

Pilch, H. 1970. *Altenglische Grammatik.* München: Hueber.

Polomé, E.C. 1983. Diachronic development of structural patterns in the Germanic conjugation system. In *Proceedings of the Ninth International Congress of Linguists, Cambridge, Mass., August 27–31, 1962,* H.G. Lunt (ed.), 870–880. The Hague: Mouton.

Prokosch, E. 1939. *A comparative Germanic grammar.* Philadelphia PA: Linguistic Society of America.

Ramat, P. 1986. *Introduzione alla linguistica germanica.* Bologna: Il Mulino.

Ramat, P. 2005. On the scalar character of (morphological) irregularity. In *Language Invariants and Mental Operations*, H. Seiler & G. Brettschneider (eds), 162–171. Tübingen: 1985, Ital. rev. transl. *Verbi forti e verbi deboli in germanico, ovvero del carattere scalare dell'irregolarità (morfologica)*, in P. Ramat, *Pagine linguistiche. Scritti di linguistica storica e tipologica*, 162–172. Bari: Laterza.

Rix, H. (ed.), 2001. *Lexikon der indogermanischen Verben (LIV). Die Wurzeln und ihre Primärstammbildungen*, 2nd edn., M. Kümmel, T. Zehnder, R. Lipp & B. Schirmer (eds). Wiesbaden: Reichert.

Ross, J.R. 1967. Der Ablaut bei den deutschen starken Verben. In *Phonologische Studien*, E.E. David, Jr. & P.B. Denes (eds), 47–118. Berlin: Akademie-Verlag.

Sapir, E. 1921. *Language*. New York NY: Harcourt, Brace.

Schmidt, G. 1991. Indogermanische Perfekta oder Aoriste mit Langvokal in der Wurzelsilbe. In *Aspekte der Albanologie – Akten des Kongresses 'Stand und Aufgaben der Albanologie heute' (3.-5. Okt. 1988)*, W. Breu, R. Ködderitzsch & H.-J. Sasse (eds), 131–143. Wiesbaden: Harrassowitz.

Seebold, E. 1970. *Vergleichendes und etymologisches Wörterbuch der germanischen starken Verben*. The Hague: Mouton.

Sievers, E. 1968. *An Old English grammar*. 1st edn., 1903. New York NY: Greenwood Press.

Silvestri, D. 2003. Aree tipologiche preistoriche. In *Dalla linguistica areale alla tipologia linguistica, Atti del Convegno della Società Italiana di Glottologia (Cagliari, 27–29 sett. 2001)*, I. Loi Corvetto (ed.), 207–227. Roma: Il Calamo.

Stark, D. 1982. *The Old English weak verbs*. Tübingen: Niemeyer.

Tellier, A. 1962. *Les verbes perfecto-présents et les auxiliaries de mode en Anglais ancien*. Paris: Klincksieck.

de Tollenaere, F. & Jones, R.L. 1976. *Word-indices and word-lists to the Gothic Bible and minor fragments*. Leiden: Brill.

Toller, T.N. 1908–21. *An Anglo-Saxon dictionary. Supplement*. Oxford: OUP.

Watkins, C. 1969. *Indogermanische Grammatik – III. Formenlehre*. Heidelberg: Winter.

Wiese, B. Forthcoming. Form and function of verbal ablaut in contemporary standard German. In *Studies in Integrational Linguistics*, R. Sackmann (ed.). Amsterdam: John Benjamins.

Relativization strategies in the languages of Europe

Sonia Cristofaro and Anna Giacalone Ramat

This paper examines the relativization patterns found in twenty-six languages of Europe, focusing on the strategies used to encode the relativized item. We provide a critical overview of extant classifications of these strategies, and discuss the distribution of these strategies across different syntactic roles. We present data on roles less accessible to relativization, such as possessors, or not included in the Accessibility Hierarchy for relativization, such as time circumstantials. These data can be accounted for in terms of a number of factors related to the syntax and semantics of the head noun, rather than the syntactic role of the relativized item as such. These factors also account for a number of recurrent parallelisms between the relativization of time circumstantials and temporal clauses.

1. Introduction

This paper deals with a number of relativization patterns found in twenty-six languages of Europe (for which see the Appendix), with particular focus on the strategies used to encode the relativized item.[1]

These strategies have been investigated in previous typological literature mainly in connection with a rare typological feature found in the languages of Europe, the presence of dedicated relative pronouns, and, in particular, relative pronouns inflected for the syntactic role of the relativized item rather than the role of the head noun (Lehmann 1984; Haspelmath 1998). Also, the distribution of these pronouns across different syntactic roles in individual languages has been shown to match Keenan and Comrie's (1977) Accessibility Hierarchy for relativization (see e.g. Fiorentino 1999 for Italian and Fleischer 2004 for German dialects).

While providing a comparative picture of the ways in which the relativized item can be encoded in the various languages, we will concentrate on a number of issues that

1. We only take into account restrictive relativization, not nonrestrictive relativization, as instantiated for example by the English sentence *This man, who works with me, is a very good friend of mine*' (for a descripion of the difference between these two relativization types, see, among others, Keenan 1985: 168–9 and Comrie 1989: 138–9).

have received comparatively little attention so far. First, the categorial status of individual relativization strategies is not always clear-cut. Relativization strategies, both in the languages of Europe and in general, are often classified in terms of two major distinctions, that between inflected and invariable relative elements and that between [+Case] and [–Case] relativization strategies (first introduced in Keenan and Comrie 1977). We will show that these distinctions are in many cases inapplicable to the languages of Europe, due to a number of (sometimes ongoing) diachronic processes involving the distribution of relativization strategies across different syntactic roles. We will therefore propose slightly modified versions of these distinctions, which, while capturing the intuitions underlying the original distinctions, are of general applicability.

Another issue we will focus on concerns the relationship between the use of individual relativization strategies and the syntactic role of the relativized item. We will present data on roles less accessible to relativization, such as possessors, or not included in the Accessibility Hierarchy, such as circumstantials formed on time nouns (henceforth, time circumstantials). These data either provide counterexamples to the Accessibility Hierarchy, or cannot be accounted for in terms of the syntactic role of the relativized item alone. We will argue that these data can be accounted for in terms of a number of factors related to the syntax and semantics of the head noun, rather than the syntactic role of the relativized item as such. This analysis also accounts for a number of recurrent parallelisms found between the relativization of time circumstantials and temporal clauses.

The languages taken into account include the major languages of Western and Eastern Europe, as well as some minority languages such as Galician and Sardinian. Although information about relativization strategies is widely available for some of these languages from both reference grammars and dedicated works, our data were mainly collected by means of questionnaires filled out by native speakers.[2] This method has at least three advantages. First, at least in principle, a picture can be obtained that is closer to actual linguistic usage than the descriptions found in reference grammars, which are often based on normative, written varieties of the language. In particular, our data are meant to cover the educated spoken varieties (both standard and colloquial) of the various languages.[3] Second, questionnaires make it possible to collect the same kind of data for all of the languages taken into account, and obtain information about parameters not taken into account in published descriptions of these languages (such as, in our case, the syntax and semantics of the head noun, for example in terms of definiteness and referentiality). Finally, published descriptions of relativization strategies often fail to include information about whether or not different relativization strategies present

2. For Italian, though, the analysis is based on our own intuitions as native speakers, as well as published descriptions of spoken Italian such as Bernini 1989, Fiorentino 1999, and Alfonzetti 2002.

3. In fact, particular relativization strategies typical of formal, possibly written varieties of individual languages (e.g. the strategies involving the relative elements *hvem* in Danish and *vilken*

in the language, and used for different syntactic roles, are used by the same speakers. This is particularly true of descriptions based on corpus, rather than elicited data (such as for example Blanche-Benveniste 1990). In this way, it is not clear whether individual speakers use different relativization strategies for different syntactic roles (a pattern that is in itself in need of explanation, and may or may not support the Accessibility Hierarchy), or they use the same strategy for all syntactic roles, but this strategy is not the same from one speaker to another (a pattern that fully conforms to the Accessibility Hierarchy). The use of questionnaires makes it possible to avoid this problem, in that questionnaires provide data about the production of the same speaker.

The paper is organized as follows. In Section 2, we provide an overview of the strategies used to encode the relativized item in the various languages, and discuss a number of problems concerning the classification of these strategies. In Section 3, we examine the distribution of these strategies across different syntactic roles, and discuss a number of cases that do not match the Accessibility Hierarchy for relativization. Section 4 addresses the issue of the relativization of time circumstantials, while Section 5 is a concluding section where the geographical distribution of the various strategies is also discussed. The discussion is supported with examples from the questionnaires.[4] For each of the examples discussed in the text, the informant that translated the corresponding sentence in the questionnaire is reported. The complete list of our informants can be found in the Acknowledgements section. The paper also includes an Appendix listing the languages taken into account and the relativization strategies we examined for each language.

2. The encoding of the relativized item: An overview

The relativized item is variously encoded in the languages of Europe. A widespread pattern involves strategies in which the syntactic role, and possibly the gender (either in terms of grammatical gender, or in terms of animacy) and number of the relativized item are indicated overtly at the morphosyntactic level. Many languages, such as Russian, have relative elements inflected for all of these features:

Russian

(1) *Muzhchina,* **kotoromu** *ya dal knigu, moy brat*
man REL.DAT.M:SG I gave book my brother
'The man I gave the book to is my brother' (Anjuta Gankicov)

in Swedish, for which see Allan, Holmes, and Lundskær-Nielsen 1995: 206 and Holmes and Hinchliffe 1997: 73 respectively) are not attested in our questionnaires, and therefore are not taken into account in this paper.

4. In the examples from the questionnaires, morphosyntactic glossing is kept to a minimum, and restricted to the elements encoding the relativized item. In the examples from published sources, on the other hand, the glossing used by the source is maintained.

Sometimes, the relative element as such is inflected for the gender and number, but not the syntactic role of the relativized item. The latter is however signaled by means of adpositions. This is for example the case in Italian:

Italian

(2) *La ragazza* **con la quale** *viaggiamo ogni mattina*
the girl with the.F.SG REL.SG we.travel every morning
è una persona molto simpatica
is a person very nice
'The girl we travel every morning with is a very nice person'

In other cases, the relative element as such is uninflected, but the syntactic role, and possibly the gender and number of the relativized item are indicated by means of a personal pronoun, or, in the case of possessor relativization, a possessive adjective:

Sardinian

(3) *s' omini* **ki dd'** *appu giau su libri esti fradi miu*
the man REL to.him AUX.1SG given the book is my brother
'The man I gave the book to is my brother' (Ignazio Putzu)

Irish

(4) *Duine an-deas is ea an cailín* **ar** *chasamar*
Person very-nice is it the girl REL.PAST we.met
lena *deartháir aréir*
with.POSS.3SG brother last-night
'The girl whose brother we met last night is a very nice person'
(Anders Alqhvist)

Relative elements can also be used that explicitly specify the syntactic role of the relativized item, but not its gender or number. For example, possessor relativization sometimes involves relative elements with adjectival properties that are inflected for the syntactic role of the relativized item, but the gender and number of the possessum ((5)). Another case in point is provided by invariable relative elements that can be used to relativize some syntactic roles only, thus providing an overt indication about these syntactic roles. This is for example the case with the locative relative elements used to relativize circumstantials in some languages. Insofar as these elements can only be used for circumstantials, they provide an overt morphosyntactic indication about the syntactic role of the relativized item, but they do not signal its gender or number ((6)).

Spanish

(5) *La chica* **cuya** *madre conocimos la pasada*
the girl REL.POSS.ADJ mother we.met the last
noche es una persona muy agradable
night is a person very nice

'The girl whose mother we met last night is a very nice person' (Francisco Gonzálvez García)

French

(6) a. *L' endroit* **où** *nous nous sommes retrouvés est*
the place where we RECPR AUX.1PL met is
au sommet de la colline.
at.the top of the hill
'The place where we met is on the top of the hill'

b. *Le jour* **où** *nous nous sommes rencontrés, il*
the day where we RECPR AUX.1PL met it
pleuvait.
rained.3SG
'On the day we met it rained' (Claudine Chamoreau)

Another relativization pattern involves strategies that provide no overt morphosyntactic indication about the syntactic role of the relativized item, nor about its gender or number. This is for example the case with invariable relative elements that provide no specification about the gender and number of the relativized item, and can be used for all syntactic roles (which means that, unlike what happens when invariable relative elements are used for some syntactic roles only, there is no indication about the syntactic role of the relativized item either). This pattern is found for example in Galician.

Galician

(7) a. *O home* **que** *viu aquí é meu irmán*
the man REL s/he.came here is my brother
'The man who came here is my brother'

b. *O día* **que** *nos coñecimos chovía*
the day REL RECPR we.met it.rained
'The day we met it rained' (Marcos Mariño, Araceli Sanchez)

Another case in point is represented by gapping strategies, as illustrated in (8) below. In this case, as the relative clause has a gap instead of the relativized item, none of the features of the relativized item is reflected overtly at the morphosyntactic level:

English

(8) a. The man we saw last night is a linguist
b. We met on the day he arrived

Existing literature on the relativization strategies just described has classified these strategies in terms of two parameters, the morphosyntactic properties of relative elements and whether or not the relativization strategy makes it possible to identify the syntactic role of the relativized item. In what follows, we will discuss a number of problems with these classifications, and suggest that they be slightly modified.

As far as the morphosyntactic properties of relative elements are concerned, inflected relative elements of the type illustrated in (1) and (2) are usually regarded as pronouns (though see van der Auwera (1985) for a number of criticisms of this analysis which regard to English). The syntactic status of invariable relative elements of the type in (7) is however more controversial, also because they display different syntactic properties from one language to another. In some analyses, they are regarded as conjunctions. In this case, if no other pronoun referring to the relativized item is present, the relativized item is argued to be represented by a gap (Kayne 1976 for French and Cinque 1978 and 1988 for Italian). In other analyses invariable relative elements are regarded as pronouns (Lehmann 1979 and 1984 for Italian), or forms having an intermediate status between conjunctions and pronouns (van der Auwera 1985 for English). As these issues are not immediately relevant to our discussion, however, we will not commit to any of these analyses, and we will just distinguish between inflected and invariable relative elements. The latter, in turn, will be distinguished from cases of gapping where no relative element is present, as in (8) above.

An important point to be stressed in this connection is however that the distinction between inflected and invariable relative elements is not always clear-cut. For example, in colloquial Czech, *co*, the neuter nominative/accusative form of an inflected relative element, can be used in isolation to relativize time circumstantials, and in combination with adpositions and personal pronouns to relativize obliques. This is illustrated in (9) below.

Czech

(9) *Ta dívka,* **co** **s** **ní** *každý ráno jezdíme, je velmi*
This girl REL with her every morning we.travel is very
milá osoba.
nice person.
'The girl we travel every morning with is a very nice person'
(Barbara Schmiedtova)

In such cases, there is a mismatch between *co* and the syntactic role, gender and number of the relativizes item. The latter may be reflected by the adposition and the personal pronoun instead, as in (9). This suggests that *co* is becoming an invariable relative element. Further evidence in support of this hypothesis comes from the fact that some speakers use *co* for all syntactic roles, and combine it with adpositions, personal pronouns or possessive adjectives to relativize indirect objects, obliques, and possessors (data from Eva Hajicova and Petr Sgall; similar phenomena are attested in Polish, as can be seen from the data in the Appendix).

From the synchronic point of view, however, forms such as *co* cannot be regarded as invariable relative elements, because they are still part of the paradigm of an inflected relative element anyway (and in fact not all speakers use them for all syntactic roles). Therefore, such cases should be kept distinct from both inflected and invariable relative elements.

Similar problems are encountered in Romance languages such as Portuguese and Spanish. These languages display an opposition between different forms of the same relative element. One form (Portuguese *que*, Spanish *que*) is used for syntactic roles not encoded by adpositions and syntactic roles encoded by adpositions when the relativized item is inanimate ((10a), (10b)), while the other form (Portuguese *quem*, Spanish *quien*) is used for syntactic roles encoded by adpositions when the relativized item is animate ((10c)).

Portuguese

(10) a. *O homem* **que** *veio aqui é meu irmão*
the man REL s/he.came here is my brother
'The man who came here is my brother'

b. *A faca* **com que** *corto o pão está na*
the knife with REL.INAN I.cut the bread is in.the
gaveta da esquerda
drawer of.the left
'The knife I cut the bread with is in the left drawer'

c. *A rapariga* **com quem** *viajamos todas as*
the girl with REL.AN we.travel all the
manhãs é muito simpática
mornings is very nice
'The girl we travel every morning with is a very nice person' (Miguel Costa)

As the relative element displays different forms, it can be regarded as inflected. On the other hand, however, it is not possible to define the parameters for which it is inflected in a context independent way, because the opposition between the various forms is only found in particular contexts. The animacy opposition is only found for the syntactic roles encoded by adpositions, and the opposition between different syntactic roles is only found when the relativized item is animate.[5]

This pattern too can be explained in diachronic terms. The relevant forms originate from the simplification of the original inflectional system of the corresponding relative element in Latin (Schafroth 1993), and it can be assumed that one of the two forms is in the process of being generalized to all cases, thus becoming a truly invariable element. This assumption is confirmed by the fact that the relevant form may be used in a variety of other syntactic environments (for example, in combination with personal pronouns, or as a general subordinating conjunction), and its cognate forms in other Romance languages function as truly invariable elements that can be used in all cases (see the Galician example in (7) above). Synchronically, however, these elements

5. French also has an opposition between different forms, *qui* and *que*, deriving from the simplification of the corresponding relative element in Latin. These forms, however, display a consistent distribution depending on the syntactic role of the relativized item. *Qui* is used for subjects, indirect objects, and obliques, while *que* is used for direct objects and time circumstantials. Thus, these forms are best regarded as inflected for the syntactic role of the relativized item. In addition to that, *qui* (as opposed to *lequel*) is only used for animates in indirect object and oblique relativization, but can also be used for inanimates in subject relativization.

should also be kept distinct both from relative elements that are consistently inflected for specific parameters (as in the Polish example in (1) above), and invariable relative elements of the type in (7).[6]

These facts show that the morphosyntactic behavior of relative elements in individual languages is the result of a number of possibly ongoing diachronic processes that make these elements not easily amenable to a bipartite classification in terms of inflected vs. invariable elements. We believe therefore that this classification should be expanded so as to distinguish between truly inflected relative elements (as illustrated for example in (1)), truly invariable relative elements (as illustrated in (7)), and relative elements that manifest inflectional oppositions in some contexts only. This is in fact the classification we adopted in presenting the data in the Appendix. This classification captures the morphosyntactic differences between individual relative elements, while at the same time accounting for the diachronic processes these elements may undergo.

The other parameter that has been used in the literature to classify relativization strategies concerns whether or not the strategy provides explicit information about the syntactic role of the relativized item. According to a distinction first introduced in Keenan and Comrie 1977, relativization strategies may be either [+Case] or [–Case]. [+Case] strategies are strategies where a nominal element unequivocally expresses which noun phrase position is being relativized, thus making it possible to recover the syntactic role of the relativized item. [–Case] strategies are strategies where this is not the case.

The application of this distinction to the relativization strategies of the languages of Europe is however problematic. The opposition between [+Case] and [–Case] refers to two different aspects of relativization strategies. On the one hand, it refers to whether or not the morphosyntactic features of the relative clause vary depending on the syntactic role of the relativized item. Thus, for example, Keenan and Comrie (1977) argue that inflected relative elements or the combination of an adposition and an inflected relative element (such as English *to which*) are [+Case], because different forms of the inflected relative elements or different adpositions are found depending on what syntactic role is being relativized.

On the other hand, the [+Case]/[–Case] distinction refers to whether or not the relativization strategy makes it possible to unambiguously identify the syntactic role of the relativized item. Thus, for example, English *who* counts as a [–Case] strategy, because it can be used for different syntactic roles.

6. Blanche-Benveniste (1990) argues that, in both Portuguese and Spanish, *que* should be kept distinct from *quem* and *quien*. As it is not inflected for animacy, *que* is a conjunction, while *quem* and *quien* are pronouns. She proposes a similar analysis for the opposition between *que* and *qui* in French. However, as all of these forms are diachronically related, and they are in complementary distribution, we believe they are best regarded as part of the same inflectional paradigm, and that absence of inflection for particular parameters in particular forms is the result of a diachronic process of reduction of this paradigm.

These two aspects are often in conflict in the relativization strategies just described for the languages of Europe. For example, a number of languages display relativization strategies in which different adpositions are used depending on the syntactic role of the relativized item, but the same adposition can be used for more than one syntactic role. This is the case in Italian, where the relative element *cui* may combine with a variety of adpositions, but individual adpositions may be used for different syntactic roles, such as for example indirect objects ((11a)) and obliques ((11b)).

Italian

(11) a. *Lo studente* **a** **cui** *ho prestato il libro è*
the student to REL AUX.1SG lent the book is
molto intelligente
very smart
'The student I lent the book to is very smart'

b. *Il convegno* **a** **cui** *siamo stati era molto interessante*
the conference to REL AUX.1PL been was very interesting
'The conference we have been to was very interesting'

The fact that individual adpositions or particular case forms of an inflected relative element can be used for more than one syntactic role can be readily accounted for in diachronic terms, in that these forms undergo a number of processes of semantic extension that have been extensively described in the literature on grammaticalization and semantic maps (see e.g. Haspelmath 1997). Also, particular forms may come to be used for more than one syntactic role due to the lower textual frequency of the category value they express (for example, the neuter as opposed to the masculine), which makes it difficult for speakers to retain different forms (such as distinct case forms) for that category value (Croft 2003). From the synchronic point of view, however, these facts pose a problem for the [+Case]/[–Case] distinction. Insofar as individual adpositions or case forms signal particular syntactic roles as opposed to others, the relevant relativization strategies should be classified as [+Case]. As the relevant case forms or adpositions can be used for more than one syntactic role, however, they provide no unambiguous indication about what syntactic role is being relativized. From this point of view, these relativization strategies should be classified as [–Case].

These facts show that the fact that a relative clause displays different morphosyntactic features depending on the syntactic role of the relativized item does not mean that the latter can be identified unambiguously, as is implied by the [+Case] vs. [–Case] distinction. These two aspects should therefore be kept distinct. For this reason, we will not use the [+Case] vs. [–Case] distinction (although we have done so in previous work, see Cristofaro and Giacalone Ramat 2002 and 2005). We will however maintain the distinction between strategies in which the syntactic role and possibly the gender and number of the relativized item are reflected overtly at the morhosyntactic level (as in Examples (1)–(6) above), and strategies where this is not the case (as in Examples (7) and (8)). This distinction captures the basic intuition underlying the [+Case] vs. [–Case] classification, namely that different relativization strategies differ in their degree of expliciteness about the syntactic role of the relativized item. At the same time, as this distinction is independent of whether or not the strategy makes it possible to unambiguously identify the syntactic role of the relativized item, it is in principle applicable to all of the relativization strategies found in the languages of Europe.

3. Relativization strategies and the Accessibility Hierarchy

Keenan and Comrie's (1977) Accessibility Hierarchy for relativization describes the possibility for a language to form relative clauses on different syntactic roles:

(12) The Accessibility Hierarchy for relativization (Keenan and Comrie 1977): Subject > Direct Object > Indirect Object > Oblique > Possessor > Object of comparison

We took into account a subset of these roles, namely subject, direct object, indirect object, oblique, and possessor. In many of the languages we examined, the same relativization strategy, such as an inflected relative element (possibly in combination with adpositions) or an invariable relative element, is used for all of these roles. This is for example the case for Slavic languages, that use an inflected relative element, and Basque, that uses gapping.

When different strategies are used for different syntactic roles, however, their distribution appears to obey a general pattern whereby, if the syntactic role and possibly the gender and number of the relativized item are indicated overtly for a particular syntactic role, then they are indicated overtly for all roles less accessible to relativization.

Moreover, strategies that provide an overt morphosyntactic indication about the syntactic role and possibly the gender and number of the relativized item are mainly used to relativize indirect objects, possessors and obliques. On the other hand, strategies that provide no such indication are mainly used to relativize subjects and direct objects.[7]

For example, Galician displays an invariable relative element that can be used for all syntactic roles that can be relativized in the language, and provides therefore no

7. The languages in our sample are all nominative-accusative, except for Basque, which is ergative-absolutive. Although subjects and direct objects may not be defined in the same way for nominative-accusative and ergative-absolutive languages (see, among others, Croft 2003), the relativization strategies we took into account for Basque apply both to the only argument of intransitive verbs and the two arguments of transitive verbs. In fact, in describing relativization in Basque, Oyarçabal (2003) speaks of subject and object relativization. Therefore, for simplicity's sake, we decided not to use a separate notation for Basque, and the relativization strategies used in this language are classified as instances of 'subject relativization' and 'object relativization' in the Appendix. This notation, however, is not meant to imply that Basque has the same grammatical relations of subject and direct object as nominative-accusative languages.

overt indication about the syntactic role (nor about the gender or number) of the relativized item (see Example (7) above). This element can be used in isolation to relativize subjects and direct objects. To relativize indirect objects and obliques, however, this element must be combined with other elements signaling the syntactic role, gender and number of the relativized item, such as adpositions, articles, and personal pronouns.

Galician

(13) a. *O home* **ao** **que** **lle** *dei o libro é*
the man to.the.M:SG REL to.him gave.1PL the book is
meu irmán
my brother
'The man I gave the book to is my brother'

b. *A rapaza* **coa** **que** *viaxamos cada mañá*
the girl with.the.F:SG REL we.travel every morning
é unha moi boa persoa
is a very nice person
'The girl we travel every morning with is a very nice person'
(Marcos Mariño, Araceli Sanchez)

Similarly, Italian displays a relative element that has different inflectional forms, *che* and *cui*, depending on the syntactic role of the relativized item (*che* is used to relativize subjects, direct objects, and time circumstantials, while *cui* is used for indirect object, oblique, and possessor relativization). In spoken colloquial Italian, *che* can also be used to relativize all syntactic roles, which suggests that the opposition between *che* and *cui* is in the process of being lost, and *che* is on its way to become a truly invariable relative element, like its counterparts in other Romance languages (as both the opposition between *che* and *cui* and the use of *che* for all syntactic roles are present in the production of the same speakers, however, *che* will be indicated as both an inflected and an invariable relative element in the Appendix). While subject and direct objects are always relativized by means of *che* alone, however, roles less accessible to relativization such as indirect objects and obliques are relativized by combining *che* with personal pronouns inflected for the syntactic role and possibly the gender and number of the relativized item. On the other hand, possessors may also be relativized by means of *che* alone, and we will come back to this pattern when discussing Examples (15) and (16) below.[8]

Italian

(14) a. *Ma tu pensa uno* **che** **gli** *cancellano il*
but you you.think somebody REL to.him they.cancel the

8. This description is based on our own intuitions as native speakers, but is in accordance with the corpus data on spoken colloquial Italian in Bernini 1989, Fiorentino 1999, and Alfonzetti 2002. Many of the cases reported in Alfonzetti 2002, however, are actually cases of nonrestrictive relatives, while we only took into account restrictive relatives.

volo *all'* *ultimo* *momento!*
flight at.the last minute
'But imagine somebody whose flight is cancelled at the last minute!'
(literally: 'But imagine somebody to whom they cancel the flight at the last minute'!')

b. *È* *una* *cosa* **che** **ci** *tiene* *moltissimo*
is a thing REL about.it cares very.much
'It's something s/he cares very much about'

In discussing the distribution of personal pronouns, which they regard as a [+Case] strategy, Keenan and Comrie (1977: 92–3) argue that, insofar as it preserves the logical structure of the relative clause, this strategy is more explicit as to the meaning of this clause, and hence it is used when this meaning is more difficult to understand (as is the case with the roles less accessible to relativization).

More generally, Hawkins (1999 and 2004) argues that, since [–Case] strategies are harder to process, they will tend to be used for syntactic roles more accessible to relativization, and if they are used for a syntactic role less accessible to relativization, then they will be used for all roles more accessible to relativization.

Although our classification of relativization strategies in the languages of Europe differs from the [+Case] vs. [–Case] distinction, this analysis fully accounts for the distribution of these strategies across different syntactic roles. Strategies that provide overt information about the syntactic role, gender and number of the relativized item are more transparent as to what role is being relativized (although they don't always make it possile to recover this role unambiguously). As a result, they tend to be used for roles less accessible to relativization, while strategies that provide no overt indication about the syntactic role, gender and number of the relativized item tend to be used for more accessible roles.

In general, relativization appears to be possible for all of the syntactic roles we took into account.[9] Some remarks are however in order about the relativization of possessors. This is one of the roles that are least accessible to relativization, and our database involves one language, Galician, where possessors cannot be relativized directly.

9. It should be observed in this connection that, while in a number of languages the same relativization strategy can be used for both animate and inanimate indirect objects, other languages associate inanimate recipients with roles other than indirect objects (e.g. direct objects). In Czech, for example, the most natural rendering of the sentence 'The plants to which I gave the mineral salts are now flourishing' is *Květiny, které jsem pohnojila, ted' kvetou,* literally 'The plants that I fertilized are now flourishing' (data from Barbara Schmiedtova). This pattern can be accounted for in terms of prototypicality. Indirect objects encode recipients of ditransitive verbs, and recipients are prototypically animate (in fact, the data in Keenan and Comrie 1977 pertain to animate indirect objects only). Because of their nonprototypical status, inanimate recipients may not be conceptualized as recipients, and therefore they may be in syntactic roles other than the indirect object. As a result, relative clauses formed on these roles are found in this case.

In other languages, as observed above (see Example (5)), a number of strategies that provide an overt indication about the syntactic role and possibly the gender and number of the relativized item are used for possessor relativization. Sardinian, however, displays a rather unusual pattern in which possessors are relativized by means of an invariable relative element, while strategies providing an overt indication about the syntactic role and sometimes the gender and number of the relativized item are used for roles more accessible to relativization (see Example (3) above). This is illustrated in (15) below.

Sardinian

(15) *Mi dd' adi nau na piccicca* **ki** *asi connosciu su*
to.me it told a girl REL AUX.2SG met the
fradi
brother
'I was told that by a girl whose brother you met' (Nicoletta Puddu)

In other cases of possessor relativization, however, the relative clause includes a lexical item specifying the role of the relativized item. For example, in (16) below, *cosa sua*, literally 'his thing' signals the possessive relation between the relativized item and the direct object *su logu* 'the position' (literally, 'the place'):

Sardinian

(16) *Su cristianu* **ki** *immoi sesi setzìu in su logu*
the person REL now AUX.2SG seated in the place
cosa sua, *fiada stimau meda*
thing his AUX.3SG valued much
'The person you got the position of was highly valued' (Ignazio Putzu)

The use of different constructions in possessor relativization seems to be related to the extent to which the possessive relation can be recovered from the context. When a possessive relation can be easily construed between possessor and possessum, as is for example the case with kinship terms, the invariable relative element is used. When the possessive relation beween possessor and possessum is less easy to construe, as is for example the case with 'person' and 'position' in (16), strategies that signal the possessive relation explicitly are used. This appears in line with the general principle that was invoked above to account for the distribution of individual relativization strategies across different syntactic roles, that is, strategies providing no overt indication abouyt the syntactic role, as well as the gender and number, of the relativized item are used when the meaning of the relative clause is easier to recover.[10]

10. In describing possessor relativization in spoken colloquial Italian, Fiorentino (1999) and Alfonzetti (2002) also mention a number of cases where the invariable relative element *che* is used in isolation (see the discussion of Example (14) above), and these are all cases where the possessive relation is fairly transparent (many, though not all cases, involve a kinship relation).

The hypothesis that higher vs. lower recoverability of the possessive relation plays a role in possessor relativization is further supported by the fact that in some languages possessors may or may not be relativized depending on whether or not the possessive relation is semantically transparent. For example, according to Oyarçabal (2003: 780) this is the factor that accounts for the ungrammaticality of (17a) as opposed to the grammaticality of (17b) in Basque. The underlying assumption here is that a possessive relationship can be more easily construed between a man and his name than between a man and a house.

Basque

(17) a. **[Etxea argazkian hartu dudan] gizona da*
house photograph.LOC take AUX.COMP man is
'It is the man (whose) house I took a photo of'

b. *[Izena ahanzi dudan] gizon batek erran dit*
name forget AUX.COMP man a.ERG tell AUX
'A man (whose) name I have forgotten told me' (Oyarçabal 2003: 780)

4. The relativization of time circumstantials

A number of languages use adpositions to relativize indirect objects, obliques, and possessors, but not time circumstantials (as instantiated in relative clauses formed on time nouns such as 'day' and 'time'). As a result, if the language uses different relative forms depending on whether or not the relevant syntactic role is encoded by adpositions (as is the case in many Romance languages), the same relative elements are used as for subject and object relativization, which also involve no adpositions (see the discussion in Section 3). For example, Catalan displays an opposition between *que*, used for subjects, direct objects and circumstantials of time, and *qui* and *què*, used for syntactic roles encoded by adpositions depending on animacy.

Catalan

(18) a. *L' home* **que** *va sopar aquí és el meu germà*
the man REL AUX.3SG dine here is the my brother
'The man who had dinner here is my brother'

b. *L' home* **que** *el meu germà està buscant és amic meu*
the man REL the my brother AUX.3SG looking.for is friend my
'The man my brother is looking for is a friend of mine'

However, Fiorentino and Alfonzetti do not specify whether the speakers that use this strategy use it for all syntactic roles (in which case the use of the strategy would be independent of possessors as such) or they use it for some syntactic roles only (in which case the nature of the possessive relation could be a relevant factor).

c. *El dia* **que** *ens vam conèixer plovia.*
the day REL RECPR AUX.1PL met it.rained
'On the day we met it rained'

d. *M' ho va dir la noia amb* **qui** *viatgem*
to.me it AUX.3SG say the girl with REL.AN we.travel
(plegats) cada dia la meva germana i jo
together every day the my sister and I
'I was told this by a girl my sister and I travel every morning with'

e. *El ganivet amb* **què** *talla el pa el meu germà*
the knife with REL.INAN cuts the bread the my brother
és en el calaix de l' esquerra.
is in the drawer of the left
'The knife my brother cuts the bread with is in the left drawer'
(César Montoliu)

This pattern has been investigated for French and Italian by Kayne (1976) and Cinque (1978, 1988) respectively, who argue that the fact that particular syntactic roles are or are not relativized by means of adpositions is related to their being encoded by means of adpositions in independent clauses, and different relative elements (such as *che* vs. *cui* in Italian) are used depending on whether or not the relevant syntactic roles are encoded by adpositions.

A first problem with this analysis is however that there are languages, such as English, where time circumstantials may be encoded by adpositions in main clauses, but not in relative clauses:

English
(19) On the day we met it rained

This shows that an analysis of relativization patterns in terms of presence vs. absence of adpositions in main clauses is not cross-linguistically valid.

Also, absence of adpositions in the relativization of time circumstantials is paralleled by other phenomena independent of adpositions as such, such as absence of an overt indication about the syntactic role, as well as the gender and number, of the relativized item.[11] These phenomena are also found in the relativization of subjects, direct objects, and time circumstantials, but not in the relativization of indirect objects, obliques, and possessors (though see the discussion of possessor relativization in Section 3). This suggests that absence of adpositions might actually be but a part of a more general pattern about the relativization of time circumstantials.

For instance, Examples (7) and (13) above show that in Galician an overt indication about the syntactic role, gender and number of the relativized item (as obtained

11. Adpositions usually provide an overt indication about the syntactic role of the relativized item, but the latter is independent of presence vs. absence of adpositions, as it can also be realized through other morphosyntactic means, such as for example inflected relative elements.

through the use of adpositions, inflected articles and personal pronouns) is found in indirect object and oblique relativization, but not in the relativization of subjects, direct objects, and time circumstantials. This pattern is also attested in Sardinian and Swiss German, as can be seen from the data in the Appendix.

Both absence of adpositions and absence of an overt indication about the syntactic role, as well as the gender and number, of the relativized item appear to be favored by a number of factors related to the semantics and syntax of the head noun, namely:

i. The fact that the head noun is nonspecific, where by specificity is meant the fact that the speaker has a particular referent in mind, and this referent is uniquely identifiable (Lyons 1999). This situation obtains for example when the head noun is accompanied by quantifiers such as 'every'.
ii. The fact that the head noun is semantically more generic, as is for example the case with nouns such as 'time' as opposed to 'day'.
iii. The fact that the head noun is in itself in a circumstantial, rather than an argument role in the main clause.

Thus, in the Italian example in (20a), the speaker is making reference to a particular day. In this case, the adposition may or may not be used. In (20b), on the other hand, the speaker has no particular day in mind, as witnessed by the quantifier 'every'. In this case, the adposition is not allowed.

In (20c), the referent of the head noun is not uniquely identifiable, in that the sentence refers to a plurality of items, as shown by the quantifier 'each'. However, 'each' differs from 'every' in that it is distributive, that is each of the items taken into account, though being part of a set, is considered individually. In this sense 'each' is more specific than 'every', though not being fully specific. In this case, again, the adposition may be used.

Italian

(20) a. *Il giorno* **che/ in cui** *ci siamo incontrati*
the day REL/ on REL RECPR AUX.1SG met
pioveva
was.raining.3SG
'On the day we met it was raining'

b. *Ogni giorno* **che** *la vedo mi sembra diversa*
every day REL her I.see to.me looks different
'Every day I see her she looks different to me'

c. *Ognuno dei giorni* **che/ in cui** *ci*
each of.the days REL/ on REL RECPR
siamo incontrati ha piovuto
we.met AUX.3SG rained
'On each of the days we met it rained'

In Spanish, nouns such as 'day' may be relativized by means of adpositions combined with the relative marker *que* (for which see the discussion in Section 2 above) when combined with the quantifier 'each' or when they are in an argument role in the main clause, but nouns such as 'time' are always relativized by means of *que* only.

Spanish

(21) a. *Todos y cada uno de los días* **que/ en que** *nos*
Each of the days REL in REL RECPR
vimos llovió
we.met it.rained
'On each of the days we met it rained'

b. *El día* **en que** *comimos fuera fue bastante cálido*
the day in REL we.ate outside was rather warm
'The day we ate outside was warm'

c. *La vez* **que** *fui allí llovió*
the time REL I.was there it.rained
'The time I went there it rained' (Francisco Gonzálvez Garcia)

Givón (1990: 679) argues that absence of adpositions in the relativization of time circumstantials is due to the fact that time nouns usually occur as circumstantials. This hypothesis appears to be based on an underlying assumption that, since circumstantials are the default role for time nouns, the occurrence of a time noun in a circumstantial role is expected and doesn't need to be signaled by any specific morphosyntactic means in either main or relative clauses.

This analysis is supported by extensive evidence showing that time nouns tend to be zero-marked cross-linguistically when occurring as circumstantials (Haspelmath 1997), and can in fact be generalized to account for the fact that time circumstantials tend to be relativized by means of strategies that provide no indication about the syntactic role, gender or number of the relativized item. As was observed in Section 3, these strategies are less explicit as to what role is being relativized, so they are used when the relativized item occurs in a default role and doesn't need to be indicated overtly.

This analysis also provides a plausible account for why quantifiers such as 'every' and generic time nouns such as 'time' favor the absence of adpositions or, more generally, the use of relativization strategies that do not signal the syntactic role, as well as the gender and number, of the relativized item. Time nouns usually do not occur as circumstantials when they designate entities relevant to ongoing discourse, and specific properties are predicated about these entities (e.g. in sentences such as 'That day was very important'). However, time nouns accompanied by quantifiers such as 'every' and generic time nouns designate nonspecific units, and it is relatively unlikely that these time units represent relevant discourse participants about which specific properties are predicated. Rather, these time units will provide a temporal setting for the events being described. As a result, in both main and relative clauses, the relevant time nouns will tend to occur as circumstantials rather than arguments (that is, in sentences such as 'every day I go there it rains' or 'the time I went there she was not in', rather than 'every day we went there was very important' or 'the time I went there was very important'). Thus, the occurrence of this type of time nouns as circumstantials is expected, and doesn't need to be indicated overtly in either main or relative clauses. In fact, Haspelmath (1997: 424) observes that zero-marking for time circumstantials is systematic when modifiers such as the quantifier 'every' are involved.

This analysis, however, does not account for the fact that the strategies used to relativize time circumstantials also depend on the circumstantial vs. argument role of the time noun in the main clause. In this analysis, the use of particular strategies to relativize time circumstantials depends on a higher vs. lower likelihood of time nouns appearing as circumstantials in both main and relative clauses. However, there appears to be no obvious reason why the fact that the time noun is in a particular syntactic role in the main clause should determine a higher or lower likelihood for it to occur as a circumstantial in the relative clause.[12]

We believe that this fact can be accounted for in terms of the discourse function of relative clauses, and that this might actually be an additional explanatory factor also for the phenomena related to the specificity and semantic generality of the head noun.

The primary discourse function of a relative clause is to identify a participant that is relevant to ongoing discourse within a set of possible referents. This function plays a central role in many analysis of relativization, such as those by Fox and Thompson (1990), Langacker (1991: 430–5), and Matsumoto (1996 and 1997). For instance, Langacker (1991) argues that a relative clause elaborates, that is, specifies, a main clause element, or, in Langacker's terms, a salient substructure of the main clause. Fox and Thompson (1990) argue that one of the primary functions of a relative clause is grounding, that is, making referents relevant to ongoing conversation by explicitly relating them to given referents in discourse.

When time nouns are used as circumstantials in the main clause, however, they usually do not function as relevant referents and topics for further conversation. For instance, in the standard reading of a sentence like 'On the day we met, it rained', the speaker's purpose is usually to establish a linkage between the meeting and the rain, not to identify some particular day with respect to others by saying that on that day it was raining. The situation here is quite different with respect to a sentence like, for

12. It has been argued (see e.g. Oyarçabal 2003: 780–1 for Basque) that the fact that the relativized item and the head noun are in the same syntactic role enhances the processability of the relative clause. This might lead to the use of strategies that provide no indication about what role is being relativized, as is the case in the relativization of circumstantials of time. In fact, this seems to be the assumption underlying Larsson's (1990) and Fiorentino's (1999) analyses of time circumstantial relativization in Italian. If this is the case, however, one would expect the relavant relativization strategies to be favored in all of the cases where the relativized item and the head noun are in the same role, not just when they are both in a circustantial role. This doesn't seem to be true for Italian, nor has such a phenomenon been observed for other languages.

instance, 'The man we met last night is a linguist', where the relative clause is actually used to identify a specific person with respect to others, and this person is going to function as a topic for further discussion. One can then assume that, since the relative clause is not being used to identify a particular entity within a set of possible referents, it is not so important to provide overt morphosyntactic specification about this entity in the relative clause. As a result, strategies that provide no such specification can be used.

On the other hand, when time nouns occur in an argument role in the main clause, e.g. in a sentence like 'The day we met was very important for us', the speaker's purpose is arguably to identify a particular temporal entity with respect to others, and this is done through the relative clause. As a result, overt specification about this entity is provided.

Similarly, as was pointed out above, time nouns accompanied by quantifiers such as 'every' and semantically generic time nouns do not refer to entities relevant to ongoing discourse. In this case too, then, when these nouns are relativized, the relative clause is not used to identify a relevant discourse topic, and thus it can be assumed that it is not important to overtly specify what role is being relativized.

Evidence in support of this analysis comes from another phenomenon quite widespread in the languages of Europe, as well as in other languages (Cristofaro and Giacalone Ramat 2002). Time circumstantials may be relativized by means of conjunctions that are also used to introduce temporal adverbial clauses, as can be seen from (22a) and (22b).

Polish

(22) a. *Tego dnia,* **kiedy/ w którym** *się*
this day when in REL.NT.SG.LOC RECPR
spotkaliśmy, padało.
we.met it.rained
'On the day we met it rained'

b. *Każdego dnia,* **kiedy** *tam jadę, pada*
every day when there I.go it.rains
'Every day I go there it rains'

c. *Dzień,* **w którym** *mi to powiedział, był*
day in REL.NT.SG.LOC to.me this he.told was
bardzo ważny dla nas obojga
very important to us both
'The day he told me that was very important for both of us'
(Agnieszka Latos)

The functional difference between adverbial clauses and relative clauses is that the former establish a link between two events, while the latter identify a participant of some event by describing some other event in which this participant is involved. This difference is neutralized in most cases of relative clauses formed on time circumstantials, because the primary discourse function of these clauses is to establish a link between two events, rather than identify some particular time unit with respect to others. Therefore, these clauses may be assimilated to temporal adverbial clauses, and the two may be expressed in the same way.

This analysis is supported by the fact that the use of temporal conjunctions, as opposed to relativization strategies proper, seems to be favored by the same factors that favor the use of strategies that provide no overt specification about the syntactic role, as well as the gender and number, of the relativized item. For example, in Polish and Bulgarian nonquantified time circumstantials are relativized by means of adpositions and pronouns inflected for the syntactic role, gender and number of the relativized item. When time nouns are combined with universal quantifiers such as 'every', however, the temporal conjunction 'when' is used ((22a), (22b), (23)). In Rumanian, time circumstantials are relativized by combining an adposition and an inflected relative element when the time noun is in an argument role in the main clause, and by using the conjunction 'when' when the time noun is in a circumstantial role in the main clause ((24)).

Bulgarian

(23) a. *V den ja,* **v kojto** *se sreštnahme valeše*
in day the in REL.NT.SG RECPR we.met it.rained
'The day we met it rained'

b. *Vseki edin ot dni te,* **v kojto** *se*
each of days the in REL.N.NOM.SG RECPR
sreštnahme valeše
we.met it.rained
'On each of the days we met it rained'

c. *Vseki den,* **kogato** *otivam tam, vali*
every day when I.go there it.rains
'Every day I go there it rains' (Svetlana Slavkova)

Rumanian

(24) a. *Ziua în* **care** *el mia spus acest lucru este*
day.the in REL he to.me.AUX.3SG told this thing is
foarte importantă pentru noi doi
very important for us both
'The day he told me that was very important for both of us'

b. *în ziua* **când** *neam întilnit ploua*
in day when we.AUX.1PL met it.rained
'The day we met it rained' (Marinella Lörinczi)

The use of temporal conjunctions and that of relativization strategies providing no specification about the syntactic role, as well as the gender and number, of the relativized item are based on the same principle. In both cases, the relative clause is not being used to provide specification about a relevant discourse referent, but rather contributes to building a temporal setting for the event described in the main clause. It comes therefore as no surprise that both phenomena are favored by the same semantic and syntactic factors.

The analysis in terms of discourse relevance is partly similar to that in terms of higher vs. lower likelihood of time nouns occurring as circumstantials. Both analyses assume that time nouns do not usually function as relevant discourse referents, and therefore are most likely to occur as circumstantials. The two analyses make however different assumptions about why time circumstantials tend to be relativized by means of strategies that provide no overt specification about the syntactic role, as well as the gender and number, of the relativized item. In one analysis, this is because the occurrence of time nouns as circumstantials is expected, and doesn't need to be signaled overtly. In the other analysis, this is because the relative clause is not being used to identify an entity relevant to ongoing discourse, and therefore no overt specification about this entity is provided. It may be the case that both of these motivations have a role in the occurrence of the relevant relativization strategies.

5. Concluding remarks

The distribution of relativization strategies in the languages of Europe is related to the syntactic role of the relativized item, and generally reflects Keenan and Comrie's (1977) Accessibility Hierarchy. The relativization of time circumstantials and, to a more limited extent, that of possessors, reveals however the interaction of a number of semantic and pragmatic factors that are independent of the syntactic role of the relativized item as such. Strategies providing no overt indication about the syntactic role, as well as the gender and number, of the relativized item are used either when the corresponding information is not communicatively relevant (as is the case in the relativization of time circumstantials), or when this information is easily recoverable from the context anyway. Both of these cases reflect the general economic principle invoked by Keenan and Comrie (1977) to account for the distribution of [+Case] and [–Case] relativization strategies, namely that overt information about the relativized item is omitted whenever the speaker can afford to do so.

Some final remarks are in order about the geographical distribution of the various relativization strategies. While the semantic and pragmatic principles underlying the observed patterns hold for all the languages taken into account, these principles are implemented in different ways from one language to another, and the way in which they are implemented in individual languages reveals genetically and geographically significant distributional patterns.

For example, the implicational pattern described in Section 3 for the distribution of strategies that provide an overt morphosyntactic indication about the syntactic role and possibly the gender and number of the relativized item allows for two language types. In the first type, these strategies are used for all of the syntactic roles included in the Accessibility Hierarchy, while in the second type these strategies are used for some syntactic roles only, depending on accessibility to relativization. The first type is attested in an area roughly covering Eastern Europe, and including Slavic languages,

Finnish, Hungarian, and Rumanian. German and Greek also follow this pattern. Languages in this area typically present an inflected relative element that can be used for all syntactic roles (see the remarks in Section 3).

The second type, on the other hand, is attested in an area that roughly corresponds to Western Europe, and includes Romance and Germanic languages (except German), Greek, and Irish. In this area, a variety of strategies are found that provide an overt indication about the syntactic role and possibly the gender and number of the relativized item, such as adpositions + invariable relative elements, adposition + inflected relative elements, adpositions + possessive adjectives, relative possessive adjectives, and invariable relative elements + personal pronouns. These strategies alternate with strategies that provide no indication about the syntactic role, gender and number of the relativized item, such as invariable relative elements and gapping. In fact, Romance languages (as well as, to a more limited extent, Czech and Polish) provide evidence about a general diachronic process involving the various relativization strategies. Typological research (e.g. Lehmann 1984) has shown that relative elements inflected for the syntactic role, gender and number of the relativized item are quite rare cross-linguistically, and typical of the languages of Europe. Romance languages show that these elements gradually give rise to invariable relative elements. At a later stage, however, the relevant elements are recombined with elements signaling the syntactic role and possibly the gender and number of the relativized item, such as adpositions, articles, and personal pronouns (see also Fiorentino 1999: Chapter 5).

It should also be pointed out that gapping (either as such, or in combination with adpositions) shows a geographically limited distribution, in that it appears to be systematically used only in English, Scandinavian languages, and Basque (as well as in a number of German dialects, for which see Fleischer 2004).

As far as the relativization of time circumstantials is concerned, the same pragmatic principle (the fact that the relative clause does not have the usual discourse function of relative clauses) arguably underlies the use of a number of different strategies, such as invariable relative elements, temporal conjunctions, and gapping. Each of these strategies, however, displays a rather clear-cut geographical distribution, in that invariable relative elements are exclusively found in Western Europe (that is, in Romance and Germanic languages, Irish, and Greek), gapping is almost exclusively found (once again) in English and Scandinavian languages, and temporal conjunctions are mainly found in Eastern Europe (that is, in Slavic Languages, Hungarian, Rumanian, as well as, once again, German).

References

Alfonzetti, G. 2002. *La relativa non-standard. Italiano popolare o italiano parlato?* Palermo: Centro di studi filologici e linguistci siciliani.

Allan, R., Holmes, P. & Lundskær-Nielsen, T. 1995. *Danish.* London: Routledge.

Bernini, G. 1989. Tipologia delle frasi relative italiane e romanze. In *L'italiano tra le lingue romanze. Atti del XX congresso della Società di Linguistica Italiana*, F. Foresti, E. Rizzi & P. Benedini (eds), 85–98. Roma: Bulzoni.

Blanche-Benveniste, C. 1990. Usages normatifs et non normatifs dans les relatives en français et en espagnol et en portugais. In *Toward a Typology of European Languages*, J. Bechert, G. Bernini & C. Buridant (eds), 317–337. Berlin: Mouton de Gruyter.

Cinque, G. 1978. La sintassi dei pronomi relativi che e il quale nell'italiano moderno. *Rivista di grammatica generativa* 3: 31–126.

Cinque, G. 1988. La frase relativa. In *Grande grammatica di consultazione*. Vol. I, L. Renzi (ed.), 443–503. Bologna: Il Mulino.

Comrie, B. 1989. *Language universals and linguistic typology*. 2nd edn., Oxford: Blackwell.

Cristofaro, S. & Giacalone Ramat, A. 2002. Relativization patterns in Mediterranean languages, with particular reference to the relativization of time circumstantials. In *Mediterranean Languages. Papers from the MEDTYP workshop, Tirrenia, June 2000*, P. Ramat & T. Stolz (eds), Bochum: Universitätsverlag Dr. N. Brockmeyer.

Cristofaro, S. Giacalone Ramat, A. 2005. Relativization in Sardinian. *Sprachtypologie und Universalienforschung* 58: 163–175.

Croft, W. 2003. *Typology and universals*. 2nd edn., Cambridge: CUP.

Fiorentino, G. 1999. *Relativa debole*. Milano: Franco Angeli.

Fleischer, J. 2004. A typology of relative clauses in German dialects. In *Dialectology meets typology: Dialect grammar from a cross-linguistic perspective*, B. Kortmann (ed.), 211–243. Berlin: Mouton de Gruyter.

Fox, B.A. & Thompson, S.A. 1990. A discourse explanation of the grammar of relative clauses in English conversation. *Language* 66: 297–316.

Givón, T. 1990. *Syntax: A functional-typological introduction*. Vol. II. Amsterdam: John Benjamins.

Haspelmath, M. 1997. *From space to time*. Munich: Lincom.

Haspelmath, M. 1998. How young is standard average European? *Language Sciences* 20: 271–287.

Hawkins, J.A. 1999. Processing complexity and filler-gap dependencies across grammars. *Language* 75: 244–285.

Hawkins, J.A. 2004. *Efficiency and complexity in grammars*. Oxford: OUP.

Holmes, P. & Hinchliffe, I. 1997. *Swedish: An essential grammar*. London: Routledge.

Kayne, R.S. 1976. French relative *que*. In *Current studies in Romance linguistics*, M. Luján & F. Hensey (eds), 255–299. Washington DC: Georgetown University Press.

Keenan, E.L. 1985. Relative clauses. In *Language Typology and Syntactic Description*, Vol. 2: *Complex constructions*, T. Shopen (ed.), 141–170. Cambridge: CUP.

Keenan, E.L. & Comrie, B. 1977. Noun phrase accessibility and universal grammar. *Linguistic Inquiry* 8: 63–99.

Langacker, R.W. 1991. *Foundations of cognitive grammar*. Vol. II: *Descriptive applications*. Stanford CA: Stanford University Press.

Larsson, L. 1990. *La sintassi dei pronomi relativi in italiano moderno*. Uppsala: Almqvist and Wiksell.

Lehmann, C. 1979. Der Relativsatz vom Indogermanischen bis zum Italienischen. *Die Sprache* 25: 1–25.

Lehmann, C. 1984. *Der Relativsatz*. Tübingen: Gunter Narr.

Lyons, C. 1999. *Definiteness*. Cambridge: CUP.

Matsumoto, Y. 1996. Interaction of factors in construal: Japanese relative clauses. In *Grammatical Constructions*, M. Shibatani & S.A. Thompson (eds), 103–124. Oxford: OUP.
Matsumoto, Y. 1997. *Noun-modifying constructions in Japanese*. Amsterdam: John Benjamins.
Oyarçabal, B. 2003. Relatives. In *A grammar of Basque*, J.I. Hualde (ed.), 762–823. Berlin: Mouton de Gruyter.
Schafroth, E. 1993. *Zur Entstehung und vergleichenden Typologie der Relativpronomina in den romanischen Sprachen*. Tübingen: Max Niemeyer.
van der Auwera, J. 1985. Relative *that*: A centennial dispute. *Journal of Linguistics* 21: 149–197.

Appendix: the relativization strategies taken into account

This appendix includes two tables. Table 1 reports the various strategies used for individual syntactic roles in each language. In Table 2, the various strategies taken into account are listed, and the languages in which each strategy is attested are reported.

The following syntactic roles are taken into account:

- Roles included within the Accessibility Hierarchy (ordered in terms of higher vs. lower accessibility to relativization): subject (S); direct object (O); indirect object (IO); oblique (Obl); possessor (Poss).
- time circumstantials with semantically more specific head nouns ('day'), in the following four cases:
  - when the head is semantically more specific ('day'), is in a circumstantial role in the main clause, and is accompanied by the universal quantifier 'every' ('every');
  - when the head is semantically more specific ('day'), is in a circumstantial role in the main clause, and is accompanied by the universal quantifier 'each' ('each');
  - when the head is semantically more specific ('day'), is in a circumstantial role in the main clause, and there are no quantifiers (HCirc);
  - when the head is semantically more specific ('day') and is in an argument role in the main clause (HArg)
- when the head is semantically more generic ('time') and is in a circumstantial role in the main clause

The following notation is used to describe the various relativization strategies:

- Adp: adposition
- Df: a different verb is selected, or the sentence is changed so as to relativize on a different syntactic role
- Ga: gapping (Example (8))
- Inflr: relative element inflected for the syntactic role, gender (either grammatical gender, or animacy) or number of the relativized item (Examples (1)–(2))
- Inflr*: specific form of an inflected relative element, used in contexts where other forms of the same element might be expected (Example (9))

- Inflr**: relative element that manifests inflectional oppositions in particular contexts only (Example (10))
- Invr: invariable relative element (Example (7)). A superscript G or R indicate that the element is not inflected for the gender (either grammatical gender or animacy) or syntactic role of the relativized item, but can only be used for certain genders or syntactic roles (Example (6)).
- PA: possessive adjective (Example (4))
- PP: personal pronoun (Example (3))
- RPA: relative possessive adjective, i.e. an element that is used for possessor relativization and has the morphopsyntactic properties of an adjective (Example (5))
- Temp: temporal conjunction also used to introduce temporal adverbial clauses (Example (22))

For each strategy, the specific relative element used in the language is reported (inflected relative elements are reported in the citation form). As specified in Section 3, Italian *che* is indicated as both an inflected and as an invariable relative element, because it appears to be used in both ways in the production of the same speakers.

Table 1. Languages and relativization strategies taken into account (ordered by language)

						Time circumstantials				
						'day'				'time'
Language	**S**	**O**	**IO**	**Obl**	**Poss**	**Every**	**Each**	**HCirc**	**HArg**	
Basque	Ga	Ga	Ga	Ga	Ga	Ga	Ga	Ga	Ga	Ga
Bulgarian	Inflr (*kojto*)	Inflr (*kojto*)	Inflr (*kojto*)	Inflr (*kojto*)	Inflr (*kojto*)	Temp (*kogato*)	Adp+ Inflr (*kojto*)	Adp+ Inflr (*kojto*)	Adp+ Inflr (*kojto*)	Adp+ Inflr (*kojto*)
Catalan	Inflr (*que*)	Inflr (*que*)	Adp+ Inflr (*que*), Infir (*que*) +PP	Adp+ InfGN (*el qual*), Adp+ Inflr (*que*)	Adp+ Inflr (*el qual*), Df, Inflr (*que*)+ PA	Inflr (*que*)	Inflr (*que*)	Inflr (*que*)	Adp+ Inflr (*que*)	Temp (*quand*)
Czech	Inflr, Inflr (*který*)	Inflr* (*co*), INflr* (*co*) + PP, Inflr (*který*)	Inflr* (*co*) + PP, Inflr (*který*)	Inflr (*který*), Inflr* (*co*)+ Adp + PP	Inflr* (*co*) + PA, Inflr (*jehož*)	Inflr* (*co*), Temp (*kdy*)	Inflr* (*co*), Temp (*kdy*)	Inflr* (*co*), Temp (*kdy*)	Inflr* (*co*), Temp (*kdy*)	Inflr* (*co*), Temp (*kdy*)
Danish	Invr (*der*, *som*)	Invr (*som*)	Invr (*som*) + Adp+ Ga, Ga	Adp+ Ga, Invr (*som*) + Adp+ Ga	Invr^{R} (*hvis*), Df	Ga, Temp (*når*)	Ga	Ga	Ga	Ga, Temp (*når*)
Dutch	Inflr (*die*)	Inflr (*die*)	Adp+ Inflr (*wie*), Adp+ Invr (*waar*)	Adp+ Inflr (*wie*), Adp+ Invr (*waar*)	Adp + Inflr (*wie*), Adp+ Invr (*waar*)	Inflr (*die*)	Inflr (*die*), Adp+ Invr (*waar*)	Inflr (*die*), Adp+ Invr (*waar*)	Inflr (*die*), Adp+ Invr (*waar*), Temp (*toen*)	Inflr (*die*), Temp (*toen*)
English	Inflr (*who*), Invr (*that*), Invr^{G} (*which*)	Ga, Inflr (*who*), Invr (*that*), Invr^{G} (*which*)	Adp+ Ga, Adp+ In-flr (*who*), Adp+ Invr^{G} (*which*)	Adp+ Ga, Adp+ Inflr (*who*), Adp+ Invr^{G} (*which*)	Adp+ Ga, Adp+ Invr^{G} (*which*), Adp+ Invr^{G} (*which*), Inflr (*who*)	Ga	Ga	Ga	Ga	Ga

Finnish	Inflr (*joka*)	Inflr (*joka*)	Inflr (*joka*)	Adp+ Inflr (*joka*), Inflr (*joka*)	Inflr (*joka*)	Temp (*kun*)	Inflr (*joka*)	Temp (*kun*)	Inflr (*joka*)	Temp (*kun*)
French	Inflr (*qui*)	Inflr (*qui*)	Adp+ Inflr (*lequel*), Adp+ Inflr (*qui*)	Adp+ Inflr (*lequel*), Adp+ Inflr (*qui*)	Invr^{R} (*dont*), Adp+ inflr (*lequel*)	Invr^{R} (*où*), Temp (*quand*)	Adp+ Inflr (*lequel*), Invr^{R} (*où*)	Invr^{R} (*où*)	Invr^{R} (*où*)	Inflr (*qui*), Invr^{R} (*où*)
Galician	Invr (*que*)	Invr (*que*)	Adp+ Inflr (*o que*) + PP	Adp+ Inflr (*o que*)	Df	Invr (*que*)	Invr (*que*)	Invr (*que*)	Invr (*que*)	Invr (*que*), Temp (*siempre que*)
German	Inflr (*der*)	Inflr (*der*)	Inflr (*der*)	Adp+ Inflr (*der*)	Inflr (*der*)	Adp+ Inflr (*der*), Temp (*als, wenn*)	Adp+ Inflr (*der*)	Adp+ Inflr (*der*), Temp (*als, wenn*)	Adp+ Inflr (*der*)	Temp (*als, wenn*)
Greek	Inflr (*opoios*), Invr (*pou*)	Inflr (*opoios*), Invr (*pou*)	Adp+ Inflr (*opoios*), Invr (*pou*) + PP	Adp+ Inflr (*opoios*), Invr (*pou*) + PP	Inflr (*opoios*), Invr (*pou*) + PP	Invr (*pou*)	Ga	Invr (*pou*)	Invr (*pou*)	Ga
Hungarian	Inflr^{G} (*aki*), Inflr^{G} (*ami*)	Inflr^{G} (*aki*), Inflr^{G} (*ami*)	Inflr^{G} (*aki*), Inflr^{G} (*ami*)	Inflr^{G} (*aki*), Inflr^{G} (*ami*)	Inflr^{G} (*aki*), Inflr^{G} (*ami*)	Temp (*amikor*)	Temp (*amikor*)	Temp (*amikor*)	Temp (*amikor*)	Temp (*amikor*)
Irish	Invr (*a*)	Invr (*a*)	Invr (*a*) + PP	Adp+ Invr (*a*) + PP	Invr (*a*) + PA	Invr (*a*)	Invr (*a*)	Invr (*a*)	Invr (*a*)	Invr (*a*)
Italian	Inflr (*che*), Invr (*che*)	Inflr (*che*), Invr (*che*)	Adp+ Inflr (*il quale*), Adp+ Inflr (*che*), Invr (*che*) + PP	Adp+ Inflr (*il quale*), Adp+ Inflr (*che*), Invr (*che*) + PP	Adp+ Inflr (*il quale*), Adp+ Inflr (*che*), RPA (*il cui*)	Adp+ Inflr (*che*), Invr (*che*)	Adp+ Inflr (*che*), Invr (*che*)	Adp+ Inflr (*che*), Invr (*che*)	Adp+ Inflr (*che*)	Adp+ Inflr (*che*), Invr (*che*)

Table 1. Continued

Language	S	O	IO	Obl	Poss	Time circumstantials				
						'day'				'time'
						Every	Each	HCirc	HArg	
Latvian	Ga, Inflr (*kas*)	Ga, Inflr (*kas*)	Ga, Inflr (*kas*)	Adp+ Inflr (*kas*)	Inflr (*kas*) (*kas*)	Temp (*kad*)	Temp (*kad*)	Temp (*kad*)	Temp (*kad*)	Temp (*kad*)
Lithuanian	Inflr (*kuris*)	Inflr (*kuris*)	Inflr (*kuris*)	Inflr (*kuris*), Adp+ Inflr (*kuris*)	Inflr (*kuris*)	Inflr (*kuris*), Temp (*kai*)	Inflr (*kuris*), Temp (*kai*)	Inflr (*kuris*), Temp (*kai*)	Inflr (*kuris*), Temp (*kai*)	Temp (*kai*)
Polish	Inflr (*który*)	Inflr (*który*)	Inflr* (*co*) + PP, Inflr (*który*)	Adp+ Inflr (*który*)	Adp+ Inflr (*który*), Inflr* (*co*) + PA, Df, Inflr (*który*)	Temp (*kiedy, gdy*)	Temp (*kiedy, gdy*)	Adp+ Inflr (*który*), Inflr, Temp (*kiedy, gdy*)	Adp+ Inflr (*który*)	Temp (*kiedy, gdy*)
Portuguese	Inflr** (*que*)	Inflr** (*que*)	Adp+ Inflr** (*que*)	Adp+ Inflr** (*que*)	RPA (*cujo*)	Inflr** (*que*)	Adp+ Inflr** (*que*), Inflr** (*que*)	Adp+ Inflr** (*que*), Inflr** (*que*)	Adp+ Inflr** (*que*), Inflr** (*que*)	Adp+ Inflr** (*que*)
Rumanian	Inflr (*care*)	Inflr (*care*)	Inflr (*care*)	Adp+ Inflr (*care*)	Adp+ Inflr (*care*), Df, RPA (*al caruia*)	Temp (*când*)	Temp (*când*)	Temp (*când*)	Inflr (*care*)	Temp (*când*)
Russian	Inflr (*kotoryj*)	Inflr (*kotoryj*)	Inflr (*kotoryj*)	Inflr (*kotoryj*), Adp+ Inflr (*kotoryj*)	Inflr (*kotoryj*)	Temp (*kogda*)	Temp (*kogda*)	Temp (*kogda*)	Temp (*kogda*)	Temp (*kogda*)

Sardinian	Invr (*ki*)	Invr (*ki*)	Adp+ Inflr, Invr (*ki*) + PP	Adp+ Inflr (*su ki*), Adp+ Invr (*ki*)	Adp+ Invr (*ki*), Adp+ Inflr (*su ki*), Invr (*ki*), Invr (*ki*) + PA	Invr (*ki*)	Invr (*ki*)	Invr (*ki*)	Invr (*ki*)	Invr (*ki*)
Serbian	Inflr (*koji*)	Inflr (*koji*)	Adp+ Inflr (*koji*)	Adp+ Inflr (*koji*)	Inflr (*koji*)	Temp (*kada*)	Temp (*kada*)	Temp (*kada*)	Temp (*kada*)	Temp (*kada*)
Spanish	Inflr** (*que*)	Adp+ Inflr** (*que*), Inflr** (*que*)	Adp+ Inflr (*el que*), Adp+ Inflr** (*que*)	Adp+ Inflr (*el que*), Adp+ Inflr** (*que*)	Df, RPA (*cuyo*)	Inflr** (*que*)	Adp+ Inflr** (*que*), Inflr** (*que*)	Inflr** (*que*)	Adp+ Inflr** (*que*), Inflr** (*que*)	Inflr** (*que*)
Swedish	Invr (*som*)	Invr (*som*), Ga	Adp+ Ga, Invr (*som*) + Adp+ Ga	Adp+ Ga, Invr (*som*) + Adp+ Ga	Invr[R] (em*vars*), DF	Ga	Ga	Ga	Ga	Ga
Swiss German	Invr (*wo*)	Invr (*wo*)	Invr (*wo*)	Invr (*wo*), Invr (*wo*) + Adp+ PP	Invr (*wo*), Invr (*wo*) + Adp+ PP	Invr (*wo*)	Invr (*wo*)	Invr (*wo*)	Invr (*wo*)	Invr (*wo*)

Table 2. Cross-linguistic distribution of individual relativization strategies

Relativization strategy	Languages
Adp + G	Danish, English, Swedish
Adp + Inflr + PP	Galician, Italian, Sardinian, Spanish
Adp + Inflr	Bulgarian, Catalan, Dutch, English, Finnish, French, German, Italian, Latvian, Lithuanian, Polish, Rumanian, Russian, Serbian
Adp + Inflr**	Portuguese, Spanish
Adp + Invr	Dutch, Sardinian, Swiss German
Adp + Invr + PP	Irish, Swiss German
Adp + Invr^{G}	English
Df	Catalan, Danish, Galician, Polish, Rumanian, Sardinian, Spanish
Ga	Basque, Danish, English, Finnish, Greek, Latvian, Swedish
Inflr	Bulgarian, Catalan, Czech, Danish, Dutch, English, Finnish, French, German, Greek, Hungarian, Italian, Latvian, Lithuanian, Polish, Rumanian, Russian, Serbian, Swedish
Inflr + PA	Catalan
Inflr + PP	Catalan, Italian, French
Inflr*	Czech
Inflr* + PA	Czech, Polish
Inflr* + PP	Czech, Polish
Inflr**	Portuguese, Spanish
Invr	Danish, Dutch, English, Galician, Greek, Irish, Italian, Sardinian, Swedish, Swiss German
Invr + Adp + Ga	Danish, Swedish
Invr + PA	Irish, Sardinian
Invr + PP	Greek, Irish, Italian, Sardinian
Invr^{G}	English
Invr^{R}	Danish, French, Swedish
RPA	Italian, Portuguese, Rumanian, Spanish
Temp	Bulgarian, Catalan, Czech, Danish, Dutch, Finnish, French, Galician, German, Hungarian, Latvian, Lithuanian, Polish, Rumanian, Russian, Serbian

Acknowledgements

We wish to thank all the people who provided us with data on the various languages, and without whom this work would not have been possible:

Basque: María-José Lopez Couso
Bulgarian: Svetlana Slavkova

Catalan: César Montoliu, Carmen Munõz
Czech: Eva Hajicova, Barbara Schmiedtova, Petr Sgall
Danish: Therese Hasforth, Janick Wrona
Dutch: Willy Vandewege
English: Kate Shyne
Finnish: Jyrki Kyherïnen, Ulrika Magnea
French: Claudine Chamoreau, Dominique Klinger
Galician: María-José Lopez Couso, Marcos Mariño, Araceli Sanchez
German: Johannes Helmbrecht, Nuria Hernandez
Greek: Dimitris Alexandrou, Costas Bachas
Hungarian: Valéria Molnár
Irish: Anders Alhqvist, Ruarí Ó hUiginn
Latvian: Ilze Milta
Lithuanian: Paulius Jurkevicius, Rasa Kliostoraityte
Polish: Agnieszka Latos, Malwina Przystalska
Portuguese: Miguel Costa
Rumanian: Marinella Lörinczi
Russian: Marina Chumakina, Anjuta Gancikov
Sardinian: Martina Fanari, Nicoletta Puddu, Ignazio Putzu
Serbian: Radmila Djordjevic, Jadranka Kratovič
Spanish: Francisco Gonzálvez García, María-José Lopez Couso, Jesus de la Villa
Swedish: Ulrika Magnea, Valéria Molnár, Johannes Nordström, Eva Wiberg
Swiss German: Michele Loporcaro

Abbreviations

ADJ	adjective
AN	animate
AUX	auxiliary
COMP	complementizer
DAT	dative
ERG	ergative
F	feminine
INAN	inanimate
LOC	locative
M	masculine
NOM	nominative
NT	neuter
PAST	past
PL	plural
POSS	possessive
RECPR	reciprocal
REL	relative
SG	singular

The spread and decline of indefinite *man*-constructions in European languages

An areal perspective[1]

Anna Giacalone Ramat and Andrea Sansò

This paper focuses on the areal distribution of indefinite *man*-constructions (i.e. impersonal active constructions in which the subject position is filled by a noun meaning 'man') in European languages. It is shown that *man*-constructions are a widespread phenomenon across Europe: they show up consistently in the so-called "Charlemagne area", and tend to diffuse eastwards to West and South Slavonic languages, whereas East Slavonic languages do not present clear instances of this construction type. This areal distribution allows us to consider these constructions as a yet unnoticed areal feature of the Standard Average European area, but they are, in a sense, a recessive areal feature, and their distribution in older times included more languages than today (especially in Germanic and Romance). On the other hand, the eastward expansion towards the Slavonic area appears to be a quite recent phenomenon, and *man*-constructions in Slavonic languages are possibly an incipient category. To cope with this apparent discrepancy, a two-wave model of diffusion is introduced, which singles out two historical periods in which the diffusion of these constructions is likely to have taken place.

Introduction

General nouns meaning *man, people, person, body* (as well as *thing, place, way*) are one of the lexical sources of indefinite pronouns across languages (Lehmann 1995: 50ff.;

1. This article is the result of joint work by the two authors. Although Andrea Sansò is responsible for the Introduction and Section 1, and Anna Giacalone Ramat is responsible for Sections 2 and 3, both authors subscribe to the general ideas presented in the article. We wish to thank the audiences at the 27th DGfS Annual Meeting (Bielefeld 2006), at the FIRB conference "Europa e Mediterraneo dal punto di vista linguistico: Storia e prospettive" (Siena 2006), and at the Colloque "La quantification en latin" (Paris, Sorbonne 2006) for valuable discussions of the ideas presented in this paper. Pierluigi Cuzzolin and two anonymous referees provided insightful comments on an earlier version of the paper.

Haspelmath 1997: 182–183; Heine and Kuteva 2002: 208). The outcome of this process of grammaticalization includes two diverse grammatical entities:

i. firstly, some of these nouns may combine with simple indefinite pronouns to form complex indefinite pronouns. This is the case of English *body*, which combines with other pronominal elements such as *some* or *any* (*somebody, anybody*). Similarly, negative indefinites may be formed by a negator plus "an element from the same source[s] that also feed the [positive] indefinites" (Lehmann 1995: 53, adapted): this happens for instance in Latin, where *nemo* goes back to *ne-hemo*, 'no-man';[2]
ii. secondly, there are languages in which indefinite pronouns consist only of such generic nouns, which do not combine with other indefinite elements. In this case, the generic noun is "first used in a noun phrase without modifiers to render meanings like 'somebody', 'something', and . . . gradually acquires phonological, morphological and syntactic features that set it off from other nouns" (Haspelmath 1997: 182), although the exact discrimination of the pronominal status of these items is a problematic issue and the differences between nouns and pronouns are often quite subtle (see Section 1.6).

The topic of this paper is a small subgroup of indefinite pronouns consisting only of generic nouns meaning 'man'. More precisely, our study deals with what we call indefinite *man*-constructions. The preliminary definition of these constructions proposed in (1) is admittedly large, in order to include in our analysis also those languages in which these constructions are not fully grammaticalized:

(1) **Definition:** *a* man-*construction is an impersonal active construction in which the subject position is filled by (an element deriving etymologically from) a noun meaning 'man'. Syntactically, this element may pattern like a full pronoun, or it may retain some or all of the syntactic properties of a noun. Semantically, the construction is an agent-defocusing strategy, i.e. it is used when the speaker wants to background the agent of an action (either because it is generic/non-identifiable, or because it is specific but unknown).*[3] *For the sake of clarity,* 'man' *or* 'man-*element' will be used throughout this paper to refer to the nominal element filling the subject position in these constructions.*

2. According to Lehmann (1995: 54), general nouns are exploited to a greater degree in the formation of negative indefinites than of positive indefinites: while English *nobody* corresponds to positive indefinites formed with the same nouns, Latin *nemo*, or *nihilum* (< *ni* + *hilum* 'fiber'), 'nothing', do not have plain indefinites formed with the same lexical sources (cf. also Haspelmath 1997: 226ff.).

3. Following a well-established tradition of the functional literature about passive and passive-like constructions (see e.g. Myhill 1997: 801), we include as "agents" transitive subjects, NPs with the same thematic role as transitive subjects in diathetical alternations, and semantically agentive NPs that occur as subjects of intransitive verbs.

Our paper focuses on European languages, many of which have such constructions. We do not discuss the pronominal status of *man*-elements for the time being (it is, however, the object of a lenghtier discussion in Section 1.6), and we will avoid using the term *pronoun* in these introductory sections to refer to the *man*-element, for it would not make any sense to exclude the non-pronominal (or less-pronominal) cases from a wide-angle, areally-driven investigation.

The remainder of this paper is organized as follows. In Sections 1.1 to 1.4, we will deal with the semantics of *man*-constructions and we will give a survey of the (subtle) semantic distinctions that they convey. Three situation types will be discussed in which the *man*-element conveys different semantic nuances, ranging from a species-generic interpretation (*man* meaning 'mankind' or 'human race') to a non-referential indefinite interpretation (*man* as an equivalent of 'one', 'anyone'), and finally to a referential indefinite interpretation (*man* as an equivalent of 'someone'). These three situation types form a grammaticalization path, which also correlates with changes in formal properties: in the more grammaticalized stages of *man*-constructions the *man*-element is more likely to behave as a full pronoun. This grammaticalization path will be introduced in Section 1.5, whereas Section 1.6 is devoted to a discussion of the formal properties of the *man*-element in *man*-constructions. Section 2 deals with the areal distribution of these constructions in Europe and neighboring areas. The results of this areal investigation show that *man*-constructions are a widespread phenomenon across Europe: these constructions show up consistently in the so-called "Charlemagne area", and tend to diffuse eastwards to West and South Slavonic languages, whereas East Slavonic languages do not present clear instances of this construction type. Moving more eastward, these constructions appear only sporadically in the languages of the Caucasus, while being absent also from Arabic varieties in the south (except Maltese). The areal distribution of *man*-constructions allows us to consider them as a yet unnoticed areal feature of the Standard Average European area. In Section 3 we take a diachronic stance on the development of these constructions, while also discussing some problems concerning their origin. It emerges clearly from our discussion that these constructions, though robustly attested throughout Europe, are, in a sense, a recessive areal feature, and their distribution in older times included more languages than today (especially in Germanic and Romance). On the other hand, the eastward expansion towards the Slavonic area appears to be a quite recent phenomenon, and *man*-constructions in Slavonic languages are possibly an *incipient category* (in the sense of Heine and Kuteva 2005: 71ff.). To cope with this apparent discrepancy, a two-wave model of diffusion is introduced, which singles out two historical periods in which the diffusion of these constructions is likely to have taken place.

1. From species-generic to referential indefinite: The semantics of *man*-constructions

Indefinite pronouns serve the function of expressing indefinite reference. A linguistic expression is indefinite if the speaker is not entitled to assume that the hearer can assign unique referential identity to it (Givón 1984: 397ff.). *Indefiniteness* (or its opposite, definiteness), however, is a complex and multi-dimensional notion, which encroaches upon another semantic dimension, namely *referentiality* (also referred to as *specificity*, see e.g. Haspelmath 1997: 37ff., Raumolin-Brunberg and Kahlas-Tarkka 1997: 26), defined as "the speaker's intent to refer to some individual" (Givón 1984: 390):[4] a linguistic expression is referential if the speaker presupposes the existence and unique identifiability of its referent. When looking at the morphosyntactic coding of definiteness and referentiality, it appears that the same coding devices (in the sense of Givón 1984: 35ff.) are used for both functional domains: articles (or absence thereof, i.e. bare nominals), demonstratives, universal and existential quantifiers, and pronouns. The *man*-element in *man*-constructions is precisely one of these coding devices: it is a semantically light (or even empty) element that can be used for both a non-referential subject (*anyone, one*) and a referential, indefinite one (*someone*). This semantic characterization of the *man*-element is in direct correlation with the general function served by *man*-constructions, namely the function of *agent defocusing* (Myhill 1997; Sansò 2006). By *agent defocusing* we mean a multi-faceted functional notion comprising (at least) the following phenomena: absence of mention of a specific agent, absence of mention of a generic agent virtually corresponding to all humanity (or a subgroup thereof), mention of an agent in a non-prominent syntactic slot, etc.

In the following sections, we will identify three typical contexts of usage for *man*-constructions, which differ in the referentiality/definiteness properties of the referent of *man*. These differences can be evaluated by assuming a definition of the domain of referentiality and (in)definiteness that does not depend on the form of linguistic expressions. The point of departure of such an analysis is Givón's (1984: 387) hierarchy of definiteness and referentiality:

(2) Generic > Non-referential indefinite > Referential indefinite > Definite

4. In some philosophical traditions there is little, if any, separation between "definite" and "having exact reference", i.e. between a hearer-based dimension (definiteness) and a speaker-based one (referentiality). For a wider discussion on the usefulness of this distinction, the reader is referred to Givón (1984: 397ff.).

This hierarchy is explicitly not devised as a characterization of linguistic forms. Rather, the categories on this scale are intended as properties of referents. A linguistic item has *generic* reference if it refers to a class of individuals (***The lion** is dangerous*/***Lions** are dangerous*);[5] it is *non-referential indefinite* if the speaker does not have a specific entity in his/her mind, and at the same time s/he does not want the hearer to infer that such a specific entity exists (*Even **a child** can understand this*). Linguistic expressions may be ambiguous as to their referentiality: an utterance such as *We are looking for **a blond girl*** is ambiguous as to the referential properties of the indefinite noun phrase *a blond girl*. A linguistic item is *referential indefinite* if it refers to a specific entity which has not been mentioned before or which cannot be identified more precisely (*He bought **a book***). Finally, an item is *definite* if the speaker assumes that the hearer knows, assumes, or can infer that particular item, even if s/he is not necessarily thinking about it (*If you see **the man** with the green hat there, tell him...*).

The three contexts of usage for *man*-constructions that will be described in detail below all involve this hierarchy: in the less grammaticalized stages of development of these constructions, *man* is used as a species-generic (§1.1), or as a non-referential indefinite (§1.2) subject, whereas in more grammaticalized instances of this construction type, the *man*-element is a referential indefinite subject roughly corresponding to English *someone* (§1.3). The discussion in the following sections will be carried out in purely semantic terms, with numerous examples drawn from both modern European languages and their older stages. The formal properties of these constructions are discussed in more detail in Section 1.6.

1.1 Man *as a species-generic element*

Like all general nouns referring to species, nouns such as *man* can be used as species-generics. There is nothing particularly interesting in this usage, which seems to be a well-attested possibility of general nouns across languages. However, this is the discourse environment in which the reanalysis of *man* as an "outil grammatical" (Meillet 1948: 277) takes place: the reanalysis is covert at this stage,

5. Generic elements occupy a peculiar position on this scale: they do not refer to items in the discourse universe, and thus they share some properties with non-referential indefinite elements. However, *genericity* (or *genericness*) is intended by Givón (1984: 265; see also Raumolin-Brunberg and Kahlas-Tarkka 1997: 26) as a third semantic/pragmatic dimension of noun phrases and pronouns along with (in)definiteness and referentiality: generic noun phrases refer to whole species or sub-species, pick out indiscriminate referents of a given class, and are accordingly placed at one extreme of the scale in (2); non-referential indefinites are, in a sense, more referential than generics because they pick out a referent without further identification (or a referent whatsoever within a well-circumscribed set of individuals).

and no overt modifications in the form of *man* reveal it. In the following examples, two interpretations are possible: one in which the noun *man* is interpreted as corresponding to *human race* or *mankind* (often opposed to God, or other species, as in (4) and (6)), and the other in which *man* can be paraphrased as *one, anyone.*

Latin

(3) *Non in solo pane vivit* ***homo*** (Matthew 4, 4)
'**Man** does not live by bread alone'[6]

(4) *Quod ergo Deus coniunxit,* ***homo*** *non separet* (Mark 10, 9)
'What God has joined together let **no man** put asunder'

Gothic (and Latin)

(5) *aiþþau ƕa gibiþ* ***manna*** *inmaidein saiwalos seinaizos? = aut quid dabit* ***homo*** *commutationem pro anima sua* (Mark 8, 37)
'There is nothing **a man / one** can give to regain his life'

Old Italian

(6) *...in questa una cosa avanza* ***l'uomo*** *tutte le bestie et animali...* (Brunetto Latini, *Rettorica*, p. 38, rr. 14–15)
'In this thing alone **the human race** overcomes all the beasts and animals'

(7) *Se alquanti di mala maniera usano malamente eloquenzia, non rimane pertanto che* ***ll'uomo*** *non debbia studiare in eloquenzia...* (Brunetto Latini, *Rettorica*, p. 36, rr. 8–10)
'If some bad people use eloquence badly, this does not mean that **all people in the world / one** should not study eloquence'

Latin

(8) *In quo mare nihil invenitur vivificatum ... neque* ***homo*** *natare potest, sed quicquid ibi iactatum fuerit, in profundum mergitur* (Antoninus Plac. 166, 10; from Salonius 1920: 246)
'In that sea nothing alive (no living creature) is found and **one** cannot swim in it, but whatever has been thrown there sinks to the bottom'

Examples (7) and (8) are particularly instructive as to the possible ambiguity in the interpretation of *man*, which triggers reanalysis. In (7), for instance, *l'uomo*, 'the man', may be interpreted as referring to the human race in general, but an interpretation in which it represents an indefinite subject (*one*) cannot be excluded (cf. Salvi, n.d.: 49).

6. The English translation of this and the following Bible examples is taken from May Metzger (1962), with some minor modifications.

1.2 Man *as a human non-referential indefinite element*

Consider now example (9). In this case, *man* cannot refer to all humanity: rather, it refers to anyone who has read what the author wrote. An interpretation of *man* as *human race, mankind* is clearly excluded in these cases. The same holds true for examples (10) and (11).

Old Italian

(9) *Potrebbe già* ***l'uomo*** *opporre contra me e dicere che*... (Dante, *Vita Nuova*, 12, 17)
'**One** could in fact argue against me (i.e. against what I said) and say that...'

(10) ...*quando* ***uomo*** *truova la donnola nella via*... (*Novellino*, 32, rr. 7–8)
'When **one** finds a weasel on his way'

(11) ...*in questo ch'è detto puote* ***uomo*** *bene intendere che*... (Brunetto Latini, *Rettorica*, p. 152, rr. 13–14)
'In (i.e. from) what has been said **one** can well understand that...'

In these examples, *man* is contextually determined, i.e. it refers to a contextually bound sub-group of humanity (people belonging to a given group, people in a given location/situation, and so on) and not to all humanity. It must be interpreted as a human non-referential indefinite element, roughly corresponding to English *one* or *anyone*. This usage correlates significantly with non-assertive contexts (i.e. irrealis, non-factual, negated, habitual, potential, and deontic contexts). That non-assertive contexts are the typical syntactic and semantic environment in which *man* starts being used as an indefinite element is not news to linguists, and has been widely recognized at least since Vendryes (1916: 186; cf. also Meillet 1948: 277). In Section 1.5 we will advance a possible explanation concerning this genesis of *man*-constructions.

This usage appears to be widespread throughout Europe, in both modern and ancient languages. The following passages are a small, non-representative sample. A detailed description of the areal distribution of *man*-constructions will be the object of Section 2.

Anglo-Saxon (and Latin)

(12) *swa* ***man*** *byrð lytle cyld = ut solet* ***homo*** *gestare parvulum filium suum* (Deut. 1, 31)
'As **a man / one** bears his little child'

Old Spanish

(13) *Non se deuie* ***el omne*** *por perdida quexar, Ca nunqua por su quexa lo puede recobrar* (*Libro de Apolonio*, 341cd., from Barrett Brown 1931: 267)
'**One** should not complain about a loss, because one would never recover (what he has lost) by means of complaints'

Medieval Occitan

(14) *aquella fazenda que* **om** *apella Massenal* (*Chartes* 377, 7, from Jensen 1986: 164)
'that farm which is called Massenal'

Slovene

(15) *V taki situaciji bi* ***človek*** *iskal drugo službo* (Martina Ožbot, p.c.)
'In such a situation **one** would look for another job'

Abruzzese

(16) ***Nome*** *magne tutta lu juorne* (D'Alessandro and Alexiadou 2006: 193)
one eats all the day
'**One** eats all day long'

At this stage, there are some formal, surface symptoms of a process of reanalysis that has already occurred covertly:[7] in some cases (as, for instance, in (10) and (11)), the *man*-element appears with no article. In Old Italian, lack of the article is impossible under a species-generic interpretation of a NP (Salvi n.d.: 49), and thus in (10) and (11) only a non-referential indefinite interpretation is possible, whereas in cases such as (9) this interpretation arises only on semantic/contextual grounds (i.e., without overt syntactic manifestations).

1.3 Man *as a human referential indefinite element*

In some languages, *man* can be used to refer to a specific human subject that the speaker does not want, or cannot, specify, i.e. as a rough equivalent of *someone*. When used in such a way, the *man*-construction functionally resembles other passive constructions (e.g. the periphrastic passive), in its capacity of backgrounding a specific agent for discourse/contextual reasons. Some examples of referential indefinite *man* are the following:

German

(17) *Aber noch in derselben Nacht schlich einer der Dörfler zum Grab des Getöteten, grub ihn aus und fraß vom Fleisch des Menschenfressers, so daß er, als* **man** *ihn faßte, gleichfalls zum Tode verurteilt wurde* (U. Eco, *Der Namen der Rose*, 247).

7. Following Timberlake (1977: 141) and Harris and Campbell (1995: 61ff.), *reanalysis* is intended here as a process directly changing underlying structures whose effects are not directly visible on the surface. Reanalysis is to be treated as distinct from *actualization*, the process by which some overt syntactic manifestations of the reanalysis emerge and "bring the surface into line with the innovative underlying structure" (Harris and Campbell 1995: 77).

'That same night, however, one man from the village went and dug up the grave of the murdered victim and ate the flesh of the cannibal, whereupon, since he was discovered, the village put him to death, too' (U. Eco, *The name of the rose*, 188).[8]

(18) ***Man** hat letzte Woche bei uns eingebrochen* (from Zifonun 2001: 237)
'Our house was burgled last week (lit.: **someone** burgled our house last week)'

French

(19) *Regarde, dit-elle, fainéant! Pendant que tu étais occupé à dormir, **on** nous a volé notre maison* (*Trésor de la langue française*, vol. 12, 498a)
'"Look", she said, "lazybones! While you were engaged in sleeping, they took away our house"'

Anglo-Saxon (and Latin)

(20) *and **man** brohte þa his heafod on anum disce and sealde þam mædene = et **allatum est** caput eius in disco, et datum est puellae* (Matthew 14, 11)
'and his head was brought on a platter and given to the girl'

Swedish

(21) ***Man** har mördat Palme* (Altenberg 2004/2005: 94)
'**Someone** murdered Palme / Palme has been murdered'

(22) *I tre veckor hade **man** haft Limpan under uppsikt i övertygelse om att han förr eller senare måste uppsöka gömstället för bytet från kuppen* (Altenberg 2004/2005: 107)
'For three weeks now, **one** (i.e., the police) had had The Breadman under constant surveillance, convinced that sooner or later he would visit the place where he had hidden the loot from the holdup'

In these examples, the action is typically a past one, bound to a specific spatio-temporal setting, and thus there must have been one or more specific agents. It appears that the languages in which *man* can be used in this way are a subset of those languages in which *man* is used as a non-referential indefinite element. As a means of backgrounding specific agents, *man* as a referential indefinite element is used as a translational equivalent of periphrastic passives, as in (17) and (20), or

8. The original version of the novel has a periphrastic passive in this passage:

(i) *Ma la notte stessa un tale del villaggio andò a scavare la fossa dell'ucciso e mangiò delle carni del cannibale, così che, **quando fu scoperto**, il villaggio condannò a morte anche lui* (U. Eco, *Il nome della rosa*, 191).

personal morphological passives, which are typically associated with the function of backgrounding specific agents (Myhill 1997; Sansò 2006: 243ff.). The following examples from Old High German, Old French, and Early Dutch show that this usage of *man* in the Charlemagne area dates back to the Middle Ages:

Early Dutch (and Latin)

(23) *enn* ***men*** *brachte hem enen boec . . . ysaie des propheten = et* ***traditus est*** *illi liber Isaiae prophetae* (Luke 4, 17, from Gray 1945: 25)
'and there was given to him the book of the prophet Isaiah'

Old French (and Latin)

(24) ***l'um*** *li menout chevals =* ***educebantur*** *equi Salomoni* (III Kings 10, 28, from Gray 1945: 28)
'horses were brought to Salomon'

Old High German (and Latin)

(25) *Thó quam hér zi Nazareth, thar hér uuas gizogan, inti ingieng after sinero giúuonu in sambaztág in thie samanunga, inti árstuont úf zi lesanne, inti* ***salta mán imo*** *then buoh thés uuizagen Esaies.* (Tatian, *Gospel Harmony*, 18, 1) = *Et venit Nazareth, ubi erat nutritus, et intravit secundum consuetudinem suam die sabbati in synagogam, et surrexit legere, et* ***traditus est illi*** *liber prophetae Esaiæ* (Luke 4, 17)
'And he came to Nazareth, where he had been brought up; and he went to the synagogue, as his custom was, on the Sabbath day. And he stood up to read; and there was given to him the book of the prophet Isaiah'

(26) *Inti uuard tho, mit diu her uuidaruuarb intfanganemo rihhe,* ***gibót tho thaz man gihaloti sine scalca*** *then her gab then scaz, thaz her uuesti uuio filu iro giuuelih giscazzot uuari.* (Tatian, *Gospel Harmony*, 151, 4) = *Et factum est, dum rediret accepto regno, et* ***iussit vocari servos*** *quibus dedit pecuniam, ut sciret quantum quisque negotiatus esset* (Luke 19, 15)
'When he returned, having received the kingly power, he commanded these servants, to whom he had given the money, to be called to him, that he might know what they had gained by trading'

1.4 Further developments

In some languages, *man* has evolved into a human referential definite pronoun, corresponding to a first person (plural and even singular) pronoun, and even to a second person. This use is sometimes labelled as "pseudo-generic" (e.g. by Altenberg 2004/2005: 95), or "4th person" (e.g. by Grafström 1969: 270, and Coveney 2000). French is the European language in which this development is most systematically found (Nyrop 1925: 385ff.; Grafström 1969; Söll 1969; Coveney 2000).

French

(27) *Au premier coup de canon qui nous a réveillés à 2 hs du matin* **on** *s'est dressé* (Grafström 1969: 272–273).
'At the first gun shot, which woke us up at 2 o'clock in the morning, **we** got dressed'

(28) ***On*** *a du pain pour nos vieux jours* (Grafström 1969: 273)
'**We**'ve got bread for our old days'

(29) ***On*** *a fait du latin ce matin?* (Nyrop 1925: 380)
'Did **you** have a Latin class this morning?'

In French "it does not seem that [+definite] *on* was general in the Paris area before the 19th century" (Coveney 2000: 450).[9] This development is somewhat different from the evolutionary process leading from a species-generic to a human (non-) referential indefinite. The latter consistently invokes a progressive switch along a single hierarchy (referentiality/definiteness), whereas the former implies a reinterpretation of an impersonal clause as a personal one:

(30) "several writers have pointed out that, even in their 'traditional' uses, there is a degree of semantic similarity between *nous* and *on*... and it is said that this has facilitated the replacement of *nous* with *on*. More specifically, both pronouns usually refer to groups of people, which vary in size and composition according to context... This semantic overlap is thought to be the reason why certain other languages similarly use an impersonal form for 4p reference" (Coveney 2000: 454).[10]

This usage is also attested in Czech and Polish (Mazon 1931: 150–151). In Polish *człowiek* (or its abridged form *człek*) is used as an equivalent of the first person (singular/plural) pronoun as early as the 18th century:

Modern Czech (Mazon 1931: 150)

(31) *rano sotva vyleze* ***člověk*** *z hnízda, uz aby se dřel, a když přijde večer, je ulahán jako mlékařčin pes...* ***Člověk*** *aby se přetrhal, a nic za to nemá!*
'à peine sorti du nid, dès l'aube, **on** doit peiner, et puis le soir on est exténué comme un chien de laitier... **On** se crève sans nul profit'

---

9. *On* has been used since Old French as a stylistically marked substitute for all the other personal pronouns (Nyrop 1925: 375ff.). The 19th century should be regarded as the period in which this usage started to appear consistently in the literature in the representation of the colloquial speech of the working class (cf. Coveney 2000: 451).

10. In Tuscan (and, to some extent, also in Standard Italian), the usage of the reflexive/middle marker *si* for 'we' has become standardised when the verb is not transitive or unergative: in these contexts, the agent may be identified as an "unspecified set of people including the speaker" (Cinque 1988: 542). This development is therefore not specific to *man*-constructions but appears to characterize other passive/impersonal construction types.

Polish (18th century, Mazon 1931: 151–152)

(32) ***Człek*** *jadł, pił, nic nie robił i suto w kieszeni*
'on mangeait, buvait son saoûl, ne faisait rien, et l'on avait la bourse pleine'

(33) ***Człowiek*** *się napracował,* ***człek*** *niemało skorzystał*
'on s'est fourbu de travail, on en a eu quelque profit'

Polish (contemporary, Stefan Dyła, p.c.)

(34) ***Człowiek*** *chce odpocząć, cieszyć się chwilą...*
man.NOM wants rest.INF cherish.INF REFL moment.INSTR
'**One** (but also: **I/we**) want(s) to rest, cherish the moment'

A similar usage is attested in Swedish (cf. (35)), where it is said to be substandard, although, as Egerland (2003: 76) puts it, "for many speakers the usage in question no longer has any particular stylistic implications":

Swedish

(35) *I går på eftermiddagen blev* ***man*** *avskedad*
yesterday afternoon was man fired
'yesterday afternoon I was fired'

1.5 *A grammaticalization path for* man*-constructions*

The grammaticalization path of *man* as an indefinite element follows Givón's hierarchy of referentiality/definiteness. The usage of *man* as a human referential indefinite subject is the most grammaticalized, while the development described in 1.4 is a somewhat heterogeneous process and is accordingly placed as an option which parallels the usage of *man* as a human referential indefinite but does not presuppose it:

(a¹) *man* as species-generic ⇨ (a²) *man* as human non-referential indefinite ⇨ (b) *man* as human referential indefinite
⬂ *(c) 1st person singular/plural*

The arrangement of situation types within this path deserves some explanation. Two facts emerge clearly from the discussion conducted thus far: firstly, the number of languages in which *man* serves as a human referential indefinite subject is a subset of those languages in which it is used as a human non-referential indefinite subject. Secondly, in these languages, *man* appears to be greatly or totally grammaticalized as a pronoun, whereas the same does not (always) hold true for those languages in which it is used as a human non-referential indefinite only. This fact alone is sufficient to motivate the arrangement proposed above. More concretely, there is a number of semantic features shared by the two leftmost situation types and only partially by *man* as a human referential indefinite which corroborate this analysis. The following table provides a synopsis of these features:

Table 1. Semantic features of the three situation types (a^1 = *man* as species-generic; a^2 = *man* as human non-referential indefinite; b = *man* as human referential indefinite; c = *man* as human specific definite).

Type	Number	Inclusion	Referentiality	Typical contexts of usage:
(a^1)	inherently plural (= 'humanity, mankind, human race')	speaker, addressee, third party	nonreferential	maxims, proverbs, generalizations
(a^2)	plural (= 'anyone')/ singular (= 'one')	speaker, addressee, third party	nonreferential	non-assertive (≅ irrealis predication)
(b)	plural/singular (= someone, be it a plurality of referents or not)	third party	referential	assertive (≅ realis predication)
(c)	1st person singular/ plural	speaker, addressee, third party	referential	irrelevant

Some of these features are fairly self-explanatory, and we do not discuss them in detail. The usages of *man*-constructions exemplified in Sections 1.1 and 1.2 do not exclude the speech act participants from predication, whereas in the examples in 1.3 *man* cannot refer to the speaker and the addressee, but is limited to a third party.[11] In the contexts exemplified in 1.1 *man* refers to the human race as opposed to something else (God, animals, etc.). Thus, the referent of *man* is plural *per se* in these cases. In the contexts exemplified in 1.2, *man* refers to a plural entity (*people in general, people in a given spatio-temporal setting*), but it can be interpreted as a singular given the appropriate hypothetic/irrealis context (*a person in a given situation* ≅ English *one*). In the contexts exemplified in 1.3, *man* may refer to both singular (*someone, specific*) and plural (*someone ≅ a specific group of people*) entities. As to the typical contexts of usage of *man* constructions, we can draw a clear-cut line opposing those cases (labelled (a^1) and (a^2) in the table) in which the predication

11. More precisely, when *man* is a species-generic, the reference normally includes the speaker/writer and the addressee; on the other hand, when *man* is used as a non-referential indefinite, reference to speech act participants may be either excluded (with a distance effect, as in *Verstehe ich auch nicht wie kann* **man** *da wohnen*, 'I don't understand how one can live there') or included (with opposite effects of proximity). For a careful consideration of the discourse effects of *man*-constructions in Swedish (and, contrastively, of the indefinite pronoun *one* in English), the reader is referred to Altenberg (2004/2005).

is non-assertive (irrealis, negated, and potential/deontic contexts, but also maxims, generalizations, proverbs, and, more generally, any action/event which either did not occur, or which is presented as occurring in a contingent, non-real world) from the examples discussed in 1.3, where *man*-constructions always depict a realis situation (i.e. one whose occurrence is actually asserted as corresponding directly to a real event).

As we have already pointed out in Section 1.2, negative, conditional and interrogative contexts are the typical discourse environments in which the reanalysis of *man* as an indefinite element takes place, and this fact has long been recognized in the literature on *man*-constructions. In the grammaticalization path sketched above, the usages of *man* as a species-generic and as a non-referential indefinite have been labelled as (a^1) and (a^2) respectively, for in many cases it is difficult to make a distinction between the two senses in written texts. General nouns referring to classes are the norm in generalizations about species. This kind of predication is usually associated with linguistic features (such as the use of a given tense or aspect) which trigger an atemporal interpretation, and is inherently non-assertive. If *man*-elements start being grammaticalized, they first spread to other non-assertive contexts. Lack of assertiveness may be triggered by other operators such as negators, temporal and hypothetical subordinators such as *if, when*, questions, etc., and thus appears to be the major feature shared by the two leftmost situation types in the grammaticalization path. In both (a^1) and (a^2), *man* has the capacity of picking out indiscriminate referents of the class of humans, indicating *any individual* within a more or less restricted class, which is determined by the operator itself and may amount to all humanity or to a subgroup thereof, according to the context. The usage of *man* as a referential indefinite subject arises through extension when it is used outside the scope of a non-assertive operator: if a given situation is presented as occurring in the real world, the most straightforward pragmatic inference that is drawn is that there must have been one or more specific agents bringing about that situation. In these cases, a semantically light or empty element such as *man* amounts to nothing but a human entity, and the assertive context forces its interpretation as a specific but indefinite human subject. Similarly, Egerland (2003: 89) argues that the arbitrary reading of *man* (i.e., in our terms, its usage as a referential indefinite), "is entirely determined by the discourse and is not restrained by any syntactic principles": whereas a generic/non-referential reading is obligatorily triggered by some syntactic operator, the "arbitrary" reading needs not to be syntactically determined, and emerges when no generic operators are available.

The data discussed here also provide some evidence that stage (c) does not necessarily presuppose stage (b). According to Mazon (1931: 150), in Czech, where *člověk* does not appear to be used as a referential indefinite, "souvent le sujet parlant, sous la forme familière de l'indéfini, se désigne lui-même (*našinec, já*)".

The same holds true for Serbo-Croat, according to Kordić (2001: 57).[12] On a merely speculative basis, we might suppose that stage (c) involves a kind of pragmatic development which is somewhat different from the processes leading from (a^1) to (a^2) and from (a^2) to (b). As already noted, the latter consistently invoke a progressive switch along a hierarchy of referentiality/definiteness, whereas the former implies a reinterpretation of an impersonal clause as a personal one.

The grammaticalization path described above is consistent with the finer-grained grammaticalization path proposed by Haspelmath (1997: 4; 149ff.) for indefinite pronouns, which proceeds from *free choice* (*any*-series) elements to more specific elements, and does not contradict the evolutionary path of impersonal pronouns envisaged by Egerland (2003): *Lexical DP > Impersonal generic pronoun > Impersonal arbitrary (i.e., specific) pronoun > referential pronoun* (but see next section for a lengthier discussion).

1.6 Man: *noun or pronoun?*

In order to single out the formal properties of *man* in *man*-constructions it might be useful to compare one case in which *man* is admittedly a full pronoun (Modern German) with a language in which *man* has not (fully) acquired the formal properties of a pronoun (Old Italian), though showing some peculiar properties that set it off from other nouns. German *man*, unlike other German pronouns, does not take modifiers such as adjectives, deictics, genitives, articles, or relative clauses (cf. (36) and (37)); Old Italian *uomo* takes modifiers such as relative clauses (cf. (38) and (39)), and adjectives (cf. (40)), and is in the overwhelming majority of cases preceded by the article; it sometimes serves as a generic placeholder (roughly corresponding to English *one*, or to indefinite *who*) in both subject and non-subject positions:

German (Ewald Lang, p.c.)

(36) *Wenn einer/ ****man**, *der die Packung aufgerissen hat, nicht bezahlt, wird er . . .*
Lit.: if someone who has opened the package does not pay, he is . . .

(37) *Ihr Idioten / Wir Studenten / ****Man** *Student*
'You idiots / we students / *man student'

12. Consider the following ambiguous example from Kordić (2001: 60), where *čovjek* is used as an equivalent of a 1st person (plural/singular), but it can be also interpreted as a generalization involving a human unidentified subject:

ii. *Tema je toliko uzvišena da čovjek ima osjećaj kako je pri dodjeli nagrade bila presudna poruka više, negoli koliko je čovjek pjesničke finoće u to unio*
‚Das Thema is dermaßen erhaben, dass **man** das Gefühl hat, die Botschaft sei bei der Preisverleihung entscheidender gewesen als die dichterische Finesse, die **man** dort eingebracht hat'

Old Italian

(38) *Sì cominciò Beatrice questo canto; / e sì com'* ***uom*** *che suo parlar non spezza, / continüò così 'l processo santo* (Dante, *Paradiso*, V, 16–18)
'So Beatrice began this canto, and as **one** who does not interrupt his speech, she thus continued her holy discourse' (Dante Alighieri, *The Divine Comedy, Paradiso*, translated, with a commentary, by Charles S. Singleton, 49. Princeton, NJ: Princeton University Press, 1977^2[1975])

(39) *per che, come fa l'****uom*** *che non s'affigge / ma vassi a la via sua, che che li appaia, / se di bisogno stimolo il trafigge, / così intrammo noi per la callaia, / uno innanzi altro prendendo la scala* (Dante, *Purgatorio*, XXV, 4–8)
'Therefore, like **one** that does not stop but, whatever may appear to him, goes on his way, if the goad of necessity prick him, so did we enter through the gap, one before the other, taking the stairway' (Dante Alighieri, *The Divine Comedy, Purgatorio*, translated, with a commentary, by Charles S. Singleton, 269. Princeton, NJ: Princeton University Press, 1977^2[1975])

(40) *Ma nulla à 'l mondo in ch'****uom saggio*** *si fide* (Petrarca, *Canzoniere*, 23, 136)
'But there's nothing **a wise man** can trust to in this world'

Moreover, *man* (as well as its relatives in other Germanic languages, and French *on*) is anaphorically referred to by *man*; *uomo* is always referred to by 3rd person singular pronouns:

German

(41) ***Man*** *muss bezahlen, wenn* ***man*** *die Packung aufreisst, um den Stoff zu prüfen*
'**One** must pay if **one** opens the package in order to examine the content'

Swedish

(42) ***Man*** *gör vad* ***man*** *kan, vecka efter vecka* (from Altenberg 2004/2005: 94)
Lit. 'One does what one can, week after week'

Old Italian

(43) *ove che l'****uom*** *vada, o stea,* ***e'*** *dee vivere onestamente* (*Pistole di Seneca*, 21)
'Wherever "man" goes or stays, **he** must live honestly'

(44) *quando* ***uomo*** *va davante a messer lo papa, certo *uomo / elli va con molta reverenzia* (Brunetto Latini, *Rettorica*, p. 156, rr. 15–17, from Salvi n.d.: 51)
'When **one** / **a man** goes to see the Pope, he goes with much awe'[13]

---

13. The same holds true for *on* in Old French (Nyrop 1925: 369ff.; Jensen 1990: 237ff.; Welton-Lair 1999: 133ff.): though being grammaticalized as a pronoun very early, *on* was often preceded by the definite article (***l'en*** *le quist, si nel pot en trover*, 'they looked for him, but they could not find him', *Saint Eustace* 12, 11), it was sometimes anaphorically referred to by *il* in coordinate structures (***on*** *chante et* ***il*** *danse*, 'there is singing and dancing'), and could be followed by a relative clause (***hum*** *qui la vait, repairier ne s'en puet*, 'nobody who goes there can come back', *Roland* 311)

These facts lead us to conclude that *(l')uomo* is a full NP in Old Italian, whereas the status of German *man* is more pronominal. A question to be posed now is what sort of pronoun German *man* is. Recall that the syntactic behaviour of *man* is significantly different from that of other pronouns in German. A full consideration of the syntactic properties of *man* in German is thus in order before answering this question.

According to Cardinaletti and Starke (1999), pronouns may be divided into two classes according to their positional and distributional properties. So-called "strong" pronouns (e.g. Italian *lui*, French *moi*, etc.) can occur in the base, or θ-position, can appear in a series of peripheral positions (e.g. dislocation), can be focussed or appear in isolation, can be coordinated, and have the same distribution of full NPs. Moreover, adverbs that modify the whole NP (e.g. French *vraiment, seulement*) may also modify strong pronouns. On the other hand, deficient pronouns (further subdivided into weak pronouns – e.g. French *il*, Italian *egli, ella* – and clitics – French *le*, Italian *lo, la*) cannot occur in the base, or θ-position, cannot appear in peripheral positions, cannot be focussed, cannot appear in isolation, cannot be coordinated, and modified by any type of modifiers. The properties of *man* in some of these syntactic environments, exemplified in (45)–(47) below, show that German *man* is a weak pronoun, unlike *er, sie, jemand, einer*, etc., which are strong pronouns:

German (Ewald Lang, p.c.)

(45) *Er / Sie / *Man und Vater haben das so vereinbart*
'He / She / *One and (his/her) father have agreed about this'

(46) *Vorsicht, da kommt wer / jemand / einer / *man*
'Be careful, someone is coming'

(47) *Du / *Man, glaube ich, hast / hat es gewußt*
'You / *One, I think, have / has come to know it'

Under this classification, Old Italian *(l')uomo*, along with other *man*-elements in other languages (e.g. *maður* in Icelandic, cf. Egerland 2003: 81), are to be considered as full lexical NPs.

Two generalizations can now be advanced concerning the formal properties of *man*-constructions. The first one has been already alluded to somewhat surreptitiously in the discussion so far:

(48) **Generalization #1**: The more grammaticalized a generic noun such as *man* is, the more it behaves like a pronominal or pronoun-like element

This generalization emerges clearly from the distribution of *man*-constructions in European languages: whenever a language has a grammaticalized *man*-construction, the *man*-element within this construction assumes the syntactic properties of a weak pronoun. Of course, further data from many more languages are needed in order to validate this generalization, possibly also beyond the European area.

The second generalization is *per se* less evident and straightforward, and deserves a more careful explanation. In the initial stages of grammaticalization, *man* elements are likely to appear with indefinite value also in non-subject positions. The history of the *man*-construction in Germanic languages is instructive in this respect. If we consider the evolution of *man*-constructions from Gothic to Modern German, the possibility of having *man* in non-subject positions in the older languages emerges immediately:

Gothic

(49) *ƕa auk boteiþ* ***mannan****, jabai gageigaiþ þana fairƕu allana jah gasleiþeiþ sik saiwalai seinai? = quid enim proderit* ***homini*** *si lucretur mundum totum et detrimentum faciat animae suae* (Mark 8, 36)
'For what does it profit **a man**, to gain the whole world and forfeit his life?'

(50) *qiþands: staua was sums in sumai baurg, guþ ni ogands jah* ***mannan*** *ni aistands = dicens iudex quidam erat in quadam civitate qui Deum non timebat et* ***hominem*** *non verebatur* (Luke 18, 2)
'He said, "In a certain city there was a judge who neither feared God nor regarded **man**"'

(51) *qaþuþ-þan þatei þata* ***us mann*** *usgaggando þata gamaineiþ* ***mannan*** *= dicebat autem quoniam quae* ***de homine*** *exeunt illa communicant* ***hominem*** *= ἔλεγεν δὲ ὅτι τὸ ἐκ τοῦ ἀνθρώπου ἐκπορευόμενον ἐκεῖνο κοινοῖ τὸν ἄνθρωπον* (Mark 7, 20)

Old High German

(52) *uuaz biderbô ist* ***manne****, oba her alla uuerlt in êht gihalôt* (Mark 8, 36)
'For what does it profit **a man**, to gain the whole world?'

(53) *ih nalles uon* ***manne*** *giuuizscaf infâhu = ego autem non* ***ab homine*** *testimonium accipio* (John 5, 34)
'Not that the testimony which I receive is **from man**'

(54) *Fon herzen uzgangent ubila githanca, manslahti, uorligiri, huor, thiuba, luggiu giuuiznissu, girida, balarati, feichan, uncusgida, ubil ouga, bismarunga, ubarhuht, tumpnissi. Thisiu sint thiu dar unsubrent man, nalles mit ungiuuasganen hantun ezzan ni unsubrit* ***man*** (Tatian 84, 9) = *De corde enim exeunt cogitationes malae homicidia adulteria fornicationes furta falsa testimonia avaritia nequitiae dolus inpudicitia oculus malus blasphemia superbia stultitia. Hae sunt quae coinquinant* ***hominem****, non lotis autem manibus manducare non coinquinat* ***hominem*** (Matthew 15, 19–20)
'For out of the heart come evil thoughts, murder, adultery, fornication, theft, false witness, slander. These are what defile **a man**; but to eat with unwashed hands does not defile **a man**'

(55) *Quad thô zi in glîhnessi inti bilidi, bithiu uuanta gilimphit simbolun zi betonne, nalles zi bilinnenne. Sum tuomo uuas in sumero burgi, thie ni forhta got inti* ***man*** *ni intriet* (Tatian 122, 1) = *Dicebat autem et parabolam ad illos, quoniam oportet semper orare et non deficere. Iudex quidam erat in quadam civitate, qui deum non timebat et* ***hominem*** *non verebatur* (Luke 18, 2)
'And he told them a parable, to the effect that they ought always to pray and not lose heart. He said, "In a certain city there was a judge who neither feared God nor regarded ***man***"'

Modern German

(56) *Ich habe* ****man/einen*** *getroffen*
'I met someone'

Although advanced on the grammaticalization path (see examples (25) and (26) above), *man* in Old High German can still be used with indefinite sense in non-subject positions. This possibility is definitely ruled out in Modern German, where in non-subject positions only *einem/einen* are possible. Thus, the generalization can be formulated as follows:

(57) **Generalization #2**: The more a generic noun such as *man* has grammaticalized as an indefinite element, the less likely it is to appear also in non-subject positions[14]

This generalization equally applies to French (**J'ai rencontré on*) and Abruzzese (**So' viste nome*, 'I have seen somebody', D'Alessandro and Alexiadou 2006: 203), two languages in which *man*-constructions are advanced on the grammaticalization path.

A detailed explanation of this peculiarity of *man*-constructions is beyond the purposes of this paper. Nonetheless, keeping in line with some formal proposals such as Egerland's (2003), we might tentatively propose that the grammaticalization path sketched above corresponds to a progressive loss of the lexical features of *man*, so that in the final stage *man* is void of lexical features, whereas in stage (a^2) it still retains some lexical content that allows it to appear in non-subject positions. Non subject-positions are generally filled only by pronouns that are inherently specified for the semantic features of person, number, gender and case as encoded in words such as nouns and pronouns: the more empty a (pronominal) element is, the less likely it is that it will appear as an internal argument of a predicate. In less formal terms, pronouns in object positions are possible only if they maintain

14. Albeit formulated differently, this generalization corresponds to generalization III in Egerland (2003: 92): "Impersonal pronouns that are exclusively generic may appear syntactically as both subjects and objects (*maður* and *you*). Impersonal pronouns that can be used both arbitrarily and generically can only appear as syntactic subjects (*man, on*, and *si*)".

some informational content allowing the identifiability of their intended referent (even in very general terms). French *on* and German *man* are definitely excluded from object position because they do not have such an informational content: they are underspecified with respect to number (being inherently ambiguous between plural and singular), person (allowing both inclusive and exclusive readings), and gender (applying also to feminine referents), they do not bear any case marker, cannot be anaphorically linked to previous linguistic material, and their referent cannot be directly referred back to (i.e. they are discursively inert elements, cf. Koenig 1999: 241ff.; Los 2005: 285ff.).[15] The present suggestion must be intended as merely speculative at this stage, because it rests only on a limited number of languages. Moreover, it is important to note that the loss of lexical features is not an abrupt process, and it is possible that more grammaticalized stages of the construction coexist with the possibility of having *man* in syntactic positions other than the subject: *man* in Old High German is a case in point, given examples such as (25)–(26) contrasting with (52)–(55).

2. The areal distribution of *man*-constructions in Europe

In the following sections, we address the issue of the distribution of *man*-constructions across Europe. The basic data for the following discussion come mainly from primary and secondary literature, but native speakers have been systematically resorted to

---

15. The loss of lexical features in *man*-constructions can be properly evaluated by resorting to formal criteria. One criterion which is crucially indicative of the pronominalization of *man* is the possibility of plural agreement (Egerland 2003: 77ff.). In French, examples such as iii are possible, in which *on* is compatible with plural (and feminine) agreement:

French

iii. *Quand* *on* *est* *belles*, . . . (Egerland 2003 : 79)
when MAN is beautiful[PL.F]

Similarly, in Swedish singular agreement appears to be the norm with *man*, but cases such as iv are perfectly acceptable under the appropriate context (e.g. when the context excludes a singular reading of *man*):

Swedish

iv. *Trots bevisföringen* *var* *man* *inte helt* *övertygad*/*övertygade*
despite the evidence was MAN not fully convinced[SG]/[PL]
om hans skuld (Egerland 2003: 80)
about his guilt
'In spite of the evidence, people were not convinced about his guilt'

in order to obtain a realistic picture of the contexts of usage of *man*-constructions in each language. Native speakers have been particularly helpful to clarify the range of uses of *man*-constructions in Slavonic languages, where they appear to be an emergent category, and as such they are often ignored by both descriptive and normative grammars.

The areal scenario emerging from the following discussion is suggestive of an eastward expansion of this construction type across Europe, but this is only one part of the story. This expansion is paralleled by the decline of these constructions in a number of Romance languages and in English, and thus the Standard Average European character of this construction must be confronted with a model of expansion accounting for both spread and decline. Such a model will be the topic of Section 3.2, whereas speculations about the origin of this construction are presented in Section 3.1.

2.1 Romance languages

Among Romance languages, *man*-constructions enjoyed much wider currency in older stages than today, French and Abruzzese being the only modern languages in which the construction is still alive.[16] The construction in question is also attested in contemporary Catalan, where it is said to be bookish (Kaufmann 2002; Carmen Muñoz, p.c.), and in Corsican (cf. Marchetti 2001), a conservative Italo-Romance variety in which the Old Tuscan situation appears to be well-preserved.

Corsican

(58) ***Ómu** s'annóia à ùn fà nunda*
Lit.: 'One annoys himself at not doing anything'

Catalan

(59) ***Hom** procedí a interrogar els testimonis esmentats* (*La Veu de Catalunya. Diari antifeixista*, 1937)
'They proceeded to examine the aforementioned witnesses'

16. In Sardinian, according to Jones (1993: 212), *sa pessone*, lit. 'the person', can be used impersonally; this fact is not confirmed by native speakers, who also point out that *omine*, 'man', is very limitedly (if ever) used in generic/impersonal contexts (Ignazio Putzu, p.c.; Nicoletta Puddu, p.c.). In Modern Occitan the usage of *om* is not very frequent, and appears to be recessive with respect to other impersonalizing strategies (cf. Meyer-Lübke [1900: 107]: "Mais en somme, à l'époque ancienne et moderne, cet emploi de *om* n'est pas bien frequent; on lui préfère *se*... ou bien la troisième ou, comme nous l'avons déjà dit, la deuxième personne du pluriel"). Some sporadic attestations of the indefinite usage of *homem* in Old Portuguese are given by Meyer-Lübke (1900: 109).

(60) *Durant molt de temps* **hom** *s'ha complagut a citar aquelles llengües a les quals manquen els termes per a expressar conceptes tals com arbre o animal* (Miquel Martí i Pol, *El pensament salvatge*, 1971)
'For a long time people have taken pleasure of citing those languages that lack terms expressing concepts such as "tree" or "animal"'

In older languages, especially in Italo-Romance varieties but also in Old Spanish[17] (cf. Barrett Brown 1931), the construction is widely attested, although there are no formal clues to assume that *man* was grammaticalized as a pronoun in these varieties.[18]

Old Spanish

(61) *Con ellos* **ombre** *non puede beuir* (*Arcipreste de Talavera* 243, from Barrett Brown 1931: 269)
'**One** cannot drink with them'

Old Abruzzese

(62) *Se boy che* **ll'omo** *crédate, dì se[m]pre veritate* (*Proverbia*, 39; from Ugolini 1959: 72)
'If you wish to be believed, always tell the truth'

Old Salentino

(63) *si illi maniasse de quillo chi* **l'omo** *appella fructu / de vita, mai no 'nvecharia et non infirmarebe* (*Libro di Sidrac Salentino* 5v10–11; from Sgrilli 1983: 206)
'If he could eat what is called the fruit of life, he would never grow old and fall sick'

Old Veneto

(64) *E quando* **l'omo** *se parte de Ciarciam, ello va .v. çornate per sablone là o è aqua amara e pesima* (*Il Milione* [translation in Old Veneto], 19, 59; from von Wartburg 1946: 38)
'And when **one** leaves Ciarciam, for 5 days one goes through a desert where water is bitter and very bad'

17. The life span of this usage of *hombre* (and its variants) in Old Spanish ranges from the middle of the 13th century to 1580 (Barrett Brown 1931: 270ff.).

18. In some varieties (cf. e.g. exx. (61) and (65)–(68)) *uomo/omo/om* may appear without any articles. The postverbal position of *omo/on* in (65) and (66) cannot be taken as a positional criterion for establishing the pronominal status of *omo* and *on* in Old Romanesco and Old Lombard respectively: although there are no comprehensive descriptions of word order in these two varieties, it does not appear that they distinguish between nouns and pronouns in subject inversion, which typically occurs when a constituent other than the subject is fronted (as in (65) and (66)).

Old Romanesco

(65) *Quanno li ambasciatori fuoro entrati in Verona, tutta Verona curre a vederli. Così li guardava* **omo** *fitto como fussino lopi* (Anonimo Romano, *Vita di Cola di Rienzo,* 8, 10)
'When the ambassadors entered Verona, the whole town hastens to see them. So, people fixed their gaze on them as if they were wolves'

Old Lombard

(66) *ben saver dev'***on** *c'aluminadho fo de salvacion* (Uguçon, 222, from Rohlfs 1949: 272)
'It should be well-known (one should know well) that he was enlightened by salvation'

Old Ligurian

(67) *mester è c'***omo** *li caze* (Monaci 1955: 441)
'It is necessary to chase them'

Old Sicilian

(68) *quannu* **homu** *è assai rebelli* (Monaci 1955: 547)
'when one is a real rebel'

Old Campanian

(69) *se* ***ll'ommo*** *avesse pustule* (*Bagni di Pozzuoli* v. 32, from Rohlfs 1949: 272)
'if one had pustules'

2.2 Germanic languages

Germanic languages show clear instances of *man*-constructions in which *man* is fully grammaticalized as a weak pronoun. Besides German and Swedish, whose constructions have been extensively exemplified in the preceding sections, highly grammaticalized *man*-constructions are attested in almost all of the modern European varieties, and in most cases they are already present in older stages. Icelandic is unique among Germanic languages in that *maður*, 'man', is used only as a non-referential indefinite (cf. (70)) and maintains nominal features.[19]

Icelandic

(70) *Á Íslandi vinnur* **maður** *til 65 ára aldurs*
'In Iceland one works until 65 years of age'

19. Faroese uses *man* as a Danicism according to Lockwood (1955). Afrikaans does not retain Dutch *men* and uses the colloquial Dutch *'n mens* (McWhorter 2004: 42).

The loss of the indefinite pronoun *man* in English dates back to the 15th century (McWhorter 2004: 42–43; Los 2002, 2005 and references therein). *Man* in Middle English was sometimes phonetically eroded to *me*, and was grammaticalized enough to be used as a referential indefinite.[20]

Old/Middle English

(71) *ða gebrohte* **man** *him to, tomiddes þam folce, ænne dumne*
then brought one him to among the people a dumb
mann, & se wæs eac swilce deaf (Æhom 18, 25, from Los 2005: 279)
man and he was also likewise deaf
'then was brought to him / then people brought to him, among the people, a man who was dumb, and also deaf'

(72) *Ac* **me** *ne auh to bien hersum bute of gode* (McWhorter 2004: 42)
but one NEG ought to be obedient except in good
'But one should not be obedient except in good things'

Several scenarios accounting for this disappearance have been proposed in the literature. Two of them are worth mentioning here, although they are hardly compatible with one another. The first systemic scenario (Los 2002, 2005) leaves no role to language contact, and invokes the weakness of *man/me(n)* in clause-initial subject position to explain its disappearance. This weakness is not shared by cognates of *man* in other Germanic languages, for in these languages a strong constraint on V2 has been retained. In English, on the contrary, this restriction was lost, and this has eroded the "niche" of *man*-uses:

(73) "there are two important factors that appear to have been overlooked: one is the competition between subjunctive *that*-clauses and *to*-infinitives, which affected *man* in that it entailed competition between the indefinite pronoun in such clauses and generic (or arbitrary) PRO. The result was a decline in the occurrence of *man* in subclauses. There was also a decline in main clauses due to the loss of verb-second in the course of the fifteenth century, after which only subjects could be 'unmarked themes' in an information-structural sense. The indefinite pronoun *man/me(n)* is unlikely to occur in this position as it cannot provide an anaphoric link with previous material, and its niche was increasingly taken over by the impersonal passive" (Los 2002: 181)

20. In Old and Middle English *man* is also preceded by indefinite elements such as *some, any, every, each,* and *no*. These forms date back to the earliest Old English texts, and are weakly grammaticalized as indefinite pronouns according to Raumolin-Brunberg and Kahlas-Tarkka (1997: 19ff., and 71ff.).

The second scenario explicitly invokes the role of language contact and foreign influence throughout the history of English. According to McWhorter (2004: 54), some Old English features "were ripe for marginalization in a contact situation, because they occurred only variably". Indefinite *man* is precisely one of these features, and its loss may have been favoured by the lack of a fully grammaticalized *man*-construction in the Scandinavian varieties which had a significant impact on English in the ninth and tenth centuries:[21]

(74) "Icelandic and Faroese lack a *man*-cognate and already in Old Norse it was recessive, ... generally replaced by impersonal verb constructions or third person verbs without pronouns. This may possibly have set in motion a *de*-emphasis on the use of Old English's *man*-cognate that eventually resulted in its disappearance early in Middle English" (McWhorter 2004: 51)

2.3 Slavonic languages

In the Slavonic area *man*-constructions, though often ignored by grammars, enjoy wide currency, especially in South and West Slavonic languages.[22] Statements such as (75) are typical of descriptive studies of *man*-constructions in Slavonic, and are confirmed by native informants:

(75) "l'emploi de *člověkŭ* avec la valeur d'indéfini s'observe sur une grande partie du domaine, à savoir en tchèque, en sorabe, en polonais, en slovène, en serbo-croate et en bulgare. Cette valeur, assurément, est plus ou moins sensible au sujet parlant, et **tel pourra la contester là où tel autre la reconnaît**" (Mazon 1931: 149, our emphasis)

Mazon significantly alludes to the controversial status of these constructions in Slavic (*tel pourra la contester là où tel autre la reconnaît*). Even more significantly, some grammars label these constructions as emerging structures (e.g. Feuillet 1996: 253 on Bulgarian: "Le bulgare ne possède pas de forme specifique pour *on*, **encore qu'on voie se multiplier les emplois de човéк dans ce sens**").

21. The temporal mismatch between the Scandinavian invasions (9th–10th centuries) and the disappearance of *man* in English (15th century) is not explicitly addressed by McWhorter, who, however, claims that "there is no stipulation that the features would vanish immediately. Instead, non-native acquisition would initiate a decline in frequency of occurrence which would *eventually* weaken and eliminate the sufficient 'trigger' ... for its transmission to new generations" (McWhorter 2004: 54, our emphasis).

22. In Old Church Slavonic, *člověkŭ* is systematically employed to translate Greek ἄνθρωπος in its indefinite usages. There are no clear cases in which it is used with indefinite meaning independently from the Greek source (Pierluigi Cuzzolin, p.c.).

The following sentences exemplify the range of uses of *man*-constructions in Slavonic languages:[23]

Bulgarian

(76) ***Chovek*** *ne* *znae* *nakade* *da* *gleda* (Olga Mladenova, p.c.)
man NEG know.IND.PRS.3SG where COMP look.IND.PRS.3SG
'**One** does not know where to look'

Slowak

(77) ***Chlovek*** *nikdy nepochopii, o chom to hovorii* (Marian Sloboda, p.c.)
Lit.: 'Man (will) never understand what is (s)he talking about'

Serbo-Croatian

(78) *Ne može* ***čovjek*** *tu da se odmori* (Danko Sipka, p.c.)
'One cannot take a rest here'

(79) (Interviewed woman:) ... *Split, u kojem sam rođena i u kojem sam provela godine kada se* ***čovjek*** *zapravo formira, toliko je snažna sredina da vas obilježi za cijeli život, bez obzira na to gdje kasnije živjeli* (Kordić 2001: 65)
‚Split, wo ich geboren bin und wo ich die Jahre verbracht habe, in denen man geformt wird, ist ein so starkes Umfeld, dass es Sie für das ganze Leben prägt, ohne Rücksicht darauf, wo Sie später leben mögen'

Polish

(80) *Jak* ***człek*** *raz na koń siędzie, to z takimi kompanami, jak ty i Michał, na kraj świata jechać gotów* (*Potop*, tom III, PIW 1982)
'When **one** mounts a horse with companions such as you and Michael, one is willing to go everywhere'

Upper Sorbian

(81) *To* ***čłowjek*** *njewě* (Eduard Werner, p.c.)
'Man weiß nie'

Slovene

(82) ***Človek*** *ne ve, kaj naj si mišli* (Martina Ožbot, p.c.)
'**One** does not know what to think about it'

---

23. We would like to acknowledge the kind help of the following native speakers and language experts who have discussed the status of *man*-constructions in Slavonic with us: Olga Mladenova, Ljuba Veselinova, Olga Arnaudova (Bulgarian); Francesca Fici, Wim Honselaar, Timur Maisak (Russian); Hana Skoumalová, Marian Sloboda, Jakub Dotlačil, Neil Bermel (Czech); Marian Sloboda (Slowak); Stefan Dyła, Agnieszka Latos (Polish); Danko Sipka (Serbo-Croatian); Eduard Werner (Upper Sorbian); Martina Ožbot, Don Reindl (Slovene).

(83) ***Človek** bi rekel, da o tem nimajo pojma* (Don Reindl, p.c.)
'**One** would say that they don't have any idea'

Russian does not present clear instances of non-referential indefinite *man* (Weiss 1997). There is substantial agreement among grammars, dictionaries and native speakers in admitting that the only contexts in which *chelovek* is used impersonally are predications about species, which are presumably universal. Besides them, *chelovek* is occasionally used as an equivalent of a personal pronoun, with distance or proximity effects determined by the context, as in (84).

Russian

(84) ***Chelovek** ustal, a vy pristaete s pustjakami*
'A person is tired (but also I am tired, he is tired), and you are bothering him with nonsense'

All in all, *man*-constructions in the Slavonic domain show up only in South and West Slavonic languages. In some cases grammars signal that these constructions arise by contact with German.[24] The spread of *man*-constructions to Slavonic appears to be a quite recent development (Mazon 1931, Feuillet 1996), although a precise dating of the beginning of this process is not possible yet, because of the lack of relevant historical data. What can be said is that in some languages these constructions arose as early as the 15th century (Czech), whereas in South Slavonic varieties this process started later, and is still in progress.

The status of these constructions in (at least part of) the Slavonic area is that of an incipient category in the sense of Heine and Kuteva (2005: 71ff.). Incipient categories are constructions which emerge in a language as a result of language contact. They often involve a grammaticalization process in the target language which is a result of syntactic calquing from the source language, in which the grammaticalization process appears either to be complete or to be more firmly established.

---

24. It is worth recalling that the possibility of a German influence on the development of such constructions and of an areal pattern of diffusion from west to east has been already admitted by Mazon (1931: 154–155), who, however, discards it in favour of a polygenetic process independent of any German influence (cf. Mazon 1931: 155 and *passim*):

v. "Ainsi la tendance à employer le nom de l'homme en fonction d'indéfini se manifeste dans toutes les langues slaves à des degrés divers et que, sauf pour le tchèque, on ne peut guère encore évaluer exactement . . . cette tendance atteint son plus grand développement dans les langues de l'Ouest, accuse une extension moindre dans les langues du Sud et est à peine sensible dans le domaine russe. Ne s'agirait-il pas, dans ces conditions, d'un calque grammatical de l'allemand *man* venu des confins slavo-germaniques?"

Their use is generally optional in that they may but need not be used. Moreover, they are used less frequently than the corresponding categories of the model languages, and they are not generally recognized by speakers (or grammarians) of the language as distinct entities of grammar. The question of whether they have any existence of their own tends to be a matter of controversy, and "purist" grammarians and language planning organizations are likely to deny their existence, while discouraging their use in formal education.

2.4 Other languages

Man-constructions are attested in a handful of other European languages. In Maltese, for instance, the nouns *bniedem* 'man' and *proxxmu* 'neighbour' can be used non-specifically. In Albanian, *njerí* is used mainly in negative / non-assertive clauses (Buchholz and Fiedler 1987: 307; Gray 1945: 31).

Maltese

(85) *Jekk jiġi* ***proxxmu*** *fuqek tagħtihx wiċċ* (Borg and Azzopardi-Alexander 1997: 201)
If comes neighbour on-PRO.2SG give.2SG-PRO.3SG.M NEG-face
'If **someone** comes up to you, don't take any notice of him'

Albanian

(86) *kur vlónet* ***njerí***
'quand ***on*** se fiance'

The construction is attested also in Celtic languages. Some examples from Old and Middle Irish, and from Medieval Welsh are given below (cf. (87)–(89)). In Modern Irish the noun meaning *man* (*duine*) is often reinforced with *éigin* ('certain') or *ar bith* ('on world'). The usage of *(an) den* in Breton appears to be similar to French *personne* in that it can occur only in negative contexts.

Old and Middle Irish

(87) *Is i liss fo leith ro alt conachacced fer di Ultaib hí cosín n-úair no foad la Conchobar, ocus ni búi* ***duine*** *no leicthe issin leis sin acht a haiti si a mummi* (*Ir. Texte* I, 71, from Vendryes 1916: 187)
'Elle (Derdriu) fut élevée dans une enceinte à part, a fin que nul homme (*fer*) des Ulates ne la vît, jusqu'au moment où elle coucherait avec Conchobar; et il n'y eut personne (*duine*) qui fût admis dans cette enceinte sauf son père nourricier et sa nourrice'

(88) *A ndorigne do fertaib ní fail* ***duine*** *doddecha* (*Thes. Pal.-hib.* II, 346, from Vendryes 1916: 187)
'Ce qu'elle a accompli de miracles, il n'est personne qui puisse le raconter'

Medieval Welsh

(89) *ny welsei* ***dyn*** *wenyth degach* (*W.B.*, col. 74, l. 13, from Vendryes 1916: 188)
'personne n'avait vu plus beau blé'

Modern Irish

(90) *Dúirt* ***duine*** ***éigin*** *liom* *é* (from Haspelmath 1997: 279)
told person certain to:me it
'Somebody told me'

(91) *An* *bhfeiceann* *tú* ***duine*** ***ar*** ***bith*** *ansin* *thall?* (from Haspelmath 1997: 279)
Q see you person on world there over
'Do you see anyone over there?'

Breton

(92) *n'euz* ***den*** *enn ti*
'il n'y a personne à la maison'

3. The spread and decline of *man*-constructions in Europe: An areal account

Map 1 summarizes the present-day distribution of *man*-constructions in Europe. Although it is evident that *man*-constructions do not all mean the same thing in different languages, being at different stages in the grammaticalization process, their areal distribution across Europe unveals a core area corresponding to the nucleus of Standard Average European (the so-called "Charlemagne area", cf. van der Auwera 1998: 823ff.; Haspelmath 2001: 1493) plus Mainland Scandinavian languages and, perhaps, the Romance South-West (Catalan and Occitan), where the construction is said to be at risk of disappearing.

In three areas, *man*-constructions are limited to the expression of a non-referential indefinite subject in non-assertive contexts. Languages belonging to these three areas have been possibly influenced by languages in the core: French and English have presumably influenced the emergence of *man*-constructions in Celtic, German is probably the main responsible for the establishing of these constructions in Slavonic, whereas the presence of *man*-constructions in Maltese and Albanian could be considered speculatively as the result of contact with Romance varieties. In historical times, the area of *man*-constructions was significantly larger, including Italian and Italo-Romance varieties, Spanish and English.

On a global perspective, *man*-constructions are unevenly distributed in the languages of the world. In Haspelmath's (1997) 100-language sample, *man*-constructions

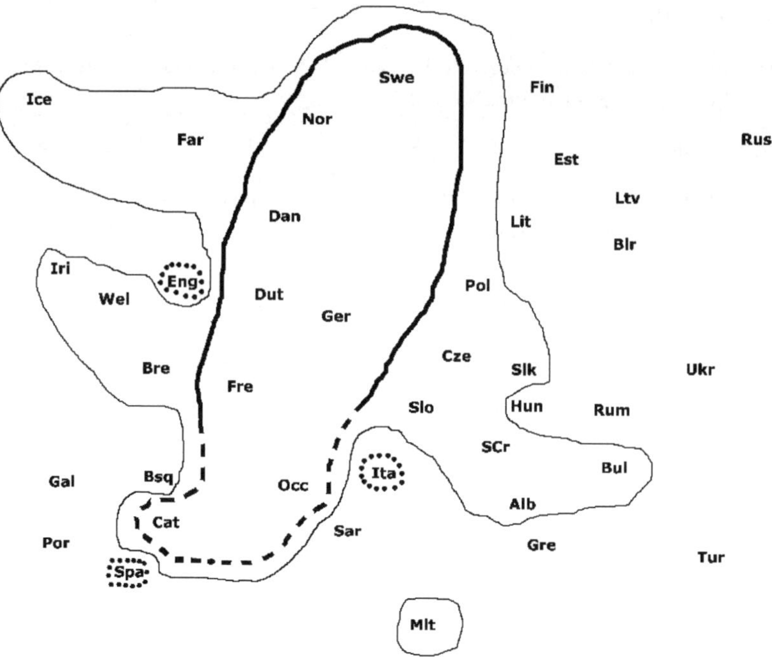

Map 1. The present-day distribution of *man*-constructions in Europe. The bold line surrounds the area in which *man*-constructions are fully grammaticalized. Dotted circles represent those languages in which a *man*-construction is attested in historical times.

are attested in 23 languages, which tend to cluster in two areas of the globe besides Europe, namely Africa and South-East Asia. *Man*-constructions are virtually absent in the Americas and appear sporadically in the Caucasus. Map 2, drawn from the World Atlas of Language Structures (Haspelmath et al. 2005), depicts the distribution of generic-noun based indefinite pronouns vs. interrogative-based indefinite pronouns.[25]

3.1 *The origin of* man*-constructions*

A widely held view identifies the source of *man*-constructions in Semitic. The indefinite usage of *ἄνθρωπος* in Greek (Thackeray 1909, Blass and Debrunner 1961, Bonfante 1980, among others), according to this view, emerged through syntactic

25. Any generalization based on this map should be taken with a pinch of salt, because under the label "Generic-noun based strategy" cases of grammaticalization of nouns such as *thing, place*, and the like are also included. However, the finer-grained picture emerging from Haspelmath's (1997) sample, though smaller, confirms the existence of three areas in which *man*-constructions are attested with significant frequency.

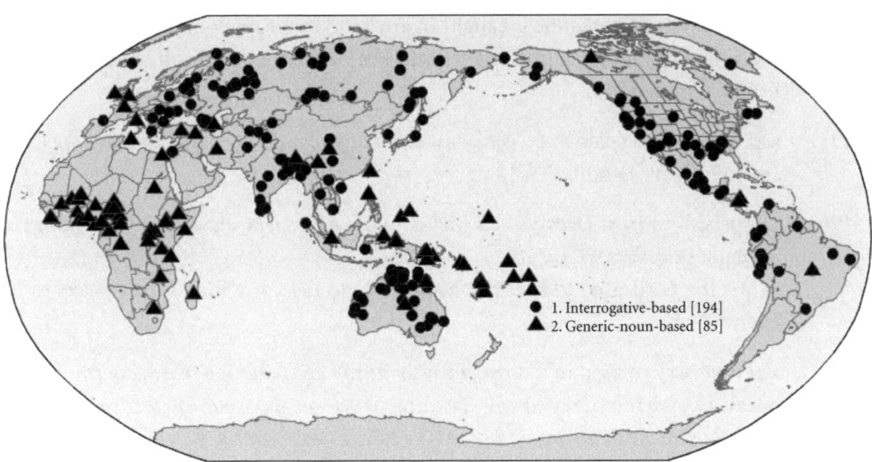

Map 2. Interrogative-based vs generic-noun based strategies for indefinite pronouns (Source: *WALS*, Haspelmath et al. 2005).

calquing from a Semitic language, and then became the source for a parallel change in Latin, where *homo* starts being used as an indefinite element in the language of religious texts (Salonius 1920; Leumann, Hofmann, and Szantyr 1965). This hypothesis is surely correct, but nonetheless it accounts only for the emergence of the indefinite usage of *ἄνθρωπος* in Greek (i.e. for the prehistory of *man*-constructions).[26]

Interestingly, the Latin construction with *homo* is used more frequently than its cognate Greek construction with *ἄνθρωπος*. Along with cases such as (93)–(94), in which *homo* corresponds to Greek *ἄνθρωπος*, there are many instances of indefinite *homo* corresponding to other Greek indefinite pronouns (*τις*, *ἕκαστος*; cf. (95)–(98)).

Greek and Latin

(93) *᾿Αδελφοί, ἐὰν καὶ προλημφθῇ* ***ἄνθρωπος*** *ἔν τινι παραπτώματι, ὑμεῖς οἱ πνευματικοὶ καταρτίζετε τὸν τοιοῦτον ἐν πνεύματι πραΰτητος, σκοπῶν σεαυτόν, μὴ καὶ σὺ πειρασθῇς* (Galatians 6,1)

(94) *fratres et si praeoccupatus fuerit* **homo** *in aliquo delicto vos qui spiritales estis huiusmodi instruite in spiritu lenitatis considerans te ipsum ne et tu tempteris* (=(93))

26. In Contemporary Hebrew (Glinert 1982: 461ff.) *iš*, 'anyone', formally identical with the word for 'man', is not found in assertive contexts. It displays some behavioural properties of a pronoun (it allows a partitive phrase, as in *iš mehem lo hešiv*, 'no one of them replied'; it precludes modification, **lo haya šam iš meyuxad*, 'no one special was there').

'My brothers, if **someone** is caught in any kind of wrongdoing, those of you who are spiritual should set him right. And keep an eye on yourself so that you will not be tempted, too'

(95) *καὶ ἐλάλησεν κύριος πρὸς Μωυσῆν ἐνώπιος ἐνωπίῳ, ὡς εἴ τις λαλήσει πρὸς τὸν ἑαυτοῦ φίλον* (Exodus, 33, 11)

(96) *Loquebatur autem Dominus ad Moysen facie ad faciem, sicut solet loqui* ***homo*** *ad amicum suum* (=(95))
'Thus the Lord used to speak to Moses face to face, as **a man** / **one** speaks to his friend'

(97) *καὶ ἁγιάσετε τὸ ἔτος τὸ πεντηκοστὸν ἐνιαυτὸν καὶ διαβοήσετε ἄφεσιν ἐπὶ τῆς γῆς πᾶσιν τοῖς κατοικοῦσιν αὐτήν· ἐνιαυτός ἀφέσεως σημασία αὕτη ἔσται ὑμῖν, καὶ ἀπελεύσεται* ***εἷς ἕκαστος*** *εἰς τὴν κτῆσιν αὐτοῦ, καὶ ἕκαστος εἰς τὴν πατρίδα αὐτοῦ ἀπελεύσεσθε* (Leviticus 25, 10)

(98) *Sanctificabisque annum quinquagesimum, et vocabis remissionem cunctis habitatoribus terrae tuae; ipse est enim jubilaeus. Revertetur* ***homo*** *ad possessionem suam et unusquisque rediet ad familiam pristinam* (=(97))
'And you shall hallow the fiftieth year, and proclaim liberty throughout the land to all its inhabitants; it shall be a jubilee for you, when each of you / **anyone** shall return to his property, and each of you shall return to his family'

3.2 *The spread (and decline) of* man*-constructions: A two-wave model*

A full discussion of the historical scenario behind the emergence and spread of these constructions is perhaps still premature, and is beyond the purposes of this paper. Greek and Latin data, however, point to a path of diffusion of these constructions that has Late Latin as its irradiation point. Romance varieties are likely to have further developed this possibility. This hypothesis was firstly proposed by Schrijnen (1939), who rejects a biased and simplistic polygenetic hypothesis for these constructions and at the same time regards the European *koiné* of Late Latin times and the peculiar language of religious texts as the fertile ground for the spread and the (perhaps partly independent) adoption of this construction type in many Romance varieties:

(99) „Es will mir vorkommen, dass wir in den verschiedenen Sprachen mit einer analogen Begriffsentwicklung zu tun haben, welche überall zu ähnlichen Ergebnissen geführt hat. Wir können im Griechischen wohl auf semitischen Einfluss schliessen, im Lateinischen auf griechischen, im Italienisch mit Meyer-Lübke auf französischen, im Französischen und Slavischen auf germanische Einwirkung, und in bestimmten Fällen und selbst in bestimmten Perioden kann dieses auch tatsächlich der Fall gewesen sein. Aber die analoge Schwächung von hebr. *'iš*, eigentlich „Mann", dann „man", gr. *ἄνθρωπος*, lat. *homo*, got. *manna* und slav.

člověkŭ, redet doch eine deutliche Sprache. Wir haben hier mit einer Reihe von Wörtern zu tun, **welche naturgemäss zum Indefinitum führen können**... (Schrijnen 1939: 369, our emphasis)

(100) Das Romanische geht auf das Vulgärlatein zurück, d.h. auf die Koinè, welche seit dem 5. Jahrhundert in sämtlichen, dem römischen Imperium angehörigen lateinischen Sprachgebieten gesprochen wurde. Aber diese Koinè war eben das altchristliche Latein, das sich immer mehr verbreitet hatte und sich so von Sondersprache zur Gemeinsprache ausgebildet hatte“ (Schrijnen 1939: 370)

What remains to be determined is precisely what contact situation(s) gave rise to *man*-constructions throughout Europe. In this section, we briefly restate the main chronological and substantive facts that have emerged clearly from our analysis, and then discuss some of its implications. In summary, the results of our analysis include the following:

a. In the core area on Map 1, *man*-constructions appear to be well-established in medieval times. This means that the first wave of diffusion of this construction type had already exhausted itself when the vernacular varieties began to appear in written records, at the end of the first millennium CE.[27] Thus, the first wave of diffusion should be dated to "the time of the great migrations at the transition between antiquity and the Middle Ages" (Haspelmath 2001: 1507; cf. also Haspelmath 1998). It should be emphasized that Latin, the official language of Western Europe in the Middle Ages and the language of holy texts, has probably played a non-secondary role in the adoption of these structures in those languages where they existed already as possible variants: remember also the extensive role played by Latin as a written language on popular varieties in the Romance territories and in the Western German territories, where the oldest documents are adaptations of religious texts such as Heliand and Otfrid (Auerbach 1958, Banniard 1992).
b. The hypothesis of a French influence on Italo-Romance vernacular varieties, while being perfectly reasonable in some cases (e.g. Old Tuscan, Old Sicilian, Old Northern Italian varieties), should be downplayed to some extent as the construction type appears to be well-established in varieties (e.g. Old Abruzzese, Old Romanesco) which were neither in direct nor in indirect contact with French.
c. The hypothesis of a German influence on French (defended, among others, by Nyrop 1925: 368, Schrijnen 1939, and Harris 1978) should be reformulated in

27. It is worth recalling that an instance of *man*-construction is attested already in the Strasbourg oaths:

vi. *Si cum* **om** *per dreit son fradra salvar dift* <--> *sôso* **man** *mit rehtu sînan bruodher scal* (Strasbourg Oaths)
'as a man / one should rightly save his brother'

terms of a common European culture within the Holy Roman Empire and intensive and effective language contact during the great migrations.

d. The decline of *man*-constructions in a number of Romance varieties and in English is surprisingly coincidental. In all these varieties, the construction was already marginal and literary by the dawn of the 15th century (Los 2005, Barrett-Brown 1931, 1936). Interestingly enough, the decline of the construction appears to be still in progress in other Romance varieties (Catalan and Modern Occitan).

e. The spread of *man*-constructions to the Slavonic area follows an eastward path and starts in the early Renaissance as a by-product of intensive German influence on West and South Slavonic languages. The status of *man*-constructions in some Slavonic languages is still controversial, and our data show that their spread is still in progress, at least in some Slavonic varieties.

These facts challenge any rigid, monodimensional model of diffusion. The diffusion of linguistic traits throughout Europe is always a multi-layered process, in which different ages and factors may play a role, and in which the possibility that some developments are independent or due to some coincidental parallelism cannot be ruled out. If it is true that the dating of the main Europeanisms to Late Antiquity / Early Middle Ages is able to explain the syntactic commonalities among languages belonging to the core Charlemagne area, it should also be recognized that in more recent times other areal phenomena have taken place as well. The reciprocal reinforcing of *man*-constructions in the Charlemagne area (plus Mainland Scandinavia) significantly resembles processes of convergence identified for other grammatical constructions (e.g. the perfect-to-preterite evolution in French, German, Dutch and Northern Italian varieties, see Giacalone Ramat to appear and references therein), but at the same time the loss of *man*-constructions in other Romance and Germanic languages points towards the possible existence of "recessive" phenomena among Europeanisms. Whether an areal explanation is tenable for the loss of *man*-constructions cannot be determined exactly yet (but recall McWhorter's 2004 discussion of the loss of *man* in English). Nonetheless, our study shows that even recessive features have the potential for expansion well beyond the chronologically rigid limits of Late Antiquity and the Early Middle Ages. Finally, the role of syntactic calquing in translations (and particularly in the translation of peculiar texts such as religious texts) should be taken into account more seriously than has been the case in the current literature on SAE. Refinements of the historical scenario behind the emergence and spread of *man*-constructions will be possible and even needed, as soon as more historical studies are available. We only hope to have demonstrated that (i) these constructions are to be considered as a Europeanism in its own right, and (ii) that their diffusion patterns in a complex, often unpredictable way, which calls into question the linearity of the current modelling of areal diffusion in Europe.

References

Altenberg, B. 2004/2005. The generic person in English and Swedish. A contrastive study of *one* and *man*. *Languages in Contrast* 5: 93–120.

Auerbach, E. 1958. *Literatursprache und Publikum in der lateinischen Spätantike und im Mittelalter*. Bern: Francke.

Banniard, M. 1992. *Viva voce. Communication écrite et communication orale du IVe au IXe siècle en Occident latin*. Paris: Institut des Études Augustiniennes.

Barrett Brown, C. 1931. The disappearance of the indefinite *hombre* from Spanish. *Language* 7: 265–277.

Barrett Brown, C. 1936. *Uomo* as an indeterminate pronoun. *Language* 12: 35–44.

Blass, F. & Debrunner, A. 1961. *A Greek grammar of the New Testament and other early Christian literature*. Chicago IL: The University of Chicago Press. (English translation of Blass F. & Debrunner, A. 1931. *Grammatik des neutestamentlichen Griechisch*. Göttingen: Vandenhoeck & Ruprecht).

Bonfante, G. 1980. The origin of the type French *on dit*, German *man sagt*, etc. *Word* 31: 69–71.

Borg, A. & Azzopardi-Alexander, M. 1997. *Maltese*. London: Routledge.

Buchholz, O. & Fiedler, W. 1987. *Albanische Grammatik*. Leipzig: Enzyklopädie.

Cardinaletti, A. & Starke, M. 1999. The typology of structural deficiency. A case study of the three classes of pronouns. In *Clitics in the languages of Europe*, [EALT-Eurotyp 20–5], H. van Riemsdijk (ed.), 145–233. Berlin: de Gruyter.

Cinque, G. 1988. On 'Si' constructions and the theory of 'Arb'. *Linguistic Inquiry* 19: 521–581.

Coveney, A. 2000. Vestiges of *nous* and the 1st person plural verb in informal spoken French. *Language Sciences* 22: 447–481.

D'Alessandro R. Alexiadou, A. 2006. The syntax of the indefinite pronoun *nome*. *Probus* 18: 189–218.

Egerland, V. 2003. Impersonal pronouns in Scandinavian and Romance. *Working Papers in Scandinavian Syntax* 71: 75–102.

Feuillet, J. 1996. *Grammaire synchronique du bulgare*. Paris: Institut d'Études Slaves.

Giacalone Ramat, A. To appear. Areal convergence in grammaticalization processes. In *New reflections on grammaticalization* 3, E. Seoane-Posse & M. J. López-Couso (eds). Amsterdam: John Benjamins.

Givón, T. 1984. *Syntax. A functional-typological introduction*. Vol. I. Amsterdam: John Benjamins.

Glinert, L. 1982. Negative and non-assertive in contemporary Hebrew. *Bulletin of the School of Oriental and African Studies* XLV: 434–470.

Grafström, Å. 1969. *On* remplaçant *nous* en français. *Revue de Linguistique Romane* 33: 270–298.

Gray, L. H. 1945. *Man* in Anglo-Saxon and Old High German Bible-texts. *Word* 1: 19–32.

Harris, A. & Campbell, L. 1995. *Historical syntax in cross-linguistic perspective*. Cambridge: CUP.

Harris, M. 1978. *The evolution of French syntax*. London: Longman.

Haspelmath, M. 1997. *Indefinite pronouns*. Oxford: Clarendon Press.

Haspelmath, M. 1998. How young is Standard Average European? *Language Sciences* 20 (Special issue on Areal Typology, guest editor P. Ramat): 271–287.

Haspelmath, M. 2001. The European linguistic area: Standard average european. In *Language typology and language universals. An international handbook*. Vol. 2, M. Haspelmath, E. König, W. Österreicher & W. Raible (eds), 1492–1510. Berlin: Walter de Gruyter.

Haspelmath, M., Dryer, M., Gil, D. & Comrie, B. (eds). 2005. *The World Atlas of Language Structures*. Oxford: OUP.

Heine, B. & Kuteva, T. 2002. *World lexicon of grammaticalization.* Cambridge: CUP.

Heine, B. & Kuteva, T. 2005. *Language contact and grammatical change.* Cambridge: CUP.

Jensen, F. 1986. *The syntax of Medieval Occitan.* Tübingen: Niemeyer.

Jensen, F. 1990. *Old French and comparative Gallo-Romance syntax.* Tübingen: Niemeyer.

Jones, M. A. 1993. *Sardinian syntax.* London: Routledge.

Kaufmann, A. B. 2002. La passiva i les construccions que s'hi relacionen. In *Gramàtica del català contemporani,* Vol. 2: *Sintaxi,* J. Solà, M.-R. Lloret, J. Mascaró, M. Pérez Saldanya (eds), 2111–2179. Barcelona: Empúries.

Koenig, J.-P. 1999. *On a tué le président!* Ultra-indefinites and the nature of passives. In *Cognition and function in language,* B. Fox, D. Jurafsky & L. Michaelis (eds), 235–251. Stanford CA: CSLI.

Kordić, S. 2001. *Wörter im Grenzbereich von Lexikon und Grammatik im Serbokroatischen.* Munich: Lincom.

Lehmann, Ch. 1995. *Thoughts on grammaticalization.* Munich: Lincom.

Leumann, M., Hofmann, J. B. & Szantyr, A. 1965. *Lateinische Grammatik.* Vol. II: *Syntax und Stilistik.* München: Beck.

Lockwood, W. B. 1955. *An introduction to modern Faroese.* Copenhagen: Munksgaard.

Los, B. 2002. The loss of the indefinite pronoun *man.* Syntactic change and information structure. In *English historical syntax and morphology. Selected papers from 11 ICEHL, Santiago de Compostela, 7–11 September 2000,* T. Fanego, M. J. López-Couso & J. Pérez-Guerra (eds), 181–202. Amsterdam: John Benjamins.

Los, B. 2005. *The rise of the* to-*infinitive.* Oxford: OUP.

Marchetti, P. 2001. *L'usu córsu. Dizionario dei vocaboli d'uso e dei modi di dire di Corsica settentrionale e centrale con i corrispondenti delle lingue italiana e francese.* Ajaccio: Imprimerie Pierre-Dominique-Sammarcelli.

May, H. G. Metzger, B. M. (eds). 1962. *The Holy Bible. Revised standard version containing the Old and the New Testaments.* New York NY: OUP.

Mazon, A. 1931. L'emploi indéfini du nom de l'homme en slave. In *Mélanges de philologie offerts a M.J.J. Mikkola, professeur de philologie slave à l'Université de Helsinki, à l'occasion de son soixante-cinquième anniversaire le 6 juillet 1931,* 146–156. Helsinki.

McWhorter, J.H. 2004. What happened to English? In *Focus on Germanic typology* [Studia Typologica 6], W. Abraham (ed.), 19–60. Berlin: Akademie.

Meillet, A. 1948. *Linguistique historique et linguistique générale.* Paris: Librairie Ancienne Honoré Champion.

Meyer-Lübke, W. 1900. *Grammaire des langues romanes.* Tome troisième: *Syntaxe* (French translation of *Grammatik der Romanischen Sprachen,* Dritter Band: *Syntax,* Leipzig, Reisland, 1899). Paris: Welter.

Monaci, E. 1955. *Crestomazia italiana dei primi secoli con prospetto grammaticale e glossario.* Nuova edizione riveduta e aumentata. Città di Castello: Dante Alighieri.

Myhill, J. 1997. Toward a functional typology of agent defocusing. *Linguistics* 35: 799–844.

Nyrop, K. 1925. *Grammaire historique de la langue française,* Tome V. Copenhagen: Gyldendalske Boghandel Nordisk Forlag.

Raumolin-Brunberg, H. Kahlas-Tarkka, L. 1997. Indefinite pronouns with singular human reference. In *Grammaticalization at work. Studies of long-term developments in English,* M. Rissanen, M. Kytö & K. Heikkonen (eds), 17–85. Berlin: de Gruyter.

Rohlfs, G. 1949. *Historische Grammatik der Italienischen Sprache und ihrer Mundarten,* Bd. II: *Formenlehre und Syntax.* Bern: Francke.

Salonius, A. H. 1920. *Vitae Patrum. Kritische Untersuchungen über Text, Syntax und Wortschatz der Spätlateinischen Vitae Patrum.* Lund: Gleerup.

Salvi, G. n.d. La realizzazione sintattica della struttura argomentale. Manuscript. Progetto *ItalAnt – Grammatica dell'italiano antico*: http://ludens.elte.hu/~gps/konyv/indice.html.

Sansò, A. 2006. 'Agent defocusing' revisited. Passive and impersonal constructions in some European languages. In *Passivization and typology: Form and function*, W. Abraham & L. Leisiö (eds), 229–270. Amsterdam: John Benjamins.

Schrijnen, J. 1939. Homo im altchristlichen Latein. In *Collectanea Schrijnen. Verspreide opstellen van Dr. Jos. Schrijnen*, Ch. Mohrmann, J. Meertens & W. Roukens (eds), 364–372. Nijmegen: Dekker & van de Vegt.

Sgrilli, P. (ed.). 1983. *Il "Libro di Sidrac" salentino. Edizione, spoglio linguistico e lessico.* Pisa: Pacini.

Söll, L. 1969. Zur Situierung von *on* "nous" im neuen Französisch. *Romanische Forschungen* 81: 535–549.

Thackeray, H. 1909. *A grammar of the Old Testament in Greek.* Cambridge: CUP.

Timberlake, A. 1977. Reanalysis and actualization in syntactic change. In *Mechanisms of syntactic change*, C.N. Li (ed.), 141–177. Austin TX: University of Texas Press.

Ugolini, F. A. 1959. *Testi volgari abruzzesi del Duecento.* Torino: Rosenberg & Sellier.

van der Auwera, J. 1998. Conclusion. In *Adverbial constructions in the languages of Europe*, J. van der Auwera (ed.), 813–836. Berlin: de Gruyter.

Vendryes, J. 1916. Sur deux faits de syntaxe celtique. *Mémoires de la Société de Linguistique de Paris* XX (4): 179–189.

Wartburg, W. von. 1946. *Raccolta di testi antichi italiani.* Bern: Francke.

Weiss, D. 1997. Russisch человек: Versuch eines referentiellen Porträts. In *Slavistische Linguistik 1996. Referate des XXII. Konstanzer Slavistischen Arbeitstreffens, Potsdam, 17.-20.9.1996*, P. Kosta & E. Mann (eds), 309–365. München: Otto Sagner.

Welton-Lair, L. K. 1999. The evolution of the French indefinite pronoun *on*: A corpus-based study in grammaticalization. PhD dissertation, Cornell University.

Zifonun, G. 2001. ‚*Man lebt nur einmal*'. Morphosyntax und Semantik des Pronomens *man*. *Deutsche Sprache* 3: 232–253.

Corpora

Corpus ItalNet (*Tesoro della lingua italiana delle origini*): http://ovisun198.ovi.cnr.it/italnet/OVI/

The Pelcra Reference Corpus of Polish: http://korpus.ia.uni.lodz.pl/

Corpus Textual Informatitzat de la Llengua Catalana: http://pdl.iec.es/home/index.asp

Titus (*Thesaurus Indogermanischer Text- und Sprachmaterialien*): http://titus.uni-frankfurt.de

Mediating culture through language

Contact-induced phenomena in the early translations of the Gospels

Silvia Luraghi and Pierluigi Cuzzolin

The paper aims to show how translation can transfer certain culture-specific concepts into a different culture, possibly modifying it. It concentrates on the translation of the Greek preposition *epí* into Latin, Gothic, and Old Church Slavonic in Luke's Gospel. We argue that, to various extents, translators incorporated results of theological discussion into their language (obviously, this is most clear for Latin, where constructions such as *confido in* 'trust in' and *fleo super* 'cry over' were created, that did not exist in Classical Latin and still survive in the Romance languages). Through carefull analysis of the various translations found, we show that even in Late Antiquity and Early Middle Ages cultural contact was a privileged vehicle for linguistic contact.

Introduction

The present paper aims to show how translation can transfer certain culture-specific concepts into a different culture, into which they may be integrated, and which they may possibly modify. Our case study concerns translations of Luke's Gospel into Latin, Gothic, and Old Church Slavonic. We will concentrate especially on the translation of the preposition *epí*.

As shown by Jerome's *Letter on Translation* (Nergaard 1993, Ceresa-Gastaldo 1975; Valgiglio 1985; Vineis 1988; Traina 1989; 101–102), ancient translation theories were based on word rather then text (*verbum de verbo* 'word from word') (see further Brock 1979). In the case of prepositions, this means that the translator tried to establish a (couple of) translation equivalent(s), and use them as extensively as possible. It also means that a translation involving another preposition appeared preferable to a translation involving a case-marked noun phrase without preposition. As we will show in the course of the paper, the translations of *epí* are interesting in several respects.

In the first place, while it can be remarked that the three target languages had one (or two) preferred prepositions that translated *epí*, it is also clear that the strategy of establishing a unique translation equivalent left out a number of occurrences, that had to be translated in some other way. However, the tendency to keep the same number of words as the original, i.e. not to translate a prepositional phrase by means of a noun phrase, thus leaving out the preposition, was strong in all translations, especially Latin. Besides, some usages of *epí* in Luke's Gospel (and in general in New Testament Greek as well as in the *Septuagint*) were not attested in Classical Greek (Blass/Debrunner/Rehkopf 2001: 186–188; Regard 1919: 417–466). Some of these new usages occur in expressions that reflect the religious thought expressed in the text.

1. Luke's Gospel and its early translations

1.1 The Greek text

Luke's Gospel was written in Greek, presumably in the 1st century CE, by a speaker of L2 Greek living in Palestine, whose mother tongue must have been Aramaic, a Semitic language related to, but for some features rather different from, Biblical Hebrew. Greek as L2 was commonly spoken by literate people in this area. In general, the authors of the New Testament, considered one of the most important documents of *koiné* Greek (i.e. in spite of possible Semitic influence), had a good knowledge of the language, and apparently wrote in a variety that was close to the spoken Greek of the time. As for their literary models, an important role must have been played by the Greek version of the Bible, the *Septuagint*, which they must have known and mastered on account of their cultural and religious background. In the field of prepositions, certain features of New Testament Greek, such as the instrumental meaning of *en*,[1] can also be found in the Old Testament. This means that, besides the possible influence of their mother tongue, the writers of the New Testament could also be influenced by their knowledge of Biblical Greek.

1.2 Latin translations

1.2.1 *The* Vetus Latina

The name *Vetus Latina* does not refer to a single Latin translation, but to a collection of several different versions, mostly written in the 2nd century CE, containing both the Old and the New Testament. An often quoted passage by Augustin attests to an extremely large number of Latin translations, at least of the Old Testament

1. On the instrumental usage of *en* as typical of New Testament Greek, see Blass/Debrunner/Rehkopf (2001: 178) and Regard (1919: 328–329). However, the latter correctly points out that the frequency of *en* was also decreasing (1919: 326): indeed, as we will see in the course of this paper, the extent to which the instrumental usage of *in* developed in Christian Latin is unmatched in Greek.

(but there is no reason to doubt that the number of translations of the New Testament was comparably high). The numerous manuscripts that have reached us are variously grouped, in an attempt to reconstruct different regional traditions, the most important being the *Vetus Itala*, used in Italy (but the name, again taken from Augustin, is sometimes used as a quasi-synonym of *Vetus Latina*); there are also attempts to reconstruct a *Vetus Hispana*, while an important group of manuscripts attests to a separate tradition from North Africa, the so-called *Afra*.

Problems arising from relations among different translations lie outside the scope of the present paper; the early Latin versions of the New Testament are relevant here only insofar as they may have influenced Jerome's new Latin translation (the *Vulgate*) and Wulfila's Gothic translation of Luke's Gospel. Indeed, as we will see below, there are passages in which Wulfila's translation does not correspond to the Greek text, but has a correspondent in one or another of the pre-Jerome Latin translations. As for the *Vulgate*, Jerome, too, knew and used the available Latin translations. In the field of prepositions, his choices do not coincide with the choices of any specific manuscript; however, it is remarkable that in almost every case he does not find new solutions, but rather chooses a translation that had already been used before: the novelty lies in the overall combination all possible translations, rather than in the search for new ones.

1.2.2 *The* Vulgate

As we pointed out in the previous section, when Jerome embarked on the translation of the Old and New Testament in the early 5th century CE, several Latin translations were available. These translations were highly unsatisfactory because translators, in an attempt to avoid introducing changes to the original meaning, often came up with grammatically incorrect and in some cases barely comprehensible Latin. With respect to the Old Testament, the poor quality of Latin translations (which were based on the *Septuagint*) was partly due to either textual problems in the Greek text, or problems inherent to the Greek translation. Therefore Jerome understood that a new translation, written in a language that could easily be understood by Latin speakers, had to be based on the Hebrew original. A cursory glance through the Old Testament shows that Jerome's translation, though taking the translation found in the *Septuagint* into account, is often independent of it. This means that when Jerome tackled the translation of the Gospels he already had an idea of how Greek prepositions were used (or misused) in the *Septuagint*, and that peculiarities in his use of Latin prepositions were partly based on his own translation of the Hebrew Bible.

Jerome's Latin was hardly comparable to the language of classical prose writers (or contemporary patristic literature), but still it was a language that could look back to a long written tradition. Besides, as remarked in § 1.2.1, Jerome relied on several centuries of translation practice for both the Old and the New Testament. This makes the Latin translation radically different to the Gothic and Slavonic ones.

1.3 Gothic

The Gothic translation of Luke's Gospel was part of a complete translation from the Greek of the Old and New Testament by Wulfila in the 4th century CE. Most of the translation of the Old Testament is now lost, as are parts of the translation of the New Testament: in particular, as regards Luke's Gospel, we have only books 1 through 10 and 14 through 20.

Like most cultured people of his time, Wulfila could speak Greek, and his translation shows a good understanding of the original text (which, as is well known, does not exactly correspond to any of the Greek texts that have reached us). Living in a multilingual environment, Wulfila also made limited use of the early Latin translations of the New Testament (*Vetus Latina*). Unlike Jerome, he could not rely on a literary tradition for his translation, because Gothic had never been a written language. As a consequence, his effort to create a written standard was all the greater, and it is more difficult for us to gauge the extent of Greek influence on his language (Keidan 2001).

1.4 Old Church Slavonic

"Old Church Slavonic is the language extrapolated from a small corpus of probably late tenth-century copies, mainly of translations made about a century earlier of Greek ecclesiastical texts. These Slavonic texts contain mainly Balkan dialectal features, have an admixture of Moravianisms, since the first translations were used for missionary activity in Greater Moravia, where further translations and copies were made, beginning from about 863." (Huntley 1993: 125). Like Gothic, Old Church Slavonic did not rely on any previous written tradition. Moreover, extant texts are not amenable to a single translation or at least to a single tradition, but result from a mixture incorporating different dialectal features, giving birth to a rather artificial language. A linguistic evaluation of the material grouped under the label Old Church Slavonic is still an open issue in the field of Slavistics. Since the majority of manuscripts transmitting the different ecclesiastical texts started being copied in various centres in Croatia, Bulgaria and Macedonia, linguistic features of local varieties crept into the different traditions, thus giving rise to several branches in the philological tradition: Czecho-Moravian, Bulgaro-Macedonian, Bulgarian, Serbian, Croatian (Taseva & Vos 2005; Ziffer 2005). Strikingly enough, monks who translated the Greek text were often apparently unable to understand it correctly and consequently provided many completely mistaken and misleading translations (all examples collected in *Staroslavjanskij slovar' (po rukopisjam X-XI vekov)*), which makes it even more difficult to provide a consistent picture of Old Church Slavonic.

The text on which the present investigation is based is preserved in the *Codex Zographensis*, a manuscript in Glagolitic, a script devised by Constantine and Methodius and used in the earliest Slavonic texts, written around the late 10th and early 11th century CE, containing the four Gospels.[2] The text of Luke's Gospel is missing at three points: 4.5–27, 12.28–14.2 (10 verses), and 24.30–44.

It is difficult to identify the exact location where the manuscript was written, but the most likely is Bulgaria or Macedonia. In any case, the manuscript displays many linguistic features that are indisputably South-Western, even though the linguistic and cultural environments where these texts were first transmitted are frequently uncertain.

2. The meaning of *epí* in Luke's Gospel and in New Testament Greek

The preposition *epí* is fairly frequent in the New Testament, and it is the only one which is well attested with all three cases, even if the accusative is by far more frequent than the genitive and the dative (see Regard 1919).[3] Its spatial meaning is 'on', 'over', and, limited to the accusative, 'towards', 'against'. When denoting spatial relations located on the vertical axis, *epí* often signals contact, as opposed to *hupér*, which never does. With the accusative, *epí* often denotes relations that are located on the horizontal axis; in such cases it often signals lack of contact ('towards', rather than 'into'), but see 12.11, discussed below as example (33). Temporal usage of *epí* is limited, but attested with all cases, and essentially denotes location in time. On the abstract plane, *epí* can denote metaphorical location ('over'); it may express cause or reason with verbs of emotion (with the dative, as pointed out in Blass/Debrunner/Rehkopf (2001: 188): "Am häufigsten bezeichnet ἐπί den Grund"), and in a case it denotes means (again with the dative, see 4.4 in example (13)). The genitive mostly denotes a static relation, and occurs with the verb 'be' or other verbs of rest; the dative is also attested with verbs of rest, but it most often occurs in abstract contexts.

The accusative often occurs with motion verbs, but verbs of rest are not infrequent. In a few occurrences, one has the feeling that, in spatial expressions, the difference between the dative and the accusative was not completely clear to the author, because the two cases occur in identical expressions, in:

(1) 12.53–54 *diameristhḗsontai, patḕr epì huiôi kaì huiòs epì patrí, mḗtēr epì thugatéra kaì thugátēr epì tḕn mētéra, pentherà epì tḕn númphēn autês kaì númphē epì tḕnántherán*

2. For a description of the *Codex Zographensis* see Jagić (1954: V-XXXVI; *CC*: 13–14); for related editorial and linguistic problems, see the fundamental contribution by Garzaniti (2001: 306–310).

3. The description in this paragraph is based on Luke's Gospel. For the meaning and use of *epí* in Classical Greek, see Luraghi (2003: 298–313), for other parts of the New Testament, see the references given in § 0.

'they will be divided, father against son, and son against father; mother against daughter, and daughter against her mother; mother-in-law against her daughter-in-law, and daughter-in-law against her mother-in-law'

The accusative also occurs in a few other passages where one would expect the genitive or the dative, as in the expression *eph' hò katékeito* 'that which he was laying on' in 5.25, or where it depends on the verb 'be'. Note however, that the extension of the accusative with this preposition is not remarkable, and the relative frequency of cases is similar to what one can find in Attic prose writers.

Apart from the occurrences mentioned above, the spatial meaning of *epí* in New Testament Greek does not display major differences with respect to Classical Greek, and similarly, the few occurrences of *epí* in time expressions have correspondences in the classical language. On the contrary, abstract usage of *epí* with the dative, and to a limited extent with the accusative (cause or reason), is an innovation; we will come back to it in the next section. Besides, two expressions that we can regard as typical idioms of the New Testament deserve to be mentioned, i.e. *ep'alētheías* 'of a truth', with the genitive, and *epì tôi onómati* (*tinós*) 'in the name (of …)', with the dative.

The preposition *epí* occurs 159 times in Luke's Gospel, 25 with the genitive, 34 with the dative, and 100 with the accusative. Before discussing individual translations, we provide correspondences in the four languages. We do not include the *Vetus Latina*, which is not a text but a collection of texts with numerous variants.

Table 1. Translations of *epí* in Latin

LATIN	genitive	dative	accusative
in abl.	12	22	7
in acc.		2	32
ad	1		21
super abl.		4	
super acc.	4	4	25
supra	3	1	6
sub abl.	2		
per			1
secus	1		
ab	1		
adversus			1
contra			1
ablative		1	1
accusative			1
dative			3
adverb	1		1

Note that the number of occurrences in Gothic is considerably smaller than the number of occurrences in the other languages, because the text is incomplete (see above, § 1.3).

Table 2. Translations of *epí* in Gothic

GOTHIC	genitive	dative	accusative
ana dat.	10	6	16
ana acc.	1		19
uf dat.	1		
at dat.	1		1
bi dat.	1	1 (?)	
bi acc.		4	2
in dat.	2		
in gen.	3		
du dat.		2	6
afar dat.		2	1
ufar dat.			4
ufaro dat.			1
accusative			3
dative			1
genitive		1 (?)	
adverb		1	3
not translated			1

Table 3. Translations of *epí* in Old Church Slavonic (OCS)

OCS	accusative	dative	genitive
na + acc.	39	5	1
na + loc.	12	1	14
kŭ + dat.	11		
vŭ + acc.	3	3	2
vŭ + loc.	3		
nadŭ + str.	3	3	1
o + loc.	3	12	
po + loc.	1	1	
otŭ + gen.			1
pri + loc.			2
u + gen.	1		
dative	1		
accusative		1	
instrumental		1	
adverb	2		
not translated	1		

3. The translation of *epí* in Latin

3.1 *The* Vulgate[4]

As remarked in § 2, Greek featured an opposition between contact and lack of contact when denoting spatial relations holding on the vertical axis. Latin did not feature this distinction: in principle, the preposition *super* can denote both contact or lack of contact, even if the latter case was perhaps more frequent. In cases in which contact is the most relevant feature of the spatial relation, the closest correspondent of *epí* is *in*. Accordingly, Latin occurrences are divided into two main groups, one that contains *in* (41 occurrences with the ablative and 34 with the accusative), and another one with *super* or the related adverb *supra* (33 occurrences with the accusative, 4 with the ablative, and 10 of *supra*). Another significant group of occurrences contains *ad*, used almost exclusively as a translation of *epí* with the accusative in cases in which *epí* denotes motion (or, less frequently, location) towards or in the vicinity of an entity. Below are some examples:

(2) 2.14 gen. *kaì epì gês eirḗnē / et in terra pax*
'and on earth peace'

(3) 21.6 dat. *ouk aphethḗsetai líthos epì líthōi / non relinquetur lapis super lapidem*
'there will not be left one stone on another'

(4) 5.12 acc. *pesṓn epì prósōpon / procidens in faciem*
'falling on his face'

(5) 10.6 acc. *eph'humâs anakámpsei / ad vos revertetur*
'it will return to you'

Clearly, there is no single preposition in Latin that can translate the Greek *epí*; judging the relative frequency, it appears that Jerome chose *in* as the closest correspondent. Even in the domain of spatial relations, this choice is not always devoid of problems: often, especially in the case of *epí* with the accusative, Jerome comes up with a type of usage that either is far from the norm of classical prose writers, or does not entirely reflect the meaning of the original text. The latter problem can also be created by the use of *ad*. Consider, for example:

(6) 10.9 *ḗggike eph'humâs hē basileía toû theoû*
appropinquavit in vos regnum dei
'the Kingdom of God has come near to you'

4. We discuss the *Vulgate* before earlier Latin translations for two reasons. In the first place, as we remarked earlier, the *Vetus Latina* is not a single text, but rather a collection of several translations based on different traditions; in the second place, after it was written, the *Vulgate* remained the only Latin translation officially in use.

(7) 22.52 *hōs epì lēistḗn exḗlthate metà makhairôn kaì xúlōn;*
quasi ad latronem existis cum gladiis et fustibus?
'have you come out as against a robber, with swords and clubs?'

Following the classical usage, one would rather expect the opposite translation, i.e. *ad* in example (6) ('towards'), and *in* in example (7) ('against').

Things become more complicated when one moves on to an analysis of abstract contexts. In the first place, there are occurrences which look quite similar in Greek, where Jerome chooses quite different Latin translations, thus opting for different meanings:

(8) 2.25 *kaì pneûma ên hágion ep' autón / et Spiritus Sanctus erat in eo*
'and the Holy Spirit was on him'
2.40 *kaì kháris Theoû ên ep' autó / et gratia Dei erat in illo*
'and the grace of God was upon him'

(9) 4.18 *pneûma Kuríou ep' emé / Spiritus Domini super me*
'the Spirit of the Lord is upon me'

Whatever the Greek text may be taken to mean, the Latin translation in (9) says something different from what is said in (8). Note that *epí* with the accusative did not normally occur with the verb 'be' (or in nominal sentences) in Classical Greek; so Jerome had no pattern to follow from Classical Greek.[5]

The same happens in a much more striking way when we turn to occurrences of *epí* with the dative, which mostly denote abstract relations. Here, Jerome mostly uses *in*, but occasionally also *super*, in a way that is unparalleled in classical Latin prose. Let us consider some examples:

(10) 1.14 *kaì polloì epì têi genései autoû kharḗsontai*
et multi in nativitate eius gaudebunt
'and many shall rejoice at his birth'

(11) 2.47 *exístanto dè pántes hoi akoúsantes autoû epì têi sunései kaì taîs apokrísesin autoû*
stupebant autem omnes qui eum audiebant super prudentia et responsis eius
'and all that heard him were astonished at his understanding and answers'

(12) 9.43 *pántōn dè thaumazóntōn epì pâsin hoîs epoíei*
omnibusque mirantibus in omnibus quae faciebat
'while they all wondered at all things which he did'

In passages such as the above, *epí* denotes reason or cause. In Classical Greek, verbs such as *khaírein* 'rejoice' and *thaumázein* 'wonder' would have taken an

5. As we will see below, § 3.2, the difference between the two passages in (8) and the one in (9) was partly established in the pre-Jerome tradition of Latin translations: while *epí* is translated with various prepositions (including *in*, *super*, and *cum* in (8), all translations agree on *super* in (9)).

instrumental dative. As is well known, the instrumental dative was becoming obsolete in the *koiné*, and was being substituted by various prepositional phrases. In Classical Latin, one could have used the instrumental ablative, or, with a verb such as *miror* 'wonder', some other type of prepositional phrase. Here, Jerome (as well as other Latin translators; see § 3.2) is confronted with several problems. In the first place, he had to translate a non-classical usage of *epí*; in the second place, he tried to conform to the original as far as the number of words was concerned, which prevented him from using a plain case instead of a prepositional phrase. He chose to extend the meaning of the two Latin prepositions *in* and *super* to the same abstract relations denoted by *epí*, based on the consideration that *in* and *super* were the closest correspondent of *epí* in the domain of spatial relations. However, he did not follow this procedure to the same extent for both prepositions: *super* occurs only three times in passages comparable to example (11) (moreover, the same verb is also attested with *in*); elsewhere it either occurs in concrete spatial expressions (see example (3) above), or in passages in which the occurrence of the verb 'be' renders the spatial metaphor more readily accessible.

Let us now turn to another passage that deserves to be mentioned, again with *epí* plus the dative:

(13) 4.4 *ouk ep' ártōi mónōi zḗsetai* [*all' en pantì rḗmati Theoû*]
non in pane solo vivet homo sed in omni verbo Dei
'man shall not live by bread alone, but by every word of God'

Example (13) is of particular interest, because it shows how the same Latin preposition, *in*, was used for two Greek prepositions, *epí* and *en*.[6] Neither preposition would have been appropriate in Classical Greek, where one would have found *apó* in both cases. As already remarked in relation to example (10), the passage in (13), too, would have contained an instrumental ablative in Classical Latin. Jerome did not depend on the original for the translation of prepositions, and was able to use expressions that he found more appropriate to Latin; however, he consistently tried to avoid leaving out a word from his translation. Indeed, this could have been a problem with many of the examples discussed in this section, had he used the plain ablative. Limiting the observation to the New Testament, for which he had only the Greek text, Jerome was also confronted with another problem: the use of *epí* was not clearly attested in the literary language in similar contexts. Consequently, he tried to be innovative in much the same way as he felt the Greek text was, as we have

6. It also points to an inconsistency in the use of these prepositions in Biblical Greek: i.e. both *epí* and *en* could translate two different Hebrew prepositions, i.e. *'al*, 'over', and *b* 'in', 'with'. The passage in (13), a quotation from the Old Testament, contains two occurrences of *'al* in Hebrew. The Greek text of the New Testament contains only the first part of the quotation (the part given here in square brackets is omitted).

remarked above. It must be mentioned, as we will see in more detail below, § 3.2, that *in* was the translation that had already been used for both *epí* and *en* in this passage by all earlier Latin translators of the Gospel. So Jerome's choice was not directly based on evidence of the same preposition, *'al*, occurring in the Hebrew text of the Old Testament. He may have found that current Latin translations were confirmed by the Hebrew original, and consequently, were better than the Greek translation.

Note that the effect of Jerome's decision to use *in* as most frequent translation of *epí*, especially in abstract contexts, made the instrumental meaning of this preposition far more relevant, which is considered a peculiar feature of Christian Latin, and is commonly associated with the influence of Hebrew *b*, a preposition that could mean both 'in' (location) and 'with' (instrument). As example (13) shows, the matter is not irrelevant, given the fact that *in* corresponds to Hebrew *'al* in this passage.

With the accusative, *epí* also denotes cause with the verb 'cry'. In Luke's Gospel this construction occurs in two passages, one of which is quoted below, as example (42). The other occurrence is:

(14) 19.41 *idṑn tḕn pólin éklausen ep' autḗn*
videns civitatem flevit super illam
'he beheld the city, and wept over it'

The verb *klaíein* 'cry' did not take *epí* in Classical Greek (with this verb, cause was expressed with *diá* and the accusative, as expected). However, this Greek construction was already attested in the *Septuagint.* If one examines the Hebrew text, it can be seen that the verb 'cry' occurs with the preposition *'el* 'to' 'towards', which, in its concrete spatial meaning, corresponds to Greek *eis* or *epí* plus the accusative. Jerome also used *super* in similar contexts in the translation of the Old Testament. In this case, his use of *super* seems to be influenced by the Greek translation: Jerome opts to extend the meaning of *super* to the same abstract contexts to which the meaning of *epí* had been extended in the *Septuagint.* Far from being his own choice, though, the usage of *super* with *fleo* 'cry' was already established in the Christian tradition, as we will see in § 3.2.

Finally, a few particular cases are worth mentioning because they contain meanings of *epí* that could not be rendered by means of the most frequent prepositions used in Latin translations. For example, temporal usage, as in *epì tḕn aúrion, altera die* in 10.35, representing one of the few cases in which Jerome translates with a plain ablative (see further 4.25), thus omitting a word, and:

(15) 3.2 *epì arkhieréōs Ánna kaì Kaïápha*
sub principibus sacerdotum Anna et Caiapha
'Annas and Caiaphas being the high priests'

(see further 4.27; this usage of *epí* is translated with the ablative absolute in the *Afra*).

We would also like to mention the passages in (16) and (17). In the first, Jerome used the infrequent preposition *secus*, a translation which also occurs in the so-called manuscript *aureum* of the *Vetus Latina*, while in the second he uses *ad*, a translation that does not correspond to earlier versions (*in* is also attested in some manuscripts of the *Vulgate*, as it is in the *Vetus Latina*):

(16) 20.37 *Mōüsês emḗnusen epì tês bátou*
Moses ostendit secus rubum
'Moses showed at the bush'

(17) 9.62 *oudeìs epibalṑn tēn kheîra autoû ep' árotron*
nemo mittens manum suam ad aratrum
'no man, having put his hand to the plow'

3.2 Earlier translations

One can only give a general overview of the tendencies found in earlier Latin manuscripts containing the translation of Luke's Gospel. They are obviously not homogeneous and reflect different choices. In general, *super* is used for the translation of *epí* with the genitive and the dative more frequently than by Jerome; however, when Jerome uses *in*, the same preposition also occurs in at least one other manuscript. The manuscript that most often has *super* in such occurrences is *e*, the principal manuscript of the *Afra*. The relative frequency of *super* is higher than in the *Vulgate* both in cases in which the preposition denotes a spatial relation, and in cases in which the meaning is abstract: for example, in 2.14 (example (2) above) several manuscripts have *super*, either with the accusative or with the ablative, while very few others have *in*.[7] In 1.14 (quoted in example (10)) most manuscripts have *in* as the *Vulgate*, but *super* is also attested, as in other passages in which *epí* denotes cause or reason. As a general remark, it can be stated that, even if Jerome's translations can almost always be found in earlier manuscripts, it was he who decided to use *in* to denote cause or reason much more frequently than *super*.

In this context, it is remarkable that there are passages in which all the manuscripts agree on the translation *in*. In such passages the preposition does not refer to a spatial relation. They are:

a. 20.21, which contains the phrase *ep'alētheías* 'of a truth',[8]
b. 4.4 quoted above as example (13),

7. The use of cases with prepositions is much less accurate in earlier translations than it is in the *Vulgate*, which usually conforms to the classical norm.

8. Two other passages contain this expression in Luke's Gospel; in the first (4.25), all manuscripts have *in* except *f* and *e*, that have *veritatem (dico vobis)* 'the truth (I tell you)' and *Amen* respectively; in the second (22.59) the *Vulgate* has *vere* 'truly', as do the majority of other Latin translations, while only *d* has *in*.

c. all occurrences of *epì tôi onómati* 'in the name', and
d. 11.22, that we will discuss below.

Occurrences in (a)–(c) contain a special use of *in*, that constitutes a peculiar feature of the language of the New Testament: in particular, (a) and (c) are idiomatic expressions of Christian religious discourse,[9] while (b), discussed here at length in § 3.1, is a passage in which Greek has both *epí* and *en*, while Latin translators decided to unify their version using *in*.

Let us now examine the passage mentioned above under (d):

(18) 11.22 *tḕn panoplíān autoû aírei eph' hē̃i epepoíthei*
universa arma eius aufert in quibus confidebat
'he takes from him all his armor wherein he trusted'

This is a typical example of the tendency already noted above, related to passages that should have contained a dative (and a noun phrase without preposition in Latin): *peíthein epí* in the sense of 'rely on', 'trust', is first attested in the New Testament; in much the same way, *confido* 'trust' did not occur with *in* in Classical Latin. Here all Latin translators agree against using *super*, which most likely would have been unclear. Note that this construction remains in the Romance languages, as do those in (a) and (c) above.[10] Here again it is worth noticing what verb and what type(s) of construction correspond to *confido in* in the Old Testament. The Hebrew verb *bṭḥ*, whose meaning is glossed as "firmae spei plaenus fuit", "be full of firm hope" in Zorell's lexicon, is translated into Greek with either *peíthein* 'trust' or *elpízein* 'hope', and into Latin with either *confido* 'trust' or *spero* 'hope' (the choice of either verb in Latin does not always correspond to Greek, and in general *confido* seems more frequent than *peíthein*). In Hebrew, it may take *b*, *'al*, or *'el*, while Jerome generally uses *in*.[11] In this case, Latin displays a tendency toward unifying various

9. The religious relevance of the expression *in nomine* 'in the name' in Latin is also demonstrated by the fact that another occurrence of *epì tôi onomáti* (1.59), in which the expression has a different meaning (*ekáloun autò epì tôi onomáti toû patròs autoû* "and they called him [Zacharias], after the name of his father") is translated with the plain ablative by Jerome: this is one of the few cases where Jerome chooses to leave out a word, and he does so in order to avoid using a religiously meaningful expression in the wrong context.

10. The verb *confido* 'trust' also occurs in 18.9 with the reflexive pronoun; in this passage, the *Vulgate* has *in*, as does manuscript *f* of the *Vetus Latina*, but the majority of other translations have *sibi*, following the classical usage. In this case, too, Jerome makes use of an already existing translation in a way that gives greater unity to his own grammatical usage.

11. An analysis of the Greek translation of the Old Testament goes far beyond the scope of the present paper. At least in the New Testament, Latin *in* with *confido* 'trust' corresponds to *epí*, *eis*, and *en* in Greek.

possible prepositions in a single consistent usage, which constituted an innovation with respect to the classical norm. Note that neither Greek nor Latin offered a precise and always satisfying equivalent of the Hebrew verb, so both the meanings of the verbs used for translation and the meanings of the prepositions are extended under the influence of the original.

Let us now turn to the translation of *epí* with the accusative in the *Vetus Latina*. Again, we find variation, but the most frequent translations are still *in*, *super/supra*, and *ad*, with a distribution that resembles that of the *Vulgate* more closely than the distribution of possible translations for *epí* with the genitive and the dative. Most cases in which all translations agree contain spatial expressions; some interesting passages are 4.18, quoted above as Example (9) (see further fn. 5), and:

(19) 6.35 *hóti autòs khrēstós estin epì toùs akharístous kaì ponēroús*
quia ipse benignus est super ingratos et malos
'for he is kind unto the unthankful and to the evil'

In this passage, *in* would have been hardly understandable, given the fact that it usually means 'against' with nouns with human referents. The Greek adjective *khrēstós* 'kind' occurs with *epí* only in the New Testament: again, the Latin translators are confronted with the problem of translating an expression for which they have no classical models, and again they decide to keep the same number of words and create a new expression in Latin, too, extending the meaning of the Latin preposition to the same abstract meaning to which Greek *epí* had been extended (*benignus* occurs with the dative and with *erga* in classical authors).

Another case in which all translations agree is 19.41, quoted above as Example (14), that contains the expression *flere super* 'cry over' plus accusative. As in the case of *confido* 'trust', here, too, we find a new construction of a verb, already common in Christian Latin before Jerome, which spread to the spoken languages, as evidenced by the fact that it remains in the Romance languages (and has spread to English and German, too).

4. The translation of *epí* in Gothic

Wulfila was a cultured man, living in a multilingual society, who, as contemporary sources tell us, could preach in Gothic as well as in Greek and in Latin. Even if his translation is based on the original Greek text of the Gospel, it is likely that he also consulted available Latin translations. Indeed, in a couple of passages in which his translation does not correspond to the Greek text, one can find the exact correspondence in some Latin manuscripts. As an example, consider the following:

(20) 1.29 *hē dè epì tôi lógōi dietarákhthē*
iþ si gasaiƕandei gaþlahsnoda bi innatgahtai
'she was troubled at his saying'

A number of Latin manuscripts have *turbata est in introitu eius* "she was troubled at his coming in", which corresponds to *bi innatgahtai.*[12] This may either mean that Wulfila and some of the Latin translators used a Greek text that is now lost, or it may indicate that Wulfila preferred to follow a Latin translation.[13] However, as we will see below, little Latin influence is detectable in the translation of prepositions.

The most frequent preposition used by Wulfila to translate *epí* is *ana*. Besides, when denoting space, *epí* with the accusative signalling motion toward an entity can be translated with *du*; in some occurrences we also find *ufar*, but this is infrequent: in fact, spatial meaning of *ana* must have been similar to that of *epí* in the feature of implying contact, while *ufar* should have been more similar to *hupér* (these remarks are partly based on the existence of pairs of prepositions such as *on/over* and *an/über* in other Germanic languages).

In general, *ana* seems to offer a better equivalent of Greek *epí* than any other Latin preposition. In expressions denoting space, both concrete or abstract, Wulfila's use of *ana* is more consistent than Jerome's use of either *in* or *super*, as shown by passages in 2.25, 2.40, and 4.18 (see examples (8) and (9) discussed above, § 3.1), all containing *ana* with the dative (apparently, any differences that may have been detected by Latin translators were not relevant to Wulfila).

Outside spatial expressions, Wulfila sometimes seems more dependent on the Greek text than Jerome, while other times he seems to depart more from Greek. Consider the following examples:

(21) 9.48 *hòs eàn déxētai toûto tò paidíon epì tôi onómatí mou*
quicumque susceperit puerum istum in nomine meo
saƕazuh saei andnimiþ þata barn ana namin meinamma
'whosoever shall receive this child in my name receiveth me'

(22) 4.25 *ep' alētheías dè légō humîn*
in veritate dico vobis
bi sunjai qiþa izwis
'but I tell you of a truth'

12. See also 19.23, where Greek has *édōkás mou tò argúrion epì trápezan?* "wherefore then gavest not thou my money into the bank?" and Jerome translates *ad mensam* 'to the table', while the Gothic translation *du skattjam* 'to the bankers' rather corresponds to *nummolariis* 'to the bankers' in manuscripts *f* and *e* of the pre-Jerome translations.

13. Note further that the Greek text given here does not contain an equivalent of *gasaiƕandei* either. The *Vulgate* contains the clause *Quae cum audisset* "as she heard those things", but some other manuscripts contain the verb 'see', as does Gothic.

Example (21) contains the expression *epì tôi onómati* 'in the name', which is apparently equivalent to the much more frequent *en (tôi) onómati.*[14] Jerome translates both expressions using *in*. As we have seen in § 3.2, this translation was not his own, but followed an already established norm, according to which Latin always had *in* with *nomine*. Wulfila uses *ana* here, while he normally uses *in namin* for *en tôi onómati*. It is not clear why he chose to make this difference, whether he reproduced equivalent spatial metaphors for the two prepositions in an attempt to avoid changing the meaning of the source text, or whether he wanted to convey different meanings in the translation. Again, one must remember that the difference between Wulfila and Jerome was that the former was translating into Gothic (and indeed using a written variety of Gothic) for the first time, while the *Vulgate* was part of an already rich tradition of Latin translations. Similar to Gothic, the Slavonic translation, too, has two different prepositions corresponding to Greek *epí* and *en* with the word 'name'. We will come back to this point below, § 5.

Example (22) contains a specular situation. The expression *ep' alētheías* 'of a truth' in the Gospels seems to be equivalent to the (again much more frequent) *alēthôs* 'truly'. Jerome uses the adverb *vere* 'truly' for the latter, while he prefers to use a prepositional phrase in this and most cases of *ep' alētheías*, thus preserving the same number of words as the source text (there are few exceptions, one of which is mentioned above in fn. 8). On the other hand, Wulfila usually translates both expressions with the prepositional phrase *bi sunjai*. Again, this situation overlaps with the Slavonic one.

As for the translation of 4.4 discussed above as example (13), in Gothic we find:

(13') *ni bi hlaib ainana libaid manna, ak bi all waurde gudis*
'man shall not live by bread alone, but by every word of God'

The preposition *bi* with the accusative in its abstract meaning is glossed as 'inbetreff, um, über' by Streitberg: in this case, Wulfila did not try to keep the same spatial metaphor used in Greek to express means (remember further that Greek had two different prepositions here, *epí* and *en*). In this connection, it is interesting to observe further that *bi* is also used to express cause with the verb 'cry', that we have discussed above in § 3.1. and 3.2: so in 19.41 (example (14) above) we find:

(14') *gasaiƕands þo baurg gaigrot bi þo*
'he beheld the city, and wept over it'

Here, Wulfila chooses to translate on the basis of the function of *epí*, rather than extending the meaning of some preposition that corresponded to *epí* in the domain of spatial relations.

14. This phrase has its origin in Biblical Hebrew (from *bisem*: Blass/Debrunner/Rehkopf 2001: 168).

In general, the translation of *epí* with the dative denoting abstract relations is problematic for Wulfila, who makes use of various prepositions. With verbs of emotion, we find *in* with the dative once (1.14), *du* with the dative twice (1.47, 7.13), *ana* with the dative twice (2.33, 18.7), and *bi* with the accusative three times (4.22, 4.32, 9.43). With the same verbs, Latin has only two possible prepositions, either *in* or *super*.[15] Below are some examples:

(10') 1.14 *jah managai in gabaurþai is faginond*
'and many shall rejoice at his birth'

(23) 1.47 *kaì ēgallíasen tò pneûmá mou epì tôi Theôi tôi sotêrí mou*
et exultavit spiritus meus in Deo salutari meo
jah swegneid ahma meins du guda nasjand meinamma
'and my spirit hath rejoiced in God my Savior'

(24) 2.33 *thaumázontes epì toîs laloúménois*
mirantes super his quae dicebantur
sildaleikjandona ana þaim þoei rodida wesun
'they marvelled at those things which were spoken of him'

(25) 4.22 *kaì ethaúmazon epì toîs lógois*
et mirabantur in verbis
jah sildaleikidedun bi þo waurda
'and they wondered at the words'

Comparing the Gothic and the Latin translation, we can note two things: (a) the usage of *in* as a translation for the abstract meaning of *epí* was much better established in Jerome than the usage of any unique or quasi-unique equivalent in Wulfila; (b) Latin sometimes made use of a metaphor based on vertical orientation, as shown by the use of *super* in (19) and similar occurrences, while Gothic did not.[16] Both remarks can further be developed in the light of what we said in § 3.1 and 3.2. As we have repeatedly shown above, the usage of *in* and *super* in specific contexts corresponding to Greek *epí* was a typical feature of Latin translations of the Gospels already before Jerome: we may assume that it had become a typical feature of Christian Latin outside translation as well. Consequently Jerome, who was writing his translation three centuries after the earlier ones, could extend its usage, presumably following an established norm of his time. As for the spatial metaphor, we have remarked that Jerome (partly following the earlier translators) decided to extend the meaning of *in* and *super* to the same non-spatial meanings of Greek *epí*.

15. Two other passages (1.29 and 20.26) cannot be used, because they apparently translate a Greek text which does not correspond to ours, see above the discussion of example (20).

16. The Gothic translation of 6.35 quoted in example (19) has the plain dative, rather than a prepositional phrase.

Let us now turn to the two verbs for which Latin translators had devised special constructions, i.e. *confido* 'trust' and *fleo* 'cry'. In the case of *peíthei epí* 'trust in', the passage quoted in example (18) is lost in Gothic; in 18.9 we find the reflexive pronoun without prepositions:

(26) 18.9 *eîpen dè kaì prós tinas toùs pepoithótas eph' heautoîs*
dixit autem et ad quosdam qui in se confidebant
qaþ þan du sumaim, þaiei silbans trauaidedun
'and he said this unto certain which trusted in themselves'

As we have mentioned in § 3.2, fn. 10, some of the earlier Latin translations also had *sibi*, the reflexive pronoun in the dative. Since in all other occurrences of *peíthei epí* 'trust in', including another one with a reflexive pronoun, Wulfila has *du*, the absence of preposition here might be connected with his knowledge of the Latin text (although it may well have been his own decision not to use a preposition). In the case of *klaíein epí* 'cry over', we have already remarked that Gothic did not extend the meaning of *ana* or *ufar* in a way similar to what Latin translators did with *super*. In this case, Wulfila's translation seems to be independent of the form displayed by both Greek and Latin, while it rather conforms to the meaning of the source text.

5. The translation of *epí* in Old Church Slavonic

Looking at Table 3 in comparison with Table 2, it is clear that Old Church Slavonic displays a broader range of possible translations for the Greek preposition *epí* than Gothic, not to mention Latin. In addition, the preposition is translated mainly according to the case accompanying it in the original. This means that *epí* plus accusative most frequently corresponds to *na* plus accusative (39 times out of 80), *epí* plus dative is mainly translated by *o* plus locative (12 times out of 27) and *epí* plus genitive mainly by *na* plus locative (14 times out of 21). However, even though some choices in rendering the preposition occur more frequently than others, an automatic rule can hardly be found: very often, in fact, similar, or even almost identical examples, are translated by means of different prepositions. This seems to reflect the situation already occurring in Greek, where the preposition does not always display clear-cut meaning differences.

As already mentioned above, *epí* plus genitive is usually employed to express location, preferably with contact. *Na* plus locative is the most frequent choice to translate *epí* plus genitive:

(2') 2.14 *i na zemi mirŭ vŭ čel'ověxŭ blagovolenie*
'and on earth peace, good will toward men'

Many occurrences exhibit a local and static meaning: 5.18 *epì klínēs / in lecto / na odrě* 'on the bed'; 6.17 *epì tópou pedinoû / in loco campestri / na městě ravĭně* 'in the plain'; 12.3 *epì tōn domátōn / in tectis / na krověxŭ* 'on the roof'; in some cases also depending on verbs which involve movement, as in:

(27) 8.16 *epì lykhnías títhēsin*
supra candelabrum ponit
na svěščĭnikŭ vŭzlagaetŭ
'setteth it on a candlestick'

In 3.2, where *epí* plus genitive has a temporal meaning, it is translated with *pri* plus locative, the usual way of rendering temporal expressions:

(15') 3.2 *pri arxierei Anně i Kaiěfě*
'Annas and Caiaphas being the high priests'

The same preposition *pri* seems to have a quite exceptional spatial meaning in example (28). As remarked above, § 3.1., *secus* is rather infrequent in Latin and the translator seems to employ an unusual preposition in order to match the unusual lexical choice of the source text:

(28) 20.37 *epì tês bátou / secus rubum / pri kǫpině*
'at the bush'

In this case Matthew's Gospel deserves a mention: the preposition *secus* for *epí* also occurs in Matth. 13.48 in the phrase *secus litus* 'by a stone', corresponding to Old Church Slavonic *na krai.*

In Luke's Gospel, most occurrences of *epí* plus dative express cause or reason and are translated by means of *o* plus locative:

(29) 1.29 *epì tôi lógōi dietarákhthē*
turbata est in sermone eius
sŭmęte sę o slovesi ego
'she was troubled at his saying'

In five occurrences the spatial value of *epí* plus dative is rendered by *na* plus locative and twice by *nadŭ* plus instrumental, as in 23.38:

(30) 23.38 *ên dè kaì epigraphè ep' autôi*
erat autem et superscriptio scripta super eum
bě že i nap'sanĭe napisano nadŭ nimŭ
'and a superscription also was written over him in'

As already observed above, *na* plus accusative is the most frequent choice to translate *epí* plus accusative, even though the fluctuation between the accusative and the locative mirrors the situation of Greek (partly already present in Homeric and Classical Greek, in which a few verbs, such as *títhēmi* 'put', could take *epí* with either the accusative or the genitive). The preposition usually indicates a movement towards somebody or something, as in 10.9, quoted above in example (6), in which we find *na vy* 'over you' (accusative) as a translation of *eph'humâs*. Motion can also be abstract:

(31) 1.17 *Epistrépsai kardías patérōn epí tékna*
Ut convertat corda patrum in filios
Obratiti srdĭca ocmŭ na čęda
'to turn the hearts of the fathers to the children'

(32) 1.35 *pneûma hágion epeléusetai epí sé*
Spiritus sanctus superveniet in te
Douxŭ svęnty naidetŭ na tę
'the Holy Ghost shall come upon thee'

However, albeit infrequently, *epí* can also have the meaning of 'into', as is clear from the following example:

(33) 12.11 *hótan dè eisphérōsin humâs epì tàs sunagōgàs kaì tàs arkhàs kaì tàs exousías*
cum autem inducent vos in synagogas et ad magistratus et potestates
egda že privedǫtŭ vy na sŭnŭmišta i vlasti i vladyčĭstviě
'and when they bring you unto the synagogues, and unto magistrates, and powers'

This usage of *epí* is not found in Classical Greek, where *eis*, rather than *epí*, has the meaning 'into'. In the Liddell-Scott Lexicon, similar examples are quoted, but this is the only one that clearly means not only 'towards' but 'into' (even in the Gospels). Interestingly, cases employed with the preposition *na* reflect such a difference: the word *sŭnŭmišta* 'synagogues' is in the accusative, while *vlasti* 'magistrates' and *vladyčĭstviě* 'powers' are in the locative case. In example (33), Greek makes no distinction between the meanings 'towards' and 'into', whereas Latin explicitly makes such a distinction by using two different prepositions, *in* with the accusative and *ad*, and Old Church Slavonic uses the same preposition, as Greek does, but with two different cases, i.e. the accusative for the meaning 'into' and the locative for 'towards'.

Frequently, *epí* signals final contact with something after a movement. This happens, for instance, with verbs of locating or falling (in 6.48 quoted below, *na* takes the locative case):

(34) 6.48 *éthēken themélion epì tḕn pétran*
posuit fundamentum super petram
položi osnovanie na kamene
'aid the foundation on a rock'

In such cases, too, movement can be abstract:

(35) 1.12 *kaì phóbos epépesen ep'autón*
et timor irruit super eum
i straxŭ napade na nĭ
'and fear fell upon him'

In two occurrences (5.12 quoted in example (4) and 17.16, below) the expression *píptein epì prósōpon* 'to fall on one's face' is rendered by the adverb *nicĭ* 'down':

(36) 17.16 *kaì épesen epì prósōpon parà toùs pódas autoû*
et cecidit in faciem ante pedes eius
i pade nicĭ na nogou ego
'and fell down on his face at his feet'

It is remarkable that in this example Slavonic, while translating the phrase *epì prósōpon* 'on his face' by means of an adverb of space, uses the preposition *na* plus locative (in the dual number) to translate *parà toùs pódas* 'at his feet', turning out to be less precise in providing spatial information than both Greek and Latin.

An example similar to (35), in which the Greek verb *egéneto* 'come into being' is translated with the verb 'be' in Slavonic, that does not imply any movement, also exhibits *na* plus locative:

(37) 1.65 *kaì egéneto epì pántas phóbos*
et factus est timor super omnes
i by na vsexŭ straxŭ
'and fear came on all'

Contact after movement is also involved in the following example, where Latin translates with *ad*:

(38) 5.11 *katagóntes tà ploîa epì tḕn gē̂n*
et subductis ad terram navibus
i izvezŭšče korabĭ na souxo
'and when they had brought their ships to land'

It is also noteworthy that in example (38) the Greek phrase *epì tḕn gē̂n* 'to land', almost automatically translated by *na zemli* in the Gospel, regardless of whether the expression involves movement or not, is rendered through a non-literal, less frequent expression.

However, if movement towards an entity does not imply final contact, a possible solution is *kŭ* plus dative, frequent with persons, with the meaning 'in(to) the presence of', often corresponding to Latin *ad*:

(39) 23.1 *ḗgagon autòn epì tòn Pilâton*
duxerunt eum ad Pilatum
privedosę i kŭ Pilatu
'they led him unto Pilate'

(40) 24.12 *édrame epì tò mnēmeîon*
cucurrit ad monumentum

teče kŭ grobu
'he ran unto the sepulcher'

With the accusative, *epí* can also have a causal meaning as in example (41): in this case it is usually translated by *o* plus locative and it regularly occurs with the verb 'cry' (see above, § 3.1 and 4, examples (14) and (14') with discussion), even though this verb can also take other prepositions such as *za* or plain cases like the genitive in other manuscripts:

(14") 19.41 *viděvŭ gradŭ plaka sę o nemĭ*
'he beheld the city, and wept over it'

(41) 23.28 *mē klaíete ep' emé*
nolite flere super me
ne plačite sę o mně
'do not weep for me'

O plus locative is also used to translate the equivalent of the verb 'live on', as in the following example (see above example (13) and discussion); unfortunately, the rest of the text is missing:

(13") 4.4 *ěko ne o xlěbě edinomĭ živŭ bǫ* †…†
'shall not live by bread alone'

In the case in which the event takes place within a delimited space, *epí* plus accusative is rendered by *po* plus dative:

(42) 23.44 *skótos egéneto eph' hólēn tèn gền*
tenebrae factae sunt in universam terram
tŭma by po vsei zemli
'there was a darkness over all the earth'

A major problem concerning Old Church Slavonic is the difficulty in identifying the linguistic model on which it depends. One of the basic assumptions in the history of Slavistics was that Old Church Slavonic was rigidly dependent on its Greek model. However, the results of numerous detailed investigations show that linguistic features typical of the areas where the manuscripts were written or proper to the variety spoken by copyists crept into the manuscripts. Besides, given the strong influence exerted by the Roman Church, the idea that monks translated exclusively from Greek models has to be reassessed.

Below, we analyze some passages from the Zographensis that deserve special discussion. In part, they may seem independent of the text they translate and rather show that specific linguistic patterns were spreading among languages because of their prestige; some occurrences are connected with grammatical peculiarities of the linguistic systems involved. For convenience, such passages are divided into three categories:

a. the Slavonic translation does not correspond to the original Greek word by word: in general new words are added but in some infrequent cases words are left out. In the following example:

(20') 1.29 *epì tôi lógōi dietarákhthē*
turbata est in sermone eius
sŭmęte sę o slovesi ego
'she was troubled at his saying'

the pronoun in the genitive case *ego* 'his' is added to the noun *slovesi* 'words'. In this case, Slavonic and Latin agree (see also the discussion about Gothic above, § 4), but this does not necessarily imply that they derive from a common source, even if this possibility cannot be ruled out *a priori*. The tendency to add a genitive or a possessive adjective in such a context is common among languages, and could be ascribed to the grammatical system the two target languages;

b. Slavonic and Latin agree in a very particular reading: in such cases, it is more difficult to think of independent innovations in the two target languages, than to assume that Latin itself was the source of the Slavonic translation (see on this yet unsolved problem Garzaniti 2001). A very interesting example is represented by the verse 12.54:

(43) 12.54 *hótan idēte nephélēn anatéllousan epì dysmôn*
cum videritis nubem orientem ab occasu
egda uzrĭte oblakŭ vŭsxodęštĭ otŭ zapadŭ
'when ye see a cloud rise out of the west'

where most likely the expression *epì dysmôn* 'on the west', not even attested in Classical Greek (where the equivalent expression is *pròs dysmôn / pròs dysmaîs* 'from the west'), probably unclear to the translator, was replaced by the translation provided by the Latin text, which perfectly corresponds to the Slavonic text.[17]

c. the third group consists of the expressions *ep'alētheías* 'of a truth', and *epì tôi onómati* 'in the name', that we have discussed in the preceding paragraphs. In the case of *ep'alētheías*, Gothic and Slavonic agree in using a prepositional phrase (*vŭ* plus accusative in Slavonic: *vŭ istinǫ*) both for the prepositional phrase and for the adverb *alēthôs* 'truly' (while Latin often has *vere*). In the case of *epì tôi onómati*,

17. The fact that the Greek expression was unclear is also evidenced by various attempts to render it in different ways by pre-Jerome Latin translators.

which, as we have seen, alternates with *en tôi onómati*, Slavonic again agrees with Gothic in using two different prepositions, as shown in the following examples:

(44) 21.8 *epì tôi onómatí mou / in nomine meo / vŭ imę moe*

(45) 10.7 *en tôi onómatí sou / in nomine tuo / o imeni tvoemĭ*

In this case, too, Slavonic and Gothic do not agree with Latin, in which we find the preposition *in* with the ablative for both types of occurrence, both in the *Vulgate* and in the earlier translations.

6. Conclusions

In our paper, we have focussed on the translation of the Greek preposition *epí* in three different languages: Latin, Gothic, and Old Church Slavonic. Among them, only Latin could rely on a well known earlier literary tradition; besides, Latin continued in the Romance languages, while Old Church Slavonic did not directly give rise to any language, but exerted a strong influence on the literary tradition of many (especially South-Eastern) Slavonic languages. Since Gothic died out, its influence is hardly detectable in any language.

In Luke's Gospel, occurrences that prove interesting from the point of view of translation involve usages of *epí* that were not attested in Classical Greek, and most often occur in contexts relevant for religious thought. In such occurrences, Latin differs from the other two languages, because the translation of the New (and Old) Testament was a much more widespread practice, that had already generated several grammatical usages which became unique to Christian Latin. Among them we discussed the instrumental usage of *in*, and constructions of the verbs *confido in* 'trust in' and *fleo super* 'cry over'. These latter constructions, that did not exist in Classical Latin, still survive in the Romance languages. They depend on the Greek model to a limited extent: in part they go back to Biblical Hebrew (or some other Semitic language),[18] but to some extent, they are also an independent creation of Latin translators (possibly taking into account prevailing theological discussion).

In the same occurrence, Gothic and Slavonic display a larger number of different translations for *epí*. This points to an expectedly low degree of theological culture.[19]

18. See further the case of *gloria* as discussed in Sznajder (2005).

19. However, when Gothic and Slavonic exhibit corresponding translations, it is impossible to assess any influence of Gothic on Slavonic, because there is no positive evidence that Slavic translators knew the Gothic text. In addition, given the theological authoritativeness of the Greek (and Latin) text, and since Goths were Arians, it is methodologically more accurate to suppose that only Greek and possibly Latin were the sources of the Slavonic translation.

Limited refinement of linguistic means is arguably reflected in the way in which an adverb such as *alēthôs* 'truly' is translated. As we have shown in § 4 and 5, both Gothic and Slavonic could apparently only make use of a prepositional phrase. Indeed, manner adverbs are a comparatively complex category, which is likely to develop late.

Our paper shows that even in Late Antiquity and Early Middle Ages cultural contact was a privileged vehicle for linguistic contact.

References

Biblia Hebraica Stuttgartensia, 1977. Herausgegeben von Karl Elliger und Wilhelm Rudolph. 5. Auflage. Stuttgart: Deutsche Bibelgesellschaft.

Die gotische Bibel. Herausgegeben von Wilhelm Streitberg [Germanische Bibliothek, 2. Abteilung, 3. Band]. 1919. 1. Teil: *Der gotische Text und seine griechische Vorlage. Mit Einleitung, Lesarten und Quellennachweisen sowie den kleineren Denkmälern als Anhang.* Heidelberg, Carl Winter. 1910. 2. Teil: *Gotisch-griechisch-deutsches Wörterbuch.* Heidelberg: Carl Winter.

Itala. Das Neue Testament in Altlateinischer Überlieferung. 1954. Bd. 3: *Lukas Evangelium.* Herausgegeben von Adolf Jülicher. Berlin: de Gruyter.

Lexicon hebraicum et aramaicum Veteris Testamenti. 1940. Edidit Franciscus Zorell. Romae: Pontificium Institutum Biblicum.

Novum Testamentum Graece et Latine apparatu critico instructum. Edidit Augustinus Merk S.J. 1984. Editio decima. Romae: Pontificium Institutum Biblicum.

Quattuor evangeliorum Codex Glagoliticus olim Zographensis nunc Petropolitanus characteribus cyrillicis transcriptum notis criticis prolegomenis appendicibus auctum edidit V. Jagić. 1954. Graz, Akademische Druck- u. Verlagsanstalt. [Unveränderter Abdruck der 1879 bei Weidmann, Berlin erschienenen Ausgabe].

Staroslavjanskij slovar' (po rukopisjam X-XI vekov). 1994. Pod redakcieĭ R.M. Ceĭtlin, R. Večerki i E. Blagovoĭj. Moskva: Russkij jazyk.

Blass, F., Debrunner, A. & Rehkopf, F. 2001. *Grammatik des neutestamentlichen Griechisch.* 18th edn., Göttingen: Vandenhoeck & Ruprecht.

Brock, S. 1979. Aspects of translation technique in antiquity. *Greek, Roman and Byzantine Studies* 20: 69–87.

Ceresa-Gastaldo, A. 1975. *Il latino nelle antiche versioni bibliche.* Roma: Studium.

Garzaniti, M. 2001. *Die altslavische Version der Evangelien.* Köln: Böhlau.

Huntley, D. 1993. Old Church Slavonic. In *The Slavonic languages*, B. Comrie & G.C. Corbett (eds), 125–187. London: Routledge.

Keidan, A. 2001. Il gotico di Wulfila: Tra diacronia e retorica. *AIΩN* 23: 49–105.

Liddell, H.G. & Scott, R. 1996. *Greek-English lexicon.* 9th edn., Oxford: Clarendon Press.

Luraghi, S. 2003. *On the meaning of prepositions and cases – The expression of semantic roles in ancient Greek.* Amsterdam: Benjamins.

Nergaard, S. 1993. *La teoria della traduzione nella storia.* Milano: Bompiani.

Regard, P. 1919. *Contribution à l'étude des prépositions dans la langue du Nouveau Testament.* Paris: Leroux.

Sznajder, L. 2005. *Gloria* dans la Vulgate ou le double poids de la traduction biblique latine. Lecture held at the 13. International Colloquium on Latin Linguistics. Brussels, 4–9 April 2005.

Taseva, L. & Vos, C. 2005. Altkirchenslavische Übersetzungen aus dem Griechischen. *Incontri Linguistici* 28: 101–117.

Traina, A. 1989. Le traduzioni. In *Lo spazio letterario di Roma antica.* Vol. II. *La circolazione del testo,* 93–123. Roma: Salerno.

Valgiglio, E. 1985. *Le antiche versioni latine del Nuovo Testamento. Fedeltà e aspetti grammaticali.* Napoli: D'Auria.

Vineis, E. 1988. Le antiche versioni latine dei Vangeli. In *Storia e preistoria dei Vangeli,* A. Ceresa-Gastaldo (a cura di), 61–90. Genova: Dipartimento di archeologia e Filologia Classica.

Ziffer, G. 2005. Lo slavo ecclesiastico antico: Questioni vecchie e nuove. *Incontri Linguistici* 28: 119–125.

Inalienability and emphatic pronominal possession in European and Mediterranean languages

Morphosyntactic strategies and historical changes

Gianguido Manzelli

Although possession is one of the most widely studied topics in linguistics, this is not true of pronominal possession and emphatic pronominal possession. The present paper is a survey of the different morphosyntactic strategies adopted to express both emphatic pronominal possession and inalienability in a representative sample of European and Mediterranean languages. The primary focus is to investigate possible connections among areally contiguous languages which belong to different groups and families and are often typologically distant.

1. Introduction

Possession in general is a favourite topic in linguistic typology (e.g. Ivanov 1989; Heine 1997; Baron, Herslund and Sørensen 2001; Pamies 2002), especially as regards nominal possessors (e.g. Koptjevskaja-Tamm 2001; Koptjevskaja-Tamm 2003). A less studied issue consists of possessive constructions with pronominal possessor (e.g. Manzelli 1990; Hölker 1996; Grassi, Sobrero and Telmon 1997: 122–125; Rijkhoff 2001: 196–200;[1] Stolz and Gorsemann 2002), although there is much interest in inalienable possession (e.g. Diem 1986; Chappell and McGregor 1996; Velázquez-Castillo 1996; Pérez-Leroux, Schmitt and Munn 2004; Stolz 2004) and in kinship terms (e.g. Hölker 1998, Dahl and Koptjevskaja-Tamm 2001).

Some studies have a theory-centric approach, e.g. Cardinaletti and Starke (1995) have a generative point of view in their interesting proposal for classifying possessives into clitic, weak and strong pronouns. In this paper I shall examine empirical data drawn from a sample of European and Mediterranean languages in

1. "Attributive possessor pronouns" (Rijkhoff 2001: 196).

order to highlight what is common and what is different in these languages as far as inalienable and emphatic possession is concerned.

2. Why inalienability and emphasis together?

Inalienable possession and emphatic possession can be considered together because there are many instances in which the same morphosyntactic means are used either to encode emphasis on possessor or inalienability. One of these instances is the double marking of the possessor (see below, 11.), which in Colloquial Modern Greek can characterize a kinship term whereas in Hungarian it can only express a strong emphasis on the possessor, cf.:

Modern Greek

Eména	*o giós* ***mou***	*eínai pénte mēnṓn*	'my son is five months old'
Pro.Acc	Art N Poss		

Hungarian

Az én	*fiam*	*öt hónapos*	'*my* son is five months old'
Art Pro.Nom	N-Poss		

The Modern Greek sentence is drawn from Stanitsas (1989: 59), who claims that the use of the accusative of the personal pronoun (*eména* 'me') before a possessee (a noun with a postposed clitic *mou* 'my'[2]) is a "pléonasme de la langue familière", cf. Macedonian *majka* ***mi moja*** 'my mummy' (Koneski 1954: 100) or French ***ma*** *petite maman à moi* 'my mummy' (Manzelli 1990: 68 and 81, Table 15). On the contrary, in Hungarian the nominative of the personal pronoun (*én* 'I') before a possessee (with possessive suffix *-am* 'my') can only convey a strong contrastive value ('*mine*, not yours'), cf. Manzelli (1990: 68 and 80, Table 13).

3. Words, clitics and affixes

From a morphological viewpoint pronominal possessors can be expressed by full words (PossW), mainly inflected forms of personal pronouns, clitics (PossC), short

2. The postnominal clitic *mou* (an old unstressed form of the genitive of the first person personal pronoun) 'my' occurred already in the Greek koine (3rd c. BC), e.g. *ho patḗr* ***mou*** (Art N Poss) 'my father' in place of the prenominal possessive adjective *emós* 'my' (still preserved in some modern Pontic dialects), e.g. *ho* ***emòs*** *patḗr* (Art Poss N) 'my father': postnominal position with the definite article had an emphatic value, e.g. *ho patèr ho* ***emós*** (Art N Art Poss) '*my* father' (see Schwyzer and Debrunner 1950: 201–202).

or weak forms of the preceding, and affixes (PossA). In the majority of cases possessive affixes are postnominal, i.e. suffixes, but North West Caucasian languages have possessive prefixes (see 3.2.). Cf. the following examples:

Russian	***mojá*** *mat'*	(PossW N)	'my mother'	
Latvian	***mans*** *tēvs*	(PossW N)	'my father'	
West Frisian	***ús*** *heit*	(PossW N)	'my father'	
Dutch	***mijn*** *moeder*	(PossW N)	'my mother'	
German	***meine*** *Mutter*	(PossW N)	'my mother'	
French	***ma*** *maison*	(PossC N)	'my house'	
Badiot	***mia*** *uma*	(PossW N)	'my mother'	(or PossC N ?)
Gardenese[3]	***mi*** *oma*	(PossC N)	'my mother'	
Neapolitan	*pate**mo***	(N-PossC)	'my father'	(Hölker 1998: 574)
Sicilian	***ma*** *patri*	(PossC N)	'my father'	(Lehmann 1998: 32)
Romanian	*cartea* ***mea***	(N-Art PossW)	'my book'	
Romanian	*tata-**mi***	(N-PossC)	'my father'	
Modern Greek	*to paidáki* ***mou***	(Art N PossC)	'my child'	
Macedonian Greek	*tou pidoúdi**m***[4]	(Art N-PossA)	'my child'	
Cappadocian Greek	*gardáši**m***[5]	(N-PossA)	'my brother'	(Janse 2004: 16)
Lovari (Romani)[6]	***muro*** *dad*	(PossW N)	'my father'	(Papp 2002: 12)
Hungarian	*a ház**am***	(Art N-PossA)	'my house'	
Estonian	***mun*** *maja*	(PossC N)	'my house'	

It must be added that it is not always an easy task to distinguish between full words and clitics (and sometimes between clitics and real suffixes).

3.1 Possessive suffixes

In *The World Atlas of Language Structures* Dryer (2005: 234–237) deals with pronominal possessive affixes and in the linguistic map of Europe (Dryer 2005: 236) Breton appears to have possessive suffixes like Hungarian and the other Finno-Ugric languages and like Turkic languages. It seems to me that this tenet can be proven false in that Breton has prenominal (clitic) possessive pronouns (*ma* 'my', *da* 'your', *e* 'his' etc., cf. ***ma*** *zad* 'my father', ***da*** *dad* 'your father', ***on*** *tad* 'our father' etc.) and possession can be strengthened ("renforcée") either by postnominal personal

3. Badiot, spoken in Badia Valley, and Gardenese, spoken in Gardena Valley (Bolzano/Bozen province, Alto Adige/Südtirol, Italy), are Ladin dialects (of so – called central Rhaeto-Romance).

4. Athanasios Andoulas's (Salonika) personal communication.

5. South Cappadocian dialect of Ulağaç: *gardáš* 'brother' is a borrowing from Turkish *kardaş* 'brother' (Janse 2004: 16).

6. Lovari is a Romani (Gypsy) dialect spoken in Hungary.

pronouns (*me* 'I', *te* 'you', *eñ* 'he' etc.) or by the preposition *da* 'to' + personal suffixes, here ProA ("préposition conjuguée": *din* 'to me', *dit* 'to you', *dezañ* 'to him' etc., Trépos 1994: 195), with a double marking of the possessor, cf. the following examples drawn from Morvannou (1978: 58) and Trépos (1994: 124):

Breton
***ma** zud*[7] *-me, kenavo* (PossC N Pro.Nom) 'my parents, goodbye'
***ma** buoh din a zo klañv* (PossC N Prep-ProA) 'my cow is ill'

As regards emphasis, these constructions seem to be ambiguous: in the first case the double marking of the possessor can be considered a matter of redundancy expressing affection, whereas in the second case emphasis cannot be excluded. Possessive suffixes do exist in Breton but only for the first and second singular person. They are in fact reduced forms ("non-syllabiques") of prenominal possessive pronouns and have a very restricted distribution, cf. after the conjunction *ha* 'and' (from Trépos 1994: 123):

Breton
***ma** hoar ha **'m** breur* = ***ma** hoar ha **ma** breur* 'my sister and my brother'

This is absolutely different from the use of possessive suffixes in Hungarian. If we compare the double marking of the possessor in Breton (from Trépos 1994: 121) and in Hungarian (see, e.g. Rijkhoff 2001: 197; Knittel 1998: 88–89; Ihsane 2001: 49) the difference is apparent:

Breton
***da** dad-te* [± emph] (PossC N Pro.Nom) 'your father'

Hungarian
a te apád [+ emph] (Art Pro.Nom N-PossA) '*your* father'

Also Lappish (Sami) is recorded in the map of Europe in Dryer (2005: 236) as a language characterized by possessive suffixes. This is, however, only partially true. In Norwegian Lappish (spoken in Norway, Sweden and Finland) the pronominal possessor is mainly expressed by the genitive of personal pronouns in prenominal position. Possessive suffixes express coreference with the subject. Only in case of inalienability (kinship terms and words like *olmmái* 'mate' or *ustit* 'friend') can possessive suffixes of first and second person occur more freely. Double marking of the possessor also occurs, cf. (from Nickel 1990: 98 and 109):

Norwegian Lappish
dat lea mu girji (Pro.Gen N) 'that is my book'
mun lean áhčistan ožžon skeaŋkka (N-Loc-PossA) 'I have got a present from my father'

---

7. Breton *tud* means here 'father and mother', but basically its meaning is 'people' (French *gens*).

gos áhččát lea?	(N-PossA)	'where is your father?'
váldde <u>du</u> biergasiiddát! [+ emph]	(<u>Pro.Gen</u> N-PossA)	'take *your* things!'

3.2 Possessive prefixes

Among the European languages only North-West Caucasian languages[8] seem to have real possessive prefixes, whereas North-East Caucasian (Nakh-Daghestanian) languages have prenominal genitive personal pronouns,[9] i.e. full words or clitics. Adyghe, a West Circassian (North West Caucasian) language, has two complete sets (combining 6 persons and 2 numbers) of possessive prefixes with a distinction between alienable possession (Russian *otčuždaemaja prinadležnost'*) and inalienable possession (Russian *neotčuždaemaja prinadležnost'*), cf. (from Kumaxov 1999: 96):

Adyghe

	[+ alien]	[– alien]	
1SG	*si-*	*s(y)-, s(a)-*	'my'
2SG	*ui-*	*u(y)-, u(a)-, p-, pI-*[10]	'your'
3SG	*jy-*	*y-*	'his/her'
1PL	*di-*	*t(y)-, t(a)-, tI-*	'our'
2PL	*š"ui-*	*š"u(y)-, š"u(a)-*	'your'
3PL	*ji-*	*a-*	'their'

Thus a distinction is made between body parts and kinship terms on the one hand and all the other possessees on the other, cf. (from Kumaxov 1989: 41 and 321):

Adyghe

š"x'ė	'head'	→ *sš"x'ė*	[– alien]	'my head'
unė	'house'	→ *siun*	[+ alien]	'my house'

8. In Manzelli (1990), where I sought to describe possessive adnominal modifiers "in all European languages" (and my list was strongly criticized), I did not include Caucasian languages but in the Eurotyp research project North-West and North-East (Nakh-Daghestanian) Caucasian languages were considered European languages.

9. This is not always the case, e.g. in Tsakhur, Tsakh dialect, *jišda balkan* 'our horse' (Ibragimov 1990: 93) the possessive pronoun *jišda* 'our' is made of a prefix *ji-* (Ibragimov 1990: 104), a *š*-morph connected with personal pronoun *ši* 'we', and a class concord morph *–da* (*balkan* 'horse' belongs to the 3rd class).

10. I transliterated Adyghe from Cyrillic script: capital letter *I* (Russian *paločka* 'small stick') involves glottalization from a phonetic point of view.

This distinction is unknown to Chechen (a Nakh or North-Central Caucasian language), cf. (from Dešerieva 1999: 178):

Chechen	
x'an *ku'g*	'your hand'
x'an *kniga*	'your book'

3.3 Zero morphs

Inalienable possession can be characterized by a zero morph in the case of first person possessor, a fact that can be considered trivial, cf. English *Father's house* = ***my*** *father's house*, cf. Chuvash (a Turkic language spoken in the Volga basin, Benzing 1959: 726, Krueger 1961: 113, Andreev 1966: 488, Andreev 1997: 484–485, Clark 1998: 437–438) and Corsican (from Durand 2003: 210), with an optional possessive, and Berber (Kabyle of Algeria) in which first person possessor cannot be expressed with kinship terms (from Sahki 1998: 68–69 and 111):[11]

Chuvash				
atte	(N)	'my father'	= *atte**m***	(N-PossA)
*a**śu***	(N-PossA)	'your father'		
*a**śšě***	(N-PossA)	'his father'		
Corsican				
babbu	(N)	'my father'	= ***me*** *babbu*	(PossC N)
*babbi**tu***	(N-PossC)	'your father'	= ***to*** *babbu*	(PossC N)
u babbu	(Art N)	'his father'	= *u* ***so*** *babbu*	(Art PossC N)
Kabyle				
baba	(N)	'my father'		
*baba**k***	(N-PossA)	'your (m.) father'		
*baba**m***	(N-PossA)	'your (f.) father'		
*baba**s***	(N-PossA)	'his father'		

In Berber nouns (except kinship terms) require a first person possessor expressed mainly by a preposition + a possessive suffix, e.g. (Tamazight) *en-u* or (Kabyle) *in-u* 'my' from the preposition *en* 'of' + first person personal suffix *–u*/*-w*, or *iw* 'my' from the preposition *ei* 'for' + *-u*/*-w*, cf. (from Sahki 1998: 110):

Kabyle		
a xxam ***in-u***	(Art N Prep-ProA)	'my house'
a xxam ***iw***	(Art N Prep-ProA)	'my house'

11. Durand (1998: 68) gives examples of Moroccan Berber dialects where first person possessor can be expressed even with kinship terms.

A zero morph for the first person singular ("first-person singular enclitic", Thackston 1999: 19) occured also in Syriac (Aramaic), e.g. *bayt* 'my house' (from *baytā* 'house, home'), but it was not restricted to inalienable possession and it was the result of a merely phonetic accident with complete loss of a former suffix. Neo-Aramaic languages have restored a first person suffix. Thus, among the Eastern Neo-Aramaic languages, Turoyo (Tur Abdin, Turkey) has *emi* 'my mother' (from *emo* 'mother') and Hertevin (Siirt province, Turkey) *beti* 'my house' (from *beta* 'house'), whereas Western Neo-Aramaic Ma'lula (spoken near Damascus, Syria) has both *tarb* (with zero morph) and *tarbi* 'my way, my path' (from *tarba* 'way, path'), see Jastrow (1997: 337 and 355).[12]

4. Word Order

In Manzelli (1990: 71, 75 and 84–90. Table 16) I claimed that Poss + N (Poss = pronominal possessive modifier) is a dominant word order in European languages, while N + Poss is marginal, regional or substandard. If we include the Mediterranean area, there is no doubt that a N + Poss word order plays a more crucial role. Word order can be strategically used to turn an unemphatic pronominal possessor into an emphatic one, for instance in Macedonian ("mise en relief", Foulon-Hristova 1998: 285):

Macedonian			
***moja**ta tatkovina*	[– emph]	(PossW-Art N)	'my country'
bratučetkata ***moja***	[+ emph]	(N-Art PossW)	'*my* cousin'

5. Focalization, contrastive emphasis and vocative

Possessive pronouns can vary according to pragmatic needs. Bulgarian has short and long forms of possessives which have a different function. Short forms are unemphatic and the absence of a postnominal definite article means inalienability (but the presence of a definite article is normal with some kinship terms), cf. (from Maslov 1981: 301; Holman and Kovatcheva 1993: 48):

Bulgarian			
baštá ***mi***	[– alien]	(N PossC)	'my father'
mŭžǘt ***mi***	[– alien]	(N-Art PossC)	'my husband'
žená ***mi***	[– alien]	(N PossC)	'my wife'
sinǘt ***mi***	[– alien]	(N-Art PossC)	'my son'

12. Cf. also Turoyo *wăxt* ***diδi*** 'my time' with a PossW in which *diδ-* is called by Jastrow (1997: 355) "a special morpheme expressing relation".

Long forms are used for focalization, cf. (from Maslov 1981: 307):

Bulgarian

kakvó ti pádna?		'what has fallen down?'
šápkata ***mi*** *pádna*	(N-Art PossC)	'my *cap* has fallen down'
čijá šápka pádna?		'whose cap has fallen down?'
mója*ta šápka pádna*	(PossW-Art N)	'*my* cap has fallen down'

Long forms are used also for contrastive emphasis, cf. (from Holman and Kovatcheva 1993: 142):

Bulgarian
Mó*ite kúfari sa golémi,* ***tvó****ite sa málki* '*my* cases are big, *yours* are small'
(PossW-Art N)

Finally long forms are used in vocative phrases, cf. (from Ghinina, Nikolova and Sakazova 1970: 139):

Bulgarian
Obíčam te, ***móe*** *otéčestvo* (PossW N) 'I love you, my country'

In Colloquial Welsh the full form *fy* 'my' is reduced to *'y* followed by nasal mutation and the personal pronoun *i* 'I, me' is put after the possessee (double marking of the possessor), but with kinship terms of close relationship only for emphasis; with any other noun the clitic pronoun *i* can be stressed for emphasis, whereas prenominal *'y* can be elided, especially after a vowel, cf. the following examples with *pensil* 'pencil' and *tad* 'father' (from Rhys Jones 1977: 88–89):

Colloquial Welsh

'y mhensil ***i***		'my pencil'
'mhensil ***i*** *yw hwn?*		'is this my pencil?'
'y 'mhensil ['] ***i*** *yw hwn*		'this is *my* pencil'
'y nhad > 'nhad	[– emph]	'my father'
'nhad!	[+ emph]	'Father! Daddy!'
'y nhad ***i*** *> 'nhad* ***i***	[+ emph]	'*my* father'

As for vocative phrases in Scandinavian languages, the use of possessive pronouns with terms of abuse is quite peculiar (Haugen 1976: 83):

Icelandic	*bjáninn* ***þinn!***	
Faroese	***tín*** *býttlingur!*	
Danish	***din*** *idiot!*	'you idiot!'

In Portuguese the vocative form is not different from the neutral form, except that the latter may have an optional definite article, in contrast with word order of Italian which does not admit a definite article before a singular inalienable possessee, cf.:

Portuguese

(*a*) ***minha*** *filha*	[– emph]	'my daughter'
minha *filha!*	[+ emph]	'my daughter!'

Italian
mia figlia [– emph] 'my daughter'
*figlia **mia**!* [+ emph] 'my daughter!'

A postnominal emphatic possessive is however admitted also in Portuguese, cf. (from Cunha and Lindley Cintra 1989: 229):

Portuguese
*tu és digna filha **minha**!* [+ emph] 'you are my worthy daughter!'

In Spanish, which has unemphatic clitic prenominal possessives, a postnominal accented possessive is normal in vocative phrases with some exceptions:[13]

Spanish

*Juan es **mi** amigo*	[– emph]	(Poss C N)	'Juan is my friend'
*Juan, ¡amigo **mío**!*	[+ emph]	(N PossW)	'Juan, my friend!'
*Sí, ¡**mi** coronel!*	[+ emph]	(PossC N)	'Yes sir, my colonel!'

In Catalan clitic prenominal possessives are restricted to inalienable nouns with singular possessor, cf. (from Yates 1975: 68, 291 and 292):

Catalan
*porto el **meu** pasaport a la butxaca* [– emph] 'I am carrying my passport in my pocket' (Art PossW N)
***ma** mare i **ton** avi eren cosins* (PossC N) [– alien] 'my mother and your grandfather were cousins'
*tot això ès teu, fill **meu*** (N PossW) [+ emph] 'all this is yours, my son'

Compare with the slightly different variety of Catalan spoken in the Balearic Islands (from Radatz 1999: 89 and 108):

Majorca Catalan

*es **meu** homo*	[– emph]	(Art PossW N)	'my husband'
*Dèu **meu**!*	[+ emph]	(N PossW)	'my God!'
***mum**pare!*	[+ emph, – alien]	(PossC-N)	'Daddy!'

In a West Friulan dialect like Folpo (spoken in Cordenons, Pordenone province, Italy), possessives in vocative phrases vary both in position and in form (from Cozzarin 2005: 303):

Folpo (West Friulan)

***me'** mari*	[– emph]	(PossC N)	'my mother'
*mari **méc**!*	[+ emph]	(N PossW)	'my mother!'

13. In Latin postnominal accented possessives were unemphatic, whereas a prenominal position meant emphasis on the possessor. Clitic forms were used only in vocative phrases both before and after nouns, cf. in Plautus *ō **mī** ere* and *ere **mī*** 'my master!' (see Lehmann 2005).

6. Alienability vs. inalienability

From a syntactic viewpoint, inalienability plays a much more relevant role than is usually presumed in European and Mediterranean languages. Swedish dialects (on the basis of Pamp 1978: 32)[14] show an interesting case of different word order based on the [± alienable] feature:

	'my father'		'my house'	
Standard Swedish	***min** far* [– alien] (PossW N)	= ***mitt** hus* [+ alien]	(PossW N)
North Swedish	*far **min*** [– alien] (N PossW)	= *huset **mitt*** [+ alien]	(N-Art PossW)
South Swedish	*far **min*** [– alien] (N PossW)	≠ ***mitt** hus* [+ alien]	(PossW N)

Subtle nuances can be observed in regional varieties of Romance languages. In Asturian-Leonese (North West of Spain) possessive clitics can have prenominal or postnominal position and in the second case the preposition *de* 'of' may be inserted before the possessive clitic, which thus becomes a stressed pronoun, cf. in Leonese (from an Internet site, see Leonese 2006):

Leonese		
*el **tou** fiyu*	[– alien] (Art PossC N)	'your son'
*fiyu **tou***	[– alien] (N PossC)	'your son'
*fiyu **de tou***	[– alien] (N Prep PossW)	'your son'

Some native speakers of Asturian claim that a different word order and a different use of the definite article depend on the degree of kinship, cf. (from an Internet site, see Andrés 2006):

Asturian			
ascending kinship	***mio** pa*	'my father'	(PossC N)
descending kinship	*el **mio** fiu*	'my son'	(Art PossC N)
same level kinship	*el **mio** hermano*	'my brother'	(Art PossC N)
	***mio** hermano*	'my brother'	(PossC N)

As for kinship terms, Albanian has a different syntactic behaviour as far as word order is concerned (postnominal possessive pronouns require nouns with final article), depending on specific lexical items, cf. (from Buchholz and Fiedler 1987: 289):

Albanian				
frequency	example	PossC N	N-Art PossC	
equal	*gjyshe* 'granny'	***ime** gjyshe*	*gjusha **ime***	'my grandmother'

14. I have deduced the schema from what Pamp (1978: 32) says about North Swedish *boka **min*** (N-Art PossW) = Standard Swedish ***min** bok* (PossW N) 'my book' and about kinship terms (*släktskapsord*) in South Swedish, as in *pågen **min*** (N-Art PossW) = Standard Swedish ***min** pojke, **min** son* (PossW N) 'my child, my son'.

prevailing[15]	*atë*	'father'	***im*** *atë*	*ati* ***im***	'my father'
exclusive	*më*	'mother'	***ime*** *më*	—	'my mother'
rare	*baba*	'father'	(***im*** *baba*)	*babai* ***im***	'my father'

7. Semitic languages (Arabic and Hebrew)

7.1 Arabic dialects

On the Southern coast of the Mediterranean Sea Arabic dialects (languages) present characteristics unknown to Coranic or Classical Arabic, which is the basis of Modern Standard Arabic, cf. what Kaye and Rosenhouse (1997: 299) claim:

> Most of the dialects developed analytical possessive particles from various nouns, which led to a functional distinction between the construct state and phrases with the genitival exponent. Most dialects prefer the construct state with inherent possession of body and kinship members; [...] and lexicalized compounds; [...] The more "external" or "temporary" possession is indicated by the genitival exponent. This is useful to: (1) control each noun for definiteness, ***emphasis*** [bold is mine], adding adjectives or a personal pronoun to the whole compound or any of its parts; (2) form genitival phrases with more than two words (the "default" in a construct state); and (3) use the construct state with words which have irregular syllabic structure often due to their foreign origin.

I collected data from various sources (not quoted here) to show the different constructions that can be found in modern Arabic dialects. When considering the following example, it must be taken into account that words for 'house' can be ambiguous as far as alienability vs. inalienability is concerned because an emotional content can be added to them:

Arabic dialect (language)	N-PossA 'my house'	Art-N PossW 'my house'
Classical Arabic	*baytī* (*dārī*)	—
Moroccan Arabic	*dāri*	*əd-dār* ***dyāli*** *əd-dār* ***mtā'i***
Western Algerian Arabic	*dāri*	*əd-dār* ***dyāli***
Eastern Algerian Arabic	*dāri*	*əd-dār* ***mtā'i***
Tunisian Arabic	*dāri*	*ed-dār* ***əmtā'i***
Maltese	*dari*	*id-dar* ***tiegħi***

15. Here "prevailing frequency" means that the construction with a prenominal possessive pronoun is the dominant word order. Below "exclusive frequency" means that PossC N is the only word order admitted, whereas "rare frequency" means that prenominal position occurs quite rarely.

Lybian Arabic	*ḥōši*	*el-ḥōš* ***mtā'i***
Egyptian Arabic	*bēti*	*il-bēt* ***bitā'i***
Palestinian Arabic	*bēti*	—
Syrian Arabic	*bēti*	—

Possessive words (PossW) are made of a 'particle' (see Fischer and Jastrow 1980: 93–99, 220 and 259) + a possessive suffix.

Emphasis on possession can be expressed by a postnominal personal pronoun as in Moroccan Arabic, cf. (from Ben Alaya 1999: 31):[16]

Moroccan Arabic

l-wālida	***dyālna***	*ḥnāya*	*māši*	*hōn!*	[+ emph]
Art-N	PossW	Pro.Nom	Neg	Adv	
the-mother	our(s)	we[17]	not	here	

'*our* mother is not here!'

This is quite different from the topicalization (*mubtada'*) in Classical Arabic, with prenominal personal pronoun, cf.:

Classical Arabic

naḥnu,	*wālidatu-**nā***	*hunā*	'as for us, our mother is here'
Pro.Nom	N-PossA	Adv	
we	mother-our	here	

As for Maltese, the matching of construct state with inalienable possession vs. possessive pronouns (preposition *ta'* + enclitic pronouns[18]) with alienable possession is exemplified by Borg and Azzopardi-Alexander (1997: 113) in the following sentences where Maltese *koxxa* (from Italian *coscia* 'thigh', Aquilina 1987, I: 694) means either '(one's own) thigh' [– alien] or 'drumstick' [+ alien]:

Maltese

kemm	*hi*	*tajba*	*koxxti*		[– alien] (N-PossA)
how much	she	good	thigh-my		

'how sound is my thigh!'

kemm	*hi*	*tajba*	*l-koxxa*	***tiegħi***	[+ alien] (Art-N PossW)
how much	she	good	the-thigh	mine	

'how tasty is this leg'

16. "Oft wird das Besitzverhältnis betont, indem das entsprechende persönliche Fürwort wiederholt wird. Das ist eine sehr geläufige und beliebte Spielart der Umgangssprache" (Ben Alaya 1999: 31).

17. Arabic personal pronouns as full words have only the nominative form.

18. The definitions of *ta'* as a preposition and of *–i* 'my', *-ek* 'your' etc. as enclitic pronouns are by Borg and Azzopardi-Alexander (1997: 206): I consider *–i* 'my', *-ek* 'your' etc. as suffixes (PossA).

According to Mitchell (1956: 25, n. 1) Egyptian Arabic distinguishes two uses of *sitt* 'lady' as a kinship term:

Egyptian Arabic		
sítti	[– alien] (N-PossA)	'my grandmother'
'is-sittĭ ***bta'ti***	[+ alien] (Art-N PossW)	'my wife'

According to Nallino (1939: 34) the use of *bitā'* is obligatory with foreign words as in *el-bālṭū bitā'ī* 'my overcoat' (cf. French *paletot* 'overcoat' via Italian *paltò* or Turkish *palto* 'overcoat, coat'). As in Moroccan Arabic, emphasis is obtained by a postnominal personal pronoun as exemplified by Nallino (1939: 36):

Egyptian Arabic				
dā	*suġlī*	*anā*	[+ emph]	'this is my own business'
Dem	N-PossA	Pro.Nom		
this	work-my	I		

The use of analytical possessive particles (cf. above Kaye and Rosenhouse 1997: 299) seems to be confined to foreign words in Palestinian and Syrian Arabic, as can be seen in the following Palestinian Arabic examples drawn from Elihai (1985: 261):

Palestinian Arabic		
'emmi	[– alien] (N-PossA)	'my mother'
bēti	[+ alien] (N-PossA)	'my house'
er-rádyo ***tába'i***	[+ alien] (Art-N PossW)	'my radio'

7.2 Hebrew

Quite surprisingly, if we consider its different history, Hebrew had a development similar to Modern Arabic dialects (languages). In Modern Hebrew (Ivrit), especially in colloquial language, the use of the old pronominal suffixes is restricted mainly to kinship terms (Ajxenval'd 1990: 49), as in:

Modern Hebrew		
avi	[– alien] (N-PossA)	'my father'

What is now dominant is the use of *šel* 'of', called *nota genitivi* in Ajxenval'd (1990: 86), with the following possible difference in meaning as far as the construct state is concerned:

Modern Hebrew		
sifri	[– alien] (N-PossA)	'my book (I have written)'
sefer ***šeli***	[+ alien] (N PossW)	'my book (belonging to me)'

The first case can be regarded as a peculiar instance of inalienable possession for obvious reasons: the authorship of a book cannot be sold, at least from an intellectual point of view. However the distinction between inalienability and alienability is neutralized in colloquial speech even with kinship terms (Schwarzwald 2001: 43 and 52):

Modern Hebrew

dodi	[– alien] (N-PossA)	'my uncle'
ha-dod ***šeli***	[– alien] (Art-N PossW)	'my uncle'

The use of a double pronoun is emphatic and more formal (Glinert 1989: 35):

Modern Hebrew

dirata	***šela***	[+ emph] (N-PossA PossW)	'*her* apartment'

From a historical viewpoint the preference for the particle *šel* (*šæl* in Sáenz-Badillos 1993: 173) 'of' is a trait of Rabbinic Hebrew, even though preceded by examples in Biblical Hebrew: it is a reduced form of the relative pronoun *'ăšèr* (*'*^{a}*šær* in Sáenz-Badillos 1993: 173) 'that, who, which' + the preposition *le* 'to', cf. Akkadian *àšar* 'where', a grammaticalized form from *àšrum* 'place' (Lancellotti 1996: 115).

8. Emphatic pronouns

Special emphatic possessive (i.e. genitive personal) pronouns occur in Basque (Rebuschi 1995). In Modern Northern Basque when a genitive (personal) pronoun modifies one argument (direct or indirect object) of a predicate and is or is not coreferential with the other argument (subject) a three-way distinction is possible, with a weak (*haren* in the singular), an emphatic (*haren beraren* or simply *beraren*), or a strong (*bere*, reflexive) form, according to Rebuschi (1995: 316–317):

Basque

haurrak$_i$	***haren***$_j$	*anaia*	*jo du*	(weak)	'the child$_i$ has hit his/her$_j$ brother'
haurrak$_i$	***beraren***$_j$	*anaia*	*jo du*	(emphatic)	'the child$_i$ has hit his/her$_j$ brother'
haurrak$_i$	***bere***$_i$	*anaia*	*jo du*	(strong)	'the child$_i$ hit his/her$_i$ brother'

In the first two cases the second argument is someone else's brother, in the third case it is the subject's own brother. Three and a half centuries ago Classical Labourdin Basque (1600–1650 ca.) had complete paradigms (seven combinations of person and number), whereas the distinction is only operative in the third person in Modern Northern Basque (Rebuschi 1995: 320). So, for example, for the first person singular Classical Labourdin could choose among a strong form of the genitive personal pronoun *neure*, a weak form *nire* (the only one surviving), and an emphatic form *neronen* 'my' (Rebuschi 1995: 321).

9. Emphatic particles

Emphatic particles are a common trait of Goidelic languages, cf.:

Irish		
mo *mhac*	[– emph]	'my son'
mo *mhacsa*	[+ emph]	'*my* son'

In Old Irish there were more different forms of the "emphasizing particles" (Thurneysen 1946: 252), varying according to person and number: these forms are connected with Proto-Indo-European **so*, cf. English *she* etc. (MacBain 1911: 298), cf. (from Thurneysen 1946: 277):

Old Irish		
mo béssi-se	[+ emph]	'*my* manners'

10. Lexical emphatic modifiers

Emphasis on possession can be expressed by lexical means in many European and Mediterranean languages belonging to different linguistic families (Indo-European, Finno-Ugric, Turkic):

Kazan Tatar	***üz*** *öjem*	[+ emph]	'my own house'
Finnish	***oma*** *taloni*	[+ emph]	'my own house'
Hungarian	*a* ***saját*** *házam*	[+ emph]	'my own house'
German	***mein eigenes*** *Haus*	[+ emph]	'my own house'
Modern Greek	*to* ***dikó mou*** *spíti*	[+ emph]	'my own house'
Italian	*la* ***mia propria*** *casa*	[+ emph]	'my own house'
Campidanese[19]	*s'idea* ***cosa mia***	[+ emph]	'just *my* idea'

11. Double marking of the possessor[20]

Double marking of the possessor is a well known strategy in quite different languages of the area, but often with different functions. In Spanish (but also in other Romance languages), for instance, double marking is used in third person singular to disambiguate the gender of the possessor:

Spanish			
su *madre de él*	[– emph]	(PossC N Prep Pro)	'his mother'
su *madre de ella*	[– emph]	(PossC N Prep Pro)	'her mother'

19. Corda (1989: 20): Campidanese is a variety of Sardinian spoken in the southern half of Sardinia.

20. Cf. "Doubling of the possessor pronoun" (Rijkhoff 2001: 190).

A similar situation is known in substandard German with the third person, but with an emphatic value (Seiler 1983: 71):

Substandard German

*ihm **sein** Haus*	[+ emph]	(Pro.Dat PossW N)	'*his* house'
*mir **mein** Haus	[+ emph]	(Pro.Dat PossW N)	*'*my* house'

In Finnish double marking is obligatory in the third person when the possessee is a subject. In the first and second person double marking expresses emphasis on the possessor (Lehtinen 1963: 134–135), but possessive suffixes are omitted in Literary Finnish when it is not a matter of real possession (Whitney 1956: 53), whereas in Colloquial Finnish they are preserved only with kinship terms and in set phrases (Leney 1993: 110), cf.:

Finnish

***äitini** on Suomessa*	[– emph]	(N-PossA)	'my mother is in Finland'
*hänen **äitinsä** on Suomessa*	[– emph]	(Pro.Gen N-PossA)	'his/her mother is in Finland'
*tarvitsen sinun **autosi***	[+ emph]	(Pro.Gen N-PossA)	'I need *your* car'
meidän kylän pojat	[– emph]	(Pro.Gen N) [Lit.]	'the boys of our village'
minun kirja	[– emph]	(Pro.Gen N) [Coll.]	'my book'

In Turkish double marking can be used for emphasis, but the difference in the third person is neutralized and in the colloquial speech of some provinces the possessive suffix can be dropped, cf. (from Lewis 2000: 66):

Turkish

*ev**imiz***	[– emph]	(N-PossA)	'our house'
*bizim ev**imiz***	[+ emph]	(Pro.Gen N-PossA)	'*our* house'
bizim ev	[± emph]	(Pro.Gen N) [informal]	'our/*our* house'
*onun ad**ı***	[± emph]	(Pro.Gen N-PossA)	'his/*his* name'
onun ad	[± emph]	(Pro.Gen N) [regional]	'his/*his* name'

Some differences can be shown if we compare Turkish, which is an Oghuz Turkic language, with a Kypchak Turkic language like Bashkir spoken in European Russia near the Southern Ural Mountains, cf. (from Juldašev 1997: 211, Juldašev 1981: 122, and Poppe 1964: 84):

Bashkir

*öjö**böδ***	[– emph]	(N-PossA)	'our house'
mineŋ malaj	[– emph]	(Pro.Gen N)	'my boy'
*byl kül mineŋ haraj**ym***	[– emph]	(Pro.Gen N-PossA)	'this lake [is] my palace'
*at**ym** mineŋ juyaldy*	[+ emph]	(N-PossA Pro.Gen)	'my horse [believe it] got lost'

In Old Turkic or Old Uyghur (since the 8th c. AD), between present-day Mongolia and present-day Xinjiang (Chinese Turkestan), double marking of the possessor was already usual ("gewöhnlich", Gabain 1974: 97), besides simple marking with possessive suffix, whereas the use of genitive personal pronouns without possessive suffixes was an unusual but probably older expression of possession ("ungewöhnliche (frühe?) Ausdruckweise", Gabain 1974: 170), cf.:

Old Turkic		
qanïm	(N-PossA)	'my father'
mäniŋ süm	(Pro.Gen N-PossA)	'my troops'
mäniŋ är	(Pro.Gen N)	'my men'

In the only Mongolic language of Europe, i.e. Kalmuck, spoken near the shores of the Caspian Sea, the situation is similar to Turkic languages, although peculiar semantic nuances do not emerge from the data drawn from Pjurbeev (1997: 79) and Iliškin and Muniev (1977: 747), cf.

Kalmuck		
avym	(N-PossA)	'my uncle'
mini degtr	(Pro.Gen N)	'my book'
mini mörm sääxn	(Pro.Gen N-PossA)	'my horse [is] beautiful'

In Classical Mongolian (16th–19th c. AD) there were no possessive suffixes[21] and the genitive of personal pronouns was used in prenominal and postnominal position with possessive meaning, cf. in *Altan Tobči* (The Golden Button, 17th c.) from Orlovskaja (1984: 215):

Classical Mongolian		
minu arban köbegüdün dotura [...]	(Pro.Gen Num N)	'of my three sons ...'
köbegüni minu Tömüčini [...]	(N Pro.Gen)	'of my son Temüjin ...'

12. Diachronic perspectives: the case of Egyptian

In the preceding paragraphs some historical developments have been touched on when possible, for Greek (see 2.), Romance languages (5., n. 13), Aramaic (3.) and Arabic dialects (7.1.), Hebrew (7.2.), Turkic (11.) and Mongolic (11.) languages. In this paragraph I shall consider Egyptian because it has not been included in the preceding description. Egyptian in its more recent form, i.e. Coptic, is now an extinct language (it was spoken at least up to the 15th–16th c. AD), but it is still used in the Coptic Christian Church, which uses the Bohairic (Northern Coptic) dialect as a liturgical language.

21. But in Classical Mongolian there was a reflexive suffix (the same for all persons), i.e. *-iyan*, *-iyen* after a consonant, *-ban*, *-ben* or *-yan*, *-gen* after a vowel (Grønbech and Krueger 1955: 25).

Middle Egyptian or Classical Egyptian (spoken up to the middle of the 14th c. BC) had possessive suffixes, but other constructions were admitted, cf. (from Gardiner 1957: 39–40, 87 and 88, retranscribed):

Middle Egyptian			
pr-f		(N-PossA)	'his house', 'a house of his'
ţȝy-ỉ[22] *ḥm.t*		(PossW N)	'my wife'
m-ḫt ỉȝw ***n-k-ỉmy***[23]	[+ emph]	(Prep N PossW)	'after thy own old age'

In Late Egyptian or Neo-Egyptian (14th–8th BC) possessive suffixes became out of date and were replaced by prenominal possessive pronouns, cf. (from Korostovtsev 1973: 90 and 97, retranscribed):

Late Egyptian			
pȝy-ỉ *pr*		(PossW N)	'my house'
pȝ pr <u>ỉnk</u>	[+ emph]	(Art N <u>Pro.Nom</u>)	'*my* house (lit. the house I)'

In Demotic Egyptian (since the 7th c. BC up to the first centuries AD) a distinction was made between body parts and other nouns (kinship terms or lexical items such as *rn* 'name') with the old pronominal suffixes and the majority of nouns with prenominal possessive pronouns, cf. (from Bresciani 1978: 33–34):

Demotic Egyptian			
rn-f	[– alien]	(N-PossA)	'his name'
ţȝe-f *ḥm.t*	[+ alien]	(PossW N)	'his wife'

More data are available for Coptic or Christian Egyptian (since the 3rd c. AD), cf. the following examples in Sahidic (Southern Coptic, Classical Coptic) from Till (1961: 28, 30, and 71):

Coptic			
*rō**i***	[– alien]	(N-PossA)	'my mouth'
***pa**eiōt*	[– alien]	(PossC-N)	'my father'
***na**ēi*	[+ alien]	(PossC-N)	'my houses'
***ta**hre <u>anok</u>*	[+ emph]	(PossC-N <u>Pro.Nom</u>)	'*my* food (lit. my food I)'

It goes without saying that the latter construction reminds us of the Egyptian Arabic emphatic possessive noun phrases with postnominal personal pronoun (see 7.1.) and one may wonder whether this fact is due to mere chance (obviously an Egyptian

---

22. On the origin of attributive possessive pronouns from demonstrative pronouns + possessive suffixes in Egyptian see Kasser (1994).

23. Middle Egyptian emphatic *n-k-ỉmy* 'your' [+ emph] seems a compound of the preposition *n* 'of', the second person singular personal (possessive) suffix *-k* and the deictic adverb *ỉmy*, cf. Coptic *ᵉmmau* 'there' (in Gardiner 1957: 88).

substrate cannot be invoked for the analogous Moroccan Arabic emphatic construction, see 7.1.).

13. Conclusion

In this paper I have chosen to describe in detail as thoroughly as possible forms and uses of unemphatic and emphatic possessive attributive pronouns (possessive adjectives in the Romance tradition) in some European and Mediterranean languages. Special regard has been given to the issue of inalienability. Many differences emerge (e.g. emphatic pronouns in Northern Basque or emphatic particles in Goidelic languages) but there is much in common among the languages of the area. Inalienability (mainly concerning kinship terms, sometimes also body parts) is grammaticalized in different ways but it is present in more than half of the (modern) languages taken into account, see Table 1.

Table 1. Inalienability, Double marking, and emphatic double marking

phylum*, family**, group	language	inalienability	double marking	emphatic double marking
IE, Greek	Modern Greek	+ (?)	+	–
U, FU, Ugric	Hungarian	–	+	+
IE, Slavonic	Macedonian	+	+	–
IE, Romance	French	+	+	–
IE, Celtic	Breton	– (?)	+	±
U, FU, Lappic	Norwegian Lappish	+	+	+
NWCauc, Circassian	Adyghe	+	?	?
NECauc, Nakh	Chechen	–	?	?
IE, Germanic	English	+	–	–
Alt, Turk, Chuvash	Chuvash	+	+	±
IE, Romance	Corsican	+	–	–
AA, Ber	Kabyle	+	–	–
IE, Slavonic	Bulgarian	±	–	–
IE, Celtic	Welsh	+	+	+
IE, Romance	Portuguese	–	+	–
IE, Romance	Italian	+	–	–
IE, Romance	Spanish	–	+	–
IE, Romance	Catalan	+	–	–
IE, Romance	Majorca Catalan	+	–	–
IE, Romance	Folpo	+	–	–
IE, Germanic	Standard Swedish	–	–	–
IE, Germanic	North Swedish	+	–	–
IE, Germanic	South Swedish	+	–	–

Table 1. Continued

phylum*, family**, group	language	inalienability	double marking	emphatic double marking
IE, Romance	Leonese	+	?	?
IE, Romance	Asturian	+	?	?
IE, Albanian	Albanian	+	–	–
AA, Sem, Arabian	Moroccan Arabic	±	+	+
AA, Sem, Arabian	Maltese	+	–	–
AA, Sem, Arabian	Egyptian Arabic	+	+	+
AA, Sem, Arabian	Palestinian Arabic	–	?	?
AA, Sem, Hebrew	Modern Hebrew	±	+	+
Basque	Northern Basque	–	–	–
IE, Celtic	Irish	–	–	–
IE, Germanic	Substandard German	–	+	+
U, FU, Balto-Finnic	Colloquial Finnish	+	+	+
Alt, Turk, Oghuz	Turkish	–	+	+
Alt, Turk, Kypchak	Bashkir	–	+	–
Alt, Mong, Western	Kalmuck	–	+	?
AA, Eg	Coptic	+	+	+

* AA = Afro-Asiatic, Alt = Altaic, U = Uralic

** Ber = Berber, Eg = Egyptian, FU = Finno-Ugric, IE = Indo-European, Mong = Mongolic, NECauc = North-East Caucasian, NWCauc = North-West Caucasian, Turk = Turkic

Double marking (doubling) of the possessor is widespread (see Table 1.). Although such a strategy is often confined to colloquial speech and avoided in written language, the similarities are striking.

The Turkic data prove that some constructions have an old history and come from geographic areas distant from Europe and the Mediterranean basin. Some trends, however, like the loss of possessive suffixes (in Finno-Ugric, Turkic and Arabic languages) or postnominal clitics (as happens in Italian dialects), may not be fortuitous but may be evidence of the fact that so many centuries of linguistic cohabitation along the rivers of Europe and on the shores of the Mediterranean Sea have left their mark.

References

Andreev, I.A. 1966. Čuvašskij jazyk. In *Tjurkskie jazyki*, N.A. Baskakov (ed.), 43–65. Moskva: Nauka.

Andreev, I.A. 1997. Čuvašskij jazyk. In *Jazyki mira. Tjurkskie jazyki*, Ė.R. Tenišev, E.A. Poceluevskij, I.V. Kormušin & A.A. Kibrik (eds), 480–491. Biškek: Kyrgyzstan.

Aquilina, J. 1987–1990. *Maltese-English dictionary*. Vols. 1–2. Malta: Midsea Books.

Ajxenval'd [Aikhenvald], A.J. 1990. *Sovremennyj ivrit*. Moskva: Nauka, Glavnaja redakcija vostočnoj literatury.

Baron, I., Herslund, M. & Sørensen, F. (eds). 2001. *Dimensions of possession*. Amsterdam: John Benjamins.

Ben Alaya, W. 1999. *Marokkanisch-Arabisch. Wort für Wort*. 3rd, edn., Bielefeld: Reise Know-How Verlag Peter Rump.

Benzing, J. 1959. Das Tschuwaschische. In *Philologiae Turcicae Fundamenta*. Vol. 1, J. Deny, K. Grønbech, H. Scheel & Z. Velidi Togan (eds), 695–751. Aquis Mattiacis: apud Franciscum Steiner.

Borg, A. & Azzopardi-Alexander, M. 1997. *Maltese*. London: Routledge.

Bresciani, E. 1978. *Nozioni elementari di grammatica demotica*. Milano: Cisalpino-Goliardica.

Buchholz, O. & Fiedler, W. 1987. *Albanische Grammatik*. Leipzig: VEB Verlag Enzyklopädie.

Cardinaletti, A. & Starke, M. 1995. The typology of structural deficiency: On the three grammatical classes. *FAS Papers in Linguistics* 1: 1–55.

Chappell, H. & McGregor, W. (eds). 1996. *The grammar of inalienability. A typological perspective on body part terms and the part-whole relation*. Berlin: Mouton de Gruyter.

Clark, L. 1998. Chuvash. *The Turkic Languages*. L. Johanson & É.Á. Csató (eds), 434–452. London: Routledge.

Corda, F. 1989. *Saggio di grammatica campidanese*. Sala Bolognese (BO): Arnaldo Forni.

Cozzarin, R. 2005. *Vocabolariu par Cordenòns. Vocabolario e grammatica della parlata di Cordenòns*. Pordenone: Lucaprint.

Cunha, C. & Lindley Cintra, L.F. 1985. *Breve Gramática do Português Contemporâneo*. Lisboa: João Sá da Costa.

Dahl, Ö. & Koptjevskaja-Tamm, M. 2001. Kinship in grammar. In *Dimensions of possession*, I. Baron, M. Herslund & F. Sørensen (eds), 201–225, Amsterdam: John Benjamins.

Dešerieva, T.I. 1999. Čečenskij jazyk. In *Jazyki mira: kavkazskie jazyki*, M.E. Alekseev, G.A. Klimov, S.A. Starostin & Ja.G. Testelec (eds), 173–186. Moskva: Academia.

Diem, W. 1986. Alienable und inalienable Possession im Semitischen. *Zeitschrift der Deutschen Morgenländischen Gesellschaft* 136(2): 227–291.

Dryer, M.S. 2005. Position of pronominal possessive affixes. In *The World Atlas of Language Structures*, M. Haspelmath, M.S. Dryer, D. Gil & B. Comrie (eds), with the collaboration of H.-J. Bibiko, H. Jung & C. Schmidt, 234–237. Oxford: OUP.

Durand, O. 1998. *Lineamenti di lingua berbera. Varietà* tamazight *del Marocco centrale*, Roma: Università degli Studi La Sapienza.

Durand, O. 2003. *La lingua còrsa. Una lotta per la lingua*. Brescia: Paideia.

Elihai, Y. 1985. *Dictionnaire de l'arabe parlé palestinien. Français-Arabe*, Paris: Klincksieck.

Fischer, W. & Jastrow, O. (eds). 1980. *Handbuch der arabischen Dialekte*. Mit Beiträgen von P. Behnstedt, H. Grotzfeld, B. Ingham, A. Sabuni, P. Schabert, H.-R. Singer, L. Tsotskhadze & M. Woidisch. Wiesbaden: Otto Harrassowitz.

Foulon-Hristova, J. 1998. *Grammaire pratique du macédonien*, Préface d'Aleksa Poposki, Paris: Langues & Mondes-L'Asiathèque.

Gabain, A. von. 1974. *Alttürkische Grammatik*. 3rd edn., Wiesbaden: Otto Harrassowitz.

Gardiner, Sir A. 1957. *Egyptian grammar. Being an introduction to the study of hieroglyphs*. 3rd edn., revised. Oxford: Griffith Institute, Ashmolean Museum (repr. 1982).

Ghinina [Ginina], S.C., Nikolova, C.N. & Sakazova [Sakŭzova], L.A. 1970. *Manuale di lingua bulgara per stranieri*. Sofia: Nauka y izkustvo.

Glinert, L. 1989. *The grammar of Modern Hebrew*. Cambridge: CUP.

Grassi, C., Sobrero, A. & Telmon, T. 1997. *Fondamenti di dialettologia italiana*. Roma: Laterza.

Grønbech, K. & Krueger, J.R. 1955. *An introduction to Classical (literary) Mongolian. Introduction, grammar, reader, glossary*. Wiesbaden: Otto Harrassowitz.

Haugen, E. 1976. *The Scandinavian languages. An introduction to their history*. London: Faber and Faber.

Heine, B. 1997. *Possession. Cognitive sources, forces, and grammaticalization*. Cambridge: CUP.

Hölker, K. 1996. *Die Possessive des Italienischen*. Münster: Lit-Verlag.

Hölker, K. 1998. Un caso di delocutività: l'assenza dell'articolo davanti al possessivo con nome di parentela in italiano (e altre lingue romanze). In *Sintassi storica. Atti del XXX Congresso Internazionale della Società di Linguistica Italiana, Pavia 26–28 settembre 1996*, P. Ramat & E. Roma (eds), 567–576. Roma: Bulzoni.

Holman, M. & Kovatcheva, M. 1993. *Teach yourself Bulgarian. A complete course for beginners*. London: Hodder and Stoughton.

Ibragimov, G.X. 1990. *Caxurskij jazyk*. Moskva: Nauka.

Ihsane, T. 2000. Three types of possessive modifiers. *Generative Grammar in Geneva* 1: 21–54.

Iliškin, I.K. & Muniev, B.D. 1977. Kratkij grammatičeskij očerk kalmyckogo jazyka. In *Kalmycko-russkij slovar'*, B.D. Muniev (ed.), 727–764. Moskva: Russkij jazyk.

Ivanov, V.V. (ed.). 1989. *Kategorija possessivnosti v slavjanskix i balkanskix jazykax*, Moskva: Nauka.

Janse, M. 2004. Animacy, definiteness, and case in Cappadocian and other Asia Minor Greek dialects. *Journal of Greek Linguistics* 5: 3–26.

Jastrow, O. 1997. The Neo-Aramaic languages. In *The Semitic languages*, R. Hetzron (ed.), 334–377. London: Routledge.

Juldašev, A.A. (ed.). 1981. *Grammatika sovremennogo baškirskogo literaturnogo jazyka*. Moskva: Nauka.

Juldašev, A.A. 1997. Baškirskij jazyk. In *Jazyki mira: Tjurkskie jazyki*, Ė.R. Tenišev, E.A. Poceluvskij, I.V. Kormušin & A.A. Kibrik (eds), 206–216. Biškek: Kyrgyzstan.

Kasser, R. 1994. Démonstratifs et possessifs en copte. *Bulletin de l'Institut Français d'Archéologie Orientale* 94: 287–301.

Kaye, A.S. & Rosenhouse, J. 1997. Arabic dialects and Maltese. In *The Semitic languages*, R. Hetzron (ed.), 263–311. London: Routledge.

Knittel, M.-L. 1998. Structure morphosyntaxique des syntagmes nominaux possessives du hongrois. In *La grammaire de la possession*, J. Guéron & A. Zribi-Hertz (eds), 83–128. Nanterre: Publidix.

Koneski, B. 1954. *Gramatika na makedonskiot jazik*, Vol. 2. *Za formite a nivnata upotreba*. Skopje: Prosvetno Delo.

Koptjevskaja-Tamm, M. 2001. Adnominal possession. In *Language Typology and Language Universals*, M. Haspelmath, E. König, W. Oesterreicher & W. Raible (eds), Vol. 2, 960–970. Berlin: Walter de Gruyter.

Koptjevskaja-Tamm, M. 2003. Possessive noun phrases in the languages of Europe. In *Noun phrase structure in the languages of Europe*, F. Plank (ed.), 621–722. Berlin: Mouton de Gruyter.

Korostovtsev [Korostovcev], M.A. 1973. *Grammaire du néo-égyptien*. Moscou: Naouka, Departement de Litterature Orientale.

Krueger, J.R. 1961. *Chuvash manual. Introduction, grammar, reader, and vocabulary*. The Hague: Mouton.

Kumaxov, M.A. 1989. *Sravnitel'no-istoričeskaja grammatika adygskix (čerkesskix) jazykov*. Moskva: Nauka.

Kumaxov, M.A. 1999. Adygejskij jazyk. In *Jazyki mira : Kavkazskie jazyki*, M.E. Alekseev, G.A. Klimov, S.A. Starostin & Ja.G. Testelec (eds), 91–102. Moskva: Academia.

Lancellotti, A. 1996. *Grammatica dell'ebraico biblico*. A. Niccacci (ed.). Assisi: Porziuncola.

Lehmann, C. 2005. Sur l'évolution du pronom posséssif. In *Latin et langues romanes. Études linguistiques offertes à József Herman à l'occasion de son 80ème anniversaire*, S. Kiss, L. Mondin & G. Salvi (eds), 37–46. Tübingen: Max Niemeyer.

Lehmann, M. 1998. *Sizilianisch. Wort für Wort.* Bielefeld: Reise Know-How Verlag Peter Rump.

Lehtinen, M. 1963. *Basic course in Finnish.* T.A. Sebeok (ed.). Bloomington IN: Indiana University.

Leney, T. 1993. *Teach yourself Finnish. A complete course for beginners.* London: Hodder and Stoughton.

Lewis, G. 2000. *Turkish grammar.* 2nd edn., Oxford: OUP.

MacBain, A. 1911. *An etymological dictionary of the Gaelic language.* 2nd edn. (repr. Glasgow: Gairm Publications, 1982).

Manzelli, G. 1990. Possessive adnominal modifiers. In *Towards a typology of European languages*, J. Bechert, G. Bernini & C. Buridant (eds), 63–111. Berlin: Mouton de Gruyter.

Maslov, J.S. 1981. *Grammatika bolgarskogo jazyka.* Moskva: Vysšaja škola.

Mitchell, T.F. 1956. *An introduction to Egyptian colloquial Arabic.* Oxford: Clarendon Press (repr. 1978).

Morvannou, F. 1978. *Le breton sans peine.* (Nouvelle Édition). Illustrations de J.L. Gousse, Vol. 1. Chennevières sur Marne: Assimil.

Nallino, C.A. 1939. *L'arabo parlato in Egitto. Grammatica, dialoghi e raccolta di vocaboli.* Ristampa della seconda edizione aggiuntavi una appendice. Milano: Ulrico Hoepli (repr. Milano: Cisalpino-Goliardica, 1983).

Nickel, K.P. 1990. *Samisk grammatikk.* Oslo: Universitetsforlaget.

Orlovskaja, M.N. 1984. *Jazyk "Altan tobči".* Moskva: Nauka, Glavnaja redakcija vostočnoj literatury.

Pamies, A. 2002. Sémantique et grammaire de la possession dans les langues d'Europe. In *Modélisation de l'apprentissage simultané de plusieurs langues apparentées*, É. Castagne (ed.), 67–98. Nice: Université Sophia-Antipolis.

Pamp, B. 1978. *Svenska dialekter.* Stockholm: Natur och Kultur.

Papp, J. 2002. *Sityu romanes! Tanulj cigányul!* Második átdolgozott kiadás. Budapest: Gandhi Nyelvstúdió.

Poppe, N. 1964. *Bashkir manual. Descriptive grammar and texts with a Bashkir-English glossary.* Bloomington IN: Indiana University.

Pérez-Leroux, A.T., Schmitt, C. & Munn, A. 2004. The development of inalienable possession in English and Spanish. In *Romance languages and linguistic theory 2002. Selected papers from 'Going Romance', Groningen, 28–30 November 2002*, R. Bok-Bennema, B. Hollebrandse, B. Kampers-Manhe & P. Sleeman (eds), 199–216. Amsterdam: John Benjamins.

Pjurbeev, G.C. 1997. Kalmyckij jazyk. In *Jazyki mira: Mongol'skie jazyki. Tunguso-man'čžurskie jazyki. Japonskij jazyk. Korejskij jazyk*, V.M. Alpatov, I.V. Kormušin, G.C. Pjurbeev & O.I. Romanova (eds), 73–87. Moskva: Indrik.

Radatz, H.-I. 1999. *Mallorquinisch. Wort für Wort.* 2nd. edn., Bielefeld: Reise Know-How Verlag Peter Rump.

Rebuschi, G. 1995. Weak and strong genitive pronouns in Northern Basque. A diachronic perspective. In *Towards a history of the Basque language*, J.I. Hualde, J.A. Lakarra & R.L. Trask (eds), 313–356. Amsterdam: John Benjamins.

Rijkhoff, J. 2001. *The noun phrase.* Oxford: OUP.

Rhys Jones, T.J. 1977. *Living Welsh* [Teach Yourself Book]. Sevenoaks: Hodder and Stoughton.

Sáenz-Badillos, A. 1993. *A history of the Hebrew language.* Translated by J. Elwolde. Cambridge: CUP (originally published in Spanish as *Historia de la Lengua Hebrea*, Sabadell: Ausa, 1988).

Schwarzwald, O.R. 2001. *Modern Hebrew.* Munich: Lincom.

Schwyzer, E. & Debrunner, A. 1950. *Griechische Grammatik auf der Grundlage von Karl Brugmanns Griechischer Grammatik*, Vol. 1, *Syntax und syntaktische Stilistik*, München: C.H. Beck'sche Verlagsbuchhandlung (repr. 1988).

Seiler, H. 1983. *Possession as an operational dimension of language*. Tübingen: Gunter Narr.

Stanitsas, S. 1989. *J'apprends le grec moderne*. Athènes: J. Cambanas.

Stolz, T. 2004. Possessions in the far north: A glimpse of the alienability correlation in modern Icelandic. In *Dimensionen und Kontinua. Beiträge zu Hansjakob Seilers Universalienforschung*, W. Premper (ed.), 73–96. Bochum: Dr. N. Brockmeyer.

Stolz, T. & Gorsemann, S. 2002. Pronominal possession in Faroese and the parameters of alienability/inalienability. *Studies in Language* 25(3): 557–599.

Thackston, W.M. 1999. *Introduction to Syriac. An elementary grammar with readings from Syriac literature*. Bethesda MD: Ibex.

Thurneysen, R. 1946. *A grammar of Old Irish*. Revised and enlarged edn., with supplement, translated from the German by D.A. Binchy & O. Bergin. Dublin: The Dublin Institute of Advanced Studies (repr. 1980).

Till, Walter C. 1961. *Koptische Dialektgrammatik. Mit Lesestücken und Wörterbuch*. 2nd revised edn. Munich: C.H. Beck.

Trépos, P. 1994. *Grammaire bretonne*. 3rd edn., Brest: Emgleo Breiz, Brud Nevez.

Velázquez-Castillo, M. 1996. *Inalienability, incorporation, and possessor ascension in Guaraní*. Amsterdam: John Benjamins.

Whitney, A.H. 1956. *Teach yourself Finnish*. London: The English Universities Press (repr. 1968).

Yates, A. 1975. *Catalan* [Teach Yourself Books]. Sevenoaks: Hodder and Stoughton.

Internet sites

Andrés, Ramón d'. 2006. = http://asturies.com/paxina.php?paxina = bilordios0610 [last accessed July 2006].

Leonese. 2006 = http://users.servicios.retecal.es/amnuve/lleones/posesivu.htm [last accessed July 2006].

Sahki, Hacène. 1998. *T'utlayt ta mazight. La langue berbère. Analyse et Écriture*. = http://www.tawalt.com/pdf/TUTLAYT_TAMAZIGHT.pdf [last accessed July 2006].

Conjunctive, disjunctive and adversative constructions in Europe

Some areal considerations

Caterina Mauri

The aim of this paper is to show the areal distribution of the semantic and morphosyntactic features characterizing conjunctive, disjunctive and adversative constructions in the languages of Europe. The analysis will be carried out on two levels. On the one hand, I will examine the cross-linguistic variation within Europe, identifying the geographical distribution of each construction type. On the other hand, I will compare European languages with non-European languages, pointing out the features which characterize Europe as an internally homogeneous area. This paper ends with the identification of the 'And-But-Or' area, located in Western-Central Europe, where conjunctive, disjunctive and adversative constructions show the same semantic and morphosyntactic properties.

1. Introduction

This paper examines the variety of morphosyntactic constructions that the languages of Europe use to code the relations of combination ('and'), alternative ('or') and contrast ('but') between two states of affairs. The constructions encoding a relation of combination are called *conjunctive*, those encoding a relation of alternative are called *disjunctive* and, finally, the constructions encoding a relation of contrast are called *adversative* constructions.

Two aims will be pursued: first of all, the areal distribution of the different attested constructions will be shown, revealing a non-random picture of the cross-linguistic variation within Europe; secondly, European data will be compared to non-European ones, in order to identify those features that characterize the languages of Europe as a homogeneous group.

In Section 2 we will examine the definitions of conjunctive, disjunctive and adversative constructions in terms of the semantic relations they convey, and then we will go through some methodological issues, like the parameters of analysis (Sections 2.1 and 2.2) and the language sample adopted (Section 2.3).

In the following three sections, the areal distribution of the features identified in 2.2 will be shown. The same frame will be hold for each of the three construction types, for which separate sections will be made: Section 3 on conjunctive, Section 4 on disjunctive and Section 5 on adversative constructions. In each section, a first subsection will be made where the attested variation within Europe is highlighted, showing by means of maps and examples the areas where languages show similar features (Sections 3.1, 4.1 and 5.1). Then a second subsection will follow, where these data will be compared to non-European data, pointing out those features that can be identified as typically European (sections 3.2, 4.2 and 5.2).

To conclude, in Section 6 we will bring into focus the regularities found in these two parallel levels of analysis. The cross-linguistic variation within Europe shows a non-random distribution and it is possible to identify a smaller linguistic area (the 'And-But-Or Area'), where languages behave in the same way with respect to the encoding of combination, contrast and alternative relations.

2. Basic definitions and parameters of analysis

All the constructions used to express the relations of *combination, alternative* and *contrast* between functionally equivalent states of affairs (henceforth SoAs) will be called *conjunctive, disjunctive* and *adversative constructions*, respectively (Haspelmath 2004: 34; Givón 1990: 491).

By state of affairs is meant here the conception of something that can be the case in some world, and can be evaluated in terms of its existence (Siewierska 1991; Dik 1968). 'State of affairs', as Cristofaro (2003: 25) says, should be understood as a hyperonym for the entities usually called 'events', 'states', 'situations', and the like. The term 'state of affairs' is preferred because it does not characterize the entity in any particular sense, whereas 'event' or 'situation' may convey a dynamic vs. static connotation. Two SoAs are said to be *functionally equivalent* when they have autonomous cognitive profiles (no SoA is presented in the perspective of the other) and they are coded in utterances characterized by the presence of some illocutionary force (cf. Langacker 1987: 484; Verstraete 2005: 613; Cristofaro 2003: 30).

Every conjunctive, disjunctive and adversative construction has been analyzed on the basis of semantic and formal parameters, which will be the object of the next two subsections.

2.1 Semantic distinctions

Further semantic distinctions have been identified for each of the three macro-relations of combination, alternative and contrast, giving rise to what can be considered semantic sub-types of conjunctive, disjunctive and adversative constructions.

Starting from the concept of combination, it is possible to distinguish between *sequential* and *non-sequential* combination, as Payne (1985) and Langacker (1987: 84) point out. This distinction depends on the presence vs. absence of a temporal or causal sequence within which the two SoAs occur one after the other. Let us see two examples from English:

(1) *The man opened the door and went away.* → SEQUENTIAL combination
(2) *John is sick and Mary is on holiday* (so they will not come). → NON-SEQUENTIAL combination

As will be shown in Section 3.1, there are languages that use different constructions for the two types of combination. In that case, those specific constructions will be called *sequential* and *non-sequential conjunctive* constructions.

As for the alternative relation, Dik (1968: 276) and Haspelmath (to appear) point out that two subtypes can be identified, depending on the relevance of an immediate choice between the presented possibilities. Haspelmath defines as 'standard disjunction' the constructions where two SoAs are given as alternative possibilities without the need for a choice between them, and 'interrogative disjunction' the constructions where the speaker presents two SoAs as alternative possibilities and asks for an immediate choice.

Since the term '*interrogative* disjunction' could give rise to an erroneous identification of this construction type with every interrogative sentence expressing an alternative, a new terminology is proposed here, that avoids such ambiguity and defines the distinction in purely semantic terms. We will call therefore *simple alternative* any alternative relation where the speaker does not ask for a choice between the alternative possibilities, and *choice-aimed alternative* any alternative relation where a choice is needed (cf. Mauri 2007). Let us now examine three English examples, in order to make these terms clear:

(3) *Usually, I write or I read until late.* → SIMPLE alternative
(4) A. *(I am tired, I don't want to study this afternoon…) Would you go for a walk with me, or have a cup of tea, or watch a movie, or… whatever?*
B. *Ok!* → SIMPLE alternative
(5) *Do we go to school tomorrow or do we stay at home?* → CHOICE-AIMED alternative

In Examples (3) and (4) the speaker simply gives alternative possibilities, without asking his interlocutor to make a choice between them. The reason why the term 'choice-aimed alternative' is preferred here to 'interrogative alternative' is clear in (4): in this example, an interrogative sentence expressing an alternative is used, but no choice is required, since the aim of the question is to ask for company and the alternative SoAs are simply presented as possibilities. In (5), on the other hand, the interrogative illocutionary force has the aim of obtaining a choice between the two possibilities given, and this is thus a choice-aimed alternative relation.

There are languages that use different constructions for the two different types of alternative: in such languages, we will call the two specific construction types *choice-aimed disjunctive* and *simple disjunctive* constructions.

Finally, let us examine the semantic subtypes that can be identified in the concept of contrast. Here the decisive element is the *origin* of the contrast between the SoAs: it can lie in the simple semantic opposition of two parallel events (Haspelmath to appear: *oppositive* contrast, Luraghi 1990: weak adversativity, see (6)), in substituting an overtly negated element with a new one (*corrective* contrast: Rudolph 1996; Abraham 1979; Anscombre and Ducrot 1977; see (7)) or in combining two SoAs, the second of which denies an expectation generated by the first one or by the context (*counterexpectative* contrast: Scorretti 1988: 260; Lang 2000: 249; see (8)).

(6) *I worked and/while you slept!* → OPPOSITIVE contrast
(7) *Paul is not studying in his room, but (he is) playing in the garden.* → CORRECTIVE contrast
(8) *Paul is tall, but he's not good at basketball.* → COUNTEREXPECTATIVE contrast

In those languages where specific constructions for the three types of contrast are attested, the labels *oppositive adversative, corrective adversative* and *counterexpectative adversative* will be used.

Kotcheva (2005) and Givón (1990: 849) identify *discontinuity* between SoAs as a crucial constituent of the notion of contrast. Discontinuity is characterized by the absence of sequentiality (or continuity), by the parallelism of the two SoAs, and by the change of at least one of the elements constituting the action (participants and actions). For instance, the relation in (9) is discontinuous because the two SoAs are non-sequential, parallel and there is a change both of agents and patients in the two actions.

(9) *I bought a postcard and Mary bought a poster.*

The sum of the parallelism plus the change of some elements characterizing the actions causes a slightly oppositive shade, which can be strengthened by the context. Three of the subtypes identified until now within combination and contrast relations can be neatly analyzed in terms of discontinuity: non-sequential combination, oppositive contrast and corrective contrast (see examples (2), (6) and (7)).

Discontinuity can thus be seen as a bridge between combination and contrast (see also Mauri 2006), since it implies the former and is implied by the latter, being semantically more specified than simple combination and less defined than contrast.

As will be shown in Section 5.1, there are some languages, mainly in the Slavic family, that have specific connectives encoding a discontinuity between the relevant SoAs. Such connectives may be used to express at least two of the three semantic subtypes that we have just characterized in terms of discontinuity (namely non-sequential combination and oppositive contrast) and cannot be used to convey sequential combination relations. Such constructions will be called *discontinuity constructions* and will be treated together with both conjunctive and adversative ones.

Let us now move to the morphosyntactic parameters that have been examined in this analysis.

2.2 Morphosyntactic parameters

Each attested construction has been analyzed with respect to the following four parameters: presence of an *overt marker* (or connective) signalling the specific semantic relation, *morpho-phonological complexity* of this marker, *parallelism* of the verbal forms encoding the SoAs and *semantic domain* of the construction, that is, the set of semantic subtypes for which it can be used.

2.2.1 *Presence vs. absence of an overt marker*

The first parameter deals with the presence or the absence of an 'overt relational marker' (Wälchli 2005: 37) which encodes the 'specific semantic relation' (Prandi 2004: 40–43).

Constructions that signal a given semantic relation by means of an overt marker whose function is to convey that relation are said to be *syndetic constructions.* Constructions that do not show any overt marker conveying a given relation leave the interpretation to the inferential enrichment and to the context (Prandi 2004) and are said to be *asyndetic constructions.* Syndetic and asyndetic constructions may coexist as different strategies within the same language.

The following example from Chechen shows the coexistence within this language of both construction types: in (10a) the combination relation is expressed by means of an *asyndetic construction* which simply juxtaposes the two SoAs, whereas in (10b) the overt marker *'a* encodes the non-sequential combination in a *(bi)syndetic construction.*

(10) Chechen, Nakh-Daghestanian (Jeschull 2004: 252–253)

a. *Mox c'iiza byylira darc hwovziira*
Wind howl.INF start:WP blizzard turn.around:WP
'The wind started to howl and the blizzard turned around.'

b. *[...] peetar-ie juxa-vaxaniehw chai'a mer*
inn-ALL back-go:PST.COND tea:'a drink:FUT
dara, byysa'a joaqq-ur jara [...]
be:IMPF night:'a spend-FUT be:IMPF
'[...] if we had returned to the inn, we could have drunk tea and spent the night [...]'

2.2.2 *Morpho-phonological complexity of the overt markers*

For each syndetic construction, the morpho-phonological complexity of the overt marker has been considered, following Kortmann (1997) in the choice of this parameter. Three aspects will be examined: the *free or bound* nature of the marker, the *number of its syllables* and the *number of the morphemes* of which it consists.

As for the criteria adopted in establishing the *bound* or *free* nature of a marker, given the central role that prosody plays in this respect and the scarcity of prosodic data, we had to rely on descriptive grammars. The main parameter distinguishing between bound and free markers is their prosodic independence: free markers may be preceded and followed by a prosodic pause (cfr. the English sentence '*I took out my journal and, without noticing it, spent two hours turning over the leaves*'), whereas bound markers cannot form an accentual unit on their own and are always attached to the preceding or following word.

An example of bound overt marker is given in (11) from Hebrew, where the conjunctive marker *ve=* is proclitic and always bound to the following word. Examples of free markers are the great majority of European connectives, like the Finnish connectives *tai* 'or' and *ja* 'and', or the English connectives *and, but* and *or.*[1]

(11) Hebrew, Semitic, Afro-Asiatic (Hadar Mamrud, p.c.)

Harbè	*studentìm*	*lomdìm*	*bemèshex*	*ha=yòm*	*ve=ovdìm*
many	student:PL	study: PL.M	during	DEF=day	*ve*=work: PL.M

ba=èrev
at:DEF=night
'Many students study during the day and work at night.'

As for the number of syllables, the attested overt markers vary from *monosyllabic* (Italian *e, o* and *ma*), to *bisyllabic* (German *oder*, Spanish *pero* and *sino*), to *trisyllabic* (Lezgian *tax̂ajt'a* 'or').

Furthermore, polysyllabic overt markers can be *monomorphemic* or *polymorphemic.* Examples of bisyllabic monomorphemic markers are the German corrective marker *sondern* and the Danish disjunctive marker *eller*, whereas examples of polysyllabic and polymorphemic markers are the French oppositive marker *tandis que*, the Italian corrective marker *bensì* and the English oppositive marker *whereas*, whose original composite morphology is still transparent.

1. Some European markers, like English *and, but* and *or*, or Italian *e, ma* and *o* may behave as proclitics in certain prosodic contexts, since they might be pronounced together with the word that follows. However, these markers have not completely lost their prosodic independence, since they may as well be preceded and followed by a prosodic pause. Therefore, even though such markers may also behave as clitics, they are regarded here as free forms.

2.2.3 *Internal parallelism*

The third parameter that has been considered deals with the verbal forms encoding the involved SoAs. Following Stassen (1985), we can distinguish between two main types of strategy: *balancing* and *deranking* (Stassen 1985: 76–83). A verbal form is called balanced when it can occur also in independent clauses, whereas it is deranked if it cannot be found in independent clauses, because it lacks certain distinctions (such as tense, mood, aspect or person agreement) or is a special form that is not allowed in independent clauses.

A given construction is said to be internally *parallel* when the involved SoAs are encoded by the same type of verbal forms, either both deranked or both balanced. A construction is instead defined as internally *non-parallel* when one SoA is encoded by a deranked verbal form and the other by means of a balanced one.

Let us now see an example from Turkish (12), where an internally non-parallel construction is used to convey the relation of sequential combination. The first of the two SoAs is coded by a deranked verbal form, since the verb suffixed by *-Ip* cannot receive further specifications of time and depends for the expression of this category on the following verb, which occurs instead in a balanced form at the end of the sentence.

(12) Turkish (Kornfilt 1997: 110)
Hasan iş-e gid-ip ev-e dön-dü
Hasan work-DAT go-*Ip* home-DAT come-PST
'Hasan went to work and came back home.'[2]

The English translation, by contrast, is an example of an internally parallel construction, where both SoAs are coded by balancing strategies and both verbal forms could occur in independent clauses.

2.2.4 *Semantic domain*

The semantic domain is the last parameter examined and is defined as the set of semantic distinctions, or semantic subtypes, for which a given construction can be used. The semantic domain identifies *specific markers*, which express only one semantic distinction, or *general markers*, which can be used to express more than one semantic distinction.

Whereas the concept of specific marker is absolute, since it only applies to those cases where a given construction can be used in just one special situation, the concept of general marker is scalar, since there are more general and less general markers, depending on the number of semantic relations that they cover. For instance,

2. Turkish *-Ip* is usually considered a converb (see Johanson 1995), hence belonging to the verbal paradigm. It may have various functions and the conjunctive function is just one of them.

ma in Italian (just like *but* in English) is general, since it can be used for corrective contrast and counterexpectative contrast (example (13)). By contrast, *aber* in German would never be used to convey correction, which is expressed by the specific marker *sondern*, and could be used only to express the counterexpectative relation (example (14)). As can be seen in example (13), Italian also has the two specific markers *però* and *bensì*, which are equivalent to *aber* and *sondern*, although *bensì* is not very common.

(13) Italian
a. *Verrei* *volentieri* *ma/però/*bensì* *non* *posso*
come:COND:1SG with.pleasure *ma/però* NEG can:PRS:1SG
'I would love to come tonight, but I can't.'
b. *Giovanni* *mi* *ha* *detto* *non* *di* *raggiungerlo* *in* *ufficio*
John 1SG.DAT has told NEG of reach:him in office
*ma/*però/bensì* *di* *aspettarlo* *qui*
ma/bensì of wait.for:him here
'John didn't tell me to reach him in his office, but to wait for him here.'

(14) German
a. *Ich* *habe* *viel* *Durst,* *aber* *ich* *mag*
1SG have:IND.PRS.1SG a.lot.of thirst *aber* 1SG like:IND.PRS.1SG
keinen *Orangensaft*
INDEF.NEG:ACC orange.juice
'I am very thirsty, but I don't like orange juice.'
b. *Peter* *lernt* *nicht* *in* *seinem* *Zimmer,* *sondern*
Peter study:IND.PRS.3SG NEG in his:DAT room *sondern*
spielt *im* *Moment* *im* *Garten*
play:IND.PRS.3SG in:DEF.DAT moment in:DEF.DAT garden
'Peter is not studying in his room, but he's playing in the garden.'

The point of view adopted here following Gil (2004) and Prandi (2004) is that a general marker, which can be used for more than one semantic distinction, is not polyfunctional (i.e. characterized by a plurality of functions), but is instead macrofunctional, that is, it simply encodes a very broad semantic relation, leading to undercoding. Further semantic specifications are obtained by means of inferential enrichment: the more specific the encoded relation is, the less is left to inference.

Following this approach, markers with a wide semantic domain will be analyzed in terms of the general semantic relation they encode, and markers characterized by a small semantic domain (specific markers) will be treated as instances of full coding (Prandi 2004: 297), that is, as cases where the specific relation is lexicalized by the marker. Thus, asserting that the Italian *ma* is more general means that it encodes the general notion of contrast without further specifications, whereas the German *aber* is specific because it only encodes the function of counterexpectative contrast.

2.3 Language sample

Before moving to the analysis of the attested data, some remarks on the language sample must be made. Since the aim of this work is twofold, that is, to identify both the internal variation and the regularities that characterize the European languages as a diversified but homogeneous group, also the language sample needs to be twofold.

In order to have a complete picture of the European conjunctive, disjunctive and adversative constructions, a *sample of 37 European languages* has been examined (see section 'Language Sample', at the end of the paper), covering all the main linguistic families attested in this geographical region. The definition of Europe used in this work is mainly geographic: 'it is the area bounded to the East by the Ural mountains, the Caspian sea, the southern Caucasus mountains, the Black sea and the Bosporus' (Kortmann 1997: 38).

However, in order to identify what is 'specifically European', it is necessary to compare European data with data from outside Europe. For this reason, a *comparison sample* has been built, made up of *36 non-European languages*, belonging to 20 different families (see information at the end of the paper). The aim of this second comparative sample is to gather information on what is attested outside Europe, in order to be able to establish if a given cluster of features characterizes a hypothetical European type or if it is attested in many languages worldwide.

The comparison sample does not constitute a balanced and representative typological sample, even though it is studied to represent as much as possible the variation of the attested conjunctive, disjunctive and adversative constructions. The major role that the availability of good descriptive grammars has played in its construction makes it mainly a convenience sample. However, given the number of non-related languages analyzed and the number of geographical areas covered, the data gathered in the comparison sample constitute a significant indicator of 'the other side of the story', that is, of what is attested and what is not attested outside Europe.

The two samples have been analyzed with different levels of depth, depending on the availability of native speakers, good grammars and specific research on this subject. However, for each language, at least one descriptive grammar has been consulted.

In the European sample, for 31 languages out of 37 data have also been gathered by means of a questionnaire filled out by native speakers, whereas in the comparison sample this method has been possible just for 7 languages. The questionnaire consists of 36 sentences, covering all the subtypes of combination, contrast and alternative investigated (see Section 2.1). Each sentence is constructed in such a way that the context of discourse is made clear, so that speakers are able to identify as precisely as possible the semantic situation that has to be rendered in their native language.

The availability of first hand data for the European languages allows for a deep analysis of the European sample, which constitutes the core of this work. Data coming from the comparison sample are less complete, but still useful and important in the identification of a potential European language type (see also Kortmann 1997). Finally, the sum of the two samples yields a global sample of 73 languages, which is broad enough to make significant cross-linguistic generalizations.

3. Conjunctive constructions in the languages of Europe

Let us start the analysis of data by presenting the areal distribution of the different attested conjunctive constructions.

In this section we will first of all examine the cross-linguistic variation that the languages of Europe show with respect to each of the four parameters (Section 3.1). Then, in Section 3.2, a comparison will be made with the conjunctive constructions attested in non-European languages and the features that may be considered 'specifically European' will be pointed out. In Fig. 1 an areal synthetic view of the European conjunctive constructions will be given.

3.1 The cross-linguistic variation within Europe

3.1.1 *Presence vs. absence of an overt relational marker*

All 37 European languages have *at least one syndetic construction* to express the combination of two SoAs. This means that all European languages have at least one overt conjunctive marker. However, in Turkish and Chechen also asyndetic constructions are attested as normal and stylistically unmarked ways of expressing the combination of two SoAs. In Section 2.2 we already saw two examples from Chechen (10), where the syndetic and the asyndetic constructions are compared.

As Mithun (1988) points out, a lot of languages in the world lack an overt conjunctive marker and signal the semantic relations by intonation and context. Moreover, there seems to be a strict correlation between the presence of overt markers and the degree to which the language is used in written form: exclusively spoken languages tend to be simpler and information is usually linked by means of adverbs or anaphoric constructions, rather than by means of complex sentences, whereas in languages with a relevant written tradition the logical relations are made explicit by means of connectives (Mithun 1988: 356–357).

Two languages out of 37 is in any case a very low percentage, especially if we consider that both Turkish and Chechen also have the possibility of using a syndetic construction. The overwhelming predominance of overt conjunctive markers in the languages of Europe could thus be connected to the high degree of written language tradition that characterizes this area. Furthermore, it could also be a consequence of the high degree of contact among the languages, which could have caused the borrowing of overt markers in those languages that did not have any, given the fact that conjunctive markers are easily borrowed across languages (Mithun 1988: 357) (see also Section 3.2). However, such borrowing phenomena are well attested outside Europe, but no clear cases are attested within the European area.

3.1.2 *Morpho-phonological complexity of the attested conjunctive markers*

All European languages except for two, Irish and Basque, have *at least one monosyllabic conjunctive marker*. Irish and Basque use instead the bisyllabic connectives *agus* and *eta*, respectively. Moreover, no polymorphemic conjunctive marker is attested in European languages.

Such data show that conjunctive markers are very simple compared to disjunctive markers and contrastive markers, probably as a consequence of the very general relation they express. Due to the very general meaning of combination, such markers can be used in a variety of different contexts and therefore tend to occur very often in discourse. As is well known (see Zipf 1949: 66–133 and Kortmann 1997: 127–128), a high frequency of use correlates with a progressive morpho-phonological reduction, so that very frequent forms will tend to be the shortest and simplest ones. Therefore, the low morpho-phonological complexity of conjunctive markers is to be linked to the simple and general semantic content that they encode (more on the unmarkedness of conjunctive markers and on its explanations can be found in Mauri 2007).

Turning now to the free or bound nature of the markers, all European languages except for Chechen (see example (10b), where the marker *'a* is a clitic[3]) have at least one conjunctive connective which consists of a free morpheme. Dargi, Lezgian and Turkish show both types, and have the possibility to use either free morphemes or bound ones (Dargi *-ra*, Lezgian *-na* and Turkish *-Ip*).

3.1.3 *Internal parallelism of conjunctive constructions*

All European languages have at least one internally parallel conjunctive construction, where both verbal forms encoding the combined SoAs are balanced forms.

3. In Chechen *'a* cliticizes onto the element immediately to the left of the lexical verb when independent clauses are conjoined; to the subject when the finite clauses are contrasted in some sense; and to the verb itself when finite subordinate clauses are conjoined (Jeschull 2004: 252–253).

However, two languages out of 37 (Turkish and Lezgian) also show non-parallel constructions, where the first verbal form is deranked and syntactically depends on the last one. We have already seen an example from Turkish in (12); let us now examine the Lezgian construction, where the aorist converb *-na* is suffixed to the first verb and cannot receive further specifications of mood:[4]

(15) Lezgian (Haspelmath 1993: 377)
De ša, čna tadi-z fe-na am kučuk-in
PT come:IMPF we:ERG quick-ADVB go-AOC he:ABS bury-HORT
'Come on, let us go quickly and bury him.'

3.1.4 *Semantic domain: general, sequential and non-sequential conjunction*

All 37 European languages have *at least one general conjunctive connective* that can be used to convey both sequential and non-sequential combination, like English *and*, Italian *e*, Spanish *y*, Russian *i*, Finnish *ja*, and so on. These markers simply encode the general relation of combination, without further specifications on the sequentiality of the two SoAS.

Besides the general marker, however, some languages also show specific markers, which are used just for one subtype of combination. For instance, the non-parallel constructions attested in Turkish and Lezgian can only be used to express sequential combination. There are special sequential conjunctive connectives in Serbo-Croatian (*pa*) and Bulgarian (*ta/da*), too.

Other languages show markers whose meaning denote some relation between combination and contrast, whose definition is often left vague in grammars. Such markers are, for instance, *a* in Russian, Polish, Belorussian, Bulgarian and Serbo-Croatian (example (16)), *ta* in Ukrainian, *õ* in Lithuanian and *tq'a* in Chechen. Descriptive grammars usually gloss these markers with an *and/but* label, which leaves their specific function quite obscure. I prefer to follow Kotcheva (2005) in calling such cases *discontinuity* markers, because what they seem to signal is an interruption of continuity between the two SoAs, determined by a change of participants and actions. Discontinuity markers are treated in this paper within the analysis of both combination and contrast relations (see Section 2.1), for their semantics constitutes a sort of bridge between the two.

Languages with discontinuity markers also employ them in contexts where in English we would normally find a conjunctive construction (16b): the overlap of

4. Haspelmath (1993: 376): "The Aorist converb is used to express chains of actions carried out by the same subject. Such sentences often have to be translated by means of coordinate clauses in English, because the action of the converb clause is not backgrounded to the same extent as the English participle would suggest".

discontinuity and conjunctive markers is only attested in *non-sequential* contexts, since sequential combination is characterized by a continuity of action which is incompatible with the use of discontinuity markers. The reason why such markers are treated in this section is thus the fact that they may be used to express just one type of combination relation, namely the non-sequential one. Let us now examine the case of Serbo-Croatian, where *i* is the general conjunctive marker (16a), while *a* is a marker that can only be used for non-sequential combination (16b) and *pa* is the sequential conjunctive marker (16c).

(16) Serbo-Croatian
a. *Zauzet sam i ne mogu više slušati*
Busy be:1SG *i* NEG can:1SG anymore listen
'I'm busy and I can't listen anymore.' (Brown and Alt 2004: 70)
b. *Ja radim a Petar spava*
I work:1SG *a* Peter sleep:3SG
'I work and Peter sleeps.' (Momcilo Corovic, p.c.)
c. *Cuo sam grmljavinu pa je pocela kiša*
hear:PTCP.PST AUX:1SG thunder:ACC *pa* AUX:3SG begin:PTCP.PST rain
'I heard a thunder and it started to rain.' (Momcilo Corovic, p.c.)

3.1.5 *Synthesis*

In Fig. 1 a unitary picture of the European cross-linguistic variation is given.

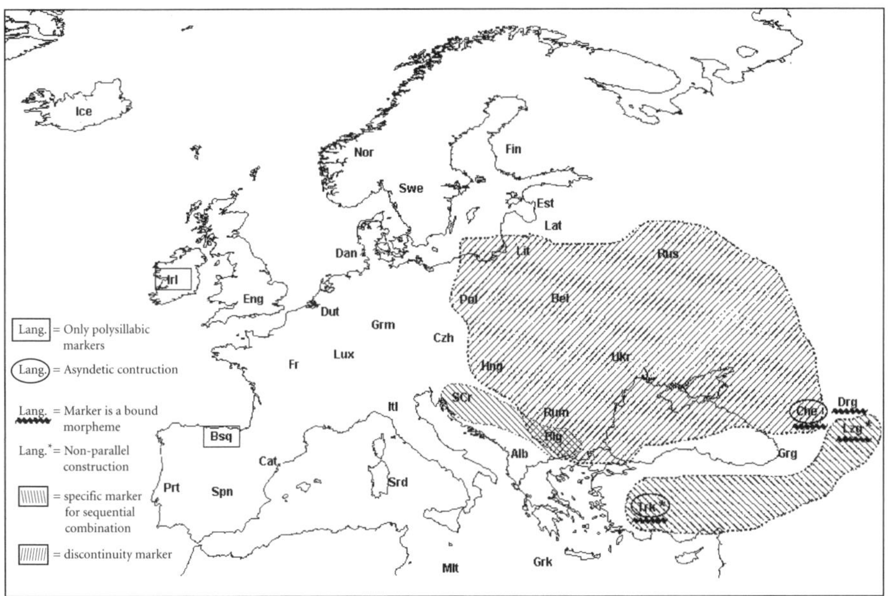

Figure 1. Conjunctive constructions in the languages of Europe

As can be seen in the figure, specific connectives, both sequential and non-sequential, are attested in the central-eastern part of Europe, whereas central-western European languages only have a general conjunctive marker. Non-parallel constructions, asyndetic constructions and bound markers are only attested in the eastern periphery of Europe as well. By contrast, the only two languages which have just bisyllabic conjunctive markers, Irish and Basque, are in the western periphery of Europe.

3.2 A glance outside Europe: what is 'typically European'?

In order to identify the features that may be considered 'typically European', let us briefly see some data from the comparison sample.

Outside Europe, asyndetic strategies seem to be very widespread. We will not focus on numbers, because, as already said, the comparison sample is mainly a convenience one and therefore cannot constitute the basis for statistical generalizations. However, 19 languages out of 36 seem to use asyndesis as a normal and unmarked strategy to convey the combination of SoAs, and this shows quite a big difference from the European data.

There is clearly a strong connection between the higher number of languages without a written tradition outside Europe and the frequency of juxtapositive conjunctive constructions. In any case, outside Europe, too, the presence of an overt marker encoding the relation of combination is well attested and often coexists with an asyndetic construction. The presence of an overt conjunctive marker thus cannot be considered a typical European feature, since it is largely attested outside Europe as well. What may be treated as a characteristic of Europe is instead the *absence of asyndetic conjunctive constructions*, since it characterizes almost all European languages in a very homogeneous and unitary way.

As for the morpho-phonological complexity of the conjunctive markers attested outside Europe, data are less uniform, but confirm the tendency already pointed out in Section 3.1. Monosyllabic and monomorphemic conjunctive markers are well attested and bisyllabic markers seem to be restricted to the expression of one of the two sub-types of combination. Moreover, the majority of the attested conjunctive markers are free morphemes. What seems to be characteristic of European conjunctive constructions is the combination of both features *monosyllabic* plus *free morpheme*. It would be risky to call it a 'typical European feature', since markers similar to English *and* are also attested in non-European languages; nonetheless, the regular occurrence of monosyllabic and free conjunctive markers characterizes almost all European languages.

Outside Europe non-parallel constructions seem to be much more widespread and, most importantly, there are a few languages in the comparison sample which do not have any parallel conjunctive construction. This deviates from the picture we have seen in Europe, where every language has at least one parallel construction. The languages which do not have the possibility to use a parallel conjunctive construction are Japanese, Tauya, Kolyma Yukaghir and Jamul Tiipay. In (17) an example from Japanese is given, where the converb *-i* encodes the combination of two SoAs and causes the syntactic dependence of the suffixed verb on the final verb.

(17) Japanese (Yoko Nishina, p.c.)
watasi-wa hatarak-i piitaa-wa neru
1SG-TOP work-*i* Peter-TOP sleep
'I work and Peter sleeps.'

Languages which show non-parallel conjunctive constructions mainly have a basic SOV order, therefore the presence of non-parallel constructions may be related to the clause combining strategies found in this language type. Lezgian and Turkish, which are the only two languages in Europe with non-parallel conjunctive constructions, have SOV basic order, whereas the rest of European languages are mostly SVO. The absence of non-parallel constructions in Europe may thus be connected to the fact that SOV languages are rare within the area and so are the clause combining strategies which are typically connected to the SOV basic order.

Finally, whereas every European language has at least one general conjunctive marker, outside Europe we find languages which do not have any general conjunctive construction, but only show specific constructions for sequential and non-sequential combination. In (18) an example from Tukang Besi is given, where the connective *kene* encodes the relation of non-sequential combination and the connective *maka* encodes the relation of sequential combination. In this language no general marker equivalent to English *and* is attested.

(18) Tukang Besi, Malayo-Polynesian, Austronesian (Donuhue 1993: 427)
a. *Te mia no-rato kene no-ganta-'e na uwe*
CORE person 3R-arrive *kene* 3R-scoop-3OBJ NOM water
'... people keep coming and fetching water ...'
b. *Jari, sa-rato-no i umbu na Ndokendoke*
So when-arrive-3POSS OBL edge NOM monkey
o-sampi-'e-mo a loka iso maka o-manga
3R-peel-3OBJ-PRF NOM banana yon *maka* 3R-eat
'So when Monkey arrived at the top he peeled the bananas and then ate them.'

Other languages in the comparison sample behave like Tukang Besi. In Tuvaluan, for instance, not only is there no general marker available, but the only attested conjunctive marker *kae* is a *discontinuity marker*, used to convey non-sequential combination and contrast relations, whereas sequential combination can only be expressed by means of a juxtapositive, thus asyndetic, strategy.

There are also non-European languages which have a general conjunctive marker, like Somali *oo*, but this is attested in only 20 languages out of 36. Considering that in Europe all languages have at least one general conjunctive marker, it makes sense to regard the presence of at least one general conjunctive marker as a typical feature of European conjunctive constructions.

3.2.1 *Conclusions*

From what we have seen throughout this section, on the basis of the variation attested in Europe and after the comparison with non-European data, we can identify the features that specifically characterize European conjunctive constructions.

European conjunctive constructions are mainly *syndetic* and *internally parallel*. Conjunctive markers tend to be *monosyllabic free morphemes*, and every language has *at least one general conjunctive marker* (specific markers are attested in Eastern Europe). Of the languages that Haspelmath (2001: 273) identifies as belonging to the nucleus of the so-called Standard Average European (SAE) area, only Polish, Serbo-Croatian and Bulgarian have specific conjunctive markers.

4. Disjunctive constructions in the languages of Europe

Let us now examine the disjunctive constructions attested in Europe. As will be evident from the next subsections, disjunctive constructions show less cross-linguistic variation than conjunctive constructions and have more or less the same formal features all over Europe (Section 4.1). On the other hand, comparing European data with data from the comparison sample, this homogeneous behavior will turn out to be a peculiarity of Europe, since in the world's languages there is much more variety in the coding of the alternative relation between SoAs (Section 4.2).

We have already seen that conjunctive constructions show a set of features that may be considered typical of Europe. In this section it will be shown that such a claim can be made with even stronger conviction for European disjunctive constructions.

4.1 The cross-linguistic variation within Europe

4.1.1 *Presence vs. absence of an overt relational marker*

All 37 European languages only use *syndetic constructions* to express the alternative between two SoAs. This means that no European language uses an asyndetic disjunctive construction and that this relation is always coded by means of an overt relational marker.

On the other hand, as will be pointed out in the course of this section, asyndetic disjunctive constructions are attested outside Europe. The complete absence of asyndetic disjunction can reasonably be treated as a typical European feature.

4.1.2 *Morpho-phonological complexity of the attested disjunctive markers*

The attested disjunctive markers are morpho-phonologically more complex than the conjunctive markers. First of all, whereas 35 languages out of 37 have at least one monosyllabic conjunctive marker, only 22 out of 37 have at least one monosyllabic disjunctive marker and 19 languages out of 37 have at least one *bisyllabic disjunctive* marker.

Examples of bisyllabic disjunctive markers are German *oder*, Swedish *eller*, Russian *ili* and Polish *albo*. In Fig. 2, where a synthetic picture of European disjunctive constructions is given, the languages with a bisyllabic disjunctive marker are signalled by a circle. Examples of monosyllabic disjunctive markers are English *or*, French *ou*, Italian *o*, Finnish *vai* and *tai*, Romanian *sau* and Maltese *jew*.

Moreover, Lezgian, Dargi and Turkish show *polymorphemic disjunctive* markers, which consist of a morpheme meaning 'and' combined with a morpheme meaning 'or', that is, alternative: Dargi *yara* (*ya-ra* 'or-and', see example 19), Lezgian *waya* (*wa-ya* 'and-or') and Turkish *veya* (*ve-ya* 'and-or'). In example (19) *yara* is glossed with as 'or-and', in order to show the transparency of its internal morphology; however, the alternative relation is encoded by the marker as a whole and *ya-*, although its meaning is that of alternative, occurs on its own only in negated sentences.

(19) Dargi, Daghestanian, Caucasic (Van den Berg 2004: 204)
ħu *džäˤäl* *ya-ra* *tuxtur.li-či* *arq'-ad,* *ya-ra*
you(ABS) tomorrow or-and doctor-SUP leave-FUT.2SG or-and
ħänči-la *dura.ulq-ad*
work-LOC go.out:M-FUT.2SG
'Tomorrow you'll either go to the doctor or you'll go to work.'

Finally, no bound disjunctive markers are attested: all European disjunctive markers are free forms. The greater morpho-phonological complexity of disjunctive markers is probably connected to the fact that they are less frequent than conjunctive markers. The lower frequency may in turn be linked to the greater semantic specificity of the relation of alternative, if compared to the very general relation of combination. In fact, the alternative relation implies at the cognitive level that of combination, in that in order to present two SoAs as alternative possibilities, they have first of all to be combined (for a detailed treatment of this hypothesis, see Mauri 2007).

4.1.3 *Internal parallelism of disjunctive constructions*

Here again, as we have seen for the first parameter, European languages behave in the same way and there is no cross-linguistic variation: all the languages in the sample use *only internally parallel disjunctive constructions.*

Non-parallel disjunctive constructions are instead attested outside Europe, as will be shown in Section 4.2. However, the number of languages using non-parallel constructions for the expression of alternative relations is very low (only three languages out of 36 in the comparison sample). Therefore internal parallelism may reasonably be considered a typical feature of the coding of alternative relations in general, rather than a feature characterizing European disjunctive constructions.

4.1.4 *Semantic domain: choice-aimed and simple disjunction*

Turning to the semantics of the attested disjunctive constructions, the picture shows some cross-linguistic variation. 29 languages out of 37 have one general disjunctive marker, which encodes the relation of alternative between two SoAs and does not specify the nature of this relation. Examples of general disjunctive markers can be found in English *or*, French *ou*, Russian *ili*, Danish *eller*, Hungarian *vagy*, and so on.

There are, however, 9 European languages which do not have any general disjunctive marker, but show only two specific markers, one for the choice-aimed alternative relation and the other for the simple alternative relation. These languages are Polish (choice-aimed: *czy*, simple: *lub/albo*), Finnish (choice-aimed: *vai*, simple: *tai*), Belorussian (choice-aimed: *ci*, simple: *abò*), Albanian (choice-aimed: *apo*, simple: *ose*), Basque (choice-aimed: *ala*, simple: *edo*), Ukrainian (choice-aimed: *cy*, simple: *abo*), Georgian (choice-aimed: *tu*, simple: *an*), Lezgian (choice-aimed: *tax̂ajt’a*, simple: *ja/wa-ja*), Dargi (choice-aimed: *ai*, simple: *ya-ra*).

In (20) an example from Georgian is given: *tu* encodes an alternative relation where a choice between the two SoAs is requested, whereas *an* is used to convey an alternative where no choice is needed, but two or more SoAs are simply presented as possibilities.

(20) Georgian, Kartvelian (Manana Topadze, p.c.)

a. *Xval sk’olaši c’avidet tu saxlši davrčet?*
tomorrow school:LOC go:1pl:OPT *tu* home:LOC stay:1PL:OPT
‘Tomorrow do we go to school or do we stay at home?’

b. *Ginda gaviseirnot ertad, an čai davliot, an k’inos*
want:2SG walk:1PL together *an* tea drink:1PL *an* movie
vuq’urot, an . . . rac ginda?
watch:1PL *an* what want:2SG
‘Would you go for a walk with me, or have a cup of tea, or watch a movie, or . . . whatever?’

Some specific choice-aimed disjunctive markers are also used as interrogative particles (cfr. Polish *czy*). However, when they are used in a pure interrogative function, these markers occur at the beginning of the clause. On the other hand, as disjunctive connectives, they are located between the clauses they link. Many disjunctive connectives indeed originate from or evolve into irrealis markers, such as interrogative particles (see Heine and Kuteva 2002: 226–227) or hypothetical forms, revealing the conceptual closeness between the meaning of alternative and hypothetical/irrealis modality (see Mauri, to appear for a detailed discussion).

Languages which have a general disjunctive marker, however, are the majority and constitute a large interconnected area, as can be seen in Fig. 2. Specific markers are attested at the periphery of Europe and in the three Slavic languages Polish, Belorussian and Ukrainian, which developed this distinction from the same forms and probably influenced one another through contact.

4.1.5 *Synthesis*

The homogeneous behavior of European languages in the coding of the alternative relation is shown in Fig. 2. Since they all have syndetic and parallel constructions, the only two parameters represented on the map are the morpho-phonological complexity of the disjunctive markers, that is, whether they are mono- or bisyllabic, and their semantic domain, distinguishing between an area with specific choice-aimed and simple markers and an area with a general disjunctive connective.

As already said, languages with specific disjunctive markers are located in the eastern part of Europe and, in any case, in the peripheral areas. Before making further generalizations, let us consider the greater cross-linguistic variation attested outside Europe.

4.2 A glance outside Europe: what is 'typically European'?

Within Europe no asyndetic disjunctive construction is attested, but in the comparison sample 12 languages out of 36 use *at least one juxtapositive strategy* to express the alternative relation between two SoAs. This is a significant difference, because a construction type which is not attested at all in Europe seems to be not unusual outside Europe.

The attested asyndetic disjunctive constructions are all characterized by some other markers which overtly signal the irrealis status of the alternatives (see Mauri, to appear): interrogative markers in the expression of a choice-aimed alternative relation (example 21) and dubitative, conditional, hypothetical markers in the expression of a simple alternative (example 22). In these constructions, the alternative relation as such is not fully encoded: what is encoded is the *possible* (or potential), rather than realis, status of the two SoAs, while the rest is left to inferential enrichment.

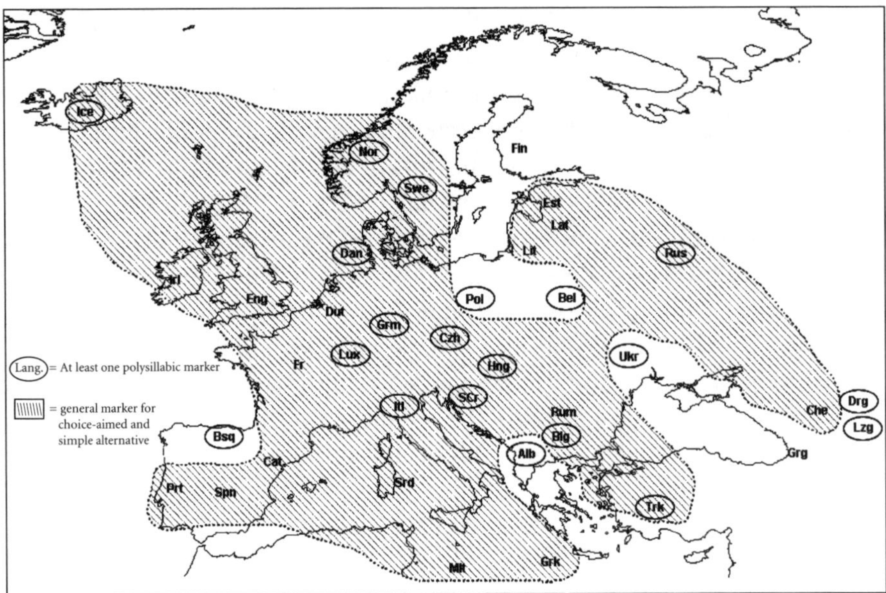

Figure 2. Disjunctive constructions in the languages of Europe

In example (21) from Korean a case of asyndetic choice-aimed disjunction is given, where the alternative is expressed by the juxtaposition of two interrogative clauses marked by the question marker *-kka.* In (22), instead, an example of asyndetic simple disjunction is give from Mangarayi, where there is no counterpart to English *or* and the alternative relation is conveyed by sequences of clauses with *maŋaya* 'perhaps' (Merlan 1982: 33).

(21) Korean, Isolate (Sohn 1994: 122)

wuli-ka	*ka-l-kka-yo?*	*salam-ul*	*ponay-l-kka-yo?*
1PL-NOM	go-PRS-Q-POL	person-ACC	send-PRS-Q-POL

'Shall we go or shall we send a person?'

(22) Mangarayi, Gunwingguan, Australian (Merlan 1982: 39)

maŋaya	*ja-Ø-ṇiŋa-n*	*maŋaya*	*ḍayi*
perhaps	3–3SG-come-PRS	perhaps	NEG

'Perhaps he'll come, perhaps not.', i.e 'it is possible that he may or may not come.'

These data show that the presence of syndetic disjunctive constructions, and even more the *absence* of asyndetic disjunctive strategies in all the languages of Europe characterizes in a unitary way the whole area.

Considering the morpho-phonological complexity of the attested disjunctive markers, the only significant difference between European and non-European languages is that in the comparison sample 5 languages out of 36 show bound disjunctive markers, whereas no such cases are attested in Europe. However, the great majority of disjunctive markers consist in free morphemes outside Europe as well.

In Section 4.1 we have seen that no European language has a non-parallel disjunctive construction, and such a uniformity is per se interesting. In the comparison sample, on the other hand, three languages do show a non-parallel disjunctive construction. These languages are Korean (example 23), Jamul Tiipaj and West Greenlandic.

Let us look at the case of Korean in (23), where the verbal suffix *-kɔna* is a specific marker of simple alternative, since it can only occur when no choice is requested between the alternative SoAs. The suffixed verb cannot receive any further specification of mood or aspect and depends for the expression of these categories on the last verb, thus causing a non-parallel structure.

(23) Korean, Isolate (Yusi Minsu Sin, p.c.)
Minsu-ka o- kɔna nae-ka ka-n-ta.
Minsu-NOM come- *kɔna* 1.SG-NOM go-INCOMP-DECL
'Minsu comes here or I go there.'

As for the semantic domain, specific constructions for the two subtypes of alternative relation are quite widespread outside Europe and only half of the sample languages have a general disjunctive marker corresponding to English *or*. The different constructions may be characterized by specific different markers or by different strategies, one syndetic and the other asyndetic. For instance, as shown in examples (21) and (23), Korean distinguishes the choice-aimed alternative from the simple alternative relation by using the juxtaposition of two interrogative sentences to express the former and an overt specific marker to express the latter (the converb *-kɔna*). The significant difference between data from the two samples is that in Europe the presence of a general disjunctive marker is attested in the great majority of languages, whereas outside Europe it is but one of the attested strategies.

4.2.1 *Conclusions*

Data presented in this section have shown the internal homogeneity attested in the European disjunctive constructions. After the comparison with non-European languages, we have found a set of features which can be said to characterize the European disjunctive constructions.

Disjunctive constructions are all *syndetic* and all *internally parallel.* Disjunctive markers are all *free morphemes, either monosyllabic or bisyllabic.* There is a large area with a *general disjunctive marker* (specific markers are attested in peripheral areas).

Among the languages that Haspelmath (2001: 273) identifies as belonging to the nucleus of SAE area, only Polish and Albanian have specific disjunctive markers.

5. Adversative constructions in the languages of Europe

After having seen the cross-linguistic variation and the regularities of European conjunctive and disjunctive constructions, let us now examine how European languages encode the different subtypes of contrast.

From a purely morphosyntactic point of view, the picture is quite homogenous, not very different from what has been said about disjunctive constructions. The semantic domain, instead, will reveal an interesting cross-linguistic variation, within which the central-western part of Europe will turn out to be once again more united in its behavior than the eastern part (Section 5.1). In Section 5.2 the European data will then be compared to the non-European data and the features characterizing the European adversative constructions will be identified.

5.1 The cross-linguistic variation within Europe

5.1.1 *Presence vs. absence of an overt relational marker*

All 37 European languages have at least one overt relational marker encoding at least one subtype of contrast. There is however one subtype of contrast, corrective contrast, which can normally be expressed in discourse by means of juxtaposition. The obligatory presence of an overt negation in the first clause and the positive polarity of the second make the contrast between the two SoAs easily inferrable, even without an overt relational marker.

Almost all languages, anyway, also show the possibility to mark this relation by means of an overt connective, as we have seen in the examples (13) from Italian and (14) from German. Two languages, however, Turkish and Georgian, do not have any syndetic strategy to express this type of contrast, but always use asyndesis. As can be seen in example (24), in Georgian the negated clause is emphasized by the emphatic particle *k'i* and then the substitute of the negated SoA is simply juxtaposed.

(24) Georgian, Kartvelian (Manana Topadze, p.c.)
Petre tavis otaxši k'i ar mecadineobs, bayši tamašobs
Peter his room:LOC EMPH NEG study:3SG garden:LOC play:3SG
'Peter is not studying in his room, but he's playing in the garden.'

5.1.2 *Morpho-phonological complexity of the attested adversative markers*

The attested adversative markers are morphologically and phonologically more complex than the conjunctive markers, whereas it is not possible to establish a hierarchical order between the attested adversative markers and the disjunctive ones, since they cross-linguistically show more or less the same morpho-phonological properties.

First of all, the attested adversative markers are all free morphemes (only Dargi shows, besides *amma*, the bound marker *-gu*). As for the number of syllables, 19 languages out of 37 show at least one polysyllabic adversative marker. Among these languages we can count German (*aber* and *sondern*), Swedish (*utan*), Spanish (*pero* and *sino*), Hungarian (*hanem*), Finnish (*mutta*), Polish (*ale*) and Greek (*αλλά*) In Fig. 3 the distribution of languages with polysyllabic adversative markers is shown. Examples of monosyllabic adversative markers are Italian *ma*, English *but*, French *mais*, Russian *no*, Danish and Norwegian *men*.

Some of the attested polysyllabic markers are also polymorphemic, like the corrective markers in Hungarian, *hanem*, and in Spanish, *sino*, which have the same internal structure of a particle meaning 'if' (*ha* and *si*) combined with a negation (*nem* and *no*).

Some morphologically complex adversative markers are attested for the expression of oppositive contrast, where we find connectives which are normally used to convey also other types of relations, mainly relations of simultaneity. Such markers have not been used by native speakers in the questionnaire, except for a few languages, and are not well described in grammars, because the semantic function of simultaneity is still felt to be the main one.

Yet, there are situations where such markers can be used to express opposition without implying the simultaneity of the linked SoAs any more. Examples of these oppositive markers are French *tandis que*, which is also polymorphemic, Italian *mentre*, English *while* and German *während*. Because of the incompleteness of data, such markers are not represented in Fig. 3, but this only means that more diachronic and typological research has to be done on this subject.

Specific corrective and oppositive markers are anyway morpho-phonologically more complex than the counterexpectative ones, and all the specific adversative markers are normally more complex than the general markers, encoding the general concept of contrast or that of discontinuity. For further details on the implicational hierarchy that can be identified within the adversative constructions, see Mauri (2006).

5.1.3 *Internal parallelism of adversative constructions*

European adversative constructions are *always internally parallel*, like the attested disjunctive constructions, analyzed in Section 4.1. The only non-parallel constructions attested in Europe are thus specific sequential conjunctive constructions. A possible explanation for this distribution may be formulated in terms of economy and recoverability of information (Haiman 1985: 159): information that is already recoverable from the context is not further specified.

The presence of an overt marker coding the sequentiality of the SoAs explicitly lexicalizes their successive location in time and their being part of the same overall macro-event. Given the temporal, aspectual and modal characterization of one of the linked SoAs, a sequential combination thus *predetermines* the temporal, aspectual and modal characterizations of the other SoA. Therefore, if one of the SoAs shows all the categories of tense, aspect and mood, the properties of the other SoA are recoverable from the context (see Mauri 2007 for further details).

5.1.4 *Semantic domain: a great variation*

In the preceding sections it has become clear that European languages show an interesting cross-linguistic variation in the coding of the different subtypes of contrast.

There are some languages with a *discontinuity marker*, which expresses both instances of non-sequential combination and oppositive contrast (see Section 2.1): for example Polish (example 25), which has the discontinuity marker *a* (shared also by Russian, Ukrainian, Bulgarian, Belorussian and Serbo-Croatian), Lithuanian (*o*), Hungarian (*meg*) and Chechen (*tq'a*).

(25) Polish (Agnieszka Latos, p.c.)
Oni płacą a my jemy.
3PL pay:3PL *a* 1PL eat:1PL
'They pay and we eat.'

In Russian, Bulgarian, Chechen and Lithuanian, this discontinuity marker is used to express also correction, as can be seen from the Lithuanian example in (26): in (26a) the discontinuity relation is further enriched by an inference of opposition, if the intonation signals some contrast, whereas in (26b) the inferential enrichment that further specifies the nature of the discontinuity is an inference of correction.

(26) Lithuanian, Baltic, Indo-European (Laura Ratautaite, p.c.)
a. *Aš dirbu õ Peter miega*
I work:PRS.1SG *õ* Peter sleep:PRS.3SG
'I work and Peter sleeps.'
b. *Peter nesimoko savo kambaryju õ žaidėia sode*
Peter NEG:study:PRS.3SG his room:LOC *õ* play:PRS.3SG garden:LOC
'Peter is not studying in his room but he's playing in the garden.'

As we have already said when talking about the morpho-phonological complexity of the adversative markers, also specific connectives for the oppositive relation are attested, which would not be used to convey a non-sequential combination or a correction: among others, we have mentioned Italian *mentre* and French *tandis que*.

Some languages have different markers for corrective and counterexpectative contrast, as already shown in example (14) from German. Such languages are, besides German, Basque (*baina* ~ *baizik*), Spanish (*pero* ~ *sino*), Swedish (*men* ~ *utan*), Finnish (*mutta* ~ *vaan*), Estonian (*aga* ~ *vaid*), Lithuanian (*bèt* ~ *õ*), Russian and Bulgarian (*no* ~ *a*), Chechen (*amma* ~ *tq'a*), Romanian (*dar* ~ *ci*), Serbo-Croatian (*ali* ~ *nȅgo/vȅc*), Icelandic (*en* ~ *heldur*) and Hungarian (*de* ~ *hanem*).

Finally, in the central-western part of Europe, many languages also have a general adversative marker used for both counterexpectative and corrective contrast: Italian (*ma*), French (*mais*), Dutch (*maar*), Luxembourgish (*mee*), English (*but*), Portuguese (*mas*), Czech (*ale*), Albanian (*por*), Greek (*αλλά*). For a detailed discussion on adversative markers and their possible semantic domains, see Malchukov (2004) and Mauri (2006 and 2007).

5.1.5 *Synthesis*

From the data presented throughout this section, the European adversative constructions show a high degree of uniformity in terms of morphosyntactic features, since they are all parallel, mostly syndetic and with free mono- or polysyllabic markers. By contrast, considering the semantic domain of the attested constructions, the languages of Europe encode the different subtypes of contrast in many different ways, using either general or specific connectives.

The attested cross-linguistic variation is shown in Fig. 3, where the areal distribution of specific markers clearly reveals a central-western area where languages behave in the same way, showing at least one general marker for the corrective and

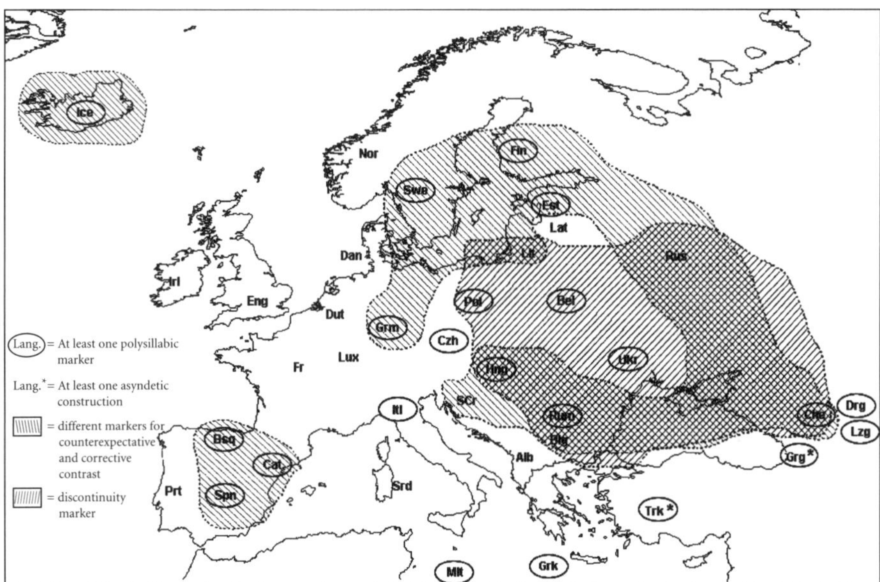

Figure 3. Adversative constructions in the languages of Europe

the counterexpectative contrast and no general marker of discontinuity (the area left white). Specific contrast markers and discontinuity markers are attested in the eastern part of Europe and in Spain, at the western periphery.

5.2 A glance outside Europe: what is 'typically European'?

The comparison sample shows some gaps in the data on adversative constructions, mainly because descriptive grammars often do not give any information about the three subtypes of contrast, and simply signal a rough translation of the English conjunction *but*. We will however try to draw a picture of what happens outside Europe, in order to put the European picture within a broader perspective and identify what may be treated as typical European.

Whereas syndesis is the most widespread strategy within the European area, outside Europe many languages use asyndetic constructions to convey the relation of contrast (11 out of 36). This usually happens in those languages where juxtaposition is a normal strategy for conjunction too, and further specifications of contrast are left to inference. Concerning the morpho-phonological complexity of the attested adversative markers, there does not seem to be a great difference between European and non-European data. In the comparison sample, too, adversative connectives are mono- and polysyllabic, showing a higher degree of complexity than the conjunctive connectives. The two samples slightly differ in the free or bound nature of the markers: in Europe, all languages have at least one free adversative morpheme and only Dargi shows the possibility of using the bound marker *-gu*; outside Europe, on the other hand, bound morphemes seem to be more common (4 languages out of 36 have bound adversative connectives).

Non-parallel adversative constructions are attested in Kolyma Yukaghir, Tauya, Korean and West Greenlandic, whereas European languages only show parallel strategies. This picture is similar to that depicted for disjunction, since in both cases Europe is characterized by the complete absence of a feature which is instead attested outside, even though in a small number of languages.

Finally, the semantic domain of the adversative constructions attested in the comparison sample could not be analyzed in depth because, as already said, descriptive grammars do not give a lot of information on the different subtypes of contrast.

There are, however, well described languages like Hebrew and Arabic, which have different specific markers for counterexpectative (Hebrew *aval*, Arabic *lākin*) and corrective contrast (Hebrew *éla*, Arabic *bal*), just like German and Spanish. By contrast, Nànáfwɛ̂ behaves like English in having only a general adversative marker used for both semantic subtypes (*sàngɛ́*).

Furthermore, languages like Tauya and Kolyma Yukaghir use Same Subject (SS) and Different Suject (DS) markers in clause chaining. The DS markers tend to cover the same semantic domain of discontinuity markers attested in Europe, mainly because they signal the discontinuity caused by the change of referents. However, more research has to be done on the possible parallelism of these two different discontinuity constructions.

5.2.1 *Conclusions*

To sum up, despite the scarcity of non-European data on adversative constructions, it is possible to identify a set of features that characterizes the European adversative constructions.

Adversative constructions are all *parallel* and mostly *syndetic*. Adversative markers consist of *free, mono- and polysyllabic* morphemes. There are *different areas*: a central area with general markers for counterexpectative and corrective contrast; an eastern area with specific markers for counterexpectative and corrective contrast, and with general markers of discontinuity; a Basque-Hispanic area to the west with specific markers for counterexpectative and corrective contrast.

6. Conclusions: 'And-But-Or' area

In the course of the paper, it has been shown that the European area shows both some internal cross-linguistic variation, mainly concerning the semantic domain of the attested constructions, and a high degree of structural homogeneity, especially if compared to non-European data gathered in the comparison sample.

In this concluding section a further generalization will be made, based on the comparison of the attested European conjunctive, disjunctive and adversative constructions. Europe has turned out to be internally quite homogeneous in the coding of each of the three analyzed semantic relations, but an even more internally consistent area can be identified within the European borders, namely what I propose to call the *'And-But-Or' area*, represented in Fig. 4.

The languages belonging to the 'And-But-Or' area encode the relations of combination, alternative and contrast in the same way. They are characterized by the following set of features:

- *syndetic* conjunctive, disjunctive and adversative constructions;
- internally *parallel* conjunctive, disjunctive and adversative constructions;
- *free* conjunctive, disjunctive and adversative markers;
- a *general* conjunctive marker ('And'), a general disjunctive marker ('Or'), a general marker for the counterexpectative and the corrective contrast ('But') and no discontinuity marker.

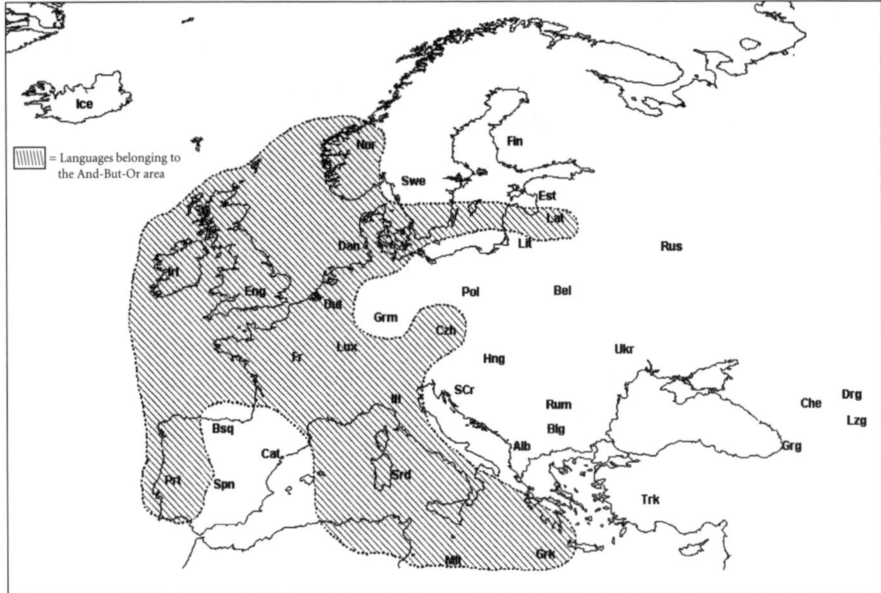

Figure 4. And-But-Or area

To this area belong all the Romance languages except for Spanish and Catalan (Italian, Sardinian, Portuguese and French), a Celtic language (Irish), all the Germanic languages except for German, Icelandic, and Swedish (Norwegian, Danish, Dutch, Luxembourgish and English), a Slavic language (Czech), Greek and finally Maltese, a non Indo-European language.

We may hypothesize reasons underlying this distribution, such as close historical and economic connections that may have caused reciprocal influences among these languages, but in that case the exclusion of German and Spanish would not be explained. On the other hand, there could be diachronic explanations in terms of the grammaticalization processes that have led to this configuration, but a comparative diachronic analysis of the conjunctive, adversative and disjunctive constructions is still missing.

The aim of this paper was to show the areal distribution of the features characterizing the European conjunctive, disjunctive and adversative constructions. However, the picture that has been drawn suggests many questions that still need an answer. The main result of this work is thus to have highlighted both some typical European features and an areal configuration of the cross-linguistic variation attested, which is far from random and may constitute a starting point for further diachronic and synchronic analysis.

Abbreviations

1	first person	ERG	ergative	PST	past		
2	second person	FUT	future	PL	plural		
3	third person	HORT	hortative	POL	polite		
ABS	absolutive	IMP	imperative	PRF	perfective		
ACC	accusative	IMPF	imperfective	PROGR	progressive		
ADVB	adverbial	INCOMP	incompletive	PRS	present		
ALL	allative	IND	indicative	PT	particle		
AOC	aorist converb	INDEF	Indefinite	PTCP	participial		
AUX	auxiliary	INF	infinitive	Q	question		
COND	conditional	LOC	locative	SG	singular		
DAT	dative	M	masculine	SUP	superior		
DECL	declarative	NEG	negative	TOP	topic		
DEF	definite	NOM	nominative	WP	witnessed		
EMPH	emphatic	OPT	optative		past		

European sample

AFRO-ASIATIC. *Semitic – Southern*: Maltese. ALTAIC *Turkic – Southern*: Turkish. ISOLATE. *Basque*: Basque. CAUCASIC. *Nakh-Daghestanian*: Chechen; *Daghestanian–Lakic*: Dargi; *Daghestanian – Lezgic*: Lezgian. INDO-EUROPEAN. *Celtic – Goidelic*: Irish; *Romance – Western*: Catalan, French, Portuguese, Spanish; *Romance – Eastern*: Italian, Romanian, Sardinian; *Germanic – Northern*: Danish, Icelandic, Norwegian, Swedish; *Germanic – Western*: Dutch, English, German, Luxembourgish; *Slavic – Western*: Czech, Polish; *Slavic – Eastern*: Belorussian, Russian, Ukrainian; *Slavic – Southern*: Bulgarian, Serbo-Croatian; *Baltic*: Lithuanian, Latvian; *Isolates*: Greek, Albanian. **Kartvelian**: Georgian. URALIC. *Balto-Finnic*: Finnish, Estonian; *Ugric*: Hungarian.
Total languages: 37. Total languages searched with questionnaires: 31.
Classification based on www.ethnologue.org, Haspelmath (1993), Nocentini (2004).

Comparison sample

AFRO-ASIATIC. *Semitic – Arabic*: Arabic; *Semitic – Canaanit*: Hebrew; *Chadic – Western*: Hausa; *Chadic – Biumandare*: Hdi; *Cushitic – Southern*: Iraqw; *Cushitic – Eastern*: Harar Oromo, Somali. AUSTRALIAN. *Gunwing-guan – Mangarayic*: Mangarayi. AUSTRO-ASIATIC. *Viet-Muong*: Vietnamese. AUSTRONESIAN. *Malayo- Polynesian*: Maori; *Polynesian*: Rapanui, Tuvaluan; *Muna-Buton*: Tukang

Besi. CHAPACURAN. *Wanham-Madeira*: Warì. CREOLE. *English based – Suriname*: Ndyuka. DRAVIDIC. *Tamil-Kannada – Tamil*: Malayalam. ESKIMO-ALEUT. *Eskimo-Inuit*: West Greenlandic. HOKAN. *Yuman – Delta-California*: Jamul Tipay. INDO-EUROPEAN. *Indo-Iranian – Persian*: Farsi; *Indo-iranian – Indo-Aryan*: Marathi. ISOLATE. Japanese. ISOLATE. Korean. MOSETENAN: Mosetén. NAD-ENE. *Nuclear – Athapaskan*: Kuskokwim. NIGER-CONGO. *Volta Congo – Kwa*: Nànáfwɛ̂; *Volta Congo – Gur*: Supyire, Koromfe; *Volta Congo – Bantu*: Kisi. NILO-SAHARAN. *Nilotic – Southern*: Lango. SINO-TIBETAN. *Tibeto-Burman – Kuki-Chin*: Hakha Lai; *Tibeto-Burman – Meithei*: Meithei; *Tibeto-Burman – Kiranti*: Dumi, Limbu. SIOUAN. *Missisippi – Winnebago*: Hocąk. TRANS NEW GUINEA. *Brahman*: Tauya. YUKAGHIR. Kolyma.
Total of languages: 36. Total of languages searched with questionnaires: 7
Classification based on www.ethnologue.org and Lyovin (1997).

Acknowledgments

I would like to express my deep gratitude to all the informants who gave me precious data about their native languages. My thanks also go to Paolo Ramat, Michele Prandi, Ewald Lang and Silvia Luraghi for reading drafts of this paper and discussing parts of it with me. I would like to thank two anonymous reviewers for their very helpful comments. Finally, my greatest thanks go to Sonia Cristofaro, who has followed this work from its very beginning with her enthusiastic support and insightful observations.

References

Abraham, W. 1979. But. *Studia Linguistica* 33(2): 89–119.

Anscombre, J. & Ducrot, O. 1977. Deux *mais* en français? *Lingua* 43: 23–40.

Brown, W. & Alt, T. 2004. *A handbook of Serbian, Bosnian and Croatian.* (http://www.seelrc.org:8080/grammar/mainframe.jsp?nLanguageID = 1): SEELRC.

Cristofaro, S. 2003. *Subordination.* Oxford: OUP.

Dik, S. 1968. *Coordination. Its implications for the theory of general linguistics.* Amsterdam: North-Holland.

Donuhue, M. 1993. *A grammar of Tukang Besi.* Berlin, New York NY: Mouton de Gruyter.

Gil, D. 2004. Riau Indonesian Sama. Explorations in macrofunctionality. In *Coordinating constructions*, M. Haspelmath (ed.), 371–424. Amsterdam: John Benjamins.

Givón, T. 1990. *Syntax: A functional-typological introduction.* Vol. II. Amsterdam: John Benjamins.

Haiman, J. 1985. *Natural syntax.* Cambridge: CUP.

Haspelmath, M. 1993. *A grammar of Lezgian.* Berlin: Mouton de Gruyter.

Haspelmath, M. 2001. The European linguistic area: Standard average european. In *Language universals and language typology: An international handbook*, M. Haspelmath, E. König, W. Österreicher & W. Raible (eds), 1492–1510. Berlin: Mouton de Gruyter.

Haspelmath, M. 2004. Coordinating constructions: An overview. In *Coordinating constructions*, M. Haspelmath (ed.), 3–39. Amsterdam: John Benjamins.
Haspelmath, M. to appear. Coordination. In *Language typology and linguistic description* (2nd edn), T. Shopen (ed.), Cambridge: CUP.
Heine, B. & Kuteva, T. 2002. *World lexicon of grammaticalization*. Cambridge: CUP.
Jeschull, L. 2004. Coordination in Chechen. In *Coordinating constructions*, M. Haspelmath (ed.), 241–265. Amsterdam: John Benjamins.
Johanson, L. 1995. On Turkic converb clauses. In *Converbs in cross-linguistic perspective*, M. Haspelmath & E. König (eds), 313–347. Berlin: Mouton de Gruyter.
Kornfilt, J. 1997. *Turkish*. London: Routledge.
Kortmann, B. 1997. *Adverbial subordination. A typology and history of adverbial subordinators based on European languages*. Berlin: Mouton de Gruyter.
Kotcheva, K. 2005. *En* as a marker of discontinuity: Evidence of runic inscriptions. MS Berlin.
Lang, E. 2000. Adversative connectors on distinct levels of discourse: A re-examination of Eve Sweetser's three level approach. In *Cause, condition, concession, contrast*, E. Couper-Kuhlen & B. Kortmann (eds), 235–256. Berlin: Mouton de Gruyter.
Langacker, R. 1987. *Foundations of cognitive grammar*. Vols. I & II. Stanford CA: Stanford University Press.
Lyovin, A.V. 1997, *An introduction to the languages of the world*, New York: OUP.
Luraghi, S. 1990. *Old Hittite sentence structure*. London: Routledge.
Malchukov, A.L. 2004. Towards a semantic typology of adversative and contrast marking. *Journal of Semantics* 21: 177–198.
Mauri, C. 2006. Combinazione e contrasto: I connettivi congiuntivi e avversativi nelle lingue d'Europa. *Archivio Glottologico Italiano* 91(2): 166–202.
Mauri, C. 2007. Coordination relations: A cross-linguistic study. PhD Dissertation, University of Pavia.
Mauri, C. to appear. The irreality of alternatives: Towards a typology of disjunction. *Studies in Language*.
Merlan, F. 1982. *Mangarayi* [Lingua Descriptive Studies 4]. Amsterdam: North Holland.
Mithun, M. 1988. The grammaticization of coordination. In *Clause combining in grammar and discourse*, J. Haiman & S. Thompson (eds), 331–60. Amsterdam: John Benjamins.
Nocentini, A. 2004. *L'Europa linguistica: profilo storico e tipologico*. Firenze: Le Monnier.
Payne, J. 1985. Complex phrases and complex sentences. In *Complex constructions*, Vol. II: *Language typology and syntactic description*, T. Shopen (ed.), 3–41. Cambridge: CUP.
Prandi, M. 2004. *The building blocks of meaning*. Amsterdam: John Benjamins.
Rudolph, E. 1996. *Contrast. Adversative and concessive expressions on sentence and text level*. Berlin: Walter de Gruyter.
Scorretti, M. 1988. Le strutture coordinate. In *Grande grammatica Italiana di consultazione*, Vol. I, L. Renzi (ed.), 227–270. Bologna: Il Mulino.
Siewierska, A. 1991. *Functional grammar*. London: Routledge.
Sohn, H.-M. 1994. *Korean*. London: Routledge.
Stassen, L. 1985. *Comparison in universal grammar*. Oxford: Blackwell.
Van den Berg, H. 2004. Coordinating constructions in Daghestanian languages. In *Coordinating constructions*, M. Haspelmath (ed.), 197–226. Amsterdam: John Benjamins.
Verstraete, J. 2005. Two types of coordination in clause combining. *Lingua* 115: 611–626.
Wälchli, B. 2005. *Co-compounds and natural coordination*. Oxford: OUP.
Zipf, G.K. 1949. *Human behaviour and the principle of least effort*. Cambridge MA: Addison-Wesley.

Complex Nominal Determiners

A contrastive study*

Ignazio Mauro Mirto and Heike Necker

This paper advances the idea that in German, Italian and English multi-word determiner phrases, termed Complex Nominal Determiners (CND), exist which are formed by at least a noun (N1) followed by a preposition (*von, di, of*). CNDs either quantify the referent of the noun they determine (N2) or simultaneously quantify *and* qualify it. Syntactic tests show that the structure of NPs with a CND can be paralleled to that of clauses with support verbs (Double Analysis) insofar as they are structurally ambiguous. N2, traditionally regarded as a dependent (*of*-phrase), can be the phrasal head. Semantic tests provide evidence that in a CND N1 carries neither referential nor lexical meaning and works as a function-word. Our study is based on data drawn from a written corpus for German and two corpora (written and spoken) for Italian. The data for English mainly comes from electronic dictionaries.

1. Introduction

A body of evidence shows that Italian noun phrases such as (1) and (2) – both sharing the linear structure in (3) – have distinct internal structures:

(1) *una marea di parenti lontani*
a tide of relatives distant
'so many distant relatives'

* Our research project began in 2003 as a result of certain remarks made by Nunzio La Fauci, to whom we heartily express our gratitude. Parts of this research were first presented at a FIRB conference (Pavia, December 2004), and then at the XXIV Lexis & Grammar Conference (Liverpool, September 2005). We would like to thank the participants for their comments and advice. Special thanks go to our colleagues from Siena: Marina Benedetti, our unit-director, Carla Bruno, Paola Dardano, Silvia Pieroni and Liana Tronci. We are also most grateful to Paolo Ramat and the FIRB for giving us the possibility to collaborate in this project and contribute to this fruitful environment. Many thanks to Catherine Camugli Gallardo and to the two anonymous reviewers for their valuable suggestions. Our grateful thanks to Mary Goggin for her help with English. All the conclusions expressed come from close collaboration between the two authors. Italian regulations on authorship require the authors to specify whichever section they are responsible for: Sections 1, 4, and 5 are the work of H. N., whilst 2 and 3 were contributed by I. M. M.

(2) *una festa di parenti lontani*
a party of relatives distant
'a party of distant relatives'

(3) <DET N1 *of* N2>

Several diagnostics point to reversed head/non-head patterns for the two phrases, as illustrated below:[1]

(4) Non-head Head
N1 = *marea* N2 = *parenti*

(5) Head Non-head
N1 = *festa* N2 = *parenti*

We suggest that a parallel distinction should be made for German pairs of phrases such as (6) and (7), which also share a <DET N1 *of* N2> linear order, but differ in a similar fashion to (1) and (2):

(6) *ein Haufen von entfernten Verwandten*
a heap of distant.DAT relatives.DAT
'so many distant relatives'

(7) *ein Fest von entfernten Verwandten*
a party of distant.DAT relatives.DAT
'a party of distant relatives'

We would like to advance the idea that in (1) the noun *marea* 'tide', unlike *festa*, can function (a) as in *La marea si abbassa* 'The tide goes out', i.e. as the head of a NP; or (b) as part of a determiner phrase that here we term CND (Complex Nominal Determiner). Likewise, the German noun *Haufen* 'heap' can be either the phrasal head, as in *Er warf alles auf einen Haufen* 'He threw everything on a heap', or part of a CND as in (6).[2]

CNDs display a <DET N1 *of*> linear structure and occupy the same position as one-word determiners, as in (8), where *una marea di* 'literally: a tide of' alternates with the quantifiers *tanti* and *molti*, both meaning 'many':

(8) *Tanti/Una marea di/Molti parenti pensavano di partire*
several relatives thought.3PL of leaving
'Several relatives thought of leaving.'

1. What we consider to be a 'head' roughly corresponds to what Nichols (1986: 57) sustains: «the head is the word which governs, or is subcategorized for – or otherwise determines the possibility of occurrence of – the other word». Broadly speaking, the term can be equated with 'predicate'.

2. An anonymous reviewer has pointed out that the behaviour of nouns within a CND differs from that of nouns in complex prepositions such as *with the intention of, with the aim of*: in her/his view the former often take on a metaphoric or metonymic meaning, the latter retain their literal meaning (see Gross and Prandi 2004).

Nouns working as *marea* 'tide' in (8) have a peculiar behaviour pattern both syntactically and semantically. Syntactically, CNDs allow for a number of uncommon phenomena, e.g. the subject-verb agreement in (8), where the verb agrees in number with N2 rather than N1. From a semantic point of view, N1 carries no lexical meaning, as does *marea* in (8), which does not take on its literal sense 'tide'. More generally, it can be shown that N1 works as a function-word rather than as a content-word.

For languages such as French and English, the syntactic and semantic behaviour of phrases with the linear structure in (3) have attracted a certain amount of attention. G. Gross (1990) applies the term 'Complex Determiners' to French phrases which are structurally equivalent to the Italian phrases above, e.g. *une averse/grêle/avalanche de coups* 'many blows/shots'. Guenthner & Blanco (2004) also briefly mention the phenomenon. Related work can be found for the so-called Complex Quantifiers (for French see Buvet 1994).[3] As for English, such phrases have been discussed under the labels 'classifier constructions' (Lehrer 1986), 'measure noun constructions' (Brems 2003), and 'measure phrases' (Dodge and Wright 2002).[4]

In both Italian and German, a wealth of CNDs can be found in everyday conversations, newspaper articles, and literary texts. In linguistic studies, however, the phenomenon has been virtually ignored. The collection of examples found in the chapters of three reference grammars of Italian (Serianni 1988, Renzi 1988 and Schwarze 1995) shows that CNDs are not treated in any specific way, as they appear only as sporadic examples. In those grammars, structures such as (8) are placed together with cases of quantification of so-called mass nouns in which countability and measurability are introduced, as in e.g. *a bottle of wine* (see Michaux 1992 for French). In 4.1 we provide evidence for setting the two cases apart.

In German, two other structures appear along with the one exemplified in (6). Both have a <DET N1 N2> structure (with no preposition), the first one with N2 always in the genitive, the second one with N1 and N2 carrying the same case marking (for a discussion of the controversial positions concerning the case marking of N2 in the literature see Hentschel 1993). As in Italian, for these structures

3. For partitive constructions of this type in the Circum-Baltic languages, see Koptjevskaja-Tamm (2001).

4. Quirk et al. (1985) classify expressions like *a lot of (furniture), a great deal of (money)* as phrasal quantifiers belonging to an open class, that in familiar spoken English also includes expressions such as *bags of (time)* and *heaps of (money)*. They write (1985: 264): «Although the quantity nouns *lot, deal*, etc. look like the head of a noun phrase, there are good grounds for arguing that the whole expression (*a lot of, a good deal of*, etc.) functions as a determiner.» The quote strengthens the head/non-head analysis given in (4) for Italian and German.

the literature provides neither systematic nor comparative analyses, except for some remarks found in Drosdowski (1995), in which the additional structures are labelled *Genitivus Partitivus* and *Partitive Apposition* respectively.

This paper focuses on Italian and German, but also includes a number of examples from English, to which, however, no specific section will be devoted in this study, since our analysis for Italian and German CNDs can be extended to their English counterparts. Of the three languages treated here only German presents a case-system.

The scope of this paper is threefold: Section 2 illustrates the syntactic properties that make CNDs peculiar in Italian and German; Section 3 provides a description of the semantics of CNDs; finally, Section 4 gives a detailed insight into our databases, and shows numbers and percentages for certain syntactic properties that characterize CNDs.

For both Italian and German we have created databases from various sources. For Italian there are two: a) a collection of 16 CDs by *la Repubblica* containing the papers published from 1985 to 2000; b) the LIP by De Mauro et al. (1993), which is a corpus of modern spoken Italian recorded from 1990 to 1992 in the areas of Florence, Milan, Naples and Rome. For German, our research is based on the online archive of the newspaper *Die Welt*.[5] The German database also contains occurrences of the *Genitivus Partitivus* and the *Partitive Apposition*, and will thus enable us to find restrictions and frequencies for the three phrase types.

Our data is classified with FileMaker, a program with a great variety of options for the creation and use of large databases, that easily allows for complex searches, and with a format that can be easily converted into other formats.

2. The syntax of CNDs

Several tests support the analysis in (4) over that in (5). With the exception of the entailment test in 2.1, which shows the need for distinct analyses of pairs of phrases such as (1)–(2) and (6)–(7), all the tests in this section are syntactic in nature.

2.1 Entailments

A noteworthy indication of the structural difference between (1) and (2) can be observed in the behaviour these NPs exhibit with regard to an entailment test. The sentences in (9) and (10) share the same subject and the same verb. Their objects

5. Freely accessible in the web for the issues from May 1995, http://www.welt.de.

are (1) and (2) respectively, so the sentences differ only in the first post-verbal noun: in (9) this noun is *marea*, in (10) it is *festa*:

(9) *Anna pensò a una marea di parenti*
Anna thought to a tide of relatives
'Anna thought about so many relatives.'

(10) *Anna pensò a una festa di parenti*
Anna thought to a party of relatives
'Anna thought about a party of relatives.'

Their structural likeness is only apparent, since they actually yield opposite results as for the entailment patterns in (11), a sentence that differs from the first two simply because its object contains N2 only, namely *parenti* 'relatives':

(11) *Anna pensò a parenti*
Anna thought to relatives
'Anna thought about relatives.'

Sentence (9) does entail (11), whilst under no interpretation can (10) entail (11) 'Anna thought about relatives'. The different entailment patterns give evidence for assigning distinct structures to (1) and (2), as a single structure could hardly explain the difference highlighted. The German counterparts (9)' *Anna dachte an einen Haufen von Verwandten* 'Anna thought about so many relatives' and (10)' *Anna dachte an ein Fest von Verwandten* 'Anna thought about a party of relatives' yield the same entailment relations with (11)' *Anna dachte an Verwandte* 'Anna thought about relatives'.

2.2 Selection restrictions

In (12) and (13) the selection restrictions of the Italian verbs *pensare* 'think' and *preoccupare* 'worry' support the analysis in (4). Both subject and object NPs are tested; sentence (12) shows what happens with the former:

(12) N1 N2
Una valanga di parenti pensava di partire
an avalanche of relatives thought.3SG of leaving
'Several relatives thought of leaving.'

The [–Animate] feature of *valanga* 'literally: avalanche' makes this noun an ineligible notional subject of the verb *pensare* 'think'. In (12), this leaves *parenti* 'relatives' as the only notional subject possible. In other words, the thematic role *pensare* assigns to its subject can only be attributed to N2. Equivalent examples can be found in German, as with *Ein Haufen von Kids versucht, Polizei-Offizier zu werden* 'literally: A heap of kids tries to become police-officer', where only N2 can receive the thematic role assigned to its subject by *versuchen*.

Turning to direct objects, consider sentence (13), in which N1 is still *valanga* 'avalanche' and N2 is *elettori* 'voters':

					N1		N2
(13)	*Le dimissioni*	*di Max*	*preoccupano*	*una*	*valanga*	*di*	*elettori*
	the resignation.PL	of Max	worry	an	avalanche	of	voters

'Max's resignation worries a lot of voters.'

Again, the selectional restrictions of *preoccupare* 'worry' fail to make N1, the [–Animate] noun *valanga*, an eligible notional object. In (13), the verb assigns its direct object thematic role to *elettori* 'voters', the N2 of a sequence such as (3). Let us then compare (13) to a German example such as *Er las Berge von Zeitungen* 'he read mountains of newspapers', where it is clearly the newspapers that are read and not the mountains.

If one shares the view that only the head of a NP receives the thematic role assigned by the verb, the selection restrictions shown above suggest that the internal structure of the subject of (12) and the direct object of (13) must be of the kind shown in (4) rather than that in (5).

2.3 Verbal number agreement

A third piece of evidence for the structure in (4) comes from number agreement. In (8) above, we showed that the verb agrees in number with N2. Agreement with the N1 *marea* 'tide', however, is less likely (see 4), but also possible:

	N1	N2		
(14)	*Una marea di*	*parenti*	*pensava*	*di partire*
	a tide of	relatives	thought.3SG	of leaving

'A considerable number of relatives thought of leaving.'

The double possibility for verbal agreement in (8) and (14) gives us a better idea of the complexity of NPs such as (1): by taking the N1 *marea* 'tide' as the head of the subject phrase, with *parenti* 'relatives' as a non-head, one correctly accounts for the singular form of the verb. The grammatical plural form of the verb, however, shows that number agreement can also be controlled by N2, the noun *parenti* 'relatives', which should then be analyzed as the phrasal head. If one supposes that a phrase can host one head only, as is generally the case, the analysis reaches an impasse. This structural ambiguity is reminiscent of that found with the Double Analysis first noticed by Maurice Gross (1981).

2.4 Paraphrases

Further evidence for considering N2 as a possible head for a complex NP like (1) emerges from paraphrasing. An experiment (related to the entailment test shown under 2.1) can be built as in the triad below, in which (15a), the source sentence, contains the direct object *un pugno di riso* 'literally: a fist of rice', whose surface structure is that of (3), susceptible to being analyzed as comprising a CND:

N1 N2
(15a) *Max mangiò un pugno di riso*
Max ate a fist of rice
'Max ate a fistful of rice.'

N1
(15b) *Max mangiò un pugno*
Max ate a fist
'Max ate a fist.'

N2
(15c) *Max mangiò riso*
Max ate rice
'Max ate rice.'

(15a) gives origin to two derived sentences whose direct object is simpler because it contains a noun only: this noun is N1 in (15b), and N2 in (15c). The translations show rather distinct semantic outcomes: the retention of N1, as in (15b), yields a (semantically deviant) derived sentence that is not a paraphrase of the initial sentence; when N2 is retained, however, the derived sentence does provide a paraphrase of (15a) (note that (15a) also entails (15c)). Together, these results qualify the noun *pugno* of (15a) as the N1 of a CND.

The paraphrase test can be performed on other grammatical relations too. However, when the alleged CND is within a subject NP and N2 is countable, unlike in (15), some changes can be necessary. The derived sentence that retains N2, i.e. (15c), is well-formed because the N2 *riso* is an uncountable direct object allowing for a zero determiner. Things are different with a countable N2 as found in a preverbal subject NP, as in (8), repeated below as (16a):

N1 N2
(16a) *Una marea di parenti pensavano di partire*
a tide of relatives thought.3PL of leaving
'Several relatives thought of leaving.'

N1
(16b) *Una marea pensava di partire*
a tide thought.3SG of leaving
'A tide thought of leaving.'

N2
(16c) *I parenti pensavano di partire*
the relatives thought.3PL of leaving
'The relatives thought of leaving.'

When this is the case, in the derived sentence where N2 is retained, this noun calls for a determiner: in (16c) a determiner (*i* 'the.PL.MASC') precedes N2, without which the sentence would be ill-formed.[6] The semantically deviant derived sentence (16b) is not a paraphrase of the source sentence (16a), as the translation clearly shows. As for (16c), if the speaker's assumptions about the relatives being known or unknown to the hearer are ignored, the sentence makes a good paraphrase of (16a). Likewise, a German example such as (16a)' *Eine Lawine von Leuten dachte/n daran, wegzufahren* 'literally: An avalanche of people was/were thinking of leaving' can be paraphrased by (16c)' *Leute dachten daran, wegzufahren* 'People were thinking of leaving', but not by (16b)' *Eine Lawine dachte daran, wegzufahren* 'literally: An avalanche was thinking of leaving'.

In one instance, the very same noun can behave as the N1 of a CND and in another as a standard referential noun. In (17), for instance, the paraphrase test shows that *granello* 'grain' is used as the N1 of a CND, given that, unlike (17b) (semantically deviant), (17c) can be a paraphrase of (17a):[7]

			N1	N2
(17a)	*Max*	*dimostrò*	*un granello di*	*buon senso*
	Max	demonstrated	a grain of	good sense
	'Max demonstrated a scrap of common sense.'			

			N1
(17b)	*Max*	*dimostrò*	*un granello*
	Max	demonstrated	a grain
	'Max demonstrated a grain.'		

			N2
(17c)	*Max*	*dimostrò*	*buon senso*
	Max	demonstrated	good sense
	'Max demonstrated common sense.'		

The complex direct object of (18a) also contains a sequence of the form found in (3) and is thus subject to being analyzed as comprising a CND.

				N1		N2
(18a)	*L'organizzazione*	*manderà*	*ogni*	*granello*	*di*	*riso*
	the organization	will send	each	grain	of	rice
	'The organization will send each and every grain of rice.'					

6. As (i) illustrates:

i.	**Parenti*	*pensavano*	*di partire*
	relatives	thought.3PL	of leaving

7. In (17a), the prenominal adjective *buon* (literally: 'good') is mandatory. Idiosyncracies such as this are rather common.

N1

(18b) *L'organizzazione manderà ogni granello*
the organization will send each grain
'The organization will send every single grain.'

N2

(18c) *L'organizzazione manderà riso*
the organization will send rice
'The organization will send rice.'

The first noun of the direct object of these three sentences is *granello* 'grain', just as in (17) above. However, the derived sentences show that *ogni granello di riso* 'each grain of rice' is not used as a CND. For *granello* to qualify as the N1 of a CND, (18c) should normally be a good paraphrase of (18a) whilst (18b) should not. This pattern is not found: (18c) does paraphrase (18a), but also (18b) – under appropriate discourse circumstances – can be understood as carrying the meaning of (18a). For example, in the case of an ellipsis in which *riso* 'rice' has already been established as the topic of conversation, and is thus thematic information that can be elided.

German exhibits the same phenomenon. As in (17), the sentence *Sein Gesicht war unter einem Berg von Schminke vergraben* 'His face was buried under a mountain of make-up' cannot be paraphrased by *Sein Gesicht war unter einem Berg vergraben* 'His face was buried under a mountain' (omission of N2, cf. 17b), though it can by *Sein Gesicht war unter Schminke vergraben* 'His face was buried under make-up' (omission of N1, cf. 17c). This confirms that in this context *ein Berg von* has to be considered a CND. On the other hand, we find German examples parallel to (18) such as *Die Tasche war unter einem Berg von Müll vergraben* 'The bag was buried under a mountain of garbage', which can be elliptically paraphrased either with *Die Tasche war unter einem Berg vergraben* 'The bag was buried under a mountain' or *Die Tasche war unter Müll vergraben* 'The bag was buried under garbage'.[8]

2.5 Partitive *ne*-cliticization

Another property characterizing CNDs is related to cases of cliticization with *ne* 'of it'. Direct objects introduced by an indefinite determiner can undergo partitive *ne*-cliticization, as in (19):

(19a) *Gianni vuole un biscotto*
Gianni wants a biscuit
'Gianni wants a biscuit.'

8. Further evidence comes from a test on anaphora. With *Sein Gesicht war unter einem Berg von Schminke vergraben* 'lit.: His face was buried under a mountain of make-up', the N1 *Berg* 'mountain' cannot work as the antecedent of an anaphor (see also fn. 11 below): **Der Berg war riesig.*

(19b) *Gianni ne vuole uno*
Gianni of.it wants one
'Gianni wants one.'

The pronominalization in (19b) brings about (a) the presence of the clitic *ne* 'of it' before the verb, and (b) the cancellation of the postverbal nominal item, though with the retention of a pronominal element (i.e. *uno* 'one', distinct from the indefinite determiner *un* 'a').

The direct objects of (20) and (21) display the surface linear sequence shown in (3). By *ne*-cliticizing these direct objects, we obtain (22) and (23) respectively:

(20) *Quei linguisti condividono un pensiero di Fodor*
those linguists share a thought of Fodor
'Those linguists share a thought of Fodor's.'

(21) *Quei linguisti condividono un sacco di onori*
those linguists share a sack of honours
'Those linguists share a shower of honours.'

(22) *Quei linguisti ne condividono uno*
those linguists of.it share one
'Those linguists share one.'

(23) *Quei linguisti ne condividono un sacco*
those linguists of.it share a sack
'Those linguists share a lot of them.'

The effects of partitive *ne*-cliticization are different. To begin with, in (23) the first noun, i.e. *sacco* 'sack', is retained, whereas in (22) this is not the case. Second, the noun undergoing *ne*-cliticization is not even the same: in (22) this is *pensiero* 'thought', namely the first noun, whilst in (23) it is the second one, i.e. *onori* 'honours'. This distinct behaviour can be explained if one assumes a reversed head/non-head pattern: the phrasal head is *pensiero* in the direct object of (20), whilst it is *onori* in the direct object of (21). The internal structure of *un pensiero di Fodor* has the structure in (5), but for *un sacco di onori* 'literally: a sack of honours' the internal structure appears to be the one given in (4), which amounts to saying that *sacco* 'sack' is the N1 of a CND.[9]

'The mountain was huge'. On the other hand, with *Die Tasche war unter einem Berg von Müll vergraben* 'The bag was buried under a mountain of garbage' both N1 and N2 can serve as an antecedent: *Der Berg stank* 'The mountain stank' or *Der Müll stank* 'The garbage stank'.

9. In Italian, some prepositional phrases introduced by *di* 'of' can also be cliticized with the pronoun *ne*, as in (i) and (ii) below:

i. *Gianni parla di Fodor*
Gianni speaks of Fodor
'Gianni speaks about Fodor.'

Additional evidence that *ne*-cliticization does have distinct effects in (20) and (21) springs from the difference in grammaticality between (24) and (25), where the post-verbal noun is left-dislocated:

(24) *Di pensieri di Fodor, quei linguisti ne condividono uno*
of thoughts of Fodor those linguists of.it share one
'As for Fodor's thoughts, those linguists share one of these.'

(25) **Di sacchi di onori, quei linguisti ne condividono uno*
of sacks of honours those linguists of.them share one

The direct object of sentence (25) contains a CND: left-dislocation of the sequence <N1 *di* N2> yields an ungrammatical outcome. Sentence (24) shows that the same operation is possible on (20).

As expected, the attempt to left-dislocate N2 only also brings about an opposite pattern of grammaticality:

(26) **Di Fodor, quei linguisti ne condividono un pensiero*
of Fodor those linguists of.it share a thought

(27) *Di onori, quei linguisti ne condividono un sacco*
of honours those linguists of.them share a sack
'As for honours, those linguists share many.'

Again, the differences in the pairs (24)–(25) and (26)–(27) prove that the internal structure of *un pensiero di Fodor* 'a thought of Fodor's' and of *un sacco di onori* 'a shower of honours' must be distinct. For the former NP, these differences corroborate the analysis shown in (5), for the latter that in (4).[10]

---

ii. *Gianni ne parla*
Gianni of.him speaks
'Gianni speaks about him.'

By cliticizing the prepositional phrase *di Fodor* in (20) as in (ii), we obtain (iii), which, on the surface, actually looks like the partitive *ne*-cliticization in (23). As (iii) is not a case of partitive *ne*-cliticization, it does not counterexemplify the test.

iii. *Quei linguisti ne condividono un pensiero*
those linguists of.his share a thought
'Those linguists share one of his thoughts.'

10. An anonymous reviewer proposes an additional test based on clitic and past participle agreement in left-dislocation (see (24) and (25)):

i. *Quella marea di parenti l'ha invitata Max*
that tide of relatives her has invited.SG.FEM Max
'As for that crowd of relatives, Max invited them.'

3. The semantics of CNDs

Nouns working as *Haufen* 'heap' in (6) or *marea* 'tide' in (8) are neither lexical nor referential.[11] Consequences of the lack of lexical meaning were observable in the triads in (15) and (16): the derived sentences in which N2 is retained are indeed paraphrases of the source sentences, whereas those in which N1 is retained are not. Such effects are also observable in English. By removing 'of N2' in the sentences below, we yield sentences that are not paraphrases of the source sentences. Occasionally, the outcome can be a sentence whose object violates the selection restrictions of the verb, as in (28b).

	N1	N2
(28a)	Tom drank a finger of whisky.	
(28b)	Tom drank a finger.	

	N1	N2
(29a)	They shared a shower of honours.	
(29b)	They shared a shower.	

---

ii. *Quella marea di parenti li ha invitati Max*
that tide of relatives them has invited.PL.MASC Max
'As for that crowd of relatives, Max invited them.'

iii. *Quella festa di parenti l'ha organizzata Max*
that party of relatives her has organised.SG.FEM Max
'As for that party of relatives, Max organised it.'

iv.* *Quella festa di parenti li ha organizzati Max*
that party of relatives them has organised.PL.MASC Max
'As for that party of relatives, Max organised them.'

In (i) and (ii), where the left-dislocated constituent contains a CND, the pronoun and the past participle can agree either with N1 or with N2. By replacing *marea* 'tide' with *festa* 'party', as in (iii) and (iv), pronominal and past participle agreement can only be controlled by N1, which is then the only phrasal head possible.

11. As one of the anonymous reviewers suggests, supplemental evidence for the non-referential nature of N1 comes from expressions such as those below:

i. They shared a shower of honours → (ii) * The shower was a mess

In (i), 'shower', the N1 of a CND, fails to establish a discourse referent. The second sentence is ill-formed because the definite NP 'the shower' lacks an eligible antecedent. This is extra evidence that the N1 of a CND is not referential, in the sense of Karttunen (1969: 5): «Let us say that the appearance of an indefinite noun phrase establishes a discourse referent just in case it justifies the occurrence of a coreferential pronoun or a definite noun phrase later in the text.» (underlining in the original). Note that in languages such as English and German, nouns (proper and common) can also commonly be part of determiner phrases (e.g. *Bob's book, my sister's watch*). In these cases, such nouns are both lexical and referential.

	N1	N2
(30a)	The lawyer has a body of evidence	
(30b)	The lawyer has a body	

On the other hand, the removal of *a finger of*, *a shower of*, and *a body of* from (28a), (29a), and (30a), respectively, does not modify the basic meaning of the sentences, in a parallel manner to the preservation of the basic meaning in case of the removal of the quantifier or the cardinal number. In both (31) and (32) the objects given are the same, i.e. 'pens':

(31) He gave me many/three pens.

(32) He gave me pens.

3.1 Translational correspondences

Further evidence for the non lexical, non-referential nature of N1 can be found in translational correspondences, which should be observed in two different ways: first, by keeping the same N1 in language A and then by finding as many translations as possible in language B. This is shown below (the data is from the dictionary *Pons*, Giacoma & Kolb 2002):

(33) Language A = Italian, fixed N1 is *marea*;
Language B = German

Italian	German
una marea di literally: a tide of	*ein Batzen* (*von*) 'lit.: a chunk of'
	ein Berg (*von*) 'lit.: a mountain of'
	eine Flut (*von*) 'lit.: a flood of'
	ein Haufen (*von*) 'lit.: a heap of'
	eine Masse (*von*) 'lit.: a mass of'
	ein Meer (*von*) 'lit.: a sea/ocean of'
	eine Menge (*von*) 'lit.: a quantity of'
	eine Stange (*von*) 'lit.: a bar of'
	ein Strom (*von*) 'lit.: a stream of'

(34) Language A = Italian, fixed N1 is *valanga*;
Language B = German

Italian	German
	ein Berg (*von*) 'lit.: a mountain of'
	eine Flut (*von*) 'lit.: a flood of'
	ein Haufen (*von*) 'lit.: a heap of'

una valanga di lit.: an avalanche of	*eine Lawine* (*von*) 'lit.: an avalanche of'
	eine riesige Menge (*von*) 'lit.: a huge quantity of'
	ein Schwall (*von*) 'lit.: a gush of'
	ein Sturm (*von*) 'lit.: a storm of'
	eine Unmenge (*von*) 'a vast amount of'

The second possibility is realized when in Language A N1 does vary a number of times, but despite such a massive variety of N1s the translation into Language B can remain the same:

(35) Language A = Italian, various N1's
Language B = German

Italian	German
un'abbondanza di 'an abundance of'	*ein Haufen* (*von*) lit.: a heap (of)
un branco di 'a flock of'	
un casino di 'a brothel of'	
un cumulo di 'a pile of'	
una marea di 'a tide of'	
un monte di 'a mountain of'	
un mucchio di 'heap of'	
un sacco di 'a sack of'	
uno sciame di 'a swarm of'	
una valanga di 'an avalanche of'	

Translational correspondences of the type shown above can be established for any pair of languages, as illustrated below for the pair Italian/English (the data is mostly drawn from the electronic dictionary *Hazon* Clic):

(36) Language A = Italian, fixed N1 is *filo*, literally 'thread, string, blade';
Language B = English

Italian	English
un filo d'acqua	*a* **drop** *of water*
un filo d'aria	*a* **breath** *of air*
un filo di giudizio	*a* **scrap** *of sense*
un filo di grasso	*an* **ounce** *of fat*
un filo di ironia	*a* **hint** *of irony*

un filo di luce	*a **scrap** of light* *a **shaft** of light* *a **pencil** of light* *a **thread** of light*
un filo d'olio	*a **drizzle** of oil*
un filo di speranza	*a **ray** of hope* *a **grain** of hope*
un filo di vento	*a **breath** of wind*
un filo di voce	*a **thready** voice*

(37) Language A = Italian, various N1s
Language B = English

Italian		English
un bordello 'brothel' *di* *una carrettata* 'cartful' *di* *un casino* 'brothel' *di* *una caterva* 'great quantity' *di* *un cumulo* 'pile' *di* *un diluvio* 'deluge' *di* *una fiumana* 'swollen river' *di* *un'infinità* 'infinity' *di* *un mare* 'sea' *di* *una marea* 'tide' *di* *una massa* 'mass' *di* *una montagna* 'mountain' *di* *un mucchio* 'heap' *di* *un oceano* 'ocean' *di* *una pletora* 'plethora' *di* *un profluvio* 'overflow' *di* *una profusione* 'profusion' *di* *un sacco* 'sack' *di* *un subisso* 'ruin' *di* *una valanga* 'avalanche' *di*	*parole*	so many words[12]

12. The translation given renders neither the "colour" lent to the expression by the CND nor the hyperbole it conveys.

The functional nature of N1 can also be revealed by the different N1s used in translational correspondences when in Language A N1 is clearly lexical and referential, as in the examples below to be compared to those in (36):[13]

(38) un filo di nylon → a nylon **thread**
un filo di paglia → a **blade** of straw
un filo di perle → a **string** of pearls

3.2 CNDs as quantifying phrases

The basically unique meaning of the three sentences in (8), repeated below in (39) for convenience, suggests that CNDs relate semantically to 'quantity':

(39) *Tanti/Una marea di/Molti parenti pensavano di partire*
several relatives thought.3PL of leaving
'Several relatives thought of leaving.'

The CND *una marea di* quantifies over the set of individuals denoted by N2, with the effect of expressing an amount comparable to that singled out by one-word quantifiers conveying the meaning 'a large number of', with the difference being that CNDs like *una marea di* create an "amplification" effect comparable to that of absolute superlatives (e.g. *tantissimi, moltissimi*).[14] The use of a CND can be characterized stylistically as a form of hyperbole (see McArthur 1992: 491).[15]

13. It could be claimed that the semantic value of N1 comes from a metaphoric process. The N1 of an expression such as *una montagna di debiti* 'literally: a mountain of debts' would thus keep (part of) its lexical meaning, conventionally extended thanks to the device at work with metaphors. In our opinion, a difference must be drawn between the meaning originating from metaphors and the meaning springing from the insertion of N1 in a CND. Only the latter allows for a potentially infinite number of paradigmatic substitutions that leave the semantic value of the expression basically unaffected (e.g. those illustrated in 37). Metaphor and metonymy may play a role in the process that leads to a CND, as they can often be considered its starting point. What we are dealing with here is the *endpoint* of this process. A CND allows us to commute words with rather "distant" lexical meanings (e.g. *mare* 'sea' and *montagna* 'mountain') with no consequences on meaning. Metaphors do not allow for this: when substitutions are possible, e.g. *l'ipotesi prende corpo* and *l'ipotesi prende sostanza*, both meaning 'the hypothesis gains credit/ground', they cannot be as numerous as those found with CNDs.

14. Absolute superlatives formed with the suffix *-issim(o)*, also called 'elatives', express an absolute degree with no reference to a comparison, which is found in relative superlatives.

15. McArthur describes the expressions *a flood of tears, loads of iron, tons of money* as "idioms". We obviously do not share this view.

Extra evidence for analyzing the observed CNDs as quantifying phrases springs from the parallel behaviour shown by the quantifier *molti* 'many' in the pair (40)–(42) and by the CND *un sacco di* 'literally: a sack of' in the pair (41)–(43):

(40) *Molti escursionisti tornarono sani e salvi*
several excursionists returned safe and sound
'Several excursionists came back safe and sound.'

(41) *Un sacco di escursionisti tornarono sani e salvi*
a sack of excursionists returned safe and sound
'Several excursionists came back safe and sound.'

(42)* *Molti 27 escursionisti tornarono sani e salvi*
several 27 excursionists returned safe and sound
'Several 27 excursionists came back safe and sound.'

(43)* *Un sacco di 27 escursionisti tornarono sani e salvi*
a sack of 27 excursionists returned safe and sound
'Several 27 excursionists came back safe and sound.'

Having the noun *escursionisti* preceded not only by the quantifier *molti*, as in the well-formed (40), but also by a cardinal number, as in (42), makes the latter sentence ungrammatical. The ill-formed (42) is probably due to the attempt to quantify the same referent twice. Notably, the same result obtains in (43), where *escursionisti* is the N2 of a CND. The identical behaviour of *molti* and *un sacco di* in (42) and (43) also lends support to the hypothesis that CNDs work as quantifiers and that their semantic value is grammatical rather than lexical. Some N1s, also belonging to other types of CND (see below), rarely occur with a cardinal number preceding N2 (in our databases we found *briciola* 'crumb', *cifra* 'figure', *groviglio* 'tangle', *gruppo* 'group', *minimo* 'minimum', *serie* 'series', *sfilza* 'succession of, series of', *valanga* 'avalanche' and for German *Batzen* 'chunk', *Berg* 'mountain', *Haufen* 'heap', *Lawine* 'avalanche', *Meer* 'sea'); the N1 *sacco*, however, is excluded.

In Italian, there are at least 80 nouns that can work as the N1 of a CND carrying the meaning 'a (very) large quantity of'. A comparable number, only slightly higher, is found of CNDs with the meaning 'a (very) small quantity of' (as in (36)), some of which are shown below:

(44) Language A = Italian, various N1s
Language B = English

Italian		English
una briciola 'crumb' *di* *un brandello* 'shred' *di* *un filo/filino* '(little) thread' *di* *un fondo* 'bottom' *di* *un frammento* 'fragment' *di* *un granello* 'grain' *di* *un minimo* 'minimum' *di* *un niente* 'nothing' *di* *un nulla* 'nothing' *di* *un'ombra* 'shadow' *di* *un pizzico* 'pinch' *di* *un po'* 'little' *di* *una punta* 'point, tip' *di* *un residuo* 'oddment' *di* *uno scampolo* 'remnant' *di* *un tantino* 'tiny bit' *di* *un tocco* 'touch' *di* *uno zinzino* 'small amount' *di*	*felicità*	a taste of happiness

CNDs meaning 'quantity', either large or small, are only a part of the total number. A CND can also: (a) metaphorically express a part-whole relationship of the type 'Portion-Mass' (see Miller 1996: 164–165) e.g. *Ugo porta una fetta di responsabilità* 'Ugo has a share of responsibility'; (b) denote a set of people or things, often negatively or derogatorily characterized, e.g. *un groviglio di idee* 'a tangle of ideas', *un'accozzaglia di cifre* 'a jumble of figures'; (c) carry an aspectual meaning, as in the re-iterated event conveyed by the subject of *Seguì una sfilza di imprecazioni* 'A string of oaths followed'; (d) for a small number of N1s, designate a quantity greater than needed or expected, e.g. *Fu sconfitto per un eccesso di sicurezza* 'He was defeated because of an excess of self-confidence', *C'era un surplus di alternative* 'There was a surplus of alternatives'.[16]

4. The databases

This section presents the results of our search on the databases, which are realized by using a record such as that shown below (the Italian sentence can be translated as 'The university is being enveloped by a cloud of suspicion':

16. With regard to some of the tests illustrated, these types of CND can react differently from those conveying large/small quantity.

```
      PHRASE una valanga di sospetti sta
             investendo l'università

      ORIGIN la Repubblica 1985 (TITOLO)

          N1 valanga
          N2 sospetti
        DET1 X INDEF
        DET2 ø
        MOD1 ø
        MOD2 ø
        NOTE
   AGREEMENT N1
   NUMBER N2 PLUR
     PATTERN 4
    POSITION PREVERBAL SUBJECT
```

Figure 1. Example of a FileMaker record in the Italian database

Firstly, the databases are numerically comparable (954 occurrences in Italian, 908 in German), but differ in at least two ways: first, the Italian occurrences come from two sources, 601 from *la Repubblica*, 353 from the LIP, whereas for German they are only drawn from the newspaper *Die Welt*. Second, the German database also includes data concerning two additional constructions, the *Genitivus Partitivus* and the *Partitive Apposition*, non-existent in Italian, which we describe in detail in the following section.

4.1 German constructions

German has two prepositionless phrase types whose functions overlap that of CNDs. The *Genitivus Partitivus*, illustrated in (45), displays the surface structure <DET N1 N2>, with N2 invariably in the genitive; in the *Partitive Apposition*, shown in (46), N1 and N2 invariably carry the same case marking (nominative in (46)), probably a case of feature spreading (see Mirto 1998):

(45) *ein großer Haufen entfernter Verwandter*
a big.NOM heap.NOM distant.GEN relatives.GEN

(46) *ein großer Haufen entfernte Verwandte*
a big.NOM heap.NOM distant.NOM relatives.NOM

Drosdowski (1995) discusses cases such as (45) and (46), but makes no mention of nominal composition, as in *ein Verwandtenhaufen* 'literally: a parents-heap'. There seem to be differences of acceptability with regard to the types of N1 compatible with each of the three structures, which are also characterized differently in relation to register and possibly regional influences. Drosdowski (1995: 646f.) points out that the genitive construction has mostly been replaced by the other structures, namely the *Partitive Apposition* and the construction with *von.*

Such surface phrase types are also found for measure phrases like those shown below. The appositional construction in (47) is rather common, whilst the type with N2 in the genitive, as in (48), is out:

(47) *eine Tasse Kaffee*
a cup.NOM coffee.NOM
'a cup of coffee'

(48)* *eine Tasse Kaffees*
a cup.NOM coffee.GEN
'a cup of coffee'

In other cases, a difference in frequency can be observed: the appositional structure in (49) is also common, whereas the corresponding genitive construction in (50) is rare:

(49) *ein Dutzend frische Eier*
a dozen.NOM fresh.NOM eggs
'a dozen fresh eggs'

(50) *ein Dutzend frischer Eier*
a dozen.NOM fresh.GEN eggs
'a dozen fresh eggs'

The appositional type in (49) is almost always used with measure nouns and quantifying phrases, in particular when N2 is singular, as pointed out in the *Duden Grammatik.* However, exceptions are found, for example when N1 is not a measure or quantity noun (e.g. *Strauß* 'bunch'), and N2 is plural. The genitive phrase type, e.g. (51), is more frequent, whereas the appositional construction, e.g. (52), is quite rare:[17]

(51) *ein Strauß duftender Rosen*
a bunch.NOM fragrant.GEN roses
'a bunch of fragrant roses'

17. To further investigate the reasons for such a variety of constructions in German, consider English, a language with the prepositional type only, as in Italian. German does possess morphological case whilst English lost it some time past. German, however, is said to be on the way to losing cases. If we reflect on the various declension classes of German nouns, we will notice that only in the plural are dative forms distinct for nearly all classes. As for the singular, in one declension class only genitive forms are distinct, in another class the nominative only is distinct, and, as is well-known, for nearly all feminine nouns we only find one singular and one plural form without formal case distinctions. So in fact we find ambiguous cases for the two prepositionless structures and the structure with feature spreading is maybe due to a process of reanalysis in the sense of Trask (1996) or Lang & Neumann-Holzschuh (1999).

(52) *ein Strauß duftende Rosen*
a bunch.NOM fragrant.NOM roses
'a bunch of fragrant roses'

A measure phrase such as that in (47) and its Italian counterpart in (53) appear to be structurally distinct from CNDs.

(53) *una tazza di caffè*
'a cup of coffee'

This can be observed in the different behaviour the two phrase types exhibit with subject-verb agreement, in passive sentences for example. In (54), the CND *una marea di persone* 'literally: a tide of people' can control verbal agreement with both N1 and N2:

(54) a. *Sono state intervistate una marea di persone.*
are been interviewed a tide of people
'Several people were interviewed.'
b. *È stata intervistata una marea di persone.*
is been interviewed a tide of people
'Several people were interviewed.'

Comparable data in German are (54a)' *Es wurden eine Unmenge von Leuten befragt* 'A vast amount of people were interviewed', and (54b)' *Es wurde eine Unmenge von Leuten befragt* 'A vast amount of people was interviewed'.

On the other hand, in (55) the measure phrase *due camion di cemento* 'literally: two trucks of cement' only allows for agreement with N1, as (55a) and (55b) illustrate:

(55) a. *Sono stati usati due camion di cemento.*
are been used two trucks of cement
'Two trucks full of cement were used.'
b.* *È stato usato due camion di cemento.*
is been used two trucks of cement
'Two trucks full of cement were used.'

In German, the counterparts of (55a) and (55b) can only be prepositionless: (55a)' *Es wurden zwei Lastwagen Zement benutzt* 'Two trucks of cement were used', (55b)' **Es wurde zwei Lastwagen Zement benutzt* 'literally: Two trucks of cement was used'.

The German prepositional construction (the same type as in Italian and English) was found in nearly 40% of the cases. This percentage varies for each

N1: we find major variations for this construction (certain N1s are never used with the prepositional construction, whilst others are used in more than 80% of the occurrences).

In the database for German, the distribution of the prepositional construction is as shown in the table below:

Table 1. Prepositional construction in German

Percentage	N1	Translation
0%	*Portion, Schuss, Stange*	'portion', 'shot', 'rod'
0,76%	*Prise*	'pinch'
7,14%	*Funken*	'spark'
12,77%	*Batzen*	'chunk'
17,65%	*Haufen*	'heap'
28,57%	*Masse*	'mass'
42,11%	*Lawine*	'avalanche'
55,66%	*Unmenge*	'vast amount'
66,67%	*Meer, Spur*	'sea, trace'
71,88%	*Flut*	'tide, flood'
76,92%	*Berg*	'mountain'
80%	*Strom*	'stream'
84,21%	*Hauch*	'breath'

Among the occurrences for the two prepositionless constructions, i.e. the remaining 60%, we find a large number of unclear cases (ca. 36% of the prepositionless constructions), i.e. occurrences where the case of N2 cannot be decided. When this is the case, it is impossible to say whether one is dealing with a genitive construction or one with apposition. For the remaining cases of the prepositionless phrase type in which the case of N2 is clearly identifiable, we find ca. 26% with N2 genitive and 38% with apposition. Some N1s incompatible with apposition are found (*Flut, Lawine, Masse, Meer, Strom*), whilst other N1s appear to prefer the appositional construction over that with N2 genitive. With the N1 *Haufen*, the genitive construction appears to be that preferred, whilst for *Unmenge* the two constructions are equally distributed.

4.2 N1 and its relation with N2

For Italian we looked into 47 N1s, whilst for German we worked on 16 N1s. The following tables present the results and provide the origin of the examples with the number of tokens and the number of N2s found with each N1. They also indicate the number of N2 (singular only, plural only, or both). The abbreviation INDECL is used when N2 is an indeclinable noun, which makes the number of occurrences uncertain.

Table 2. N1s in the Italian database[18]

N1	Origin	Tokens	Different N2s	Number of N2	Translation
abbondanza	L	1	(1)	SG	'abundance'
attimino	L	2	(2)	SG	'moment.DM'
banda	L	1	(1)	PL	'band, gang'
branco	L	4	(2)	PL	'flock, herd'
briciola	R/L	50	(47)	< SG, PL poss.	'crumb'
briciolo	R	1	(1)	SG	'bit, scrap'
casino	L	2	(2)	SG & PL	'brothel'
cifra	L	3	(3)	PL	'sum, amount'
ciurma	L	1	(1)	SG	'mob, rabble'
combriccola	L	1	(1)	PL	'gang'
complesso	L	12	(4)	PL	'whole'
completo	L	1	(1)	PL	'set'
cumulo	L	1	(1)	SG & PL	'pile'
dose	L	2	(2)	SG & INDECL	'dose'
famiglia	L	1	(1)	PL	'family'
frammento	L	1	(1)	SG	'fragment'
frazione	L	1	(1)	SG	'fraction'
gamma	L	3	(3)	PL & INDECL	'range'
gragnuòla	L	1	(1)	PL	'hail'
groviglio	R	60	(57)	< PL, SG poss.	'tangle'
gruppo	L	19	(12)	< PL, SG poss.	'group'
infinità	L	3	(3)	PL	'infinity'
insieme	L	9	(8)	< PL, INDECL	'whole'
marea	L	2	(2)	PL	'tide'
minimo	L	16	(14)	< SG, PL poss.	'minimum'
monte	L	3	(2)	PL	'mountain'
mucchio	L	1	(1)	PL	'heap'
numero	L	15	(12)	PL	'number'
ondata	L	2	(2)	PL	'wave'
pezzettino	L	2	(2)	SG	'piece.DM.DM'
pizzico	L	1	(1)	SG	'pinch'
po'	L	88	(64)	< SG, PL poss.	'little'
pochino	L	3	(2)	SG	'little.DM'
poco	L	8	(8)	< SG, PL poss.	'little'
pugno	R	33	(26)	< PL, SG poss.	'fist'
quantità	L	7	(6)	SG & PL	'quantity'
raccolta	L	4	(4)	PL	'collection'

18. Abbreviations: R = *la Repubblica*, L = LIP, SG = singular, PL = plural, INDECL = indeclinable, < = is more frequent, poss. = is possible, DM = diminutive. Indeclinable is only mentioned where we do not find singular and plural cases of N2, which might be "hidden" by the indeclinable noun.

Table 2. Continued

N1	Origin	Tokens	Different N2s	Number of N2	Translation
residuo	L	1	(1)	SG	'residue'
resto	L	6	(6)	< SG, PL poss.	'rest'
sacco	R/L	102	(55)	< PL, SG poss.	'sack'
scarica	L	2	(2)	PL	'discharge'
schiera	L	1	(1)	INDECL	'rank'
sciame	L	1	(1)	PL	'swarm'
sequenza	L	1	(1)	PL	'sequence'
serie	R/L	303	(219)	< PL, SG poss.	'series'
sfilza	R	91	(72)	< PL, SG poss.	'string, series'
valanga	R/L	81	(60)	< PL, SG poss.	'avalanche'

Table 3. N1s in the German database[19]

N1	Tokens	Different N2s	Number of N2	Translation
Batzen	47	(20)	< SG, PL poss.	'chunk'
Berg	26	(22)	< PL, SG poss.	'mountain'
Flut	32	(30)	< PL, SG poss.	'tide, flood'
Funken	14	(9)	SG	'spark'
Hauch	76	(71)	< SG, PL poss.	'breath'
Haufen	102	(83)	< PL, but also SG	'heap'
Lawine	38	(33)	< PL, SG poss.	'avalanche'
Masse	7	(7)	PL	'mass'
Meer	18	(17)	< PL, SG poss.	'sea'
Portion	59	(53)	SG	'portion'
Prise	132	(114)	< SG, PL poss.	'pinch'
Schuss	12	(12)	SG	'shot'
Spur	12	(12)	< SG, PL poss.	'trace'
Stange	1	(1)	SG	'rod'
Strom	5	(5)	PL & SG	'stream'
Unmenge	327	(261)	< PL, SG poss.	'vast amount'

4.3 Agreement

Section 2 showed that with CNDs verbal agreement can be controlled by either N1 or N2. For obvious reasons, our search only includes subject CNDs, though some cases of agreement with a participial phrase were also found. In the Italian database, only 182 CNDs (about 20%) are subjects. In 41 of such cases (about 22%) it cannot be established whether agreement is with N1 or N2 because both share

19. For the German database there is no need to indicate the origin since all the occurrences were drawn from *Die Welt.*

number and/or gender. In other 91 cases (= 50%) agreement is with N1 (in one additional case only in number, in another case in gender with N1 and in number with N2). Finally, we found agreement with N2 in 48 cases (i.e. about 26% of the cases of agreement if we exclude the already mentioned cases). These numbers are summed up in the following table.[20]

Table 4. Verbal agreement in the Italian database

Not applicable	With N1	With N2	Unclear	Total of subject CNDs
772	91 (93)	48 (49)	41	182

The non-head nature of N1 in Italian appears to be confirmed by the syntactic agreement between the verb and N2. As for German, in most of the cases where verbal agreement is visible (about 31%),[21] this is with N1 (59 cases, i.e. about 27% of the cases of agreement). Nonetheless, in 8 occurrences (about 4%) where N1 is *Hauch, Portion* or *Unmenge*, agreement is clearly with N2 rather than with N1, as illustrated in the following examples:

(56) *Die Unmenge verglimmter Zigarettenstummel sind deshalb im letzten Jahr*
the vast amount of old cigarette butts be.3PL therefore in the last year
vor und um Sankt Peter nicht wirklich weniger geworden.
in front of and around St. Peter's not really diminished
'Last year, the vast amount of old cigarette butts in front of and around St. Peter's did not really diminish.'

(57) *Gefährlich – das sind in dem Buch auch eine Unmenge anderer Gestalten*
dangerous that be.3PL in the book also a vast amount of other creatures
'Dangerous – that's what many of the other creatures also are in this book.'

(58) *Im Aromenspektrum zeigen sich heute*
in the aromatic spectrum show.3PL themselves today
ein Hauch von Honig, Passionsfrucht, Pfirsich und Ananas
a breath of honey, passion fruit, peach and pineapple
'Small amounts of honey, passion fruit, peach and pineapple show up in the aromatic spectrum today.'

20. Summing up the numbers of agreement with N1 and N2 and the unclear cases we arrive at a total of 183, but we have to consider that in one case – as already mentioned – the auxiliary agrees in number with N2, whilst the past participle agrees in gender with N1. The total number is therefore 182. The example is taken from the LIP: *pero' curandosi ci son state una serie di eh di problemi anche in famiglia* 'however in curing himself a series of problems emerged in the family'. This example is probably due to a misprint or a slip of the tongue.

21. In 149 cases (about 69% of the agreement cases) it is not decidable if agreement is with N1 or N2 since they are either both singular or both plural.

Drosdowski (1995: 702) mentions this double possibility of agreement in standard German for measure phrases that do not express a precise number. He claims that agreement with N2 is more frequent if N1 and N2 carry the same case marking (this is also the opinion that Helbig & Buscha 2002 express). Our data does not confirm this frequency.

Table 5. Verbal agreement in the German database

Not applicable	With N1	With N2	Unclear	Total of subject CNDs
692	59	8	149	216

4.4 Determination

The Italian database shows an overwhelming majority of indefinite determination: more than 84%. In only about 14% of the occurrences is determination of N1 definite (the definite article and the demonstratives were both considered as definite determination). No overt determination was found in less than 2% of the cases.

Table 6. Determination of N1 in the Italian database

Determination	Occurrences	Percentage
indefinite	802	84,07%
definite	138	14,47%
bare	14	1,47%

In German too we observe a preponderance of indefinite determination (60%) as in Italian. Nearly 28% of the occurrences have zero determination in N1 (this is largely the case when N1 is plural, as with *Batzen, Berg, Flut, Haufen, Lawine, Masse, Portion, Prise, Strom, Unmenge*, or when N1 is in a title). Definite determination takes place in only about 12% of the occurrences.

Table 7. Determination of N1 in the German database

Determination	Occurrences	Percentage
indefinite	540	59,47 %
definite	103 (4 are possessives, analyzed as articles in German)	11,34 %
bare	253	27,86 %
negative	12	1,32 %

The considerable difference between the percentages for absent determination in Italian and German might be motivated by the larger number of plural N1s in German (272 cases in German – only 9 cases in Italian).

4.5 Frequency of N1s in CNDs and elsewhere

Section 3 provided evidence for the non lexical nature of the nominal element in CNDs. Some of these nominal elements occur more frequently in CNDs than in their lexical-referential sense. Two extremely different N1-types can be opposed, as shown in the following table for the occurrences of *valanga* and *sfilza* in the newspaper *la Repubblica*:

Table 8. Literal/non-literal use in the Italian database

N1	Total occurrences in the period of time analyzed	Occurrences in CND
valanga/valanghe	205	106 (51,70 %)
sfilza/sfilze	68	68 (100 %)

The numbers for *valanga* 'avalanche' clearly indicate that in nearly 50% of cases this noun is lexical and referential, whereas those for *sfilza* 'string, series' show that it is *always* used as the N1 of a CND.

Also in the German database we find that some N1s frequently occur in CND constructions, whilst others occur more frequently in their normal lexical-referential sense. The following table illustrates two examples:

Table 9. Literal/non-literal use in the German database

N1	Total occurrences in the period of time analyzed	Occurrences in a CND
Meer/Meere/Meeres/Meeren	546	18 (3,3 %)
Unmenge/Unmengen	430	327 (76,05 %)

Only rarely does *Meer* 'sea' appear as the N1 of a CND, whilst *Unmenge* 'vast amount' occurs more frequently as the N1 of a CND than in other constructions.

5. Concluding remarks

This article distinguishes between various phrase-types displaying the <DET N1 *of* N2> linear structure. In that exemplified with *una festa di parenti* 'a party of relatives', N1 is the head and the *of*-phrase is a complement, whilst in the type illustrated with *una marea di parenti* 'literally: a tide of relatives' the entire initial sequence <DET N1 *of*> appears to work as a multi-word determiner, here labelled Complex Nominal Determiner. The N1 of a CND is non-lexical and non-referential. A number of syntactic properties suggest that either N1 or N2 can alternately work as the phrasal head. Thus, the CND phrase-type recalls Gross's (1981) Double Analysis to a certain extent, since its internal structure cannot be established once and for all.

Our study focuses on CNDs in Italian and German, with a passing glance at English, analyzed with respect to their syntactic and semantic behaviour (e.g. verbal number agreement, selection restrictions, entailments, lack of referentiality). A look at translational correspondences gives further evidence of the specific nature of CNDs.

The creation of databases for Italian and German allowed us to focus on real data, which helped verify the existence and frequency of various aspects of CNDs. In German, the existence of at least two other overlapping prepositionless constructions has to be taken into account. The match between a given N1 and the construction selected of the three available appears to be idiosyncratic since the type of selection cannot be predicted.

CNDs have been almost totally ignored in linguistic literature as a phenomenon with clearly defined boundaries. We hope to have shown that CNDs are a precisely definable group – also cross-linguistically – with a certain relevance in both spoken and written language.

Limits of space prevent us from treating other key aspects of CNDs in detail. The ways in which the type of N1 affects the choice of N2 remains to be investigated, as do the reasons that make indefinite determination preponderant both in Italian and German.

References

Brems, L. 2003. Measure noun constructions: An instance of semantically driven grammaticalization. *International Journal of Corpus Linguistics* 8(2): 283–312.

Buvet, P. 1994. Détermination: Les noms. *Lingvisticae Investigationes* XVIII: 121–150.

De Mauro, T., Mancini, F., Vedovelli, M. & Voghera, M. 1993. *LIP Lessico di frequenza dell'italiano parlato.* Milano: ETASLIBRI Fondazione IBM Italia.

Dodge, E. & Wright, A. 2002. Herds of wildebeests, flasks of vodka, heaps of trouble: An embodied constructional approach to English measure phrases. In *Proceedings of the 28th Meeting of the Berkeley Linguistic Society,* J. Larson & M. Paster (eds), 75–86. Berkeley CA: Berkeley Linguistic Society.

Drosdowski, G. (ed.). 1995. *Duden. Grammatik der deutschen Gegenwartssprache.* Mannheim: Dudenverlag.

Giacoma, L. & Kolb, S. (eds). 2002. *Wörterbuch Deutsch-Italienisch, Italienisch-Deutsch/ Dizionario tedesco-italiano, italiano-tedesco.* Bologna: Zanichelli & Klett (PONS).

Gross, G. 1990. Définition des noms composés dans un lexique-grammaire. *Langue française* 87: 84–90.

Gross, G. & Prandi, M. 2004. *La finalité: Fondements conceptuels et genèse linguistique.* Louvain-La-Neuve: De Boek Université.

Gross, M. 1981. Les bases empiriques de la notion de prédicat sémantique. *Langages* 63: 7–52.

Guenthner, F. & Blanco, X. 2004. Multi-lexemic expressions: An overview. *Lingvisticae Investigationes Supplementa*, 239–252. Amsterdam: John Benjamins.

Hazon Clic. 2001. *Dizionario interattivo Garzanti. Inglese-italiano, italiano-inglese*, CD-ROM. Torino: UTET, Garzanti Linguistica.

Helbig, G. & Buscha, J. 2002. *Deutsche Grammatik. Ein Handbuch für den Ausländerunterricht.* Berlin: Langenscheidt.

Hentschel, E. 1993. Flexionsverfall im Deutschen? Die Kasusmarkierung bei partitiven Genetiv-Attributen. *Zeitschrift für germanistische Linguistik* 21: 320–333.

Karttunen, L. 1969. *Discourse referents.* International Conference on Computational Linguistics: COLING. Proceedings of the 1969 conference on Computational linguistics. Sång-Säby, Sweden.

Koptjevskaja-Tamm, M. 2001. 'A piece of cake' and 'a cup of tea': Partitive and pseudo-partitive nominal constructions in the Circum-Baltic languages. In *The Circum-Baltic languages. Typology and contact. Volume 2. Grammar and typology*, Ö. Dahl & M. Koptjevskaja-Tamm, 523–568. Amsterdam: John Benjamins.

Lang, J. & Neumann-Holzschuh, I. (eds). 1999. *Reanalyse und Grammatikalisierung in den romanischen Sprachen.* Tübingen: Niemeyer.

Lehrer, A. 1986. English classifier constructions. *Lingua* 68: 109–148.

McArthur, T. 1992. *The Oxford companion to the English language.* Oxford: OUP.

Michaux, C. 1992. The collectives in French: A linguistic investigation. *Lingvisticae Investigationes* XVI(1): 99–124.

Miller, G.A. 1996. *The science of words.* New York NY: Scientific American Library.

Mirto, I.M. 1998. *The syntax of the meronymic construction.* Pisa: ETS.

Nichols, J. 1986. Head-marking and dependent-marking grammar. *Language* 62: 56–119.

Quirk, R., Greenbaum, S., Leech, G. & Svartvik, J. 1985. *A comprehensive grammar of the English language.* New York NY: Longman.

Renzi, L. 1988. *Grande grammatica italiana di consultazione.* Vol. I. Bologna: il Mulino.

Schwarze, C. 1995. *Grammatik der italienischen Sprache.* 2nd Revised edn., Tübingen: Niemeyer.

Serianni, L. 1988. *Grammatica italiana. Italiano comune e lingua letteraria.* Torino: Utet.

Trask, R.L. 1996. *Historical linguistics.* London: Arnold.

Relativisation strategies in insular Celtic languages

History and contacts with English[1]

Elisa Roma

In the first part of this paper I provide a description of the major relativisation patterns found in the Celtic languages of the British Isles, examining the distribution of relative markers both from a typological and from a diachronic point of view. In the second part Old and Early Middle English relativisation markers are chronologically ordered and compared to the Celtic patterns. While Celtic influence on English has been claimed for gapping and preposition stranding, the data indicate other outcomes of early contact, namely the constraint against an agreeing relative marker after an agreeing determiner on the antecedent noun, and the resumptive strategy with obliques. Finally general conclusions on the direction and typology of borrowing are drawn.

Introduction

This paper deals with relativisation patterns attested at early stages in the Celtic languages of the British Isles, and investigates aspects in the evolution of these structures that may be connected with contact phenomena in both the history of Celtic languages and the history of English.

When referring to relativisation strategies or relativisation patterns I mean basically the following typology of structures:

synthetic relative marker = relative pronoun (relative clause marker + case in one word)
analytic relative marker = relative clause and case role are disjointly or doubly marked
all-purpose relative marker = general introductory particle/connective (no overt case marking)

1. I am grateful to Paolo Ramat, Anna Giacalone Ramat, Silvia Dal Negro and two anonymous referees for useful comments on earlier drafts of the paper, to Sandro Caruana for going through my English, and to Marusca Francini for checking some glosses on Old English. Since I have not always followed their suggestions in a straightforward manner, blame for any shortcoming and error is *a fortiori* to be put solely on me.

The abbreviation RC will be used for "relative clause".

The paper is divided into three parts. Section A deals with Celtic relativisation patterns, Section B with Old and Middle English patterns, while a comparison between these patterns is carried out in Section C. Within Section A the first paragraph (A.1) is devoted to Irish, the second (A.2) to Welsh, whereas in the third paragraph (A.3) I summarise the Celtic patterns; subparagraphs refer to different strategies, for which survival, spread or loss is also accounted. While Section A slightly simplifies the situation, owing to the overwhelming variety of structures in every single stage (more examples to be found in the Pavia Database), Section B, though drawing on secondary sources, deals with a specific period in the history of English in some detail. Nevertheless, Section A is basically descriptive, while the main focus of Section B is possible contact phenomena.

Grammatical glosses generally conform to the Leipzig standard (see the List of Abbreviations).

A.1 Gaelic relativisation patterns

In Irish relative clauses are marked by any of the followings:

A.1.1 Specific **RELATIVE FORMS** (i.e. **ENDINGS**) of the verb: only non-oblique (so-called "direct") RCs. The verb does not agree with the RC antecedent in Person; Number agreement, on the other hand, was present in OI,[2] but was later lost during the Middle and Early Modern Irish period. Relative endings in OI had three forms, which were only available for non-compound verbs (OI had two inflections, basically so-called "absolute" for non-compound verbs in absolute initial position, so-called "conjunct" for compound verbs and for simple verbs in non initial position) and were only used in affirmative sentences: 3rd person SG. (ex. 1), used only when the subject of the relative clause is (3rd) SG.; 1st plural, if the subject of the relative clause is 1PL. while the antecedent is not (ex. 2); 3rd PL. (ex. 3). Later only 3rd singular relative endings has survived (see ex. 14b).

(1) *húare rocreitset* *ard-lathi* *in* *betho*
since PRF:believe.PST.3PL high+prince.PL.NOM ART.GEN world.GEN
cretfed *cách* *íarum* et *intí*
believe:FUT.3SG everyone then and ART.M.SG.NOM-DEICT
creitfes *ní* *áġathar* *á* *ngreim*
believe:FUT.3SG.REL NEG fear.PRS.3SG 3.GEN POSS.PL.power.ACC

2. See the List of Abbreviations below for standard labels associated with language periods.

'since the chief princes of the world have believed, everyone will believe then, and he who shall believe is not afraid of their power' (Wb1^{a}3 [OI]).

(2) *a* *mbás* *tíagme-ni* *do-áirci* *bethid*
ART.N.SG.NOM N.death.NOM go.PRS.1PL.REL-1PL cause.PRS.3SG life:ACC
dúib-si *.i.* *is* *ar* *bethid* *dúib-si*
to:2PL-2PL id est COP.PRS.3SG on life:ACC to:2PL-2PL
tíagmi-ni *bás*
go.PRS.1PL-1PL death.ACC
'the death to which we go causes life to you, that is, it is for the sake of life to you that we go to death' (Wb 15^{b}28 [OI])

Note how in (1) relative inflected 3rd SG. relative *cretfes* contrasts with *cre(i)tfed*, and how in (2) relative 1st plural *tíagme* contrasts with non-relative *tíagmi* (*-ni* is a clitic so-called "emphatic" pronoun used for contrast, as 2PL. *-si*; clefted Prepositional Phrases do not require a subordination marker on the following clause).

(3) *duairci* *bás* *dun* *chach*
cause.PRS.3SG death.ACC to.ART.M.SG.DAT DAT.everyone.DAT
ngaibde
NAS.take:PRS.3PL.REL
'causes death to all whom they seize' (Ml 76^{a}16 [OI])

In (3) *gaibde* is a relative form as opposed to non-relative *gaibit*; moreover, nasalisation of the initial consonant of the relative verb-form occurs (<*ng*> = /ŋ/); such mutation is usually found in OI in object RCs (as here); see below A.1.3 for initial mutations in RCs.

In OI relative endings were not available for secondary tenses (imperfect indicative and subjunctive, secondary future, which have no absolute forms), while in ModI they are available only for the present and future tense, and lenition (see below A.1.3 and ex. 14) occurs anyway on the relative verb-form, so that the verb-form is actually doubly marked as relative. Although relative endings occur in Modern Irish dialects, they have in fact been excluded from the Official Standard, with the exception of a few petrified forms.

For the highly frequent so-called "substantive verb", i.e. the existential verb, the OI relative form had a suppletive stem (see *fil* in ex. 36) which has been preserved in ModI for "indirect" RCs (see below A.1.7). A specific relative ending is attested in MW only for the verb 'to be' (*yssid*), see below A.2.1.

A.1.2 (Only OI) Specific **SET OF INFIXED OBJECT PRONOUNS**: both oblique and non-oblique RCs. Infixed object pronouns[3] in relative clauses differ from infixed pronouns used in non-relative clauses; nevertheless, only 3rd person pronouns follow the rule

3. The term "infixed pronoun" is traditional in OI grammar. Pronominal objects in OI are expressed through affixes which are not actually inserted in the verb root, but put immediately

regularly, while since the OI period both relative and non relative 1st and 2nd person infixed pronouns can be used in relative clauses. Thus
intí do-eim 'he who protects'
intí do-dom-eim (rel. infix) or *intí do-m-eim* (non rel. infix) 'he who protects me' (cp. *do-m-eim* '(he/she) protects me'), *do-dot-eim* or *do-t-eim* 'who protects you', etc., but only *do-dn-eim* 'who protects him', *do-da-eim* 'who protects her/them' (cp. *d-an-eim* '(he/she) protects him', *do-sn-eim* '(he/she) protects her/them').

This marker further testifies to the original syntax of Celtic RC markers (second position clitics;[4] see below A.2.2 on Welsh). Infixed pronouns on the other hand do not have a specific relative form in MW, in which they can mark a relative clause only when the object pronoun is resumptive; see below A.2.1, ex. 42.

In (4) below after a focussed subject antecedent (here *messe* and *mé*) the verb has relative marking in the form of the infixed object *da* in the first clause and in the relative ending in the second (see above A.1.1, *bæras* = *béras* as opposed to non-relative *béraid*). No person agreement ever occurs in relative clauses.

(4) *amal as messe du<da>forsat inna*
as COP.PRS.REL 1SG:1SG create<3PL.OBJ.REL>PRF.3SG ART.PL.ACC
dúli is mé dano bæras mes
creatures.ACC COP.PRS.3SG 1SG also bring.FUT:3SG.REL judgement.ACC
fírián foraib
just.ACC on:3PL
'As it is me that created them, the creatures, it is me also that will pass righteous judgement on them' (Ml 94^{b}7 [OI])

(5) *Caíni ailmi / ar<dom>peitet*
beautiful pines / make_music<1SG.OBJ.REL>PRS.3PL
'Beautiful are the pines which make music for me.' (Murphy, *Lyrics* 8 [OI])

---

after the first element in the verbal complex, which may be either the verb itself (in such case they are called "suffixed pronouns"), or the first preverb in a compound verb (as in (4) and (5) above), or a negative form, or a clause connective (e.g. preposition + RC marker, as in (12) above); since suffixed pronouns were already obsolete in OI, an empty preverb (*no*) is frequently used to "infix", or rather "append" a pronoun. It should be stressed, though, that preverb and verb root are often semantically interwoven to the highest degree, so that the affix inserted between these two can easily be called an "infix".

4. This is the traditional view, held among others by Thurneysen, which is challenged by Sornicola (1989). Though Sornicola is basically right in assuming a syntacticisation of initial mutations which can dispose of the reconstruction of a specific phonetic enviroment for all their contexts of occurrence, I find that her proposal is too radical. I do not agree that since it is primarily the syntacticisation of mutations (their grammaticalisation as dependency markers) that lies behind their use in relative function, this requires abandoning the reconstruction of a second position relative marker in the prehistory of Irish or Insular Celtic which should account for the development of mutations. She might be right in arguing that the Insular Celtic relative marker was not a descendant of the Indo-European stem **yo-* (a view which has been put forward by others, at least for some contexts, see Schrijver 1997: 112), but this may not concern us here.

In (5) relativisation is marked through the form of the (indirect) object infix (*dom*; non relative *ar-um-peitet* 'make music for me', compound verb *ar-peiti* 'makes music').

A.1.3 Initial consonant MUTATIONS on the verb, i.e. lenition (for "direct" RCs, i.e. subject and object RCs, see exx. 6–7) or nasalisation/eclipsis (in OI for temporal relationships, see ex. 9, optional in object RCs (ex. 8), in ModI obligatory in "indirect" relative clauses, i.e. oblique and possessor RCs, see below A.1.7).[5] Simple uncompounded verbs, i.e. verbs with no preverb, in OI usually required an empty preverb (*no*) before mutation if the conditions for specific relative ending were not met with (ex. 7), while prefixed (i.e. compound) verbs mutated the initial consonant of the verb-root (ex. 6 and 13 below); the system, though, collapsed very early, as the mutation began to occur on the initial consonant of the verb form since the OI period.

(6)

int-í	*do-thuit*	*foir*	*con-boing*	*a*
ART.M.SG.NOM-DEICT	fall.REL.PRS.3SG	on:3SG.M/N	break.PRS.3SG	3GEN

chnámi,
POSS.M.bones.ACC

int-í	*for-a*	*tuit-som*	*immurgu*
ART.M.SG.NOM-DEICT	on-REL	[NAS.]fall.PRS.DEP.3SG-3SG.M	though

atbail-side
die.PRS.3SG-3SG.M

'He who falls on it breaks his bones, but he on whom it falls dies'
(Wb $4^{d}15$ [OI])

Do-thuit in (6) has root-initial lenition (<*th*> = /θ/), while *tuit* is the prototonic form of the same verb. Prototonic forms occur after a closed set of preverbal particles (here preposition + relative marker *a*, see below A.1.4).

(7)

is	*hed*	*in-so*	*no-chairigur*	*i-tossuch*
COP.PRS.3SG	3SG.N	ART.N.NOM-DEICT	REL-LEN.blame:PRS.1SG	in-beginning.DAT

'This is what I reprimand in the first place' (Wb $11^{d}1$ [OI])

In (7) the simple verb *cairigidir* requires the empty preverb *no* before lenition (<*ch*> = /x/).

(8)

ind	*frithorcun*	*dombir-siu*	*forrun-ni*	*diar*
ART.F.SG.NOM	offence.F.NOM	give.NAS.PRS.2SG-2SG	on:1PL-1PL	to:our

forcitul
instruction.DAT

'the offence that Thou puttest upon us for our instruction' (Ml $87^{a}7$ [OI])

5. Lenition in I basically involves fricativisation of both voiced and unvoiced stops and /m/ and deletion of /f/; nasalisation involves sonorisation of unvoiced stops and /f/ and nasalisation of voiced stops. When the initial phoneme of the verb is a vowel only nasalisation can affect the verb (in such case a nasal consonant segment is added), otherwise no relative marker occurs on the verb (see A.1.2 on *do-eim*).

In (8) *m* in *dombir-siu* represents nasalisation of the initial consonant of the verb root (*dobeir* 'gives', *do* preverb + *beir* verb-root; <*mb*> = /m/).

(9) *ilardatu inna aimsire mbite-som*
multiplicity ART.F.SG.GEN time.F.GEN NAS.be.PRS.HAB:REL.3PL-3PL
isind fognam
in:ART.DAT service.DAT
'the multiplicity of the time they are in the service' (Ml 28^{b}9 [OI])

In (9) the temporal antecedent is followed by a nasalising relative clause (again <*mb*> = /m/); the verb form has relative ending (3rd PL. *-te*, corresponding non-rel. form *(bí)-t*). Later simple direct relative clause marking (either lenition or relative ending) occurs in such contexts, as well as after conjunctions such as *hóre* 'when, since', *in tan* 'when', *amal* 'as' (see ex. 4), which represent petrified case-forms of nouns (for example *hóre* was originally the gen. SG. of *úar* 'hour').

A.1.4 The **UNSTRESSED PARTICLE *a*** [ə] **(causing initial mutations)** preposed to the verb form or root. This was found in OI: a) after the preverbs *imm* 'around' and *ar* 'before' (ex. 10); b) when the relative clause was introduced by a preposition (all prepositions in OI, a few in ModI) in oblique relative clauses (exx. 11–12, see also (6) above and (19) below); c) as an antecedent for "open" relative clauses ('all that, what'), followed by a leniting relative clause (in ex. 13 *an* is followed by lenition of the initial consonant of the verb root, represented by <*ch*> = /x/ in *adchiam* and *rochluinemmar*). The particle had originally the same form as the nom.-acc. of the neuter (definite) article, and it caused nasalisation of the following word (in context (b) and (c), but not (a); in (a) it is reconstructed as an originally dative form, with vowel ending). In (b) above *a* behaved as a clitic particle and was always immediately followed by stress, which means that in OI it was followed by the so-called prototonic verb-form in its conjunct inflection (in contrast with the deuterotonic form required by the other RC markers, except negative particles, about which reference is made in A.1.5 below).

(10) *is hé in peccad rogéni a*
COP.PRS.3SG 3SG.M ART.M.SG.NOM sin.NOM(M) PRF:do.PST.3SG ART.N.SG.ACC
n-uile comaccobor .i. na comaccobor
N-all concupiscence.N.ACC id est any.N concupiscence.N.NOM
ar<a>rograd i rect
forbid<REL>PRF.DEP.PASS.SG in law
r-a-géni peccad in mé
PRF-3SG.N.OBJ-do.PST.3SG sin.NOM(M) in me
'it is sin that has wrought every concupiscence, i.e. any concupiscence that has been forbidden in the Law, sin has wrought it in me' [glossing *occasione vero accepta, peccatum per mandatum operatum est in me omne concupiscentiam*, Wb 3^{c}25 [OI]]

(11) *Cib* *cenél* *tra* *dia* *roscribad*
INDF:COP.SBJV.PRS.3SG race then to:REL PRF:write:PST.PASS.SG
ind *epistil* *so…*
ART.F.SG.NOM epistle.F.NOM DEM
'whatever be the nation to which this epistle has been written' (Wb 3^{b}20 [OI])

(12) *dona-hí* *dia-nd-rérchoíl*
to:DET.PL-DEICT to:REL-REL.3SG.N.OBJ.REL-PRF.determine.PST.3SG
int-í *Día*
ART.M.SG.NOM-DEICT God
'to those to whom he, God, had decreed it' (glossing *quibus decreverit*, Ml 46^{c}7 [OI])

In (12) relativisation is marked through (preposition +) *a* + nasalisation (<*nd*> = /n/), and through the form of the object infix, i.e. (nasalised) *d* (cp. non-relative *a* in *rag*é*ni* in ex. 10) followed by the dependent (prototonic) form of the verb (*rérchoíl* as opposed to *as-rochoili*).

(13) *is* *demniu* *liunn* *an* *adchiam* *hua*
COP.PRS.3SG certain.COMPV with.1PL DET.N.SG.NOBL see.REL.PRS.1PL from
sulib *oldaas* *an* *rochluinemmar* *hua* *chluasaib*
eye.PL.DAT than DET.N.SG.NOBL hear.REL.PRS.1PL from ear.PL.DAT
'more certain for us is what we see with eyes than what we hear with ears' (Ml 112^{b}13 [OI])

In ModI[6] the particle *a* is used in affirmative RCs before the verb with the appropriate mutation: basically, lenition for subject and object RCs, usually called "direct" RCs (see exx. 14–16) and nasalisation for oblique RCs, usually called "indirect" RCs (see ex. 17). Before the past tense the unstressed preverbal particle used for oblique relative clauses is *ar*, which is followed by lenition (see ex. 18); the initial consonant of the verb, though, is regularly lenited in the past tense as opposed to present and future tense, so that mutation is unconnected with relativisation in this case.

(14a) *An* *té* *a* *bhíonn* *amuigh* *fuaraíonn* *a* *chuid.*
ART DEM REL LEN.be.HAB.PRS outside cool:PRS 3GEN POSS.SG.M.share

(14b) *An* *té* *a* *bhíos* *amuigh* *fuaraíonn* *a* *chuid.*
ART DEM REL LEN.be.HAB.PRS.REL outside cool:PRS 3GEN POSS.SG.M.share
'Out of sight out of mind' (lit. 'who goes out, his meal cools (down)') (ModI)

6. ModI examples come from a variety of sources: if quoted from Cristofaro and Giacalone Ramat's questionnaire (this volume) they are labelled [Q]; if not otherwise specified, they are adapted from the Christian Brothers' Grammar (1962: 143–144, exx. 15, 20, 21, 30) or from Ó Dónaill's Dictionary (1977, s.v. *fuaraigh*, ex. 14). Ex. (16) is adapted from a novel by Pádraig Standún, *An t-Ainmhí*, Indreabhán 1992, p. 12.

Both versions of the proverb in (14) occur, with and without the relative ending *-s*. The heavy constituent is fronted. Note that particle (*a*) and mutation (<*bh*> representing /v/ as opposed to /b/) cooccur in both examples.

(15) *Sin é an fear a phóg an cailín.*
that 3SG.M ART.M.SG man.NGEN REL LEN.kiss.PST ART.M.SG girl.NGEN
'That's the man who kissed the girl/ whom the girl kissed.' (ModI)

The sentence in (15) is ambiguous, as shown in the translation. However, the former interpretation (subject relative clause) sounds more natural. In order to avoid ambiguity, the analytic strategy with resumptive object pronoun is used for object RC (as in (30) below), but it is to be noted that ambiguity does not rise when one element in the RC is unambiguously marked as subject, as in (16).

(16) *Is measa na rudaí a fheiceann siad ar an teilifís*
COP.PRS worse ART.PL thing:PL REL LEN.see.PRS 3PL.SBJ on ART television
ná an rud a chonaic siad trathnóna.
than ART thing REL see.PST 3PL.SBJ afternoon
'The things they watch on television are worse than what they have seen tonight.' (ModI)

Whereas example (15) is ambiguous, the sentence in (16) is not, since the pronoun *siad* can only be used as subject. The same happens with inflected forms of the verb (e.g. *an fear a charaim* 'the man I love', where *caraim* has 1st singular present ending). These are precisely the circumstances in which the gapping strategy may be used in present-day Standard English (i.e. object RC, see below B.2.1).

In (17) and (18) below the resumptive pronoun (fused with the preposition) agrees with the grammatical gender of the antecedent (see below A.1.7; <*ng*> represents the nasalised version of /g/, i.e. /ŋ/).

(17) *Tá an scian a ngearraim an t-arán léi*
be.PRS ART.F.SG knife(F) REL NAS.cut:PRS.1SG ART bread with.3SG.F
sa tarracán.
in.ART drawer
'The knife I cut the bread with is in the drawer.' (ModI [Q])

(18) *Is é mo dheartháir an fear ar thug mé*
COP.PRS 3.SG.M my brother ART man REL.OBL.PST give.PST 1SG
an leabhar dó.
ART book to.3SG.M
'The man I gave the book to is my brother.' (ModI [Q])

A.1.5 Specific **FORMS OF THE NEGATION** (*nach, nár*, OI *nád*, as opposed to non-relative *ní, níor*); typical also of Welsh; (relative) negation and relative particle are mutually exclusive.

(19) *cech tenga cen meth / forsa tardad rath,*
every tongue without failure / on:REL [NAS.]give.PRF.DEP:PASS.SG grace

cech cride fon mbith / nád chota nach mbrath
every heart through:ART N.world/ NEG.REL swear.SBVJ.PRS.DEP.3SG any N.treachery
'every tongue without fail on which grace has been granted, every heart in the world that does not swear any treachery …' (Murphy, *Lyrics* 10 [OI])

(20) *Dúirt sé rud éigin nár thuig mé.*
say.PST 3SG.M.SBJ thing INDF NEG.REL.PST understand.PST 1SG
'He said something I didn't understand.' (ModI)

(21) *Sin seomra nár chodail mé ann go fóill*
that room NEG.REL.PST sleep.PST 1SG there till now
'that's a room I haven't slept in yet.' (ModI)

In (20) and (21) note how the relative negative form *nár* in ModI requires lenition both in direct (20) and indirect (21) RCs; the same neutralisation of case contrast holds true for nasalisation after the non-past negative relative form *nach.*

A.1.6 NO (INITIAL) MARKER; this occurs in OI, MI and EMI especially with forms of the perfect or with any other conjunct verb form, for which no relative ending was available, when lenition marked the initial consonant of the verb for other reasons, since *a* was not established as a relative particle with direct RCs (ex. 22). The system was well established when the subject of the RC was the 1st or 2nd Person, and it was thus marked on the verb. In MW absence of relative marker either occurred as an archaism with compound verbs, or as a typical outcome of so-called Abnormal Sentence de-marking, as the particles used to introduce relative clauses grammaticalised into affirmative particles and afterwards also introduce main clauses, see below A.2.1.

(22) *in nuae-thintud-sa dorigenus-sa ho ebreib*
ART.NOM new+translation.NOM-DEM make.PRF.1SG-1SG from Hebrew.PL.DAT
'this new translation which I have made from the Hebrews' (Ml 2[a]6 [OI])

A.1.7 Oblique and possessor relative clauses in ModI resort to the analytic strategy, i.e. they contain an **ANAPHORIC RESUMPTIVE PRONOUN**, either a proclitic genitive pronoun (prenominal possessive) or an inflected preposition which agrees with the antecedent in Person, Number and Gender, and codes case-marking (see above exx. 17–18). The resumptive strategy is the only one attested for Genitive RCs since the oldest extant documents in both branches of Insular Celtic, while with prepositional phrases OI behaved differently both from ModI and from Welsh (see above A.1.4 and below A.2.3).

(23) *biit alaili and rofinnatar a pecthe resíu docói grád forru*
be.HAB.PRS.3PL other:PL there know.PRS.PASS.PL 3.GEN [POSS.PL]sins before go.SBJV:PRS.3SG order.NOM on:3PL
'There are others there whose sins are known before they are given any grade.' (*quorundam hominum (.i. ordinandorum) peccata manifesta sunt*), (Wb 29[a]28 [OI])

In (23) no specific relativisation marker occurs, as in conjunct inflexion (*rofinnatar*) there are no relative endings. Case is marked only on the genitive pronoun *a*, while Number agreement is expressed through mutation on the following noun (the initial <*p*> in *pecthe* is nasalised, i.e. = /b/, though this is not shown in OI writing; cp. (1) above for nasalisation after possessive *a* shown in writing on a voiced consonant).

Note that during the whole history of Irish no oblique case happens to be marked solely through nominal inflection apart from the genitive, which is an exclusively adnominal case (dative case is used almost exclusively after prepositions even in OI). There would thus be no way to mark genitive case in RCs except for a true relative pronoun (which does not exist), while for other obliques the introductory preposition is sufficient (see exx. 11–12). Possessor relativisation is usually avoided in OI,[7] but if it does occur it either lacks any marker (ex. 24) or has case-marking on anaphoric pronouns (exx. 23 and 25).

(24) *A* *rí* *rímter* *flaithe*
VOC king.VOC count:PRS.PASS.PL prince:PL.ACC
'o King whose princes are numbered' (Fél. Prol. 286 [OI])

(25) *Bied* *bess* *ngairit* *a* *ree*
be.FUT.3SG COP.FUT.3SG.REL NAS.short his period
coícuit *mblédna* *i* *mbith* *chee*
fifty NAS.year.PL.GEN in NAS.world here
'He whose time shall be short shall be fifty years in this world.' (*Murphy,* Lyrics 39 [MI])

In (25) no antecedent surfaces. Relativisation is marked through relative ending (*-s*), while case is marked only on the anaphoric genitive pronoun *a*. (This kind of "open" RC with no overt antecedent is not uncommon in OI, see Thurneysen 1946: 315–316, § 496).

In ModI both constructions are possible, the analytic one in (26) below, with indirect relative marking + resumptive pronoun, and the preposition + particle in (27). However, the first one (with resumptive pronoun) is commoner and the second option only survives for a few prepositions: *ar* 'on' (*ara*), *as* 'from' (*asa*), *do* 'to' (*dá*), *i* 'in' (*ina*), *le* 'with' (*lena*), i.e. it is a relic.

(26) *Sin* *é* *an* *fear* *ar* *thug* *mé* *céad* *punt*
that 3SG.M ART.SG.M man.M REL.OBL.PST give.PST I hundred pound
dó.
to.3SG.M
'That's the man I gave one hundred pounds to.' (ModI [Q])

7. Cp. Wb 24^{a}38 *et caeteris quorum nomina sunt in libro vitae – ní epur a n-anman sund* 'I do not say their names here'.

(27)

Sin	*é*	*an*	*fear*	*dár*	*thug*	*mé*	*céad*	*punt.*
that	3SG.M	ART.SG.M	man	to:REL.PST	give.PST	I	hundred	pound

'That's the man to whom I gave one hundred pounds.' (ModI [Q])

The resumptive pronoun strategy is very rarely attested in Old Irish for prepositional RCs, as in (28).

(28)

hua	*duemar*	*nech*	*suidigther*	*loc*
since	protect:PRS.PASS.SG	INDF.M.NOM	establish:PRS.PASS.SG.REL	place

daingen	*do*	*inna*	*agathar*	*ní*
firm	to.3SG.M	in.NEG.REL	fear.SBJV.PRS.SG.DEP	INDF.N.ACC

'since anyone is protected to whom a strong place in which he does not fear anything is established' (Ml 87^{d}15 [OI])

In (29) below lenition on the head noun (*post*, <*ph*> = /f/) after the 3rd person possessive form *a* marks Number and Gender agreement with the antecedent (non-lenition would refer to a feminine antecedent, nasalisation to a plural antecedent; see above (23) for OI).

(29)

Bhí	*ard-mheas*	*ar*	*an*	*duine*	*a*	*bhfuair*	*tú*	*a*	*phost*
be.PST	high+respect	on	ART	person	REL	NAS.got	2SG	3.GEN	POSS.SG.M.job

'The person whose position you got was highly valued' (ModI [Q])[8]

A resumptive pronoun (analytic strategy) can be used in ModI also for object RCs when they are ambiguous (for subject and object interpretation), i.e. (15) in its second meaning can be rephrased as in (30).

(30)

Sin	*é*	*an*	*fear*	*ar*	*phóg*	*an*	*cailín*	*é.*
that	3SG.M	the	man	REL.OBL.PST	kiss.PST	ART	girl	3SG.M

'That's the man whom the girl kissed.' (ModI)

Note that, when a resumptive pronoun (here *é* in its second occurrence) is inserted, the oblique relative marker occurs (relative particle *ar* instead of *a* for the past tense, see (26) above).

Place, time, cause and manner circumstantials originally displayed the same strategy as direct object RCs (for OI see A.1.3), with nasalisation, as in (9) above, and no resumptive pronoun; later lenition, i.e. non-oblique relative marker, could also be used after some temporal antecedents. In ModI the indirect RC marker is used either with or without a resumptive pronoun, as in (31) here below.

8. *Fuair* is an irregular verb-form and requires the relative particle and mutation usually selected by non-past tenses.

(31) *(Is) lá maith lá ar bith a bhfoghlaimím rudaí nua.*
(COP.PRS) day good day on world REL OBLREL.learn.PRS.1SG thing:PL new
'Any day I learn new things is a good day.' (ModI [Q])

A.1.8 A typical phenomenon should be noted about definiteness of NPs in Irish. Each NP which does not contain a PP regularly has only one definiteness marker (determiner), thus only one definite article: i.e. *the son of the King → the King's son*, that is to say (ModI) *mac an rí* not **an mac an rí*, cp. OE *þæs cynges Heanriges manna* 'king Henry's men' (which shows that the determiner belonged with the genitive noun, not with the head noun, though the head noun is thus marked as definite). The opposition can be seen in the following OI examples (32 and 33), where *dígal* 'punishment' is preceded by the definite article only when it modifies a definite head-noun, i.e. when the article is required by the head-noun:

(32) *tabair digail*
give.IMP.2SG punishment.F.SG.ACC
'inflict punishment' (Ml 27c12, a gloss on *ultor adsiste*)

(33) *tabairt inna diglae*
give.VN.NOM ART.F.SG.GEN punishment.F.SG.GEN
'the infliction of punishment' (Ml 27c21)

Nevertheless, RC antecedents are obligatorily preceded by (definite) articles or quantifiers in OI when their definiteness relies in fact on the following restrictive relative clause; the definite article alone can also be used for open antecedents, as stated above, see ex. 13 (OI examples below, see Thurneysen 1946: 296, § 471).

(34) *hore nád-mair peccad dia-forgénsam cose*
for NEG.REL-remain.PRS.DEP.3SG sin to.REL-[NAS.]serve.PRF.1PL till:DECIT
'for sin, which we have served hitherto, does not remain' (Wb 3c15, gl. *nunc autem soluti sumus a lege mortis, in qua detenebamur*)

(35) *na decad in dán doradad dó fesin*
NEG.IMP watch.IMP.3SG ART gift give.PRF.PASS.SG to.3SG.M REFL
acht dán á cheli
but gift 3.GEN POSS.SG.M.mate.GEN
'let him not regard the gift that has been given to himself, but the gift of his fellow' (Wb 23c16)

(36) *indaas ar tomus-nai .i. in tomus in chumachtai fil*
than our measure-1PL id est ART measure ART.GEN power.GEN be.PRS.SG.REL
linni is laigiu són indaas chumachtai doinachtae
with.1PL:1PL COP.PRS.3SG little.COMPV it than power.GEN manhood.GEN
Crist
Christ.GEN

'than our measure, i.e. the measure of the power that we own is less than (the measure) of the power of the manhood of Christ' (Ml 26b6, a gloss on Lat.

(de praestantiore persona) quam est nostra mensura; similarly Wb 9^c10 ***assin folud*** *apprisc inna colno* ***araróitmar*** 'out of **the** brittle **substance** of the flesh **which we have received**' to be compared with *asin folud tanidiu* ***araróit*** 'out of **the** subtle-**substance which he has received**')

The sentence in (34) contains a non-restrictive relative clause, and its antecedent *peccad* 'sin' does not require a definite article. Cp. (10) above, where *peccad* is syntactically marked as definite in its first occurrence because it is the focussed element in a cleft sentence on subject position,[9] as is clear from the lack of an article both in its second occurrence in (10) and in (34) above. In (35) *dán* 'gift' is preceded by the definite article when it represents the antecedent noun of a restrictive RC, while it lacks a definite article in its second occurrence, where its definiteness is established by the following genitive (*á cheli* 'of his mate'). In (36) the RC head noun (*tomus*) is preceded by an article it would not otherwise need (cp. in the following clause the definite NP *chumachtai doinachtae Crist* with no article, as the whole NP is marked as definite by the definiteness of the phrase-final genitive noun); cp. (36) with (9) above, where the RC antecedent is the dependent noun *amsire* (in the genitive case), and no article precedes the head noun *ilardatu*, the definiteness of which is established by *inna amsire* + RC. On the relevance of such distribution of markers on RC antecedents for Celtic-English comparison see B.1.5 and Section C.

A.2 Welsh relativisation patterns

In **Welsh** three main relativization strategies are attested, i.e. relative particle and initial mutation (A.2.1), no marker (A.2.2), relative marker and resumptive pronoun (A.2.3).[10]

A.2.1 In "direct" relative clauses, i.e. subject (37) and object (38) RCs, the UNSTRESSED RELATIVE PARTICLE ***a*** [ə] + Soft MUTATION (= Lenition) is used. As in Irish, negative RCs are introduced only by negative forms, i.e. *na(d)* (literary also *ni(d)*) in ModW, followed by Mixed Mutation on the verb, but the ordinary negation may also be used (see (43) below for MW). In the modern spoken language only Soft

9. The so-called dependent clause in a cleft sentence in Irish is always marked either as a relative clause or as a main clause, that is to say there is no ambiguity (in affirmative clauses) about the interpretation of the clause connective, as for English *that*, German *daß*, Italian *che*, etc., which also introduce non-relative subordinate clauses (cp. French *qui* in subject clefts).

10. Old and Middle Welsh examples from D. S. Evans (1964: 60–74), Isaac (1996) for CA, and *Geiriadur Prifysgol Cymru*; ModW examples mainly from T. A. Watkins (1993) and Williams (1980).

Mutation has survived after negation, due to the ultimate lack of contrastive function of Mixed Mutation.[11]

(37) *trychan meirch godrud a gryssyws ganthud*
three:hundred horses spirited REL LEN.rush:PST.3SG with.3PL
'the three hundred spirited horses that rushed forth with them' (CA 1136–37 [MW])

(38) *y march a rodyssei Teirnon idaw*
ART horse REL give:PLUPRF.3SG Teirnon to.3SG.M
'the horse which Teyrnon had given him' (PKM 25, 8 [MW])

The relative particle *a* can combine with an object pronoun (*e* in (39) below) in MW.

(39) *e vedin a-e cretei*
to LEN.army REL-3OBJ trust:SBVJ.IMPF.3SG
'to an army who would trust him' (CA 533 [MW])

Poorly documented Old Welsh also had a relative invariable particle *hai*, as illustrated in (40):

(40) *tir telih hai oid i-lau elcu filius gelhig*
land Telych REL COP.IMPF.3SG in-hand Elcu f. Gelhig
'The land of Telych which was in the hand(s) of Elgu the son of Gelli'
(Chad 2, 'Surexit memorandum'; LL, 8th–9th century [OW])

As in Modern Irish, there is no formal distinction between subject and object relativisation: both are marked with the particle *a* + lenition of the initial consonant of the verb, cp. (37) and (38); as a result of this, ambiguity may arise in some sentences, as in (41).

(41) *Hwn yw 'r dyn a welodd y ferch.*
this.M COP.PRS ART man REL LEN.see:PST:3SG ART F.girl
'The man who saw the girl/whom the girl saw is this.' (ModW)

Thus the analytic strategy for Direct Object RCs is frequently found in negative clauses in MW (ex. 42).

(42) *llyna beth ny-s gwrthodaf i*
there_is LEN.thing NEG-3OBJ refuse:FUT:1SG 1SG
'that is a thing which I will not refuse' (lit. 'that I will not refuse it')
(YCM 64, 15 [MW])

11. Lenition or Soft Mutation in W involves voicing of unvoiced stops and of the voiceless liquid /r̥/, fricativization of voiced stops and /m/, except for /g/, which is deleted; the voiceless lateral fricative /ɬ/ becomes a voiced lateral approximant /l/). When the initial phoneme of the verb is a vowel no relative marker occurs on the verb (e.g. CA (*passim*) [MW] *gwyr a aeth Gatraeth* 'the men who went to Catraeth').

In Welsh the introductory invariable particle *a* can also be used to introduce main clauses. Isaac (1996: 57) formulates the following definition of the function of the particle *a*, which introduces direct relative clauses, dependent clauses in focus constructions (i.e. cleft sentences) and main declarative clauses (in topicalising so-called Abnormal Sentences): «A declarative clause is preceded by the particle *a* when the case role of the subject or direct object of the clause is a feature of an argument preceding the clause, and there is no other particle (negative *ny(t)*, aspectual *ry*) in this position». Thus in some cases the distinction between main clause ('the man goes') and a corresponding RC ('the man who goes') relies solely on the number of predicates and their (shared) arguments in the whole sentence. Note, however, that verbs in RCs do not usually agree even in Number with the antecedent (see (37) and (43)).

Since *a* and Soft Mutation are only used for subject and object relativisation, while the oblique relative particle *y/yd* might cause no mutation (but see D. S. Evans 1964: 171, § 190 and A.2.3 below for details), one can say again that mutation also marks case.

In (43) below the negative particle subsumes the relative particle and is followed by relative lenition on the verb. Alternatively, the dependent clause negation form *na(t)* can be used, which only occurs in subordinate clauses. Note, again, that there is no Number agreement between antecedent and verb in the RC; Number agreement is optional in such cases in MW (see (44) below).

(43) *ny hu wy ny gaffo eu neges*
NEG SO 3PL NEG LEN.get.SBVJ.PRS.3SG their mission
'not so those who do not fulfil their mission' (CA 615 [MW])

In (44) below Number agreement between antecedent (*wyr*) and verb (*thechyn*) occurs. In such cases, however, the mutation required after negation is not the regular RC marker, i.e. lenition, but Spirant Mutation (fricativisation of unvoiced stops), which also occurs after negation in main clauses, as can be seen from (44) itself; thus in such cases there is no surface distinction between relative and non-relative clause (or, put differently, there is a somewhat looser connection between clauses).

(44) *ny phorthassan warth wyr ny thechyn*
NEG SM.bear:PST.3PL shame men NEG SM.flee.IMPF.3PL
'the men who would not flee bore no shame' (CA 1173 [MW])

The only specific relative verb form in Welsh is the copular form OW *issid*, MW *yssyd*, ModW *sydd* (present indicative). See (45) below and cp. similar sentences in OW Computus Fragment (10th cent.): *ir .e. hinnuith, issid diguedham oll in pagina regulari* 'that e which is the last of all in the Pagina Regularis'); see above A.1.1. on Irish.

(45) *y bont yssyd ar yr auon*
ART F.bridge be.PRS.REL on ART river
'the bridge which is over the river' (PKM 40, 20 [MW])

A.2.2 NO MARKER: this option is severely restricted, both syntactically and chronologically. It is confined to "direct" (i.e. non-oblique) RCs in OW and early MW, where it is deemed a relic due to the ancient insertion of the particle between preverb and verb stem (as preserved in OI, see above A.1.4).

(46) *Omnipotens auctor ti dicon-es*
2SG make-PST.3SG
'you (SG.) who have made' (Juvencus B 1 (9th–10th century; poetry) [OW])

(47) *Gur dicon-es remedau[t] elbid*
person make-PST.3SG wonder:PL world
a'n guor-it, a'n guor-aut.
PART-1PL.OBJ save-PRS.3SG PART-1PL.OBJ save-PST.3SG
'He who made the wonders of the world will save us, has saved us.' (Juvencus B 5 (9th–10th century; poetry) [OW])

(48) *Onid imwared-it o'r druc digon-it*
unless deliver-PRS.2SG from-ART evil make-PRS.2SG
'unless you (SG.) deliver yourself from the evil which you do' (*Black Book of Hergest* 19, 7 (HGCref. 6. 13) [MW, poetry])

In (46), (47) and (48) there is no relative particle introducing the RC (note that in (46) there is no Person agreement between antecedent and verb, as in general in the Celtic languages). This is, according to D. S. Evans (1964: 61, § 65, n. 1), an archaism, as the relative particle was originally inserted between preverb and verb stem, though no mutation is preserved on the initial consonant of the verb root.[12] In Old Welsh the "deletion" of the relative particle occurs with the following preverbs: *dy-*, *dym-*, *go-*, *ym-*. The system in fact survived in MW for negation, which was never preceded by a relative particle (see A.1.5 on Irish), and, for some time, for the preverbal particles *neu* 'or' and *ry* (see (49) below); as alluded to above, in early MW lenition of all consonants used to follow the negation only in relative position, while in non relative position either non-mutation or a different mutation (the Spirant Mutation) occurred (see ex. 44). Later Spirant Mutation for unvoiced stops and Lenition for other consonants have been generalised after negation; this is called 'Mixed Mutation' in Modern Welsh. Contrast between relative and non-relative clause marked through mutation has thus been neutralized for negative sentences (see above A.1.5 on such neutralisation in Irish).

(49) *deu oc eu tre re ry gwydyn*
two from their town swift PRF LEN.fall:IMPF.3PL
'Two which had swiftly descended from their town.' (CA 974 [MW])

12. <c> instead of <g> between preverb and verb-root in the compound verb *di-goni* in (48) could in principle reflect fricativisation and devoicing of the initial consonant of the verb root, i.e. <c> = [x], but it simply reflects an old orthographic usage, as mentioned by Evans (1964: 7).

In (49) the preverbal particle *ry* (which here has pluperfect value, but which can also have perfect value) subsumes the relative particle.

It should be noted, though, that in MW "absence" of relative marker can be considered to be more widespread, as the particles used to introduce relative clauses (i.e. *a* + lenition for "direct" relative clauses and *y(t)* for "indirect" relative clauses) can also introduce main clauses, as alluded to above; in fact they are also called affirmative particles.

A.2.3 Oblique (so-called "indirect") RCs are introduced by the **UNSTRESSED RELATIVE PARTICLE** *y* (ModW [ə]) or its allomorph MW *yt*, ModW *yr*, and contain a **RESUMPTIVE PRONOUN**, in the form of a possessive (genitive) pronoun, as in (50) and (52), or in the form of an inflected preposition (i.e. preposition + pronoun agreeing in Person, Number and Gender with the antecedent), as in (51). In (50), though, a "direct" RC marking is followed by a resumptive pronoun (see A.1.7 on Irish genitive RCs). In the modern spoken language the particle often disappears and the opposition between non-oblique and oblique RC could in principle rely exclusively on the opposition between mutation (for direct cases) and non-mutation (for indirect cases) of the initial consonant of the verb. Nevertheless, Lenition (Soft Mutation) has been generalised in all contexts, and has thus become a general RC marker.

(50) *Cledyf a uo eur neu aryant ar y aual*
sword REL LEN.be.SBJV.PRS.SG gold or silver on its pommel
'a sword on the pommel of which there is gold or silver' (LlB 98, 15–16 [MW])

(51) *y wlat yd hanwyf oheni*
ART F.land REL be_from:PRS.1SG from.3SG.F
'the land from which I come' (PKM 2, 24 [MW])

(52) *Hwn yw 'r dyn y gyrraist ei gar*
this.M COP.PRS ART man REL drive:PST.2SG 3SG POSS.M.car
'This is the man whose car you drove.' (ModW)

Preposition + demonstrative introducing a RC (as in Irish, which anyway uses an invariable form of the simple definite article, see A.1.4) can only be found in MW translated texts (D. S. Evans 1964: 66, § 70, ftn. 2), both with and without a resumptive pronoun. Note that the RC in (53) below is non-restrictive; see below A.2.5 on this issue.

(53) *Crist, y unmap ef, yn yr hwnn yd wyt ti*
Christ his only+son 3SG.M in ART DEM.M.SG REL be.PRS.2SG 2SG
yn credu idaw
in believe:VN to.3SG.M
'Christ, his only son, in whom you do believe' (B X.56.9 [MW])

The form *pieu* (lenited *bieu*), which occurs in (54) below, had grammaticalised into a possessor relativisation connective, but was originally an interrogative form, consisting of an oblique (dative) case form of *pwy* 'who?' and the 3rd SG present form of the copula.

In Modern Welsh it undergoes mutation, as any verb form in a RC, and the noun following it (originally its subject) also undergoes mutation as if it were a direct object; its preterite form (*pioedd*), though, is no longer in use (the appropriate form of the verb 'to be' preceding a petrified *biau* is used instead).

(54) *A' r iarll pieu y gaer honno goreu gwr am vwyt yw*
and ART earl whose.is ART F.fort DEM best man about food be.PRS.3SG
'And it's the earl who owns that fortress that is the best man for food'
(*Owein* 707, Isaac 1996: 59 [MW])

A.2.4 Both in Middle and in Modern Welsh place, time, cause and manner circumstantials require the oblique relative particle *y* (as for "indirect" RCs) but no resumptive pronoun (as for "direct" RCs). See (55) and (56) below for place and manner respectively.

(55) *y ford y guelyn y preideu*
ART F.way OBLREL see:IMPF.3PL ART flock.PL
'the street where they were wont to see the flocks' (PKM 51. 25–26 [MW])

(56) *Dyna'r modd y clywais i am y peth.*
that.is:ART way OBLREL hear:PST.1SG 1SG about ART thing
'That is the way I heard about the matter' (ModW)

Note that in (55) and (56) there is no mutation after the relative particle *y*.

A.2.5 In MW the demonstrative pronouns *yr hwnn, yr honn, yr hynn* 'that' (masc., fem. and neuter/ PL. respectively) can be used both as antecedents (for "open" relative clauses) and in appositive (non-restrictive) relative clauses (D. S. Evans 1964: 69, § 74) to introduce the relative clause itself, as in (57) (see also (53) for the use of such demonstrative forms in oblique relative clauses):

(57) *ny dylyut ti tremygv duw, yr hwnn ysyd*
NEG ought:SBJV:IMPF.2SG 2SG contempt:VN God ART DEM be.PRS.REL
lewenyd y dynyon ac egylyon
LEN.joy to man:PL and angel:PL
'you shouldn't despise God, who is joy to men and angels' (LlA 14.3 (D. S. Evans 1964: 69) [MW])

When the antecedent of a restrictive relative clause is a name, the definite article can precede it, as in (58):

(58) *yr Hu a gyffroes y vrenhines*
ART Hu REL LEN.move:PST.3SG ART F.queen
'the Hu that roused the queen' (B V.207.2, D. S. Evans 1964: 26 [MW])

In general, though, Welsh has the same restriction Irish has against two definiteness markers in one NP (though the rule is less strict than in Irish, which has genitive case and can thus more easily make up complex NPs with explicit dependency markers in addition to word order and mutation). The determiner agrees in Gender (though not in Case, which is overall lost in W) with the dependent noun, causing initial mutations. See A.1.8 above on Irish, B.1.5 below on Old English and Section C.

A.3 General features of RCs in Celtic

In all Medieval and Modern Celtic languages (including indeed Breton) any kind of marker always occurs on the verb or immediately before it, affecting it through initial mutations; recall that the verb is the first element of the clause (disregarding negation, subordinators and Welsh affirmative particles, which all represent at any rate a proclitic part of the verbal complex). Antecedent NP and RC tend to be adjacent; only very few words can intervene, usually in poetry (in W PPs modifying the head noun can sometimes even be delayed after the RC, e.g. PKM 4. 6-7 *y rann a dylyei uot am y hwyneb o wisc y phenn* 'the part of her headdress which should be over her face', lit. 'the part which should be over her face of the dress of her head').

In subject RCs the verb is always 3rd Person, that is it does not agree in Person (and only optionally agrees in Number in older varieties) with the antecedent.

No relative pronoun agreeing with the antecedent in grammatical features such as Gender or Number, or in any semantic feature having to do with the Animacy Hierarchy, ever appears in Insular Celtic languages. Case marking does not surface either, except in initial mutations on the verb, resumptive anaphoric pronouns or introductory prepositions (with invariable particle; this occurs only in Irish, while in Welsh preposition + demonstrative introducing RCs is only found in MW translated texts, see ex. 53). The relationship between mutation and case, though, is regularly found only in Modern Welsh (*a* + lenition for non-oblique relative clauses, *y(r)* + non-lenition for oblique relative clauses), and in Modern Irish (lenition for non-oblique relative clauses, nasalization for oblique relative clauses, but only for primary tenses, because in secondary tenses the oblique relative particle has fused with an aspectual particle and causes lenition), where case is on the other hand mainly marked on resumptive pronouns. No formal distinction usually occurs between restrictive and non-restrictive RCs, except for the use of the (definite) article before restrictive relative clauses (restrictive RC antecedents are obligatorily preceded by the article) and the use of preposition + demonstrative in MW non-restrictive relative clauses, where again definiteness effects can be seen (see above A.2.5).

The different kinds of RC markers are summarised in Table 1 and Table 2 (diachronically stable and syntactically widespread strategies in bold).

Table 1. Distribution of Insular Celtic RC markers in time

	OI	MI	ModI	OW	MW	ModW
verbal ending	YES	YES	YES	only for one verb-form		
(PART +) **mutation**	YES	YES	YES	YES	YES	YES
REL **negation**	YES	YES	YES	YES	YES	YES
no marker	YES	YES	NO	YES	YES	NO
object infix set	YES	NO	NO	NO	NO	NO
resumptive pro.	YES	YES	YES	YES	YES	YES
	(GEN)	(all obliques)		(all obliques)		

Table 2. Distribution of Insular Celtic RC markers according to case-roles (simplified: both I and W)

	SUBJ	DO	(IO +) OBLIQUES	GEN	CIRCUMSTANTIALS
verbal ending	YES	YES	NO	YES	YES
(PART+) mutation	**YES**	**YES**	**YES**	**YES**	**YES**
REL negation	**YES**	**YES**	**YES**	**YES**	**YES**
no marker	NO	YES	NO	YES/NO	NO
resumptive pro.	NO	(YES)	YES (not IO)	YES	NO
infix set (only OI)	YES	YES	YES	YES	YES

B.1 English relativisation patterns

Some scholars have suggested that gapping, as in (59)

(59) *the man I love*

and preposition stranding, as in (60)

(60) *the man I am in love with* (as opposed to so-called pied-piping, as in *the man with whom I am in love*)

in English might be due to Celtic substrate influence, as nothing similar can be found in Continental Indo-European languages (see Preusler 1956; Filppula/Klemola and Pitkänen 2002 and the literature quoted therein; White 2002: 169; on the analytic strategy for oblique relative clauses in Welsh Pokorny (1959) stated: «Evident ist die Identität der engl. Konstruktion "*the man I talked to you about*", die zweifellos aus Britischen stammt»).

Celtic and English RCs have apparently become more similar to each other during the centuries they have been in contact with one another in the British Isles, though Celtic languages still maintain their peculiarities (initial mutations in the first place). Irish has lost relative infixes (A.1.2) and relative preverbs (A.1.3 and A.1.4), and in general verb stem splitting – though this occurred earlier than any significant contact with English. Irish has also grammaticalised an unstressed invariable relative particle originally made up of a demonstrative stem (*a*), and has generalised a sort of preposition stranding (though, since prepositions are inflected in all Celtic languages, these agree in Person, Number and Gender with the antecedent and thus represent regular resumptive forms); English, on the other hand, has undergone a significant spread of an invariable marker (OE *þe*, ModE *that*), of gapping and of preposition stranding[13]

13. Poussa (2002) gives the label "particlisation" to such evolution of relative marking, and suggests that it might be related to Scandinavian influence on English; see Section C below.

(see Table 3 at the end of Section B for a diachronic summary of English patterns). On the other hand, Welsh has remained fairly stable.

Nevertheless, dating both the Celtic data and the spread of the different patterns in English provides a slightly different picture. The datings and data that will be given below for OE are based mainly on Bourcier (1977). B.1.1 below will concern RC connective choice, B.1.2 the analytic strategy, B.1.3 place and time circumstantials, B.1.4 preposition stranding. In B.1.5 I will provide a sketch of the geographical distribution of invariable vs. inflected connectives and of definiteness effects related to connective choice. Subsequently, in B.2, I will briefly examine later attested relativisation patterns in English, that is to say gapping (B.2.1), new stranding patterns (B.2.2), and inflected *wh*-pronouns (B.2.3).

B.1.1 Bourcier shows that in older OE prose texts (9th–10th cent.) the three main relativisation markers, i.e. the demonstrative pronoun *se, seo, þæt* (case-inflected and agreeing in Number and Gender with the antecedent, being an old Germanic structure), the invariable particle *þe*, and a combination of the two (*se þe*), had different distributions. *Se þe* is frequently used in "open relative clauses", i.e. where *se* is in fact the antecedent, as in (61), or when the antecedent is not adjacent to the RC (Vezzosi 1998: 239–240), but its distribution may not concern us here.

(61) *and ða ðe his beboda eallunga forseoð*
and DEM.PL.NOM REL his commands wholly despise:PRS.PL
beoð on helle besencte
be.FUT:PL on hell:DAT make_to_sink.PASS.PTCP.PL
'and whoever despises his orders shall be sunken in hell' (SCA I.28)

First of all, with 1st and 2nd person pronominal antecedents only the invariable particle could be used[14] (Bourcier 1977: 66; Vezzosi 1998: 231, 246–7), as in (62), cp. (63).

(62) *þu þe þyrstende wære monnes blodes xxx wintra,*
2SG REL thirst:PRS.PTCP be.PST.2SG man:GEN blood:GEN 30 winters
drynce nu þyne fylle.
drink:SBJV.SG now your.ACC fill
'you, that have been thirsting for man's blood for thirty winters, now drink your fill.' (KAO 76.33, Vezzosi 1998: 225)

(63) Gospels, Mathew VI.9
Corpus ms. (West-Saxon) *fæder ure þu þe eart on heofenum*
Lindisfarne ms. (Northumbrian) *fāder urer ðu arð in heofenum*
Rushworth ms. (Mercian) *fæder ure þu þe in heofenum art*

14. The only exceptions to this rule seem to be (rare) cases where the pronoun is accompanied by *eall* (Vezzosi 1998: 247), which usually requires *se þe*: BHM 145.119 ***ic eow*** *bidde* ***ealle þa þe*** *on þisse stowe syndon* 'I pray all of you that are in this place', BHM 229.20 *þu eart* ***ure ealra fultum, ða þe*** *on þe gelyfað* 'you are the support of all of us who believe in you'.

Secondly, the particle was the preferred choice when the antecedent was preceded by the demonstrative itself (*se, seo, þæt*), particularly when the antecedent was in the dative (*þæm*) or genitive case (*þæs*), and above all when the relative clause was restrictive and the antecedent and relative clause were not separated by other words (see below on this point; see also Vezzosi 1998: 251 and her text frequencies pp. 256–257). The correlation between appositive and demonstrative on the one hand and restrictive and particle on the other hand is stronger (i.e. predictive) with feminine antecedents; for neuter (and, later, inanimate) nouns *þæt* gradually took up the functions of the invariable particle *þe* (i.e. it spread to prepositional relative clauses; later it is also used with any antecedent), though *þe* still prevailed in restrictive clauses and was always chosen when the antecedent noun was preceded by *þæt*, particularly in a non-nom./acc. case form (see also Vezzosi 1998: 222 on the spread of *þæt*). The correlation between appositive and demonstrative and restrictive and particle is confirmed by the almost exclusive use of *se* and *se þe* with proper names (see Vezzosi 1998: 254: in her corpus the ratio is *se* 70%, *se þe* 25%, with *þe* used in cases like BHM 142.221, ex. (97) below). The correlation rises to functional equivalence in oblique RCs in West-Saxon texts (Bourcier 1977: 193, 233), that is to say that restrictive RCs always selected *þe* with stranded preposition.

In general, in older texts, while the particle could be used in any context, the pronoun was used mainly in non-restrictive and/or non-adjacent relative clauses, containing non-presupposed information, as in the following examples (64 and 65):

(64) *Basilius wæs gehaten sum halig biscop se wæs fram cyld-hade*
Basilius was named INDF holy bishop DEM.M.SG.NOM was from childhood
swiðe gehealdsum
very hold:ADJ
'Basilius was the name of a holy bishop, who was very temperate since childhood' (ALS 50.2, Vezzosi 1998: 250)

(65) *and æfter him se arcebiscop of Uiana wearð to Papan*
and after him DET.M.SG.NOM archbishop of Vienna become.PST.3SG to Pope
gecoren ðam wearð nama Calixtus,
choose.PASS.PTCP DEM.SG.M.DAT become.PST.3SG name C.
se siððan to Sancte Lucas mæssan
DEM.M.SG.NOM since to Saint L. mass
Euangelista com into France to Ræins
Evangelist come.PST.3SG into F. to R.
'and after him the archbishop of Wien was chosen as Pope, whose name became Calixtus, and who later came to France in Reims for St. Luke the Evangelist's Mass' (SCP (ASChron.) 40.18. Vezzosi 1998: 251)

Thirdly, in general, case-role of the antecedent both in the main and in the relative clause correlates with connective choice: going rightwards in the case hierarchy reported here below, *þe* was the most likely option, which in earlier texts is excluded from subject RCs:

subject (nominative), direct object (accusative), indirect object (dative), oblique (object of preposition), genitive

(In the plural, though, when the distinction between *þe* (particle) and *þa* (pronoun in the nominative case) is lost, the system is in fact simplified earlier for subject RCs, where in principle the opposition between pronoun and particle should have been stronger). Insertions between antecedent and RC on the other hand increase the likelihood of *se*. This is true for all the OE period in the West Saxon area (Bourcier 1977: 157–158). Thus I assume that the case-role of the antecedent is relevant here because it correlates with the likelihood for the antecedent to be adjacent to a non-embedded RC: uninflected RC markers are of course usually bound to their antecedents, while agreeing relative pronouns can more easily be separated from their antecedents. (Bourcier, though, speaks in this connection of "ending lightness vs. heaviness", particularly focussing on the antecedent determiner).

B.1.2 One of the most interesting distributions for the early period concerns oblique RCs. In some texts (KAO, KAG, 9th cent.) the **analytic strategy** is particularly frequent for indirect object (dative) and genitive RCs (Bourcier 1977: 36, 70); this strategy is also generally viewed as "frequent" in OE by Vezzosi (1998: 228, 272–273) and "not uncommon" by Mustanoja (1960: 202); see exx. 66–70.

(66) *hie weorðað besencte on*
they become.PRS.PL make_to_sink.PASS.PTCP.PL on
ða ealdan unryhtwisnesse
DET.F.SG.DAT old:F.SG.DAT injustice:DAT
ðæs lytegan fiondes ðe bi him awriten
DET.M.SG.GEN cunning:GEN enemy:GEN REL by him written_out:PASS.PTCP
is ðætte…
is that
'they will be sunk in the old injustice of the cunning enemy about whom it is written that…' (KAG 233.16, Bourcier 1977: 36)

(67) *Se þonne bið siwenige se ðe his*
DEM.M.SG.NOM then be.PRS.HAB.3SG blear-eyed DEM.M.SG.NOM REL his
andgit bið to ðon beorhte scienende
intellect be.PRS.HAB.3SG to DEM.N.SG.INS brightly shining
þæt mæge ongietan soðfæstness
that may:SBJV.3SG perceive:INF truth:ACC
'blear-eyed is he whose intellect is so brightly shining that it may understand the truth' (KAG 67.24, Bourcier 1977: 36; *Lippus quidem vero est, cujus quidem ingenium ad cogitationem veritatis emicat*)

(68) *Se* *bið* *eac* *eallenga* *healede* *se*
DET.M.SG.NOM be.PRS.HAB.3SG besides wholly ruptured DEM.M.SG.NOM
se ðe *eall* *his* *mod* *bið* *aflowen*
REL.M.SG.NOM all his mind be:PRS.HAB:3SG from:flow:PASS.PTCP
to *gægelbærnesse*
to luxury:DAT
'And altogether ruptured is he whose mind is all flown out in luxury' (KAG 73.10, Bourcier 1977: 36)

(69) *Þa* *on ðæm* *dæge* *plegedon* *hie* *of* *horsum,* *ægþer ge*
then on DEM.M.SG.DAT day:DAT play:PST:PL they of horse:PL.DAT either and
Philippus ge *Alexander, þe* *he* *his* *dohtor* *him* *sellan* *wolde*
P. and A. REL he his daughter him give:INF will.PST.3SG
'Then on that day they entertained themselves with horses, either Philippus or Alexander, to whom he would give his daughter' (KAO 118.29, Bourcier 1977: 50, 528)

(70) *and* *ic* *gehwam* *wille* *þærto* *tæcan*
and I each_one:DAT will.PRS.1SG thereto teach:INF
þe *hine* *his* *lyst* *man* *to* *witanne*
REL 3SG.M.ACC 3SG.N.GEN please.PRS.3SG IMPERS to know:INF:DAT
'and I will therefore teach to everyone who is pleased to learn' (KAO 102.24, Vezzosi 1998: 228)

According to Bourcier the analytic strategy – which he terms "décumul" – is frequent in KAO, though with indirect object RCs all three strategies can be found in this text, thus *þæm* (inflected pronoun), *þe…him* (invariable particle and resumptive pronoun) and *þe* (invariable particle alone). In BEH (see below B.1.5) it is much rarer, but it can be found for genitives (especially in the plural *þe…heora*, Bourcier 1977: 60). A few cases are registrered even for direct object RCs, and also for subject RCs, but in later texts.

Similar examples can be found also slightly later in the OE period: BHM 47.6 (10th cent., Vezzosi 1998: 228, 273; Allen 1980: 93) *forþon þe hi habbaþ manega saula on heora gewaldum* ***þe him*** *wile git God miltsian* 'because they have many souls in their power that God will yet have mercy on'; BHM 107.20 (Vezzosi 1998: 272) *worldricra manna deaþ* ***þe heora*** *lif mannum leof wære and þuhte fæger and wlitig heora lif and wynsumlic* 'the death of mighty men whose life was dear to men and whose life seemed fair and beautiful and pleasant'.

In the same contexts (genitive and indirect object relativisation) the simple particle *þe* was used sometimes, as in (71–73):

(71) *of* *þæm* *mere* *þe* *Truso* *standeð* *in* *staðe*
of DET.M.SG.DAT sea:DAT REL Truso stand:PRS.3SG in bank:DAT
'from the sea on the shore of which Truso stands' (KAO 20.9, Vezzosi 1998: 226)

(72) *þæt hie þa wæron swyþe sleande þe hie fylstan sceoldon*
that they DEM.PL.ACC were greatly strike:PRS.PTCP REL they help:INF shall.PST.PL
'so that they were severely striking those that they should help' (*fylstan* + DAT)
(KAO 158.25. Vezzosi 1998: 226)

(73) *Be þam men ðe bið husl forboden*
by DET.M.SG.DAT man:DAT REL be.PRS.HAB.3SG Eucharist forbidden
'by the man to whom Eucharist is forbidden' (ALI 170–171, Bourcier 1977: 246 – 11th cent.)

Later on in time, the analytic strategy may be found in West-Saxon texts (exx. 74–75), generally also for prepositional RCs (ex. 76):

(74) *& þæra sancta naman þe heora freols on morgen bið*
and DET.PL.GEN saints names REL 3PL.GEN festival tomorrow be.FUT.3SG
et nomina sanctorum quorum festa crastinus excipiet dies
(ERC 28.17 – 11th cent. ms., 10th cent. original? Bourcier 1977: 235; quorum > *þe heora* also in 25.20, 44.30)

(75) *And wite se ríca man þe him God hæfð*
and know:SBJV DET.M.SG.NOM rich man REL 3SG.M.DAT God have.PRS.3SG
micelne welan & æhta þyses lífes
great:M.SG.ACC wealth:ACC and possession:PL.ACC this:GEN life:GEN
to-forlǽten
to-forgive:INF
'And may you know, the rich man to whom God has to forgive many riches and possessions of this life…' (ALI 136–137, Bourcier 1977: 246 – 11th cent.)

(76) *wa þam menn þe swycdom þurh hine cymð*
WOO DET.M.SG.DAT man.DAT REL offence through 3SG.M.ACC come.PRS.3SG
'vae homini per quem scandalum venit' (Gospels (Corpus ms.) Mathew XVIII, 7, Bourcier 1977: 137)

The analytic construction is frequent (ratio 4 *þe…hiera*/1 *þara*) in the (West-Saxon) Anglo-Saxon Charters of the 9th, 10th and 11th cent. (Bourcier 1977: 288, 290 and 292): Bourcier views such later cases of "décumul" as archaisms.

In 12th cent. texts the analytic strategy seems to become rare (especially for indirect object RCs, where only *þam* and *þam þe* are to be found), but it occurs for genitives e.g. in OEH (Bourcier 1977: 316–7, 340), see (77):

(77) *ac þurh God, þe ic þurh hys willan hider asent wæs*
but through God REL I through his will here sent was
'…but through God, by whose will I was sent here' (OEH 196.8, Bourcier 1977: 572 – 12th cent.; *sed Dei voluntate huc missus sum*)

The analytic pattern was used also for locatives, as in (78):

(78) *and þa on þæm setle ðe he þær sæt*
and then on DET.N.SG.DAT settlement:DAT REL he there sit.PST.3SG
þa gefor Æþelflæd…
then travel.PST.3SG Æ.
'and then in the place where he had settled down, went also Æthelflad'
(SCP 103.57 (921), Vezzosi 1998: 265)

The truly analytic strategy (i.e. with resumptive pronoun) is mentioned even in Jespersen's grammar (1927: III, 108–111), where OE examples are given, though it is quite significant that, while quoting many languages where the construction occurs (including Spanish, Italian, Old and Modern French, Greek, Lithuanian, Modern Persian, Semitic, Egyptian and Malay), Jespersen does not mention any Celtic language at all. Visser (1963–73: 521–23, §§ 604–608) also mentions the construction and somewhat disputably suggests that the need for disambiguation – as the particle *þe* did not express case – was not the only reason for its occurrence, as it can be found in OE with the connective word *se*: Bourcier (1977: 258, n. 122; 581) finds in his large corpus only 1 example in prose texts and 1 in poetry, here reported as (79) and (80), where it should be noted that *se* is uninflected for case (see also Allen 1980: 93–4):

(79) *Eadig bið se wer se him Drihten*
blessed be.FUT.3SG DET.M.SG.NOM man REL 3SG.M.DAT Lord
synne ne getealde
sin:PL.ACC NEG reckon:PST.3SG
'Blessed will be he to whom the Lord did not impute sins' (ALI 434, ca. 1150)

(80) *Þæt is se Abraham se him engla God*
that is DET.NOM.M.SG A. REL 3SG.M.DAT angel:PL.GEN God
naman niwan asceop
name:ACC new:ACC appoint.PST.3SG
'that is the Abraham to whom the angels' God gave a new name'
(EXO 101.380 – 9th cent.)

(note the verb-final relative clause introduced by *se*; V final order is usually typical of RCs introduced by the invariable particle, see below B.1.4).

The construction has obviously been considered non-standard, and according to Visser ceased to exist in the 18th century (but see Herrmann 2005: 70 ff. on its rare occurrence in Modern British English dialects). As noted for simple *þe* above, anyway, the particle + resumptive pronoun was preferred yet again in restrictive RCs as opposed to the inflected pronoun. (Bourcier (1977: 136) quotes various instances such as *þam men, þe hine/þam men, þe him/þone mon, þe him* '(to) the man that/to whom', LWS II.62, 306 etc.). Finally it should be noted that although "reinforcements" of relative pronouns, i.e. double case-marking, or truly analytic strategies can be found in other Germanic languages, the OE pattern corresponds to the Celtic one as a simple anaphoric personal pronoun is used to mark case rather than a demonstrative/relative one: in contrast to e.g. Middle Low German *de…des, de…dem* (Rösler 2002: 53, 57) OE used *þe…his, þe…him* etc., not **þe… þæs, þe… þæm* etc. Thus the analytic strategy for locatives in (78) should be kept separate.

B.1.3 For **temporal and locative circumstantials** the OE strategy is seemingly quite similar to the Welsh one: invariable particle *þe* but no resumptive pronoun, i.e. no case marking (Bourcier 1977: 36, 50, 59, 162, 183, *passim*), see (81–82):

(81) *on þam dæge þe þæt Ebreisce folc heora*
on DET.SG.DAT day:DAT REL DET.N.SG.NOM Jewish people.N.NOM their
geares getel onginnað
year:GEN number begin.PRS.PL
'on the day when the Jewish people begin their year's count' (SCA I, 98, Vezzosi 1998: 227)

(82) *Þreo asæton on ða healfe þæs deopes ðe*
three settle.PST.PL on DET.F.SG.ACC half:ACC DET.N.SG.GEN deep.N.GEN REL
ða Deniscan scipu aseten wæron
DET.PL.NOM Danish:PL.NOM ship:PL.NOM settle:PASS.PTCP be.PST.PL
'Three settled on the half side of the sea where the Danish ships were settled' (SCP (ASChron.) 91.3, Vezzosi 1998: 227)

For locative circumstantials, though, the locative pronoun *þær* is more frequent in old texts (e.g. in BEH both *in þære stowe, þær* and *in þære stowe, þe* occur quite often, but the first one is more common); *þær* could also be used resumptively, as in (83). Later the simple stranded preposition (*in, on, to*) was usually required (Bourcier 1977: 163), as in (84):

(83) *þæt þær næs seo stow, þe he ðær*
that there NEG.be.PST.3SG DET.F.SG.NOM place.F.NOM REL he there
mihte beon on aleȝd
may.PST.3SG be.INF on place.PASS.PTCP
'that there was not the place where he might be put' (BWG 226.13)

(84) *& he þa forlet þa stowe þe he on wæs*
and he then leave.PST.3SG DET.F.SG.ACC place.F.ACC REL he on be.PST.3SG
'and he then left the place where he was' (BWG 119.18)

The similarity between W and E, though, seems trivial here (see Cristofaro and Giacalone Ramat, this volume).

B.1.4 The **stranding pattern** (with invariable particle, stranded preposition and no resumptive pronoun) occurred in OE alongside the synthetic one for prepositional RCs (preposition + appropriate inflected form of *se, seo, þæt*). Stranding was the preferred option with some prepositions (*mid, on, to, ymb*) since the oldest extant West-Saxon texts, while others (*from, þurh, be*) seem to favour the synthetic strategy (Bourcier 1977: 35); this distribution is perhaps related to the fact that the prepositions in the first set were more frequently used adverbially, i.e. as preverbs,[15] than those in the second set (that is to say, it may be viewed as an entirely "Germanic" phenomenon), as exemplified by (85):

(85) *he hie het gebindan & beforan eallum*
he 3PL.ACC command.PST.3SG tie:INF and before all.PL.DAT
þæm folce mid besman swingan & siþþan mid æxsum
DET.N.SG.DAT folk:DAT with rod:PL.DAT flog:INF and later with axe:PL.DAT
heora heafda on aceorfan.
their head:PL.ACC on cut:INF
'he ordered to bind them and to flog them with rods before all the people and then to cut off their heads with axes.' (KAO f. 24 (Bately 1980: 40.22) [OE])

Be that as it may, the stranding pattern as opposed to the synthetic one (preposition in clause-initial position) was favoured – and became later obligatory – in restrictive RCs, and particularly when nothing intervened between antecedent and relative *þe*. This distribution is older in the West-Saxon area than in the Anglian area (see below B.1.5); for example in the Vespasian Psalter (Mercian) and in the Northumbrian ms. of the Gospels (Lindisfarne) only preposition + inflected *se* occurs, while in contemporary West-Saxon texts invariable *þe/þæt* was already well established, as exemplified by (86–88).

(86) *and locian hwæþer he þæt land gecneowe þæt*
and look:INF whether he DET.N.SG.ACC land.N.ACC know.PST.3SG DEM.N.SG.ACC
hie toweard wæron
they towards be.PST.PL
'and see if he knew the land they were approaching' (KAO 202.2, Vezzosi 1998: 221) [OE])

(87) *and þone stede þe se deofol of*
and DET.M.SG.ACC place.M.SG.ACC REL DET.M.SG.NOM devil off
afeoll
fall_down.PST.3SG
'and the place the devil fell off' (SCA I, 14, Vezzosi 1998: 227)

(88) *Hē wæs swyðe spēdig man on þæm æhtum*
he was very wealthy man on DET.PL.DAT possession:PL.DAT
þe hēora spēda on beoð
REL 3PL.GEN wealth.PL.NOM on be.PRS.HAB.PL
'He was a very wealthy man in those possessions in which their wealth lies' (KAO 15, 7–8 [OE] (V-final))

15. From a diachronic point of view one may rather speak in terms of prepositional use of adverbs, but this may not concern us here.

As for word order, RCs introduced by inflected *se, seo, þæt* in OE displayed the unmarked declarative order (SVO), while RCs introduced by *þe* preserved the subordinate clause order SOV. In oblique RCs the stranded preposition was thereby not in sentence final position, as occurred later, but in preverbal position. P-V order lingered on up to the 13th cent. (see Visser 1963–73: 399; Bourcier 1977: 438–439), when V-P order became dominant. The non-V-final order in RCs introduced by *þe* first appeared with the verb *to be* (Bourcier 1977: 107–108); see above (63), Corpus ms. It is interesting to note that when *þæt* (the neuter pronoun) began to assume the functions previously held by *þe*, it could be found with V-final order (always in the West-Saxon version of the Gospels, see Bourcier 1977: 167; cp. (86) above).

B.1.5 Some geographical differences can be observed regarding RCs in OE texts. In the West-Saxon area *þe* was chosen as an unmarked connective earlier than in the Anglian (Mercian and Northumbrian) area; in particular Bede (BEH), which is thought to be copied from an Anglian original, displays a very low frequency of the invariable particle, particularly with masculine and feminine antecedents, and does not include any example of the analytic construction for obliques (Bourcier 1977: 36, 60); moreover, its conservatism is also reflected in the frequency of V-final order even in RCs introduced by inflected *se* (Bourcier 1977: 57). Similarly in the Vespasian Psalter (Mercian) only *se* and *se ðe* can be found (Bourcier 1977: 89–90), and *se* was usually more persistent in Mercian texts of the 10th cent. than in contemporary West-Saxon texts (Bourcier 1977: 116–117). Even in later texts (12th cent.) the Eastern Midlands seem to better preserve inflected *se*, though Gender and Number agreement was in fact lost (Bourcier 1977: 464–467).

More specifically, while in West-Saxon a restrictive RC usually had the structure outlined in (89) below – with the antecedent preceded by the determiner, e.g. acc. *þone* (Bourcier 1977: 124–5; direct object relative clause with antecedent in the accusative case) –, in Mercian this typically corresponded to (90):

(89) *þone* (inflected determiner) head noun *þe* (invariable relative particle)

(90) Ø (no determiner) head noun *þone* (inflected relative pronoun)

Similarly with neuter antecedents either (91) or (92) occurs in LWS (Bourcier 1977: 170):

(91) Ø head noun *þæt*

(92) *þæt* head noun *þe*

This is reflected in a sort of minimal pair in (93a-b) (Bourcier 1977: 127) and in (94) and (96) as opposed to (95) (where, however, *þe* is used: see Bourcier 1977: 193, and here below on case-attraction):

(93a) Gospels, John VII.39, Lindisfarne ms. (Northumbrian) *of gaste þone* 'of the spirit that'

(93b) Gospels, John VII.39, Corpus ms. (West-Saxon) *be þam gaste þe* 'by the spirit that'

(94) Gospels, Mathew X.6, p. 83, Rushworth ms. (Mercian)
ah mae gaþ to þæm sciopum þe
but more go.IMP.2PL to DET.PL.DAT sheep:PL.DAT REL
sed potius ite ad oves quae
to lore wyrðon huses israhela
to loss:DAT become.PST.PL house:GEN Israel:GEN
perierunt domus israhel

(95) Gospels, Matthew XV.24, p. 129, Rushworth ms. (Mercian)
ne ic wæs asended nymþe to scepum þæm þe
NEG I was send:PASS.PTCP except to sheep:PL.DAT DET.PL.DAT REL
non sum missus nisi ad oves quae
forloren wyrdon huses israheles
destroy:PASS.PTCP become.PST.PL house:GEN Israel:GEN
perierunt domus israhel

(96) Gospels, Matthew X.6, Corpus ms. (West-Saxon)
ac gað ma to þam sceapum þe forwurdon
but go.IMP.2PL more to DET.PL.DAT sheep:PL.DAT REL perish.PASS.PL
*ysrahela hywrædden*e
Israel:GEN household:GEN

Cp. also (97)

(97) *Ic eom se Andreas þe ge secaþ*
I am DET.M.SG.NOM Andreas REL 2PL seek.PRS.PL
'I am the Andreas that you are seeking' (BHM 241.221, Vezzosi 1998: 255)

There seemed to be a restriction against two inflected demonstratives (see also Mitchell 1985: II, 160 for such tendency); in West-Saxon texts such restriction had clear connections with the various functions displayed by *se, seo, þæt*, here listed in Bourcier's formulation (1977: 170):

a. il indique une détermination établie par les énoncés précédents (fléchage contextuel arrière)
b. il constitue le premier terme d'un déterminant dichotomique qui enserre le substantif, le second étant la relative (fléchage contextuel avant)
c. enfin, il peut avoir une valeur allusive (le célèbre…, le méprisable…, selon les cas), se rattachant au fléchage situationnel

In function (b), i.e. when it represents the first part of a twofold determiner which surrounds the head-noun, the second one being the RC, it agrees in Gender, Number and Case with the noun and thereby appropriates all agreement features from the relative clause connective. Cp. the following two examples, (98) and (99):

(98) *fram rome byrig to þære byrig þe is gehaten alexandria*
from Rome town to DET.F.SG.DAT town REL is called A.
'from the city of Rome to the city that is called Alexandria' (ALS 25.262, Vezzosi 1998: 257)

(99) *to grecum to atheniscre byrig seo wæs þa*
to Greek:PL.DAT to Athenian:F.DAT town DEM.F.SG.NOM was then
bremost on lare
famous:SUP on learning:DAT
'to Greece, to the city of Athens, which was then the most famous in learning'
(ALS 50.11, Vezzosi 1998: 258)

In the first example the town acquires definiteness by the following relative clause, where it is identified (*Alexandria*), while in the second example the town is named before the relative clause, which contains additional information (not relevant for its identification). Thus in (98) the structure outlined in (89) is evident. On the other hand example (99) typifies the structure illustrated in (90).

As expected, only when the head noun is preceded by an indefinite determiner, as in (100) and (101) below, can both forms occur, as in such cases the opposition between restrictive and non restrictive RC can surface (100 with *þe* vs. 101 with inflected pronoun):

(100) *and ferde ða to sumere cyrcan þe wæs to lofe*
and travel:PST.3SG then to one.DAT church:DAT REL was to glory:DAT
ðære eadigan Marian gehalgod
DET.F.SG.GEN blessed:GEN Mary:GEN consecrate.PASS.PTCP
'and then (he) went to a church that was consecrated to the praise of blessed Mary' (SCA I.448, Bourcier 1977: 573)

(101) *Ure Drihten ferde to sumere byrig*
our Lord travel.PST.3SG to one.DAT town:DAT
seo is gehaten Naim
DEM.F.SG.NOM is called N.
'Our Lord went to a town which is called Naim' (SCA I.490, Bourcier 1977: 573)

Such distribution (inflected demonstrative on the head noun selecting non-inflected relative marker, particularly if the determiner is in an oblique case) became even stronger in later texts (11th century: see Bourcier 1977: 261, 267); even in Mercian texts of the 11th cent. the inflected relative pronoun plural form *þa, þo* only appeared when the head noun had no determiner (Bourcier 1977: 285).

According to Vezzosi (1998: 250–1), *þe* was the preferred choice even when the head noun had a different determiner, i.e. a genitive noun or a possessive, as in (102) (Vezzosi, however, did not take into account any dialect distinction):

(102) *Þa cuædon hie þæt hie hie þæs ne*
then say.PST.PL they that 3PL.NOM REFL DEM.N.SG.GEN NEG
onmunden þon ma þe eowre
consider_worthy:PST.PL DET.N.SG.INS more than 2PL.POSS.PL.ACC
gerefan þe mid þam cyninge ofslægene wærun
officer:PL.ACC REL with DET.M.SG.DAT king:DAT slay:PST.PTCP:PL be.PST.PL

'then they said that they did not consider themselves entitled to accept that any more than your officers that were slain with the king' (SCP (ASChron.) 48.37)

This restriction (only one inflected determiner/demonstrative in a single NP) is unparallelled in other ancient Indo-European languages (Greek in the first place) and, most importantly, in those Germanic languages where the demonstrative stem has taken up relative functions. I believe this is one of the few points where Celtic influence is worth considering (see above A.1.8 and A.2.5 on such distribution), as the phenomenon is somehow restricted in time and does not seem to correspond to any language-internal drift (which would cancel inflection and feature-agreement on the head-noun determiner, rather than on the relative connective).

In the Mercian area, moreover, relative pronoun case attraction (i.e. transfer of case from the antecedent to the relative pronoun) is more widespread than in the West-Saxon area; and again structures like (103) (Bourcier 1977: 104, 108, 111) instead of (104) can in fact be considered similar to the previous one (N+ postposed determiner + *þe*, as in ex. 95).[16]

(103) noun (in the dative case) + *þaem* + *þe*

(104) *þam* + noun (in the dative case) + *þe*

The high frequency of the case-attraction pattern in (105) in 9th cent. and later poetry (Bourcier 1977: 382, 407) confirms its antiquity.

(105) noun (in the dative case) + *þaem* + *þe* / noun (in the genitive case) + *þara* + *þe*

Cp. also cases like (106) (Vezzosi 1998: 234–35), where the demonstrative is part of the antecedent rather than of the RC:

(106) *Wuldor sy Gode on heannessum and mannum on eorþan*
glory be.SBJV.SG God:DAT on heaven:PL.DAT and man:PL.DAT on earth:DAT
þam þe godes willan syn
DEM.DAT that good:GEN will:GEN be.SBJV.PL
'Glory be to God in heavens and to men on earth who are goodwilling'
(BHM 93.181)

It is interesting to note in this connection how in 9th cent. poetry (Vercelli) the opposition between specific and non-specific indefinite antecedents (*ænig, æghwylc, nænig*) is expressed by *þara þe* ('one/ any/ some/ none of those who') vs. simple *þætte* ('one/ any/ some such that') respectively (Bourcier 1977: 393), showing a similar opposition between demonstrative stem belonging to the antecedent and to the RC.

16. Allen's observations (1980: 86–87) ultimately lead to a similar description: «This type is called the "se ðe" type, and here the pronoun may have either the case of the relativized NP or that of the head. The pronoun optionally attracts into the case of the head noun only when the relativized item is the dative or accusative object of the higher clause».

Further to the geographical distribution, in the OE Martyrology (mixed dialect, though Mercian area) prep. + *þære* + head noun + *seo* can be found for subject relative clauses, while in the West-Saxon area *seo* never follows *þære* (Bourcier 1977: 147).

Again, as alluded to above, the particle was favoured in West-Saxon in prepositional RCs when restrictive, while in Mercian and Northumbrian texts only the synthetic strategy with preposition + inflected pronoun can be found (Bourcier 1977: 131–134). The preposition was used even with temporal antecedents, as shown by the correspondences in (107):

(107) Vespasian Psalter: *in die qua* > *in dege in ðaem*
in via hac qua > *in wege ðissum ðaem*

Later on (10th–11th cent.) the West-Saxon distribution can also be found in the Mercian area (Bourcier 1977: 252), and is firmly established in Ælfric's texts (11th cent., Bourcier 1977: 341). In Wulfstan's texts only "postpositions" (i.e. stranding patterns) are found (Bourcier 1977: 344–345).

B.2.1 The earliest examples of **gapping** are severely restricted, essentially to cases like (108) (Bourcier 1977: 55–56, 138–139; Vezzosi 1998: 295–296):

(108) SG *X…, Y wæs haten* *X, Y hatte* ('X, that Y was called')
PL *X…, Y and Z wæron hatene* *X, Y and Z hatton* ('X, that Y and Z were called')

Thus, while being lexically selected, the construction is also syntactically restricted (the predicate noun is fronted[17]). Later on the formula seems just to linger on, and is semantically confined to non-restrictive relative clauses with very loose connections between clauses; Bourcier in fact poses the following schema:

se X… þe Y… wæs haten (restrictive, focus on the antecedent)
X…, se wæs haten Y… (non-restrictive, focus on the relative clause)
X…, þe Y… wæs haten (non-restrictive, focus on the antecedent)
X… Y… wæs haten (non-restrictive, non-subordinating)

The gapping strategy then spread to other lexical elements but was still very rare and was confined to subject relative clauses, as in (109) (Bourcier 1977: 282–283; 360–362, 434, 450, but see B.2.2 below for stranding patterns). Its appearance in object RCs occurred even later.

(109) *þæt is þonne þæt ic geann ðæder into ðære halgan*
that is then that I grant.PRS.1SG thither into DET.F.SG.DAT holy:DAT
stowe anes beages is on syxtigum
place:DAT one:GEN ring:GEN is on sixty:DAT

17. Cp. Platzack (2002: 85) for a similar fronting in Old Swedish gapping construction in subject RCs.

mancussum *goldes*
mancus:PL.DAT gold:GEN
'That is then that I bestow there to that holy place one ring which is sixty mancuses of gold' (AWW 62.17, West-Saxon, 1000–1066; Bourcier 1977: 283, 566)

B.2.2 As has been illustrated earlier, stranding patterns are found both in OE and ME (Visser 1963–73: 397 ff.; Denison 1993: 130–133), but **new stranding patterns**, which were hardly found in OE but which gained ground during the ME period, are: stranding in RCs with gapping (as in (110), so – called contact clauses or apò koinoũ constructions, see Visser 1963–73: 404, 536 ff., 541–546; Denison 1993: 132), stranding in *wh*-relative clauses (as in (111), see Visser 1963–73: 400-1; Denison 1993: 132; Bourcier 1977: 470), and stranding in free relative clauses, i.e. relative clauses with open antecedents (as in (112), see Visser 1963–73: 548; Denison 1993: 132):

(110) *ic kiþe eow þat ic habbe gegefen*
I announce.PRS.1SG 2PL.DAT that I have.PRS.1SG give.PST.PTCP
Criste & Scē Petre into Westmunstre
Christ:DAT and St. Peter:DAT into Westminster:DAT
ðet cotlif ic wæs geboran inne
DET.N.SG.ACC hamlet I be.PST.1SG born in
'I proclaim to you that I have given to Christ and St. Peter in Westminster the small village I was born in' (AWH p. 369, c. 1065; Visser 1963–73: 541; Bourcier 1977: 286, 566)

(111) *& he maȝȝ wel bitacnenn himm*
and he may well point:INF 3SG.M.DAT
Whamm he stod inn to follzhenn
whom he stand.PST.3SG in to follow:INF
'And he may well mean to follow him in whom he stood' (OHW 225.6518, Ormulum; beg. 13th cent. according to Bourcier 1977: 606. ex. 1012)

(112) *Hwamse heo bisecheð fore is sikerliche iborhen*
whoever 3SG.F.NOM intercede.PRS.3SG for is certainly saved
'Whoever she intercedes for is certainly saved' (SWard 311, c. 1225; Denison 1993: 132))

Cp. (110) above with (113) below, with the invariable particle *þatt* instead of gapping; the two might differ in relation to the functions of the RCs (restrictive in (110) vs. non-restrictive in (113)):

(113) *Amang þatt Judewisshe follc þatt Crist wass borenn offe*
among DET.N.SG.ACC Jewish folk.N.ACC REL Christ was born of
'among the Jewish people whereof Christ was born' (OHW 141.4096; Ormulum; beg. 13th cent. according to Bourcier 1977: 606. ex. 1013).

If the gapping strategy could be viewed as the product of the deletion of a phonetically light invariable particle, then the Celtic and English development could be seen at best as similar processes, which do not nevertheless correspond chronologically. However, since the emergence of a well-established invariable particle for all verbs in the Celtic languages seems to have occurred later than the simple gapping strategy (i.e. zero connective, see A.1.1, A.1.6, A.2.2) for subject relative clauses, the possibility of substrate influence ought not be ruled out completely. Moreover, the OE zero pattern with subject RC, which could be claimed to be a substratal phenomenon, is not comparable to the new one with preposition stranding. On the other hand, the emergence of gapping in preposition stranding construction, and later on its restriction to object (restrictive) RCs agrees with the Celtic pattern, where

a. inflected prepositions occur in clause-final position
b. rigid word order, obligatory absence of independent subject pronouns (and in English obligatory presence of subject pronouns) allows only object RC interpretation (*the man I love*, cp. for OI (22) and for MW (48) above, see A.1.4 and A.1.6)

In my opinion, though, the issue remains unproven. In actual fact, if preposition stranding patterns in other Germanic languages are taken into account (see Platzack 2002), the Celtic contribution to English stranding constructions may seem to be negligible, as I further elaborate in the conclusions presented in Section C below.

B.2.3 *Wh*-pronouns in relative clauses are a ME development, which according to Bourcier (1977: 241) makes its earliest appearance in prose in interlinear glosses on Latin – Liber Scintillarum, 1st half of the 11th cent., West-Saxon *unusquisque in quo* > *anra gehwylc* ['each one'] ***on hwam*** – where it is a calque. Two contrasting examples (respectively (114) and (115)) in the 9th cent. poem *Elene* (Vercelli's Book) testify according to Bourcier (1977: 395) to the use of the interrogative pronoun within "non-actualising" contexts (negative main clause, non-realis modality), thus restricting the actual contribution of foreign influence in this development (see below):

(114) *Ic wat geare þæt hio wile*
I know.PRS.1SG well that 3SG.F.NOM will.PRS.3SG
secan be ðam sigebeame
seek:INF by DET.M.SG.DAT victory+tree:DAT
on ðam *þrowode þeoda waldend*
on DEM.M.SG.DAT suffer_martyrdom:PST.3SG nation:PL.GEN ruler
'I know for sure that she will seek by the cross on which the king of nations suffered…' (Elene 77, 419, Krapp, vol. II; Bourcier 1977: 584)

(115) *Ne meahte hire Iudas, ne ful gere wiste,*
NEG may.PST.3SG 3SG.F.DAT Judas NEG full well know.PST.3SG
sweotole gecyþan be ðam sigebeame,
clearly announce:PASS.PTCP by DEM.M.SG.DAT victory+tree:DAT
on hwylcne *se hælend ahafen wære,*
on which DET.M.SG.NOM saviour raise:PASS.PTCP be.PST.SBJV.3SG

sigebearn *godes,* *ær…*
victory+born:NOM God:GEN before
'Judas did not have power on her, did not know her well, clearly announced by the cross on which the Saviour would be raised, victorious child of God, before…' (Elene 90, 859, Krapp, vol. II; Bourcier 1977: 585)

Judging by Bourcier's earliest examples[18] of inflected interrogative pronouns introducing RCs, the interrogative pronoun has apparently penetrated the system starting from the lowest positions in the accessibility hierarchy, i.e. from prepositional and genitival RCs (cp. Romaine 1984).

The interrogative pronoun was typical of non-restrictive contexts: *hwas* etc. frequently resumed personal pronoun antecedents. It substituted the preposition + inflected pronoun pattern with animate antecedents: the older pattern with prep. + inflected *se, seo, þæt* was by then dying out (Bourcier 1977: 436–7; 439, 442, 450, etc.). In some 13th cent. texts this pattern contrasts with stranding (with introductory *þe* or, more frequently, *þæt*) for some prepositions. Only somewhat later does *hwat* for inanimate antecedents appear, again at first in prepositional RCs (Bourcier 1977: 451, 472; early example ARD 169.34, 13th cent., Bourcier 1977, ex. 904 *þuruh hwat*), and stranding with interrogative pronouns (13th cent., Bourcier 1977: 470, see above ex. 111). The tendency to use *wh*-pronouns in non-restrictive RCs had already been noted for ME by Mustanoja (1960: 202) and is reflected in Standard Modern English.

Table 3. English relativisation markers in time

RELATIVISATION PATTERN	EMERGENCE	SPREAD
se (inflected demonstrative)	attested since earliest documents	NO
se þe (inflected demonstrative + particle)	attested since earliest documents	NO
þe/ þæt/ that (non-agreeing invariable particle)	attested since earliest documents	YES
analytic strategy (particle + pronoun)	9th cent. (areally restricted)	up to the 12th cent.
preposition stranding	attested since earliest documents	YES
gapping	11th cent. (in non-formulaic clauses)	YES
wh-	11th cent. (in prose)	YES
preposition stranding with gapping	11th cent.	YES

18. See the following brief list: ex. 770 p. 588 PME (I) 171.201 (12th cent., South) ***for hwam***; ex. 781–782 p. 589 (Vespasian Homilies, 12th cent., South) ***of wam***; p. 428 Lawman's Brut (12th cent., South) ***wan*** (direct object), ***þorh wan***; p. 434–435 LHM (12th cent., West Midlands) ex. 818

c. Discussion and conclusions

Juan de la Cruz (1972), while allowing for a common (possibly non-Indo-European) source for stranding patterns in English and Scandinavian languages (Icelandic, Danish, Swedish and Norwegian), rules out the possibility of Celtic influence mainly because of the independent evidence in favour of Hamitic influence on Celtic (Pokorny 1959, on whose position see however the quotation in B.1 above, and Wagner 1959): « [...] given Pokorny's evidence and the internal complexity of the isogloses concerned, it is hard to indulge in the temptation of assigning a Celtic origin to the English and Scandinavian structures.» (de la Cruz 1972: 172).

As a further argument de la Cruz notes that the so-called prepositional passive (e.g. *They were looked for*), being a direct outcome of other stranding patterns, is not found in Celtic (however, in the case it is necessary to point out that Celtic languages do not have a "true passive", but only a so-called "impersonal", i.e. mainly an agent removing strategy, rather than a patient promoting one, so that one may find something corresponding to "*it was looked for them*"); nevertheless, prepositional passive constructions are attested only since ME and seem to be a later English development. As for Hamitic influence, it is not sound practice to rule out contact influence between languages whose contacts are firmly established, basing one's argument upon other assumed but not proven contacts; cp. e.g. Preusler (1956: 340) for the opposite argument about prepositionally-introduced dependent clauses (e.g. *it depends upon whether...*): «...denke ich auch hier an substratwirkung des Keltischen aufs Englische, um so mehr [emphasis mine], als ich auch für die keltische fügung nichtindogermanischen ursprung vermute».[19]

According to Preusler (1956) all Celtic traits in English emerged during the Middle English period, as substrate influence requires many generations in order to spread first in the spoken and then in the standard and written language (the only one which is accessible to us).[20] In his opinion, when Scandinavian languages, Dutch and French agree with English in any of the syntactic features of his list, this is due to their

---

p. 591 ***on hwulche***, ex. 821 p. 592 ***þurh hwam***, ex. 822 p. 592 ***hwas***; p. 436 SIA (13th cent., West Midlands) ex. 828 p. 592 ***hwas***; p. 439 HMC (13th cent., West Midlands) exx. 847, 848 and 855 p. 592, ex. 858 p. 594 ***hwas***, ex. 849 ***under hwam***, ex. 853 p. 593 ***bi hwam***, 866 p. 594 and ex. 867 p. 595 ***þurh hwam***; p. 595 LKE (13th cent., West Midlands) ex. 873 ***þurh hwam & under hwam.***

19. The point against de la Cruz's conclusions is not weakened even if one assumes Hamito-Semitic substrate to be actually present in Celtic, as such substrates of course represent different chronological and linguistic strata. Incidentally, the issue of non Indo-European substrate in Celtic has been more convincingly revived in a typological framework by Orin Gensler (1993).

20. Preusler's list of Celtic traits in English is the following:
double "be" root in the present (OE *is* vs. habitual *bið*; MW *mae* vs. habitual *bydd*); the progressive form made up of the verb "to be" plus a nominal verb-form (E *he is learning*, W *mae yn dysgu*);

common Celtic substratum. It should be noted, though, that it is now clear that syntactic phenomena which may be found in Insular Celtic languages should not be ascribed *per se* to the continental Celtic substratum of the rest of Europe. For instance, Celtiberian is now known to have had a typical Indo-European inflected relative pronoun (and even preposed RCs; see e.g. Eska/E. Evans 1993: 33, 35[21]). Secondly, it is reasonable to allow many generations, not many centuries, for contact to surface; in my opinion, contrarily to what Preusler claimed, Celtic influence on English has been overshadowed by later contact layers (precisely Scandinavian, Norman French and Flemish).

It seems better, therefore, to look for contact features that the above data highlight.[22]

a. First the all-purpose marker *þe*, and later on in time gapping (at first with preposition stranding), are associated with restrictive relative clauses. These are, presumably, the most common type of RCs in ordinary speech (in the spoken language as opposed to the literary language, see Herrmann 2005: 38 on this point).

---

the conflation of locative, instrumental and comitative values in one preposition which is also used for agents with the passive (OE *be, bi* and *mid*; W *gan(t)*, I *la*); the adverbal (i.e. not adnominal) marking of present participles objects (absence of morphological case is ascribed to Welsh; but it is hard to maintain that W has verbal rection for VNs); the aspectual distinction between perfective and non-perfective (progressive) present and past forms; the *do* periphrasis (in interrogative and negative sentences); cleft sentences; "contact clauses"; sentence-final prepositions in relative clauses; resumptive pronouns (i.e. non relative) for genitive relative clauses (OE construction found in Scottish and Irish English); prepositionally-introduced dependent clauses (*a complete proof of what we already know*); the indefinite article in classificatory copular sentences (e.g. *he is a soldier*) paralleled by Welsh *yn* in similar sentences; the order common noun – proper name, particularly in place-names (*Ælfred cyning* → *king Alfred*); constructions like *a friend of mine* (i.e. obligatory definiteness agreement between head and dependent noun when in the genitive; if the two do not correspond, a prepositional phrase must be used: ModI *cara dom* lit. 'a friend to me'); the widespread use of possessive adjectives (as in *he raised his hands*); the possessive + reflexive besides the pronoun (in the appropriate case) + reflexive (E *myself*, W *my hun, fy hun*); the use of an auxiliary (*do*) in answers and echo-forms; the combining of two comparatives to express growing degrees (*more and more*).

On the similarity of Irish and English cleft sentences (so-called "Pseudorelativierung") see also Kurzová (1981: 101). On *myself* etc. see Vezzosi (2005); Vezzosi argues that a Celtic model should be assumed for the development of intensifiers and reflexives. Her arguments, which were devised independently from the ones put forward in this paper, are nevertheless strikingly similar in nature to mine.

21. The point holds even if one does not agree on the interpretation of Celtiberian texts, see Sornicola (1989: 267).

22. On Scandinavian influence on English relative clauses see Poussa (2002: 9–10).

Some kind of formal distinction between restrictive and non-restrictive emerges at various stages in the history of English (new markers, such as *þe, þæt*, stranding, Ø, are preferably used for restrictive clauses at first):

(preferred choices)	RESTR.	NON-RESTR.	
OE	*þe*	*se, seo, þæt*	
late ME/ModE	*that*	*which/who*	(Mustanoja 1960: 190)

Such distinction seems to be linked in OE with progressive loss of a (double) agreeing determiner (both on the head noun in the main clause and as a RC marker), that is to say for the spread of the following choice for restrictive RCs: either (116a) or alternatively (116b), but not (117), which represents the older Indo-European (cp. Greek) and specifically Germanic pattern:

(116a) (agreeing) DET – N – invariable non-agreeing (in Number and Gender, though partially case-marked) RC marker

(116b) N – agreeing and case-marked RC marker (= DET)

(117) (agreeing) DET – N – agreeing and case-marked RC marker

The first pattern is the insular Celtic one (see above A.1.8, A.2.5), with agreeing determiner and invariable particle (possibly the outcome of a demonstrative-determiner petrified case-form) but partial case marking (the "direct" vs. "indirect" RC is the basic distinction); in English "partially case marking" means that some options (invariable *þe*, gapping) are increasingly available only for some syntactic roles. Celtic influence should be seen in the OE evolution whereby particle vs. inflected relative pronoun choice links up with the presence of an agreeing determiner on the head noun rather than with other factors (see B.1.5). The evolution proceeds Northwards and Eastwards (see again B.1.5), as would be consistent with Celtic influence: Celtic languages have survived after the Anglo-Saxon invasion in the South-Western part of England (cp. Jackson 1953: 221 ff. on the distribution of Celtic river names: the most Celtic-influenced area of Britain, excluding of course Cornwall and Wales, is in the South-West). As new relativisation patterns, particularly borrowed patterns (see Romaine 1984), seem to spread out starting from the lowest positions in the Accessibility Hierarchy, the fact that the pattern in (116a) is more frequent for oblique cases in the early period (see B.1.1) and that Standard Modern English preserves obligatory overt marking in restrictive RCs precisely in the highest position (subject RCs) confirms the prediction.

b. Spread of interrogative pronouns in relative function is on the other hand a non-Celtic phenomenon, which has been claimed to be influenced by Latin and French (Mustanoja 1960: 191, 196; Romaine 1984: 450; Poussa 2002: 2), but which may also reflect an internal drift (see B.2.3). On the other hand, Welsh *piau* (A.2.3) could have historical connections with English interrogative pronouns spread (which dates from the 12th cent. onwards: Mustanoja 1960: 191; cp. the high frequency of *hwas* in late OE, B.2.3 above, ftn. 18).

c. One of the most likely candidates for Celtic influence on English, excluding the pattern in (a), is the OE analytic pattern with resumptive pronoun, which occurred alongside synthetic and non-case-marking strategies and was not very frequent except in some areas and in some contexts; that is to say, it was rather restricted geographically, chronologically and syntactically. Later on in time, it was simply deemed to be non-standard (however, according to Mustanoja (1960: 202), the idiom *that* + personal pronoun is "not infrequent" in ME): again, a situation which is compatible with syntactic borrowing from a non-prestige (from the point of view of the borrower) language. Since, as noted in B.1.2, the resumptive pronoun is not the demonstrative/relative one, I venture to suggest a link between such choice and the restriction in (a) above.
d. Absence of synthetic pattern for genitive RCs in Scots and Irish English (Jespersen 1922–1931: III, 111: Scots *at* + possessive, Hiberno-English *that* + possessive) is a clearcut contact/substrate outcome;[23] recall that both Irish and Welsh had only the no-marker strategy or the resumptive one for genitive RCs since their earliest documents (see A.1.7 and A.2.3). Similarly to the evolution in point (c) above, the trend looks "natural" (a different strategy for the lowest position in the Accessibility Hierarchy), a fact which can often conceal syntactic borrowing.
e. In sub-standard ModW, on the other hand, oblique RCs occur with simple stranded prepositions (i.e. non inflected prepositions in final position), as in English, e.g. *y dyn (yr) oedd John yn sôn am* 'the man that John was talking about' (*am* simple non-inflected preposition; see T. A. Watkins 1993: 342). This seems a clear outcome of the reverse process.

At a coarse-grain level, various diachronic layers are to be envisaged for language contact between a language 1 (L1) and a language 2 (L2). When two linguistic communities meet in a given area, the languages do not maintain equal prestige, and the low prestige language L1 – which might be spoken by the majority of the population– borrows many lexical items from the high prestige L2. As (some) speakers of L1 gradually acquire the prestige language L2, the latter shows the traces of structural (mainly phonological and syntactic) borrowing from L1 (see (a) and (c) above; the most clear outcomes of such processes can be seen in so-called creolization, with typical relexification and substrate structure). When, as a consequence of long-term contact or "minorization" of L1, either the whole population becomes bilingual (e.g. in a diglossic situation) or at least most of the L1 speakers are bilingual, lexical borrowing is parallelled by structural borrowing in L1 from L2 (see (e) above; this can be assimilated to the so-called decreolization process). Language shift can in fact intervene both before

23. There may be other substratal phenomena, for which more empirical and historical data would be needed. One such phenomenon may be for example the lower frequency of *wh*-relative markers and of pied-piping in Hiberno-English as compared to British English, see Geisler (2002) on Ulster English.

and after L1 is structurally influenced by L2, or it may even never happen. It is clear that while the last kind of structural borrowing presupposes a long-lasting contact and is rooted in massive lexical borrowing, the structural borrowing in L2 from L1 is not (Thomason/Kaufman 1988: 20–21, *passim*): thus, Celtic loanwords in English are not as frequent as English loanwords in the Celtic languages, Dravidian loanwords in Indo-Aryan languages are not as numerous as Sanskrit borrowings in Dravidian languages, while on the contrary early structural transfer from Celtic in English and from Dravidian in Indo-Aryan languages represent the expected pattern. On the other hand, structural borrowing from the prestige languages English and Indo-Aryan in the Celtic and Dravidian languages respectively is more recent (Emeneau 1980, Chapter 5 [1954] and 3 [1962]; Krishnamurti 2003: 40–42; see Thomason/Kaufman 1988: 35 ff., 212). However, as I suggest above, the effects of early contacts between Celtic and English have been overshadowed by later events in the history of English.

List of abbreviations

Languages

E = English; I = Irish; W = Welsh
OE = Old English (7th–11th cent.); ME = Middle English (12th–16th cent.); ModE = Modern English
OI = Old Irish (7th–9th cent.); MI = Middle Irish (10th–12th cent.); EMI = Early Modern Irish (13th–17th cent.); ModI = Modern Irish
OW = Old Welsh (8th–12th cent.); MW = Middle Welsh (13th–16th cent.); ModW = Modern Welsh

Grammatical glosses

Glosses conform to the Leipzig Glossing Rules, accessible at www.eva.mpg.de/lingua/files/morpheme.html. Since glosses are meant to highlight morphosyntactic phenomena related to relativisation, some morphological distinctions (in particular nominal Case and Gender) were not specified occasionally, when they are irrelevant to such phenomena. Labels for specific mutations may be intentionally left as such (i.e. unglossed) in order to let the reader observe the formal side of what it is claimed that they express in the relativisation system. They are also left as such or altogether omitted when they are grammatically meaningless (that is, they resemble simple sandhi phenomena, as in exx. 39 and 57), while they may be appropriately glossed when expressing other categories (e.g. Gender in ex. 2). Contrarily to the usual practice for Indo-European languages, due to traditional labels, I have chosen the following order for nominal inflection (when cumulatively marked): Gender, Number, Case.

ABS = absolute inflection (non-compound verbs not preceded by COMP, NEG, etc.); ACC = accusative; ART = article; COMP = complementiser; COMPV = comparative;

COP = copula; DAT = dative; DEICT = deictic (particle); DET = determiner; DEM = demonstrative; DEP = dependent form (verb inflection in some subordinate or negative clauses); F = feminine; FUT = future; GEN = genitive; HAB = habitual; INDF = indefinite; IMPERS = impersonal (generic first-argument or first-argument skipping); IMP = imperative; IMPF = imperfect (habitual past); INF = infinitive; INS = instrumental; LEN = Lenition (specific mutation, in Welsh usually called Soft Mutation); M = masculine; N = neuter; N + gloss = non- (e.g. NGEN = non-genitive); NAS = Nasalisation (specific mutation); NEG = negation; NOM = nominative; OBJ = object; OBL = oblique; PART = particle (mainly introducing verbal nouns in complement clauses, cp. English *to* + infinitive); PASS = passive; PL = plural; PLUPRF = pluperfect (relative tense); POSS = possessive; POT = potential (OI *ro* prefixed to subjunctives, which has both potential and optative meaning); PRF = perfect; PRS = present; PST = past; PTCP = participle; PVB = preverb; REFL = reflexive; REL = relative; SBJ = subject; SBJV = subjunctive; SECFUT = secondary future (conditional); SG = singular; SM = Spirant Mutation (specific mutation); SUP = superlative; VN = verbal noun. Numbers refer to Persons.

Texts

The abbreviations used for texts and their edited sources refer to those in the Royal Irish Academy *Dictionary of the Irish Language* (Quin 1913–1976) for Irish, to those in *Geiriadur Prifysgol Cymru* and D. S. Evans 1964 for Welsh, and to those listed in Bourcier 1977 for English (if not quoted from a different secondary source, which is given). For easier reference, I list some of the sources below:

English

ALI = *Ancient Laws and Institutes of England*, ed. by B. Thorpe, London 1840.

ALS = *Ælfric's Lives of the Saints*, ed. by W. W. Skeat, Early English Text Society, Oxford 1881–1900.

ASC = *Anglo-Saxon Charters*, ed. by A. J. Robertson, Cambridge 1939.

BEH = *Bede's Ecclesiastical History*, ed. by Th. Miller, Early English Text Society, Oxford 1890–1898.

BHM = *The Blickling Homilies of the Tenth Century*, ed. by R. Morris, Early English Text Society, Oxford 1880.

Gospels = *The Holy Gospels in the Anglo-Saxon, Northumbrian, and Old Mercian versions*, ed. by W. W. Skeat, Cambridge 1871–87.

KAO = *King Alfred's Orosius*, ed. by H. Sweet, Early English Text Society, Oxford 1883 (Bately 1980 = *The Old English Orosius*, ed. by J. Bately, Early English Text Society, Oxford 1980).

KAG = *King Alfred's West-Saxon version of Gregory's Cura Pastoralis*, ed. by H. Sweet, Early English Text Society, Oxford 1871–72.

Krapp = *The Anglo-Saxon Poetic Records*, ed. by G. P. Krapp, vol. II, New York, Columbia University Press 1932.

LWS = *Leechdoms, Wortcunning and Starcraft of Early England*, ed. by O. Cockayne, London 1864–66.

OHW = *The Ormulum*, ed. by R. Holt and R. M. White, Oxford 1878.
SCA = *Ælfric's Homilies* (Sermones Catholici), ed. by B. Thorpe, London 1844–46.
SCP = *Two of the Saxon Chronicles Parallel*, ed. by J. Earle and C. Plummer, Oxford 1892–1899.

Irish
Ml = The Milan Glosses on the Psalms (9th cent.), ed. by W. Stokes and J. Strachan, *Thesaurus Palaeohibernicus*. Cambridge, Cambridge University Press 1901–03.
Murphy, *Lyrics* = G. Murphy, *Early Irish Lyrics*, Oxford University Press 1956.
Wb = The Würzburg Glosses on the Pauline Epistles (8th cent.), W. Stokes and J. Strachan, *Thesaurus Palaeohibernicus*. Cambridge, Cambridge University Press 1901–03.

Welsh
CA = *Canu Aneirin*, ed. by I. Williams, Cardiff 1938.
PKM = *Pedeir Keinc y Mabinogi*, ed. by I. Williams, Cardiff 1930.

References

Allen, C.L. 1980. *Topics in diachronic English syntax*. New York NY: Garland.
Ball, M.J. & Fife, J. (eds). 1993. *The Celtic languages*. London: Routledge.
Bourcier, G. 1977. *Les propositions relatives en vieil-anglais*. Paris: H. Champion.
Christian Brothers. 1962. *New Irish grammar*. Dublin: Fallons.
de la Cruz, J.M. 1972. A syntactical complex of isogloses in the north-western end of Europe (English, North Germanic and Celtic). *Indogermanische Forschungen* 77: 171–180.
Denison, D. 1993. *English historical syntax*. London: Longman.
Emeneau, M.B. 1980. *Language and linguistic area*. Selected essays introduced by A.S. Dil. Stanford CA: University Press.
Eska, J. & Evans, E.D. 1993. Continental Celtic. In *The Celtic languages*, M. J. Ball & J. Fife (eds), 26–63. London: Routledge.
Evans, D.S. 1964 [1989[5]]. *A grammar of Middle Welsh*. Dublin: Dublin Institute for Advanced Studies.
Filppula, M., Klemola, J. & Pitkänen, H. (eds). 2002. *The Celtic roots of English*. Joensuu: Faculty of Humanities.
Geiriadur Prifysgol Cymru, A dictionary of the Welsh language. 1999–2002. 4 Vols. Cardiff: University of Wales Press.
Geisler, C. 2002. Relativization in Ulster English. In *Relativisation on the North Sea littoral*, P. Poussa (ed.), 135–146. Munich: Lincom.
Gensler, O.D. 1993. A typological evaluation of Celtic/Hamito-Semitic syntactic parallels. PhD Dissertation, University of California at Berkeley.
Herrmann, T. 2005. Relative clauses in English dialects of the British Isles. In *A Comparative grammar of British English dialects. Agreement, gender, relative clauses*, B. Kortmann, T. Herrmann, L. Pietsch & Susanne Wagner (eds), 21–123. Berlin: Mouton.
Isaac, G.R. 1996. *The verb in the Book of Aneirin. Studies in syntax, morphology and etymology*. Tübingen: Niemeyer.
Jackson, K.H. 1953. *Language and history in early Britain*. Edinburgh: Edinburgh University Press.

Jespersen, O. 1922–1931. *A Modern English grammar*. Heidelberg: Carl Winter.
Krishnamurti, Bhadriraju. 2003. *The Dravidian languages*. Cambridge: CUP.
Kurzová, H. 1981. *Der Relativsatz in den indoeuropäischen Sprachen*. Hamburg: Helmut Buske.
Mitchell, B. 1985. *Old English syntax*. Oxford: Clarendon.
Mustanoja, T.F. 1960. *A Middle English syntax*. Helsinki: Société Néophilologique.
Ó Dónaill, N. 1977. *Foclóir Gaeilge-Béarla*. Dublin: An Gúm.
Platzack, C. 2002. Relativization in the Germanic languages, with particular emphasis on Scandinavian. In *Relativisation on the North Sea littoral*, P. Poussa (ed.), 77–96. Munich: Lincom.
Pokorny, J. 1959. Keltische Urgeschichte und Sprachwissenschaft. *Die Sprache* 5 : 152–164.
Poussa, P. 2002. North Sea relatives: Introduction. In *Relativisation on the North Sea littoral*, P. Poussa (ed.), 1–23. Munich: Lincom.
Preusler, W. 1956. Keltischer Einfluss im Englischen. *Revue des Langues Vivantes* 22: 322–350.
Quin, E.G. et al. (eds). 1913–76. *Dictionary of the Irish language based mainly on Old and Middle Irish materials*. 4 Vols. Dublin: Royal Irish Academy.
Romaine, S. 1984. Towards a typology of relative-clause formation strategies in Germanic. In *Historical syntax*, J. Fisiak (ed.), 437–470. Berlin: Mouton.
Rösler, I. 2002. Relative clauses in Low German (15th–16th Century). In *Relativisation on the North Sea littoral*, P. Poussa (ed.), 51–62. Munich: Lincom.
Schrijver, P. 1997. *Studies in the history of Celtic pronouns and particles*. Maynooth: Department of Old Irish.
Sornicola, R. 1989. Il relativo in irlandese antico. Una riconsiderazione II. *Indogermanische Forschungen* 94: 234–271.
Thomason, S.G. & Kaufman, T. 1988. *Language contact, creolization, and genetic linguistics*. Berkeley: University of California Press.
Thurneysen, R. 1946. *A grammar of Old Irish*. Dublin: Dublin Institute for Advanced Studies.
Vezzosi, L. 1998. *La sintassi della subordinazione in anglosassone*. Perugia: Edizioni Scientifiche Italiane.
Vezzosi, L. 2005. Areality and grammaticalization: How to solve a puzzling case in the English grammar. *Archivio Glottologico Italiano* 90: 174–209.
Visser, F.T. 1963–1973. *An historical syntax of the English language*. 4 Vols. Leiden: E. J. Brill.
Wagner, H. 1959. *Das Verbum in den Sprachen der Britischen Inseln*. Tübingen: Niemeyer.
Watkins, T.A. 1993. Welsh. In *The Celtic languages*, M.J. Ball & J. Fife (eds), 289–348. London: Routledge.
White, D.L. 2002. Explaining the innovations of Middle English. In *The Celtic roots of English*, Filppula et al. (eds), 153–174. Joensuu: Faculty of Humanities.
Williams, S.J. 1980. *A Welsh grammar*. Cardiff: University of Wales Press.

Canonical and non-canonical marking of core arguments in European languages

A typological approach*

Domenica Romagno

It is observed that the prepositional direct object phenomena are related to past participle agreement and auxiliary selection in compound tenses. The purpose of this paper is to show that verb properties and object referent properties co-occur in prepositional direct object selection. Data from Spanish, Sardinian, Sicilian, Calabrian, Maltese and Roumanian are examined. The triggering parameters are the same in all the languages that are considered: 1) object affectedness (and, consequently, verb telicity), 2) object agentivity, 3) object individuation. Each parameter represents a scale according to which verb phrases (or clauses) can be ranked and, then, objects are more or less likely to be prepositional (= non-canonically marked) or non-prepositional (canonically marked).

1. Past participle agreement and object marking

In Romagno (2005) we tried to account for the fact that past participle agreement (for example: It.[1] *la torta è stat<u>a</u> mangiat<u>a</u> da Marco* 'the cake was eaten by Mark',

---

* I would like to thank Giorgio Banti, Pierangiolo Berrettoni, Franco Fanciullo, Romano Lazzeroni, Giuseppe Longobardi, Paolo Ramat, Elisa Roma for their comments on an earlier version of this paper. On Spanish data we refer to Romagno (2005). All data from Sardinian, Sicilian, Maltese, Calabrian and Roumanian were elicited from native speakers by means of questionnaires. I wish to thank very much Milena Cocco, Mario Andrea Cau, Simone Pisano, Nino e Pino Basiricò, Sandro Caruana, Giuseppina Silvestri and Oana Uţa for answering my questions patiently and for sharing with me their native intuitions. Without them, this work would not have been possible. I would also like to thank Bruno Mazzoni, Aldo Cuneo and Ignazio Putzu who gave me some useful suggestions on Roumanian and Sardinian respectively.

1. The following abbreviations are used: It. = Italian, lit. = literally, fem. = feminine, Sp. = Spanish, PDO = prepositional direct object, PPT = past participle, VP = verb phrase, NP = noun phrase, Log = Logudorese, Camp = Campidanese, n. = note, Sard. = Sardinian, Sic. = Sicilian, sing. = singular, PL. = plural, ex. = example, Ger. = German, anc. Gr. = ancient Greek, mod. Gr. = modern Greek.

Maria è arrivata 'Mary has arrived', *Chicco ha chiusa la porta* 'Chicco closed (lit. has closed) the door', *le ho viste* 'I have seen them (fem.)') and prepositional direct object (for example: Sp. *Maria ha matado a Juan* 'Mary killed John') tend to be mutually exclusive in Romance languages. We started from the observation that prepositional direct object (henceforth PDO) also correlates with auxiliary selection in compound tenses: languages such as Spanish, Portuguese, Roumanian, etc., that have PDO, use a single auxiliary verb, i.e. HABERE or *sim.*[2](Portuguese, for instance, uses *ter* < TENERE); on the other hand languages such as Italian and French, that do not have PDO, use two auxiliary verbs (HABERE and ESSE) in paradigmatic opposition (see La Fauci 1988; Vincent 1982). We can suppose, then, that past participle (henceforth PPT) agreement and auxiliary ESSE encode the same underlying principle, that is opposite to the one governing PDO distribution.[3]

ESSE as an auxiliary verb and PPT agreement with subject occur, for instance in Italian, in unaccusative and passive constructions: *Maria è morta* 'Mary died', *Maria è arrivata a casa* 'Mary has arrived home (lit. at home)', *Maria è stata uccisa* 'Mary was killed'. The subject in these constructions corresponds to the affected entity undergoing a change of state (or location). The verb has a state predicate in its logical structure (Dowty 1979) and the state predicate argument is the syntactic subject. The formal representation of *morire* 'to die', for instance, is BECOME **state'** (x): *Maria è morta* = BECOME **morta'** (Maria); the PPT (*morta*) denotes the state of *Maria*. The PPT, then, agrees with undergoer arguments. In fact it does not agree with subjects of transitive and unergative verbs: *Maria ha rotto (*rotta) il vaso* 'Mary has broken the pot', *Maria ha camminato (*camminata) per due ore* 'Mary walked (lit. has walked) for two hours'. The subjects of those verbs are actors. As expected, HABERE is the auxiliary verb in transitive and unergative predications.

2. In Roumanian «all verbs take *a avea*, the reflex of *habere*, as their perfect auxiliary, regardless of their case structure and semantic classification.» (Vincent 1982: 87). ESSE as an auxiliary verb is used only in the passive voice: *o casă a fost zidită* 'a house has been built'. But – as it was widely noted – «sentences of this form are a modern innovation based on imitation of nineteenth-century French and Italian literary models, and the historically continuous and more typically Roumanian rendering is: *s'a zidit o casă*, with passive being expressed by the etimologically reflexive form *s'a zidit*.» (Vincent 1982: 87). In sentences like *Marco e plecat* 'Marco is away/absent' the verb functions as a copula and *plecat* as a nominal predicate (an adjective: Lombard 1974: 300). See the opposition: *Marco e plecat* vs. *Marco a plecat a casă* 'Marco has gone home'.

3. With regard to the relation between PDO and PPT agreement in European languages and to Spanish PDO we refer to Romagno (2005) for a more detailed discussion, a bigger data sample and further references. On PPT agreement at the morphology-syntax interface see Kayne (1985, 1989, 1995).

The undergoer argument in a transitive construction corresponds to the syntactic object. We can suppose, then, that PPT agrees with undergoer objects (and not only with undergoer subjects). This is what happens, for instance, in Italian, where PPT can agree with objects of transitive verbs[4]: *Mario ha chiusa/-o la porta* 'Mario closed (lit. has closed) the door', *Mario ha rotta/-o la bambola* 'Mario has broken the doll'.

Since object affectedness is strictly related to verb phrase (hencefort VP) telicity (see, among others, Verkuyl 1972; Bertinetto 1986; Tenny 1994; Slabakova 2001), we can suggest that PPT agrees only with objects in highly telic transitive constructions; PPT agreement with lowly affected – or unaffected – objects (i.e. in lowly telic – or atelic – transitive constructions) is actually «assai meno accettabile, se non addirittura impossibile» (Ramat 1984: 150): * *(? ?) Maria ha salite le scale* 'Mary has gone up the stairs'.

If it is true that object PPT agreement is residual in Italian and that prototypical categories erode starting from the periphery (the prototype is therefore the more resistant nucleus), we can state that the highly telic transitive verbs are the prototype – and probably the historical archetype (see Romagno 2005: 93) – of the category.

We conclude that PPT agrees with prototypical undergoer arguments whether in subject or in object syntactic position; PPT agreement is obligatory with passive and unaccusative subjects, because only in those cases it signals the contrast between subject syntactic role and undergoer thematic one: the prototypical subject is actor (Van Valin 1990; Van Valin & LaPolla 1997).

If it is true that unaccusative and passive subjects are objects in a deep level, we can conclude that PPT agreement always marks objects and that subject agreement reveals the underlying object.

2. Canonical vs. non-canonical object marking in Spanish: prototypical arguments and non-prototypical configurations

In Romagno (2005) we studied PDO starting from Spanish data, because «dans aucune autre langue romane occidentale, la construction n'apparaît dans une distribution aussi diversifiée» (Roegiest 1979: 38; see Romagno 2005: 96).

4. We consider here the so-called "full objects" that follow the verb. We do not consider the preceding clitics, with which PPT agrees normally in standard Italian at least. PPT agreement with full objects cannot depend on the need of denoting object gender and/or number (see Romagno 2005: 92). It is barely necessary to point out that this agreement is residual in Italian.

It is commonly said that the preposition marks animate direct objects. But cases like

(1) *la nodriza educa el niño*
'the nurse raises/educates the child'
vs.

(2) *la nodriza ha matado al niño*
'the nurse killed the child'

show that the object animacy does not suffice to predict the presence vs. absence of the preposition *a* (Romagno 2005: 96). The object is the same in (1) and in (2); what is different is the verb semantics: *matar* is a highly telic verb that affects its object to a high degree (the object of *matar* undergoes a total and definite change of state), while *educar* is a lowly telic verb, which can also leave its object unaffected (Bertinetto & Squartini 1995).

An adequate attention has never been paid yet to the fact that PDO is selected not only by referent animacy, but also by object affectedness. Since object affectedness is strictly related to VP telicity, we can say that the referent animacy and the VP telicity co-occur in PDO selection.

The prototypical object is an affected argument that undergoes an externally caused change of state (or location): its thematic role is, therefore, that of an undergoer. The object syntactic role and the undergoer thematic role contrast with an animate referent; this contrast depends on the fact that an animate entity is, typically, agentive: the prototypical agentive argument is actor and corresponds to the syntactic subject. Animacy is, therefore, an object agentivity epiphenomenon. Inanimate PDOs are, in fact, well-known not only in Spanish: an inanimate object can take the preposition if it is agentive to a certain degree. This is the case, for instance, of nouns denoting metals or plants: metals are reactive, plants take part in the biological cycle (Salcedo 1999: 1801; see below).

The traditional statement can, therefore, be corrected: the object agentivity and the VP telicity are the basic parameters governing PDO.

When the verb is highly telic and the object is highly agentive, the preposition marks the object almost without exception. This case probably represents the prototype of the morphosyntactic category; certainly, it was, historically, the archetype: «los primeros verbos con los que aparece *a* son aquellos cuyo sentido afecta al objeto directo» (Salcedo 1999: 1802).

On the periphery of the category the two parameters operate independently: a non-agentive object can take the preposition if the verb is highly telic:

(3) *Y se comen a los libros*
'and they eat the books up';

but if the verb is lower in telicity, an highly agentive object can take the preposition:

(4) *... lleva a algunos hombres a resolver con el robo sus dificultades sociales*
'(it) takes someone to solve his social difficulties with stealing'

vs.

(5) *llevar el caballo a beber*
'to take the horse for drinking',

without preposition, because animal nouns are lower than rational beings nouns on the animacy hierarchy (Silverstein 1976) that is also an agentivity hierarchy.[5]

It is, then, clear that the probability of agentive objects being marked by the preposition depends on a telicity gradient that Pottier (1968) exemplifies with an *"axe sémantique verbal"* from *matar* 'to kill', which has always PDOs, to *tener* 'to have', which never has PDOs.

The VP telicity actually can be measured not only by the verb meaning *per se*, but also by some noun phrase (henceforth NP) properties, namely individuation (Verkuyl 1972). The NP individuation can increase the VP telicity: *"Mary ate an/the apple"* is more telic than *"Mary ate apples"* (Slabakova 2001: 35–). Bare plurals (such as *apples*) and mass NPs like, for instance, *"chocolate"*, do not function as affected object but as verb meaning modifiers (Van Valin & LaPolla 1997). Object affectedness is, therefore, strictly related to object-NP individuation. It is now clear why an agentive object is as much more atypical as it is more individuated. Then a highly individuated object is more likely to be prepositional:

(6) *Achille ha matado a Hector*
'Achilles killed Hector'

vs.

(7) *Achille mata enemigos*
'Achilles kills enemies (= he is an enemies killer)'.

Object individuation is, therefore, a third parameter governing PDO. The highest elements on the individuation hierarchy (1st and 2nd person pronouns and proper names) are always marked by the preposition; 3rd person pronouns are more frequently marked by the preposition when they are specified by *mismo* 'self' (for example: 'himself', etc.), that is when they are more individuated.

5. We just want to point out that verbs like 'to take' are lower in telicity than verbs like 'to kill', 'to slaughter', etc.: only the latter imply a total and definite change of state of the object. This is the reason why object individuation and object agentivity being the same, the object of verbs like 'to kill' is more likely to be non-canonically marked than the object of verbs like 'to take': see (5) vs. (40), (56), etc. It is necessary to stress that agentivity and animacy are properties which entail each other in prototypical representations (the prototypical subject is animate and agentive, the prototypical object is inanimate and non-agentive), but they do not so in non-prototypical representations: the object remains undergoer even when it is animate, the subject remains actor even when it is inanimate. On the contrary, ontologically inanimate entities can be represented as animate (see the case of plants and metals) and therefore undergo the same morphosyntactic restrictions operating in the representations of animate entities in object syntactic role. Non-canonical object marking precisely indicates the contrast between the undergoer thematic role of the object and its agentivity.

Object individuation seems to be subordinate to object affectedness and, consequently, to lexical telicity: an highly individuated (and animate[6]) object does not take the preposition when the verb is atelic (or lowly telic):

(8) *La esposa de don Juan Carlos espera para el año próximo su tercer hijo*
'J.C.'s wife is expecting her third son for the next year'. (Pottier 1968: 90)

Since VP telicity is measured in some cases by subject agentivity (see Hopper & Thompson 1980), subject agentivity cooccurs in PDO selection: «en la mayor parte de los verbos cuyo complemento directo lleva *a*, el sujeto es o bien agente o bien causa» (Salcedo 1999: 1784):

(9) *este abogado escondió a muchos prisioneros*
'this lawyer hid many prisoners'
vs.
(10) *esta montaña escondió muchos prisioneros*
'this mountain hid many prisoners'.

Mountains are non-agentive. The VP in (10) is atelic: it functions as a state predicate denoting an accidental property of the mountain (= 'the mountain was the hiding place for many prisoners').

We conclude that PDO is governed by three parameters: 1) object agentivity, 2) object affectedness (and, consequently, verb telicity), 3) object individuation.[7] All of them are respectively present and absent in the opposite poles of a gradient: *Achille ha matado a Hector* 'Achilles killed Hector' vs. *Yo prefiero la virtud* 'I prefer the virtue'. In the former case the direct object is necessarily marked by the preposition; in the latter it is necessarily not. On the *continuum* between the two poles variations are definied by a higher or lower degree of the three above mentioned parameters.

2.1 To sum up

PPT agreement marks prototypical undergoer arguments, i.e. objects of highly telic transitive verbs and subjects of unaccusative and passive constructions. When PPT

6. Animacy hierarchy and individuation hierarchy overlap in highest and lowest positions (see Silverstein 1976; Timberlake 1977; Lazard 1984).

7. We should like to anticipate two objections. 1) An object of a telic verb can be lowly affected (or unaffected): this happens, for instance, with verbs such as 'to find', 'to lose', etc. that, in fact, frequently reject PDO in the languages we examined. But, if it is possible to have a telic verb with an unaffected object, it is impossible to have an affected object with an atelic verb: the object affectedness implies the VP telicity. 2) If it is true that the object individuation can increase the VP telicity with verbs that can be [± telic], like, for instance, 'to eat', 'to drink', etc., it is also true that a highly individuated object can be connected to an inherently atelic verb: in this case, the verb generally does not take non-canonical marking (see (8)).

agrees with unaccusative and passive subjects, subject agreement encodes an underlying object and signals the contrast between subject syntactic role and undergoer thematic role.

PDO encodes a non-prototypical configuration of a prototypical object: the preposition signals the contrast between an agentive referent and an undergoer argument in object syntactic position. Unlike PDO, PPT agreement does not depend on referent inherent properties: in fact, PPT agrees both with personal and inanimate nouns.

The two strategies are not ontologically incompatible (they, actually, coexist in transitional stages), but they are cognitively in contrast to each other: in both of them thematic role is pertinent, but referent properties are pertinent in one case and they are not in the other. This is the reason why they tend to be mutually exclusive.

3. Canonical vs. non-canonical object marking in other European and Mediterranean languages

In this paper we are going to verify our hypothesis by further investigations into other languages, in order to find out if the three parameters we have shown governing Spanish PDO also operate in other languages which have PDO. [8]

8. We just want to point out that PDO can depend also on different (i.e. pragmatic, historical, etc.) factors that only marginally affect core arguments encoding and, then, are not examined in this paper. Therefore, we do not consider here the following cases: 1) non-canonical marking of leftwards dislocated objects: that marking is governed by pragmatic features overlapping the parameters which are studied here only for the fact that in both cases the object is *"mis en relief"* (in one case because the object referent is atypical, in the other because the object position is atypical); but their distribution is not the same: Western Tuscan marks dislocation *(a me mi ha rovinato la guerra* 'the war damaged me'), but it does not have PDO in other cases (Berretta 1989). 2) Non-canonical object marking depending on the so-called *"intensité subjective"* (Pottier 1968: 91), topicalization, *et sim.* 3) Non-canonical object marking depending on Latin verb constructions (for further details refer to Romagno 2005: 109, n. 20). The geographical arrangements of the PDO phenomena can be accounted for considering the variations of the hierarchical order of the parameters that select PDO (see below). We do not consider here the possible diastratic and diaphasic variations that can be found in particular in Italian dialects because of the contact with the standard language. What interests here is to observe that the alternation between canonical and non-canonical object marking corresponds to a parameters selection. If this is the case, we can suppose that the disappearance of the preposition under the influence of the standard language went an orderly way, from the periphery to the center of a scalar category. Finally, we do not discuss the diachronic matter of the origin of PDO. On that topic see, among others, Sornicola 1997 and 2000; Reichenkron 1951; Melis 1995; Pensado 1995; Nocentini 1985.

3.1 Sardinian

Logudorese and Campidanese Sardinian are examined: the two Sardinian varieties do not show differences in PDO selection.

Inherently atelic verbs never take PDOs, independently from referent properties:

(11) Log *Considero Maria una pisedda educada*
Camp *Consideru Maria una piciocca educada*
'I consider Mary a polite girl': highly individuated and highly agentive object;

(12) Log *Considero custa azione spregevole*
Camp *Consideru custa azioni indigna*
'I consider this action despicable': highly individuated but lowly agentive object;

(13) Log *Considerat troppu sos amigos*
Camp *Considerada troppu is amigus*
'(he/she) considers his/her (lit. the) friends too much': lowly individuated but highly agentive object;

(14) Log *Considerat troppu sos perigulos*
Camp *Considerada troppu is perigulus*
'(he/she) considers the risks too much': lowly individuated and lowly agentive object.

See also:

(15) Log *Maria tenet tres fizos*
Camp *Maria tenidi tres fillus*
'Mary has three children'

(16) Log *Maria tenet unu fizu de nomene Marco*
Camp *Maria tenidi unu fillu chi di nanta Marco*
'Mary has a child whose name is Mark'

(17) Log *Maria tenet unu bellu cane*
Camp *Maria tenidi unu bellu cani*
'Mary has a beautiful dog'

(18) Log *Maria tenet una domo meda accogliente*
Camp *Maria tenidi una domu meda bella*
'Mary has a very comfortable house'

(19) Log *Maria disizzat una domo pius manna*
Camp *Maria disigiada una domu prus manna*
'Mary would like a bigger house'

(20) Log *Maria disizzat su discu nou de A. S.*
Camp *Maria disigiada su discu nou de A. S.*
'Mary wants the new disc by A. S.'

(21) Log *Maria disizzat unu maridu piagherosu*
Camp *Maria disigiada unu pobiddu bonu*
'Mary would like a kind husband'

(22) Log *ti deghet calchiunu menzus*
Camp *ti descidi cuncunu mellus*
'you merit someone better'

Verbs such as 'to consider', 'to have', 'to want', 'to like', 'to desire', 'to merit', etc. are inherently atelic: they do not affect their objects and, therefore, they never take PDOs.

The same happens in Spanish (Romagno, 2005: 102, see above).

On the other hand, with a highly telic verb a lowly individuated and lowly agentive object can take the preposition:

(23) Log *...E si papan a sos libros*
Camp *...E si papan a is librus*
'...And they eat the books up'.

In (23) the object NP has a plural and inanimate referent.

Like in Spanish, both specified and bare plural objects are usually non-prepositional; but the probability of plural objects being marked by the preposition increases when they are affected:

(24) Log *s'Accademia hat designadu battoro membros*
Camp *s'Accademia hadi designau quattru membrus*
'The Academy designated four members'

(25) Log *hat mandadu infermieris*
Camp *hadi mandau infermieris*
'(he/she) sent nurses'

vs.

(26) Log *sos nazistas bochian a sos pitzinnos*
Camp *is nazistas bocianta a is pippius*
'the Nazis killed the children'

(27) Log *S'invidia leat a medas omines*
Camp *S'invidia pigada a medas omines*
'The envy takes[9] many people'.

Verb properties (i.e. telicity) and object referent properties (i.e. individuation and agentivity) co-occur in PDO selection; but the verb telicity, that is measured by the

9. In Spanish *coger* takes PDO more frequently than *tomar* (Roegiest 1998). Both means 'to take', but *coger* implies a higher object affectedness. When the subject of 'to take' is the illness, the envy, *et sim.*, *coger* is used, because a change of state is caused to the object (see Romagno 2005: 104, n. 13).

object affectedness, seems to be the basic feature in Sardinian. Let us consider the following examples:

(28) Log *Sa balia creschet su pitzinnu*
Camp *Sa balia crescidi su pipiu*
'the nurse looks after/raises the child'

(29) Log *Sa balia educat/imparat a su pitzinnu*
Camp *Sa balia educada a su pipiu*
'the nurse educates the child'

(30) Log *Sa balia hat bochidu a su pitzinnu*
Camp *Sa balia hadi bociu a su pipiu*
'the nurse killed the child'.

The object has the same referent in the three sentences above, but only in (29) e (30) it is marked by the preposition. (28) differs from (29) and (30) in object affectedness: 'to kill' is an inherently telic verb, that totally affects its object, in that a definite change of state is caused to it; 'to educate' affects its object, but in a lower degree than 'to kill'; 'to look after/to raise' denote a state of affairs or an event without a specified endpoint, then the object can be totally unaffected (Bertinetto & Squartini 1995). The following examples show to what extent the object referent properties affect the PDO choice depending on the verb type:

(31) Log *Achille hat bochidu a Ettore*
Camp *Achille hadi bocciu a Ettore*
'Achilles killed Hector'

(32) Log *Achille hat bochidu a sos inimigos*
Camp *Achille hadi bocciu a is nemigus*
'Achilles killed the enemies'

(33) Log *Achille bochit a inimigos*
Camp *Achille bocidi a nemigus*
'Achilles kills enemies (= he is an enemies killer)'.

With 'to kill', the object is prepositional also when it is a bare plural (that is very lowly individuated) and the VP denotes an attitudinal/habitual action of the subject, therefore describing a subject feature (Van Valin & LaPolla, 1997: see (33)).

(34) Log *Sa balia creschet a Maria*
Camp *Sa balia crescidi a Maria*
'the nurse looks after/raises Mary'

(35) Log *sa balia creschet sos pitzinnos*
Camp *sa balia crescidi is pippius*
'the nurse looks after/raises the children'

(36) Log *sa balia creschet pitzinnos*
Camp *sa balia crescidi pippius*
'the nurse looks after/raises children (= the nurse's occupation is to raise/to look after children)'.

The verb that means 'to look after/to raise' takes PDO only when the object NP is a proper name (that is very highly individuated: see (34)).

(37) Log *Sa balia educat a Maria*
Camp *Sa balia educada a Maria*
'the nurse educates Mary'

(38) Log *sa balia educat a sos pitzinnos*
Camp *sa balia educada a is pippius*
'the nurse educates the children'

(39) Log *sa balia educat pitzinnos*
Camp *sa balia educada pippius*
'the nurse educates children (= the nurse is a children educator)'.

Unlike 'to kill', 'to educate' (less telic than 'to kill'), does not have PDO when the object is a bare plural and the VP indicates a subject property (see (39)).

Verbs like 'to kill', 'to slaughter', 'to butcher', etc. select PDOs also when the objects are not at the top of the agentivity hierarchy, for example with animal nouns:

(40) Log *Marco hat bochidu a su porcu*
Camp *Marco hadi bociu a su procu*
'Mark slaughtered the pig'.

But when the VP does not denote a concrete telic event (that is when it indicates an attitudinal/habitual action of the subject, therefore describing a subject feature), the lowly individuated object is non-prepositional if it is also lowly agentive:

(41) Log *Marco bochit porcos*
Camp *Marco bocidi procus*
'Mark slaughters pigs (= he is a pigs slaughterer)'.

On the other hand, a highly individuated and highly agentive object does not take the preposition when the verb is inherently atelic:

(42) Log *s'isposa de don Juan Carlos ispettat pro s'annu chi benit su terzu fizu sou*
Camp *sa sposa de don Juan Carlos apettada po s'annu chi benidi su terzu fillu suu*
'J.C.'s wife is expecting her third son for the next year' (see also (11), (16)).

Personal pronouns (the highest individuated/agentive arguments) are regularly non-canonically marked, also with atelic verbs:

(43) Camp *Maria disigiada a tui/a mimi/a issu*
'Mary wants you/me/him'.

With verbs like 'to want' the 3rd person pronoun *issu* does not take the preposition when it precedes the verb:[10]

(44) Camp *issu du disigiada*
'(she) wants him'.

Instead, with inherently telic verbs like 'to kill', *issu* is marked by the preposition also when it precedes the verb:

(45) Camp *a issu d'hadi bociu*
'(she/he) killed him'.

A final remark. Like in Spanish, «los nombres que designan objetos dotados de autonomía en su funcionamiento tales como los nombres que designan metales, y los nombres de máquinas se comportan como animados» (Salcedo 1999: 1801):

(46) Log *S'acidu guastat a sos metallos*
Camp *S'acidu guastada a is metallus*
'the acid affects the metals'

(47) Log *un'autobus at rugadu a s'automobile de Luca*
Camp *una corriera hadi investiu a sa macchina de Luca*
'a bus knocked Luca's car down'.

Inanimate object that are agentive to a certain degree can be non-canonically marked (note that the verb is highly telic in (46) and (47)). Sardinian data, then, confirm the statement that the referent animacy is an epiphenomenon of the object agentivity: an undergoer object is prototypically non-agentive. When it is agentive, it takes non-canonical marking (= *a*).

3.2 Sicilian

Sicilian data are from Erice, Valderice and the neighbourhood.

Like in Spanish and Sardinian, inherently atelic verbs ('to have', 'to want', etc.) normally reject PDOs, independently from referent properties:

(48) *Maria avi un figghiu chi si chiama Marcu*
'Mary has a child whose name is Mark'

(49) *Maria avi ṭṛi figghi*
'Mary has three children'

(50) *Maria avi un beḍḍu cani*
'Mary has a nice dog'

10. 1st and 2nd person pronouns also have clitic forms, that precede the verb and are, obviously, non prepositional: Camp *mi disigiada, ti disigiada* '(she/he) wants me/you'.

(51) *Maria avi 'na casa commira assai*
'Mary has a very comfortable house'.[11]

On the other hand, unlike Spanish and Sardinian, objects that have inanimate referents are usually non-prepositional, also with highly telic verbs:

(52) *i libbra si li mancianu*
'they eat the books up' (see (3), (23))

(53) *fari la turri chiù auta di lu munnu*
'to build the highest tower in the world'.

Then, the object affectedness (as effect of the verb telicity: see (48)–(51)) and the object agentivity (see (52), (53)) are required for PDO selection.

We are going to show now how the object individuation co-occurs with the verb telicity. See the following examples:

(54) *Achille ammazzau a Ettore/a li nimici*
'Achilles killed Hector/the enemies'

(55) *Achille ammazza nimici*
'Achilles kills enemies (= he is an enemies killer)'

(56) *Marcu ammazzau a lu porcu*
'Mark slaughtered the pig'

(57) *Marcu ammazza porci*
'Mark slaughters pigs (= he is a pigs slaughterer)'.

'to kill', 'to slaughter', etc. are inherently telic verbs that affect their objects in that a total and definite change of state is caused to them. The object individuation can change the VP telicity. When the object NP is a bare plural (= lowly individuated: see (55) and (57)), the VP does not denote a concrete telic event, but it indicates an attitudinal/habitual action of the subject, describing so a subject feature: the object is, therefore, non-prepositional. Note that, unlike Sardinian, but like Spanish, this happens with personal and animal nouns.

11. In some cases, also with atelic verbs, when the object NP is a proper name, it tends to be shifted leftwards at the beginning of the sentence and then replaced with a clitic pronoun. In those cases the object is non-canonically marked: *A Maria la cunsideru 'na picciotta arucata* 'I consider Mary a polite girl'. A topicalized object, an object at the beginning of a sentence or, more generally, an object preceding the verb is frequently prepositional (on pragmatic factors determining non-canonical marking see note 8). A highly agentive and highly individuated object, such as a proper name, tend to be non-canonically marked; when it is lowly affected (or unaffected), it is usually placed in such atypical syntactic position that it requires non-canonical marking.

Bare plurals are generally non-prepositional: *mannau 'nfirmera* '(he/she) sent nurses', *curau malati* '(he/she) treated patients', etc. Personal pronouns, on the opposite pole of the individuation hierarchy, are always prepositional:

(58) *taliavanu tutti a mia*
'all of them were looking at me'

(59) *a mia 'ncasa m'aspittavanu*
'they were waiting for me at home'
(from G. Basiricò, *Lezione di siciliano. Atto unico in dialetto e lingua*).

The probability of a more or less individuated object being non-canonically marked depends on the verb telicity (measured by the object affectedness):

(60) *A nurizza ammazzau o*[12] *picciriḍḍu*
'the nurse killed the child'

vs.

(61) *A nurizza 'nzigna/nunṭṛica o/u picciriḍḍu*
'the nurse educates/looks after/raises the child';

(62) *I nazisti ammazzanu e*[13] *picciriḍḍi*
'the Nazis kill the children'

vs.

(63) *A nurrizza 'nzigna/nunṭṛica e/i picciriḍḍi*
'the nurse educates/looks after/raises the children'.

The same object can be only prepositional when the verb is inherently telic (see (60), (62)), both prepositional and non-prepositional with less telic verbs (see (61), (63)). With verbs like 'to educate', 'to look after', etc. the object NP is always non-canonically marked only if it is a personal pronoun or a proper name (that is at the top of the individuation/agentivity scale): *a nurrizza 'nzigna/nunṭṛica a Maria* 'the nurse educates/looks after/raises Mary'.

On the other hand, an inherently atelic verb does not take PDO, also if the object is highly individuated (and highly agentive):

(64) *A mugghiera di don Batassanu pi l'annu chi veni aspetta u terzu figghiu*
'B.'s wife is expecting her third son for the next year' (see (8), (42)).

Obviously, also when the low telicity (or the atelicity) is a compositional property of sentences and VPs, and not a property of the verb meaning *per se* (Verkuyl 1972: see above), the object is non-prepositional:

(65) *A nurrizza 'nzigna/nunṭṛica picciriḍḍi*
'the nurse educates/looks after/raises children (= the nurse is a children educator, etc.)': see (36), (39).

12. *O* = preposition *a* + singular masculine definite article *u*.

13 *E* = preposition *a* + plural masculine definite article *i*.

A more affected but less individuated object is more likely to be prepositional than a less affected but more individuated object:

(66) *a 'miria pigghia a tanti omini*
'the envy takes many people' (see (27); n. 8)
vs.

(67) *annu a pigghiari un prufissuri di disignu*
'they have to take an art teacher'.

The generic plural (= very lowly individuated) object in (66) is regularly marked by the preposition because it undergoes a change of state (men become envious). The object in (67) (*un prufissuri di disignu* 'an art teacher') is more individuated than the object in (66), but it is non-prepositional because it is less affected (it does not change its state).

When in a lowly telic sentence like (67) the object is specified by a surname (that is, it is monoreferential), it can be both prepositional and non-prepositional:

(68) *annu a pigghiari o/u prufissuri Rossi*
'they have to take teacher Rossi'.

Unlike Spanish (see above, (9), (10)), the subject agentivity is not pertinent to PDO selection. The choice between canonical and non-canonical object marking with a telic verb like 'to hide', which has PDO also with a lowly individuated object, is not connected with subject properties:

(69) *st'avvucatu/sta muntagna ammucciàu a na' copu di priggiuneri*
'this lawyer/this mountain hid many prisoners'.

Like in Spanish (see Romagno 2005: 104), verbs such as 'to send', 'to see', etc., on the periphery of the telicity gradient, have both prepositional and non-prepositional objects, independently from the referent properties.

3.3 Maltese

The non-canonical object marker in Maltese is the preceding particle *lil*. This particle is traditionally often associated with the preposition *lil* 'to'. The particle *lil* is subject to morphophonemic variation triggered by the surrounding context.[14]

Non-canonical object marking in Maltese is very common, but the choice between prepositional and non-prepositional object seems to be free in most cases. However, we can pick out the prototypes of PDO and non-PDO respectively:

(70) *Akille qatel lil Ettore*
'Achilles killed Hector'

---

14. *lil* becomes *lill-* if the object takes the definite article. The definite article *l-* is assimilated to the consonants known as *Xemxin* ("Sun-Letters"), which are *ċ, d, n, r, s, t, x, ż, z*. The shortened form is *'il* before a consonant or *'l* before a word beginning with a vowel (Aquilina 1987).

vs.

(71) *Nippreferi il-virtù*
'I prefer the virtue'.

In (70) the object is highly affected (the verb is inherently telic), highly individuated and highly agentive: then, it is always prepositional. In (71) the object is unaffected (because the verb is inherently atelic), non-individuated and non-agentive (it is an abstract noun): then, it is always non-prepositional (see Sp. *yo prefiero la virtud*; Sard. Camp *deu preferru sa virtudi*, Log *deo preferro sa virtude*; Sic. *preferisciu la virtù*).

Proper names of persons, that are very highly individuated and very highly agentive, can be both prepositional and non-prepositional when the verb is inherently atelic (non-canonical marking is, however, the most common):

(72) *Maria tixtieq lil Mario/Mario*
'Mary wants Mario'.

Less individuated objects both with animate and inanimate referents are, normally, non-prepositional when the VP is atelic:

(73) *kien qed iżomm t-tifel/tifel minn idu*
'(he/she) was holding the/a child by the hand'

(74) *Maria tixtieq raġel iktar ġentili*
'Mary would like a kinder husband'

(75) *Maria tixtieq dar ikbar*
'Mary would like a bigger house'.

The probability of lowly individuated objects (for instance, plural nouns) being non-canonically marked is directly proportional to the objects affectedness (and, consequently, to the VPs telicity):

(76) *l-Akkademja ħatret erba' membri*
'the Academy designated four members'

(77) *bagħat in-nurses (? lin-nurses)*
'(he/she) sent nurses'

vs.

(78) *lest li joqtol lin-nies/in-nies bla ħniena*
'disposed to annihilate human people without mercy'

(79) *fejjaq lil morda (? fejjaq morda)*
'(he/she) cured patients'

(80) *in-Nażisti kienu joqtlu lit-tfal/t-tfal*
'the Nazis killed the children'.

On the other hand, a highly individuated (and highly agentive) object is non-prepositional if the verb is inherently atelic:

(81) *il-mara ta' don J.C. qed tistenna it-tielet tarbija tagħha għas-sena d-dieħla*
' J.C.'s wife is expecting her third son for the next year' (see (8), (42), (64)).

Like in the other languages examined above, verb properties (i.e. telicity) and object referent properties (i.e. individuation and agentivity) co-occur in PDO selection.

The probability of the same object being prepositional is related to its affectedness:

(82) *l-omm qatlet lit-tifel/it-tifel*
'the mother killed the child'

(83) *l-omm teduka lit-tifel/it-tifel*
'the mother educates the child'

(84) *l-omm trabbi it tifel (? lit-tifel)*
'the mother looks after/raises the child'.

(84) differs from (82) and (83) in object affectedness. As we noted above (see (28)–(30)), 'to kill' is an inherently telic verb, that totally affects its object; 'to educate' affects its object, but in a lower degree than 'to kill'; 'to look after/to raise' denote an event without a specified endpoint, in that the object can be totally unaffected (Bertinetto & Squartini 1995). The following examples show to what extent the object referent properties affect the PDO choice depending on the verb type:

(85) (= 70) *Akille qatel lil Ettore*
'Achilles killed Hector'

(86) *Akille qatel lill-għedewwa/l-għedewwa*
'Achilles killed the enemies'

(87) *Akille joqtol lil-għedewwa/għedewwa*
'Achilles kills enemies (= he is an enemies killer)'.

With verbs like 'to kill', the object can be prepositional also when it is a bare plural (that is very lowly individuated) and the VP denotes an attitudinal/habitual action of the subject (see (87)). Obviously, when the object is a proper name (= highly individuated and highly agentive: see (85)), it is regularly prepositional.

(88) *l-omm trabbi lil Maria*
'the mother looks after/raises Mary'

(89) *l-omm trabbi t-tfal (? lit-tfal)*
'the mother looks after/raises the children'

(90) *l-omm trabbi tfal*
'the mother looks after/raises children (= the mother's occupation is to look after/to raise children)'.

With verbs like 'to look after, to raise' the object is normally prepositional only when it is a proper name.

(91) *l-omm teduka lil Maria*
'the mother educates Mary'

(92) *l-omm teduka lit-tfal/t-tfal*
'the mother educates the children'

(93) *l-omm teduka tfal*
'the mother educates children (= she is a children educator)'.

Unlike 'to kill', 'to educate' (less telic than 'to kill'), does not take PDO when the object is a bare plural and the VP indicates a subject property (see (93)).

When the object does not have a personal referent, for instance when it denotes an animal, it is usually non-prepositional, also if the verb is highly telic:

(94) *Mario qatel il-ħanżir (??lil-ħanżir)*
'Mario slaughtered the pig'.

If the object NP is a bare plural, it is, obviously, always non-prepositional:

(95) *Mario qatel il-ħnieżer*
'Mario slaughters pigs (= he is a pig slaughterer)' (see (41), (57)).

A more affected but less individuated object is more likely to be prepositional than a less affected but more individuated object:

(96) *l-għira taħkem lil ħafna irġiel/ħafna irġiel*
'the envy takes many people'

vs.

(97) *imisshom jsibu professur ta' l-arti*
'they have to take an art teacher'

The generic plural (= very lowly individuated) object in (96) can be non-canonically marked because it undergoes a change of state (it becomes envious). The object in (97) ('an art teacher') is more individuated than the object in (96), but it is canonically marked because it is less affected (it does not change its state).

When in a lowly telic sentence like (97) the object is specified by a surname (that is it is monoreferential), it can be both prepositional and non-prepositional:

(98) *imisshom jieħdu l-professur Rossi/lill-professur Rossi*
'they have to take teacher Rossi' (see (66), (67), (68)).

Like in other languages we examined, verbs such as 'to send', 'to see', etc. on the periphery of the telicity gradient have both prepositional and non-prepositional objects, independently from the referent properties.

Like in Spanish (see (9), (10)), in some cases, the subject agentivity co-occurs with the other features in PDO selection:

(99) *dan l-avukat ħeba ħafna priġunieri/lil ħafna priġunieri*
'this lawyer hid many prisoners'

vs.

(100) *din il-muntanja ħbiet ħafna priġunieri/??lil ħafna priġunieri*
'this mountain hid many prisoners'.

Mountains are non-agentive. The VP in (100) is atelic: it functions as a state predicate denoting an accidental property of the mountain (= 'the mountain was the hiding place for many prisoners').

Nouns denoting metals or plants, which are inanimate, but agentive to a certain degree (metals are reactive, plants take part in the biological cycle) can be PDO:

(101) *l-aċdu jgħarraq lill-/il-metall*
'the acid affects the metals'

(102) *mod biex tiskopri l-mard li jattakka lill-/il-planti*
'a way to find out the diseases affecting the plants'.

Note that the verb is highly telic in (101) and (102).

Then, Maltese data – like Spanish and Sardinian data – confirm the statement that the referent animacy is an object agentivity epiphenomenon (Romagno 2005: 99).

Finally, personal pronouns in object position are always prepositional:

(103) *Luigi jhobb lilha/lili/lilek*
'Luigi loves she/me/you'.

The particle *lil* is grammaticalized in the object personal pronouns: they are formed by the preceding particle *lil* + an enclitic pronominal suffix added to *lil*.

3.4 Calabrian

Calabrian data are from Verbicaro (Cosenza).

Non-canonical marking pertains highly agentive objects only.

Objects having inanimate referents are non-prepositional, independently from the verb semantics:

(104) *Maria a ruttə sa 'ncidda*
'Mary has broken this pot'

(105) *ruinə i fjirrə*
'(it) damages the metals'

(106) *Maria tena nna casa proprij bella*
'Mary has a very nice house'.

But also animal nouns are normally non-prepositional, with more or less telic verbs:

(107) *Mario ad ammazzatə u maialə*
'Mario slaughtered the pig'

(108) *Mario a lassatə u kuanə*
'Mario left the dog'.

Essentially, the opposition between PDO and non-PDO cuts the animacy hierarchy between human nouns and non human nouns.

Then, personal pronouns and proper name, that are at the top of the agentivity/individuation scale (see Lazard 1984), are always prepositional:

(109) *Luigi vodə/ad ammazzatə a Maria/a ghjidda/a mmia/a ttia*
'Luigi wants/killed Mary/she/me/you'.

Like in the other languages examined above, inherently atelic verbs normally reject PDOs both with individuated and non-individuated objects:

(110) *Maria tena nu fuigghjə kə sə kiama Marcə*
'Mary has a child whose name is Mark'

(111) *Maria tena abbojə figghji*
'Mary has many children'.

The probability of a very lowly individuated object being non-canonically marked depends on the verb type. With a lowly telic verb, it is non-prepositional:

(112) *a mannatə mbərmjirə*
'(he/she) sent nurses'.

With a highly telic verb, it is prepositional:

(113) *a sanatə a tantə malatə*
'(he/she) healed many patients'.

On the other hand, a highly individuated (and highly agentive) object is non-prepositional when the verb is atelic:

(114) *a mugghjera i don Giuwannə aspettədə u tuerzə fuigghjə*
'G.'s wife is expecting her third son' (see (8), (42), (64), (81)).

To be noted the difference between (a) *aspettədə u tuerzu fuigghiə* ' [she] is expecting her third son' and (b) *aspettədə allu tuerzu fuigghiə* '[she] is waiting for her third son'. The predicate is atelic and the object is animate in both sentences. The absence of the preposition in (a) can be related to the fact that in many languages the foetus (and also the child) are considered lowly agentive.[15]

15. Cf. the gender of Ger. *das Kind*, anc. Gr. τὸ τέκνον, mod. Gr. το παιδί, etc.

Let us consider now the following examples:

(115) *Akillə ad ammazzatə a Təruccia/allu kuatrarjiddə/allə*[16] *nəmicə*
'Achilles killed T./the child/the enemies'
vs.

(116) *Akille ammazza nnəmicə*
'Achilles kills enemies (= he is an enemies killer)';

(117) *a tata kresciadə a Maria/allu kuatrarjiddə/allə kuatrarjiddə*
'the nurse raises/educates Mary/the child/the children'
vs.

(118) *a tata kresciadə kkuatrarjiddə*
'the nurse educates/raises children (= she is a children educator, etc.)'.

When the VP does not indicate a concrete telic event, but an attitudinal/habitual activity of the subject (that is when it corresponds to an atelic predicate), the object is non-prepositional (see (116), (118)).

Finally, like in Spanish (see (9), (10)) and in Maltese (see (99), (100)), a sentence like:

(119) *savvukuatə ad ammucciatə ad abbojə karcəratə*
'this lawyer hid many prisoners'

has PDO; on the opposite side,

(120) *sa muntagna ad ammucciatə abbojə karcəratə*
'this mountain hid many prisoners (= this mountain was the hiding place for many prisoners)'

does not.

3.5 Roumanian

The non-canonical object marker in Roumanian is the preposition *pe* (Spitzer 1928; Puşcariu 1937; Niculescu 1959; Manoliu-Manea 1989).

Personal pronouns[17] and proper names, the highest elements both on the individuation and on the agentivity scale, are always prepositional, independently from verb type:

(120) *Ahile l*[18]*-a omorât pe Hector*
'Achilles killed Hector'

---

16. Non-canonical marker *a* becomes *allu/allə* (sing./PL.) when the object takes the definite article, *ad* when the object-NP begins with a vowel.

17. Relative and interrogative pronouns *care, cine* and demonstrative pronouns tend to be non-canonically marked, independently both from object referent properties and verb properties. Demonstrative pronouns are highly individuated (because their referents are known both to hearer and speaker) and, then, more likely to be prepositional. Non-canonical marking for relative and interrogative pronouns depends, presumably, on pragmatic factors (see above notes 8 and 11).

18. A clitic pronoun – the so-called *"pronom personnel conjoint"* (Lombard 1974) – anticipates or replaces frequently the object when the object is non-canonically marked.

(121) *doica o educă/o crește pe Maria*
'the nurse educates/raises Mary'

(122) *o consider pe Maria o fat ă binecrescut ă*
'I consider Mary a polite girl'.

Obviously, when a common noun is specified with, for instance, a surname (that is when it has a single referent), it is non-canonically marked:

(123) *trebuie s ă-l ia pe profesorul Rossi*
'they have to take teacher Rossi'.

A less individuated object can be both prepositional and non-prepositional:

(124) a. *doica a omorât/educă/crește copilul/copiii*, but also
b. *doica îl/ îi a omorât/educă/crește pe copil/pe copii*
'The nurse killed/educates/raises the child/the children'.[19]

Very lowly individuated objects, such as bare plurals, are usually non-prepositional:

(125) *a trimis infirmieri*
'(he/she) sent nurses'

(126) *se dedică r ăpirii fetelor tinere*
'he gives himself up to abduct young girls'.

On the other hand, a highly individuated and highly agentive object is non-prepositional when the verb is atelic:

(127) *soția lui don Juan Carlos așteaptă al treilea fiu anul viitor*[20]
'J.C.'s wife is expecting her third son for the next year' (see (8), (42), (64), (81), (114)).

Inherently atelic verbs normally reject PDO (unless the object is a proper name or personal pronoun: see above):

(128) *Maria are un fiu care se numește Marco/trei copii/un câine frumos/o casă mai mare*
'Mary has a child whose name is Mark/three children/a nice dog/a very comfortable house'.

---

19. An anonymous reviewer notes that (124)a. and (124)b. are in complementary distribution: (124)a. [+ standard], (124)b. [+ popular].

20. In a lower variety the construction with anticipated clitic pronoun is also acceptable: *soția lui don Juan Carlos îl așteaptă pe al treilea fiu anul viitor.* The so-called *"pronom personnel conjoint"* selects the non-canonically marked object (see n. 18).

Also when the atelicity depends not only on the verb meaning *per se*, but it is compositional (Verkuyl 1976; Slabakova 2001: see above), objects are canonically marked:

(129) *Ahile omoară duşmani*
'Achilles kills enemies (= he is an enemies killer)'

(130) *doica educă/creşte copii*
'the nurse educates/raises children (= the nurse's occupation is to raise/to educate children)'.

On the other hand, a highly telic verb can take non-canonical marking also when the object referent is lowly individuated or inanimate:

(131) *jandarmii l-au prins în flagrant delict pe unul*
'the guard caught somebody red-handed'

(132) *únde e prăjitùra? – Am mîncát-o pe toată* (Lombard 1974: 226)
'where is the gâteau? – I ate it up';

(133) a. *ai citít aceste cărți? – Le-am citit pe toate* (Lombard 1974: 225)
'did you read these books? – I finished reading all of them'
vs.
b. *am citit numai unele* (Lombard 1974: 211)
'I read only some of them', without *pe*.

4. Conclusions: phenomenical diversity and underlying principles. Beyond the traditional theory

In Romagno (2005) it was shown that – contrary to what is commonly said – Spanish PDO is governed not only by object referent properties, but also by verb properties.

The three parameters we showed governing the choice between canonical object marking (namely non-PDO) and non-canonical object marking (namely PDO) in Spanish are the same that determine object marking in Sardinian, Sicilian, Maltese, Calabrian and Roumanian.

The parameters are: 1) object affectedness (and, consequently, verb telicity); 2) object agentivity; 3) object individuation.

Obviously, canonical and non-canonical object marking do not require that all the three parameters are always necessarily absent or present respectively. Each parameter suggests a scale according to which VPs (or clauses) can be ranked and, then, objects are more or less likely to be canonically or non-canonically marked.

The only considerable difference among languages we examined regards the agentivity scale.

In Spanish, Sardinian and Roumanian, a lowly agentive object can be non-canonically marked, if the VP is highly telic (Romagno 2005: 100–; see above (3), (23), (131), (132), (133) a). Moreover, in Roumanian, lowly agentive but highly individuated objects, such as, for instance, demonstrative pronouns denoting inanimates, can be prepositional also when they are lowly affected (see n. 17).

In Sicilian, Maltese and Calabrian, object affectedness and object individuation being treated alike, only highly agentive objects require non-canonical marking. But, in Sicilian, non-canonical object marking cuts the animacy hierarchy (that functions here as an agentivity hierarchy: see above) between animate and inanimate nouns: animal nouns, in fact, can be PDOs (see (56)). On the other hand, in Maltese and Calabrian, the "cut-off point" is between human and non human nouns: animal nouns are, in fact, canonically marked (see (94), (107), (108)).

Moreover – unlike Sicilian and Calabrian, but like Spanish and Sardinian – in Maltese, nouns denoting metals, plants, *et sim.*, that is inanimate referents that are agentive to a certain degree (metals are reactive, plants take part in the biological cycle, etc.), can be non-canonically marked (see (46), (47), (101), (102)).[21]

4.1 Towards a typology of the Mediterranean area?

The alternation between non-canonical and canonical object marking as "accusative vs. Ø" (what we called PDO vs. non-PDO) seems to be largely widespread: a great number of genetically, areally and typologically disparate languages offer evidences for both object marking strategies (see Moravcsik 1978; Nocentini 1992; Bossong 1998).

What is relevant here is that the three parameters we showed to determine non-canonical object marking in Mediterranean languages and in Roumanian (that probably was linked to Mediterranean area by Balkan Romance varieties) operate also outside this area.

We are going now to consider – just to give an example – non-canonical object marking in Persian.

Non-canonical marker is the postposition *râ* (Lazard 2001a/b). The probability of a given object being marked by the postposition – without considering pragmatic factors that may not concern us here – depends on: 1) object individuation (*"degré de définitude"*, in Lazard's terms), 2) object agentivity (*"degré*

21. Nouns denoting metals or plants are lower than animal nouns on the agentivity hierarchy. If a language has non-canonical marking of metal or plant nouns in certain conditions, in the same conditions (i.e. object affectedness and object individuation being equal) animal nouns (and all nouns preceding metal and plant nouns on the agentivity hierarchy) are, obviously, non-canonically marked.

d'humanitude"), 3) both lexical and compositional telicity ("*degré de plénitude du verbe*" and "*distance sémantique entre le verbe et l'objet*"). Inherently atelic verbs (such as *dâštan* 'to have'), that do not affect their objects, tend to reject non-canonical marking (Lazard 2001a: 335). On the other hand, a highly telic verb takes non-canonical marking also if the object is lowly individuated (Lazard 2001a: 328, ex. 1). «On pourrait formuler la règle dans les termes suivants: toutes choses égales d'ailleurs, l'emploi de *râ* est d'autant plus probable que le processus exprimé par le verbe affecte davantage son objet» (Lazard 2001b: 382). Totally affected objects take *râ*, objects that are not totally affected do not (Lazard 2001a: 344–).

Nevertheless, it is peculiar that among European languages the alternation between PDO and non-PDO is attested only in the Romance area around the Mediterranean, from the Iberian peninsula to Sicily, and in Roumanian, that was presumably linked to Mediterranean languages by Balkan Romance varieties.

Finally, Maltese object marking is particularly interesting in the Mediterranean context. Maltese Arabic has historically been exposed to a massive Romance – particularly Sicilian – influence spanning many centuries. On the other hand, PDO is attested in Eastern Arabic modern dialects, and in Biblical Aramaic and Late Biblical Hebrew (Borg & Mifsud 2002).

«Classical Arabic marked direct objects via a case inflection [. . .]. In general, subjects take the nominative with *-u*, objects the accusative with *-a*. [. . .] However, in the less frequent uses where a verbal noun takes an object, it is also possible to have object marking via the presence of the preposition *li* 'to'» (Borg & Mifsud 2002: 36–37; see also Wright 1967, III, §29).

Arabic data that were made available by studies on this topic (Khan 1984; Bossong 1998; Borg & Mifsud 2002) do not allow us to say whether non-canonical object marking is determined by the same parameters which govern object marking in the languages we examined above, among which there is Maltese. But, data collected by Farina (2005) seem to show that, at least in Late Biblical Hebrew, PDO is selected by the three parameters triggering PDO in European and Mediterranean languages investigated in this paper.

References

Aquilina, J. 1987. *Maltese.* Valletta: Progress Press.

Berretta, M. 1989. Sulla presenza dell'accusativo preposizionale in italiano settentrionale: Note tipologiche. *Vox Romanica* 48: 13–37.

Bertinetto, P.M. 1986. *Tempo, aspetto e azione nel verbo italiano.* Firenze: Accademia della Crusca.

Bertinetto, P.M. & Squartini, M. 1995. An attempt at defining the class of 'gradual completion verbs'. In *Temporal reference. Aspect and actionality*, Vol. 1, P.M. Bertinetto, V. Bianchi, J. Higginbotham & M. Squartini (eds), 11–26. Torino: Rosenberg & Sellier.

Borg, A. & Mifsud, M. 2002. Maltese object marking in a Mediterranean context. In *Mediterranean languages. Papers from the MEDTYP workshop, Tirrenia, June 2000,* P. Ramat & T. Stolz (eds), 33–46. Bochum: Universitätverlag Brockmeyer.

Bossong, G. 1998. La marquage différentiel de l'objet dans les langues d'Europe. In *Actance et valence dans les langues de l'Europe,* J. Feuillet (ed.), 193–258. Berlin: Mouton de Gruyter.

Dowty, D.R. 1979. *Word meaning and Montague grammar.* Dordrecht: Reidel.

Farina, M. 2005. La particella 'et in ebraico biblico. Unpublished Thesis, University of Pisa.

Hopper, P.J. & Thompson, S.A. 1980. Transitivity in grammar and discourse. *Language* 56: 251–299.

Kayne, R.S. 1985. L'accord du participe passé en français et en italien. *Modèles Linguistiques* 7: 73–90.

Kayne, R.S. 1989. Facets of romance past participle agreement. In *Dialect variation and the theory of grammar,* P. Benincà (ed.), 85–103. Dordrecht: Foris.

Kayne, R.S. 1995. Agreement and verb morphology in three varieties of English. In *Studies in Comparative Germanic Syntax,* H. Heider, S. Olsen & S. Vikner (eds), 159–165. Dordrecht: Kluwer.

Khan, G.A. 1984. Object markers and agreement pronouns in semitic languages. *Bulletin of the School of oriental and African Studies* 47: 468–500.

La Fauci, N. 1988. *Oggetti e soggetti nella formazione della morfosintassi romanza.* Pisa: Giardini.

Lazard, G. 1984. Actance variations and categories of the object. In *Objects,* F. Plank (ed.), 269–292. London: Academic Press.

Lazard, G. 2001a. Le morphème *râ* en persan et les relations actancielles. In *Études de linguistique générale,* G. Lazard (ed.), 327–355. Leuven: Peeters.

Lazard, G. 2001b. Le *râ* persan et le *ba* chinois. In *Études de linguistique générale,* G. Lazard, 379–386. Leuven: Peeters.

Lombard, A. 1974. *La Langue Roumaine.* Paris: Klincksieck.

Manoliu-Manea, M. 1989. Rumänisch: Morphosyntax. In *Lexikon der Romanistischen Linguistik* (ed.), III, G. Holtus, M. Metzeltin & C. Schmitt (eds), 101–114. Tübingen: Niemeyer.

Melis, C. 1995. El objeto directo personal en *El Cantar de Mio Cid.* Estudio sintáctico-pragmático. In *El complemento directo preposicional,* C. Pensado (ed.), 133–163. Madrid: Visor.

Moravcsik, E.A. 1978. On the case marking of objects. In *Universals of human language,* Vol. 4, J.H. Greenberg (ed.), 249–289. Stanford CA: University Press.

Niculescu, A. 1959. Sur l'objet direct prépositionnel dans les langues romanes. In *Recueil d'études romanes, publié à l'occasion du IXe Congrès international de Linguistique romane à Lisbonne du 31 mars au 3 avril 1959,* 167–185. Bucarest: Éditions de l'Académie de la République Populaire de Roumanie.

Nocentini, A. 1985. Sulla genesi dell'oggetto preposizionale nelle lingue romanze. In *Studi linguistici e filologici per Carlo Alberto Mastrelli,* L. Agostiniani, V. Grazi & A. Nocentini (eds), 299–312. Pisa: Pacini.

Nocentini, A. 1992. Oggetto marcato vs. oggetto non marcato: Stato ed evoluzione di una categoria nell'area euroasiatica. In *L'Europa linguistica: contatti, contrasti, affinità di lingue, Atti del XXI Congresso internazionale della SLI,* A.G. Mocciaro and G. Soravia (eds), 227–246. Roma: Bulzoni.

Pensado, C. 1995. La creación del complemento directo preposicional y la flexión de los pronombres personales en las lenguas románicas. In *El complemento directo preposicional,* C. Pensado (ed.), 179–233, Madrid: Visor Libros.

Pottier, B. 1968. L'emploi de la préposition *a* devant l'objet en espagnol. *Bulletin de la Société de Linguistique de Paris* 63: 83–95.

Puşcariu, S. 1937. Au sujet de *p(r)e* avec l'accusatif. In *Études de linguistique roumaine*, 439–457. Cluj-Bucareşti: Imprimeria Naţională.

Ramat, P. 1984. *Linguistica Tipologica.* Bologna: Il Mulino.

Reichenkron, G. 1951. Das präpositionelle Akkusativ-Objekt im ältesten Spanish. *Romanische Forschungen* 63: 342–397.

Roegiest, E. 1979. A propos de l'accusatif prépositionnel dans quelques langues romanes. *Vox Romanica* 38: 37–54.

Roegiest, E. 1998. Variación del objeto directo español y dinamicidad verbal. In *Estudios en honor del Profesor Josse De Kock*, N. Delbecque & C. De Paepe (eds), 469–488. Leuven: University Press.

Romagno, D. 2005. La codificazione degli attanti nel Mediterraneo romanzo: Accordo del participio e marcatura dell'oggetto. *Archivio Glottologico Italiano* 90: 90–113.

Salcedo, E.T. 1999. El complemento directo preposicional. In *Gramática descriptiva de la lengua Española*, Real Academia Española, 2, I. Bosque & V. Demonte (eds), 1779–1803. Madrid: Espasa Calpe.

Silverstein, M.1976. Hierarchy of features and ergativity. In *Grammatical categories in Australian languages*, R.M.W. Dixon (ed.), 112–171. Canberra: Australian Institute of Aboriginal Studies.

Slabakova, R. 2001. *Telicity in the second language.* Amsterdam: John Benjamins.

Sornicola, R. 1997. L'oggetto preposizionale in siciliano antico e in napoletano antico. Considerazioni su un problema di tipologia diacronica. *Italienische Studien* 18: 45–59.

Sornicola, R. 2000. Processi di convergenza nella formazione di un tipo sintattico: La genesi ibrida dell'oggetto preposizionale. In *Les nouvellevs ambitions de la linguistique diachronique, Actes du XXIIe Congrès International de Linguistique et de Philologie Romanes (Bruxelles 23–29 Juillet 1998)*, II, A. Englebert et al. (eds), 419–427. Tübingen: Max Niemeyer.

Spitzer, L. 1928. Rum. *p(r)e*, span. *a* vor persönlichem Akkusativobjekt. *Zeitschrift für Romanische Philologie* 48: 423–432.

Tenny, C.L. 1994. *Aspectual roles and the syntax-semantics interface.* Dordrecht: Kluwer.

Timberlake, A. 1977. Reanalysis and actualization in syntactic change. In *Mechanisms of syntactic change*, C.N. Li (ed.), 141–177. Austin TX: University of Texas Press.

Van Valin, R.D. Jr. 1990. Semantic parameters of split intransitivity. *Language* 66: 221–260.

Van Valin, R.D. Jr. & LaPolla, R.J. 1997. *Syntax: Structure, meaning & function.* Cambridge: CUP.

Verkuyl, H.J. 1972. *On the compositional nature of the aspects.* Dordrecht: Reidel.

Vincent, N. 1982. The development of the auxiliaries *habere* and *esse* in Romance. In *Studies in the Romance verb*, N. Vincent & M. Harris (eds), 71–96. London: Croom Helm.

Wright, W. 1967. *A grammar of the Arabic language*, 3rd edn., Cambridge: CUP.

Re: duplication

Iconic vs counter-iconic principles (and their areal correlates)

Thomas Stolz

This article provides a new vista of an old problem, viz. the supposed counter-iconic nature of a variety of reduplicative patterns which encode categories such as diminution, attenuation, etc. It is argued that even these categories are iconically represented by reduplication because iconicity is not tied to an increase in size of the entities referred to by the reduplicative construction. Iconicity applies if the semantic description of the quality encoded by reduplication is more complex than the one necessary for the description of the non-reduplicated pattern. This new understanding of iconicity is illustrated by examples of total reduplication drawn from a world-wide convenience sample of languages. Circum-Mediterranean languages are given special emphasis in the final discussion.

1. Introduction

Contemporary linguistics[1] has re-discovered reduplication as an intriguingly interesting topic whose adequate description is not only a demanding empirical and methodological task but also an undertaking which promises many important insights into the nature of human language(s) in general. In the wake of Moravcsik's

1. This contribution is part of a research program on *The areality of a universal: total reduplication* at the *University of Bremen*/Germany financed by the *Deutsche Forschungsgemeinschaft* (DFG). This particular text has grown out of a seminar on reduplication I taught at the *Università degli Studi di Pavia*/Italy in April 2006. I am grateful to Paolo Ramat and Anna Giacalone Ramat for giving me the opportunity to work in the intellectually stimulating surroundings of the *Dipartimento di Linguistica*. Likewise, I want to express my gratitude to the participants of my seminar. Ewald Lang was helpful in bibliographical matters. Two anonymous readers, Sonia Cristofaro, Andrea Sansò, Nataliya Levkovych, Andreas Ammann and Elisa Roma commented on my ideas and their suggestions have somehow made it into my mind (and thus presumably also into my text – at least partially). Nevertheless, I take full responsibility for everything that is said in this paper.

(1978) groundbreaking article, adherents to different schools of thought have looked more closely at reduplication and related issues in numerous publications. Kouwenberg (2003), Müller (2004), Hurch (2005) and Inkelas/Zoll (2005) mark the most recent development in this field. The oft-cited prime mover in the realm of reduplication research by Pott (1862) and to a lesser extent also Brandstetter (1917) were already full-blown cross-linguistic studies of all kinds of phenomena which may be subsumed under the heading of repetition. Among these, reduplication in the strict sense constitutes only a sub-set with specific properties, cf. the captions in (1).

(1) The proper place of reduplication

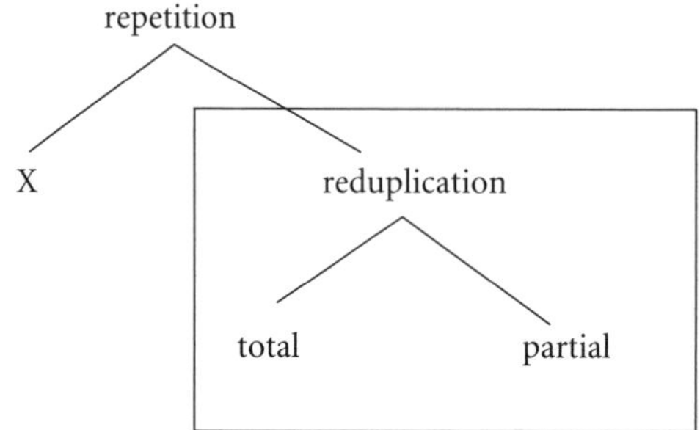

The variable X in the above diagram may be spelled out in various ways. Depending on the theoretical prerequisites of the observer's approach to the issue, X may stand for seemingly disparate phenomena such as syntactic and/or semantic parallelism, co-compounds, cognate objects, segmental gemination, morphological agreement, etc. all of which are touched upon in the contributions to Hurch (2005). Moreover, Inkelas/Zoll (2005: 212) claim that "reduplication forms a natural class with antonym constructions". Gil (2005) demonstrates that there is a continuum which ranges from stylistic repetition to grammatical reduplication with a large greyish in-between area for which the classification is not straightforward.

For practical reasons, I will disregard the unclear fringes of repetition and concentrate on bona fide cases of grammatical reduplication without denying that a thorough investigation of what occurs outside the realm of grammar will reveal more about the structural and conceptual foundations of reduplication itself. I also take a relatively traditional stance when I require reduplication to involve the copying of segmental material of an independently existing morpheme (in the widest possible sense of the term), whereas the model of Morphological Doubling (Inkelas/Zoll 2005: 25) starts from a completely different angle, which allows for purely semantic reduplication. This rather selective look at the phenomenology is justified because my contribution focuses on the very basic problem of motivation of form, i.e., I tackle the question of whether or not it is possible to identify a common semantic or conceptual background for functionally dissimilar categories which cross-linguistically go together well with reduplicative constructions as their grammatical expression. With a view to determining to what extent iconicity can be held responsible as driving force for reduplication, it is advisable to operate on the basis of largely uncontroversial examples which resemble each other as to their degree of grammaticalisation. Wherever possible I will extend the discussion to cover also areas situated beyond this borderline. Methodologically, I approach the issue at hand according to common functional-typological practice. The empirical basis consists of data drawn from a wide variety of languages some of which are spoken in the Mediterranean region and its vicinity. Many data stem from languages situated in different parts of the globe. Moreover, no special sampling procedure has been applied, nor have I taken measures to avoid any of the usual biases. The presentation is predominantly synchronic. In Section 2, I briefly review the controversy over the role of iconicity. This includes a survey of pertinent cases in 2.1 followed by the presentation of more problematic instances in 2.2. In Section 3, general principles of iconicity and markedness are discussed (for this purpose, examples from outside the realm of reduplication are analysed for both markedness proper and local markedness). Section 4 is devoted to the re-interpretation of the controversial facts of reduplication in terms of a revised model of iconicity. The conclusions in Section 5 are meant to evaluate my findings in the larger framework of typology and universals research (with special emphasis on areal linguistics).

2. Iconic or not?

Right on the first page of his treatise on reduplication and related issues, Pott (1862: 1) observes that "solche Doppelung [...] gar mancherlei Functionen ausübt und demzufolge begrifflich in sehr verschiedener Geltung auftritt".[2] This relatively vague statement suggests that there is no common semantic bond between the various linguistic categories expressed by reduplication. Much in the same vein, Brandstetter (1917: 32) concludes that one may ask whether there is a psycholinguistic basis for reduplication phenomena: "In vielen Fällen ist der Grund ohne weiteres ersichtlich, in manchen kann man ihm durch Erwägungen nahekommen, oft bleibt er dunkel".[3] This translates into the absence of properties on the content side shared by all instances of reduplication. Since the early students of

2. My translation: "this kind of doubling [...] fulfils a wide variety of functions and thus is attested with notionally rather different values".

3. My translation: "In many cases, the motivation [for reduplication] is directly obvious, in some cases one may approach it by reasoning, often it remains opaque".

reduplication adopted an all-embracing holistic approach to the phenomenon which extended over the full range of repetition in language, their inability to identify a semantic link between the various uses to which reduplication is put in the languages of the world might have to do with their lumping together strictly grammatical and purely stylistic aspects. We owe to Sapir (1921: 79) the observation that, functionally, reduplication displays "self-evident symbolism". However, Moravcsik (1978: 316), who looks exclusively at grammatical reduplication in the sense of inflectional and derivational categories also insists that there is no special qualification of reduplicative constructions for the expression of certain meanings and functions. To her mind, reduplication escapes being assigned a higher degree of motivation and thus behaves like any other morphological technique. Rubino's (2005: 19–22) survey of functions fulfilled by reduplication in the languages of the world, however, indirectly shows that certain areas of grammar are practically never associated with reduplication while for others, reduplicative patterns abound. As yet, I have not found convincing examples of reduplication being employed to mark gender, person or case distinctions,[4] for instance. On the other hand, many of the tasks carried out by reduplication have to do with semantic augmentation and related phenomena (cf. below).

Moreover, Abbi (1992: 29) discusses the areally wide-spread total reduplication in South Asia and emphasises that the constructions she reviews "are relatively non-arbitrary. They are not truly iconic [...]. They are not completely arbitrary because in spite of the varied range of meanings [...] they have a kernel semanteme." Kiyomi (1995: 1163) claims that reduplication has a "fuzzy status in which form and meaning are either motivated or arbitrary". More recently, Inkelas/Zoll (2005: 14) observe with regard to reduplication that "[t]he prevalence of semantically iconic reduplication can readily be seen [...]. Iconic semantics is not, however, the general rule. Reduplication, especially partial reduplication, is associated cross-linguistically with all sorts of meaning, both inflectional and derivational, whose degree of iconicity is often negligible". Interestingly, those who are sceptical about the iconicity of reduplication express their doubts especially in connection with partial reduplication (Moravcsik 1978; Inkelas/Zoll 2005), whereas Abbi (1992) whose main concern is with total reduplication allows for an at least mild degree of motivation (and so does Kiyomi (1995)).

In the light of this disagreement, one might get the impression that the two kinds of reduplication – total vs. partial – constitute two distinct phenomena,

4. Rubino (2005: 21) mentions one example where case-marking by reduplication could be involved (so-called absolutives in Chukchi). On closer inspection however, the evidence is weak and the word-forms most probably call for a different analysis (namely: pure number distinction [cf. below]).

which obey different principles including semiotic ones (Mayerthaler 1977: 28). Apart from the fact that Mayerthaler's idea to ascribe different semiotic potential to partial and total reduplication creates more problems than it solves (Hurch/Mattes 2005: 146), his solution is at odds with the currently prevailing idea that the description of all kinds of repetition phenomena should be integrated in one model (Inkelas/Zoll 2005). A look at the many contributions to Kouwenberg (2003), however, reveals that even for languages which, like the vast majority of Creoles world-wide, overwhelmingly employ total reduplication, the pertinent descriptions distinguish (not always consistently) between iconic and non-iconic types of reduplication. Abraham (2005) attempts to reconcile iconic and non-iconic interpretations of reduplication with each other. He criticises Kiyomi (1995) for her "strict adherence to the iconistic principle" (Abraham 2005: 554 and 558) in order to explain the co-existence of semantically diametrically opposed functions of reduplication even in one and the same language. Admittedly, Kiyomi's (1995: 1163) so-called semantic principle of "higher/lower degree of X" is problematic because the way it is applied to the structural facts is largely arbitrary. However, in the subsequent sections I will demonstrate that Kiyomi (1995) actually has a point when she tries to subsume iconic and non-iconic structures under one roof.

Hurch/Mattes (2005: 147) do not believe that this is possible when they demand that one should "auch andere Erklärungen suchen, statt die Interpretation der Funktionen von Reduplikation unbedingt in ein Korsett der Ikonizität zu zwingen."[5] Nevertheless, I go beyond Kiyomi's claim and assume that much of what passes as counter-iconic in the literature can be re-interpreted as an instance of iconicity - **under a particular reading of the term**. Before I can present my evidence and explain the special reading of iconicity, it is in order to recapitulate first what is commonly understood as iconic in reduplication research (Section 2.1). Then we have to understand what is meant by counter-iconic structures (Section 2.2).

2.1 What is iconic?

In modern linguistics, iconicity is associated with scholars such as Mayerthaler (1981), Haiman (1985), Givón (1995), Dressler (1985), and more recently Rivas (2004: 251–67). For the present purpose, I take Dressler's approach as my starting point. According to the adaptation of Peircean semiotics by the proponents of Natural Morphology, iconicity is the semiotic principle according to which the degree of complexity on the content side of a linguistic sign is reflected by the degree of complexity on the expression side of the same sign in a parallel fashion

5. My translation: "also look for different explanations in lieu of forcing the interpretation of the functions of reduplication by all means into the straight-jacket of iconicity."

(Dressler 1985: 281–5). Simplifying, more content requires more expression, less content goes along with less expression as schematically shown in (2).

(2) Iconic relation

	linguistic sign 1	linguistic sign 2
content	X	XX
expression	X	XX

Iconicity in this sense is thus a relational concept which requires two entities (= linguistic signs) to be interrelated such that linguistic sign 1 is semantically less complex than sign 2. If the asymmetric complexity of the signata of both signs corresponds to an equally asymmetric complexity of their respective expressions (= signantia), then the relation between linguistic sign 1 and linguistic sign 2 is iconic. The assumed differences in complexity are indicated by the number of Xs used in the above schema. Ideally, linguistic sign 2, which is characterised by a relatively higher degree of complexity, represents the marked member of an opposition of categories whereas its competitor (= linguistic sign 1) is associated with the status of unmarked member. The issue of markedness will concern us again below.

Reduplication – be it total or partial – always displays a gain in complexity on the expression side in comparison to the related non-reduplicated construction.[6] Thus, reduplication at least intuitively invites the interpretation of conveying more meaning than the simple form. Accordingly, reduplicative constructions can be expected to serve the expression of marked categories. This pattern is indeed widely attested. In the next sections, I survey a selection of pertinent categories for which reduplicative constructions are reported to be iconic. These cover typically verbal categories in the realm of the imperfective aspect, intensification of adjectives/adverbs, nominal and verbal number marking, etc. (Abraham 2005: 550–1). For expository reasons, I start with the latter categories although cross-linguistically, they are not the most common case.

2.1.1 *Number marking on nouns*

The paradigm case of markedness relations is the singular-plural distinction. It is common knowledge in linguistics that plurals are typologically marked in comparison to the singular. This observation is easy to translate into conceptual terms if we understand the plural concept as necessarily including the one of the singular.

6. For obvious reasons, I cannot discuss at length the issue raised by Inkelas/Zoll (2005), according to whom partial reduplication is derived from an underlying pattern of total reduplication. For a different viewpoint, I refer the reader to Hurch/Mattes (2005: 148–53).

Thus, it is to be expected that in a language where singular and plural receive morphologically distinct expressions which differ in complexity, it will be the plural which takes the more complex one (cf. below). If the morphological differences are based on reduplication, the reduplicative construction represents the plural. A pertinent example is provided by the Indonesian sentences in (3).[7]

(3) Indonesian

(3.1) Singular Noun [LPP Indonesian 11]

Dan ***orang*** *dewasa itu merasa sangat puas mengenal*
and **human** grown that feel very content know
*se-se**orang*** *yang berdudi seperti itu*
one-some**one** who minded like that
'And the grown-up **person** was very content to know someone who was like himself.'

(3.2) Plural Noun [LPP Indonesian 10]

Aku sering hidup di antara ***orang-orang*** *dewasa*
I often live in among **human-human** grown
'I have lived for a long time with grown-up **persons**.'

The relevant nominal lexeme is *orang* 'human being'. In (3.1), *orang* occurs on its own because singular is the intended meaning. If plural is to be encoded, the preferred strategy is to apply total reduplication to the singular form - as *orang-orang* 'human beings' in (3.2). The relationship between the Indonesian singular and plural forms is perfectly iconic not only because the expression of the plural is more complex than the one of the singular but also because the plural expression includes the singular expression. This is reflected by the diagram in (4). *Orang-orang*, in a way, could be interpreted as 'more than one instance of *orang*', i.e. more of the same content is expressed by making use of more of the same expression.

(4) Iconic inclusion

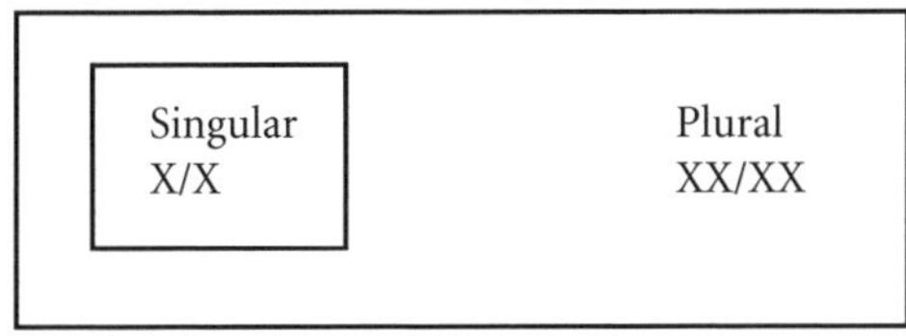

7. These are the conventions I use in the examples. In the original, the transmorphemisation and the English translation, boldface identifies those elements of an utterance which are focused upon in the ensuing discussion. I restrict the morphological analysis of the examples to a minimum. Only where reduplicative techniques are involved do I provide detailed information about morpheme boundaries, etc. Where the orthography of my sample languages treats reduplicative constructions as tight or loose compounds (one word vs. hyphenated word), I always employ a hyphen in the original and the transmorphemisation. Elsewhere, the two elements of total reduplicative patterns are presented as two separate words.

This pattern is applicable to other cases as well, for instance to partial reduplication as in Tahitian singular *'ōfa'i* 'stone' → plural *'ōfafa'i* 'stones' (Coppenrath/Prevost 1974: 46), where the stressed syllable $/fa/$ of the lexical morpheme is copied to yield the plural form, i.e. the expression of the singular is included in the expression of the plural. Reduplication may only affect an attribute as in Tahitian *te mau 'umara maitata'i* {DEF.PL} {PL} {potato} {good:RED} 'the good potatoes', where the stressed syllable $/ta/$ of the lexical morpheme of the adjective is copied to yield the plural form whereas the noun itself remains uninflected (with plural being indicated by the preceding article and number-marking particle) (Coppenrath/Prevost 1974: 66). Again the singular form is included in the expression of the plural. In all of these cases, the increase in complexity on the content side is mapped unto the expression side.[8]

Elsewhere we find similar constructions whose function is not the expression of the plural proper but nevertheless involves the basic meaning of the plural. This is the case with count nouns in Quechua (Ayacuchano), for instance. The Spanish-derived noun *ubiha* 'sheep' is the singular citation form. This is made plural by adding the plural suffix *–kuna* to the basic form: *ubihakuna* 'sheep (plural)'. Alongside the singular-plural distinction, there is also a third possibility to refer to sheep in this variety of Quechua, namely by totally reduplicating the citation form (Hartmann 1987: 158). *Ubiha ubiha* '(many) sheep (collective/plural of abundance)' can be used with reference to a flock of sheep whereas the morphological plural may embrace a given number of individual heads of sheep (not necessarily belonging to the same flock). These differences in meaning notwithstanding, both collective and plural share the property of referring to more than a single head of sheep. In a way, the collective implies the meaning of the plural. Similarly, there are other usages of total reduplication, which, on superficial inspection, might seem to be too remote from number marking to have anything to do with plural or related categories. In Hindi, total reduplication is frequently employed – but never for the formation of nominal plurals in the strict sense of the term. The noun *baccaa* 'child' is pluralised regularly by replacive bound morphology: *bacce* 'children'. However, both singular and plural forms may be reduplicated though with clear differences in meaning, cf. (5).

8. The same holds for those cases where reduplication alone is not sufficient to mark number distinctions and thus goes along with other mainly affixal strategies as in Classical Aztec singular *cōhuā-tl* {snake}-{ABS} 'snake' → plural *cō-cōhua-ʔ* {RED}-{snake}-{PL} 'snakes' (Launey 1981: 28) where reduplication of the leftmost CV-chain is accompanied by substitutive suffixation of a dedicated plural marker. The plural form does not contain the entire singular form, but it is still segmentally and morphologically more complex.

(5) Hindi (Abbi 1980: 1)

(5.1) Totality

baccaa	***baccaa***	*uskii*	*maut*	*par*	*royaa*
child	**child**	POR.3	death	on	cry:PAST

'**Every child** wept on his death.'

(5.2) Exclusiveness

bacce	***bacce***	*melaa*	*dekhne*	*gaye*
children	**children**	fair	see	go:PAST

'**Only the children** went to see the fair.'

The total reduplication of the singular form yields *baccaa baccaa* 'all children/ every child' – a construction which encodes totality. Again, totality is inherently related to the plural as the construction only makes sense when it refers to more than one child. All children automatically means more than one child. Likewise, the total reduplication of the plural of the same noun has a meaning component which links the construction to the plural concept. *Bacce bacce* 'only/ exclusively (the) children' displays connections with plurality for two reasons. One is rather trivial because the reduplicated noun itself is overtly marked for plural and thus invites a plural reading. The other is less obvious. The construction *bacce bacce*, in a way, is the mirror image of *baccaa baccaa*: the latter comprises all entities to which the classification as child applies (and nothing else) whereas the former excludes all entities to which the classification as child fails to apply (but does not necessarily hold for all children). In this way, *bacce bacce* singles out a group of potential referents and is thus valid for more than just one instance of *baccaa*. Totality and exclusiveness count as inherently associated with plurality although they are not genuine strategies of marking the plural *tout court*.

The situation is very similar in the case of the distributive. In the Afro-Asiatic language Maltese, total reduplication of nouns is employed for various purposes among which distributive is prominent. High animacy of nouns is no obstacle to their being reduplicated (as in [6]).

(6) Maltese

(6.1) Animate distributive [Na 5]

l-għalliem	*u*	*s-Surmast*	*bd-ew*	*i-dur-u*
DET-teacher	and	DET-headmaster	start.PERF-3PL	3-go_around.IMPERF-PL

tifel	***tifel***
boy	**boy**

'The teacher and the headmaster began to walk **from boy to boy**.'

(6.2) Inanimate distributive [Mq 92]

Dak	*il-ħin*	*ftakar*	*kif*	*kien*
this:F	DET-time	remember.PERF:REF	how	be.PAST

i-dur	*ir-raħal*	*triq*	*triq*	*i-ħabbat*
3SG.M-go_around.IMPERF	DET-village	**street**	**street**	3SG.M-knock.IMPERF

bieb	*bieb*	*u*	*ji-t-karrab*	*għal-l-flus*
door	**door**	and	3SG.M-REF-sigh	for-DET-money

'At that time he remembered how it was to walk ***from street to street***, knock on **every door** and beg for money.'

In (6.1), the noun *tifel* 'boy; child' occurs twice in its singular form. However, the total reduplication *tifel tifel* 'from boy to boy' should not be mistaken for the plural formation strategy. The plural proper is formed morphologically by introflexion (= *tfal* 'children') or suppletion (= *subien* 'boys'). The reduplicative construction refers to a path along a variety of entities which belong to the same ontological class – in this case the class BOY, i.e., plurality is involved as the construction makes sense only if at least two members of the same class are present.[9] The same applies to the two inanimate nouns which are used for the distributive in (6.2). *Triq* 'street' and *bieb* 'door' are the singular forms of the lexemes under scrutiny. The regular plurals are *toroq* 'streets' and *bibien* 'doors', respectively. Again, the distributive is conceptualised as a path along several streets and several doors and thus, plurality is also indirectly co-present as a semantic component of the distributive.

In sum, there is a variety of major and minor nominal number categories whose common bond is their connection to plurality. Wherever plurality is included in the spell-out of semantic features of a category, the principles of iconicity as depicted by (4) apply: total or partial reduplication employed as expression of collective, totality, exclusion, and distributive. It is iconic because it maps the higher degree of semantic/conceptual complexity of these categories unto the expression side of the linguistic sign. The higher degree of semantic/conceptual complexity inter alia rests on the fact that these categories have affinities to the plural and just like the plural differ from the conceptually more basic singular in the complexity of their means of expression.

2.1.2 *Verbal plurality and aspectual distinctions*

With verbs too, reduplication often indicates plurality. However, in contrast to nouns, the interpretation of verbal number marking is less straightforward as the so-called plural may have a wide range of readings (Dressler 1968). Classical Aztec is a case in point. There are three types of reduplication, all of which affect verbs though to different extent. Alongside the types (C)V- (= reduplication of the body of the initial syllable of the lexical morpheme with obligatorily short vowel) and

9. A relatively unlikely alternative would require one boy to be extraordinarily large or, supposed he is in a lying position uncommonly tall such that the headmaster and the teacher would have to walk all along this boy to reach some other goal.

(C)V:- (= reduplication of the body of the initial syllable of the lexical morpheme with obligatorily short vowel), there is the type (C)Vʔ-, which consists of a copy of (mostly!) the body of the initial syllable of the lexical morpheme with an obligatory glottal plosive in coda position (Launey 1981: 264–8). Launey (1981: 265) states that the latter type "marque plutôt sa dispersion [= of the process described by the lexical morpheme]: les effets du processus sont répartis sur divers objets ou dans divers lieux.[10]" Owing to the fact that in Classical Aztec, inanimate nouns are usually transnumeral (or neutral as to number) and therefore escape the formal number distinction of singular vs. plural, the dispersive may be used as an indirect means to encode plurality of an inanimate participant. In (7), a minimal pair of sentences demonstrates how the major types of reduplication on verbs differ from each other functionally.

(7) Classical Aztec (Launey 1981: 265)

(7.1) (C)V:- frequentative

*mo-***tlā***-tlapohua* *in* *puerta*
REFL-RED-open DET door
'The door opens **frequently/all the time**.'

(7.2) (C) Vʔ- totality/dispersive

*mo-***tlà***-tlapohua* *in* *puerta*
REFL-RED-open DET door
'**All** the doors open/doors open **everywhere**.'

As is clear from the two alternative translations of (7.2), the (C)Vʔ-reduplication invites at least two interpretations, namely one which focuses on the multitude of referents ("many" or "all doors") and the other focussing on the spatial dispersion of similar events involving similar participants ("everywhere", "all over the place"). No matter which interpretation is more likely to apply in a given case, plurality (of locations or participants) will always be involved. For both interpretations (and both aspects), the non-reduplicated simple verb form *motlapohua* (*in puerta*) '(the door) opens' refers to one specific occasion and is thus close to a semelfactive interpretation. That's why the dispersive fits in well with the above observations as to the iconicity of the major and minor number categories in the nominal realm.

This viewpoint can be easily extended to cover other instances of reduplication for instance in Classical Aztec. The frequentative exemplified in (7.1) implies that a given event pattern is repeated time and again (mostly by the same primary participant encoded as subject). The examples in (8) demonstrate how one and the same verb can undergo different types of reduplication processes. In contradistinction

10. My translation: "[it] rather marks its dispersion: the effects of the process are distributed over several objects or several locations."

to the minimal pair in (7), however, the dispersive function of the (C)Vʔ-reduplication precludes the identification of a location as in (8.1).

(8) Classical Aztec

(8.1) (C)V:- frequentative (Launey 1981: 264)
n-on-ī-ichtequi in cuezcoma-c
1SG-DIR-RED-steal DET silo-LOC
'I **frequently** go to steal from the silo.'

(8.2) (C)Vʔ- totality/dispersive (Launey 1981: 265)
n-on-ì-ichtequi
1SG-DIR-RED-steal
'I go about stealing **here and there/everywhere**.'

In both cases, the action of stealing repeats itself over time. This is clear for the frequentative, but it is also implied in the very concept of the dispersive: stealing in various locations is tantamount to stealing repeatedly i.e. on spatio-temporally distinct occasions (although the dispersive clearly highlights the spatial distribution whereas the frequentative focuses on the frequency of identical events). Events which recur on more than one occasion are at the basis of aspectual distinctions within the realm of the imperfective under which notions as e.g. iterative and habitual can be subsumed. In all of these cases, events are repeated and thus statements are made about a plurality of events. The reduplicated verb forms represent this plurality whereas the simple verb forms do not (normally) invite a reading associated with plurality (= Classical Aztec *nonichtequi* 'I go out to steal', meaning on this particular occasion only). This is absolutely in line with the basic idea of iconicity presented in the foregoing section.

However, reduplication is also made use of to encode aspectual distinctions which do not correspond to a plurality of events. Paradigm cases of these categories are durative and progressive. What distinguishes these sub-categories of the imperfective from the ones mentioned above is the fact that they refer to a single event whereas their counterparts obligatorily cover several events (although the number of repetitions remains indefinite). The frequentative and associated categories depict an event as recurring in certain intervals. This recurrence translates into extension over time, meaning: the event type may be activated repeatedly in an extended period. Extension over time is exactly what is highlighted by the durative and similar aspectual categories. There are no intervals of activation, in a manner of speaking, but one single realisation of a given event type is portrayed as requiring time. Being more extended in terms of time is tantamount to a higher degree of complexity on the conceptual level as the duration of the event/process has to be represented specifically. Simplifying, this duration exceeds the one of other say, punctual events. If we accept a point on the time arrow as the representation of a punctual event, then the durative and sundry categories of the imperfective require a line for their representation. The line is more complex than the point because the line covers a more extended segment on the time arrow. Schematically, this difference can be represented in the form of the diagram in (9).

(9) Extension over time

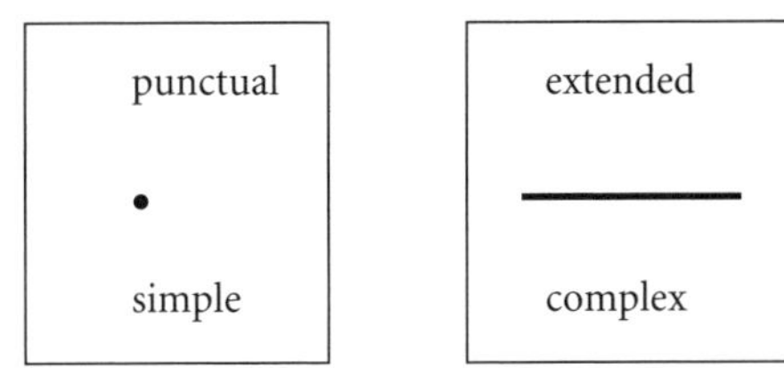

Iconicity applies if the expression of the category belonging to the range of the imperfective is more complex than the one which encodes punctual. Length differences on the conceptual and referential level are mapped unto the length of the *signantia* in terms of segmental material. Reduplicative constructions are segmentally more extended than their non-reduplicated bases. The examples in (10) illustrate this difference.

(10) Chamorro (Topping 1980: 55)

(10.1) Perfective

mañocho

man-chocho hit gi restaurant

PL-eat 1PL.ABS in restaurant

'We **ate/have eaten** in a restaurant.'

(10.2) Imperfective

mañochocho

*man-***cho***-chocho hit gi restaurant*

PL-RED-eat 1PL.ABS in restaurant

'We **are eating** in a restaurant.'

The Austronesian language Chamorro employs partial reduplication (of stressed syllables) to indicate extension over time (in this case: the progressive), whereas the non-reduplicated form has a perfective meaning, i.e., the event or process is treated as bounded or restricted in extension. The segmentally more complex form – the reduplicative *mañochocho* – represents the category which refers to extension over time, whereas the simpler form *mañocho* refers to a temporally bounded event.

Total reduplication is also used for the purpose of symbolising extraordinarily long extension over time as in Example (11) from West-Greenlandic, a member of the Eskimo-Aleutan phylum.[11]

11. The number 4 refers to the so-called fourth person aka obviative, which is required in this type of complex sentences.

(11) West-Greenlandic (Fortescue 1984: 280–1)
Muluguni *muluguni* *tikissaaq*
stay_away:4SG.COND **stay_away:4SG.COND** come:FUT:3SG
'After **staying away** (from home) **for a long time**, he would come (back to them).'

One instance of *muluguni* 'he stayed away' would have sufficed to render the utterance grammatically acceptable but total reduplication of the finite verb is needed to represent the additional idea of a very long absence from home. As it is still largely unclear whether the strategy of total reduplication is systematically employed for this purpose, the best we can do is classifying it as a possibly iconic means to represent differences in the extension over time of events and processes. Clearly, the West-Greenlandic case comes close to a durative.

Similary, in Maltese, verbs and especially infinite forms of verbs can be totally reduplicated to indicate long duration or continuation of processes as in (12).

(12) Maltese [Aħ 6]
U *jiena* *wkoll* *in-ħoss-ni* ***nieżel*** ***nieżel***
and I also 1SG-feel.IMPERF-1SG.O **descend.PART** **descend.PART**
lejn *Wied* *l-Ispirt-i*
towards river DET-ghost-PL
'And I too felt like **continuously descending** towards the River of the Ghosts.'

The sentence would be perfectly well-formed with only one participle *nieżel* 'descending', however it would loose the meaning component of long duration. One participle alone indicates that the participant is on his way down to the river, two identical participles invoke the temporal extension of the process of reaching the river (and indirectly also suggest that the path itself is rather long and thus the construction has both temporal and spatial implications).

This section has shown that not only plurality is iconically represented by reduplication but also long duration. Plurality and long duration have in common that both are conceptually more of what is associated with singular and short duration (or punctual aspect, for that matter). This additional element leads to a more complex meaning which is expressed by more complex *signantia.* This parallel behaviour of the two sides of the linguistic sign is iconic. The subsequent section highlights a semantic property which connects plurality to long duration and these two to other categories expressed by reduplication.

2.1.3 *Intensity*

There is a third area for which reduplication is most commonly employed in the languages of the world, namely intensification. As a matter of fact, it is exactly this function which is cross-linguistically so wide-spread that it approaches the status of a universal. Its potential universality makes intensification a good candidate for the prototypical function of reduplicative constructions from which other functions (such as the ones discussed above) are derived. Before elaborating on this issue, I discuss a selection of pertinent cases of intensification.

In Classical Aztec, the (C)V:-reduplication pattern is not only used to mark the frequentative (as in [7.1] and [8.1]) but it also invites a qualitative reading: "On a alors des verbes 'intensifs' qui marquent une appréciation quantitative ou qualitative ('faire qqch. fortement, ou fréquamment, ou avec application, ou avec une intention particulière') (Launey 1981: 264)".[12] In (13), the two readings of the reduplicated verb form are given as alternatives. The unreduplicated verb form *tzàtzi* would just mean 'he cries', in combination with *huel* 'well' it would render the meaning of 'he cries well; he knows how to cry' (Launey 1981: 113).

(13) Classical Aztec (Launey 1981: 264)
Huel *tzā-tzàtzi*
well RED-cry
'He cries very **loudly/often**.'

For the same purpose, total reduplication of finite verbs is employed in Maltese. This strategy is illustrated by Example (14).

(14) Maltese [Mq 12]
daħl-et *t-għaġġel* *t-għaġġel*
enter.PERF-3SG.F 3SG.F-**hasten**.IMPERF 3SG.F-**hasten**.IMPERF
'She went inside **very quickly**.'

Information about the manner in which a movement is executed is very often provided by a separately inflected finite verb (mostly in the imperfective), which accompanies the primary predicate (often in the perfective), which in turn provides information about the movement in general and/or the directionality. The order of these predicates is fixed with secondary predication following primary predication. The finite verb *daħlet* 'she entered' is a full-blown grammatically correct sentence. With the addition of *tgħaġġel* 'she hastens', the action of entering is depicted as happening quickly. The total reduplication of the secondary predication indicates that the speed with which the agent entered (the room) exceeds the norm associated with quickness – ergo: very quickly. The meaning of quickly is thus intensified via reduplication along the same lines as the meaning of crying is intensified in (13).

Doing something more intensively than normally would be the case implies that the conceptual basis associated with the norm is made more complex. In a manner of speaking, intensification extends the meaning associated with the

12. My translation: "Thus, there are 'intensive' verbs which mark a quantitative or qualitative evaluation ('to do sth. strongly or often or diligently or with a special intention')."

norm and thus there is more of what the norm represents. This observation also holds for those word-classes or syntactic functions for which reduplication is attested abundantly, viz. adjectives, adverbs or – where these word-classes do not exist independently – (adnominal and adverbal) modifiers in general.[13] In (15), adjectival and adverbial instances of total reduplication are illustrated by examples from Welsh. Partial reduplication in Chamorro follows in (16).

(15) Welsh

(15.1) Adjectival [LPP Welsh II, 15]

Achos	*mai*	*lle*	***bach***	***bach***	*sy*	*gen*	*i*
reason	that.is	place	**small**	**small**	REL.is	with	1SG

'Because it is a **very small** place that I have.'

(15.2) Adverbial [HP Welsh, 167]

Cerddai	*'n*	***gyflym***	***gyflym***
go:IMPER.3SG	in	**speedy**	**speedy**

'He went **very quickly**.'

Both *bach* 'small' and *cyflym* 'speedy' are adjectives but *cyflym* is regularly adverbialised by the free morpheme *'n* (< *yn* 'in'), which also causes the initial consonant of the following word to be lenited. In both sentences, total reduplication is not needed to make the constructions grammatically acceptable. One instance of *bach* alone suffices to characterise *lle* 'place' as small. Likewise, one instance of *cyflym* is enough to give the idea of something being done quickly. However, if intensified meaning is intended, then total reduplication is called for. The double occurrences of *bach* and *cyflym* emphasise that the place is very small and that the person moved very quickly, respectively. In a way, *bach bach* encodes more of *bach* i.e. of smallness whereas *gyflym gyflym* encodes more of *gyflym* i.e. of speediness.

In (16), the situation of modern Chamorro is surveyed.

13. In a variety of cases, the resulting constructions are vague as to the scope of the reduplication. In Hungarian for instance, the nominal adverbial in (i) consists of the total reduplication of a case-inflected noun.

i. Hungarian [LPP Hungarian XXVI, 2]

Erre	*elkezdenek*	*ágálni*	*és*	*csak*	*forognak*	***kör-be* = *kör-be***
then	start:3PL	complain:INF	and	only	turn:3PL	**circle**-INESS = **circle**-INESS

'Then they start complaining and turn **round and round** (lit. **in circle in circle**).'

The total reduplication of *körbe* 'in (a) circle' may have two effects: first of all, it signals that the circular motion is repeated giving rise to several circles (note that the regular plural *körökbe* 'in circles' is not used here); secondly, the verb is modified adverbially such that an iterative/frequentative meaning is added.

(16) Chamorro (Topping 1973: 183)

simple		reduplicated	
ñalang	'hungry'	*ñá**la**lang*	'very hungry'
dánkolo	'big'	*dánkolo**lo***	'very big'
metgot	'strong'	*métgo**go**t*	'very strong'
bunita	'pretty'	*buníta**ta***	'very pretty'

In contrast to the progressive, which requires the reduplicated (C)V-sequence to copy part of the stressed syllable of a word (cf. [10.2] above), the so-called intensifier reduplication affects the last possible CV-sequence of a word independent of stress-site. The reduplicated word forms exceeds the length of the simple forms by one syllable. In addition, their semantics is such that reference is made to a higher degree of the quality represented by the simple form.

If we compare the three major patterns of iconic reduplication, we immediately recognise the conceptual parallels which connect them to each other, cf. (17).

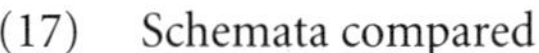

(17) Schemata compared

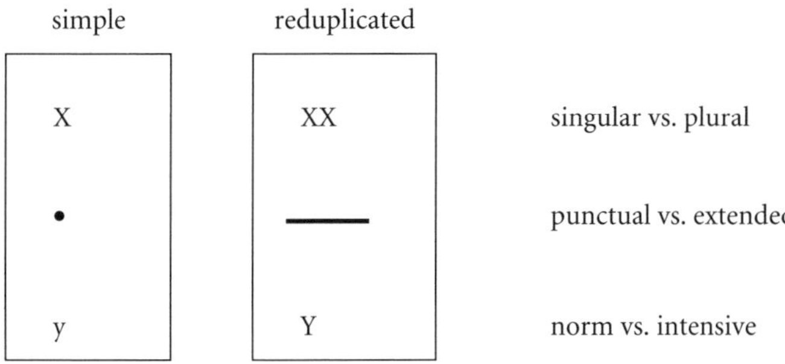

On the left, the concepts associated with the non-reduplicated forms are represented whereas the ones expressed by reduplication are placed to the right. It strikes the eye that simple form goes along with simple concepts. Complex form, however, fits complex concepts. What unites the complex concepts is the fact that, one way or the other, they contain more of what is in the respective simple counterpart. Therefore, it is justified to subsume the three above iconic relations under one common pattern (Stolz 2006: 123). For expository reasons, the simplest representation for all three is identical to the one put forward for number distinctions where one X stands for the simple concept and XX accordingly represents the complex concept. In this way, the unified schema (18) resembles the one for iconicity in general in (2).

(18) Unified schema

	simple	reduplicated
concept	X	XX

The idea suggests itself to equate the higher degree of conceptual complexity of those categories which are expressed by reduplicative constructions with a general property intensity. Trivially, intensification is the prototypical realisation of this property. Moreover, plural and temporal extension can also be understood as instances of intensification albeit in a slightly metaphorical way: what is more of X is also intensively X. The combination of more of content X and more of expression X instantiates iconicity if less of content X also goes along with less of expression X. However, this golden rule appears to be violated by a variety of cases as the subsequent section demonstrates.

2.2 What fails to be iconic...

There are two relational patterns which counterbalance iconicity. Pairs of linguistic signs whose *signantia* and/or *signata* are equally complex classify as non-iconic, cf. (19). Wherever the conceptually less complex category receives the more complex expression of two linguistic signs, counter-iconicity applies, cf. (20). Since the latter constellation more seriously challenges the idea that iconicity motivates the use of reduplicative structures (Stolz 2006: 126–9), I will focus on them in what follows. The discussion of non-iconic cases will be reserved for a later occasion.

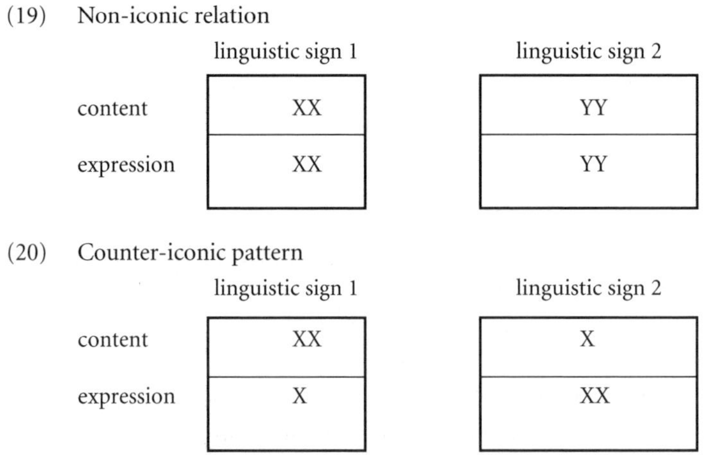

For practical reasons, I dwell especially on diminution (and related categories like attenuation) as the most prominent representative of counter-iconicity. Hurch/ Mattes (2005: 146) argue that iconicity cannot be the sole driving force for reduplicative patterns, although it may be cognitively dominant. Imitative (= the category with which similarity but not identity is encoded), certain tenses/aspects, diminution, and attenuation as categories expressed by reduplication are said to run counter to iconicity-based models of reduplication. The counter-evidence speaking against iconicity is not particularly convincing when it comes to analysing tense/aspect categories as the examples provided by the above scholars are fully in line with the schema in (9): frequentative, successive action, iterative etc. are aspectual distinctions all of which involve plurality of events. Owing to the fact that no deviant theory of aspect is provided, I consider this part of the argument of Hurch/Mattes (2005: 150–2) beside the point (except perhaps Tagalog future).[14] This is different however with the remainder of their data which thus deserve to be looked at more closely especially because, in cross-linguistic perspective, diminution is so frequently encoded by reduplication that it cannot be declared an exception (Hurch/Mattes 2005: 146).

For a start, I briefly mention the notorious examples for reduplicative diminution in colloquial French (Rainer 1998: 280): *bête* 'daft' → *bébête* 'a little daft', *fils* 'son' → *fifils* 'little son', *lapin* 'hare' → *pinpin* 'pet hare', *mère* 'mother' → *mémé* 'dear mother', etc. These cases attest to partial reduplication – sometimes accompanied by the loss of segmental material of the non-reduplicated form. Since reduplication is employed to signal diminution (mostly with hypochoristic connotations), we are facing a paradox in terms of iconicity: more form is used to express less content – that is at least what comes to mind first if one interprets the diminutive to mean less of the quality expressed by the non-reduplicated form. Whether or not this is the correct way of seeing things will be discussed below. Suffice it here to question that a little son is less of a son. However, is a little son perhaps more of a son? With a view at better understanding the potential counter-examples, I continue the survey with examples from attenuation. Consider the Hindi examples in (21). Two adjectives – *kaccaa* 'raw' and *niilii* 'blue' – are totally reduplicated. However, the meaning ascribed to the reduplicative construction surprisingly is not 'very raw' nor 'very blue'. In lieu of intensification *kaccaa kaccaa* and *niilii niilii* represent diminution or attenuation, i.e., the meaning of the simple adjective is depicted as applying only to a lesser degree: slightly raw is less than raw just as bluish is less than blue.

(21) Hindi

(21.1) Taste and ripeness (Abbi 1980: 94)

kaccaa	***kaccaa***	*amruud*	*laanaa*
raw	**raw**	guava	bring

'Bring a **slightly raw** guava!'

(21.2) Colours (Abbi 1980: 95)

uske	*paas*	*ek*	***niilii***	***niilii***	*ṭopii*	*hai*
he	have.3SG	one	**blue**	**blue**	cap	be.3SG

'He has a **bluish** cap.'

14. On the other hand, I absolutely agree with Hurch/Mattes (2005: 153–4) on their most important claim according to which not all cases of partial reduplication can be diachronically derived from total reduplication via grammaticalisation – a point of view which also takes issue with Inkelas/Zoll (2005), though only indirectly.

Superficially, more expression material is used for less content and thus we are facing counter-iconicity. Total reduplication is employed to encode that what is mentioned twice is there to a degree which fails to reach the level of the norm. In point of fact, attenuation via reduplication is a pattern which is attested in a wide variety of languages world-wide. There are areal hotbeds: Abbi (1992: 69–73), for instance, has found evidence for attenuative reduplication in practically all phyla of the Indian sub-continent: in her sample, Indo-Aryan languages (Hindi, Punjabi, Dogri), Austro-Asiatic languages (Kharia, Khasi), Dravidian languages (Telugu, Kurukh) and Tibeto-Burman languages (Meitei) employ total reducplication for the purpose of attenuation. However, as Abbi (1992: 73) emphasises "it is only certain kinds of nominal modifiers which can be used for attenuation/approximation when reduplicated," namely those which refer to taste and/or colour. Similar phenomena can be observed in many languages spoken outside the South Asian region. According to Bakker (2003: 76), all colour terms of the English-based creole Saramaccan may be attenuated via total reduplication: *geli* 'yellow' → *geli-geli* 'yellowish', *guun* 'green' → *guun guun* 'greenish', *weti* 'white' → *weti weti* 'whitish', etc. Furthermore, Kouwenberg/LaCharité (2003: 9–10) provide a long list of non-iconic/counter-iconic cases of reduplication in Caribbean creoles among which diminution is relatively wide-spread. Especially intriguing are those relatively frequent cases where segmentally identical patterns of reduplication have two different readings whose disambiguation often depends on prosodic properties. Sentence (22) from the French-based creole Haitian is a case in point: the adjective *dus* 'sweet' is subject to total reduplication. If the lexical tone of *dus* remains unaffected by the reduplication, the meaning is intensification. However, if reduplication is accompanied by falling intonation, attenuation applies.

(22) Haitian (Sylvain 1979: 42)
Mãžé-sa-a **dus-dus**
food-DEM-DET **sweet-sweet**
'This food is (a) **very sweet**/(b) **sweetish**.'

This vagueness/ambiguity of the reduplicative construction on the segmental level seems to support the idea that iconicity is not as important as assumed for reduplication. If we disregard suprasegmentals for the sake of the argument, two widely divergent meanings can be associated with the same chain of segments – and only one of these meanings implies the increase of the property expressed by the non-reduplicated form whereas the competing reading invokes the opposite, namely the decrease of the same property. As will be shown below (Section 4), this potential counter-evidence can be turned into supporting evidence for iconicity exactly because two divergent meanings are involved.

Besides diminution and attenuation, the similative/imitative belongs to the functional domain of reduplication in a variety of languages. Behind this category, there are two notions, namely similarity and pretension. The similative/imitative expresses that something is similar to but not identical with something else. The category indicates that what is expressed is not the real thing, in a manner of speaking. Thus, reduplication appears to be used counter-iconically because more expressive material is employed in order to highlight the fact that the content of the simple non-reduplicated form does not fully apply. For Riau Indonesian, Gil (2005) identifies reduplicative patterns which invite a reading that connects to playfulness and pretension. Example (23) illustrates this.

(23) Riau Indonesian (Gil 2005: 59)
saya ***ti****-tidur* *saya* *tahu*
1:SG RED-sleep 1:SG know
'I was **only pretending** to sleep, I knew [what she was doing].'

The partial reduplication of the verb *tidur* 'sleep' indicates that what actually happened was not sleeping. The speaker pretended to be asleep while he observed what someone else was doing. The meaning component of pretence is introduced via additional segmental material. More segments, more syllables and more morphs are necessary to encode less than the meaning of the lexical morpheme – if we accept that pretending to sleep is somehow less of sleeping. The same applies to those cases in which reduplication encodes resemblance as in Saramaccan, cf. (24). In most of the cases, the reduplicative similitive construction can be replaced by a prepositional phrase containing *kuma* 'as, like' → *kuma X* 'like X' (Bakker 2003: 76).

(24) Saramaccan (Bakker 2003: 76)

simple	meaning	reduplicated	meaning
baafu	'soup'	*baafu-baafu*	'soup-like'
puili	'powder'	*puili-puili*	'powder-like'
fania	'rice-meal'	*fania-fania*	'medicine'
dombo	'clot'	*dombo-dombo*	'clotty'
wara	'water'	*wata-wata*	'watery'

The simple forms indicate the norm whereas the reduplications are used to characterise the property as not being identical to the norm. Being soup-like is tantamount to failing to be soup. Soup-like stuff is not really soup. Again, the constellation of simple and reduplicated forms and their distribution over functions and meanings is suggestive of counter-iconicity because the more complex construction is employed to express the fact that some entity lacks a number of traits which are needed however to make this entity conform to the norm. In a way, more expression marks the lack of content units.

Diminution, attenuation, similative and imitative share one important element. In all of these categories, the fact is highlighted that a given entity falls short of fulfilling the required criteria to pass as what is indicated by the non-reduplicated form.

Thus, there is always not enough of property X. The lack of X is highlighted by these reduplicative constructions. At the same time, the expressions employed for this purpose are more complex than the ones used for the norm. In (25), I try to capture the convergence between the counter-iconic patterns.

(25) Schemata of counter-iconicity

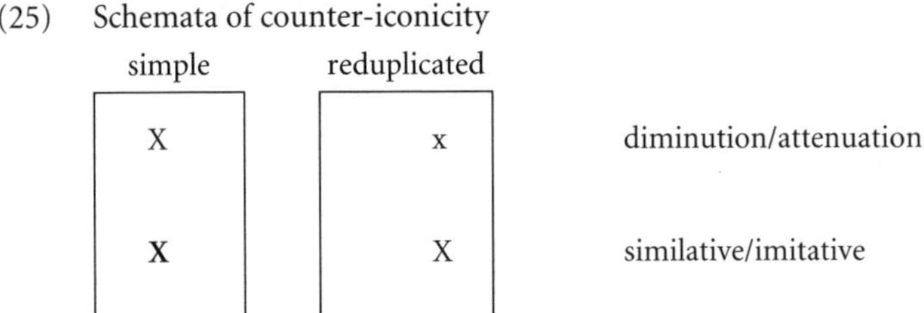

The difference in size of the symbols is meant to reflect the difference between norm and diminutive/attenuative. For the similative and imitative, the lack of boldface is indicative of the absence of one essential property which defines the norm. As a matter of fact, the schemata can be unified easily because both associate with the absence of some property.

Another remarkable instance of (apparent) counter-iconicity is the use of total reduplication to mark the singular in one class of nouns in Itelmen.[15] The table in (26) contains the nominative and locative case forms in the singular and the plural of four nouns. Throughout the singular, the lexical morpheme is reduplicated, whereas in the plural, the lexical morpheme occurs only once. Given that both singular and plural forms of these nouns are always morphologically complex, one cannot consider the plural forms to represent the simpler alternative. Nevertheless, the presence of total reduplication in the category, which is normally the conceptually basic one, calls for an explanation.

(26) Itelmen (Georg/Volodin 1999: 63)

Nominative		Locative		meaning
SG	PL	SG	PL	
tam-tam	*tam-əʔn*	***tam-tam**-ank*	*tam-əʔn-k*	deformity
k’uf-k‘uf	*k’f-əʔn*	***k’uf-k’uf**-enk*	*k’f-əʔn-k*	agnail
lop-lop	*lop-aʔn*	***lop-lop**-ank*	*lop-aʔn-k*	joint
ç’u-ç‘u	*ç’u-ʔn*	***ç’u-ç’u**-nk*	*ç’u-ʔn-k*	salmon

The reduplicated *tam-tam* associates automatically with the singular whereas simple *tam* has a plural meaning. The number distinction goes along with a counter-iconic

15. For similar phenomena in the related language Chukchi, see Rubino (2005: 18).

use of expressive means: the more complex construction represents the conceptually basic category – at least on superficial inspection. On this basis, it is possible to add the Itelmen case to the inventory of schemata in (25). As the schema for the Itelmen number hierarchy is the inverse of the one included in (17), we may subsume all counter-iconic patterns under (27), which is the opposite of the unified schema of iconic relation in (18).

(27) Unified schema (counter-iconicity)

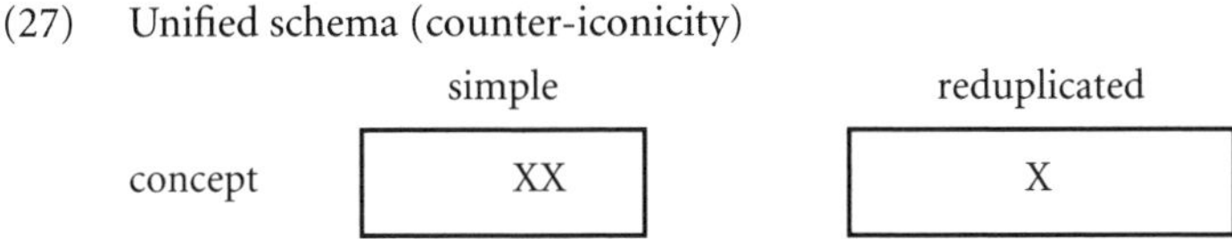

In sum, the evidence adduced above suggests that the principles developed on the basis of bona fide instances of iconic relations cannot simply be applied to the cases discussed in this section. This impossibility has given linguists food for thought. As mentioned already in Section 2, various attempts have been made to explain the co-existence of conceptually divergent functions within the domain of one and the same construction type. The positions reach from denying that iconicity has a say in the grammar of reduplication at all via hypotheses according to which iconicity is restricted to one particular segment of the functional domain of reduplication to those viewpoints which try to find a common denominator for iconic, non-iconic and counter-iconic patterns. For the present purpose, I side with the latter group. In the subsequent section, I briefly address the issue of local markedness in order to demonstrate that what appears to be counter-iconic might as well be just another instance of iconicity.

3. Markedness

The Itelmen example in (26) is a good starting point for developing my argument. What we see in the table in (26) is just a fragment of the entire number-marking system of Itelmen (Stolz 2006: 124–5). Reduplication as a number-marking device is attested only for a relatively restricted group of nouns (about 100 according to Georg/Volodin 1999: 62), whereas elsewhere in the system the singular-plural distinction is marked by bound affixal morphology. Both numbers are normally marked by suffixes. However, only the singular allows for a zero-allomorph. Interestingly, the singular affixes are at times morphologically more complex expressions than the ones used for the plural: SG = {0, *-m, -n, -ŋ, -ç, -lŋin, -miŋ*} vs. PL = {*-ʔ, -ʔn, -sx*} (Georg/Volodin 1999: 64). Thus, beside iconic patterns like SG *pahel* 'cap' → PL *pahel-ʔ* 'caps' and SG *kamlo-n* 'grand-child' → PL *kamlo-ʔn* 'grand-children', there are also non-iconic or counter-iconic ones as, e.g., SG *kḷime-lŋin* 'kidney' → PL *kḷime-ʔn* 'kidneys', although iconic patterns (with plural predominantly marked by *-ʔn*) seem to be more frequent (Georg/Volodin 1999: 64–7). In addition to the bipartite singular-plural distinction, Itelmen also has a collective in *–al* which interacts with the two aforementioned numbers in peculiar ways, cf. SG *wa-ç* 'stone' → PL *wa-ʔn* 'stones' → COLL *waw-al* 'stony place' (Georg/Volodin 1999: 68). The presence of a potential third number collective is suggestive of the existence of a fourth distinction, viz. the singulative. Since the distribution of Itelmen nouns over number distinctions is not sufficiently clear, I illustrate the workings of a number system which combines singular-plural and singulative-collective distinctions with material drawn from a better known language.

Local markedness is a well-known phenomenon (Tiersma 1999). Certain lexico-semantic areas behave differently from the bulk of the lexicon when it comes to applying grammatical rules. This observation is at the heart of lexical typology. The paradigm-case of what Mayerthaler (1981) calls markedness reversal – a terminological alternative for local markedness – is number marking in systems which distinguish collective from singulative. In Welsh, collective-singulative distinctions co-exist and interact paradigmatically with singular-plural distinctions (Cuzzolin 1998). While the latter correspond relatively closely to what the iconic patterns discussed in Section 2.1 look like (SG *peth* 'thing' → PL *peth-au* 'things', for instance), the collective-singulative opposition turns the relation upside down – or so it seems. The expression referring to a single individual is more complex than the one which refers to groups of such entities (generically or collectively). As a rule, the collective is morphologically simple or less complex than the singulative. The singulative, on the other hand, is always morphologically more complex than the collective as it contains the additional gender-sensitive number affix *–yn/-en*. An absolutely incomplete list of pertinent examples is provided in (28).

(28) Welsh (Stolz 2001: 65–70)

simple		complex	
collective	meaning	singulative	meaning
picwn	'wasps'	*picwnen*	'wasp'
egnod	'fleas'	*egnodyn*	'fleas'
mogrug	'ants'	*mogrugyn*	'ant'
moch	'pigs'	*mochyn*	'pig'
dincod	'seeds'	*dincodyn*	'a grain of seed'
blew	'hair(s)'	*blewyn*	'a hair'
llwch	'dust'	*llychyn*	'a grain of dust'
bedw	'birches'	*bedwen*	'birch-tree'
celfi	'furniture'	*celficyn*	'a piece of furniture'

The number of nouns which partake in the collective-singulative system is considerably larger than (28) suggests. Moreover, it is also possible to make semantically-based predictions about which nouns allow for a formal distinction of collective and singulative and which ones fail to do so. The distinction is rule-governed, systematic and productive (Stolz 2001: 68–9). As a matter of fact, the semantic diversity of the nouns listed above is no obstacle to identifying conceptual affinities which link them to one another. All of the nouns refer to entities which normally come in great numbers or large amounts. Wasps, fleas, ants, pigs and sundry animals more often than not live in swarms, flocks and herds. Thus, one conceives of these animate beings as (members of) collectives. There needs to be a special reason to individualise a member of these collectives. The same applies to the remaining cases: seeds, dust, hair are again entities whose expected "life-form" is collective – a single grain of dust, for instance, is already something out of the ordinary. This extraordinary status is perhaps less evident for trees and pieces of furniture, although one may assume that the normal way in which birches (or other trees) grow is in grove-like groups (as the opposition COLL *coed* 'wood, forest' → SGL *coed-en* 'a tree' suggests). This argumentation can be extended to furniture because we normally expect one's lodgings to be made comfortable with a number of pieces of furniture.[16]

If we reformulate conceptual complexity along the lines of default expectancy, we can postulate a large group of nouns for which the individual item is the expected form of the referent. This group may compete with those nouns for which the collective is most representative of the typical form in which the referents occur. This is schematically represented in (29).

(29) Collective vs singulative - conceptually

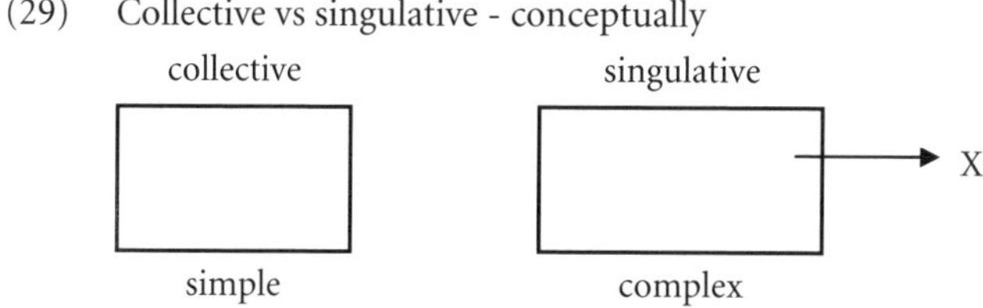

The singulative highlights ("singles out") one segment of the referents covered by the concept underlying the collective and therefore involves an additional conceptual

16. A trickier case is the one example of a human noun that still forms part of the collective-singulative system: COLL *plant* 'offspring' → SGL *plent-yn* 'a child'. Presently, families tend to be rather small in comparison to what was the norm in the (not too distant) past. Even though this is somewhat speculative, I dare to hypothesise that in former times an only child was somewhat odd, whereas more extended families with a lot of offsprings were considered normal. In this way, the collective-singulative opposition may also be a relic of a period in which the formal expression was motivated by culturally-based expectancy.

element which singles out a member of the collective. The singulative is conceptually more complex than the collective and accordingly requires the more complex expression. Thus, the collective is the unmarked member of the pair of categories as opposed to the singulative whereas the singular is the unmarked number in contrast to the plural wherever these conceptual differences translate into hard grammatical facts in a given language. Of course, this statement of relatively well-known facts does not solve our original problem. Local markedness – in this case the lower degree of expectancy for individuals of a certain class to occur – does not make the observed patterns more iconic as long as iconicity is equated with a difference in size and number such that the conceptually more complex category is associated with more of what is implied by the conceptually basic category. In Section 4, I will argue for a revision of this quantity-oriented understanding of iconicity.

4. Iconicity revisited

In Section 2.2, I discussed a small selection of examples from Creole languages which employ segmentally identical reduplicative constructions for two rather diverse functions. Intensification (or augmentation) and diminution/attenuation are often expressed by identical chains of segments which, however, tend to be prosodically distinct (although we still lack sufficient information about the suprasegmental facts of many of these languages). A language which also allows for divergent functions to associate with the same reduplicative patterns without, however, resorting to suprasegmental means of disambiguation is the Austronesian language Paiwan spoken on Taiwan. Egli (1990: 31) reports that the functional domain of reduplication comprises pluralisation, diminution/attenuation, emphasis (= intensification), distributive, and progressive/iterative/durative. Reduplication can be partial or total in Paiwan. In addition, reduplication very often co-occurs with affixation. Since pluralisation, intensification and diminution affects members of the same word-classes ("nouns" and "adjectives"), these two functions are given prominence here. The table in (30) provides a selection of reduplicative patterns which invite two readings each.

(30) Two readings per pattern (Egli 1999: 35–46)

lexeme	meaning	reduplication	iconic	counter-iconic
quma	'field'	*quma-quma*	'fields'	'little field'
berhung	'hole'	*berhung-berhung*	'holes'	'small hole'
umaq	'house'	*uma-umaq*	'houses'	'small house'
sikau	'net bag'	*sikau-kau*	'net bags'	'small net bag'
ngatsi	'flask'	*ngatsi-ngatsi*	'flasks'	'small flask'

vulavan	'silver pot'	*vulava-lavan*	'silver pots'	'small silver pot'
alak	'child'	*alak-alak*	'children'	'infant; doll'
kudrar	'big'	*kudra-kudrar*	'very big'	'biggish'
kedri	'small'	*kedri-kedri*	'very small'	'smallish'
qujil	'red'	*qujil-jil*	'very red'	'reddish'
rajai	'sharp'	*raja-jai*	'very sharp'	'sharpish'
vurung	'old'	*vuru-vurung*	'very old'	'somewhat old'

In the absence of suprasegmental markers, the correct interpretation of the reduplicative patterns depends crucially on contextual information. There must be contexts in which only one of the two possible readings makes sense. What is important to know is whether or not the reduplicative pattern is polysemous and thus both meanings co-exist as such on the content side of the linguistic sign. If so, the context activates the meaning which fits semantically. According to this idea, iconicity would apply in some contexts only whereas counter-iconicity applies elsewhere. The semantic ambiguity would also imply that different degrees of iconicity reside in the same linguistic sign waiting for a trigger. Another possibility which does not solve the problem because it just postpones the necessity to explain: homophony of two distinct linguistic signs with different iconic potential.

However, it is also possible to resort to semantic vagueness and assume that the two readings can be derived from a semantically less specified common core meaning. This common meaning is deviation from X (Pott 1862: 102). With a view to explaining what is meant by this, I have to call to mind an idea put forward by Ewald Lang (adopted by Wurzel 1987: 477–82). He provides a formal account of the increasing conceptual complexity of categories in extended paradigms such as the comparative systems of adjectives. In this treatment, counter-iconicity is prevented from becoming an obstacle mainly by avoiding diagrammaticity as basic principle of iconicity. Thus, constructions may be in an iconic relation although their segmental complexity does not invite an iconic interpretation. Iconicity still applies because the "semantische Repräsentation wird komplexer in dem Maße, wie der Spielraum ihrer Interpretationsmöglichkeiten auf der Ebene der konzeptuellen Struktur als Reflex grammatischer Strukturbildung systematisch eingeschränkt wird" (Lang [Wurzel 1987: 482]).[17] Even though this idea cannot be applied fully to the above cases, there is one important element in the quote which may lead to a solution of the general problem outlined in the foregoing sections, namely the

17. My translation: "semantic representation becomes more complex to the extent to which its range of possible interpretations on the level of conceptual structure as a reflex of grammatical structuring is systematically subject to restriction."

fact that the range of possible interpretations is said to be shrinking constantly – implying that the stronger the restrictions the higher the degree of markedness. The restrictions have to be specified in the conceptual representation and thus make the representations of the more marked categories more complex. Therefore, iconicity is primarily a matter of conceptual complexity, its representation and ease of processing. In the case of apparent counter-iconicity however, it is still possible to operate on the basis of diagrammaticity – in addition to Lang's idea of restricted range of interpretation making it necessary to add elements to the conceptual representation of categories.

Consider the examples in (30) again. What have plurals and diminutives in common? They are both marked categories: the plural is the marked partner of the singular, the diminutive is the marked partner of the derivational basis. In both cases, the unmarked partner is represented by a morphologically simple word form whereas the marked members of the oppositions require reduplicative constructions. If we accept the idea that the non-reduplicated form represents a kind of norm or prototype, then both plural and diminutive count as deviations from the norm/prototype. The fact that there is a deviation from a norm/prototype affects the conceptual representation of the categories because the concepts of plural and diminutive require two components in lieu of one: in addition to what constitutes the concept of the prototype there must also be information about the failure to coincide fully with the norm. This situation is reflected schematically by (31).

(31) Conceptual representation

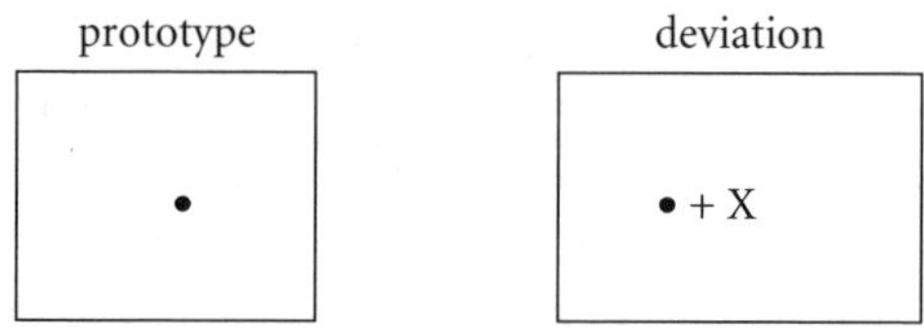

With a view to representing a deviation, the norm from which something deviates has to be co-present in the concept of the category to which deviation can be ascribed. This additional element X may have various spell-outs. In the case of the plural, X stands for a perhaps infinite replication of what is the norm/prototype, i.e., the content of X is additive (and thus determines to what degree the deviation exceeds the norm). For the diminutive, the picture is different to the extent that X is basically subtractive in the sense that it indicates that the deviation falls short of fulfilling the expectations associated with the norm/prototype. At this point, Lang's model comes in handy as it dissociates iconicity from diagrammaticity – at least as diagrammaticity is most commonly understood, namely that there must be more of a property Y expressed by more segmental material as opposed to another linguistic sign. Indeed, diminution does not imply the increase of the features which belong to the semantic matrix of the derivational basis. In spite of this failure to replicate features which are already present in the prototype/norm, the diminutive nevertheless calls for a conceptual representation which is more complex than the one of the derivational basis. What is iconic in this respect is the relation that holds between the linguistic sign representing the derivational basis and the linguistic sign representing the diminutive because the latter is conceptually more complex and at the same time also receives the more complex expression. This analysis can be applied to the plural, too, without necessarily resorting to the replication of features of the prototype. If both diminutive and plural are deviations from a norm/prototype, then it is sufficient to explain their parallel behaviour with one and the same principle – in this case with the fact that their conceptual representation is more complex than the one of the norm/prototype. (32) is an attempt to illustrate this parallel behaviour schematically.

(32) Conceptual representation

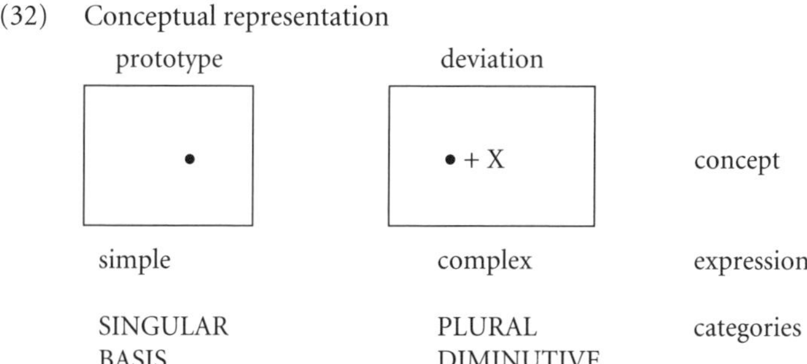

This deviation-based model is easily applicable to those cases of iconicity and counter-iconicity discussed in Sections 2.1–2.2. For all categories which are traditionally viewed as instances of iconicity, it can be assumed that their content implies a deviation from a given prototype or norm. In these cases, the deviation corresponds to a surplus of the content associated with the prototype. Wherever counter-iconicity is reported to apply according to the usual criteria of determining iconicity, these cases can be re-interpreted along the lines of the Paiwan diminutive – meaning: similative, attenuative and singulative are categories whose conceptual representation involves the prototype plus an element X with subtractive content. In this way, it is possible to extend the domain of iconicity such that it comprises not only relations which involve an increase of those features which are already present in the basic category but also relations for which deviation has to be specified. Counter-iconicity thus, turns into a variant of iconicity in the sense that the deviation from the norm/prototype is conceptually represented by an element X which has subtractive content in lieu of additive content.

5. Areas and beyond

If we take reduplication to mean exact copying of segmental material, then, from a Mediterranean point of view, there is hardly any reason to search for an integrative model of iconicity of the kind exposed in Section 4. Owing to the almost total absence of systematic cases of non-iconic and counter-iconic reduplication in the Circum-Mediterranean languages,[18] the traditional understanding of iconicity would suffice to describe the situation in this area. Admittedly, genuine instances of plural marking via reduplication have not been reported so far. However, distributives of the kind illustrated by Example (6) from Maltese are well-attested in practically all languages spoken along the shores of the Central and Eastern Mediterranean no matter to which phylum they belong (Stolz 2004: 37–42). The use of total reduplication for the function of intensification, however, has a much wider geographic distribution and reaches far into other European territories to the North of the Mediterranean basin (Stolz 2004: 31–5). Diminution and sundry seemingly problematic categories do not qualify as Mediterraneanisms.

The situation changes as soon as we allow for segmental modification to accompany the reduplication process. In the Levant and neighbouring regions, reduplication-cum-variation on the copy is an areal feature whose origins are still a matter of debate (Müller 2004). The typical pattern is well known from Turkish – but it also occurs productively in Georgian, Armenian, Kurdish, Abkhaz, Lezgian, Lebanese Arabic, Arumanian as well as in historical or non-standard varieties of Bulgarian, Macedonian, Neo Greek, Rumanian, Persian (Stolz/Sansò in press), cf. (33).

(33) Turkish (Ersen-Rasch 1984: 326)
bira mira *iç-me-d-im*
beer "m-eer" drink-NEG-PAST-1SG
'I didn't drink **beer or the like**.'

In this example, the reduplication of the noun *bira* 'beer' consists of the copy of all segments but the initial one which is regularly replaced by the bilabial nasal /m/. The resulting word-form *mira* does not have a meaning of its own, i.e., its interpretation is completely dependent on the co-presence of *bira*. What those m-initial copies encode, however, is the deviation of the additional referents from the prototype determined by the basic noun. The meaning range of *mira* in combination with *bira* are all beverages which share with *bira* the fact of being alcoholic but fail to qualify as proper instances of beer. It is logical to consider this pattern of reduplication even more iconic than the ones discussed above because the

18. There are some relics of a previously more widely used pattern of diminutive partial reduplication in modern Hebrew, which have been inherited as lexicalised forms from Old Hebrew.

deviation in conceptual properties is reflected by the deviation on the segmental level: since the initial consonant of the basic noun is not copied but replaced by something different, the copy also deviates from the original. One segment is not faithfully copied – and this is indicative of a subtractive content of the additional component X needed for the conceptual representation of what is encoded by the reduplicative pattern. Interestingly, in those languages which employ m-initial reduplication patterns, total reduplication without segmental modification is functionally confined to iconic relations in the traditional sense of the term – notably distributive reduplication and intensification.

The evidence from the Eastern part of the Mediterranean has a remarkable parallel in the areally wide-spread patterns of reduplication-cum-variation in the languages of South Asia (especially India) as described by Abbi (1992). The differences in phonological qualities of the replacive segments notwithstanding, Mediterranean and South Asian patterns concur in so far as their functions are concerned. In both areas, reduplication-cum-variation refers to list-like groups of potential referents which resemble the one represented by the non-reduplicated word but fail to qualify as an instantiation of the same ontological class. The list-like character of the construction is clearly associated to pluralisation (section 2.1) and thus motivates the use of reduplication. The variation of initial segments on original and copy, however, is indicative of deviation. In contrast to the Levant, South Asian languages employ reduplication without variation not only for distributive but also for attenuation/diminution in certain lexico-semantic fields (cf. examples in [21]).

Thus, some areas prefer to distinguish formally those reduplicative patterns which encode additive content from others whose conceptual representation includes an element with subtractive content. Elsewhere, additive and subtractive components do not trigger different expressions or reduplicative patterns. The fact that both can be expressed by the same means speaks in favour of a common conceptual background. In the above discussion, I have identified this shared component as an element that indicates deviation from a norm or prototype. The conceptual bridge deviation allows us to formulate an integrative account for both iconic and counter-iconic relations which, according to the traditional viewpoint, do not lend themselves to being united under one roof. To my mind, iconicity is a principle which cannot be reduced to situations in which a difference in size/amount is made larger. Iconicity also applies if the conceptual representation of differences between the contents of two linguistic signs requires additional components in one of them – and at the same time affects the expression side such that the more complex concept goes along with the more complex expression. Viewed from this angle, the supposed dichotomy of iconic vs. counter-iconic relations dissolves into different realisations of iconicity.

It remains to be seen whether this new understanding of iconicity can also be extended to non-iconic relations. Moreover, it is likewise necessary to check the deviation-based model of iconicity against a much richer empirical basis which should also include diachronic evidence. I do not claim that each and every formally encoded relation in language follows the semiotic principles of iconicity. However, I am convinced that much of what is commonly believed to be counter-evidence against the workings of iconicity in the realm of reduplication is in fact the opposite, namely proof of the fact that various relations can be iconic – not only those which invoke the concrete meaning of 'more'.

Abbreviations

ABS = absolutive, C = consonant, COLL = collective, COND = conditional, DEF = definite, DET = determiner, DIR = directional, F = feminine, FUT = future, IMPERF = imperfective, LOC = locative, M = masculine, O = object, PART = participle, PAST = past, PERF = perfective, PL = plural, RED = reduplication, REF = reflexive, REL = relative, SG = singular, SGL = singulative, V = vowel.

Sources

Antoine de Saint-Exupéry, *Le Petit Prince* – translated:

LPP Hungarian: György Rónay (trans.), *A Kis Herceg*. Budapest: Móra.

LPP Indonesian: Ratti Affandi et al. (transl.), *Pangeral kecil*. Jakarta: Pustaka Jaya.

LPP Welsh: Llinos Iorweth Dafis (transl.), *Y Tywysog Bach*. Lerpwl: Cyhoeddiadau Modern Cymreig, s.a.

J. K. Rowling, *Harry Potter and the Philosopher's Stone* - translated

HP Welsh: Emily Huws (transl.), *Harri Potter a Maen yr Athronydd*. Llundain: Bloomsbury.

Maltese

Aħ: James Fennimore Cooper [Michael Grech, transl.]. 1985. *L-Aħħar Moħoki*. Malta: Klabb kotba Maltin.

Mq: Tusè Costa. 1998. *Il-Ġimgħa Mqaddsa tal-Kappillan*. San Ġwann: PEG.

Na: Trevor Żahra. 1993. *Ġrajjiet in-Nannu Ċens*. Malta: Merlin Library Ltd.

References

Abbi, A. 1980. *Semantic grammar of Hindi. A study in reduplication.* New Dehli: Bahri.

Abbi, A. 1992. *Reduplication in South Asian languages. An areal typological and historical study.* New Dehli: Allied Publishers.

Abraham, W. 2005. Intensity and diminution triggered by reduplicating morphology: Janus-faced iconicity. In Hurch 2005, 547–68.

Bakker, P. 2003. Reduplication in Saramaccan. In Kouwenberg 2003, 73–82.

Brandstetter, R. 1917. *Die Reduplikation in den indianischen, indonesischen und indogermanischen Sprachen.* Luzern: Kantonsschule.

Coppenrath, H. & Prevost, P. 1974. *Grammaire approfondie de la langue tahitienne (ancienne et moderne).* Papeete: Pureora.

Cuzzolin, P. 1998. Sull'origine del singolativo in celtico, con particolare riferimento al medio gallese. *Archivio Glottologico Italiano* 83(2): 121–49.

Dressler, W.U. 1968. *Studien zur verbalen Pluralität.* Wien: Österreichische Akademie der Wissenschaften.

Dressler, W.U. 1985. *Morphonology. The dynamics of derivation.* Ann Arbor MI: Karoma.

Egli, H. 1990. *Paiwangrammatik.* Wiesbaden: Harrassowitz.

Ersen-Rasch, M. I. 1984. *Türkisch für Sie. Grammatik.* Munich: Hueber.

Fortescue, M. 1984. *West-Greenlandic.* London: Croom Helm.

Georg, S. & Volodin, A.P. 1999. *Die itelmenische Sprache. Grammatik und Texte.* Wiesbaden: Harrassowitz.

Gil, D. 2005. From repetition to reduplication in Riau Indonesian. In Hurch 2005, 31–64.

Givón, T. 1995. *Functionalism and grammar.* Amsterdam: John Benjamins.

Haiman, J. (ed.) 1985. *Iconicity in syntax.* Amsterdam: John Benjamins.

Hartmann, R. 1987. *Rimaykullayki. Unterrichtsmaterialien zum Quechua Ayacuchano.* Berlin: Reimer.

Hurch, B. (ed.) 2005. *Studies on reduplication.* Berlin: Mouton de Gruyter.

Hurch, B. & Mattes, V. 2005. Über die Entstehung von partieller Reduplikation. In *Sprache und Natürlichkeit. Gedenkband für Willi Mayerthaler*, G. Fenk-Oczlon & C. Winkler (eds), 137–56. Tübingen: Narr.

Inkelas, S. & Zoll, S. 2005. *Reduplication. Doubling in morphology.* Cambridge: CUP.

Kiyomi, S. 1995. A new approach to reduplication: A semantic study of noun and verb reduplication in the Malayo-Polynesian languages. *Linguistics* 33: 1145–67.

Kouwenberg, S. (ed.) 2003. *Twice as meaningful. Reduplication in Pidgins, Creoles and other contact languages.* Westminster: Battlebridge.

Kouwenberg, S. & LaCharité, D. 2003. The meanings of "more of the same". Iconicity in reduplication and the evidence for substrate transfer in the genesis of Caribbean Creole languages. In Kouwenberg 2003, 7–18.

Launey, M. 1981. *Introduction à la langue et à la littérature aztèques.* Tome I: *Grammaire.* Paris: L'Harmattan.

Mayerthaler, W. 1977. *Studien zur theoretischen und französischen Morphologie. Reduplikation, Echowörter, morphologische Natürlichkeit, Haplologie, Produktivität, Regeltelescoping, paradigmatischer Ausgleich.* Tübingen: Niemeyer.

Mayerthaler, W. 1981. *Morphologische Natürlichkeit.* Wiesbaden: Athenaion.

Moravcsik, E. 1978. Reduplicative constructions. In *Universals of Human Language.* Vol. III: *Word structure*, J.H. Greenberg (ed.), 297–334. Stanford: Stanford University Press.

Müller, H.-G. 2004. *Reduplikationen im Türkischen. Morphophonologische Untersuchungen.* Wiesbaden: Harrassowitz.

Pott, A.F. 1862. *Doppelung (Reduplikation, Gemination) als eines der wichtigsten Bildungsmittel der Sprache.* Lemgo: Meyer'sche Hofbuchhandlung.

Rainer, F. 1998. La réduplication française du type fifille d'un point de vue diachronique. In *Atti del XXI Congresso Internazionale di Linguistica e Filologia Romanza. Centro di studi filologici siciliani, Università di Palermo 18–24 settembre 1995. Sezione 1: Grammatica storica delle lingue romanze,* G. Ruffino (ed.), 279–90. Tübingen: Niemeyer.

Rivas, J. 2004. *Clause structure typology. Grammatical relations in cross-linguistic perspective.* Lugo: Tristram.

Rubino, C. 2005. Reduplication: Form, function and distribution. In Hurch 2005 (ed.), 11–30.

Sapir, E. 1921. *Language. An introduction to the study of speech.* New York NY: Harcourt, Brace & World.

Stolz, T. 2001. Singulative-collective: Natural morphology and stable classes in Welsh number inflection on nouns. *Sprachtypologie und Universalienforschung* 54(1): 52–76.

Stolz, T. 2004. A new Mediterraneanism. Word iteration in areal perspective. *Mediterranean Language Review* 15: 1–47.

Stolz, T. 2006. (Wort-)Iteration: (k)eine universelle Konstruktion. In *Konstruktionsgrammatik. Von der Anwendung zur Theorie,* K. Fischer & A. Stefanowitsch (eds), 105–32. Tübingen: Stauffenburg.

Stolz, T. & Sansò, A. In press. The Mediterranean area revisited. Word-iteration as a potential Mediterraneanism. *Orbis* 40.

Sylvain, S. 1979. *Le créole haïtien.* Genève: Slatkine.

Tiersma, P.M. 1999. *Frisian reference grammar.* Ljouwert: Fryske Akademie.

Topping, D. 1973. *Chamorro reference grammar.* Honolulu HI: University of Hawaii Press.

Topping, D. 1980. *Spoken Chamorro.* Honolulu HI: University of Hawaii Press.

Wurzel, W.U. 1987. Zur Morphologie der Dimensionsadjektive. In *Grammatische und konzeptuelle Aspekte von Dimensionsadjektiven,* M. Bierwisch & E. Lang (eds), 459–516. Berlin: Akademie.

Index of Languages

Index of Names

Index of Subjects

Studies in Language Companion Series

A complete list of titles in this series can be found on the publishers' website, *www.benjamins.com*

89 **STARK, Elisabeth, Elisabeth LEISS and Werner ABRAHAM (eds.):** Nominal Determination. Typology, context constraints and historical emergence. vii, 359 pp. + index. *Expected August 2007*

88 **RAMAT, Paolo and Elisa ROMA (eds.):** Europe and the Mediterranean as Linguistic Areas. Convergencies from a historical and typological perspective. 2007. xxv, 364 pp.

87 **VERHOEVEN, Elisabeth:** Experiential Constructions in Yucatec Maya. A typologically based analysis of a functional domain in a Mayan language. 2007. xiv, 380 pp.

86 **SCHWARZ-FRIESEL, Monika, Manfred CONSTEN and Mareile KNEES (eds.):** Anaphors in Text. Cognitive, formal and applied approaches to anaphoric reference. 2007. xvi, 282 pp.

85 **BUTLER, Christopher S., Raquel HIDALGO DOWNING and Julia LAVID (eds.):** Functional Perspectives on Grammar and Discourse. In honour of Angela Downing. xxiv, 468 pp. + index. *Expected July 2007*

84 **WANNER, Leo (ed.):** Selected Lexical and Grammatical Issues in the Meaning–Text Theory. In honour of Igor Mel'čuk. 2007. xviii, 380 pp.

83 **HANNAY, Mike and Gerard J. STEEN (eds.):** Structural-Functional Studies in English Grammar. In honour of Lachlan Mackenzie. 2007. vi, 393 pp.

82 **ZIEGELER, Debra:** Interfaces with English Aspect. Diachronic and empirical studies. 2006. xvi, 325 pp.

81 **PEETERS, Bert (ed.):** Semantic Primes and Universal Grammar. Empirical evidence from the Romance languages. 2006. xvi, 374 pp.

80 **BIRNER, Betty J. and Gregory WARD (eds.):** Drawing the Boundaries of Meaning. Neo-Gricean studies in pragmatics and semantics in honor of Laurence R. Horn. 2006. xii, 350 pp.

79 **LAFFUT, An:** Three-Participant Constructions in English. A functional-cognitive approach to caused relations. 2006. ix, 268 pp.

78 **YAMAMOTO, Mutsumi:** Agency and Impersonality. Their Linguistic and Cultural Manifestations. 2006. x, 152 pp.

77 **KULIKOV, Leonid, Andrej MALCHUKOV and Peter de SWART (eds.):** Case, Valency and Transitivity. 2006. xx, 503 pp.

76 **NEVALAINEN, Terttu, Juhani KLEMOLA and Mikko LAITINEN (eds.):** Types of Variation. Diachronic, dialectal and typological interfaces. 2006. viii, 378 pp.

75 **HOLE, Daniel, André MEINUNGER and Werner ABRAHAM (eds.):** Datives and Other Cases. Between argument structure and event structure. 2006. viii, 385 pp.

74 **PIETRANDREA, Paola:** Epistemic Modality. Functional properties and the Italian system. 2005. xii, 232 pp.

73 **XIAO, Richard and Tony McENERY:** Aspect in Mandarin Chinese. A corpus-based study. 2004. x, 305 pp.

72 **FRAJZYNGIER, Zygmunt, Adam HODGES and David S. ROOD (eds.):** Linguistic Diversity and Language Theories. 2005. xii, 432 pp.

71 **DAHL, Östen:** The Growth and Maintenance of Linguistic Complexity. 2004. x, 336 pp.

70 **LEFEBVRE, Claire:** Issues in the Study of Pidgin and Creole Languages. 2004. xvi, 358 pp.

69 **TANAKA, Lidia:** Gender, Language and Culture. A study of Japanese television interview discourse. 2004. xvii, 233 pp.

68 **MODER, Carol Lynn and Aida MARTINOVIC-ZIC (eds.):** Discourse Across Languages and Cultures. 2004. vi, 366 pp.

67 **LURAGHI, Silvia:** On the Meaning of Prepositions and Cases. The expression of semantic roles in Ancient Greek. 2003. xii, 366 pp.

66 **NARIYAMA, Shigeko:** Ellipsis and Reference Tracking in Japanese. 2003. xvi, 400 pp.

65 **MATSUMOTO, Kazuko:** Intonation Units in Japanese Conversation. Syntactic, informational and functional structures. 2003. xviii, 215 pp.

64 **BUTLER, Christopher S.:** Structure and Function – A Guide to Three Major Structural-Functional Theories. Part 2: From clause to discourse and beyond. 2003. xiv, 579 pp.

63 **BUTLER, Christopher S.:** Structure and Function – A Guide to Three Major Structural-Functional Theories. Part 1: Approaches to the simplex clause. 2003. xx, 573 pp.

62 **FIELD, Fredric:** Linguistic Borrowing in Bilingual Contexts. With a foreword by Bernard Comrie. 2002. xviii, 255 pp.

61 **GODDARD, Cliff and Anna WIERZBICKA (eds.):** Meaning and Universal Grammar. Theory and empirical findings. Volume 2. 2002. xvi, 337 pp.

60 **GODDARD, Cliff and Anna WIERZBICKA (eds.):** Meaning and Universal Grammar. Theory and empirical findings. Volume 1. 2002. xvi, 337 pp.

59 **SHI, Yuzhi:** The Establishment of Modern Chinese Grammar. The formation of the resultative construction and its effects. 2002. xiv, 262 pp.

58 **MAYLOR, B. Roger:** Lexical Template Morphology. Change of state and the verbal prefixes in German. 2002. x, 273 pp.

57 **MEL'ČUK, Igor A.:** Communicative Organization in Natural Language. The semantic-communicative structure of sentences. 2001. xii, 393 pp.

56 **FAARLUND, Jan Terje (ed.):** Grammatical Relations in Change. 2001. viii, 326 pp.

55 **DAHL, Östen and Maria KOPTJEVSKAJA-TAMM (eds.):** Circum-Baltic Languages. Volume 2: Grammar and Typology. 2001. xx, 423 pp.

54 **DAHL, Östen and Maria KOPTJEVSKAJA-TAMM (eds.):** Circum-Baltic Languages. Volume 1: Past and Present. 2001. xx, 382 pp.

53 **FISCHER, Olga, Anette ROSENBACH and Dieter STEIN (eds.):** Pathways of Change. Grammaticalization in English. 2000. x, 391 pp.

52 **TORRES CACOULLOS, Rena:** Grammaticization, Synchronic Variation, and Language Contact. A study of Spanish progressive -ndo constructions. 2000. xvi, 255 pp.

51 **ZIEGELER, Debra:** Hypothetical Modality. Grammaticalisation in an L2 dialect. 2000. xx, 290 pp.

50 **ABRAHAM, Werner and Leonid KULIKOV (eds.):** Tense-Aspect, Transitivity and Causativity. Essays in honour of Vladimir Nedjalkov. 1999. xxxiv, 359 pp.

49 **BHAT, D.N.S.:** The Prominence of Tense, Aspect and Mood. 1999. xii, 198 pp.

48 **MANNEY, Linda Joyce:** Middle Voice in Modern Greek. Meaning and function of an inflectional category. 2000. xiii, 262 pp.

47 **BRINTON, Laurel J. and Minoji AKIMOTO (eds.):** Collocational and Idiomatic Aspects of Composite Predicates in the History of English. 1999. xiv, 283 pp.

46 **YAMAMOTO, Mutsumi:** Animacy and Reference. A cognitive approach to corpus linguistics. 1999. xviii, 278 pp.

45 **COLLINS, Peter C. and David LEE (eds.):** The Clause in English. In honour of Rodney Huddleston. 1999. xv, 342 pp.

44 **HANNAY, Mike and A. Machtelt BOLKESTEIN (eds.):** Functional Grammar and Verbal Interaction. 1998. xii, 304 pp.

43 **OLBERTZ, Hella, Kees HENGEVELD and Jesús SÁNCHEZ GARCÍA (eds.):** The Structure of the Lexicon in Functional Grammar. 1998. xii, 312 pp.

42 **DARNELL, Michael, Edith MORAVCSIK, Michael NOONAN, Frederick J. NEWMEYER and Kathleen M. WHEATLEY (eds.):** Functionalism and Formalism in Linguistics. Volume II: Case studies. 1999. vi, 407 pp.

41 **DARNELL, Michael, Edith MORAVCSIK, Michael NOONAN, Frederick J. NEWMEYER and Kathleen M. WHEATLEY (eds.):** Functionalism and Formalism in Linguistics. Volume I: General papers. 1999. vi, 486 pp.

40 **BIRNER, Betty J. and Gregory WARD:** Information Status and Noncanonical Word Order in English. 1998. xiv, 314 pp.

39 **WANNER, Leo (ed.):** Recent Trends in Meaning–Text Theory. 1997. xx, 202 pp.

38 **HACKING, Jane F.:** Coding the Hypothetical. A comparative typology of Russian and Macedonian conditionals. 1998. vi, 156 pp.

37 **HARVEY, Mark and Nicholas REID (eds.):** Nominal Classification in Aboriginal Australia. 1997. x, 296 pp.

36 **KAMIO, Akio (ed.):** Directions in Functional Linguistics. 1997. xiii, 259 pp.

35 **MATSUMOTO, Yoshiko:** Noun-Modifying Constructions in Japanese. A frame semantic approach. 1997. viii, 204 pp.

34 **HATAV, Galia:** The Semantics of Aspect and Modality. Evidence from English and Biblical Hebrew. 1997. x, 224 pp.

33 **VELÁZQUEZ-CASTILLO, Maura:** The Grammar of Possession. Inalienability, incorporation and possessor ascension in Guaraní. 1996. xvi, 274 pp.

32 **FRAJZYNGIER, Zygmunt:** Grammaticalization of the Complex Sentence. A case study in Chadic. 1996. xviii, 501 pp.